Your Companion Site —
Even more help for studying!

W9-BKT-067

bedfordstmartins.com/mckaywest

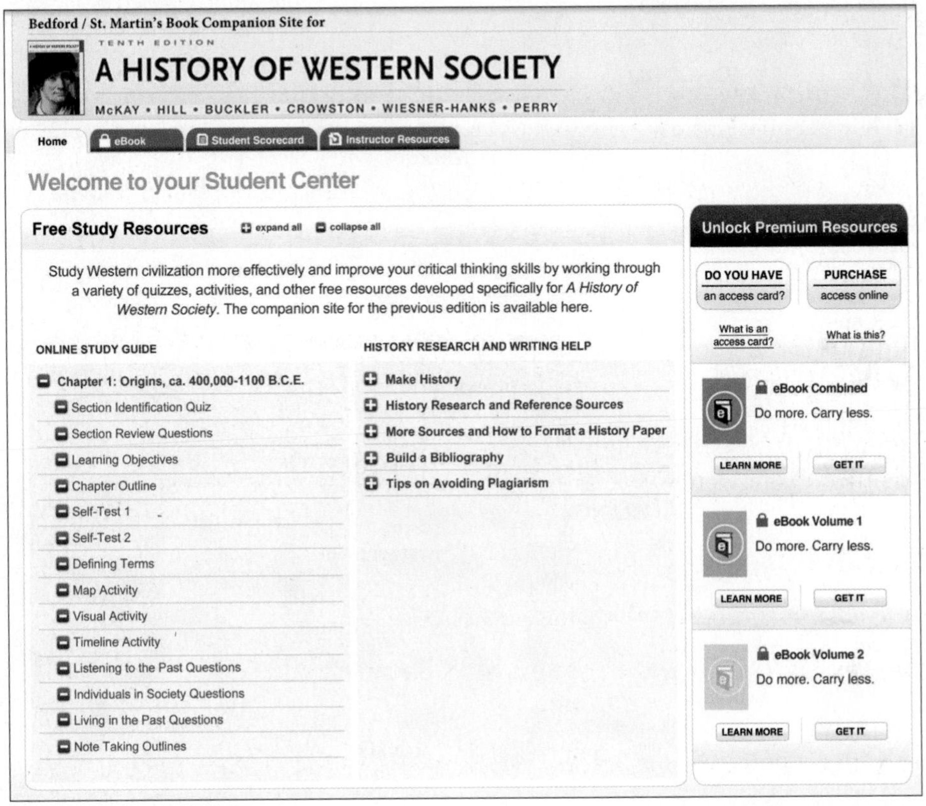

Bedford / St. Martin's Book Companion Site for

TENTH EDITION

A HISTORY OF WESTERN SOCIETY

McKAY • HILL • BUCKLER • CROWSTON • WIESNER-HANKS • PERRY

| Home | eBook | Student Scorecard | Instructor Resources |

Welcome to your Student Center

Free Study Resources ⊞ expand all ⊟ collapse all

Study Western civilization more effectively and improve your critical thinking skills by working through a variety of quizzes, activities, and other free resources developed specifically for *A History of Western Society*. The companion site for the previous edition is available here.

ONLINE STUDY GUIDE

⊟ Chapter 1: Origins, ca. 400,000-1100 B.C.E.
- Section Identification Quiz
- Section Review Questions
- Learning Objectives
- Chapter Outline
- Self-Test 1
- Self-Test 2
- Defining Terms
- Map Activity
- Visual Activity
- Timeline Activity
- Listening to the Past Questions
- Individuals in Society Questions
- Living in the Past Questions
- Note Taking Outlines

HISTORY RESEARCH AND WRITING HELP
- Make History
- History Research and Reference Sources
- More Sources and How to Format a History Paper
- Build a Bibliography
- Tips on Avoiding Plagiarism

Unlock Premium Resources

| DO YOU HAVE | PURCHASE |
| an access card? | access online |

What is an access card?   What is this?

🔒 eBook Combined
Do more. Carry less.
LEARN MORE   GET IT

🔒 eBook Volume 1
Do more. Carry less.
LEARN MORE   GET IT

🔒 eBook Volume 2
Do more. Carry less.
LEARN MORE   GET IT

FREE Online Study Guide — Improve your performance!
Get immediate feedback on your progress with

- Quizzing
- Key terms review
- Map and visual activities
- Timeline activities
- Note-taking outlines

FREE History Research and Writing Help
Refine your research skills, evaluate sources, and organize your findings with

- *Make History* maps, documents, images, and Web sites
- History Research and Reference Sources
- More Sources and How to Format a History Paper
- Build a Bibliography
- Tips on Avoiding Plagiarism

CONTEMPORARY EUROPE

ATLANTIC OCEAN

NORWAY
Bergen
Oslo

SWEDEN
Stockholm
Göteborg

North Sea

Baltic Sea

DENMARK
Aarhus
Copenhagen

RUSSIA
Kaliningrad

SCOTLAND
Edinburgh
Glasgow

NORTHERN IRELAND
Belfast

IRELAND
Dublin

Cork

UNITED KINGDOM
Liverpool
Birmingham

WALES
ENGLAND
Thames R.
London

English Channel

NETHERLANDS
Amsterdam
Rotterdam

Antwerp
Brussels
BELGIUM

Luxembourg
LUXEMBOURG

Elbe R.
Berlin

GERMANY
Frankfurt

Rhine R.

Prague
CZECH REP.
Brno

Gdańsk
Vistula R.

POLAND
Warsaw
Oder R.
Kraków

SLOVAKIA
Miskol
Vienna
Bratislava

Seine R.

Paris

FRANCE

Loire R.

Lyons

Rhône R.

LIECHTENSTEIN
Zürich
Vaduz
Bern
SWITZERLAND

Munich
Innsbruck
AUSTRIA
Graz

Danube R.

Milan

A L P S

Po R.

Budapest
HUNGARY

SLOVENIA
Ljubljana

Zagreb
CROATIA

Belgrade

BOSNIA AND HERZEGOVINA
Sarajevo
SERBIA

Bay of Biscay

PORTUGAL
Oporto
Lisbon

Madrid

SPAIN
Barcelona

ANDORRA
Andorra la Vella

P Y R E N E E S

Ebro R.

Marseilles
MONACO

Corsica

San Marino
SAN MARINO

APENNINES

Adriatic Sea

Rome
ITALY

Naples

Split

Podgorica
MONTENEGRO

Tiranë
ALBANIA

Seville

Gibraltar (Gr. Br.)

Balearic Is.

Sardinia

Tyrrhenian Sea

Ionian Sea

Palermo
Sicily

Algiers

Rabat

Tunis

Valletta
MALTA

MOROCCO

TUNISIA

Mediterranean

ALGERIA

Tripoli

LIBYA

Elevation

Feet	Meters
Over 13,120	Over 4,001
6,561–13,120	2,001–4,000
1,641–6,560	501–2,000
661–1,640	201–500
0–660	0–200
Below sea level	Below sea level

⊛ National capital
• Major city

0   150   300 miles
0   150   300 kilometers

A History of Western Society

■ Roger van der Weyden, *Portrait of a Woman with a White Headdress*, ca. 1435.

A History of Western Society

VOLUME 1

From Antiquity to the Enlightenment

Tenth Edition

John P. McKay
University of Illinois at Urbana-Champaign

Bennett D. Hill
Late of Georgetown University

John Buckler
University of Illinois at Urbana-Champaign

Clare Haru Crowston
University of Illinois at Urbana-Champaign

Merry E. Wiesner-Hanks
University of Wisconsin–Milwaukee

Joe Perry
Georgia State University

BEDFORD/ST. MARTIN'S

Boston • New York

FOR BEDFORD/ST. MARTIN'S

Publisher for History: Mary Dougherty
Director of Development for History: Jane Knetzger
Executive Editor for History: Traci Mueller Crowell
Senior Developmental Editor for History: Laura Arcari
Senior Production Editor: Christina Horn
Senior Production Supervisor: Nancy Myers
Executive Marketing Manager: Jenna Bookin Barry
Associate Editor: Lynn Sternberger
Production Assistant: Alexis Biasell
Senior Art Director: Anna Palchik
Text Design: Brian Salisbury
Copyeditor: Sybil Sosin
Map Editor: Charlotte Miller
Indexer: Leoni Z. McVey
Page Layout: Boynton Hue Studio
Photo Research: Carole Frohlich and Elisa Gallagher, The Visual Connection Image Research, Inc.

Cover Design: Billy Boardman
Cover Art: Roger van der Weyden, *Portrait of a Woman with a White Headdress,* ca. 1435. Oil on oak, 47 × 32 cm. Photo: Gemäldegalerie, Staatliche Museen Berlin/Bildarchiv Preussischer Kulturbesitz, Art Resource, NY.
Cartography: Mapping Specialists, Ltd.
Composition: NK Graphics
Printing and Binding: RR Donnelley and Sons

President: Joan E. Feinberg
Editorial Director: Denise B. Wydra
Director of Marketing: Karen R. Soeltz
Director of Editing, Design, and Production: Susan W. Brown
Assistant Director of Editing, Design, and Production: Elise S. Kaiser
Managing Editor: Elizabeth M. Schaaf

Library of Congress Control Number: 2010920486

Manufactured in the United States of America.

1 2 3 4 5 6   14 13 12 11 10

For information, write: Bedford/St. Martin's, 75 Arlington Street, Boston, MA 02116 (617-399-4000)

ISBN-10: 0-312-68773-7   ISBN-13: 978-0-312-68773-1 (combined edition)
ISBN-10: 0-312-64059-5   ISBN-13: 978-0-312-64059-0 (Vol. 1)
ISBN-10: 0-312-64060-9   ISBN-13: 978-0-312-64060-6 (Vol. 2)
ISBN-10: 0-312-64061-7   ISBN-13: 978-0-312-64061-3 (Vol. A)
ISBN-10: 0-312-64062-5   ISBN-13: 978-0-312-64062-0 (Vol. B)
ISBN-10: 0-312-64063-3   ISBN-13: 978-0-312-64063-7 (Vol. C)
ISBN-10: 0-312-63827-2   ISBN-13: 978-0-312-63827-6 (Since 1300)
ISBN-10: 0-312-64058-7   ISBN-13: 978-0-312-64058-3 (Since 1300 for Advanced Placement)

Published and distributed outside North America by:
PALGRAVE MACMILLAN
Houndmills, Basingstoke, Hampshire RG21 6XS
Companies and representatives throughout the world.
ISBN-10: 0-230-12102-0   ISBN-13: 978-0-230-12102-7 (combined edition)
ISBN-10: 0-230-12103-9   ISBN-13: 978-0-230-12103-4 (Vol. 1)
ISBN-10: 0-230-12104-7   ISBN-13: 978-0-230-12104-1 (Vol. 2)
ISBN-10: 0-230-12105-5   ISBN-13: 978-0-230-12105-8 (Since 1300)
A catalogue record for this book is available from the British Library.

◾ Brief Contents

▪ Contents

1 Origins
ca. 400,000–1100 B.C.E.   2

2 Small Kingdoms and Mighty Empires in the Near East
ca. 1100–513 B.C.E.   32

3 The Development of Classical Greece
ca. 2000–338 B.C.E.   56

4 The Hellenistic World
336–30 B.C.E.   90

5 The Rise of Rome
ca. 750–31 B.C.E.   118

6 The Pax Romana
31 B.C.E.–284 C.E.   144

7 Late Antiquity
250–600   174

8 Europe in the Early Middle Ages
600–1000 206

9 State and Church in the High Middle Ages
1000–1300 238

10 The Life of the People in the High Middle Ages
1000–1300   272

11 The Creativity and Challenges of Medieval Cities
1100–1300   302

12 The Crisis of the Later Middle Ages
1300–1450   338

13 European Society in the Age of the Renaissance
1350–1550   372

14 Reformations and Religious Wars
1500–1600   406

15 European Exploration and Conquest
1450–1650   442

16 Absolutism and Constitutionalism
ca. 1589–1725   478

17 Toward a New Worldview
1540–1789   518

Maps, Figures, and Tables

Maps

Figures and Tables

Living in the Past

Listening to the Past

Individuals in Society

▪ Preface

With this, the tenth edition of *A History of Western Society*, we invite our colleagues and current and past adopters to join us in seeing the book as if for the first time. For us, this edition—undertaken at a new publishing house—has been an opportunity to revisit our original vision and to thereby realize the most thorough reconsideration of our text since we first began. *A History of Western Society* grew out of the initial three authors' desire to infuse new life into the study of Western Civilization. We knew that historians were using imaginative questions and innovative research to open up vast new areas of historical interest and knowledge. At that point, social history was dramatically changing the ways we understood the past, and we decided to create a book that would re-create the lives of ordinary people in appealing human terms, while also giving major economic, political, cultural, and intellectual developments the attention they unquestionably deserve. The three new authors who have joined the original author team—and who first used the book as students or teachers—remain committed to advancing this vision for today's classroom. With its new look, line-by-line edits aimed at increasing the book's readability and accessibility, reinvigorated scholarship, and broader definition of social history that reflects where instructors and students are now, we've rethought every element of the book to bring the original vision into the twenty-first century and make the past memorable for a new generation of students and instructors.

History as a discipline never stands still, and over the last several decades cultural history has joined social history as a source of dynamism. Because of its emphasis on the ways people made sense of their lives, *A History of Western Society* has always included a large amount of cultural history, ranging from foundational works of philosophy and literature to popular songs and stories. The focus on cultural history has been heightened in this tenth edition in a way that highlights the interplay between men's and women's lived experiences and the ways men and women reflect on these experiences to create meaning. The joint social and cultural perspective requires—fortunately, in our opinion—the inclusion of objects as well as texts as important sources for studying history, which has allowed us to incorporate the growing emphasis on material culture in the work of many historians.

These new directions have not changed the central mission of the book, which is to introduce students to the broad sweep of Western Civilization in a fresh yet balanced manner. Every edition has incorporated new research to keep the book up-to-date and respond to the changing needs of readers and instructors, and we have continued to do this in the tenth edition. As we have made these changes, large and small, we have sought to give students and teachers an integrated perspective so that they could pursue—on their own or in the classroom—the historical questions that they find particularly exciting and significant.

Textual Changes

For the tenth edition we took the time to revisit, reconsider, and revise every paragraph of the book. We paid painstaking attention to the writing, and we're proud of the results. Informed by recent scholarship, every chapter was revised with an aim toward readability and accessibility. Several main lines of revision have guided our many changes. In particular, as noted above, we have broadened the book's focus on social history to include a greater emphasis on cultural history. This increased emphasis is supported in every chapter by the use of artifacts that make history tangible and by the new Living in the Past visual feature, described below, that demonstrates the intersection between society and culture. In addition, the social and cultural context of Western Civilization has been integrated throughout the narrative, including expanded and new sections on Egyptian life, common people in Charlemagne's empire, artistic patronage during the Renaissance, identities and communities of the Atlantic world, eighteenth-century education, nineteenth-century family life, consumer society between the two world wars, life under Nazi occupation, and state and society in the East Bloc, among others.

The tenth edition continues to reflect Europe's interactions with the rest of the world and the role of gender in shaping human experience. The global context of European history is reflected in new scholarship on the steppe peoples of Central Asia, Muslim views of the Crusades, the Atlantic world, decolonization, and globalization. New scholarship on gender is woven throughout the book and is included in sections on Frankish queens, medieval prostitution, female humanists, politics and gender during the French Revolution, and gender roles during industrialization.

These major aspects of revision are accompanied by the incorporation of a wealth of new scholarship and subject areas. Additions, among others, include material on Paleolithic and Neolithic life (Chapter 1); the Neo-Babylonians (Chapter 2); the later period of the Roman Empire in the West (Chapter 7); the bubonic plague in eastern Europe (Chapter 12); the Jesuits (Chapter 14); the limits of enlightened absolutism (Chapter 17); eighteenth-century beliefs and practices (Chapter 19); expanded coverage of the peasant revolt (Chapter 20); sections on the Battle of the Somme, waging total war, and the human costs of World War I (Chapter 26); popular support for National Socialism (Chapter 27); the affluent society (Chapter 30); and up-to-date coverage of the economic downturn in Europe, the Iraq War, and the global recession (Chapter 31).

Organizational Changes

To meet the demands of the evolving course, we took a close and critical look at the book's organization, and have made several major changes in the organization of chapters to reflect the way the course is taught today. Chapter 7 now begins in 250 with the reforms of Diocletian and Constantine, and includes material on the debate over the decline of the Roman Empire in the West as well as a more comprehensive discussion of the barbarian migrations. To increase clarity, we've combined the separate chapters on absolutism in western and eastern Europe into a single chapter on absolutism and constitutionalism. Volume 2 also features a completely revised and updated post-1945 section featuring a third, new, postwar chapter, "Europe in an Age of Globalization, 1990 to the Present." In response to the growth in new and exciting scholarship for this period, the postwar chapters have been completely rewritten by new author Joe Perry with new scholarship on decolonization, consumerism as an aspect of the Cold War, new patterns of immigration and guest worker programs, the growth and decline of the welfare state in eastern and western Europe, and Europe's place in an era of increasing globalization, including the challenges to liberalism mounted by new social movements.

Features

We are proud of the diverse special features that expand upon the narrative and offer opportunities for classroom discussion and assignments, and in the new edition we have expanded our offerings to include a brand new feature created in response to current research trends that is sure to get students and instructors talking. This **NEW** visual feature, **Living in the Past**, uses social and cultural history to show how life in the past was both similar to and different from our lives today. Focusing on relatively narrow aspects of social and cultural history to write compelling stories that would encourage students to think about the way the past informs the present was both a challenge and a pleasure. The resulting thirty-one essays—one in each chapter—introduce students to the study of material culture, encourage critical analysis, and engage and inform with fascinating details about life in the past. Richly illustrated with images and artifacts, each feature includes a short essay and questions for analysis.

We use these features to explore the deeper ramifications of things students might otherwise take for granted, such as consumer goods, factories, and even currency. Students connect to the people of the past through a diverse range of topics such as "Assyrian Palace Life and Power," "Roman Table Manners," "Foods of the Columbian Exchange," "Coffeehouse Culture," "The Immigrant Experience," "A Model Socialist Steel Town," and "The Supermarket Revolution."

In our years of teaching Western Civilization, we have often noted that students come alive when they encounter stories about real people in the past. To give students a chance to see the past through ordinary people's lives, each chapter includes one of the popular **Individuals in Society** biographical essays that offer brief studies of individuals or groups, informing students about the societies in which they lived. This feature grew out of our long-standing focus on people's lives and the varieties of historical experience, and we believe that readers will empathize with these human beings as they themselves seek to define their own identities. The spotlighting of individuals, both famous and obscure, perpetuates the book's continued attention to cultural and intellectual developments, highlights human agency, and reflects changing interests within the historical profession as well as the development of "micro-history." **NEW** features include essays on Cyrus the Great; Queen Cleopatra; the Venerable Bede; Meister Eckhart; Rose Bertin, "Minister of Fashion"; Josiah Wedgwood; Germaine de Staël; and Armando Rodrigues, West Germany's "One-Millionth Guest Worker."

Each chapter also continues to include a primary source feature titled **Listening to the Past**, chosen to extend and illuminate a major historical issue through the presentation of a single original source or several voices. Each opens with an introduction and closes with questions for analysis that invite students to evaluate the evidence as historians would. Selected for their interest and importance and carefully fitted into their historical context, these sources allow students to hear the past and to observe how history has been shaped by individuals. **NEW** topics include "Cicero and the Plot to Kill Caesar," "Augustus's *Res Gestae*," "Eirik's Saga," "Perspectives on Humanist Learning and Women," "Denis Diderot's 'Supplement to Bougainville's Voyage,'" "Contrasting Views on the Effects of Rural Industry," "Abbé de Sieyès, 'What Is the Third Estate?,'" "Herder and Mazzini on the Development of Nationalism," "Lin Zexu and Yamagata Aritomo, Confronting Western Imperialism," and "The Nixon-Khrushchev 'Kitchen Debate.'" In addition to using documents as part of our special feature program, we have quoted extensively from a wide variety of primary sources in the narrative, demonstrating that such quotations are the "stuff" of history. We believe that our extensive program of using primary sources as an integral part of the narrative as well as in extended form in the "Listening to the Past" chapter feature will help readers learn to interpret and think critically.

With the goal of making this the most student-centered edition yet, we paid renewed attention to the book's pedagogy. To help guide students, each chapter opens with a **chapter preview with focus questions** keyed to the main chapter headings. These questions are repeated within the chapter and again in **NEW chapter reviews**. Many of the questions have been reframed for this edition, and new summary answers have been added to the chapter review. Each chapter review concludes with a carefully selected list of annotated **suggestions for further reading**, revised and updated to keep them current with the vast amount of new work being done in many fields.

To help students understand the material and prepare for exams, each chapter includes **NEW Looking Back, Looking Ahead** conclusions. Replacing the former chapter summaries, each conclusion provides an insightful synthesis of the chapter's main developments, while connecting to events that students will encounter in the chapters to come. In this way students are introduced to history as an ongoing process of interrelated events.

To promote clarity and comprehension, boldface **key terms** in the text are defined in the margins and listed in the chapter review. **NEW phonetic spellings** are located directly after terms that readers are likely to find hard to pronounce. The **chapter chronologies**, which review major developments discussed in each chapter, have been improved to more closely mirror the key events of the chapter, and the number of topic-specific **thematic chronologies** has been expanded, with new chronologies on "Art and Philosophy in the Hellenic Period" and "Major Figures of the Enlightenment," among others. Once again we also provide a **unified timeline** at the end of the text. Comprehensive and easy to locate, this useful timeline allows students to compare developments over the centuries.

The high-quality art and map program has been thoroughly revised and expanded. The new edition features more than **600 contemporaneous illustrations**. To make the past tangible, and as an extension of our enhanced attention to cultural history, we include over **100 artifacts**—from swords and fans to playing cards and record players. As in earlier editions, all illustrations have been carefully selected to complement the text, and all include captions that inform students while encouraging them to read the text more deeply. Completely redesigned and reconceptualized for the new edition, **87 full-size maps** illustrate major developments in the narrative. In addition, **61 NEW spot maps** are embedded in the narrative to show areas under discussion. **NEW** maps in the tenth edition highlight such topics as the Persian wars, the Hanseatic League, the Russian civil war, the Holocaust, Cold War Europe, pollution in Europe, and the Soviet war in Afghanistan, among others.

We recognize students' difficulties with geography and visual analysis, and the new edition includes the popular **Mapping the Past map activities** and **NEW Picturing the Past visual activities**. Included in each chapter, these activities give students valuable skills in reading and interpreting maps and images by asking them to analyze the maps or visuals and make connections to the larger processes discussed in the narrative. All these activities can be completed online and submitted directly to instructors at the free online study guide.

To showcase the book's rich art program and to signal our commitment to this thorough and deep revision, the book has been completely redesigned. The dynamic new contemporary design engages and assists students with its clear, easy-to-use pedagogy.

Acknowledgments

It is a pleasure to thank the many instructors who read and critiqued the manuscript through its development:

Georgia Bonny Bazemore, Eastern Washington University
John Beeler, University of Alabama
Dudley R. Belcher, Tri-County Technical College
Stephen A. Beluris, Moorpark College
Nancy B. Bjorklund, Fullerton College
Paul Bookbinder, University of Massachusetts, Boston
Edward A. Boyden, Nassau Community College
Harry T. Burgess, St. Clair County Community College
Jacqueline de Vries, Augsburg College
Daniel Finn, Valencia Community College
Jennifer Foray, Purdue University
Gary Forsythe, Texas Tech University
Lucille M. Fortunato, Bridgewater State College
Robert Genter, Nassau Community College
Stephen Gibson, Allegany College of Maryland
Andrew L. Goldman, Gonzaga University
Anthony Heideman, Front Range Community College
Jason M. Kelly, Indiana University
Keith Knutson, Viterbo University
Lynn Lubamersky, Boise State University
Susan A. Maurer, Nassau Community College
Greg Mauriocourt, Technical College of the Lowcountry
Jennifer McNabb, Western Illinois University
Elisa Miller, Rhode Island College
James M. Mini, Montgomery County Community College
Mary Lou Mosley, Paradise Valley Community College
Lisa Ossian, Des Moines Area Community College
Scott W. Palmer, Western Illinois University
Dennis Ricci, Community College of Rhode Island and Quinsigamond Community College
James Robertson, Montgomery County Community College
Daniel Robison, Troy University
Jahan Salehi, Guilford Tech Community College
Carol Longenecker Schmidt, Tri-County Technical College
Robert Shipley, Widener University
Karen Sonnelitter, Purdue University
Donathan Taylor, Hardin-Simmons University
Norman R. West, SUNY at Suffolk
Shelley Wolbrink, Drury University
Robert Zajkowski, Hudson Valley Community College

It is also a pleasure to thank the many editors who have assisted us over the years, first at Houghton Mifflin and now at Bedford/St. Martin's. At Bedford/St. Martin's, these include senior development editor Laura Arcari, with assistance from Beth Welch, for developing the new "Living in the Past" features; freelance development editor Michelle McSweeney; associate editors Lynn Sternberger and Jack Cashman; executive editor Traci Mueller Crowell; director of development Jane Knetzger; publisher for history Mary Dougherty; map editor Charlotte Miller; photo researcher Carole Frohlich; text permissions editor Sandy Schechter; and Christina Horn, senior production editor, with the assistance of Alexis Biasell and the guidance of managing editor Elizabeth Schaaf and assistant managing editor John Amburg. Other key contributors were designer Brian Salisbury, page makeup artist Cia Boynton, copyeditor Sybil Sosin, proofreaders Andrea Martin and Angela Hoover Morrison, indexer Leoni McVey, and cover designer Billy Boardman. We would also like to thank editorial director Denise Wydra and president Joan E. Feinberg.

Many of our colleagues at the University of Illinois, the University of Wisconsin–Milwaukee, and Georgia State University continue to provide information and stimulation, often without even knowing it. We thank them for it. We also thank the many students over the years with whom we have used earlier editions of this book. Their reactions and opinions helped shape the revisions to this edition, and we hope it remains worthy of the ultimate praise that they bestowed on it, that it's "not boring like most textbooks." Merry Wiesner-Hanks would, as always, also like to thank her husband Neil, without whom work on this project would not be possible. Clare Haru Crowston thanks her husband Ali and her children Lili, Reza, and Kian, who are a joyous reminder of the vitality of life that we try to showcase in this book. John McKay expresses his deep appreciation to JoAnn McKay for her keen insights and unfailing encouragement. Joe Perry thanks Andrzej S. Kaminski and the expert team assembled at Lazarski University for their insightful comments and is most grateful to Joyce de Vries for her unstinting support and encouragement.

Each of us has benefited from the criticism of our coauthors, although each of us assumes responsibility for what he or she has written. John Buckler has written the first six chapters; building on text originally written by Bennett Hill, Merry Wiesner-Hanks has assumed primary responsibility for Chapters 7 through 14; building on text originally written by Bennett Hill and John McKay, Clare Crowston has assumed primary responsibility for Chapters 15 through 20; John McKay has written and revised Chapters 21 through 25; and Joe Perry has written and revised Chapters 26 through 31, building on text originally written by John McKay.

A History of Western Society is supported by numerous resources — study tools for students, materials for instructors, and many options for packaging the book with documents readers, trade books, atlases, and other guides — that are free or available at a substantial discount. Descriptions follow; for more information, visit the book's catalog site at **bedfordstmartins.com/mckaywest/catalog**, or contact your local Bedford/St. Martin's sales representative.

Available Versions of This Book

To accommodate different course lengths and course budgets, *A History of Western Society* is available in several different formats, including three-hole punched loose-leaf Budget Books versions and e-books, which are available at a substantial discount.

- Combined edition (Chapters 1–31): available in hardcover, loose-leaf, and e-book formats
- Volume 1, From Antiquity to the Enlightenment (Chapters 1–17): available in paperback, loose-leaf, and e-book formats
- Volume 2, From the Age of Exploration to the Present (Chapters 15–31): available in paperback, loose-leaf, and e-book formats
- Volume A, From Antiquity to 1500 (Chapters 1–13): available in paperback
- Volume B, From the Later Middle Ages to 1815 (Chapters 12–20): available in paperback
- Volume C, From the Revolutionary Era to the Present (Chapters 20–31): available in paperback
- Since 1300 (Chapters 12–31): available in paperback and e-book formats
- Since 1300 for Advanced Placement (Chapters 12–31): available in hardcover and e-book formats

Our innovative e-books give your students the content you want in a convenient format at about half the cost of a print book. **Bedford/St. Martin's e-Books** have been optimized for reading and studying online. **CourseSmart e-Books** can be downloaded or used online, whichever is more convenient for your students.

Companion Site

Our new companion site at **bedfordstmartins.com/ mckaywest** gathers free and premium resources, giving students a way to extend *A History of Western Society* online. This book-specific site provides a single destination that students can use to practice, read, write, and study, and to find and access quizzes and activities, study aids, and history research and writing help.

FREE Online Study Guide. Available at the companion site, this popular resource provides students with self-review quizzes and activities for each chapter, including a multiple-choice self-test that focuses on important concepts; an identification quiz that helps students remember key people, places, and events; a flash-card activity that tests students' knowledge of key terms; and map activities to strengthen students' geography skills. Instructors can monitor students' progress through an online Quiz Gradebook or receive e-mail updates.

FREE History Research and Writing Help. Also available at the companion site, this resource includes **History Research and Reference Sources**, with links to history-related databases, indexes, and journals; **More Sources and How to Format a History Paper**, with clear advice on how to integrate primary and secondary sources into research papers and how to cite and format sources correctly; **Build a Bibliography**, a simple Web-based tool that generates bibliographies in four commonly used documentation styles; and **Tips on Avoiding Plagiarism**, an online tutorial that reviews the consequences of plagiarism and features exercises to help students practice integrating sources and recognize acceptable summaries.

Instructor Resources

Bedford/St. Martin's has developed a wide range of teaching resources for this book and for this course. They range from lecture and presentation materials and assessment tools to course management options. Most can be downloaded or ordered at **bedfordstmartins.com/mckaywest/catalog**.

HistoryClass for *A History of Western Society*. HistoryClass, a Bedford/St. Martin's Online Course Space, puts the online resources available with this textbook in one convenient and completely customizable course space. There you can access an interactive e-book and primary sources reader; maps, images, documents, and links; chapter review quizzes; interactive multimedia exercises; and research and writing help. In HistoryClass you can get all our premium content and tools and assign, rearrange, and mix them with your own resources. For more information, visit **yourhistoryclass.com**.

Bedford/St. Martin's Course Cartridges. Whether you use Blackboard, WebCT, Desire2Learn, Angel, Sakai, or Moodle, we have free content and support available to help you plug our content into your course management system. Registered instructors can download cartridges with no hassle and no strings attached. Content includes our most popular free resources and book-specific content for *A History of Western Society*. Visit **bedfordstmartins.com/cms** to see a demo, find your version, or download your cartridge.

Instructor's Resource Manual. The instructor's manual offers both experienced and first-time instructors tools for presenting textbook material in engaging ways. It includes chapter review material, teaching strategies, and a guide to chapter-specific supplements available for the text.

Guide to Changing Editions. Designed to facilitate an instructor's transition from the previous edition of *A History of Western Society* to the current edition, this guide presents an overview of major changes as well as of changes in each chapter.

Computerized Test Bank. The test bank includes a mix of fresh, carefully crafted multiple-choice, definition, short-answer, and essay questions for each chapter. The questions appear in Microsoft Word format and in easy-to-use test bank software that allows instructors to easily add, edit, re-sequence, and print questions and answers. Instructors can also export questions into a variety of formats, including WebCT and Blackboard.

PowerPoint Maps, Images, Lecture Outlines, and i>clicker Content. These presentation materials are downloadable individually from the Media and Supplements tab at bedfordstmartins.com/mckaywest/catalog and are available on *The Bedford Lecture Kit Instructor's Resource CD-ROM*. They include ready-made and fully customizable PowerPoint multimedia presentations built around lecture outlines with embedded maps, figures, and selected images from the textbook and with detailed instructor notes on key points. Also available are maps and selected images in JPEG and Power-Point formats; content for i>clicker, a classroom response system, in Microsoft Word and PowerPoint formats; the Instructor's Resource Manual in Microsoft Word format; and outline maps in PDF format for quizzing or handing out. All files are suitable for copying onto transparency acetates.

Overhead Map Transparencies. This set of full-color acetate transparencies includes 130 maps for the Western Civilization course.

Make History: Free Documents, Maps, Images, and Web Sites. Finding the source material you need is simple with Make History. Here the best Web resources are combined with hundreds of carefully chosen maps and images and helpfully annotated. Browse the collection of thousands of resources by course or by topic, date, and type. Available at bedfordstmartins.com/makehistory.

Videos and Multimedia. A wide assortment of videos and multimedia CD-ROMs on various topics in Western Civilization is available to qualified adopters through your Bedford/St. Martin's sales representative.

Packaging Opportunities

Save your students money and package your favorite text with more! For information on free packages and discounts of up to 50 percent, visit bedfordstmartins.com/mckaywest/

catalog, or contact your local Bedford/St. Martin's sales representative.

e-Book. The e-book for this title can be packaged with the print text at no additional cost.

***Sources of Western Society*, Second Edition**. This primary-source collection—available in Volume 1, Volume 2, and Since 1300 versions—provides a revised and expanded selection of sources to accompany *A History of Western Society*, Tenth Edition. Each chapter features five or six written and visual sources by well-known figures and ordinary individuals alike. Now including nineteen visual sources and 30 percent more documents, this edition offers both breadth and depth. A new Viewpoints feature highlights two or three sources that address the same topic from different perspectives. Document headnotes and reading and discussion questions promote student understanding. Available free when packaged with the text.

***Sources of Western Society* e-Book**. The reader is also available as an e-book. When packaged with the print or electronic version of the textbook, it is free.

Rand McNally Atlas of Western Civilization. This collection of over fifty full-color maps highlights social, political, and cross-cultural change and interaction from classical Greece and Rome to the postindustrial Western world. Each map is thoroughly indexed for fast reference. Available for $3.00 when packaged with the text.

The Bedford Glossary for European History. This handy supplement for the survey course gives students historically contextualized definitions for hundreds of terms—from *Abbasids* to *Zionism*—that they will encounter in lectures, reading, and exams. Available free when packaged with the text.

The Bedford Series in History and Culture. More than one hundred titles in this highly praised series combine first-rate scholarship, historical narrative, and important primary documents for undergraduate courses. Each book is brief, inexpensive, and focused on a specific topic or period. For a complete list of titles, visit bedfordstmartins.com/bshc. Package discounts are available.

Trade Books. Titles published by sister companies Hill and Wang; Farrar, Strauss and Giroux; Henry Holt and Company; St. Martin's Press; Picador; and Palgrave Macmillan are available at a 50 percent discount when packaged with Bedford/St. Martin's textbooks. For more information, visit bedfordstmartins.com/tradeup.

The Social Dimension of Western Civilization. Combining current scholarship with classic pieces, this reader's forty-eight secondary sources, compiled by Richard M. Golden, hook students with the fascinating and often surprising details of how everyday Western people worked, ate, played, celebrated, worshiped, married, procreated, fought, persecuted, and died. Package discounts are available.

The West in the Wider World: Sources and Perspectives. Edited by Richard Lim and David Kammerling Smith, the first college reader to focus on the central historical question "How did the West become the West?" offers a wealth of written and visual source materials that reveal the influence of non-European regions on the origins and development of Western Civilization. Package discounts are available.

A Pocket Guide to Writing in History. This portable and affordable reference tool by Mary Lynn Rampolla provides reading, writing, and research advice useful to students in all history courses. Concise yet comprehensive advice on approaching typical history assignments, developing critical reading skills, writing effective history papers, conducting research, using and documenting sources, and avoiding plagiarism — enhanced by practical tips and examples throughout — have made this slim reference a bestseller. Package discounts are available.

A Student's Guide to History. This complete guide provides the practical help students need to be successful in any history course. In addition to introducing students to the nature of the discipline, author Jules Benjamin teaches a wide range of skills from preparing for exams to approaching common writing assignments, and explains the research and documentation process with plentiful examples. Package discounts are available.

1
Origins

ca. 400,000–1100 B.C.E.

The civilization and cultures of the modern Western world, like great rivers, have many sources. These sources have flowed from many places and directions. Early peoples in western Europe developed numerous communities uniquely their own but also sharing some features. Groups developed their own social organizations and religious practices, and they mastered such diverse subjects as astronomy, mathematics, geometry, trigonometry, and engineering. The earliest of these peoples did not record their learning and lore in systems of writing. Their lives and customs are consequently largely lost to us.

Other early peoples confronted many of the same basic challenges as those in Europe. They also made progress, but they took the important step of recording their experiences in writing. The most enduring innovations occurred in the ancient Near East, a region that includes the lands bordering the Mediterranean's eastern shore, the Arabian peninsula, parts of northeastern Africa, and above all Mesopotamia, the area of modern Iraq. Fundamental to the development of Western civilization and culture was the invention of writing by the Sumerians, which allowed knowledge of the past to be preserved and facilitated the spread of learning, science, and literature. Ancient Near Eastern civilizations also produced the first written law codes, as well as religious concepts that still permeate daily life.

How do we know and understand these things? Before embarking on the study of Western history, it is necessary to ask what it is. Only then can the peoples and events of tens of thousands of years be placed into a coherent whole. ■

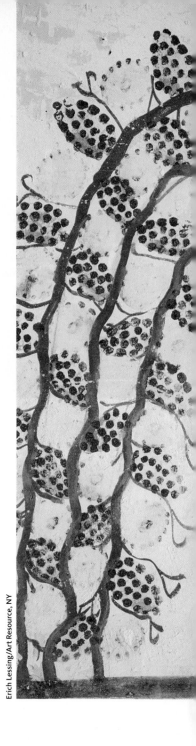

Life in Early Egypt. The lives of early Egyptians revolved around the seasons and their crops. This wall painting depicts workers picking bunches of grapes for winemaking.

CHAPTER PREVIEW

Understanding Western History
■ What factors are key to understanding the meaning of "the West" and Western civilization?

From Caves to Towns
■ How did early peoples evolve from bands of hunter-gatherers to settled farming communities?

Mesopotamian Civilization
■ What were some of the enduring accomplishments of Mesopotamian civilization?

The Spread of Mesopotamian Culture
■ How did the Babylonians unite Mesopotamia politically and culturally and spread that culture to the broader world?

Egypt, the Land of the Pharaohs, 3100–1200 B.C.E.
■ How did Egypt's geography contribute to the rise of a unique culture, and what was the role of the pharaoh in this society?

The Hittites and the End of an Era, ca. 1640–1100 B.C.E.
■ How did the Hittites rise to power, and how did they and other civilizations of the Near East fare in response to the attack of foreign invaders?

Understanding Western History

What factors are key to understanding the meaning of "the West" and Western civilization? ■

Most human groups have left some record of themselves. Some left artifacts, others pictures or signs, and still others written documents. In many of these records, groups set out distinctions between themselves and others. Some of these distinctions are between small groups such as neighboring tribes, some between countries and civilizations, and some between vast parts of the world. One of the most enduring of the latter are the ideas of "the West" and "the East."

Describing the West

What do we mean by "the West"? Everyone has an answer, but these answers vary widely. Ideas about the West and the distinction between West and East derived originally from the ancient Greeks. Greek civilization grew up in the shadow of earlier civilizations to the south and east of Greece, especially Egypt and Mesopotamia. Greeks defined themselves in relation to these more advanced cultures, which they saw as "Eastern." Greeks were also the first to use the word *Europe* for a geographic area, taking the word from the name of a minor goddess. They set Europe in opposition to "Asia" (also named for a minor goddess), by which they meant both what we now call Asia and what we call Africa. Later Europeans divided certain regions of the world into the "Near East" of the eastern Mediterranean, Arabian peninsula, and northeastern Africa and the "Far East" of Asia.

The Greeks passed this conceptualization on to the Romans, who saw themselves clearly as part of the West. For some Romans, Greece remained in the West, while other Romans came to view Greek traditions as vaguely "Eastern." To Romans, the East was more sophisticated and more advanced, but also decadent and somewhat immoral. Roman value judgments have continued to shape preconceptions, stereotypes, and views of differences between the West and the East—which were also called the "Occident" and the "Orient"—to this day. We can see them reflected in comments about the "mysterious East" and "oriental ways of thinking."

Greco-Roman ideas about the West were passed on to people who lived in western and northern Europe, who saw themselves as the inheritors of this classical tradition and thus as the West. When these Europeans established colonies outside of Europe beginning in the late fifteenth century, they regarded what they were doing as taking Western culture with them, even though many aspects of Western culture, such as Christianity, had actually originated in what Europeans by that point regarded as the East. With colonization, Western came to mean those cultures that included significant numbers of people of European ancestry, no matter where on the globe they were located.

In the early twentieth century educators and other leaders in the United States became worried that many people, especially young people, were becoming cut off from European intellectual and cultural traditions. They encouraged the establishment of college and university courses focusing on "Western civilization," the first of which was taught at Columbia University in 1919. In designing the course, the faculty included cultures that as far back as the ancient Greeks had been considered Eastern, such as Egypt and Mesopotamia, describing them as the "cradles of Western civilization." This conceptualization and the course spread to other colleges and universities, evolving into what became known as the introductory Western civilization course, the staple of historical instruction for generations of college students. After World War II divisions between the West and the East changed again. Now there was a new division between East and West within Europe, with Western coming to imply a capitalist economy and Eastern the Communist Eastern bloc. Thus, Japan became Western, and some Greek-speaking areas of Europe became Eastern. The collapse of communism in the Soviet Union and eastern Europe in the 1980s brought yet another refiguring, with much of eastern Europe joining the European Union, originally a Western organization.

At the beginning of the twenty-first century, "Western" still suggests a capitalist economy, but it also has certain cultural connotations, such as individualism and competition, which some see as negative and others as positive. Islamic radicals often describe their aims as an end to Western cultural, economic, and political influence, though Islam itself is generally described, along with Judaism and Christianity, as a Western monotheistic religion. Thus, throughout its long history, the meaning of "the West" has shifted, but in every era it has meant more than a geographical location.

What Is Western Civilization, and Why?

Just as the meaning of the word "Western" is shaped by culture, so is the meaning of the word "civilization." The word **civilization** comes from the Latin adjective *civilis,* which refers to a citizen, either a citizen of a town or of a larger political unit. In the ancient world,

civilization A large-scale system of human political, economic, and social organizations; civilizations include laws that govern, a code of manners and social conduct, and scientific, philosophical, and theological beliefs that explain the larger world.

residents of cities generally viewed themselves as more advanced and sopisticated than rural folk—a judgment that has not disappeared in today's world. They saw themselves as more "civilized" and those who lived outside cities as more backward and primitive.

This division between civilized and uncivilized was gradually extended to whole societies. Civilizations were those human societies in which political, economic, and social organizations operated on a large scale, not primarily through families and kin groups. Civilizations had cities, laws that governed human relationships, codes of manners and social conduct that regulated how people were to behave, and scientific, philosophical and theological beliefs that explained the larger world. Generally only societies that used writing were judged to be civilizations. Human societies in which people were nomadic or lived in small villages without formal laws, and in which traditions were passed down orally, were not regarded as civilizations. They were often seen as inferior by those who lived within civilizations, just as urban residents saw rural people as inferior.

The idea of a civilization came to mean more than a system of political and social organization. It also meant a particular way of thinking and believing, a particular style of art, and other facets of culture. Civilizations thus had different sizes. For example, when discussing the ancient city of Athens, some historians spoke of Athenian civilization and others Greek civilization. As discussed above, others came to view Athens as part of Western civilization, a very large division of human society.

Since the idea of Western civilization was first developed, people have debated its geographical extent and also debated what its core values are. Are there certain ideas, customs, concepts, and institutions that set Western civilization apart from other civilizations, and if so, when and how did these originate? How were these values and practices transmitted over space and time, and how did they change? No civilization stands alone, and each is influenced by its neighbors. Whatever Western civilization was—and is—it is shaped by interactions with other societies, cultures, and civilizations. Though "civilization" and "citizen" are related linguistically, the idea of civilization is much fuzzier than the narrower concept of citizen. It is so nebulous, in fact, that some historians have given up using broad terms like "Western civilization," but the idea that there are basic distinctions between the West and the rest of the world in terms of cultural values has been very powerful for thousands of years, and it still shapes the way many people view the world.

Chronology

ca. 400,000 B.C.E.	Primitive stone tools begin to be used
400,000–11,000 B.C.E.	Paleolithic period
11,000–4,000 B.C.E.	Neolithic period
ca. 7000 B.C.E.	Domestication of plants and animals
ca. 3100 B.C.E.	Unification of Upper and Lower Egypt
ca. 3000 B.C.E.	Establishment of first Mesopotamian cities; development of wheeled transport and cuneiform writing
3000–1600 B.C.E.	Erection of the Stonehenge monument
2500 B.C.E.	Scribal schools flourish in Sumer
2331 B.C.E.	Establishment of the Akkadian empire
ca. 2000 B.C.E.	Indo-Europeans arrive in the Near East
ca. 1800 B.C.E.	Hyksos people settle in the Nile Delta; Hittites expand eastward
1792–1750 B.C.E.	Hammurabi rules Babylon
1367–1350 B.C.E.	Akhenaten imposes monotheism in Egypt
ca. 1200–1000 B.C.E.	Sea Peoples destroy the Hittite and Egyptian empires

From Caves to Towns

How did early peoples evolve from bands of hunter-gatherers to settled farming communities? ▪

Virtually every year brings startling news about the path of human evolution. Humans evolved first in Africa and migrated from there around the world. By at least 400,000 B.C.E. humans were making basic stone tools, a technology that gave its name to the earliest period of human history, the **Paleolithic** (Old Stone) **period**, which lasted until about 11,000 B.C.E. The Paleolithic is thus by far the longest period of human history. During this era, people lived by gathering and hunting, adapting their tools and styles of living to every type of environment. About 11,000 B.C.E., people in some parts of the world

Paleolithic period The time between 400,000 and 11,000 B.C.E., when early peoples began making primitive stone tools, survived by hunting and gathering, and dwelled in temporary shelters.

Neolithic period The period between 11,000 and 4000 B.C.E., when the development of agriculture and the domestication of animals enabled peoples to establish permanent settlements.

LIVING IN THE PAST

ON SEPTEMBER 19, 1991, TWO GERMAN VACATIONERS climbing in the Italian Alps came upon a corpse lying face-down and covered in ice. Scientists determined that the Iceman, as the corpse is generally known, dates to the Neolithic period, having died 5,300 years ago. He was between twenty-five and thirty-five years old at the time of his death, and he stood about five feet two inches tall. An autopsy

revealed much about the man and his culture. The bluish tinge of his teeth showed a diet of milled grain, which proves that he came from an environment where crops were grown. The Iceman hunted as well as farmed: he was found with a bow and arrows and shoes of straw, and he wore a furry cap and a robe of animal skins that he had stitched together with thread that he had made from grass.

The equipment discovered with the Iceman demonstrates his mastery of several technologies. He carried a hefty copper ax, indicating a knowledge of metallurgy. He relied chiefly on archery to kill game. In his quiver were numerous wooden arrow shafts and two finished arrows. The arrows had flint heads, a sign of stoneworking, and feathers were attached with resin-like glue to the ends of the shafts. He knew the value of feathers to direct the arrows; thus he had mastered the basics of ballistics. His bow was made of yew, a relatively rare wood in central Europe that is among the best for archers.

Yet a mystery still surrounds the Iceman. When his body was first discovered, scholars assumed that he was a hapless traveler overtaken in a fierce snowstorm. But the autopsy found an arrowhead lodged under his left shoulder. The Iceman was not alone on his last day. Someone was with him, and that someone had shot him from below and behind. The Iceman is the victim in the first murder mystery of Western civilization, and the case will never be solved.

began settling into communities sustained by agriculture and domestic animals, beginning an era labeled the **Neolithic** (New Stone) **period**, which lasted until roughly 4000 B.C.E.

Paleolithic Life

Paleolithic peoples were gatherers and hunters, and they used pointed flaked stones for a wide variety of tasks. Most of their diet came from plants, supplemented by insects, shellfish, small animals caught in traps, and fish caught in nets. They did hunt large game, but hunting was difficult and less reliable as a food source. The most important element of early human success was flexibility and adaptability. (See "Living in the Past: The Iceman," above.)

The basic social unit of Paleolithic societies was probably the family, but family bonds were no doubt stronger and more extensive than those of families in modern, urban, industrialized societies. Paleolithic peoples depended on the extended family for cooperative work and mutual protection. The ties of kinship probably also extended beyond the family to the tribe, a group of families led by a patriarch, a dominant male who governed the group. Most tribes probably consisted of thirty to fifty people.

Group members had to cooperate to survive. There was probably some type of division of labor by sex, and also by age, with children and older people responsible for different tasks from those of adult men or women. Obtaining food was a constant preoccupation, but it was not a constant job, for hunter-gatherers generally

The artifacts found with the body tell scientists much about how the Iceman lived. The leather quiver with wooden arrows tipped with flint show that the Iceman worked with stone. The Iceman made his own ax, but bartered for the copper head, indicating a society beginning to rely more heavily on metal. His shoes, made with a twine framework stuffed with straw and covered with skin, indicate that he used all parts of the animals he hunted. (corpse: Courtesy, Roger Teissl; quiver: S.N.S./Sipa Press; ax and shoes: South Tyrol Museum of Archaeology, http://www.iceman.it)

QUESTIONS FOR ANALYSIS

1. What do these images demonstrate about the Iceman's knowledge of his environment?

2. What does the Iceman reveal about the society in which he lived?

need only about twenty hours a week to find food. Paleolithic peoples thus had time for sharing stories, ideas, and traditions.

Some of the most striking accomplishments of Paleolithic peoples were intellectual. They used reason to govern their actions. Thought, language, and cave paintings—the world's first art—permitted the lore and experience of the old to be passed on to the young. Paleolithic peoples developed the custom of burying their dead and leaving offerings with the body, perhaps in the belief that somehow life continued after death.

Neolithic Life

The real transformation of human life occurred when hunters and gatherers gave up their nomadic way of life to depend primarily on the grain they grew and the animals they domesticated. Agriculture made for a more stable and secure life. Neolithic peoples thus flourished, fashioning an energetic and creative era. They were responsible for many fundamental inventions and innovations that the modern world takes for granted. First, obviously, was systematic agriculture, the primary economic activity of the entire ancient world and the basis of all modern life. The settled routine of Neolithic farmers led to the evolution of towns and eventually cities. Farmers usually raised more food than they could consume, and their surpluses permitted larger and healthier populations. Since surpluses of food could also be bartered for other commodities, the Neolithic era witnessed the beginning of large-scale trade.

The transition to settled life also had a profound

impact on the family. The shared needs and pressures that make for strong extended-family ties in nomadic societies are less prominent in settled societies. Bonds to the extended family weakened. In towns and cities, the nuclear family—father, mother, and children—was more dependent on its immediate neighbors than on kinfolk.

At one time scholars thought that agriculture originated in the ancient Near East and gradually spread elsewhere. Contemporary work, however, points to a more complex pattern of development. For unknown reasons, people in various parts of the world all seem to have begun domesticating plants and animals at roughly the same time, around 7000 B.C.E. Four main points of origin have been identified. In the Near East, people at sites as far apart as Tepe Yahya in modern Iran, Jarmo in Iraq, Jericho in Palestine, and Hacilar in modern Turkey raised wheat, barley, peas, and lentils. They also kept herds of sheep, pigs, and possibly goats. In western Africa, Neolithic farmers domesticated many plants, including millet, sorghum, and yams. In northeastern China, peoples of the Yangshao culture developed techniques of field agriculture, animal husbandry, pottery making, and bronze metallurgy. Innovations in the New World were equally striking. Indians in Central and South America domesticated a host of plants, among them corn, beans, and squash. From these far-flung areas, knowledge of farming techniques spread to still other regions.

Once people began to rely on farming for their livelihood, they settled in permanent villages and built houses. Early farmers chose places where the water supply was constant and adequate for their crops and flocks. At first, villages were small, consisting of a few households. As the population expanded and prospered, villages usually developed into towns. Towns also became vulnerable to outside attack, and the townspeople responded by building walls. Besides providing protection, walls permitted a more secure and stable way of life than that of the nomad. They also prove that towns grew in size, population, and wealth, for these fortifications were so large that only a big, dependable labor force would have raised them. They also indicate that towns were developing social and political organizations. The walls were the work of the whole community, and they would have been impossible without central planning.

Prosperity had two other momentous consequences. First, grain became an article of commerce. The farming community traded surplus grain for items it could not produce itself. The community thus obtained raw materials such as precious gems and metals. The early towns in Mesopotamia imported copper from the north, and eventually copper replaced stone tools and weapons. Trade also brought Neolithic communities in touch with one another, making possible the spread of ideas and techniques.

Second, agricultural surplus made possible the division of labor. It freed some members of the community from the necessity of raising food. Some men and women devoted their attention to making the new stone tools farming demanded—hoes and sickles for field work, and mortars and pestles for grinding the grain. Other artisans began to shape clay into pottery vessels, which were used to store grain, wine, and oil, and which served as kitchen utensils. Still other artisans wove baskets and cloth. People who could specialize in particular crafts produced more and better goods than any single individual could.

Prosperity and stable conditions nurtured other innovations and discoveries. Neolithic farmers improved their tools and agricultural techniques. They domesticated bigger, stronger animals, such as the bull and the horse, to work for them. To harness the power of these animals, they invented tools like the plow, which came into use by 3000 B.C.E. The first plows had wooden shares and could break only light soils, but they were far more efficient than stone hoes. By 3000 B.C.E. the wheel had also been invented, and farmers devised ways of hitching bulls and horses to wagons. Using animals and machines to do a greater proportion of the work enabled Neolithic farmers to raise more food more efficiently and easily than ever before.

The development of systematic agriculture in the Neolithic period was a fundamental turning point in the history of civilization. Farming gave rise to stable societies that enjoyed considerable prosperity. It made possible an enormous increase in population. Some inhabitants of the budding towns turned their attention to the production of goods that made life more comfortable. Settled circumstances and a certain amount of leisure made the accumulation and spread of knowledge easier. Finally, sustained farming prepared the way for urban life.

Many scholars consider walled towns the basic feature of Neolithic society. Yet numerous examples prove that some Neolithic towns existed without stone or mud-brick walls. For instance, at Stonehenge in England the natives erected wooden palisades for safety. At Unteruhldingen in Germany the community established its unwalled town just offshore on a lake and let nature defend them. The most concentrated collection of walled towns is found in Mesopotamia. Since generations of archaeologists and historians have concentrated their attention on this region, they have considered it typical. Yet they have failed to properly appreciate circumstances elsewhere. The fundamental point about the Neolithic period is that men and women created stable communities based on agriculture. They defended their towns in various ways by common consent and effort. This organized communal effort is far more important than the types of defenses they built.

Stonehenge Megaliths (large stone structures) like the one shown here at Stonehenge can still be seen across the British Isles and in France. A Neolithic society laboriously built this circle to mark the passing of the seasons. (© Frank Siteman/Science Faction/Corbis)

Stonehenge presents an example of how the unique context of a Neolithic group influenced the communal efforts of its people. Remnants of this Neolithic society can still be seen today in industrial England. Named after the famous stone circle built approximately 3000–1600 B.C.E., this culture spread throughout the British isles and northwestern France. Because the people who built Stonehenge left no written records, the magnificent circle provides only silent insights into their Neolithic culture.

Like other similar structures, Stonehenge is a large ring of huge worked stones weighing many tons. It marks the movement of the sun, moon, and stars. It was also a place of ritual ceremony celebrating the renewal of life. Just as the celestial bodies had their annual cycles, the Stonehenge people had their cycles of life and death — and continuity.

The construction of the great circle tells much about the people who built it. Only a relatively large and stable population could provide a workforce able to devote so many years to its erection. The people first had to quarry the stones and in many cases haul them over long distances. They crossed their neighbors' lands, which indicates shared customs and beliefs. Other circles such as at nearby Avebury housed religious centers in the shape of two large inner circles. Artifacts discovered there suggest that the people worshiped an earth-goddess who symbolized life. She brought fertility to the land, a fundamental need for an agricultural society. Many other structures contained the simple homes of permanent settlers, and still others were fortified enclosures that protected

Well-established agricultural area
Megalithic monument

North Sea

Stonehenge

ATLANTIC OCEAN

The British Isles, ca. 2500 B.C.E.

the inhabitants. These sites served various social functions, and they reveal the existence of relatively prosperous, well-organized, and centrally led communities. They also prove cooperation among similarly constituted groups. None of them individually could have built these monuments.

The people themselves lived in the countryside in communities of perhaps fifty families. They farmed the land, kept animals, and made their own pottery. As in other early societies, headmen and groups of elders probably made up a simple communal leadership that discussed matters with members of the community to make decisions. Skeletons show that the villagers' average height was about five feet five inches, and their build slender. They lived an average of thirty-five years and suffered from various diseases. Broken bones prove their hard labor. Yet the Stonehenge people also knew how to mend bones and had some rudimentary knowledge of medicine.

Despite short lives and hard work, the Stonehenge people enjoyed a surprisingly rich intellectual life. Their stone circles alone prove that they had mastered astronomy, mathematics, and engineering. They intimately knew their environment and cherished a simple religion. Their society enjoyed long peaceful periods in which to live and work. Most notably, these people used part of their time over many years to preserve and pass along to future generations the detailed building techniques and mathematics to raise Stonehenge. The elders likewise taught the young the traditions and lore of the past. Yet despite their many wonderful achievements, the Stonehenge people did not develop writing. Without literacy they failed to hand their legacy to others beyond their own culture. Thus all of their learning died with them. Literacy proved one of the supreme advances in history. That breakthrough came in Mesopotamia.

Mesopotamian Civilization

What were some of the enduring accomplishments of Mesopotamian civilization? ■

The origins of Western civilization are generally traced to an area that is today not seen as part of the West: Mesopotamia (mehs-oh-puh-TAY-mee-uh), the Greek name for the land between the Euphrates (you-FRAY-teez) and Tigris (TIGH-gris) Rivers. There the arid climate confronted people with the hard problem of farming with scant water supplies. Farmers learned to irrigate their land and later to drain it to prevent the buildup of salt in the soil. **Irrigation** on a large scale, like building stone circles in western Europe, demanded organized group effort. That in turn underscored the need for strong central authority to direct the effort. This corporate spirit led to governments in which individuals subordinated some of their particular concerns to broader interests. These factors made urban life possible in a demanding environment. By about 3000 B.C.E. the Sumerians, whose origins are mysterious, established the first cities in the southernmost part of Mesopotamia, which became known as Sumer (Map 1.1). The fundamental innovation of the Sumerians was the creation of writing, which helped unify this society culturally and opened it to the broader world that we still share today.

irrigation A system of watering land and draining it to prevent buildup of salt in the soil; the solution to the problem of arid climates and scant water supplies.

Environment and Mesopotamian Development

From the outset, geography had a profound effect on the evolution of Mesopotamian civilization. In this region agriculture is possible only with irrigation. Consequently, the Sumerians and later civilizations built their cities along the Tigris and Euphrates Rivers and their branches. In addition to water, the rivers supplied fish, a major element of the Sumer diet. The rivers also provided reeds and clay, which the Sumerians used as building materials. Since this entire area lacks stone, mud brick became the primary building block of Mesopotamian architecture.

Although the rivers sustained life, they acted simultaneously as a powerful restraining force, especially on Sumerian political development. They literally made

Sumer a geographical maze. Between the rivers, streams, and irrigation canals stretched open desert or swamp, where hostile nomadic tribes often roamed. Communication between cities was difficult and at times dangerous. City was isolated from city, each in its own locale. Thus each Sumerian city became a state, independent of the others and protective of its independence. Any city-state that tried to unify the country was resisted by the others. As a result, the political history of Sumer is one of almost constant warfare. The experience of the city of Nippur is an example of how bad conditions could become. At one point in its history, Nippur was conquered eighteen times in twenty-four years. Although Sumer was eventually unified, unification came late and was always tenuous.

The harsh environment fostered a grim, even pessimistic, spirit among the Sumerians and other Mesopotamians. They especially feared the ravages of flood. The Tigris can bring quick devastation, as it did to Baghdad in 1831, when flood waters destroyed seven thousand homes in a single night. Similar tragedies occurred often in antiquity. The chronicle of King Hammurabi (see page 17) recorded years when floods wiped out whole cities. Vulnerability to natural disaster deeply influenced Mesopotamian religious beliefs.

The Mesopotamians considered natural catastrophes the work of the gods. The Sumerians described their chief god, Enlil, as "the raging flood which has no rival." The gods, they believed, used nature to punish the Mesopotamians. According to the myth of the Deluge, which gave rise to the biblical story of Noah:

> A flood will sweep over the cult-centers;
> To destroy the seed of mankind . . .
> Is the decision, the word of the assembly of the gods.[1]

The myth of Atrahasis describes the gods' annoyance at the prosperity of mankind and tells how Enlil suggests sending a drought to destroy human life:

> Oppressive has become the clamor of mankind.
> By their uproar they prevent sleep.
> Let the flour be cut off for the people,
> In their bellies let the greens be too few.[2]

In the face of harsh environmental conditions, the Mesopotamians considered themselves weak and insignificant as compared to the gods. In response to natural disaster, people could only pray to the gods for relief.

The Invention of Writing and the First Schools

The origins of writing probably go back to the ninth millennium B.C.E., when Near Eastern peoples used clay tokens as counters for record keeping. By the fourth millennium, people had realized that drawing pictures of the tokens on clay was simpler than making tokens. This breakthrough in turn suggested that more information

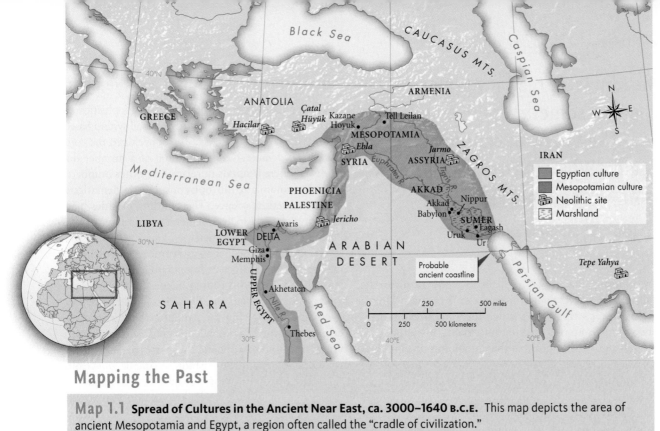

Map 1.1 Spread of Cultures in the Ancient Near East, ca. 3000–1640 B.C.E. This map depicts the area of ancient Mesopotamia and Egypt, a region often called the "cradle of civilization."

ANALYZING THE MAP What geographical features of this region naturally suggest the direction in which civilization spread?

CONNECTIONS Why did Mesopotamia and Egypt earn the title of "cradle of civilization"? Why did the first cultures of Mesopotamia spread farther than the culture of Egypt?

To complete this activity online, go to the Online Study Guide at bedfordstmartins.com/mckaywest.

could be conveyed by adding pictures of still other objects. The result was a complex system of pictographs in which each sign pictured an object. These pictographs were the forerunners of a Sumerian form of writing known as **cuneiform** (kyou-NEE-uh-form), from the Latin term for "wedge shaped," used to describe the strokes of the stylus, or pen.

How did this pictographic system work, and how did it evolve around 3000 B.C.E. into cuneiform writing? At first, if a scribe wanted to indicate a star, he simply drew a picture of it (line A of Figure 1.1) on a wet clay tablet, which became rock-hard when baked. This complicated and laborious system had serious limitations. It could not represent abstract ideas or combinations of ideas.

Scribes overcame this problem by combining signs to express meaning. To refer to a slave woman, for example, the scribe used the sign for woman (line B) and the sign for mountain (line C)—literally, "mountain woman" (line D). Because the Sumerians regularly obtained their slave women from the mountains, this combination of signs was easily understandable.

The next step was to simplify the system. Instead of drawing pictures, scribes developed signs that represented ideas. Thus the signs became *ideograms*: they symbolized ideas. The sign for star could also be used to indicate heaven, sky, or even god. The real breakthrough came when the scribes started using signs to represent sounds. For instance, two parallel wavy lines indicated the word *a* or "water" (line E). Besides water, the word *a* in Sumerian also meant "in." The word *in* expresses a

cuneiform Sumerian form of writing; the term describes the wedge-shaped strokes of the stylus.

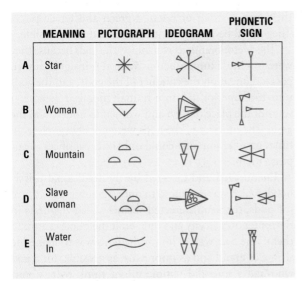

Figure 1.1 Sumerian Writing

❝ My headmaster read my tablet, said: 'There is something missing,' caned me. The fellow in charge of silence said: 'Why did you talk without permission,' caned me. **❞**

—ANONYMOUS SUMERIAN SCRIBE

relationship that is very difficult to represent pictorially. Instead of trying to invent a sign to mean "in," some clever scribe used the sign for water because the two words sounded alike in Sumerian. This phonetic use of signs made possible the combining of signs to convey abstract ideas.

The Sumerian system of writing was so complicated that only professional scribes mastered it, and even they had to study it for many years. By 2500 B.C.E. scribal schools flourished throughout Sumer. Most students came from wealthy families and were male. Each school had a master, teachers, and monitors. Discipline was strict, and students were caned for sloppy work and misbehavior. One graduate of a scribal school had few fond memories of the joy of learning:

> My headmaster read my tablet, said:
> "There is something missing," caned me.
>
> . . .
>
> The fellow in charge of silence said:
> "Why did you talk without permission," caned me.
> The fellow in charge of the assembly said:
> "Why did you stand at ease without permission,"
> caned me.[3]

The Sumerian system of schooling set the educational standards for Mesopotamian culture; the Akkadians and, later, the Babylonians adopted its practices and techniques. Mesopotamian education always had a practical side because of the economic and administrative importance of scribes. Most scribes took administrative positions in the temple or palace, where they kept records of business transactions, accounts, and inventories. But scribal schools did not limit their curriculum to business affairs; they were also centers of culture and scholarship. Topics of study included mathematics, botany, and linguistics. Advanced students copied and studied the classics of Sumerian literature. Talented students and learned scribes wrote compositions of their own. As a result, many literary, mathematical, and religious texts survive today, giving a full picture of Mesopotamian intellectual and spiritual life.

polytheism The worship of several gods; this was the tradition of the Mesopotamian and Egyptian religions.

Mesopotamian Thought and Religion

The Mesopotamians made significant and sophisticated advances in mathematics using a numerical system based on units of sixty, ten, and six. They developed the concept of place value—that the value of a number depends on where it stands in relation to other numbers. The Mesopotamians did not consider mathematics a purely theoretical science. The building of cities, palaces, temples, and canals demanded practical knowledge of geometry and trigonometry.

Mesopotamian medicine was a combination of magic, prescriptions, and surgery. Mesopotamians believed that demons and evil spirits caused sickness and that magic spells could drive them out. Physicians could help force a demon out by giving the patient a foul-tasting prescription. As medical knowledge grew, some prescriptions were found to work and thus were true medicines. In this slow but empirical fashion, medicine grew from superstition to an early form of rational treatment.

Mesopotamian thought had a profound impact in theology and religion. The Sumerians originated many beliefs, and their successors added to them. The Mesopotamians practiced **polytheism**, that is, they believed that many gods ran the world. They did not consider all gods and goddesses equal. Some deities had very important jobs, taking care of music, law, sex, and victory, while others had lesser tasks, overseeing leatherworking and basket weaving. The god in charge of metalworking, for example, was hardly the equal of the god of wisdom.

Mesopotamian gods were powerful and immortal, but otherwise lived their lives much as human beings lived theirs. Unlike men and women, they could make themselves invisible, but like humans, they celebrated with food and drink, and they raised families. They enjoyed their own Garden of Eden, a green and fertile place. They could be irritable, vindictive, and irresponsible.

The Mesopotamians worshiped the gods because they were mighty. Human beings were too insignificant to pass judgment on the conduct of the gods, and the gods were too superior to honor human morals. Likewise, it was not the place of men and women to understand the gods. The motives of the gods were not always clear. In times of affliction, one could only offer sacrifices to appease them.

Encouraged and directed by the traditional priesthood, which was dedicated to understanding the ways of the gods, the people erected shrines called ziggurats in the center of each city and then built their houses around them. The best way to honor the gods was to make the shrine as grand and as impressive as possible, for a god who had a splendid temple might think twice about sending floods to destroy the city.

The Mesopotamians had many myths to account for the creation of the universe. According to one Sumerian myth (echoed in Genesis, the first book of the Bible), only the primeval sea existed at first. The sea produced heaven and earth, which were united. Heaven and earth gave birth to Enlil, who separated them and made possible the creation of the other gods. The later Babylonian culture (page 16) had similar beliefs. In the beginning was the primeval sea, the goddess Tiamat, who gave birth to the gods. When Tiamat tried to destroy the gods, Marduk, the chief god of the Babylonians, proceeded to kill her and divide her body and thus created the sky and earth. These myths are the earliest known attempts to answer the question, "How did it all begin?"

In addition to myths, the Sumerians produced the first epic poem, the *Epic of Gilgamesh* (GIL-guh-mesh), which evolved as a reworking of at least five earlier myths. (See "Listening to the Past: Gilgamesh's Quest for Immortality," page 14.) An epic poem is a narration of the achievements, the labors, and sometimes the failures of heroes that embodies a people's or a nation's conception of its own past. Historians can use epic poems to learn about various aspects of a society, and to that extent epics can be used as historical sources. The Sumerian epic recounts the wanderings of Gilgamesh—the semihistorical king of Uruk (OO-rook)—and his search for eternal life. The *Epic of Gilgamesh* shows the Sumerians grappling with such enduring questions as life and death, humankind and deity, and immortality. Despite its great antiquity, it addresses questions of importance to people today.

Sumerian Social and Gender Divisions

Sumerian society was a complex arrangement of freedom and dependence, and its members were divided into four categories: nobles, free clients of the nobility, commoners, and slaves. Nobles consisted of the king and his family, the chief priests, and high palace officials. Generally, the king rose to power as a war leader; elected by the citizenry, he established a regular army, trained it, and led it into battle. The might of the king and the frequency of warfare quickly made him the supreme figure in the city, and kingship soon became hereditary. The symbol of royal status was the palace, which rivaled the temple in grandeur.

The king and the lesser nobility held extensive tracts of land that were, like the estates of the temple, worked by slaves and clients. Clients were free men and women who were dependent on the nobility. In return for their labor, the clients received small plots of land to work for themselves. Although this arrangement assured the clients of a livelihood, the land they worked remained the possession of the nobility or the temple. Thus, not only did the nobles control most—and doubtless the best—land, but they also commanded the obedience of a huge segment of society. They were the dominant force in Mesopotamian society.

Commoners were free and independent of the nobility. They belonged to large families that owned land in their own right. Commoners could sell their land if the family approved, and even the king could not legally take their land without their approval. Male commoners, unlike women, had a voice in the political affairs of the city and full protection under the law.

At the bottom rung of society were slaves. Some Sumerian slaves were prisoners of war and criminals who had lost their freedom as punishment for their crimes. Still others served as slaves to repay debts. These were more fortunate than the others, because the law

Ziggurat The ziggurat is a stepped tower that dominated the landscape of the Sumerian city. Surrounded by a walled enclosure, it stood as a monument to the gods. Monumental stairs led to the top, where sacrifices were offered for the welfare of the community. (Charles & Josette Lemars/Corbis)

LISTENING TO THE PAST

The human desire to escape the grip of death, to achieve immortality, is one of the oldest wishes of all peoples. The Sumerian Epic of Gilgamesh *is the earliest recorded treatment of this topic. The oldest elements of the epic go back at least to the third millennium* B.C.E. *According to tradition, Gilgamesh was a king of Uruk whom the Sumerians, Babylonians, and Assyrians considered a hero-king and a god. In the story, Gilgamesh and his friend Enkidu set out to attain immortality and join the ranks of the gods. They attempt to do so by performing wondrous feats against fearsome agents of the gods, who are determined to thwart them.*

During their quest Enkidu dies. Gilgamesh, more determined than ever to become immortal, begins seeking anyone who might tell him how to do so. His journey involves the effort not only to escape from death but also to reach an understanding of the meaning of life.

The passage begins with Enkidu speaking of a dream that foretells his own death.

" Listen, my friend [Gilgamesh], this is the dream I dreamed last night. The heavens roared, and earth rumbled back an answer; between them I stood before an awful being, the sombre-faced manbird; he had directed on me his purpose. His was a vampire face, his foot was a lion's foot, his hand was an eagle's talon. He fell on me and his claws were in my hair, he held me fast and I smothered; then he transformed me so that my arms became wings covered with feathers. He turned his stare towards me, and he led me away to the palace of Irkalla, the Queen of Darkness [the goddess of the underworld; in other words, an agent of death], to the house from which none who enters ever returns, down the road from which there is no coming back. **"**

At this point Enkidu dies, whereupon Gilgamesh sets off on his own. During his travels he meets with Siduri, the wise and good-natured goddess of wine, who gives him the following advice.

" Gilgamesh, where are you hurrying to? You will never find that life for which you are looking. When the gods created man they allotted to him death, but life they retained in their own keeping. As for you, Gilgamesh, fill your belly with good things; day and night, night and day, dance and be merry, feast and rejoice. Let your clothes be fresh, bathe yourself in water, cherish the little child that holds your hand, and make your wife happy in your embrace; for this too is the lot of man. **"**

Ignoring Siduri's advice, Gilgamesh continues his journey, until he finds the god Utnapishtim (oot-nuh-PISH-tim). Like Gilgamesh, he was once a mortal, but the gods so favored him that they put him in an eternal paradise. Gilgamesh puts to Utnapishtim the question that is the reason for his quest.

" Oh, father Utnapishtim, you who have entered the assembly of the gods, I wish to question you concerning the living and the dead, how shall I find the life for which I am searching?

Utnapishtim said, "There is no permanence. Do we build a house to stand forever, do we seal a contract to hold for all time? Do brothers divide an inheritance to keep forever, does the floodtime of rivers endure? . . . What is there between the master and the servant when both have fulfilled their doom? When the Anunnaki [the gods of the underworld], the judges, come together, and Mammetun [the goddess of fate] the mother of destinies, together they decree the fates of men. Life and death they allot but the day of death they do not disclose.

---

required that they be freed after three years. But all slaves were subject to whatever treatment their owners might mete out. They could be beaten and even branded. Yet they received at least some legal protection. Slaves engaged in trade and made profits. They could borrow money, and many slaves were able to buy their freedom.

Each of these social categories included both men and women, but their experiences were not the same, for Sumerian society made clear distinctions based on gender. Sumerian society—and all Western societies that followed, until very recently—was **patriarchal** (PAY-tree-AR-kuhl), a system in which most power rests with older adult men. The patriarch of a tribe led the families that made up the tribe, but he cooperated with the heads of other related families. He was supposed to govern wisely and in accordance with custom and family tradition. A good patriarch directed family affairs justly. All members of the tribe

patriarchal Societies in which most power is held by older adult men, especially those from the elite groups.

Then Gilgamesh said to Utnapishtim the Faraway, "I look at you now, Utnapishtim, and your appearance is no different from mine; there is nothing strange in your features. I thought I should find you like a hero prepared for battle, but you lie here taking your ease on your back. Tell me truly, how was it that you came to enter the company of the gods and to possess everlasting life?" Utnapishtim said to Gilgamesh, "I shall reveal to you a mystery, I shall tell you a secret of the gods." **"**

Utnapishtim then tells Gilgamesh of a time when the great god Enlil had become angered with the Sumerians and encouraged the other gods to wipe out humanity. The god Ea, however, warned Utnapishtim about the gods' decision to send a great flood to destroy the Sumerians. He commanded Utnapishtim to build a boat big enough to hold his family, various artisans, and all animals in order to survive the flood that was to come. Although Enlil was infuriated by the Sumerians' survival, Ea rebuked him. Then Enlil relented and blessed Utnapishtim with eternal paradise. After telling the story, Utnapishtim foretells Gilgamesh's fate.

"Utnapishtim said, "...The destiny was fulfilled which the father of the gods, Enlil of the mountain, had decreed for Gilgamesh: In netherearth the darkness will show him a light: of mankind, all that are known, none will leave a monument for generations to compare with his. The heroes, the wise men, like the new moon have their waxing and waning. Men will say, Who has ever ruled with might and power like his? As in the dark month, the month of shadows, so without him there is no light. O Gilgamesh, this was the meaning of your dream [of immortality]. You were given the kingship, such was your destiny, everlasting life was not your destiny. Because of this do not be sad at heart, do not be grieved or oppressed; he [Enlil] has given you power to bind and to loose, to be the darkness and the light of mankind. He has given unexampled supremacy over the people, victory in battle from which no fugitive returns, in forays and assaults from which there is no going back. But do not abuse

Gilgamesh from a decorative panel of a lyre unearthed at the Sumerian city of Ur. (The University Museum, University of Pennsylvania, neg. T4-108)

this power, deal justly with your servants in the palace, deal justly before the face of the Sun." **"**

Source: *The Epic of Gilgamesh*, translated with an introduction by N. K. Sanders. Penguin Classics 1960, Third edition, 1972, pp. 89–116. Copyright © N. K. Sanders, 1960, 1964, 1972. Used with permission of Penguin Group (UK).

QUESTIONS FOR ANALYSIS

1. What does the *Epic of Gilgamesh* reveal about Sumerian attitudes toward the gods and human beings?
2. At the end of his quest, did Gilgamesh achieve immortality? If so, what was the nature of that immortality?
3. What does the epic tell us about Sumerian views of the nature of human life? Where do human beings fit into the cosmic world?

and family had various rights and responsibilities. Everyone had a recognized place in the social order. The patriarch generally provided all members with a secure family life.

Scholars debate the origins of patriarchy, for a hierarchy based on gender was already in place by the time the first written records appear. It may have been linked to the private ownership of property for agriculture. Men generally did the plowing and cared for animals, which led to boys' being favored over girls for the work

they could do for their parents while young and the support they could provide in their parents' old age. Boys became the normal inheritors of family land. Women could sometimes inherit if there were no sons in a family, but they did not gain the political rights that came with land ownership for men.

The city-states that developed in the ancient Middle East, beginning with Sumer, further heightened gender distinctions. Sumer was dominated by hereditary aristocracies, whose members became concerned with

Sumerian Harpist A seated woman plays a simple harp. Her fashionable dress and hat indicate that she is playing at the royal court. Other scenes from art prove that music played a vital part in the lives of all Sumerians. (Erich Lessing/ Art Resource, NY)

maintaining the distinction between themselves and the majority of the population, and by male property owners who wanted to be sure the children their wives bore were theirs. These concerns led to attempts to control women's reproduction. Laws governing sexual relations and marriage practices set up a very unequal relationship between spouses. In most states, laws mandated that women be virgins on marriage and imposed strict punishment for a married woman's adultery; sexual relations outside of marriage on the part of husbands were not considered adultery. Concern with family honor thus became linked to women's sexuality in a way that it was not for men; men's honor revolved around their work activities and, for more prominent families, around their performance of public duties, including keeping written records, in the expanding government bureaucracies.

These economic and political developments were accompanied and supported by cultural norms and religious concepts that heightened gender distinctions. In some places, heavenly hierarchies came to reflect those on earth, with the gods arranged in a hierarchy dominated by a single male god, who was viewed as the primary creator of life. Because other hierarchies such as those of the hereditary aristocracy privileged the women connected to powerful or wealthy men, women did not see themselves as part of a coherent group and often supported the institutions and intellectual structures that subordinated them.

The Spread of Mesopotamian Culture

How did the Babylonians unite Mesopotamia politically and culturally and spread that culture to the broader world? ▪

The Sumerians established the basic social, economic, and intellectual patterns of Mesopotamia, but the Semites played a large part in spreading Sumerian culture far beyond the boundaries of Mesopotamia. The interaction of the Sumerians and Semites, in fact, gives one of the very first glimpses of peoples of different origins coming together. The outcome was the evolution of a new culture that consisted of two or more old parts. In 2331 B.C.E. the Semitic chieftain Sargon conquered Sumer and created the Akkadian empire. The symbol of his triumph was a new capital, the city of Akkad (AH-kahd). Sargon, the first "world conqueror," led his armies to the Persian Gulf. Although his empire lasted only a few generations, it spread Mesopotamian culture throughout the Fertile Crescent. This legacy would be carried on by the Babylonians, who under Hammurabi would unite Mesopotamia politically and culturally.

The question is why Mesopotamian culture had such an immediate and wide appeal. In the first place, it was successful and enjoyed the prestige of its success. Newcomers wanted to find a respectable place in this old and venerated culture. It also provided an easy means of communication among people on a broad scale. Culture ignores borders. Despite local variations, so much common ground existed that similar political and economic institutions, exchange of ideas and religious beliefs, methods of writing, and a shared etiquette served as links among all who embraced Mesopotamian culture.

The Triumph of Babylon

Although the empire of Sargon was extensive, it was short-lived, and within two hundred years it collapsed. The Akkadians, too, failed to solve the problems posed by Mesopotamia's geography and population pattern. It was thus left to the Babylonians to unite the city-states of Mesopotamia politically and culturally.

The Babylonians were Amorites (AM-uh-rites), a Semitic people who had migrated from Arabia and settled on the site of Babylon along the middle Euphrates, where that river runs close to the Tigris. Babylon enjoyed an excellent geographical position and was ideally suited to be the capital of Mesopotamia. It dominated trade on the Tigris and Euphrates Rivers: all commerce to and from Sumer and Akkad had to pass by its walls. It also looked beyond Mesopotamia. Babylonian merchants followed the Tigris north to Assyria (uh-SEER-ee-uh) and Anatolia. The Euphrates led merchants to Syria, Palestine,

Sargon of Akkad This bronze head, with elaborately worked hair and beard, portrays the great conqueror Sargon of Akkad. The eyes were originally inlaid with precious jewels, which have since been gouged out. This head was found in the ruins of the Assyrian capital of Nineveh, where it had been taken as loot. (Bildarchiv Hansmann/Interfoto)

lonians made their own contribution to Mesopotamian culture—a culture vibrant enough to maintain its identity while assimilating new influences. Hammurabi's conquests and the activity of Babylonian merchants spread this enriched culture north to Anatolia and west to Syria and Palestine.

Life Under Hammurabi

One of Hammurabi's most memorable accomplishments was the proclamation of a law code that offers a wealth of information about daily life in Mesopotamia. Hammurabi's was not the first law code in Mesopotamia; the earliest goes back to about 2100 B.C.E. Like the codes of the earlier lawgivers, **Hammurabi's law code** proclaimed that he issued his laws on divine authority "to establish law and justice in the language of the land, thereby promoting the welfare of the people." Hammurabi's code inflicted such penalties as mutilation, whipping, and burning. Despite its severity, a spirit of justice and a sense of responsibility pervade the code. Hammurabi genuinely felt that his duty was to govern the Mesopotamians as righteously as possible.

The Code of Hammurabi has two striking characteristics. First, the law differed according to the social status and gender of the offender. Nobles were not punished as harshly as commoners, nor commoners as harshly as slaves. Certain actions that were crimes for women were not crimes for men. Second, the code demanded that the punishment fit the crime. It called for "an eye for an eye, and a tooth for a tooth," at least among equals. However, a noble who destroyed the eye of a commoner or slave could pay a fine instead of losing his own eye. Otherwise, as long as criminal and victim shared the same social status, the victim could demand exact vengeance.

> **Hammurabi's law code** A proclamation in the language of the land issued by the Babylonian king Hammurabi to establish law and justice; it inflicted harsh punishments, but was pervaded by a sense of responsibility to the people.

Hammurabi's code began with legal procedure. There were no public prosecutors or district attorneys, so individuals brought their own complaints before the court. Each side had to produce written documents or witnesses to support its case. In cases of murder, the accuser had to prove the defendant guilty; any accuser who failed to do so was put to death. This strict law was designed to prevent people from lodging groundless charges. Another procedural regulation covered the conduct of judges. Once a judge had rendered a verdict, he could not change it. In this way, the code tried to guarantee a fair trial and a just verdict.

The code suggests that Mesopotamians were worried about witchcraft and sorcery. Anyone accused of witchcraft, even if the charges were not proved, underwent an ordeal by water. The defendant was thrown into the Euphrates, which was considered the instrument of the

and the Mediterranean. The city grew great because of its commercial importance and sound leadership.

Babylon was fortunate to have a farseeing and able king, Hammurabi (hahm-moo-RAH-bee) (r. 1792–1750 B.C.E.). Hammurabi set out to do three things: make Babylon secure, unify Mesopotamia, and make Babylon the center of Mesopotamian civilization. The first two he accomplished by conquering Assyria in the north and Sumer and Akkad in the south. Then he turned to his third goal.

Politically, Hammurabi consolidated his power by utilizing the Semitic concept of the tribal chieftain and the Sumerian idea of urban kingship. Culturally, he encouraged the spread of myths that explained how Marduk (MAHR-dook), the god of Babylon, had been elected king of the gods by the other Mesopotamian deities. Hammurabi's success in making Marduk the god of all Mesopotamians made Babylon the religious center of Mesopotamia. Through Hammurabi's genius the Baby-

gods. A defendant who sank was guilty; a defendant who floated was innocent.

Consumer protection is not a modern idea; it goes back to Hammurabi's day. Merchants had to guarantee the quality of their goods and services. A boat builder who did sloppy work had to repair the boat at his own expense. A boatman who lost the owner's boat or sank someone else's boat replaced it and its cargo. House builders guaranteed their work with their lives. If inhabitants died in a house collapse, the builder was put to death. A merchant who tried to increase the interest rate on a loan forfeited the entire amount. Hammurabi's laws tried to ensure that consumers got what they paid for and paid a just price.

Because farming was essential to Mesopotamian life, Hammurabi's code dealt extensively with agriculture. Tenants faced severe penalties for neglecting the land or not working it at all. Since irrigation was essential to grow crops, tenants had to keep the canals and ditches in good repair. Otherwise the land would be subject to floods, and farmers would face crippling losses. Anyone whose neglect of the canals resulted in damaged crops had to bear all the expense of the lost crops. Those tenants who could not pay the costs were forced into slavery.

Hammurabi gave careful attention to marriage and the family. As elsewhere in the Near East, marriage had aspects of a business agreement. The prospective groom or his father and the father of the future bride arranged everything. The groom offered the father a bridal gift, usually money. If the man and his bridal gift were acceptable, the father provided his daughter with a dowry. After marriage the dowry belonged to the woman (although the husband normally administered it) and was a means of protecting her rights and status. Once the two men agreed on financial matters, they drew up a contract; no marriage was considered legal without one. Either party could break off the marriage, but not without paying a stiff penalty. Fathers often contracted marriages while their children were still young, and once contracted, the children were considered to be wed even if they did not live together.

The wife was expected to be rigorously faithful. The penalty for adultery, defined as sex between a married woman and a man not her husband, was death. According to Hammurabi's code, "If the wife of a man has been caught while lying with another man, they shall bind them and throw them into the water."[4] There was no corresponding law for married men. The husband had the power to spare his wife by obtaining a pardon for her from the king. He could, however, accuse his wife of adultery even if he had not caught her in the act. In such a case she could try to clear herself before the city council that investigated the charge. If she was found innocent, she could take her dowry and leave her husband. If a woman killed her husband, she was impaled.

The husband had virtually absolute power over his household. He could even sell his wife and children into slavery to pay debts. Sons did not lightly oppose their fathers, and any son who struck his father could have his hand cut off. A father was free to adopt children and include them in his will. Artisans sometimes adopted children to teach them the family trade. Although the father's power was great, he could not disinherit a son without just cause. Cases of disinheritance became matters for the city to decide, and the code ordered the courts to forgive a son for his first offense. Only if a son wronged his father a second time could he be disinherited.

Prostitution, both male and female, was as common in Mesopotamia as it is today. Though disreputable, it was not illegal in Mesopotamia and was instead taxed. Prostitutes, like Mesopotamians in general, differed in social status. A "temple prostitute" performed sexual acts in the temple as part of her sacred duties. The money went to the maintenance of the temple. Other women lived as courtesans, sexual partners and social companions to wealthy and powerful men, who generally had wives and children as well. Prostitutes and courtesans differed from concubines, who were women who lived with men without marriage. All of them lived under the protection of the law.

Hammurabi's law code took magic as a fact of life. Magic was often associated with religion and medicine. Mesopotamians genuinely believed that supernatural

Law Code of Hammurabi Hammurabi ordered his code to be inscribed on a stone pillar and set up in public. At the top of the pillar Hammurabi is depicted receiving the scepter of authority from the Shamash, the god of justice. (Réunion des Musées Nationaux/ Art Resource, NY)

forces could directly and benevolently intervene on their behalf. In devout belief they used chants and incantations to call on higher unseen powers to bring them happiness.

Law codes, preoccupied as they are with the problems of society, provide a bleak view of things, but other Mesopotamian documents give a happier glimpse of life. Although Hammurabi's code dealt with marriage in a hard-fisted fashion, countless wills and testaments show that husbands habitually left their estates to their wives, who in turn willed the property to their children. Hammurabi's code restricted married women from commercial pursuits, but financial documents prove that many women engaged in business without hindrance. Some carried on the family business, while others became wealthy landowners in their own right.

Marriage was primarily an arrangement between families, but evidence of love has also survived. A Mesopotamian poem tells of two people meeting secretly in the city. Their parting is delightfully romantic:

> *Come now, set me free, I must go home,*
> *Kuli-Enlil . . . set me free, I must go home.*
> *What can I say to deceive my mother?*[5]

Mesopotamians found their lives lightened by holidays and religious festivals. Traveling merchants brought news of the outside world and swapped marvelous tales. Despite their pessimism, the Mesopotamians enjoyed a vibrant and creative culture that left its mark on the entire Near East.

The practical impact of Hammurabi's code is much debated. There is disagreement about whether it recorded laws already established, promulgated new laws, or simply proclaimed what was just and proper. It is also unknown whether Hammurabi's proclamation was legally binding on the courts. Nevertheless, Hammurabi's code gives historians a valuable view into the lives of the Mesopotamians.

Egypt, the Land of the Pharaohs, 3100–1200 B.C.E.

How did Egypt's geography contribute to the rise of a unique culture, and what was the role of the pharaoh in this society? ■

The Greek historian and traveler Herodotus (heh-RAHD-uh-tuhs) in the fifth century B.C.E. called Egypt the "gift of the Nile." No other single geographical factor had such a fundamental and profound impact on the shaping of Egyptian life, society, and history as the Nile (Map 1.2). The Egyptians never feared the relatively tame Nile in the way the Mesopotamians feared the Tigris. Instead, they sang its praises:

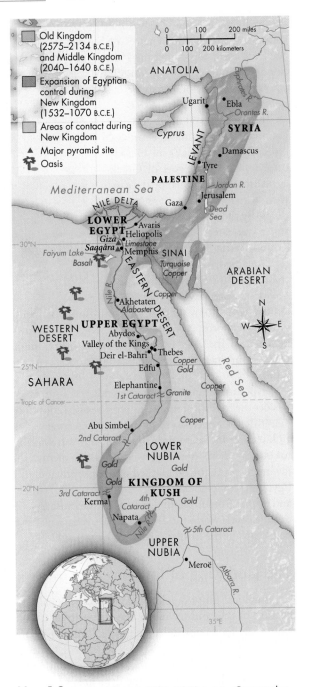

Map 1.2 Ancient Egypt, 2575–1070 B.C.E. Geography and natural resources provided Egypt with centuries of peace and abundance.

> *Hail to thee, O Nile, that issues from the earth and*
>   *comes to keep Egypt alive! . . .*
> *He that waters the meadows which Re [Ra] created,*
> *He that makes to drink the desert . . .*
> *He who makes barley and brings emmer [wheat] into*
>   *being . . .*
> *He who brings grass into being for the cattle . . .*
> *He who makes every beloved tree to grow . . .*
> *O Nile, verdant art thou, who makest man and cattle*
>   *to live.*[6]

To the Egyptians, the Nile was the supreme fertilizer and renewer of the land. Each September the Nile floods its valley, transforming it into a huge area of marsh or lagoon.

The annual flood made growing abundant crops almost effortless, especially in southern Egypt. Herodotus, used to the rigors of Greek agriculture, was amazed by the ease with which the Egyptians raised crops. By the end of November the water retreated, leaving behind a thin covering of fertile mud ready to be planted with crops. The extraordinary fertility of the Nile Valley made it easy to produce an annual agricultural surplus, which in turn sustained a growing and prosperous population. The Nile also unified Egypt. The river was the region's principal highway, promoting easy communication throughout the valley.

Egypt was fortunate in that it was nearly self-sufficient. Besides the fertility of its soil, Egypt possessed enormous quantities of stone, which served as the raw material of architecture and sculpture. Abundant clay was available for pottery, as was gold for jewelry and ornaments. The raw materials that Egypt lacked were close at hand. The Egyptians could obtain copper from Sinai (SIGH-nigh) and timber from Lebanon. They had little cause to look to the outside world for their essential needs, a fact that helps explain the insular quality of Egyptian life.

The God-King of Egypt

Geographical unity quickly gave rise to political unification of the country under the authority of a king whom the Egyptians called "pharaoh." The Egyptians themselves told of a great king, Menes (MEH-neez), who united Upper Egypt—the upstream valley in the south—and Lower Egypt—the delta area of the Nile that empties into the Mediterranean Sea—into a single kingdom around 3100 B.C.E. Thereafter the Egyptians divided their history into dynasties, or families of kings. For modern historical purposes, however, it is more useful to divide Egyptian history into periods (see chronology above). The political unification of Egypt in the Archaic period (3100–2660 B.C.E.) ushered in the period known as the Old Kingdom (2660–2180 B.C.E.), an era remarkable for prosperity, artistic flowering, and the evolution of religious beliefs.

Like the Mesopotamians, the Egyptians were polytheistic in that they worshiped many gods, some mightier than others. They developed complex, often contradictory, ideas of their gods that reflected the world around

Periods of Egyptian History

Dates	Period	Significant Events
3100–2660 B.C.E.	Archaic	Unification of Egypt
2660–2180 B.C.E.	Old Kingdom	Construction of the pyramids
2180–2080 B.C.E.	First Intermediate	Political chaos
2080–1640 B.C.E.	Middle Kingdom	Recovery and political stability
1640–1570 B.C.E.	Second Intermediate	Hyksos "invasion"
1570–1075 B.C.E.	New Kingdom	Creation of an Egyptian empire; Akhenaten's religious policy
1100–653 B.C.E.	Third Intermediate	Political fragmentation and decline of empire

them. The most powerful of these gods was Amon (AH-muhn), a primeval sky-god, and Ra, the sun-god. Amon created the entire cosmos by his thoughts. He caused the Nile to flood and the northern wind to blow. He brought life to the land and its people, and he sustained both. The Egyptians cherished Amon because he championed fairness and honesty, especially for the common people. The Egyptians called him the "vizier of the humble" and the "voice of the poor." He was also a magician and physician who cured ills, protected people from natural dangers, and protected travelers. The Egyptians considered Ra the creator of life. He commanded the sky, earth, and underworld. This giver of life could also take it without warning. Ra was associated with the falcon-god Horus, the "lord of the sky," who served as the symbol of divine kingship. Horus united Egypt and bestowed divinity on the pharaoh. The obvious similarities between Amon and Ra eventually led the Egyptians to combine them into one god, Amon-Ra. Yet the Egyptians never fashioned a formal theology to resolve these differences. Instead they worshiped these gods as different aspects of the same celestial phenomena.

The Egyptians likewise developed views of an afterlife that reflected the world around them. The dry air of Egypt preserves much that would decay in other climates. Thus there was a sense of permanence about Egypt: the past was never far from the present. The dependable rhythm of the seasons also shaped the fate of the dead. According to the Egyptians, Osiris (oh-SIGH-ruhs), a fertility god associated with the Nile, died each year, and each year his wife, Isis (EYE-suhs), brought him back to life when the Nile flooded. Osiris eventually became king of the dead, and he weighed human beings' hearts to determine whether they had lived justly enough to deserve everlasting life. Osiris's care of the dead was shared by Anubis, the jackal-headed god who annually helped Isis resuscitate Osiris. Anubis was the god of mummification, so essential to Egyptian funer-

Ra and Horus The god Ra was the most powerful of the Egyptian gods. Here he takes on the form of Horus, the falcon-god (left). The red circle over Ra's head identifies him as the sun-god. In this scene Ra also assumes characteristics of Osiris, god of the underworld. He stands in judgment of the dead woman on the right. She meets the god with respect but without fear, as he will guide her safely to a celestial heaven. (Egyptian Museum, Cairo)

ary rites. The Egyptians preserved these ideas in the ***Book of the Dead***, which explained that the soul left the body to become part of the divine after death. It entered gladly through the gate of heaven and remained in the presence of Aton (AHT-on) (a sun-god) and the stars. Thus the Egyptians did not draw a firm boundary between the human and the divine, and life did not end with death.

The focal point of religious and political life in the Old Kingdom was the **pharaoh** (FAY-roh), who commanded the wealth, resources, and people of all Egypt. The pharaoh was so powerful that the Egyptians considered him to be Horus in human form, a living god on earth, who became one with his father Osiris after death. His wife was associated with Isis, for both the queen and the goddess were viewed as protectors. The pharaoh was not simply the mediator between the gods and the Egyptian people. Above all, he was the power that achieved the integration between gods and human beings, between nature and society, and that ensured peace and prosperity for the land of the Nile. The pharaoh was thus a guarantee to his people, a pledge that the gods of Egypt (strikingly unlike those of Mesopotamia) cared for their people.

The pharaoh's surroundings had to be worthy of a god. Only a magnificent palace was suitable for his home; in fact, the word *pharaoh* means "great house." Just as the pharaohs occupied a great house in life, so they reposed

in great pyramids after death. Built during the Old Kingdom, these massive stone tombs contained all the things needed by the pharaoh in his afterlife. The walls of the burial chamber were inscribed with religious texts and spells relating to the king's journeys after death. The pyramid also symbolized the king's power and his connection with the sun-god. After burial the entrance was blocked and concealed to ensure the pharaoh's undisturbed peace. (Contrary to common belief, no curses for violation of pyramids have been found.) To this day the great pyramids at Giza near Cairo bear silent but magnificent testimony to the god-kings of Egypt.

The Life of the Pharaoh's People

Egyptian society reflected the pyramids that it built. At the top stood the pharaoh, who was traditionally endowed with absolute power over everyone in the kingdom. In reality he relied on a sizable circle of high officials and their literate staffs to administer his vast lands.

Book of the Dead An Egyptian book that preserved ideas about death and the afterlife; it explains that the soul leaves the body to become part of the divine after death.

pharaoh The leader of religious and political life in the Old Kingdom, he commanded the wealth, resources, and people of Egypt.

King Menkaure and Queen The pharaoh and his wife represent all the magnificence, serenity, and grandeur of Egypt. (Old Kingdom, Dynasty 4, reign of Mycerinus, 2532–2510 B.C.; Greywacke; H × W × D: 54¹¹⁄₁₆ × 22³⁄₈ × 2¹⁵⁄₁₆ in. [139 × 57 × 54 cm]. Harvard University–Museum of Fine Arts Expedition, 11.1738. Museum of Fine Arts, Boston)

order—harmony among themselves, nature, and the divine. They were in effect ruled by a god. If the pharaoh was weak or allowed anyone to challenge his unique and sacred position, he opened the way to chaos. Twice in Egyptian history the pharaoh failed to maintain rigid centralization. During these two eras, known as the First (2180–2080 B.C.E.) and Second Intermediate (1640–1570 B.C.E.) periods, Egypt was exposed to civil war and invasion. Yet the monarchy survived, and in each period a strong pharaoh arose to crush the rebels or expel the invaders and restore order.

In the minds of the Egyptians, the Nile formed an essential part of this cosmic harmony. The river made them farmers and divided their year into three seasons, beginning with its flooding from June to September. During this time farmers were free to work on the pharaoh's building programs. When the water began to recede in October, they diverted some of it into ponds for future irrigation and began planting wheat and barley for bread and beer. A farmer needed only a flimsy wooden plough to part the soft mud. From October to February farmers harvested crops. Reapers with wooden sickles fixed with flint teeth cut the grain high, leaving long stubble. Women with baskets followed behind to gather the cuttings. Last came the gleaners—women, children, and old men who gathered anything left behind. Harvest time generally brought farmers joy, but in Egypt it brought the tax collector. One scribe described the worst that could happen:

> And now the scribe lands on the river bank is about to register the harvest-tax. The janitors carry staves and the Nubians rods of palm, and they say, Hand over the grain, though there is none. The farmer is beaten all over, he is bound and thrown into a well, soused and dipped head downwards. His wife has been bound in his presence and his children are in fetters.[7]

That was an extreme situation, but it illustrates the plight of commoners.

The lives of all Egyptians centered around the family. Marriage was a business arrangement, just as in Mesopotamia, arranged by the couples' parents. The couple was expected to have children as quickly as possible. They especially wanted boys. Boys continued the family line, and only they could perform the proper burial rites for their father. Yet the family also wanted girls, and the Egyptians did not practice infanticide. As in other cultures, the children played together and with their parents. The children were especially taught to honor and love their mother. All Egyptians tried to educate their children so that they could prosper, and for that they began with writing. The goal for most ordinary Egyptians was to become scribes.

Wealthy Egyptians lived in spacious homes with attractive gardens and walls for privacy. Such a house had an ample living room and a comfortable master bed-

High priests also shouldered much of the religious burden of performing necessary rituals and running the lands donated to the various gods. A numerous peasantry made up the broad base of the social pyramid.

The vision of thousands of people straining to build the pyramids and countless artists adorning the pharaoh's tomb brings to the modern mind a distasteful picture of absolute power. Indeed, the Egyptian view of life and society is alien to those raised with modern concepts of individual freedom and human rights. Yet to ancient Egyptians the pharaoh embodied the concept of **ma'at**, a cosmic harmony that embraced truth, justice, and moral integrity. Ma'at gave the pharaoh the right, authority, and duty to govern. To the people the pharaoh personified justice and

ma'at The Egyptian belief in a cosmic harmony that embraced truth, justice, and moral integrity; it gave the pharaohs the right and duty to govern.

Pyramids of Giza Giza was the burial place of the pharaohs of the Old Kingdom and of the aristocracy, whose smaller rectangular tombs surround the two foremost pyramids. (Jose Fuste Raga/Corbis)

room with an attached bathroom. Smaller rooms served other purposes, including housing family members and servants, and providing space for cows, poultry, and storage. Poorer people lived in cramped quarters. Excavations at Tell el Amarna show that their houses were sixteen and one-half feet wide by thirty-three feet long. The family had narrow rooms for living, including two small rooms for sleeping and cooking. Worst of all, the very poor lived in hovels with their animals. Most families kept cats for pets and to catch mice and other pests. Whether rich or poor, the Egyptians kept their houses clean.

Life in Egypt began at dawn with a bath and clean clothes. The Egyptians bathed several times a day because of the heat and used soda for soap. Rich and poor alike used perfumes as deodorants. They left the house scantily clad, again because of the heat. Men often wore only a kilt and women a sheath. They all preferred linen clothes because they were cool.

Ordinary women lived a curious combination of restraint and freedom in a male-oriented society. While they obeyed their fathers, husbands, and other men, they possessed considerable rights. Marriage serves as an example. Nothing indicates that any ritual or religious act played any part in it. Marriage seems to have been purely a legal contract in which a woman brought one-third of her family's property to the marriage. The property continued to belong to her, though her husband managed it. She could obtain a divorce simply because she wanted it. If she did, she took her marriage portion with her and could also claim a share of the profits made during her marriage. Women could own land in their own names and operated businesses. The income gave them a strong

Shabti Figurines The Egyptians believed in an afterlife in which earthly work must go on. They made Shabti figurines for their tombs that could be called magically to life to do that work for them, just as their servants had done during their life on earth. The figurines fulfilled in death the tasks that ordinary human beings did in life. (Courtesy of the Trustees of the British Museum)

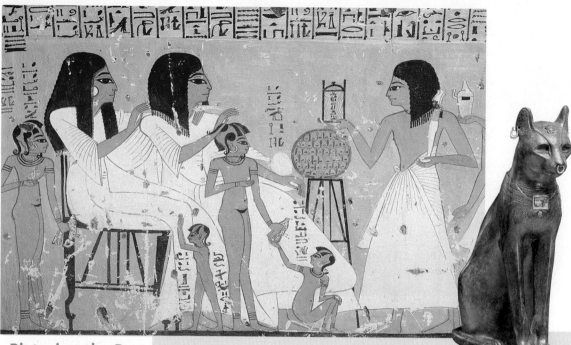

Picturing the Past

Egyptian Home Life This grave painting depicts an intimate moment in the life of an aristocratic family. As in life, the deceased father sits at the center of his household. Often found in Egyptian tombs are statuettes of cats (inset), family pets, and the symbol of the goddess Bastet. (family: Gianni Dagli Orti/The Art Archive; cat: Courtesy of the Trustees of the British Museum)

ANALYZING THE IMAGE How many different types of people are shown in this scene? How do the depictions of the different groups relate to their status in this household?

CONNECTIONS Based on your reading, do you find this depiction of Egyptian home life accurate? How might an image of a poor family differ from this depiction?

To complete this activity online, go to the Online Study Guide at bedfordstmartins.com/mckaywest.

voice in all family affairs. Women could testify in court and bring legal action against men. These economic factors protected women and gave them an enhanced station in society.

Yet for all of women's economic powers, they held a curious position in marriage. The husband could keep several wives or concubines. One wife, however, remained primary among the others. A husband could order his wife to her quarters and even beat her. But if a man treated his wife too violently, she could take him to court. If she won, her husband received 100 lashes from a whip and surrendered his portion of their joint property to her. A man could dispense with his wife for any reason, just as she could leave him. While a husband went unpunished for adultery, the wife suffered death. Many of these instances must have been extreme because if a husband treated his wife too brutally, she could always take her dowry and leave.

Information from literature and art depicts a world in which ordinary husbands and wives enjoyed each others' company alone and together with family and friends.

They held parties together, and together accepted invitations to parties. They both participated in the festivities after dinner. Egyptian tomb monuments often show the couple happily standing together, arms around each other. In short, despite constraints that many modern people find distasteful, Egyptian families ordinarily led happy lives.

The Hyksos in Egypt

While Egyptian civilization flourished behind its bulwark of sand and sea, momentous changes were taking place in the ancient Near East, changes that would leave their mark even on rich, insular Egypt. These changes involved enormous and remarkable movements, especially of peoples who spoke Semitic tongues.

The original home of the Semites was perhaps the Arabian peninsula. Some tribes moved into northern Mesopotamia, others into Syria and Palestine, and still others into Egypt. Shortly after 1800 B.C.E. people whom the Egyptians called Hyksos, which means "rulers of the uplands," began to settle in the Nile Delta. The movements of the Hyksos were part of a larger pattern of migration of peoples during the First and Second Intermediate periods. The history of Mesopotamia records many such wanderings of people in search of better homes for themselves. Such nomads normally settled in and accommodated themselves with the native cultures. The process was mutual, for each group had something to give to and to learn from the other.

So it was in Egypt, but the historical record, as shown by this description of the events as later recorded by the priest Manetho in the third century B.C.E., depicted the coming of the Hyksos as a brutal invasion:

> In the reign of Toutimaios—I do not know why—the wind of god blew against us. Unexpectedly from the regions of the east men of obscure race, looking forward confidently to victory, invaded our land, and without a battle easily seized it all by sheer force. Having subdued those in authority in the land, they then barbarously burned our cities and razed to the ground the temples of the gods. They fell upon all the natives in an entirely hateful fashion, slaughtering them and leading both their children and wives into slavery. At last they made one of their people king, whose name was Salitis. This man resided at Memphis, leaving in Upper and Lower Egypt tax collectors and garrisons in strategic places.[8]

The Hyksos Settlement of Egypt, ca. 1640–1570 B.C.E.

Although the Egyptians portrayed the Hyksos as a conquering horde, they were probably no more than nomads looking for good land. Their entry into the delta was probably gradual and generally peaceful.

The Hyksos created a capital city at Avaris, located in the northeastern Nile Delta, but they probably exerted direct rule no farther south. The Hyksos brought with them the method of making bronze and casting it into tools and weapons that became standard in Egypt. They thereby brought Egypt fully into the **Bronze Age** culture of the Mediterranean world, a culture in which the production and use of bronze implements became basic to society. Because bronze tools were sharper and more durable than the copper tools they replaced, they made farming more efficient than ever before. The Hyksos's use of bronze armor and weapons as well as horse-drawn chariots and the composite bow, made of laminated wood and horn and far more powerful than the simple wooden bow, revolutionized Egyptian warfare. However much the Egyptians learned from the Hyksos, Egyptian culture eventually absorbed the newcomers. The Hyksos

came to worship Egyptian gods and modeled their monarchy on the pharaonic system.

The New Kingdom: Revival and Empire

Politically, Egypt was only in eclipse. The Egyptian sun shone again when a remarkable line of kings, the pharaohs of the Eighteenth Dynasty, arose to challenge the Hyksos. These pharaohs pushed the Hyksos out of the delta, subdued Nubia in the south, and conquered Palestine and parts of Syria in the northeast. In this way, Egyptian warrior-pharaohs inaugurated the New Kingdom—a period in Egyptian history from 1570 to 1075 B.C.E. characterized by enormous wealth and imperialism. During this period, probably for the first time, widespread slavery became a feature of Egyptian life. The pharaoh's armies returned home leading hordes of slaves who constituted a new labor force for imperial building projects.

The pharaohs of the Eighteenth Dynasty created the first Egyptian empire. They ruled Palestine and Syria through their officers and incorporated the neighboring region of Nubia into the kingdom of Egypt. Egyptian religion and customs flourished in Nubia, making a huge impact on African culture there and in neighboring areas. The warrior-pharaohs celebrated their success with monuments on a scale unparalleled since the pharaohs of the Old Kingdom had built the pyramids. Even today the colossal granite statues of these pharaohs and the rich tomb objects of Tutankhamon ("King Tut") testify to the might and splendor of the New Kingdom.

One of the most extraordinary of this line of pharaohs was Akhenaten (ah-keh-NAH-tuhn) (r. 1367–1350 B.C.E.), a pharaoh more concerned with religion than with conquest. Nefertiti (nef-uhr-TEE-tee), his wife and queen, encouraged his religious bent. (See "Individuals in Society: Nefertiti, the 'Great Wife,'" page 27.) The precise nature of Akhenaten's religious beliefs remains debatable. The problem began during his own lifetime. His religion was often unpopular among the people and the traditional priesthood, and its practice declined in the later years of his reign. After his death, it was condemned and denounced; consequently, not much is known about it. Most historians, however, agree that

Bronze Age The period in which the production and use of bronze implements became basic to society; bronze made farming more efficient and revolutionized warfare.

Tutankhamon as Pharaoh This painted casket depicts the pharaoh as the defender of the kingdom repulsing its invaders. Tutankhamon rides into battle under the signs of the sun-disk and the vulture-goddess, indicating that he and Egypt enjoy the protection of the gods. (Egyptian Museum, Cairo)

Akhenaten and Nefertiti practiced **monotheism** (mahn-uh-THEE-i-zuhm); that is, they believed that there was only one universal god—the sun-god Aton, whom they worshiped. They considered all other Egyptian gods and goddesses frauds and disregarded their worship.

Akhenaten's monotheism, imposed from above, failed to find a place among the people. The prime reason for Akhenaten's failure is that his god had no connection with the past of the Egyptian people, who trusted the old gods and felt comfortable praying to them. Average Egyptians were no doubt distressed and disheartened when their familiar gods were outlawed, for those gods were the heavenly powers that had made Egypt powerful and unique. The fanaticism and persecution that accompanied the new monotheism were in complete defiance of the Egyptian tradition of tolerant polytheism, or worship of several gods. Thus, when Akhenaten died, his religion died with him.

monotheism The belief in one universal god.

Indo-European Peoples who speak a language from a large family of languages that includes English, most of the languages of modern Europe, Greek, Latin, Persian, and Sanskrit.

The Hittites and the End of an Era, ca. 1640–1100 B.C.E.

How did the Hittites rise to power, and how did they and other civilizations of the Near East fare in response to the attack of foreign invaders? ▪

At about the same time the Hyksos entered the Nile Delta, the Hittites, who had long been settled in Anatolia (modern Turkey), became a major power in that region and began to expand eastward. The Hittites were the first Indo-Europeans to become important throughout the region. The term **Indo-European** refers to people who speak a language from a large family of languages that includes English, most of the languages of modern Europe, including Greek and Latin, and languages as far afield as Persian and Sanskrit, spoken in ancient Turkey and India. During the eighteenth and nineteenth centuries, European scholars learned that peoples who spoke Indo-European languages had migrated as far west as Ireland and as far east as Central Asia. Archaeologists were subsequently able to assign rough dates to these migrations and to put them into their historical context. As a result, historians learned that around 2000 B.C.E.

Nefertiti, the "Great Wife"

INDIVIDUALS IN SOCIETY

THE EGYPTIANS CALLED THE PHARAOH'S WIFE the "great wife," somewhat in the way that Americans refer to the president's wife as the "first lady." The great wife legitimized her husband's exercise of power through religious beliefs. The Egyptians believed that she was divinely born and that the god Amon took the human form of her husband, impregnated her, oversaw the development of the child in her womb, and ensured

a healthy delivery. Thus the child was the offspring of both the god and the pharaoh. The great wife could not legally be pharaoh, for only a male could exercise that power. Yet only she could make legitimate the pharaoh's right to power. The Egyptians literally and formally considered hers the throne of power, although her power was passive rather than active.

So stood things until Nefertiti, who was an exceptional great wife. Unlike her predecessors, she was not content to play a passive role in Egyptian life. Like her husband, Akhenaten, she passionately embraced the worship of Aton. She used her position to support her husband's zeal to spread the god's worship. Together they built a new palace at Akhetaten, the present Amarna, away from the old centers of power. There they developed and promulgated the cult of Aton to the exclusion of the traditional deities. Nearly the only literary survival of their religious belief is the "Hymn to Aton," which declares Aton to be the only god. It also mentions Nefertiti as "the great royal consort whom he !Akhenaten! loves, the mistress of the Two Lands !Upper and Lower Egypt!"

Until recently historians have thought that Akhenaten divorced and exiled Nefertiti. Scholars now, however, have uncovered a very different and remarkable story of her later life. Instead of rejecting her, Akhenaten made Nefertiti his co-regent. She now jointly ruled Egypt with her husband. After his death, she governed the kingdom in her own right. Yet her rare accession to the sole power came at a dark time in Egyptian history. Hostile neighbors threatened the Egyptian-held Syrian border, among them the Hittites. In a daring move Nefertiti sent a letter to Suppiluma, the Hittite king, offering to marry one of his sons. The king was stunned, but Nefertiti's move was brilliant. By joining the enemy, she would create a Hittite-Egyptian superpower. Intrigued by the idea, the Hittite king sent her his son Zannanza, but an Egyptian assassinated him, causing the plan to collapse. Nefertiti nonetheless kept Egypt independent and died peacefully, leaving the throne to her son Tutankhamon.

Nefertiti played a novel role in Egyptian art. In funerary and temple art, she is usually depicted with Akhenaten and their daughters. This practice went against the tradition of presenting the royal couple as austere and aloof. Instead, Nefertiti and Akhenaten were portrayed as an ordinary family. Their daughters often appear playing on their parents' laps or with one another. Even Nefertiti's own appearance in Egyptian art was a departure from tradition. As the illustration here shows, the famous bust of her is a realistic, not idealized, portrait. The face is one of grace, beauty, and dignity. It is the portrait of an individual, not a type.

Nefertiti's bust has its own story. When Akhenaten's successor abandoned the palace at Amarna, the site was ignored, except as a source for building materials. Nefertiti's bust remained in the sculptor's workroom, which eventually caved in. There it lay, undamaged, for more than three thousand years. On December 6, 1912, a German archaeological team discovered it intact and sent it to Germany. The authenticity of the bust has recently been challenged, but on flimsy grounds. After World War II, the bust was moved to its current home outside Berlin, where Nefertiti can still be admired today.

The long-lost bust of the queen of Egypt. (Bildarchiv Preussischer Kulturbesitz/Art Resource, NY)

QUESTIONS FOR ANALYSIS

1. What were Nefertiti's religious beliefs, and how did she demonstrate them?

2. In what ways was Nefertiti unique among "great wives"?

27

Indo-Europeans migrated into Anatolia where, after conquering and mingling with the local people, they founded a new kingdom. The Hittites left a lasting imprint on the Near East before the empires of the whole region suffered the shock of new peoples and widespread disruption.

The Rise of the Hittites

The rise of the Hittites to prominence in Anatolia is reasonably clear. During the nineteenth century B.C.E. the native kingdoms in the area engaged in suicidal warfare that left most of Anatolia's once-flourishing towns in ashes and rubble. In this climate of destruction, the Hittite king Hattusilis I built a hill citadel at Hattusas from which he led his Hittites against neighboring kingdoms (Map 1.3). Around 1595 B.C.E., Hattusilis's grandson and successor, Mursilis I, extended the Hittite conquests as far as Babylon. Upon his return home, the victorious Mursilis was assassinated by members of his own family, an act that plunged the kingdom into confusion and opened the door to foreign invasion. Mursilis's career is representative of the success and weakness of the Hittites. They were extremely vulnerable to attack by vigilant and tenacious enemies. Yet once they were united behind a strong king, the Hittites were a power to be reckoned with.

The Hittites, like the Egyptians of the New Kingdom, produced an energetic and able line of kings who built a powerful kingdom. Perhaps their major contribution was the introduction of iron into warfare and agriculture in the form of weapons and tools. In 1274 B.C.E. the Hittite king Muwattalli attacked the Egyptian army of Rameses II at the Battle of Kadesh in Syria. In hard fighting the Hittites stopped the Egyptian advance, inflicting heavy casualties on the Egyptians. In defeat, Rameses retreated to Egyptian-held territory, leaving the Hittites in control of northern Syria. This battle could have led to further warfare, but instead the Hittites offered the Egyptians peace and then alliance. Formal friendship followed alliance, and active cooperation followed friendship. They next included the Babylonians in their alliance. All three empires developed an official etiquette in which they treated one another as "brothers," using this familial term to indicate their connection. They made alliances for offensive and defensive protection and swore to uphold one another's authority. Hence, the greatest powers of the period maintained peace.

In northwestern Anatolia the Hittites came into contact with Greeks moving into Greece and western Anatolia. The Greeks migrating east were less advanced than the Hittites. They settled among other Indo-European people, such as the little-known Luwians, and established the small kingdom of Wilusa with a capital at Taruisa. Recent scholars have reasonably identified these two places as the Ilion and Troy of the Homeric *Iliad* (see

Map 1.3 Balance of Power in the Near East, ca. 1300 B.C.E. This map shows the regions controlled by the Hittites, Egyptians, and Babylonians at the height of their power. The yellow area within the brown ribbon represents the part of Mesopotamia conquered by the Hittites during their expansion eastward.

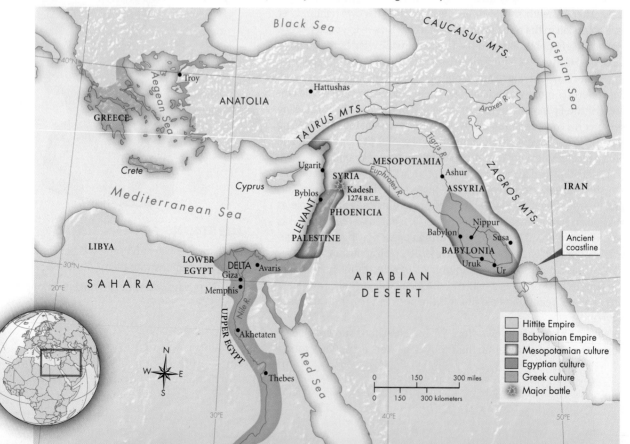

Chapter 3). The Greeks came under the shaky control of the Hittites, but more importantly, they became absorbed into the more advanced culture around them. The Hittites thereby helped to bring the sophisticated culture of the East to the emerging culture of the West.

While the Hittites never created a high culture of their own with art and philosophy, they preserved, nourished, and passed on the venerable customs, knowledge, and traditions of the Near East to their successors. Thanks to them, people from the eastern Mediterranean to Central Asia shared in these gifts through years of uninterrupted peace, until hordes of raiders brought devastating raids from the sea.

The Fall of Empires and the Survival of Cultures

The Battle of Kadesh ushered in a welcome period of peace and stability in the Near East that lasted until the thirteenth century B.C.E. Then, however, foreign invaders destroyed both the Hittite and the Egyptian empires. The most famous of these marauders, called the **Sea Peoples** by the Egyptians, launched a series of stunning attacks from about 1200 to 1000 B.C.E. that brought down the Hittites and drove the Egyptians back to the Nile Delta. They did not penetrate inland to disrupt the Babylonian kingdom. Nor did the Sea Peoples and other dimly known peoples do serious damage to the social and cultural advances made by their predecessors.

The basic social, economic, and cultural patterns of the Near East not only survived the onslaught, but also maintained their hold on the entire area. The disrupted peoples and newcomers followed the same pattern of cultural accommodation as the Sumerians, Hyksos, Hittites, and other groups described earlier in this chapter. Yet it is a mistake to think that the Egyptian and Hittite civilizations survived to face a cultural vacuum.

The Egyptians took the lead in the recovery by establishing commercial contact with their new neighbors. With the exchange of goods went ideas. Both sides shared practical concepts of shipbuilding, metal technology, and methods of trade that allowed merchants safely and efficiently to transact business over long distances. They all—old-timers and newcomers—began to establish and recognize recently created borders, which helped define them geographically and politically. One of the most striking and enduring of these developments was the cultural exchange among them.

When the worst was over, the Egyptians reached beyond their greatly reduced territory to engage in trade with the Semitic peoples of Palestine and Syria whom they found living in small walled towns. Farther north, they encountered the Phoenicians (fih-NEE-shuhnz), a people who combined sophisticated seafaring with urban life.

The situation in northern Syria reflected life in the south. Small cities in all these places were mercantile centers rich not only in manufactured goods but also

Hittite Merchants The peace brought by Hittite kings encouraged trade and economic growth. Although most merchants paid for goods in money, many others still relied on barter to negotiate their deals. Here two Hittite merchants show each other samples of their goods. (Gianni Dagli Orti/The Art Archive)

in agricultural produce, textiles, and metals. The cities flourished under royal families that shared power and dealt jointly in foreign affairs. These northerners relied heavily on their Mesopotamian heritage, which was a product of overland trade with Babylon. While adopting Babylonian writing to communicate with their more distant neighbors to the east, they also adapted it to write their own north Semitic language. Their texts provide a wealth of information about their life. At the same time they welcomed the knowledge of Mesopotamian literature, mathematics, and culture. They worshiped both their own and Mesopotamian deities. The cultural exchange remained a mixture of adoption, adaptation, contrast, and finally balance, as the two cultures came to understand and appreciate each other.

Southern Anatolia presented a similar picture. The Hittite kingdom dissolved after repeated attacks. The remaining settlements consisted of trading colonies and small agricultural communities. Thousands of cuneiform tablets testify to commercial and cultural exchanges

> **Sea Peoples** Foreign invaders who destroyed the Hittite and Egyptian empires in the thirteenth century B.C.E.

with Mesopotamia. Here also the Hittite heritage sturdily lived on, especially in politics and social relations. In Anatolia kingship and temple were closely allied, but the government was not a theocracy (rule by a religious authority). A city assembly of adult free men worked together under the king, and a prince administered the cit-

ies. Thus some men who were not members of the elite had a voice in political and social affairs. The world of these people rested on a mixture of the Hittite past and their own native achievements. This combination enabled them to create an environment uniquely their own.

LOOKING BACK LOOKING AHEAD

THROUGH CENTURIES the peoples of Europe and the ancient Near East progressed from dwelling in caves to dwelling in cities. The development of agriculture allowed Neolithic groups to prosper and to fashion a broad cultural life. The result was more complex and prosperous communities. These developments led to the first genuine urban societies in Mesopotamia. The Sumerian development of writing enabled Mesopotamian culture to be passed on to others. Neighboring peoples adopted their advances in writing, arts and sciences, literature, and religion, thereby spreading it through much of the Near East.

In Egypt another strong culture developed, one that made an impact in Africa, the Near East, and, later, Greece. The Egyptians' pharaonic system and religious beliefs influenced the lives of their neighbors. Into this world came the Hittites, an Indo-European people who learned from their neighbors and rivals. Their political system and alliances would bring peace to the region and influence later peoples.

After a period of devastating raids in the west, the Hittite Empire collapsed, leaving a greatly reduced Egypt in the eastern Mediterranean and a stable, but somewhat distant Babylonia in Mesopotamia. The surviving settlements shared the benefits of their societies with the newcomers, who stayed and intermingled with the cultures of the Near East. The newcomers contributed to the advance of Egyptian and Mesopotamian cultures by introducing new technologies and religious ideas. The result was the emergence of a huge group of communities, including the Phoenicians, Hebrews, and Syrians, that enjoyed their own individual character, while at the same time sharing many common features with their neighbors.

CHAPTER REVIEW

■ What factors are key to understanding the meaning of "the West" and Western civilization? (p. 4)

Before studying the history of Western people, historians had to decide what they meant by "the West" and "Western civilization": what made it integral while distinct from other cultures. The ancient Greeks were the first to make a distinction between the West and the East. The Romans would adopt this conceptualization, considering the East as both more advanced and slightly immoral. Later Europeans would embrace this classical model, though over time just what was considered part of the East and West would shift according to the political, cultural, and social climate. The notion of Western civilization has likewise changed over time. Western civilization now refers to the ideas, customs, and institutions of Europe, the Americas, and their colonies. Because many of the roots of this civilization can be traced to Asia and Africa, the concept of a distinct Western civilization remains controversial.

■ How did early peoples evolve from bands of hunter-gatherers to settled farming communities? (p. 5)

For thousands of years Paleolithic peoples moved from place to place in search of food. Only in the Neolithic era—with the invention of new stone tools, a reliance on sustained agriculture, and the domestication of animals—did people begin to live in permanent locations. Villages evolved into towns, where people began to create new social bonds and political organizations. Stonehenge is one example of the collective effort and imagination of a Neolithic community.

■ What were some of the enduring accomplishments of Mesopotamian civilization? (p. 10)

The area where these developments first led to genuine urban societies is Mesopotamia. Here the Sumerians and then other Mesopotamians developed writing, which enabled their culture to be passed on to others. Their religious beliefs reflected a pessimistic view of the world in which the gods could bring destruction without concern for human life. The great Sumerian poem, the *Epic of Gilgamesh*, shows them grappling with questions of life and death that are still of importance today. The beginnings of patriarchy and social class inequalities can also be seen in their culture.

■ How did the Babylonians unite Mesopotamia politically and culturally and spread that culture to the broader world? (p. 16)

The Sumerians established the basic social, economic, and intellectual patterns of Mesopotamia, but the Semites played a large part in spreading Mesopotamian culture to the broader world through both conquest and commercial exchange. First the Akkadians and then the Babylonians came to power in the region. Under Hammurabi, the Babylonians were able to unify Mesopotamia politically and culturally. The law code of Hammurabi illustrates the king's intentions to regulate the lives of his people and promote social harmony.

■ How did Egypt's geography contribute to the rise of a unique culture, and what was the role of the pharaoh in this society? (p. 19)

The fertile Nile Valley and other natural resources contributed to the rise of a wealthy and insular culture in Egypt. The Egyptians developed their own writing system and religious beliefs, and they undertook monumental building projects that required sophisticated organizational and intellectual skills. Under the strong central leadership of the pharaoh, Egyptian life was stable and predictable.

■ How did the Hittites rise to power, and how did they and other civilizations of the Near East fare in response to the attack of foreign invaders? (p. 26)

The Hittites, an Indo-European people, entered the Near East from eastern Europe. They rose to prominence in the wake of warfare between local groups that had left the towns of Anatolia ruined. The Hittites introduced iron tools and weapons to the region and developed an alliance with the Egyptians and Babylonians that facilitated the exchange of goods and ideas throughout the Near East. Only Egypt survived the attacks of the hostile invaders beginning around the thirteenth century B.C.E., but key social, economic, and cultural patterns survived to enrich future generations.

Suggested Reading

Bryce, Trevor. *The Kingdom of the Hittites*, new ed. 2005. The definitive study of the Hittites.

Bryce, Trevor. *The Trojans and Their Neighbors*. 2006. Examines the arrival of the Greeks in Asia Minor (Anatolia) and their associations with native peoples.

Burl, Aubrey. *The Stonehenge People*. 1987. An examination of the people and their monuments by the leading expert on the topic.

David, A. Rosalie. *Pyramid Builders of Ancient Egypt*, 2d ed. 1996. Studies the lives of the people who labored to build the pyramids for their pharaohs.

Golden, Jonathan M. *Ancient Canaan and Israel*. 2009. A new and solid introduction to the Canaanite influence on early Hebrew culture.

Harding, A. F. *European Societies in the Bronze Age*. 2000. A comprehensive survey of developments in Europe during the Bronze Age.

Hawass, Zahi. *Silent Images: Women in Pharaonic Egypt*. 2000. Blends text and pictures to draw a history of ancient Egyptian women.

Kuhrt, Amelie. *The Ancient Near East*, 2 vols. 1995. Covers the region from the earliest time to Alexander's conquest.

Leick, Gwendolyn. *The Babylonians*. 2002. An introduction to all aspects of Babylonian life and culture.

McDowell, A. G. *Village Life in Ancient Egypt: Laundry Lists and Love Songs*. 1999. A readable study of the basic social and economic factors of the entire period.

Oren, E. D. *The Hyksos*. 1997. Studies the archaeological evidence for the Hyksos.

Reeves, Nicholas. *Akhenaten*. 2001. Gives a detailed account of the pharaoh, Nefertiti, and their world.

Saggs, H. W. F. *The Babylonians*. 2002. An account of all the eras of Mesopotamian history.

Silverman, David P. *Ancient Egypt*. 1997. A good general account of the region.

Snell, Daniel. *Life in the Ancient Near East, 3100–332 B.C.E.* 1995. Covers the social history of the ancient Near East.

Visicato, Giuseppe. *The Power and the Writing: The Early Scribes of Mesopotamia*. 2000. Studies the practical importance of early Mesopotamian scribes.

Key Terms

civilization (p. 4)
Paleolithic period (p. 5)
Neolithic period (p. 6)
irrigation (p. 10)
cuneiform (p. 11)
polytheism (p. 12)
patriarchal (p. 14)
Hammurabi's law code (p. 17)
Book of the Dead (p. 21)
pharaoh (p. 21)
ma'at (p. 22)
Bronze Age (p. 25)
monotheism (p. 26)
Indo-European (p. 26)
Sea Peoples (p. 29)

Notes

1. Quoted in J. B. Pritchard, ed., *Ancient Near Eastern Texts*, 3d ed. (Princeton, N.J.: Princeton University Press, 1969), p. 44. *Note:* John Buckler is the translator of all uncited quotations from a foreign language in Chapters 1–6.

2. Ibid., p. 104.

3. Quoted in S. N. Kramer, *The Sumerians: Their History, Culture, and Character*, p. 238. Copyright © 1963 by The University of Chicago. All rights reserved. Used by permission.

4. Pritchard, p. 171.

5. Kramer, p. 251.

6. Pritchard, p. 372.

7. Quoted in A. H. Gardiner, "Ramesside Texts Relating to the Taxation and Transport of Corn," *Journal of Egyptian Archaeology* 27 (1941), pp. 19–20.

8. Manetho, *History of Egypt*, frag. 42, pp. 75–77.

For practice quizzes and other study tools, visit the Online Study Guide at **bedfordstmartins.com/mckaywest**.

For primary sources from this period, see **Sources of Western Society**, Second Edition.

For Web sites, images, and documents related to topics in this chapter, visit Make History at **bedfordstmartins.com/mckaywest**.

2
Small Kingdoms and Mighty Empires in the Near East

ca. 1100–513 B.C.E.

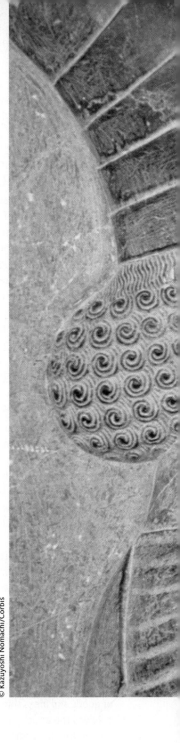

The migratory invasions that brought down the Hittites and stunned the Egyptians in the late thirteenth century B.C.E. ushered in an era of confusion and weakness. Although much was lost in the chaos, the old cultures of the ancient Near East survived to nurture new societies. In the absence of powerful empires, the Phoenicians, Hebrews, and many other peoples carved out small independent kingdoms until the Near East was a patchwork of them. During this period Hebrew culture and religion evolved under the influence of urbanism, kings, and prophets.

In the ninth century B.C.E. this jumble of small states gave way to an empire that for the first time embraced the entire Near East. Yet the same ferocity of the Assyrian Empire that led to its rise contributed to its downfall only two hundred years later. The Chaldeans, a Semitic-speaking people who had long dwelt in northern Mesopotamia, now became strong enough to create a new, strong kingdom in Babylon. In 550 B.C.E. the Persians and Medes (meeds), Indo-Europeans who had migrated into Iran, created a "world empire" stretching from Anatolia in the west to the Indus Valley in the east. For over two hundred years, the Persians gave the ancient Near East peace and stability. ∎

Life in an Empire. The kings subject to the Persians brought tribute to King Darius at his palace at Persepolis. Here a Phoenician king bears his gift of loyalty.

CHAPTER PREVIEW

Disruption and Diffusion
■ How did the Nubians, Kush, and Phoenicians respond to the power vacuum in Egypt and the western Near East?

The Children of Israel
■ How did the Hebrew state evolve, and what were the unique elements of Hebrew religious thought?

Assyria, the Military Monarchy
■ What enabled the Assyrians to conquer their neighbors, and what finally caused their undoing?

The Empire of the Persian Kings
■ How did the Persians rise to power and control and influence the subjects of their extensive empire?

How did the Nubians, Kush, and Phoenicians respond to the power vacuum in Egypt and the western Near East? ▪

If the fall of empires was a time of massive political disruption, it also ushered in a period of cultural diffusion, an expansion of what had already transpired in the broad region. Even though empires expired, many small kingdoms survived, along with a largely shared culture. These small states and local societies had learned much from the great powers, but they nonetheless retained their own lore and native traditions, which they passed on to their neighbors, thus diffusing a Near Eastern culture that was slowly becoming common. The best-known examples can be found along the coast of the eastern Mediterranean, where various peoples—some of them newcomers such as the Philistines—created homes and petty kingdoms in Phoenicia and Palestine.

The End of Egyptian Power

The invasions of the Sea Peoples brought the great days of Egyptian power to an end. The long wars against invaders weakened and impoverished Egypt, causing political upheaval and economic chaos. One scribe left behind a somber portrait of stunned and leaderless Egypt:

> The land of Egypt was abandoned and every man was a law to himself. During many years there was no leader who could speak for others. Central government lapsed, small officials and headmen took over the whole land. Any man, great or small, might kill his neighbor. In the distress and vacuum that followed ... men banded together to plunder one another. They treated the gods no better than men, and cut off the temple revenues.[1]

No longer able to dream of foreign conquests, Egypt looked to its own security from foreign invasion. Egyptians suffered four hundred years of political fragmentation, a new dark age known to Egyptian specialists as the Third Intermediate Period (ca. 1100–653 B.C.E.).

In southern Egypt, meanwhile, the pharaoh's decline opened the way to the energetic Nubians, who extended their authority northward throughout the Nile Valley. Since the imperial days of the Eighteenth Dynasty (see Chapter 1), the Nubians had adopted many

features of Egyptian culture. Now Nubian kings and nobles embraced Egyptian culture wholesale. Libyans from North Africa also filtered into the Nile Delta, where they established independent dynasties. From 950 to 730 B.C.E. northern Egypt was ruled by Libyan pharaohs. The Libyans built cities, and for the first time a sturdy urban life grew up in the delta. Although the coming of the Libyans changed the face of the delta, the Libyans, like the Nubians, eagerly adopted Egypt's religion and way of life. Thus the Nubians and the Libyans repeated an old Near Eastern phenomenon: new peoples conquered old centers of political and

Nubian Cylinder Sheath
The purpose of this sheath is unknown, but it and many others were found in the tombs of the kings of Kush in the Sudan. The winged goddess at the bottom stands between two figures of the Egyptian god Amon-Ra. The sheath plainly shows the Nubian debt to Egyptian religion and art. (Nubian, Napatan Period, reign of King Amani-natakelebte, 538–519 B.C. Findspot: Sudan, Nubia, Nuri, Pyramid 10. Gilded silver, colored paste inclusions. Height × diameter: 12 × 3.1 cm [4¾ × 1¼ in.]. Museum of Fine Arts, Boston. Harvard University–Boston Museum of Fine Arts Expedition, 20.275)

military power but were assimilated into the older culture.

The reunification of Egypt occurred late and unexpectedly. With Egypt distracted and disorganized by foreign invasions, an independent African state, the kingdom of Kush, grew up in the region of modern Sudan with its capital at Nepata. Like the Libyans, the Kushites worshiped Egyptian gods and used Egyptian hieroglyphs (HIGH-ruh-glihfs). In the eighth century B.C.E. their king, Piankhy, swept with his army through the entire Nile Valley. United once again, Egypt enjoyed a brief period of peace during which Egyptians continued to assimilate their conquerors. Nonetheless, reunification of the realm did not lead to a new Egyptian empire.

Yet Egypt's legacy to its African neighbors remained vibrant and rich. By trading and exploring southward along the coast of the Red Sea, the Egyptians introduced their goods, religion, and ideas as far south as Ethiopia. Egypt was also the primary civilizing force in Nubia, which became another version of the pharaoh's realm, complete with royal pyramids and Egyptian deities.

The Rise of Phoenicia

One of the sturdy peoples who rose to prominence in the wake of the Sea Peoples' attacks were the Phoenicians, Semitic-speakers who had long inhabited several cities along the Mediterranean coast of modern Lebanon. Although they had lived during the great days of the Hittites, Egyptians, and Babylonians, in this period the Phoenicians came into their own. Now fully independent, they put their freedom to excellent use. Unlike the Philistine newcomers, who turned from seafaring to farming, the Phoenicians took to the sea. They were master shipbuilders, and with their stout ships, between about 900 and 550 B.C.E. they became the seaborne merchants of the Mediterranean. With the Greeks, one of their early customers, they traded their popular purple and blue textiles, from which originated their Greek name, Phoenicians, meaning "Purple People."

The growing success of the Phoenicians, combined with peace in the Near East, brought them prosperity. In addition to textiles and purple dye, they began to

ca. 1100–653 B.C.E.	Third Intermediate Period in Egypt
ca. 965–925 B.C.E.	Hebrew kingdom unified under Solomon
ca. 950–800 B.C.E.	Beginning of the Hebrew Bible
ca. 900–612 B.C.E.	Assyrian Empire
ca. 900–550 B.C.E.	Phoenician seafaring and trading in the Mediterranean
722 B.C.E.	Israel destroyed by the Assyrians
ca. 710–550 B.C.E.	Creation of the Persian Empire
626–539 B.C.E.	Neo-Babylonian Empire
ca. 600 B.C.E.	Introduction of Zoroastrianism
587 B.C.E.	Judah destroyed by the Neo-Babylonians
587–539 B.C.E.	Babylonian Captivity of the Hebrews
ca. 550–513 B.C.E.	Expansion of Persia from a subject people to world empire

Phoenician Ships These small ships seem too frail to breast the waves. Yet Phoenician mariners routinely sailed them, loaded with their cargoes, to the far ports of the Mediterranean. (British Museum/Michael Holford)

manufacture goods for export, such as metal tools, weapons, and cookware. They also expanded their trade to Egypt, where they mingled with other local traders. Moving beyond Egypt, they struck out along the coast of North Africa to establish new markets in places where they encountered little competition. This route led them to establish Carthage (meaning "new city" in Phoenician), which prospered to become the leading city in the western Mediterranean.

Although the Phoenicians did not found colonies, as did the later Greeks, they planted trading posts and small farming communities along the coast. From them they shared the vital culture of the more developed Near East with less urbanized peoples. Yet they did not impose their culture, preferring instead to let the natives adopt whatever they found desirable. In this peaceful fashion the Phoenicians spread their trade and something of their customs. But they did so as merchants, not missionaries. Their trade routes eventually took them to the far western Mediterranean and beyond to the Atlantic Ocean.

Phoenician culture was urban, based on the prosperous commercial centers of Tyre, Sidon, and Byblos, all cities still thriving today. The Phoenicians' overwhelming cultural achievement was the development of an alphabet (Figure 2.1): unlike other literate peoples, they used one letter to designate one sound, a system that vastly simplified writing and reading. The Greeks would later modify this alphabet and use it to write their own language.

The Children of Israel

How did the Hebrew state evolve, and what were the unique elements of Hebrew religious thought? ■

The fall of the Hittite Empire and Egypt's collapse created a vacuum of power in the western Near East that allowed for the rise of numerous small states. South of Phoenicia arose a small kingdom, the land of the ancient Hebrews. It is difficult to say precisely who the Hebrews were and what brought them to this area, because virtually the only written source for much of their history is the Hebrew Bible, which is essentially a religious document. Moreover, it was compiled at different times, with the earliest parts dating to between about 950 and 800 B.C.E.

Early Jewish history, like that of most other peoples, is compounded of myths, legends, and facts. While the Hebrew Bible preserves many stories of events that defy the laws of nature, historians and archaeologists have been able to verify other aspects of the Bible. A conflict has arisen between those who accept the Bible as truth and those who demythologize it. Myth often contains grains of truth, but just as important, myth represents what people believe happened. Pitting myth against history, therefore, is the wrong approach. It is preferable to understand what both contribute to our understanding of the past.

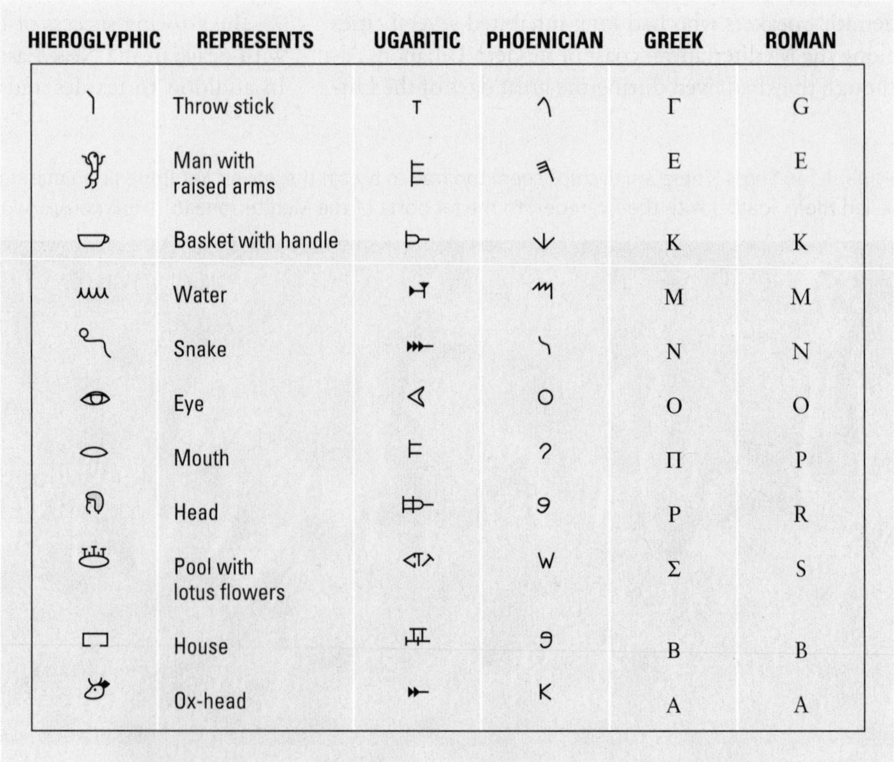

Figure 2.1 Origins of the Alphabet This figure shows the origin of many of the letters of our alphabet. As peoples encountered a form of writing, each altered the sign without changing its value.

(Source: A. B. Knapp, *The History and Culture of Ancient Western Asia and Egypt*, Chapter IV, Chart 4-1, p. 191. Copyright © 1988 Wadsworth, a division of Cengage Learning, Inc. Reproduced by permission, www.cengage.com/permissions.)

The Hebrew State

Earlier Mesopotamian and Egyptian sources refer to people called the Hapiru, independent nomads who roamed the Near East in search of pasturage for their flocks. According to Hebrew tradition, the followers of Abraham migrated from Mesopotamia around 2184 B.C.E., and Egyptian documents record Hapiru already in Syria and Palestine in 2000 B.C.E. The Hebrews are believed to have been a part of this group. Together with other semi-nomadic peoples, they migrated into the Nile Delta seeking good land. There the Egyptians enslaved them.

The period of enslavement and the subsequent release of the Hebrews, Passover and the Exodus, form a pivotal episode in their history, though historians have yet to find proof of a large-scale exodus. According to the Hebrew Bible, Moses threatened the pharaoh with the death of all first-born sons of the Egyptians. He instructed the Hebrews to prepare a hasty meal of a sacrificed lamb eaten with unleavened bread. The blood of the lamb was painted over the doors of Hebrew houses. At midnight the Hebrew God **Yahweh** (YAH-way) spread death over the land, but he passed over the Hebrew houses with the blood-painted doors. This was literally the Passover of Yahweh. The next day a terrified pharaoh ordered the Hebrews out of Egypt. Moses then led them in search of the Promised Land, a period known as the Exodus. During the Exodus Yahweh summoned Moses to Mount Sinai, where he made a covenant with the Hebrews as his

chosen people (see page 38). After forty years of wandering in the desert, Yahweh led the Hebrews to the holy land. While the story of their flight has not been substantiated, we do know that the Hebrews finally settled in Palestine in the thirteenth century B.C.E.

In Palestine the Hebrews encountered the Philistines (FIL-uh-steens); the Amorites, relatives of Hammurabi's Babylonians; and the Semitic-speaking Canaanites. Despite numerous wars, contact between the Hebrews and their new neighbors was not always hostile. The Hebrews freely mingled with the Canaanites, and some went so far as to worship Baal, an ancient Semitic fertility god represented as a golden calf. Despite the anger expressed in the Bible over Hebrew worship of Baal, there is nothing surprising about the phenomenon. Once again, newcomers adapted themselves to the culture of an older, well-established people.

The greatest danger to the Hebrews came from the Philistines, whose superior technology and military organization at first made them invincible. In Saul (ca. 1000 B.C.E.), a farmer of the tribe of Benjamin, the Hebrews found a champion and a spirited leader. In the biblical account Saul and his men battled the Philistines for control of the land, often without success. In the meantime Saul established a monarchy over the twelve Hebrew tribes.

Saul's work was carried on by David of Bethlehem, who pushed back the Philistines and waged war against his other neighbors. To give his kingdom a capital, he captured the city of Jerusalem, which he enlarged, fortified, and made the religious and political center of his realm. David's military successes won the Hebrews unprecedented security, and his forty-year reign was a period of vitality and political consolidation. His work in consolidating the monarchy and enlarging the kingdom paved the way for his son Solomon.

Possible Route of the Hebrew Exodus, ca. 1250 B.C.E.

Yahweh The Hebrew god that appeared to Moses on Mount Sinai and made a covenant with the Hebrews; in Medieval Latin he became known as Jehovah.

The Golden Calf According to the Hebrew Bible, Moses descended from Mount Sinai, where he had received the Ten Commandments, to find the Hebrews worshiping a golden calf, which was against Yahweh's laws. In July 1990 an American archaeological team found this model of a gilded calf inside a pot. The figurine, which dates to about 1550 B.C.E., is strong evidence for the existence of the cult represented by the calf in Palestine. (Courtesy of the Leon Levy Expedition to Ashkelon. Photo: Carl Andrews)

Solomon (ca. 965–925 B.C.E.) applied his energies to creating the nation of Israel out of a collection of tribes ruled by a king. He divided the kingdom into twelve territorial districts, cutting across the old tribal borders. To bring his kingdom up to the level of its more sophisticated neighbors, he set about a building program to make Israel a respectable Near Eastern state. Work was begun on a magnificent temple in Jerusalem and on cities, palaces, fortresses, and roads. Solomon dedicated the temple in grand style and made it the home of the Ark of the Covenant, the cherished chest that contained the holiest of Hebrew religious articles. The temple in Jerusalem was intended to be the religious heart of the kingdom and the symbol of Hebrew unity. Yet Solomon's efforts were hampered by strife. In the eyes of some people, he was too ready to unite other religions with the worship of the Hebrew god Yahweh. The financial demands of his building program drained the resources of his people, and his use of forced labor for building projects further fanned popular resentment. However, Solomon turned a rude kingdom into a state with broad commercial horizons and greater knowledge of the outside world.

At his death, the united state of Israel broke into two parts, with one part retaining the name Israel (Map 2.1). A rough analogy comes from the U.S. Civil War, when the North continued to be the United States of America and the South became the Confederate States of America. The northern part of the kingdom of David and Solomon became Israel, with its capital at Samaria. The southern half was Judah, and Jerusalem remained its center. With political division went a religious rift: Judah worshiped Yahweh alone, while Israel, the northern kingdom, established rival sanctuaries for gods other than Yahweh. War soon broke out between them, as recorded in the Bible. Evidence of this warfare came to light in August 1993 when an Israeli archaeologist found an inscription that refers to the "House of David." The stone celebrates an Israelite victory from the early ninth century B.C.E. This discovery is the first mention of King David's royal family outside the Bible and helps confirm the biblical account of the fighting between the two kingdoms.

Eventually, in 722 B.C.E., Israel was wiped out by the Assyrians (see page 43), but Judah survived numerous calamities until the Neo-Babylonians crushed it in 587 B.C.E. The survivors were sent into exile in Babylonia, a period of exile commonly known as the **Babylonian Captivity**. In 538 B.C.E., after the Persians defeated the Babylonians, King Cyrus (SIGH-russ) the Great permitted

Babylonian Captivity Period from 587 to 538 B.C.E. during which the survivors of a Babylonian attack on the southern kingdom of Judah were exiled in Babylonia.

Covenant A formal agreement between Yahweh and the Hebrew people that if the Hebrews worshiped Yahweh as their only god, he would consider them his chosen people and protect them from their enemies.

Map 2.1 **Small Kingdoms of the Near East, ca. 800 B.C.E.** This map illustrates the political fragmentation of the Near East after the great wave of invasions that occurred during the thirteenth century B.C.E.

some forty thousand exiles to return to Jerusalem. During and especially after the Babylonian Captivity, the exiles redefined their beliefs and practices and thus established what they believed was the law of Yahweh. Those who lived by these precepts came to be called Jews.

The Evolution of Jewish Religion

Hand in hand with their political evolution, the Hebrews were evolving their spiritual ideas. Their chief literary product, the Hebrew Bible, has fundamentally influenced both Christianity and Islam and still exerts a compelling force on the modern world.

Fundamental to an understanding of the Jewish religion is the concept of the **Covenant**, a formal agreement between Yahweh and the Hebrew people. According to the Bible, the god Yahweh appeared to Moses on Mount Sinai. There Yahweh made a covenant with the Hebrews: if the Hebrews worshiped Yahweh as their only god, he would consider them his chosen people and protect them from their enemies. The Hebrews believed that Yahweh had led them out of bondage in Egypt and had helped them conquer Israel, the Promised Land. In return, the Hebrews worshiped Yahweh alone and obeyed his Ten Commandments, an ethical code of conduct revealed to them by Moses.

Unlike Akhenaten's Egyptian brand of monotheism (see Chapter 1), Hebrew monotheism became the religion of a whole people, deeply felt and cherished. Some might fall away from Yahweh's worship, and various holy men had to exhort the Hebrews to honor the Covenant, but on the whole the people clung to Yahweh. Yet the Hebrews did not consider it their duty to spread the belief in the one god, as later Christians did. As the chosen people, their chief duty was to maintain the worship of Yahweh as he demanded. That worship was embodied in the Ten Commandments, which forbade the Hebrews to steal, murder, lie, or commit adultery. The Covenant was a constant force in Hebrew life. (See "Listening to the Past: The Covenant Between Yahweh and the Hebrews," page 40.)

From the Ten Commandments evolved Hebrew law. The earliest part of this code, the Torah or Mosaic law, was often as harsh as Hammurabi's code (see Chapter 1), which had a powerful impact on it. Later tradition, largely the work of prophets who lived from the eleventh to the fifth centuries B.C.E., put more emphasis on righteousness than on retribution.

The uniqueness of the Hebrews' religion can be seen by comparing the essence of Hebrew monotheism with the religious outlook of the Mesopotamians. Whereas the Mesopotamians considered their gods capricious, the Hebrews believed that their god would protect them and make them prosper if they obeyed his commandments. The Jews strenuously condemned everyone and everything connected with invoking the intervention of forces from the other world. They felt that magicians, witches, astrologers, and soothsayers harmfully and wrongly usurped powers that properly belonged to Yahweh. The Mesopotamians, however, accepted magic as a natural part of their religious life. The Mesopotamians thought human beings insignificant compared to the gods, so insignificant that the gods might even be indifferent to them. The Hebrews, too, considered themselves puny in comparison with Yahweh. Yet they believed that they were Yahweh's chosen people, whom he had promised never to abandon. Finally, though the Mesopotamians believed that the gods generally preferred good to evil, their religion did not demand ethical conduct. The Hebrews could please their god only by living up to high moral standards as well as worshiping him.

Yahweh is a single god, not surrounded by lesser gods and goddesses; there is thus no female divinity in Judaism, though occasionally aspects of God are described in feminine terms, such as Sophia, the wisdom of God. Though Yahweh is conceptualized as masculine, he did not have sexual relations as Mesopotamian, Egyptian, and Greek male deities did. His masculinity was spiritualized, and human sexual relations were considered a source of ritual impurity. Despite this, sex itself was basically good because it was part of Yahweh's creation, and the bearing of children was seen in some ways to be a religious function. In the codes of conduct written down in the Hebrew Bible—which Christians adopted and later termed the "Old Testament"—sex between a married woman and a man not her husband was an abomination, as were incest and sex between men. Men were free to have sexual relations with concubines, servants, and slaves, as well as with their wives. The possibility of divorce was also gender-specific: a man could divorce his wife unilaterally (though community norms frowned on divorce for frivolous reasons), but a wife could not divorce her husband, even for desertion. In general Judaism frowned on celibacy, and almost all major Jewish thinkers and rabbis were married.

Religious leaders were important in Judaism, but not as important as the Torah and the Talmud they interpreted; these texts came to be regarded as the word of Yahweh and thus had a status other writings did not. The most important task for observant Jews was studying religious texts, an activity limited to men until the twentieth century. Women were obliged to provide for men's physical needs so that they could study, which often meant that Jewish women were more active economically than their contemporaries of other religions. Women's religious rituals tended to center on the home, while men's centered on the temple. The reverence for a particular text or group of texts was passed down from Judaism to the other Western monotheistic religions that grew from it, Christianity and Islam, which has given the statements about gender in these texts particular power.

The Lives of the Hebrews

The nomadic Hebrews first entered Palestine as tribes, numerous families who thought of themselves as all related to one another. At first, good farmland, pastureland, and freshwater sources were held in common by the tribe. Common use of land was—and still is—characteristic of nomadic peoples. Typically each family or group of families in the tribe drew lots every year to determine who worked which fields. But as formerly nomadic peoples turned increasingly to settled agriculture, communal use of land gave way to family ownership. In this respect, the experience of the ancient Hebrews seems typical of that of many early peoples. Slowly the shift from nomad to farmer affected far more than just how people fed themselves. Family relationships reflected evolving circumstances. With the transition to settled agriculture, the tribe gradually became less important than the extended family. As in Mesopotamia, land was handed down within families, generally from father to son.

The Covenant Between Yahweh and the Hebrews

LISTENING TO THE PAST

These passages from the Hebrew Bible address two themes important to Hebraic thinking. The first is the meaning of kingship; the second is the nature of the Covenant between the Hebrews and their God, Yahweh. The background of the excerpt is a political crisis that has some archaeological support. The war with the Philistines put a huge strain on Hebrew society. The passage below describes an incident when Nahash,

the king of the Ammonites, threatened to destroy the Hebrews. New and effective political and military leadership was needed. The elders of the tribes had previously chosen judges to lead the community only in times of crisis. The Hebrews, however, demanded that a kingship be established, even though Yahweh was their king. They turned to Samuel, the last of the judges, who anointed Saul as the first Hebrew king. In this excerpt Samuel reviews the political, military, and religious situation confronting the Hebrews, reminding them of their obligation to honor the Covenant and expressing hesitation in naming a king.

❝ Then Nahash the Ammonite came up and encamped against Jabeshgilead: and all the men of Jabesh said unto Nahash, Make a covenant with us, and we will serve thee. And Nahash the Ammonite answered them, On this condition will I make a covenant with you, that I may thrust out all your right eyes, and lay it for a reproach upon all Israel. And the elders of Jabesh said unto him, Give us seven days' respite, that we may send messengers unto all the coasts of Israel: and then, if there be no man to save us, we will come out to thee.

Then came the messengers to Gibeah of Saul, and told the tidings in the ears of the people: and all the people lifted up their voices, and wept. And, behold, Saul came after the herd out of the field; and Saul said, What aileth the people that they weep? And they told him the tidings of the men of Jabesh. And the Spirit of God came upon Saul when he heard those tidings, and his anger was kindled greatly. And he took a yoke of oxen, and hewed them in pieces, and sent them throughout all the coasts of Israel by the hands of messengers, saying, Whosoever cometh not forth after Saul and after Samuel, so shall it be done unto his oxen. And the fear of the Lord fell on the people, and they came out with one consent. And when he numbered them in Bezek, the children of Israel were three hundred thousand, and the men of Judah thirty thousand. And they said unto the messengers that came, Thus shall ye

say unto the men of Jabeshgilead, To morrow, by that time the sun be hot, ye shall have help. And the messengers came and shewed it to the men of Jabesh; and they were glad. Therefore the men of Jabesh said, To morrow we will come out unto you, and ye shall do with us all that seemeth good unto you. And it was so on the morrow, that Saul put the people in three companies; and they came into the midst of the host in the morning watch, and slew the Ammonites until the heat of the day: and it came to pass, that they which remained were scattered, so that two of them were not left together.

And the people said unto Samuel, Who is he that said, Shall Saul reign over us? bring the men, that we may put them to death. And Saul said, There shall not a man be put to death this day: for to day the Lord hath wrought salvation in Israel. Then said Samuel to the people, Come, and let us go to Gilgal, and renew the kingdom there. And all the people went to Gilgal; and there they made Saul king before the Lord in Gilgal; and there they sacrificed sacrifices of peace offerings before the Lord; and there Saul and all the men of Israel rejoiced greatly.

And Samuel said unto all Israel, Behold, I have hearkened unto your voice in all that you said to me, and have made a king over you. And now, behold, the king walks before you; and I am old and grayheaded; and behold, my sons are with you: and I have walked before you from my childhood until this day. Behold, here I am: witness against me before the Lord, and before his anointed: whose ox have I taken? or whose ass have I taken? or whom have I defrauded? whom

For women, the evolution of Jewish society led to less freedom of action, especially in religious life. At first women served as priestesses in festivals and religious cults. Over the course of time, however, the worship of Yahweh became more male-oriented and male-dominated. Women were seen as ritually impure because of menstruation and childbirth, and as a result their role in religion was much reduced. Even when they did participate in religious rites, they were segregated from

the men. For the most part, women were largely confined to the home and the care of the family.

The typical marriage in ancient Israel was monogamous, and a virtuous wife was revered and honored. Perhaps the finest and most fervent song of praise to the good wife comes from the book of Proverbs in the Hebrew Bible:

Who can find a virtuous woman? for her price is far above rubies. . . . Strength and honour are her clothing; and she

have I oppressed? or of whose hand have I received any bribe to blind my eyes with it? and I will restore it to you.

And they said, You have not defrauded us, nor oppressed us, neither have you taken anything from any man's hand. And he said to them, the Lord is witness against you, and his anointed is witness this day, that you have not found anything in my hand. And they answered, he is witness. And Samuel said unto the people, It is the Lord that advanced Moses and Aaron, and that brought your fathers up out of the land of Egypt. Now therefore stand still, that I may reason with you before the Lord of all the righteous acts of the Lord, which he did to you and your fathers. **"**

At this point Samuel reminds the Hebrews of their Covenant with Yahweh. He lists the times when they had broken that Covenant, the times when they had served other gods. He also reminds them of Yahweh's punishment for their backsliding. He tells them frankly that they are wrong to demand a king to rule over them, for Yahweh was their lord, god, and king. Nonetheless, Samuel gives way to their demands.

" Now therefore behold the king whom you have chosen, and whom you have desired! and behold, the Lord has set a king over you. If you will fear the Lord, and serve him, and obey his voice, and not rebel against the commandment of the Lord, then shall both you and also the king who reigns over you continue following the Lord your God: But if you will not obey the voice of the Lord, but rebel against the commandment of the Lord, then shall the hand of the Lord be against you, as it was against your fathers. Now therefore stand and see this great thing, which the Lord will do before your eyes. Is it not wheat harvest today? I will call to the Lord, and he shall send thunder and rain; that you may perceive and see that your wickedness is great, which you have done in the sight of the Lord, in asking you a king. So Samuel called to the Lord; and the Lord sent thunder and rain that day: and all the people greatly feared the Lord and Samuel. And all the people said to Samuel, pray for your ser-

Ark of the Covenant depicted in a relief from a synagogue in Capernaum, second century C.E. (Ancient Art & Architecture Collection)

vants to the Lord your God, so that we will not die: for we have added to all of our sins this evil, to ask us for a king. And Samuel said to the people, Fear not: you have done all this wickedness; yet turn not aside from following the Lord, but serve the Lord with all your heart; And do not turn aside; for then should you go after vain things, which cannot profit nor deliver; for they are vain. For the Lord will not forsake his people for his great name's sake: because it pleases the Lord to make you his people. Moreover, as for me, God forbid that I should sin against the Lord in ceasing to pray for you: but I will teach you the good and the right way: Only fear the Lord, and serve him in truth with all your heart: for consider how great things he has done for you. But if you shall still act wickedly, you will be consumed, both you and your king. **"**

Source: 1 Samuel 11:1–15; 12:1–7, 13–25. Abridged and adapted from *The Holy Bible*, King James Version.

QUESTIONS FOR ANALYSIS

1. How did Samuel explain his anointment of a king?
2. What was Samuel's attitude toward kingship?
3. What were the duties of the Hebrews toward Yahweh? How might those duties conflict with those toward the secular king? How might the Hebrews avoid the conflict?

shall rejoice in time to come. She openeth her mouth with wisdom; and in her tongue is the law of kindness. She looketh well to the ways of her household, and eateth not the bread of idleness. Her children arise up, and call her blessed; her husband also, and he praiseth her. . . . Favour is deceitful, and beauty is vain: but a woman that feareth the lord, she shall be praised. (Proverbs 31:10, 25–30)

The commandment "honor thy father and thy mother" was fundamental to the Mosaic law. The wife

" Who can find a virtuous woman? for her price is far above rubies. . . . Strength and honour are her clothing; and she shall rejoice in time to come. **"**

—**BOOK OF PROVERBS, HEBREW BIBLE**

Hebrew Archer Although graven images were taboo to the Hebrews, Israeli archaeologists recently found this black seal depicting an archer shooting an arrow. The inscription beside him means *for Hagab*. The children of Hagab were among those whom King Cyrus returned from Babylonia (Ezra 2:46). (Photo: Clara Amit. Courtesy, Israel Antiquities Authority)

was a pillar of the family, and her work and wisdom were respected and treasured. The newly married couple was expected to begin a family at once. Children, according to the Book of Psalms, "are a heritage of the lord, and the fruit of the womb is his reward" (Psalms 128:3). The desire for children to perpetuate the family was so strong that if a man died before he could sire a son, his brother was legally obliged to marry the widow. The son born of the brother was thereafter considered the offspring of the dead man. If the brother refused, the widow had her revenge by denouncing him to the elders and publicly spitting in his face.

The early education of children was in the mother's hands. She taught her children right from wrong and gave them their first instruction in the moral values of society. As boys grew older, fathers instructed them in religion and the history of their people. Many children were taught to read and write, and the head of each family was probably able to write. Fathers also taught sons the family craft or trade.

The development of urban life among the Jews created new economic opportunities, especially in crafts and trades. People specialized in certain occupations, such as milling flour, baking bread, making pottery, weaving, and carpentry. All these crafts were family trades. Sons worked with their father, daughters with their mother. If the business prospered, the family might be assisted by a few paid workers or slaves. The practitioners of a craft usually lived in a particular section of town, a custom still prevalent in the Middle East today. Commerce and trade developed later than crafts. Trade with neighboring countries was handled by foreigners, usually Phoenicians. Jews dealt mainly in local trade, and in most instances craftsmen and farmers sold directly to their customers.

Daily life was governed by the law laid out by the Torah and the Talmud, a later work that records civil and ceremonial law and Jewish legend. The dietary rules of the Jews provide an excellent example of both the relationship between the Torah and the Talmud and their effect on ordinary life and culture. According to the Torah, people were not to eat meat that they found in the field. This very sensible prohibition protected them from eating dangerous food. Yet if meat from the countryside could not be eaten, some rules were needed for meat in the city. The solution found in the Talmud was a set of regulations for the proper way to conduct ritual slaughter and to prepare food. Together these two works regulated and codified Jewish dietary customs.

Assyria, the Military Monarchy

What enabled the Assyrians to conquer their neighbors, and what finally caused their undoing? ■

Small kingdoms like those of the Phoenicians and the Hebrews could exist only in the absence of a major power. The beginning of the ninth century B.C.E. saw the rise of such a power: the Assyrians of northern Mesopotamia, whose chief capital was at Nineveh (NIN-uh-vuh) on the Tigris River. The Assyrians were a Semitic-speaking people heavily influenced, like so many other peoples of the Near East, by the Mesopotamian culture of Babylon to the south. They were also one of the most warlike peoples in history. Living in an open, exposed land, the Assyrians experienced frequent and devastating attacks by the wild, war-loving tribes to their north and east and by the Babylonians to the south. The constant threat to survival experienced by the Assyrians promoted political cohesion and military might. (See "Living in the Past: Assyrian Palace Life and Power," page 44.) Yet they were also a mercantile people who had long pursued commerce with both the Babylonians in the south and the peoples of northern Syria in the north.

The Power of Assyria

The Assyrians had inhabited northern Mesopotamia since the late third millennium B.C.E. For over two hundred years they labored to dominate the Near East. In 859 B.C.E., the new Assyrian king, Shalmaneser (shal-muh-NEE-zuhr), unleashed the first of a long series of attacks on the peoples of Syria and Palestine. These ominous events inaugurated two turbulent centuries marked by Assyrian military campaigns, constant efforts by Syria and the two Jewish kingdoms to maintain or recover their independence, and eventual Assyrian conquest of Babylonia and northern Egypt. In addition, periodic political instability occurred in Assyria itself, which prompted stirrings of freedom throughout the Near East.

Under the Assyrian kings Tiglath-pileser III (TIG-lath-pih-LEE-zuhr) (744–727 B.C.E.) and Sargon II (r. 721–705 B.C.E.), both mighty warriors, the Near East trembled as never before under the blows of Assyrian armies. The Assyrians stepped up their attacks on Anatolia, Syria, and Palestine. The kingdom of Israel and many other states fell; others, like the kingdom of Judah, became subservient to the warriors from the Tigris. In 717 to 716 B.C.E. Sargon led his army in a sweeping attack along the Philistine coast, where he defeated the pharaoh. Sargon also lashed out at Assyria's traditional enemies to the north and then turned south against a renewed threat in Babylonia. By means of almost constant warfare, Tiglath-pileser and Sargon carved out an Assyrian empire that stretched from east and north of the Tigris River to central Egypt (Map 2.2). Revolt against the Assyrians inevitably promised the rebels bloody battles and cruel sieges followed by surrender accompanied by systematic torture and slaughter.

Though atrocity and terrorism struck unspeakable fear into Assyria's subjects, Assyria's success was actually due to sophisticated and effective military organization. By Sargon's time, the Assyrians had invented the might-

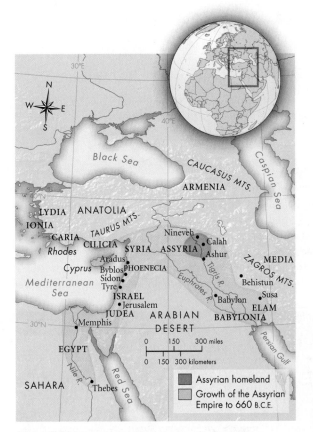

Map 2.2 Expansion of the Assyrian Empire, ca. 900–660 B.C.E. The Assyrian Empire at its height (ca. 660 B.C.E.) included almost all of the old centers of power in the ancient Near East.

iest military machine the ancient Near East had ever seen. The mainstay of the Assyrian army was the infantryman armed with spear and sword and protected by helmet and armor. The Assyrian army also featured archers, some on foot, others on horseback, and still others

Surrender of the Jews
The Jewish king Jahu finally surrendered to the Assyrians. Here his envoy kneels before the Assyrian king Shalmaneser III in total defeat. Although the Assyrian king treated Jahu well, his people were led off into slavery. (British Museum/Michael Holford)

LIVING IN THE PAST

IN 1854 THE BRITISH ARCHAEOLOGIST W. K. Loftus uncovered the palace of the Assyrian king Ashurbanipal (669–626 B.C.E.) at Nineveh in modern Iraq. Among its treasures he found carved reliefs that stunningly illustrated royal life and Assyrian power. The friezes shown here decorated the walls of the palace where visitors to Ashurbanipal's court would see them.

The relief on the left shows Ashurbanipal and his queen enjoying a tranquil banquet in the shade of an arbor. Elegantly clothed, they drink first to the gods. Servants fan them. The king reposes on a lavish couch covered with expensive rugs. The queen sits beside him on an ornate chair, and servants carry in an opulent meal. Other servants play music for the royal couple. In true Assyrian style the seemingly peaceful scene gives a bald message of victory and power. Hanging from the tree on the left is the head of Teumann, king of Elam, whom Ashurbanipal has just defeated in battle. The servants are Teumann's captured sons.

A frieze of a royal hunt (right) depicts a different display of royal power. Ashurbanipal routinely hunted lions, but only partly as sport. Hunting also enabled him to display symbolically his role as the protector

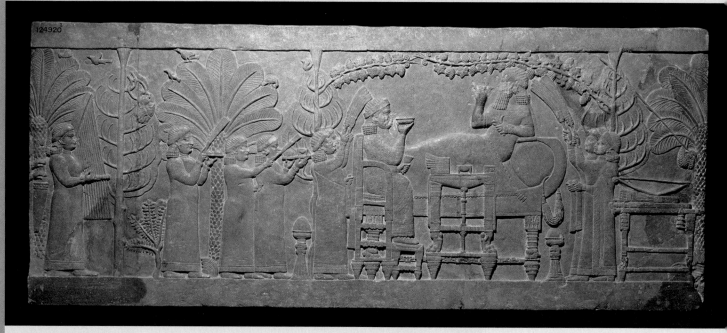

Ashurbanipal and his queen enjoying a banquet. (Courtesy of the Trustees of the British Museum)

in chariots—the latter ready to wield lances once they had expended their supply of arrows. Some infantry archers wore heavy armor. These soldiers served as a primitive field artillery whose job was to sweep the enemy's walls of defenders so that others could storm the defenses. Slingers (warriors who used slingshots, like David in the Old Testament) also served as artillery in pitched battles. For mobility on the battlefield, the Assyrians organized a corps of chariots.

Assyrian military genius was remarkable for the development of a wide variety of siege machinery and techniques, including excavation to undermine city walls and battering rams to knock down walls and gates. Never before in the Near East had anyone applied such technical knowledge to warfare. The Assyrians even invented the concept of a corps of engineers, who bridged rivers with pontoons or provided soldiers with inflatable skins for swimming. And the Assyrians knew how to coordinate their efforts, both in open battle and in siege warfare. Assyrian king Sennacherib's account of his siege of Jerusalem in 701 B.C.E. is a vivid portrait of the Assyrian war machine:

As to Hezekiah, the Jew, he did not submit to my yoke, I laid siege to 46 of his strong cities, walled forts and to the

of his people. The hunts often took place in the extensive parks that surrounded the royal court. Part of an elaborate ritual, the lions were let loose from pens. When ready, the king advanced either on foot or horseback. When on foot, he was armed with bow or lance and accompanied only by a shield-bearer. Like a toreador in a bullfight, the king had to face the lion alone. Here King Ashurbanipal is mounted on a stallion that is wide-eyed from fear of the lion beside him. The king wears only a richly embroidered jacket, a kilt, and riding boots. As the lion lunges, he plunges his spear down the lion's throat in a public display of his bravery and skill.

QUESTIONS FOR ANALYSIS

1. How realistic are these depictions? Based on what you know about the Assyrians, do you think they offer accurate depictions of palace life?

2. Consider the purpose of these two images. What did the king hope to convey with these depictions of himself? How might the reactions of subjects and foreigners have varied?

A royal lion hunt. (Courtesy of the Trustees of the British Museum)

countless small villages in their vicinity, and conquered them by means of well-stamped earth-ramps, and battering rams brought thus near to the walls combined with the attack by foot soldiers, using mines, breaches as well as sapper work. . . . Himself I made prisoner in Jerusalem, his royal residence, like a bird in a cage. I surrounded him with earthwork in order to molest those who were leaving his city's gate.[2]

The Jews recorded this same incident, and historians find it interesting to see how two different peoples interpreted the same event. The Jews ignored political and military events and insisted that the siege of

❝ Himself I made prisoner in Jerusalem, his royal residence, like a bird in a cage. I surrounded him with earthwork in order to molest those who were leaving his city's gate. ❞

—**KING SENNACHERIB**

45

Jerusalem resulted from Hezekiah's disbelief that Yahweh could repel the Assyrian invasion. For the Assyrians, the conquest was proof of military superiority. For the Jews, it stood as a symbol of the fate of those who mistrusted their god.

Assyrian Rule and Culture

Not only did the Assyrians know how to win battles, but they also knew how to use their victories to consolidate their power. As early as the reign of Tiglath-pileser III, the Assyrian kings began to organize their conquered territories into an empire. The lands closest to Assyria became provinces governed by Assyrian officials. Kingdoms beyond the provinces were not annexed but became dependent states that followed Assyria's lead. The Assyrian king chose their rulers either by regulating the succession of native kings or by supporting native kings who appealed to him. Against more distant states the Assyrian kings waged frequent war in order to conquer them outright or make the dependent states secure.

In the seventh century B.C.E. Assyrian power seemed firmly established. Yet the downfall of Assyria was swift and complete. Babylon finally won its independence from Assyria in 626 B.C.E. and joined forces with the Medes, an Indo-European-speaking folk from Persia (modern Iran). Together the Babylonians and the Medes destroyed

Picturing the Past

Assyrian Battle Scene Art here serves as a textbook of Assyrian warfare. While some Assyrian troops attack the city wall, archers clear the parapets, and Assyrian combat engineers undermine the foundations of the wall. (British Museum. Photo © Michael Holford)

ANALYZING THE IMAGE How many means of attack do the Assyrians use against the besieged city? Can the defenders repel them all?

CONNECTIONS The Assyrians, with their military might, greatly expanded their empire. Yet they were unable to hold onto their gains. Why do you think their downfall was so swift?

To complete this activity online, go to the Online Study Guide at bedfordstmartins.com/mckaywest.

"Nineveh is laid waste: who will bemoan her?"

—NAHUM

the Assyrian Empire in 612 B.C.E., paving the way for the rise of the Persians. The Hebrew prophet Nahum (NAY-uhm) spoke for many when he asked, "Nineveh is laid waste: who will bemoan her?" (Nahum 3:7). Their cities destroyed and their power shattered, the Assyrians disappeared from history, remembered only as a cruel people of the Old Testament who oppressed the Hebrews. Two hundred years later, when the Greek adventurer and historian Xenophon (ZEH-nuh-fuhn) passed by the ruins of Nineveh, he marveled at the extent of the former city but knew nothing of the Assyrians. The glory of their empire was forgotten.

Modern archaeology has brought the Assyrians out of obscurity. In 1839 the intrepid English archaeologist and traveler A. H. Layard began the most noteworthy excavations of Nineveh. His findings electrified the world. Layard's workers unearthed masterpieces, including monumental sculpted figures—huge winged bulls, human-headed lions, and sphinxes—as well as brilliantly sculpted friezes. Equally valuable were the numerous Assyrian cuneiform documents, which ranged from royal accounts of mighty military campaigns to simple letters by common people. Among the most renowned of Layard's finds were the Assyrian palace reliefs, whose number has been increased by the discoveries of twentieth-century archaeologists. Assyrian kings delighted in scenes of war, which their artists depicted in graphic detail. By 668 B.C.E. Assyrian artists had hit on the idea of portraying a series of episodes—a visual narrative of events that had actually taken place. Scene followed scene in a continuous frieze, so that the viewer could follow the progress of a military campaign from the time the army marched out until the enemy was conquered.

Assyrian art fared better than Assyrian military power. The techniques of Assyrian artists influenced the Persians, who adapted them to gentler scenes. In fact, many Assyrian innovations, military and political as well as artistic, were taken over wholesale by the Persians. Although the memory of Assyria was hateful throughout the Near East, the fruits of Assyrian organizational genius helped the Persians to bring peace and stability to the same regions where Assyrian armies had spread terror.

The Neo-Babylonian Empire

The decline of Assyria allowed the Babylonians to create a new dynasty of kings and priests known as the Chaldeans. The Neo- (or new) Babylonian empire they created was marked by the restoration of past Babylonian greatness. The Chaldeans were Semitic-speaking tribes that settled in southern Mesopotamia, where they established their rule, later extending it farther north. They grew up strong enough to overthrow Assyrian rule in 626 B.C.E. with the help of another new people, the Indo-European Medes, who had established themselves in modern western Iran (see page 48). Their most famous king, Nebuchadnezzar (ne-buh-kuhd-NEH-zuhr) (r. 604–562 B.C.E.), thrust Babylonian power into Syria and Judah, destroying Jerusalem and deporting the Hebrews to Babylonia.

The Neo-Babylonian Empire, ca. 560 B.C.E.

The Chaldeans focused on solidifying their power and legitimizing their authority. Kings and priests consciously looked back to the great days of Hammurabi. They instituted a religious revival that included restoring old temples and sanctuaries, as well as creating new ones in the same tradition. Part of their effort was commercial, as they sought to revive the economy in order to resurrect the image of Babylonian greatness. In their hands Babylonia itself became one of the wonders of the ancient world. They preserved many basic aspects of Babylonian law, literature, and government. Yet they failed to bring peace and prosperity to Mesopotamia. Loss of important trade routes to the north and northeast, combined with catastrophic inflation, reduced income. Additional misfortune came in the form of famine and plague. The Chaldean kings had to some degree created a situation that ultimately led to their downfall in 539 B.C.E. It would come not from internal rebellion, but rather from two groups of Iranian newcomers: the Medes and the Persians.

The Empire of the Persian Kings

How did the Persians rise to power and control and influence the subjects of their extensive empire? ■

Like the Hittites before them, the Iranians were Indo-Europeans from central Europe and southern Russia. They migrated into the land between the Caspian Sea and the Persian Gulf. Like the Hittites, they then fell under the spell of the more sophisticated cultures of their Mesopotamian neighbors. Yet the Iranians went on to create one of the greatest empires of antiquity, one that encompassed scores of peoples and cultures. The Persians, the most important of the Iranian peoples, had a farsighted conception of empire. Though as conquerors they willingly used force to accomplish their ends, they normally preferred to depend on diplomacy to rule. They usually respected their subjects and allowed them to practice their native customs and religions. Thus the Persians gave the Near East both political unity and cultural diversity. Never before had Near Eastern people viewed empire in such intelligent and humane terms.

The Land of the Medes and Persians

Persia—the modern country of Iran—is a stark land of towering mountains and flaming deserts with a broad central plateau in the heart of the country. Between the Tigris-Euphrates Valley in the west and the Indus Valley

in the east rises an immense plateau that cuts the interior from the sea. Iran's geographical position and topography explain its traditional role as the highway between East and West. Throughout history, wild nomadic tribes migrating from the broad steppes of Russia and Central Asia have streamed into Iran. Confronting the uncrossable salt deserts of Iran, most of them have turned either eastward or westward, moving until reaching the advanced and wealthy urban centers of Mesopotamia and India. Where cities emerged along the natural lines of east-west communications, Iran became the area in which nomads met urban dwellers, an area of unique significance for the civilizations of both East and West.

The Iranians entered this land around 1000 B.C.E. as part of the vast movement of Indo-European-speaking peoples whose wanderings took them from Europe to India (see Chapter 1). These Iranians were nomads who migrated with their flocks and herds. They were also

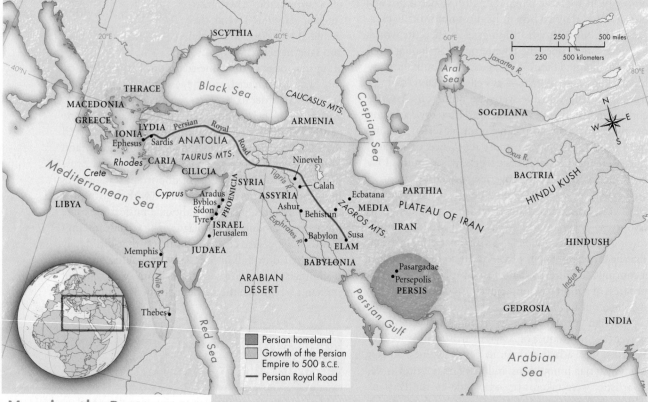

Mapping the Past

Map 2.3 **Expansion of the Persian Empire, ca. 1000–500 B.C.E.** Compare this map showing the extent of the Persian Empire with Map 1.3 on page 28, which shows the earliest political extent of the Near East, and Map 2.2 on page 43.

ANALYZING THE MAP What new areas have opened to the old Mesopotamian cultures shown on Map 1.3? What cultures have been consumed by the growth of Assyria and Persia?

CONNECTIONS What do these maps suggest about the shift of power and the spread of civilization in the ancient Near East?

To complete this activity online, go to the Online Study Guide at bedfordstmartins.com/mckaywest.

horse breeders, and the horse gave them a decisive military advantage over the native peoples of Iran. Centuries of immigration saw constant cultural interchange between conquering newcomers and conquered natives.

Two groups of Iranians gradually began coalescing into larger units. The Persians settled in Persia, in southern Iran (Map 2.3). Their kinsmen, the Medes, occupied Media in the north. The Medes united under one king around 710 B.C.E. They next extended their control over the Persians to the south. In 612 B.C.E. they joined the Babylonians to overthrow the Assyrian Empire. With the rise of the Medes, the balance of power in the Near East shifted east of Mesopotamia for the first time.

The Rise of the Persian Empire

In 550 B.C.E. Cyrus the Great (r. 559–530 B.C.E.), king of the Persians and one of the most remarkable statesmen of antiquity, conquered the Medes. (See "Individuals in Society: Cyrus the Great," page 50.) Cyrus's conquest of the Medes resulted not in slavery and slaughter but in the union of the Iranian peoples. Having united Persia and Media, Cyrus set out to achieve two goals. First, he wanted to win control of the West and thus of the terminal ports of the great trade routes that crossed Iran and Anatolia. Second, he strove to secure eastern Iran from the pressure of nomadic invaders.

In a series of major campaigns, Cyrus achieved his goals. He swept into Anatolia, easily overthrowing the young kingdom of Lydia. His generals subdued the Greek cities along the coast of Anatolia, thus gaining him important ports on the Mediterranean. From Lydia, Cyrus marched to the far eastern corners of Iran and conquered the regions of Parthia and Bactria. Internal discord had weakened the Babylonians, and they welcomed him as a liberator when his soldiers moved into their kingdom in 539 B.C.E., overthrowing the Chaldean kings. With these victories, Cyrus demonstrated to the world his benevolence as well as his military might. He spared the life of Croesus (KREE-suhs), the conquered king of Lydia, who then served him as a friend and adviser. He allowed the Greeks to live according to their customs, thus making possible the spread of Greek culture. Cyrus's humanity likewise extended to the Jews, whom he found enslaved in Babylonia. He returned their sacred objects to them and allowed them to return to Jerusalem and rebuild the temple.

Cyrus's successors Darius (dah-REE-uhs) (r. 521–486 B.C.E.) and Xerxes (ZERK-sees) (r. 486–464 B.C.E.) rounded out the Persian conquest of the ancient Near East. Within thirty-seven years (550–513 B.C.E.), the Persians had transformed themselves from a subject people to the rulers of an empire that included Anatolia, Egypt, Mesopotamia, Iran, and western India. They had created a world empire encompassing all the oldest and most honored kingdoms and peoples of the ancient Near East. Never before had this region been united in a single vast political organization (see Map 2.3).

The Persians knew how to preserve the peace. Unlike the Assyrians, they did not resort to royal terrorism to maintain order. Instead, the Persians built an efficient administrative system to govern the empire, based in the capital city of Persepolis (puhr-SEH-puh-lihs), near modern Schiras, Iran. From Persepolis they sent directions to the provinces and received reports from their officials. To do so they maintained a sophisticated system of roads linking the empire. The main highway, the famous **Royal Road**, spanned some 1,677 miles (see Map 2.3). Other roads branched out to link all parts of the empire from the coast of Asia Minor (Anatolia) to

Royal Road The main highway created by the Persians; it spanned 1,677 miles from Greece to Iran.

Funeral Pyre of Croesus This scene, an excellent example of the precision and charm of ancient Greek vase painting, depicts the Lydian king Croesus on his funeral pyre. He pours a libation to the gods, while his slave lights the fire. The Greek historian Herodotus has a happier ending, saying that Cyrus the Great set fire to the pyre, but that Apollo sent rain to put it out. (Louvre/Réunion des Musées Nationaux/Art Resource, NY)

Cyrus the Great

INDIVIDUALS IN SOCIETY

CYRUS (559–530 B.C.E.), KNOWN TO HISTORY AS "THE GREAT" and the founder of the Persian Empire, began life as a subject of the Medes, an Iranian people very closely related to the Persians. Legend records that Astyages, king of the Medes, ordered the infant Cyrus killed to eliminate him as a future threat. Cyrus, like the biblical Moses, escaped the plot and went on to rule both his own Persians and the Medes.

Cyrus was a practical man of sound judgment with a good sense of humor. He was merciful but strict with his counselors and generals. He was also broad-minded and keenly interested in foreign peoples and their ways of life. Legend tells how Cyrus's intelligence and good qualities, such as those shown while a boy, later won him the kingship of the Persians. Herodotus tells how Cyrus's playmates chose him king. He assigned them specific duties; and when one aristocratic boy refused to obey his orders, Cyrus had him "arrested." The boy's father later demanded that Cyrus explain his haughty behavior. Cyrus replied that the other boys had chosen him king, and he did his duty justly, as a king should. He told the man that if he had done anything wrong, he was there to take his punishment. The man and the other boys admired his calm sense of duty and responsibility.

Astyages eventually marched against the grown Cyrus and was defeated. Instead of enslaving the Medes, Cyrus accepted them as cousins and included them in the new kingdom of Persia, thus demonstrating his magnanimous concept of rule. Unlike the Assyrians, Cyrus was building an empire based on Persian rule of faithful subjects.

Cyrus's assumption of the kingship was an irreversible step: Persia held too important a strategic position for its neighbors to leave it alone. Croesus, king of the Lydians, who considered Cyrus an immediate threat, planned to cross his eastern border at the Halys River to attack Cyrus. Legend has it that Croesus consulted the Delphic oracle about the invasion, and Apollo told him, "If you make war on the Persians, you will destroy a mighty empire."* Thinking that the oracle meant the Persian Empire, Croesus went ahead and was defeated; the oracle meant that he would destroy his own kingdom.

Cyrus's victory brought the Greeks of Asia Minor under his rule. They had loyally obeyed Croesus and resisted Cyrus, but he won their friendship by treating them mildly. They dutifully paid the royal taxes, in return for which they enjoyed peace, political stabil-

Cyrus's tomb, though monumental in size, is rather simple and unostentatious. The cylinder (below) is a historical text, written in Babylonian, that defended the legitimacy of Cyrus's rule and announced the return to traditional political life and religious practices. (tomb: Christina Gascoigne/ Robert Harding World Imagery/Alamy; cylinder: Erich Lessing/Art Resource, NY)

the valley of the Indus River. This system of communications enabled Persian kings to keep in close touch with their subjects and officials. They were thereby able to make the concepts of right, justice, and good government a practical reality.

Persian Religion

Iranian religion was originally tied to nature. Ahuramazda (ah-HOOR-uh-MAZ-duh), the chief god, was the creator and benefactor of all living creatures. Mithra, the sun-god whose cult would later spread throughout the Roman Empire, saw to justice and redemption. As in ancient India, fire was a particularly important god. The sacred fire consumed the blood sacrifices that the early Iranians offered to all their deities. A priestly class, the Magi, developed among the Medes to officiate at sacrifices, chant prayers to the gods, and tend the sacred flame. In time the Iranians built fire temples for their sacrifices and rites.

Around 600 B.C.E. a preacher named Zarathustra (zar-uh-THUH-struh) — better known as Zoroaster (zo-roh-ASS-tuhr) — introduced new spiritual concepts to the people of Iran. Zoroaster taught that life is a constant battleground for the two opposing forces of good and evil. The Iranian god Ahuramazda embodied good and truth, but was opposed by Ahriman (AH-ree-mahn), a hateful spirit who stood for evil and lies. Ahuramazda and Ahriman were locked together in a cosmic battle for the human race, a battle that stretched over thousands of years.

Zoroaster emphasized the individual's responsibility to choose between good and evil. He taught that people possessed the free will to decide between Ahuramazda and Ahriman and that they must rely on their own conscience to guide them through life. Their decisions were crucial, Zoroaster warned, for there would be a time of reckoning. The victorious Ahuramazda, like the Egyptian god Osiris, would preside over a last judgment to determine each person's eternal fate. Those who had lived according to good and truth would enter a divine kingdom. Liars and the wicked, denied this blessed immortality, would be condemned to eternal pain, darkness, and punishment. Thus Zoroaster preached a last judgment that led to a heaven or a hell.

Zoroaster's teachings converted Darius, who did not, however, try to impose the beliefs on others. Under the protection of the Persian kings, **Zoroastrianism** (zo-ro-ASS-tree-uh-nihz-uhm) swept through Persia, winning converts and sinking roots that sustained healthy growth for centuries. Zoroastrianism survived

> **Zoroastrianism** Persian religion whose gods, Ahuramazda, god of good and light, and Ahriman, god of evil and dark, were locked in a battle for the human race; the religion emphasized the individual's responsibility to choose between good and evil.

ity, and prosperity. Greek subjects continued to practice their religion with the same freedom as other Persian subjects. They also enjoyed the liberty to continue their intellectual pursuits.

Cyrus went on to conquer Babylon in 539 B.C.E., where he was received as a liberator. Cyrus wrote of his victory: "When I entered Babylon as a friend, and when I established the seat of government under jubilation and rejoicing, Marduk, the great lord, induced the magnanimous inhabitants of Babylon to love me. . . . My numerous troops walked around Babylon in peace. I did not allow anybody to terrorize the country of Sumer and Akkad."† He restored civil government and religious cult centers that had fallen into ruin. He particularly honored the traditional Babylonian god Marduk. In addition he freed the Jews from their Babylonian Captivity and permitted them to return to their homeland. Cyrus paid for the rebuilding of their temple in Jerusalem and returned sacred vessels that the Babylonians had seized. The Hebrew Bible states that Yahweh made Cyrus his anointed and supported all his efforts.

Cyrus died in 530 B.C.E. while campaigning in Central Asia. Though much of his life was spent at war, he knew how to govern conquered peoples benevolently. He honored and protected their religions and saw to the maintenance of their temples. He allowed them to live according to their own customs and local laws. Like other kings, he taxed them, but without oppressing them. The epitaph on his simple tomb read: "O man, I am Cyrus the son of Cambyses. I established the Persian Empire and was King of Asia. Do not begrudge me my memorial."‡

QUESTIONS FOR ANALYSIS

1. What were the keys to Cyrus's success as a ruler?
2. How did Cyrus's rule compare to that of the Assyrians?

* Herodotus 1.53.3.

†James B. Pritchard, ed., *The Ancient Near East*, vol. I (Princeton: Princeton University Press, 1958), p. 207.

‡Arrian, *The Anabasis of Alexander*, 6.29.9.

the fall of the Persian Empire to influence liberal Judaism, Christianity, and early Islam, largely because of its belief in a just life on earth and a happy afterlife that satisfied the longings of most people. Good behavior in the world, even though unrecognized at the time, would receive ample reward in the hereafter. Evil, no matter how powerful in life, would be punished after death. In some form or another, Zoroastrian concepts still pervade the major religions of the West and every part of the world touched by Islam.

Persian Art and Culture

The Persians carried on the cultural work of the Hittites, their predecessors in Central Asia. They cultivated native customs and beliefs, while freely adopting aspects of the venerable civilizations of peoples farther west. They both welcomed and respected new religious beliefs. They saw in the older creeds another long-established way of worshiping the gods. To these older faiths they contributed their own religious beliefs, enriching them with the moral concepts of Zoroastrianism. The importance of truth and the promise of a happy life after death reinforced the precepts of traditional religions like those of the Egyptians and Hebrews. The Persians thereby enriched the beliefs of all, while blending their ideas with older moral concepts.

The Persians made significant contributions to art, culture, and peoples' ways of life. In art they took the Assyrian tradition of realistic monumental sculpture, but ennobled it. Instead of gory details of slaughter, they portrayed themselves as noble and their subjects as dignified. They also depicted foreigners realistically. They noted and carved the physical features of their subjects, the way they wore their hair, their clothing, their tools and weapons. Their art expressed their power not by portraying bloody warfare but by emphasizing the benign peace shared by all their subjects.

The Persians encouraged their subjects to live according to their own social and religious customs. They did not unnecessarily interfere with their subjects' daily lives. Their rule resulted in an empire that brought people together in a new political system while honoring traditional local ways of life. Although some peoples, notably the Egyptians, sometimes rebelled against Persian rule, most subjects enjoyed uninterrupted lives. Above all, the Persians gave the Near East two centuries of peace and stability.

Median Religious Ritual This gold plaque shows a Median priest carrying a bundle of sacred twigs called a *barsom*. In a simple ceremony he will light the barsom to burn the sacrifice about to be offered to the god. (Courtesy of the Trustees of the British Museum)

The Impact of Zoroastrianism The Persian kings embraced Zoroastrianism as the religion of the realm. This rock carving at the Persian city of Behistun records the bond. King Darius I (left center) is seen trampling on one rebel; other rebels are lined up behind him. Above is the sign of Ahuramazda, the god of truth and guardian of the Persian king. (Robert Harding World Imagery)

LOOKING BACK LOOKING AHEAD

DURING THE CENTURIES following the Sea Peoples' invasions, natives and newcomers brought order to life across the ancient Near East. As Egypt fell, small kingdoms, including Israel and Phoenicia, grew and prospered. These fortunate circumstances enabled a comfortable life to develop once again. Yet a dark side of life emerged when the Assyrians created a cruel military monarchy in Mesopotamia. The Near East saw a period of harshness and oppression that only the triumph of the Persians ended. This Iranian people spread a broad and humane empire across the area. They gave the region general peace and opened avenues to both the West and the East. That to the West became particularly important because it introduced them to the Greeks. This step led to the enrichment of life for Greeks and Easterners alike. The world was becoming much larger.

Since the early Greeks had already settled in the areas of modern Turkey and Greece, they had absorbed numerous aspects of the advanced cultures they had encountered. They learned of Near Eastern religious myths and the sagas of heroic wars. They also acquired many of the advanced technologies that they encountered. They combined these borrowings with their own intrinsic talents to create their own distinct civilization, one that fundamentally shaped the subsequent development of Western society.

CHAPTER REVIEW

■ How did the Nubians, Kush, and Phoenicians respond to the power vacuum in Egypt and the western Near East? (p. 34)

During the centuries following the Sea Peoples' invasions, the African kingdoms of the Nubians and the Kush extended their power northward into Egypt and adopted elements of Egyptian culture such as hieroglyphs and pyramids. In Anatolia the Phoenicians took advantage of the fall of the Hittites and the weakness of Egyptian power in the Nile Delta to spread commodities and ideas through trade.

■ How did the Hebrew state evolve, and what were the unique elements of Hebrew religious thought? (p. 36)

Another group to benefit from the absence of a major power in the region were the Hebrews, who created a small kingdom in Palestine. Later split into two halves, Israel and Judah, the Hebrew kingdom was short-lived, but its religious beliefs and written codes of law and custom proved to be long lasting. Judaism, the Hebrews' monotheistic religion, continues as a vibrant faith today and was an important source for Christianity and Islam. The Egyptian enslavement of the Hebrews, Passover, and the Exodus are central events in both Hebrew history and religious thought.

■ What enabled the Assyrians to conquer their neighbors, and what finally caused their undoing? (p. 42)

The Assyrians' superior military organization enabled them to conquer many small kingdoms. Their experience on the battlefield led to the development of new and effective siege machinery and techniques. They spread their power by brutal conquests, forging an extensive empire ruled by terror. Their aggression created many enemies who ultimately joined to defeat them. Assyrian rule ended swiftly in 612 B.C.E. after the Babylonians and Medes joined together to defeat them.

■ How did the Persians rise to power and control and influence the subjects of their extensive empire? (p. 47)

The Persians assimilated the best of the civilizations that they found around them. Through conquest that was mild compared with that of the Assyrians, they broadened the geographical horizons of the ancient world. Their empire looked west to the Greeks and east to the peoples of the Indus Valley, and they gave the Near East a long period of peace. The Persians, whose empire far surpassed that of the Assyrians, had a farsighted conception of empire. Though as conquerors they willingly used force to accomplish their ends, they preferred to depend on diplomacy to rule. They usually respected their subjects and allowed them to practice their native customs and religions. Thus the Persians gave the Near East both political unity and cultural diversity. Through their religion Zoroastrianism, they also introduced the concept of life as a battleground between good and evil.

Suggested Reading

Alon, Gedaliah. *The Jews in Their Land*. 1989. Covers the Talmudic period.

Assman, Jan. *Moses the Egyptian*. 1997. A study of monotheism.

Boyce, Mary. *Zoroastrianism*. 1979. The best introduction to the essence of Zoroastrianism.

Briant, Pierre. *From Cyrus to Alexander*. 2002. A superb treatment of the entire Persian Empire.

Brosius, Maria. *The Persians: An Introduction*. 2006. Covers the essentials of Persian history.

Edwards, David N. *The Nubian Past*. 2004. Studies the history of Nubia and the Sudan, incorporating archaeological evidence to supplement historical sources.

Gates, Charles. *Ancient Cities: The Archaeology of Urban Life in the Ancient Near East and Egypt, Greece, and Rome*. 2003. Provides a survey of ancient life primarily from an archaeological point of view, but one that includes cultural and social information.

Hoffmeier, James K. *Israel in Egypt: The Evidence for the Authenticity of the Exodus Tradition*. 1997. Discusses evidence for the account in Hebrew Scripture concerning the Exodus.

Markoe, Glenn E. *The Phoenicians*. 2000. A fresh investigation of the Phoenicians at home and abroad in the western Mediterranean over their long history, with many illustrations.

Morkot, Robert G. *The Black Pharaohs: Egypt's Nubian Rulers*. 2000. Examines the growth of the Kushite kingdom and its rule over pharaonic Egypt in the eighth century B.C.E.

Niditch, Susan. *Ancient Israelite Religion*. 1997. A brief but broad interpretation of Jewish religious developments.

Pastor, Jack. *Land and Economy in Ancient Palestine*. 1997. Discusses the basics of economic life of the period.

Redford, Donald B. *Egypt, Canaan, and Israel in Ancient Times*. 1992. A study of political, cultural, and religious relationships among the peoples of Egypt, Assyria, and the Near East during thousands of years of history.

Saggs, H. W. F. *Everyday Life in Babylonia and Assyria*, rev. ed. 1987. Offers a general and well-illustrated survey of Mesopotamian history from 3000 to 300 B.C.E.

Key Terms

Yahweh (p. 37)
Babylonian Captivity (p. 38)
Covenant (p. 38)
Royal Road (p. 49)
Zoroastrianism (p. 51)

Notes

1. James H. Breasted, *Ancient Records of Egypt*, vol. 4 (Chicago: University of Chicago Press, 1907), para. 398.
2. J. B. Pritchard, ed., *Ancient Near Eastern Texts*, 3d ed. (Princeton, N.J.: Princeton University Press, 1969), p. 288.

For practice quizzes and other study tools, visit the Online Study Guide at **bedfordstmartins.com/mckaywest**.

For primary sources from this period, see *Sources of Western Society*, **Second Edition**.

For Web sites, images, and documents related to topics in this chapter, visit Make History at **bedfordstmartins.com/mckaywest**.

3

The Development of Classical Greece

ca. 2000–338 B.C.E.

The people of Greece developed a culture that fundamentally shaped Western civilization. They were the first to explore most of the questions that continue to concern Western thinkers to this day. Going beyond mythmaking, the Greeks strove to understand the world in logical, rational terms. The result was the birth of philosophy and science — subjects that were as important to most Greek thinkers as religion. The concept of politics evolved through Greek philosophy. Greek contributions to the arts and literature were equally profound.

The history of the Greeks is divided into two broad periods: the Hellenic (heh-LEH-nihk) period (the subject of this chapter), roughly the time between the arrival of the Greeks (approximately 2000 B.C.E.) and the victory over Greece in 338 B.C.E. by Philip of Macedonia; and the Hellenistic (hehl-luh-NIHS-tik) period (the subject of Chapter 4), the age beginning with the remarkable reign of Philip's son, Alexander the Great (336–323 B.C.E.) and ending with the Roman conquest of the Hellenistic East (200–146 B.C.E.). ■

Life in Classical Greece. Religion was central to Greek life. This detail from a vase shows Greek men and women approaching a temple at the left. There, the priestess, with a bough in hand, greets them.

CHAPTER PREVIEW

Hellas: The Land
■ When the Greeks arrived in Hellas, how did they adapt themselves to their new landscape?

The Polis
■ What was the origin of the polis, and what types of governments were established to rule it?

The Archaic Age, 800–500 B.C.E.
■ What major developments mark the Archaic Greek period in terms of spread of culture and the growth of cities?

The Classical Period, 500–338 B.C.E.
■ What were the major developments in literature, philosophy, religion, and art, and how did war affect this intellectual and social process?

The Final Act
■ How did the Greek city-states meet political and military challenges, and how did Macedonia become dominant?

Hellas: The Land

When the Greeks arrived in Hellas, how did they adapt themselves to their new landscape? ■

Hellas, as the Greeks still call their land, encompassed the Greek peninsula, the islands of the Aegean (ah-GEE-uhn) Sea, and the lands bordering the Aegean, an area known as the Aegean basin (Map 3.1). Mountains divide the land, leaving few plains and rivers that are generally no more than creeks, most of which go dry in the summer. Greece is, however, blessed with good harbors, the most important of which look to the east. The islands of the Aegean serve as steppingstones to Asia Minor (Anatolia), the lands of western Turkey.

The major regions of Greece were Thessaly (THEH-suh-lee) and Boeotia (bee-OH-shuh) in the north and center, lands marked by fertile plains that helped to sustain a strong population capable of serving as formidable cavalry and infantry. Immediately to the south of Boeotia is Attica (A-teh-kuh), an area of thin soil that is home to the olive and the vine. Its harbors looked to the Aegean, which invited its inhabitants, the Athenians, to concentrate on maritime commerce. Still farther south, the Peloponnesus (peh-luh-puh-NEE-suhs) was a patchwork of high mountains and small plains that divided the area into several regions.

The geographical fragmentation of Greece encouraged political fragmentation. Communications were extraordinarily poor. Rocky tracks were far more common than roads, and the roads were seldom paved. These conditions prohibited the growth of a great empire like those of the Near East.

Minoan A flourishing and vibrant culture on Crete around 1650 B.C.E.; the palace was the center of political and economic life, the most important one being Knossos.

Mycenaean A Greek society that developed around 1650 B.C.E. when a powerful group centered at Mycenae spread its culture over the less advanced native population.

The Minoans and Mycenaeans

The origins of Greek civilization are complicated, obscure, and diverse. During the Bronze Age, Neolithic peoples built prosperous communities in the Aegean, but not until about 2000 B.C.E. did they establish firm contact with one another. By then artisans had discovered how to make bronze, which gave these Stone Age groups more efficient tools and weapons. With the adoption of metallurgy came even greater prosperity. Some Cretan (KREE-tuhn) farmers and fishermen began to trade their surpluses with their neighbors. The central position of Crete (kreet) in the eastern Mediterranean made it a crucial link in this trade. The Cretans voyaged to Egypt, Asia Minor, other islands, and mainland Greece.

They thereby played a vital part in creating an Aegean economy that brought them all into close contact. These favorable circumstances produced the flourishing and vibrant **Minoan** culture on Crete, named after the mythical King Minos.

As seen in Chapter 1, only literacy can lead to history, so while the Minoans created a script now called Linear A, none of it can be read, so much of how the Minoans lived remains lost to us. Instead, archaeology and art offer some glimpses of life on Crete. The palace was the political and economic center of Minoan society. About 1650 B.C.E. Crete was dotted with palaces, but the palace at Knossos (NO-suhs) towered above all others in importance. Few specifics are known about Minoan life except that at its head stood a king and his nobles. Minoan society was wealthy and, to judge by the absence of fortifications on the island, relatively peaceful. Minoan artistic remains, including frescoes and figurines, show women as well as men leading religious activities, watching entertainment, and engaging in athletic competitions, such as leaping over a bull. Yet these scenes probably depict aristocratic ladies rather than ordinary women.

This situation continued until the arrival of Greek-speaking peoples in the Balkans around 2000 B.C.E. They came gradually as individual groups who spoke various dialects of the same language. They nonetheless considered themselves a related people. More culturally advanced than the natives, they easily took control of the land. By about 1650 B.C.E. one group had founded a powerful kingdom at Mycenae (migh-SEE-nee). The experience of the **Mycenaeans** differed from that of their distant kinsmen who were simultaneously settling in northwestern Anatolia. There the Greeks became absorbed by the superior native culture around them. In the west the Mycenaeans spread their advanced culture over less developed people.

Early Mycenaean Greeks raised other palaces and established cities at Thebes (theebz), Athens, and elsewhere. As in Crete, the political unit was the kingdom. The king and his warrior aristocracy stood at the top of society. The seat and symbol of the king's power was his palace, which was also the economic center of the kingdom. Within its walls royal artisans fashioned jewelry and rich ornaments, made and decorated fine pottery, forged weapons, prepared hides and wool for clothing, and manufactured the other goods needed by the king and his retainers. Palace scribes kept records in Greek with a script known as Linear B, which was derived from Minoan Linear A. The Mycenaean economy was marked by an extensive division of labor, all tightly controlled from the palace. At the bottom of the social scale were male and female slaves, who were normally owned by the king and aristocrats but who also worked for ordinary people.

Contacts between the Minoans and Mycenaeans were originally peaceful, and Minoan culture flooded the Greek mainland. But around 1450 B.C.E. the Mycenaeans attacked Crete, destroying Knossos. For about the next fifty years, the Mycenaeans ruled much of the island until a further wave of violence left Knossos in ashes.

Whatever the explanation of these events, Mycenaean kingdoms in Greece benefited from the fall of Knossos, quickly expanding commercially throughout the Aegean. Palaces became grander, and citadels were often protected by mammoth stone walls. Prosperity, however, did not bring peace, and between 1300 and 1000 B.C.E. kingdom after kingdom suffered attack and destruction. Although later Greeks accused the Dorians (DOR-ee-uhns) of overthrowing the Mycenaean kingdoms, these centers undoubtedly fell because of mutual discord.

The fall of the Mycenaean kingdoms ushered in a period of such poverty, disruption, and backwardness that historians usually call it the "Dark Age" of Greece (ca. 1100–800 B.C.E.). Even literacy, which was not widespread in any case, was a casualty of the chaos. Nonetheless, the Greeks survived the storm to preserve their culture and civilization. Greece remained Greek; nothing essential was swept away. Greek religious cults remained vital to the people, and basic elements of social organization continued to function effectively. It was a time of change and challenge, but not of utter collapse.

The disruption of Mycenaean societies caused the widespread and prolonged movement of Greek peoples. They dispersed beyond mainland Greece farther south to Crete and in greater strength across the Aegean to the shores of Anatolia. They arrived during a time when traditional states and empires had collapsed. Economic hardship was common, and various groups wandered for years. Yet by the conclusion of the Dark Age, the Greeks had spread their culture throughout the Aegean basin.

Chronology

ca. 2000 B.C.E.	Greeks arrive in the Balkans
ca. 1650 B.C.E.	Founding of the kingdom of Mycenae; establishment of Minoan palaces
ca. 1100–800 B.C.E.	Dark Age; Greek migrations within the Aegean basin; poems of Homer and Hesiod
ca. 800–500 B.C.E.	Archaic age; rise of Sparta and Athens
ca. 750–550 B.C.E.	Greek colonization of the Mediterranean
ca. 735 B.C.E.	Sparta begins expansion by going to war against Messenia
508 B.C.E.	Cleisthenes begins democratic reforms in Athens
500–338 B.C.E.	Classical period; major intellectual and artistic achievements
499–479 B.C.E.	Persian wars
459–445 B.C.E.	War between Sparta and Athens
447 B.C.E.	Construction of the Parthenon begins
431–404 B.C.E.	Peloponnesian War
404–338 B.C.E.	Spartan and Theban hegemonies; success of Philip of Macedonia
399 B.C.E.	Socrates executed
386 B.C.E.	First Common Peace
371–362 B.C.E.	Thebes, with an alliance of city-states, rules Greece
359 B.C.E.	Philip II ascends Macedonian throne
338 B.C.E.	Philip II wins Battle of Chaeronea; gains control of Greece

Mycenaean Dagger Blade The Mycenaeans were a robust, warlike people who enjoyed the thrill and danger of hunting. This scene on the blade of a dagger depicts hunters armed with spears and protected by shields defending themselves against charging lions. (National Archaeological Museum/Archaeological Receipts Fund)

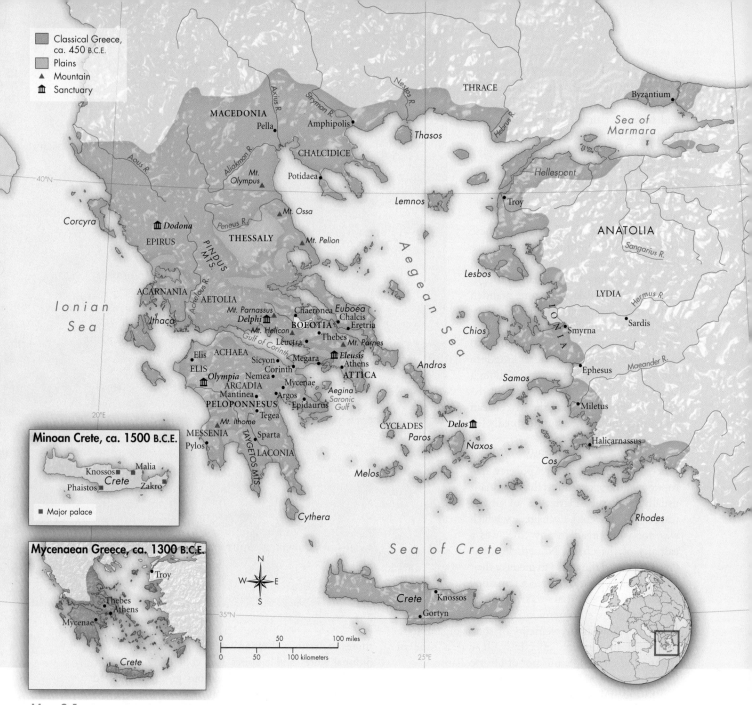

Map 3.1 Classical Greece, 500–338 B.C.E. In antiquity, the home of the Greeks included the islands of the Aegean and the western shore of Turkey as well as the Greek peninsula itself.

Homer, Hesiod, and the Epic

Much of what we know of the Dark Age comes from Greek literature. The Greeks, unlike the Hebrews, had no sacred book that chronicled their past. They had Homer's *Iliad* and *Odyssey* to describe a time when gods still walked the earth. These epics are poetic tales of the heroic deeds of legendary heroes. They also learned about the origin and descent of the gods from the *Theogony* (thee-AH-guh-nee), an epic poem by Hesiod (HEH-see-uhd). The poems of Homer and Hesiod offered the Greeks an ideal past, a legendary Heroic Age. In terms of pure history, these works contain scraps of informa-tion about the Bronze Age, much about the early Dark Age, and some about the poets' own era.

The *Iliad*'s tale of war belongs to the Troy of the late Bronze Age. Homer's *Iliad* recounts the Mycenaean Greek expedition to besiege Troy to retrieve Helen, who was abducted to Troy by Paris, the king's son. The heart of the *Iliad*, however, concerns the quarrel between Agamemnon, the king of Mycenae, and the tragic hero of the poem, Achilles (uh-KIL-eez), and how their quarrel brought suffering to the Achaeans, the name Homer gives to the Mycenaeans. The poem explores the greatness and the pettiness of mighty Achilles and Agamemnon, and exhibits their tragic flaws.

Homer's *Odyssey* (AH-duh-see) records the adventures of Odysseus (oh-DIH-see-uhs), a wise and fearless hero of the war at Troy, during his ten-year voyage home to his wife Penelope. He encounters many dangers, storms, and adventures, but with wisdom and steady courage he finally reaches his home and Penelope, the ideal wife, dedicated to her husband, family, and home.

Both of Homer's epics portray engaging but flawed characters who are larger than life, yet typically human. Homer was also strikingly successful in depicting the great gods, who generally sit on Mount Olympus (oh-LIM-puhs) and watch the fighting at Troy like spectators at a baseball game, although they sometimes participate in the action. Homer's deities are reminiscent of Mesopotamian gods and goddesses: raucous, petty, deceitful, and splendid. In short, they are human.

Hesiod, who lived somewhat later than Homer, made the gods the focus of his epic poem, the *Theogony*. Hesiod was influenced by Mesopotamian myths, which the Hittites had adopted and spread to the Aegean. Like the Hebrews, Hesiod envisaged his cosmogony—his account of the way the universe developed—in moral terms. Zeus, the son of Cronus (CROH-nuhs), defeated his evil father and took his place as king of the gods. He then sired Lawfulness, Right, Peace, and other powers of light and beauty. Thus, in Hesiod's conception, Zeus was the god of righteousness who loved justice and hated wrongdoing.

The Polis

What was the origin of the polis, and what types of governments were established to rule it? ■

After the upheavals that ended the Mycenaean period and the slow recovery of prosperity during the Dark Age, the Greeks developed the **polis** (PAH-luhs). The term *polis* (plural *poleis*) is generally interpreted as "city-state," although the word is basically untranslatable. While "city-state" does not capture how integral the countryside was to the community, it is at least a generally understood and accepted term.

The polis was far more than a political institution. Above all it was a community of citizens whose customs comprised the laws of the polis. Even though the physical, religious, and political form of the polis varied from place to place, it was the very badge of Greekness.

Origins of the Polis

Recent archaeological expeditions and careful study have done much to clarify the origins of the polis. Even during the late Mycenaean period, towns had grown up around palaces. These towns and even smaller villages performed basically local functions. The first was to administer the ordinary political affairs of the community. The village also served a religious purpose in that each, no matter how small, had a local cult to its own deity. The exchange of daily goods made these towns and villages economically important, if only on a small scale. These settlements also developed a social system that was particularly their own. They likewise had their own views of the social worth and status of their inhabitants and the nature of their public responsibilities. In short, they relied on custom and mutual agreement to direct their ordinary affairs.

The coming of the Dorians did not significantly change this political evolution, but it had two effects. In some cases it disrupted the task of rebuilding and consolidating some of the developing communities. The Dorians at times carved out territory for themselves at the expense of the natives, but they also assimilated the culture around them. This process actually strengthened the sense of identity among the local people. The situation could have been cataclysmic, but for the most part it was not. The native inhabitants acknowledged their differences with the newcomers. They maintained their traditional religion, albeit sometimes in altered form, but they also accepted the religious validity of new cults. In addition, they looked upon the Dorians as fellow Greeks. Recent archaeological and historical studies reveal a picture of continuity and assimilation.

When fully developed, each polis normally shared a surprisingly large number of features with other poleis. Physically a polis was a society of people who lived in a city (*asty*) and cultivated the surrounding countryside (*chora*). The city's water supply came from public fountains, springs, and cisterns. By the fifth century B.C.E. the city was generally surrounded by a wall. The city contained a point, usually elevated, called the acropolis (uh-KRAH-puh-luhs) and a public square or marketplace called the *agora* (AH-guh-ruh). On the **acropolis**, which in the early period was a place of refuge, stood the temples, altars, public monuments, and various dedications to the gods of the polis. The **agora** was the political center of the polis. In the agora were shops, public buildings, and courts.

The countryside was essential to the economy of the polis and provided food to sustain the entire population. But it was also home to sanctuaries for the deities of the polis and the site of important religious rites. The sacred buildings, shrines, and altars were physical symbols of a polis, uniting country and city dwellers. The religious dedications in them were the possessions not only of the gods but also of the polis, reflecting its power and prestige.

polis Generally interpreted to mean city-state, it was the basic political and institutional unit of Greece.

acropolis An elevated point within a city on which stood temples, altars, and public monuments.

agora A public square or marketplace that was a political center of Greece.

The Sanctuary of Apollo at Delphi The Greeks worshiped Apollo at Delphi, a somewhat remote spot on Mount Parnassus (see Map 3.1). As seen from a higher slope, the theater overlooks the temple of Apollo, which is approached by the Sacred Way that leads up to it. (Steve Vidler/SuperStock)

The average polis did not have a standing army. Instead it relied on its citizens for protection. Very rich citizens often served as cavalry, which was, however, never as important as the heavily armed infantry, or **hoplites**, who were the backbone of the army. Hoplites wore metal helmets and body armor, carried heavy, round shields, and armed themselves with spears and swords. In some instances the citizens of a polis hired mercenaries to fight their battles. Mercenaries were expensive, untrustworthy, and willing to defect to a higher bidder. Even worse, they sometimes seized control of the polis that had hired them.

Governing Structures

Greek city-states had several different types of government. **Monarchy**, rule by a king, was prevalent during the Mycenaean period but afterward declined. While Sparta boasted of two kings, they were only part of a more broadly based constitution. From about 500 B.C.E. Greek states were either democracies or oligarchies. Sporadic periods of violent political and social upheaval often led to a third type of government—tyranny. **Tyranny** was rule by one man who had seized power by unconstitutional means, generally by using his wealth to win a political following that toppled the existing legal government.

The most popular and lasting of these political ideals were democracy and oligarchy (O-luh-gahr-kee). In principal, **democracy** meant that all people, without respect to birth or wealth, administered the workings of government. In reality, Greek democracy meant the rule of citizens, not "the people" as a whole, and citizenship was drastically limited. While Athens presents the best example of democracy in action, Greek democracies were in fact little more than expanded oligarchies. **Oligarchy**, which literally means "the rule of the few,"

hoplites The heavily armed infantry who were the backbone of the Greek army.

monarchy Type of government in which a king rules; common during the Mycenaean period.

tyranny Rule by one man who used his wealth or other powers to seize the government unconstitutionally.

democracy A type of Greek government in which all people, without regard to birth or wealth, administered the workings of government; in practice, only people granted citizenship participated.

oligarchy A type of Greek government in which a small group of wealthy citizens, not necessarily of aristocratic birth, ruled.

federalism A political system developed by Greek states that banded together in leagues and marshaled their resources to defend themselves from outside interference, while remaining independent in their internal affairs.

was government by a small group of wealthy citizens. None of the Greek democracies reflects the modern concept that "all men are created equal." All democracies, Athens included, jealously guarded political rights. Only free adult men who had lived in the polis a long time were citizens. The remaining free men and all women were not active citizens of the democracy. Resident foreigners and slaves were also excluded from citizen rights, except for protection under the law. Still, democracy was attractive because it permitted certain male citizens to share equally in the determination of diplomatic and military policy of the polis. Even though noncitizens lived in a democratic polis, only the citizens were sovereign.

Many Greeks preferred oligarchic constitutions. Oligarchy was the government of the prosperous but it left the door open to political and social advancement. Greek oligarchy was not generally oppressive, and it possessed a democratic aspect. All members of an oligarchic government held a passive citizenship in which they enjoyed civil rights. If members of the polis could meet property or money qualifications, they could enter the governing circle. Thus oligarchy provided an avenue for political and social advancement. Moreover, oligarchs listened to the will of the people, a major factor in their long success. Oligarchy was also popular because it provided political stability.

Although each polis was normally jealous of its independence, some Greeks banded together to create leagues of city-states. Here was the birth of **federalism**, a political system in which several states formed a central government while remaining independent in their internal affairs. United in a league, a confederation of city-states was far stronger than any of its individual members and was better able to withstand external attack.

Even federalism could not overcome the passionate individualism of the polis, which proved to be a serious weakness. The citizens of each polis were determined to remain free and autonomous. Rarely were the Greeks willing to unite in larger political bodies. The political result in Greece, as earlier in Sumer (see Chapter 1), was almost constant warfare. The polis could dominate, but unlike Rome, it could not incorporate.

The Archaic Age, 800–500 B.C.E.

What major developments mark the Archaic Greek period in terms of spread of culture and the growth of cities? ■

The Archaic (ahr-KAY-ik) age was one of the most vibrant periods of Greek history, an era of extraordinary expansion geographically, artistically, and politically. During this period the Greeks recovered from the downfall of the Mycenaean kingdoms and continued the advances made during the Dark Age. Greeks ventured as far east as the Black Sea and as far west as Spain. Politically these were the years when Sparta and Athens—the two poles of the Greek experience—rose to prominence.

Overseas Expansion

During the years 1100–800 B.C.E. the Greeks not only recovered from the breakdown of the Mycenaean world but also grew in wealth and numbers. This prosperity brought new problems. The increase in population meant that many families had very little land or none at all. The resulting social and political tensions drove many Greeks to seek new homes outside of Greece. Other factors, largely intangible, played their part as well: the desire for a new start, a love of excitement and adventure, and natural curiosity about what lay beyond the horizon.

From about 750 to 550 B.C.E., Greeks from the mainland and Asia Minor traveled throughout the Mediterranean and even into the Atlantic Ocean in their quest for new land (Map 3.2). They sailed in the greatest numbers to Sicily and southern Italy, where there was ample space for expansion. In Sicily they found the Sicels, who had adopted many

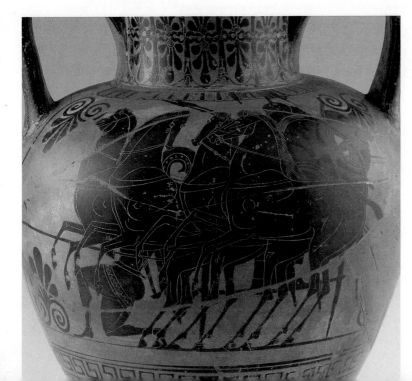

Early Greek Warfare Before the hoplites became the backbone of the army, wealthy warriors rode into battle in chariots, dismounted, and engaged the enemy. This scene, from the side of a vase, shows on the left the warrior protecting the chariot before it returns to the rear. The painter has caught the lead horses already beginning the turn. (Courtesy of the Ure Museum of Greek Archaeology, University of Reading)

Gold Comb This gold comb is a remarkable combination of Greek and Eastern details. The mounted horseman is clothed with largely Greek armor, but he attacks an Eastern enemy. The horseman's companion is also Eastern. This piece testifies to the exchange of artistic motifs and styles in the eastern Mediterranean basin. (The State Hermitage Museum, St. Petersburg. © The State Hermitage Museum)

European peoples. They welcomed Greek culture, and the Greeks found it easy to establish prosperous cities without facing significant local hostility.

Some adventurous Greeks sailed farther west to Sardinia, France, Spain, and even the Canary Islands. In Sardinia they established trading stations for bartering with the natives. Commerce was so successful that some Greeks established permanent towns there. From these new outposts Greek influence extended to southern France. The modern city of Marseilles, for example, began as a Greek colony and later sent settlers to southern Spain.

Colonization changed the entire Greek world, both at home and abroad. In economic terms the expansion of the Greeks created a much larger market for agricultural and manufactured goods. From the east, especially from the northern coast of the Black Sea, came wheat. In return flowed Greek wine and olive oil, which could not be produced in the harsher climate of the north. Greek-manufactured goods, notably rich jewelry and fine pottery, circulated from southern Russia to Spain. During this same period the Greeks adopted the custom of minting coins. Over time coinage would replace the barter system, in which one person exchanges one good for another without the use of money. Thus Greek culture and economics, fertilized by the influences of other societies, spread throughout the Mediterranean basin.

Carthaginian customs, including a new urban culture. Fiercely independent, they greeted the coming of the Greeks just as they had the arrival of the Phoenician Carthaginians. They welcomed Greek culture but not Greek demands for their land. Nonetheless, the two peoples made a somewhat uneasy accommodation, and there was some intermarriage among them. In southern Italy the Greeks encountered a number of Indo-

Colonization presented the polis with a huge challenge, for it required organization and planning on an

Map 3.2 Colonization of the Mediterranean, ca. 750–550 B.C.E. Though the Greeks and Phoenicians colonized the Mediterranean basin at about the same time, the Greeks spread much farther.

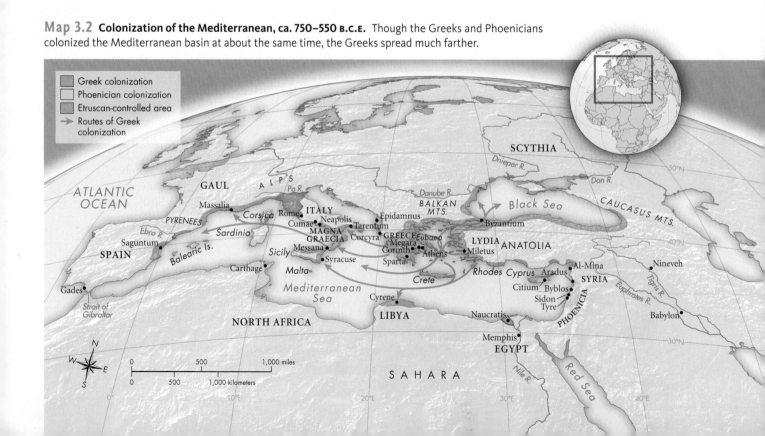

unprecedented scale. The colonizing city, called the *metropolis*, or mother city, first decided where to establish the colony, how to transport colonists to the site, and who would sail. Then the metropolis collected and stored the supplies that the colonists would need both to feed themselves and to plant their first crop. The metropolis also had to provide adequate shipping for the voyage. All preparations ready, a leader, called an *oikist*, ordered the colonists to sail. The oikist was then in full command of the band until the colony was established in its new site and capable of running its own affairs. A significant aspect of colonizing ventures was that all free male colonists were considered political equals and were expected to have a voice in the new colony.

Once the colonists landed, the oikist laid out the new polis, selected the sites of temples and public buildings, and established the government. Then he surrendered power to the new leaders. The colony was thereafter independent of the metropolis. For the Greeks, colonization had two important aspects. First, it demanded that the polis assume a much greater public function than ever before, thus strengthening the city-state's institutional position. Second, colonization spread the polis and its values far beyond the shores of Greece. Even more important, colonization on this scale had a profound impact on the course of Western civilization. It meant that the prevailing culture of the Mediterranean basin would be Greek, the heritage to which Rome would later fall heir.

The Growth of Sparta

During the Archaic period the Spartans expanded the boundaries of their polis and made it the leading power in Greece. Like other Greeks, the Spartans faced the problems of overpopulation and land hunger. Unlike other Greeks, they solved these problems by conquest, not by colonization. To gain more land, the Spartans set out in about 735 B.C.E. to conquer Messenia (muh-SEE-nee-uh), a rich, fertile region in the southwestern Peloponnesus. This conflict, the First Messenian War, lasted for twenty years and ended in a Spartan triumph. The Spartans appropriated Messenian land and turned the Messenians into **helots** (HEH-luhts), or state serfs.

In about 650 B.C.E. Spartan exploitation and oppression of the Messenian helots led to a helot revolt so massive and stubborn that it became known as the Second Messenian War. The Spartan poet Tyrtaeus, a contemporary of these events, vividly portrays the ferocity of the fighting:

Spartan Expansion, ca. 735–500 B.C.E.

For it is a shameful thing indeed
When with the foremost fighters
An elder falling in front of the young men
Lies outstretched,
Having white hair and grey beard,
Breathing forth his stout soul in the dust,
Holding in his hands his genitals
stained with blood.[1]

Confronted with such horrors, Spartan enthusiasm for the war waned. Finally, after some thirty years of fighting, the Spartans put down the revolt. Nevertheless, the political and social strain it caused led to a transformation of the Spartan polis. After the victory non-noblemen, who had done much of the fighting, demanded rights equal to those of the nobility. The agitation of these non-nobles disrupted society until the aristocrats agreed to remodel the state.

The "Lycurgan regimen," as the reforms were called after a legendary lawgiver, was a new political, economic, and social system. Political distinctions among Spartan men were eliminated, and all citizens became legally equal. Actual governance of the polis was in the hands of two kings who were primarily military leaders. The kings and a group of elders made up a council that deliberated on foreign and domestic matters and prepared legislation for the assembly, which consisted of all Spartan citizens. The real executive power of the polis was in the hands of five ephors (EH-fuhrs), or overseers, elected from and by all the citizens. In effect, the Lycurgan regimen did nothing more than broaden the aristocracy, while at the same time setting limits on its size. Social mobility was for the most part abolished, and instead an aristocratic warrior class governed the polis.

To provide for their economic needs, the Spartans divided the land of Messenia among all citizens. Helots worked the land, raised the crops, provided the Spartans with a certain percentage of their harvest, and occasionally served in the army. The Spartans kept the helots in line by means of systematic brutality and oppression.

In the Lycurgan system every citizen owed primary allegiance to Sparta. Suppression of the individual together with emphasis on military prowess led to a barracks state. Family life itself was sacrificed to the polis. Once Spartan boys reached the age of seven, they were enrolled in separate companies with other boys their age. They lived in this setting for part of their lives. They slept outside on reed mats and underwent rugged physical and

helots State serfs who worked the land.

military training until age twenty-four, when they became frontline soldiers. For the rest of their lives, Spartan men kept themselves prepared for combat. Their military training never ceased, and the older men were expected to be models of endurance, frugality, and sturdiness. In battle Spartans were supposed to stand and die rather than retreat. An anecdote frequently repeated about one Spartan mother sums up Spartan military values. As her son was setting off to battle, the mother handed him his shield and advised him to come back either victorious, carrying the shield, or dead, being carried on it. In the Lycurgan regimen, Spartan men were expected to train vigorously, disdain luxury and wealth, do with little, and like it.

Similar rigorous requirements applied to Spartan women, who were unique in all Greek society. They were prohibited from wearing jewelry or ornate clothes. They too exercised strenuously in the belief that hard physical training promoted the birth of healthy children. Yet they were hardly oppressed. They enjoyed more active and open public life than most other Greek women. They were far more emancipated than many other Greek women in part because Spartan society felt that mothers and wives had to be as hardy and independent as their sons and husbands. Sparta was not a place for weaklings, male or female. Spartan women saw being the mothers and wives of victorious warriors as a privilege, and on several occasions their own courage became legendary. The Spartan woman had a reputation for an independent spirit and self-assertion. While nominally under the guidance of a male guardian, she often managed her own financial affairs and owned her own land. Unlike other women in Greece, she could own property; Aristotle testified that at one point women owned two-fifths of the land in Sparta. For all of these reasons, Spartan women shared a footing with Spartan men that most other Greek women lacked.

Along with the emphasis on military values for both sexes, the Lycurgan regimen served to instill in society the civic virtues of dedication to the state and a code of moral conduct. These aspects of the Spartan system were generally admired throughout the Greek world.

The Evolution of Athens

Like Sparta, Athens faced pressing social and economic problems during the Archaic period, but the Athenian response was far different from that of the Spartans. Instead of creating an oligarchy, the Athenians extended to all citizens the right and duty of governing the polis. The Athenian democracy was one of the most thoroughgoing in Greece.

For Athens the late seventh century B.C.E. was a time of turmoil, the causes of which are virtually unknown. In 621 B.C.E. Draco (DRAY-koh), an Athenian aristocrat, doubtless under pressure from the peasants, published the first law code of the Athenian polis. His code was thought harsh, but it nonetheless embodied the ideal that the law belonged to the citizens. Nevertheless, peasant unrest continued.

By the early sixth century B.C.E. social and economic conditions led to another explosive situation. The aristocrats owned the best land, met in an assembly to govern the polis, and interpreted the law to their advantage.

Spartan Hoplite The bronze figurine portrays an armed soldier about to strike an enemy. His massive helmet with its full crest gives his head nearly complete protection, while a corselet covers his chest and back, and greaves (similar to today's shin guards) protect his shins. In his left hand he carries a large round shield. Hoplites were the backbone of all Greek armies. (Bildarchiv Preussischer Kulturbesitz/Art Resource, NY)

Noble landowners were forcing small farmers into economic dependence. Many families were sold into slavery; others were exiled, and their land was mortgaged to the rich. Poor farmers who had borrowed from their wealthy neighbors had to put up their land as collateral. If a farmer was unable to repay the loan, his creditor put a stone on the borrower's field to signify his indebtedness and thereafter took one-sixth of the annual yield until the debt was paid. If the farmer had to borrow again, he pledged himself and sometimes his family. If he was again unable to repay the loan, he became the slave of his creditor.

In many other city-states, conditions like those in Athens led to the rise of tyrants. One person who recognized these problems clearly was Solon (SOH-luhn), himself an aristocrat. Like Hesiod, Solon used his poetry to condemn the aristocrats for their greed and dishonesty. Solon recited his poems in the Athenian agora, where anyone could hear his relentless call for justice and fairness. The aristocrats realized that Solon was no crazed revolutionary, and the common people trusted him. Around 594 B.C.E. the nobles elected him *archon* (AHR-kahn), chief magistrate of the Athenian polis, and gave him extraordinary power to reform the state.

Solon immediately freed all people enslaved for debt, recalled all exiles, canceled all debts on land, and made enslavement for debt illegal. He also divided society into four legal groups on the basis of wealth. In the most influential group were the wealthiest citizens, but even the poorest and least powerful men enjoyed certain rights. Solon allowed them into the old aristocratic assembly, where they could take part in the election of magistrates.

Although Solon's reforms solved some immediate problems, they did not bring peace to Athens. Some aristocrats attempted to make themselves tyrants, while others banded together to oppose them. In 546 B.C.E. Pisistratus (pigh-SIHS-trah-tuhs), an exiled aristocrat, returned to Athens, defeated his opponents, and became tyrant. Pisistratus reduced the power of the aristocracy while supporting the common people. Under his rule Athens prospered, and his building program began to transform the city into one of the splendors of Greece. His reign as tyrant promoted the growth of democratic ideas by arousing rudimentary feelings of equality in many Athenian men. But Athenian acceptance of tyranny did not long outlive Pisistratus, for his son Hippias ruled harshly, committing excesses that led to his overthrow.

Democracy took shape in Athens under the leadership of Cleisthenes (KLIGHS-thuh-neez), a wealthy and prominent aristocrat who had won the support of lower-status men and emerged triumphant in 508 B.C.E. Cleisthenes created the *deme* (deem), a local unit that kept the roll of citizens, or *demos*, within its jurisdiction. All the demes were grouped in tribes, which thus formed the link between the demes and the central government.

The democracy functioned on the idea that all full citizens were sovereign. Because not all citizens could take time from work to participate in government, they delegated their power to other citizens by creating various offices meant to run the democracy. The most prestigious was the board of ten archons, who were charged with handling legal and military matters.

Legislation was in the hands of two bodies, the boule (BOO-lee), or council, composed of five hundred members, and the ecclesia (ee-KLEE-zhee-uh), the assembly of all citizens. By supervising the various committees of government and proposing bills to the ecclesia, the boule guided Athenian political life. It received foreign envoys and forwarded treaties to the ecclesia for ratification. It oversaw the granting of state contracts and was responsible for receiving many revenues. It held the democracy together. Nonetheless, the ecclesia had the final word. Open to all male citizens over eighteen years of age, it met at a specific place to vote on matters presented to it. The ecclesia could accept, amend, or reject bills put before it. Every member could express his opinion on any subject on the agenda, and a simple majority vote was needed to pass or reject a bill.

Athenian democracy proved to be an inspiring ideal in Western civilization. It demonstrated that a large group of people, not just a few, could efficiently run the affairs of state. Because all citizens could speak their minds, they did not have to resort to rebellion or conspiracy to express their desires. Like all democracies in ancient Greece, however, Athenian democracy was limited. Slaves, women, recent migrants, and foreigners could not be citizens; their opinions about political issues were not taken into account or recorded.

The Classical Period, 500–338 B.C.E.

What were the major developments in literature, philosophy, religion, and art, and how did war affect this intellectual and social process? ◼

In the years 500 to 338 B.C.E., Greek civilization reached its highest peak in politics, thought, and art. In this period the Greeks beat back the armies of the Persian Empire. Then, turning their spears against one another, they destroyed their own political system in a century of warfare. Some thoughtful Greeks felt prompted to record and analyze these momentous events. Herodotus (ca. 485–425 B.C.E.), from Asia Minor, traveled the Greek world to piece together the course of the Persian wars. Although he consulted documents when he could find them, he relied largely on the memories of

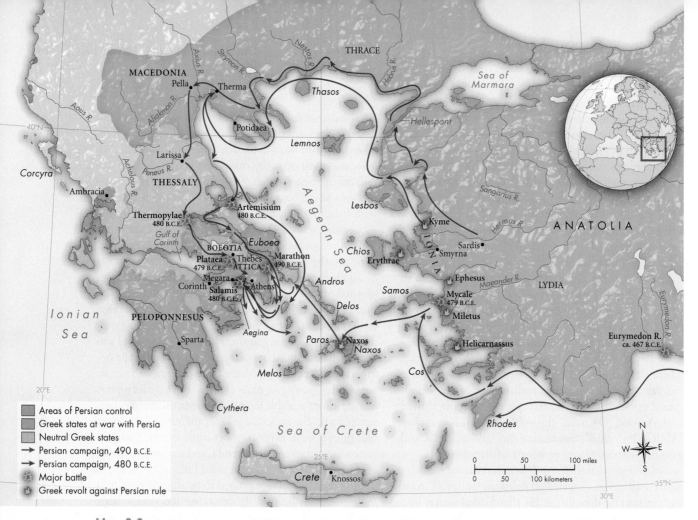

Map 3.3 **The Persian Wars, 499–479 B.C.E.** Begun initially as a local conflict between the Ionian Greeks and the Persians, the war eventually spread to involve a coalition of Greek forces who were able to defeat the Persians.

the participants. Not only is he the "father of history"; he is also the first oral historian. Next came Thucydides (thoo-SIHD-ih-dees) (ca. 460–ca. 399 B.C.E.), whose account of the Peloponnesian (puh-luh-puh-NEE-zhuhn) War remains a classic of Western literature. Unlike Herodotus, he was often a participant in the events that he described.

This era also saw the flowering of philosophy, as thinkers in Ionia and on the Greek mainland began to ponder the nature and meaning of the universe and human experience. The Greeks invented drama, and the Athenian tragedians Aeschylus (ES-kuh-luhs), Sophocles (SOF-uh-kleez), and Euripides (you-RIP-uh-deez) explored themes that still inspire audiences today. Greek architects reached the zenith of their art and created buildings whose ruins still inspire awe. Because Greek intellectual and artistic efforts attained their fullest and finest expression in these years, this age is called the "classical period." Few periods in the history of Western society can match it in sheer dynamism and achievement.

The Persian Wars

One of the hallmarks of the classical period was warfare. In 499 B.C.E. the Ionian Greeks, with the feeble help

of Athens, rebelled against the Persian Empire, which at its zenith controlled part of Ionia, Thrace, and Macedonia (Map 2.3, page 48). The rebellion failed, and the Ionians remained under Persian rule. Yet in 490 B.C.E. the Persians struck back at Athens, only to be defeated at the Battle of Marathon, a small plain in Attica (Map 3.3). This victory taught the Greeks that they could defeat the Persians and successfully defend their homeland. Despite the rebuff, the Persians renewed the attack. In 480 B.C.E. the Persian king Xerxes led a mighty invasion force into Greece. In the face of this emergency, many of the Greeks united and pooled their resources to resist the invaders. The Spartans provided the overall leadership and commanded the Greek armies. The Athenians, led by Themistocles (thuh-MIHS-tuh-kleez), provided the heart of the naval forces with their fleet of triremes, oar-propelled warships. (See "Living in the Past: Triremes and Their Crews," page 70.)

The first confrontations between the Persians and the Greeks occurred at the pass of Thermopylae (thuhr-MOP-uh-lee) and in the waters off Euboea. At Thermopylae the Greek hoplites, heavily armed foot soldiers, showed their mettle. Before the fighting began, a report came in that when the Persian archers shot their bows the arrows darkened the sky. According to Herodotus,

Statue of Leonidas Found at Sparta, this statue is commonly thought to represent Leonidas, the Spartan king who died valiantly at Thermopylae. With its careful rendering of the muscles and face, the statue reflects the Spartan ideal of the strong, intelligent, and brave warrior. (Vanni/Art Resource, NY)

one gruff Spartan replied merely, "Fine, then we'll fight in the shade."[2] The Greeks at Thermopylae fought heroically, but the Persians won the battle. In 480 B.C.E. the Greek fleet met the Persian armada at Salamis, an island just south of Athens. Though outnumbered, the Greek navy won an overwhelming victory. The remnants of the Persian fleet retired, and with them went all hope of Persian victory. In the following year, a coalition of Greek forces, commanded by the Spartan Pausanias with assistance from the Athenian Aristides, smashed the last Persian army at Plataea, a small polis in Boeotia. Greece remained free.

The significance of these Greek victories is nearly incalculable. By defeating the Persians, the Greeks ensured that they would not be taken over by a monarchy, which they increasingly viewed as un-Greek. The decisive victories meant that Greek political forms and intellectual concepts would be handed down to later societies.

Growth of the Athenian Empire

The defeat of the Persians had created a power vacuum in the Aegean, and the Athenians took advantage of the situation. The Athenians and their allies, again led by Aristides, formed the **Delian League**, a grand naval alliance aimed at liberating Ionia from Persian rule. The league took its name from the small island of Delos, on which stood a religious center sacred to all parties. The Delian (DEE-lee-uhn) League was intended to be a free alliance under the leadership of Athens. Athenians provided most of the warships and crews and determined how many ships or how much money each member of the league should contribute to the allied effort.

The Delian League, ca. 478–431 B.C.E.

The Athenians, supported by the Delian League and led by the young aristocrat Cimon (KEY-muhn), carried the war against Persia. But Athenian success had a sinister side. While the Athenians drove the Persians out of the Aegean, they also became increasingly imperialistic. Athens began reducing its allies to the status of subjects. Tribute was often collected by force, and the Athenians placed the economic resources of the Delian League under tighter and tighter control. Dissident governments were put down, and Athenian ideas of freedom and democracy did not extend to the citizens of other cities.

Athens justified its conduct by its successful leadership. In about 467 B.C.E. Cimon defeated a new and huge Persian force at the Battle of the Eurymedon River in Asia Minor, once again removing the shadow of Persia from the Aegean. But as the threat from Persia waned and the Athenians treated their allies more harshly, major allies such as Thasos (THAH-saws) revolted (ca. 465 B.C.E.), requiring the Delian League to use its forces against its own members.

Delian League A free naval alliance under the leadership of Athens aimed at liberating Ionia from Persian rule.

The expansion of Athenian power and the aggressiveness of Athenian rule also alarmed Sparta and its allies. While relations between Athens and Sparta cooled, Pericles (PEHR-uh-kleez) (ca. 494–429 B.C.E.), an aristocrat of solid intellectual ability, became the leading statesman in Athens. Like the democracy he led, Pericles was aggressive and imperialistic. At last, in 459 B.C.E. Sparta and Athens went to war over conflicts between Athens and some of Sparta's allies. Though the Athenians conquered Boeotia, Megara (MEG-uhr-uh), and Aegina

Triremes and Their Crews

LIVING IN THE PAST

MEN PULLING LONG OARS PROPELLED GREEK WARSHIPS IN BATTLE. These ancient mariners were free men who earned good wages; some became professionals who hired themselves out to any military leader. An experienced rower was valuable because he had learned how to row in rhythm with many other men. The trireme usually carried 186 rowers, 14 marines, a steersman who also served as navigator, and a captain.

The hull, or frame, for the trireme was long and narrow like a stiletto blade, and the ship was built for speed, not comfort. A bronze battering ram capped the bow, or front of the ship. In battle the crews rowed as hard as possible to ram enemy ships. After smashing the enemy's hull, the marines swept over the side to capture the ship. Rowers often had to pull their oars hurriedly in reverse to free themselves from sinking enemy triremes.

Life aboard a trireme was cramped and uncomfortable. The crew sat about eight feet above the waves, and storms proved a constant danger. One captain described a particularly hard night at sea: "It was stormy, the place offered no harbor, and it was impossible to go ashore and get a meal. . . . So we were forced to ride at anchor all night long in the open sea without food and sleep. . . . It was our lot to have by night rain and thunder and a violent wind."* Surviving a naval battle held its own dangers, for a trireme had no space for lifeboats. One sailor described his escape from a sinking ship: "One man said that they had been saved by clinging to a barrel. Others who were drowning told him, if he got away safely, to report that the admirals were doing nothing to rescue men who had fought most gallantly for their country."† Despite such discomforts and dangers, these oared ships and their men ruled the

A modern trireme reconstructed from ancient evidence.
(Paul Lipke/Trireme Trust USA)

*Pseudo-Demosthenes 50.22–23.
†Xenophon, *Hellenika* 1.7.11.

(ih-JIGH-nuh) in the early stages of the war, they met defeat in Egypt and later in Boeotia. The war ended in 445 B.C.E. with no serious damage to either side and nothing settled. But it divided the Greek world between the two great powers.

Athens continued its severe policies toward its subject allies and came into conflict with Corinth, one of Sparta's leading supporters (see Map 3.3). In 433 B.C.E. Athens sided with Corcyra against Corinth in a dispute between the two. Together with the Corcyraean fleet, an Athenian squadron defeated the Corinthian navy in open combat. The next year Corinth and Athens collided again, this time over the Corinthian colony of Potidaea, in a conflict the Athenians also won. In this climate of anger and escalation, Pericles took the next step. To punish Megara for alleged sacrilege, Pericles in 432 B.C.E. persuaded the Athenians to pass a law, the Megarian Decree, that excluded Megarians from trading with Athens and

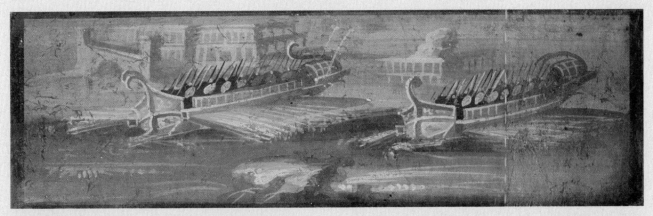

Mediterranean throughout classical antiquity. Greek and later Roman naval architects designed them expertly, and their crews routinely manned them with skill and courage.

Two triremes with full crews race, which was good training for the attack. (© Ministero per I Beni e le Attivita Culturali—Soprintendenza archeologica di Napoli)

QUESTIONS FOR ANALYSIS

1. What skills did a rower need for the various aspects of his job?

2. What do these images reveal about conditions aboard a trireme?

3. Compare the design of the trireme to the Phoenician ship shown on page 35. What advantages did this design have over the older design of Phoenician ships?

Source: J. S. Morrison, *Greek and Roman Oared Warships 399–30 B.C.E.* (Oxbow Books, 1996).

A side view of an ancient battering ram found off Israel. (William Murray)

its empire. In response the Spartans convened a meeting of their allies, whose complaints of Athenian aggression ended with a demand that Athens be stopped. Reluctantly the Spartans agreed to declare war. The real reason for war, according to the Athenian historian Thucydides, was simple: "The truest explanation, though the one least mentioned, was the great growth of Athenian power and the fear it caused the Lacedaemonians [Spartans], which drove them to war."[3]

The Peloponnesian War

At the outbreak of the Peloponnesian War the Spartan ambassador Melesippus warned the Athenians: "This day will be the beginning of great evil for the Greeks." Few men have ever prophesied more accurately. The Peloponnesian War lasted a generation and brought in its wake fearful plagues, famine, civil wars, widespread destruction, and huge loss of life.

Map 3.4 **The Peloponnesian War, 431–404 B.C.E.** This map shows the alignment of states during the Peloponnesian War.
ANALYZING THE MAP Where geographically do the major battles and sieges take place? What does this suggest about the spread of this conflict?
CONNECTIONS What does this map tell us about the growing political disintegration of Greece?

To complete this activity online, go to the Online Study Guide at bedfordstmartins.com/mckaywest.

After a Theban attack in 431 B.C.E. on the nearby polis of Plataea (plah-TEE-uh), the Peloponnesian War began in earnest (Map 3.4). In the next seven years, the army of Sparta and its Peloponnesian allies invaded Attica five times. The Athenians stood behind their walls, but in 430 B.C.E. the cramped conditions nurtured a dreadful plague, which killed huge numbers, eventually claiming Pericles himself. (See "Listening to the Past: Thucydides on the Great Plague at Athens, 430 B.C.E.," page 74.) The death of Pericles opened the door to a new breed of politicians, men who were rash, ambitious, and more dedicated to themselves than to Athens. Under Cleon (KLEE-on), the Athenians counterattacked and

defeated the Spartans at Pylos (PIE-lohs), a rocky peninsula. In response, the Spartan commander Brasidas widened the war in 424 B.C.E. by capturing Amphipolis, one of Athens's most valuable subject states. Two years later, both Cleon and Brasidas were killed in a battle to recapture the city. Recognizing that ten years of war had resulted only in death, destruction, and stalemate, Sparta and Athens concluded the Peace of Nicias (NI-shee-uhs) in 421 B.C.E.

The Peace of Nicias resulted in a cold war. But even cold war can bring horror and misery. Such was the case when in 416 B.C.E. the Athenians sent a fleet to the neutral island of Melos with an ultimatum: the Melians could surrender or perish. The Melians resisted. The Athenians conquered them, killed the men of military age, and sold the women and children into slavery.

The cold war grew hotter, thanks to the ambitions of Alcibiades (al-suh-BIGH-uh-dees) (ca. 450–404 B.C.E.), an aristocrat, a kinsman of Pericles, and a student of the philosopher Socrates (SOK-ruh-teez). A shameless opportunist, Alcibiades widened the war to further his own career and increase the power of Athens. He con-

❝ Infantry, fleet, and everything else were utterly destroyed, and out of many few returned home. ❞

—THUCYDIDES

vinced the Athenians to attack Syracuse, the leading polis in Sicily. His only valid reason was that such an operation would cut the grain supply from Sicily to the Peloponnesus. The undertaking was vast, requiring an enormous fleet and thousands of sailors and soldiers. In 414 B.C.E. the Athenians laid siege to Syracuse. The Syracusans fought back bravely and in 413 B.C.E. succeeded in crushing the Athenians. Thucydides wrote the epitaph for the Athenians: "infantry, fleet, and everything else were utterly destroyed, and out of many few returned home."[4]

The disaster in Sicily ushered in the final phase of the war, which was marked by three major developments: the renewal of war between Athens and Sparta, Persia's intervention in the war, and the revolt of many Athenian subjects. The year 413 B.C.E. saw Sparta's declaration of war against Athens and widespread revolt within the Athenian Empire. Yet Sparta still lacked a navy, the only instrument that could take advantage of the unrest of Athens's subjects, most of whom lived either on islands or in Ionia. The sly Alcibiades, now working for Sparta, provided a solution: the Persians would build a fleet for Sparta, and in return, the Spartans would give Ionia back to Persia. Now equipped with a fleet, the Spartans challenged the Athenians in the Aegean, the result being a long roll of inconclusive naval battles.

The strain of war prompted the Athenians in 407 B.C.E. to recall Alcibiades from exile. He cheerfully double-crossed the Spartans and Persians, but even he could not restore Athenian fortunes. In 405 B.C.E. Spartan forces destroyed the last Athenian fleet at the Battle of Aegospotami, after which the Spartans blockaded Athens until it was starved into submission. After twenty-seven years the Peloponnesian War was over, and the evils prophesied by the Spartan ambassador Melesippus in 431 B.C.E. had come true.

Athenian Arts in the Age of Pericles

In the last half of the fifth century B.C.E. and prior to the outbreak of the Peloponnesian War, Pericles turned Athens into the showplace of Greece. He appropriated Delian League funds to pay for a huge building program, planning temples and other buildings to honor Athena (uh-THEE-nuh), the patron goddess of the city, and to display to all Greeks the glory of the Athenian polis. To build support, Pericles also pointed out that his program would employ many Athenians and bring economic prosperity to the city. Thus began the undertaking that

Art and Philosophy in the Hellenic Period

Period	Significant Events	Major Writers/ Philosophers
Bronze Age 2000–1100 B.C.E.	Arrival of the Greeks in Greece	
Dark Age 1100–800 B.C.E.	Evolution of the polis Rebirth of literacy	Homer Hesiod
Archaic Age 800–500 B.C.E.	Rise of Sparta and Athens Colonization of the Mediterranean basin Flowering of lyric poetry Development of philosophy and science in Ionia	Anaximander Heraclitus Sappho Solon Thales
Classical Period 500–338 B.C.E.	Persian wars Peloponnesian War Rise of drama and historical writing Flowering of Greek philosophy Conquest of Greece by Philip of Macedonia	Aeschylus Aristophanes Aristotle Euripedes Herodotus Plato Socrates Sophocles Thucydides

turned the Acropolis into a monument for all time. Construction of the Parthenon (PAHR-thuh-non) began in 447 B.C.E., followed by the Propylaea, the temple of Athena Nike (Athena the Victorious), and the Erechtheum (Map 3.5).

Although anyone could visit the Acropolis, the Athenians normally hiked up the long approach only for religious festivals. The most important and joyous of them was the Great Panathenae. Every four years all Athenians and legal residents formed a huge procession to bring the statue of Athena in the Parthenon an exquisite robe, richly embroidered with mythological scenes. A few marshals directed the procession, which was more fun than formality. At the head of the procession walked an aristocratic young maiden carrying an offering basket. More richly dressed women followed her, most carrying gold and silver vessels containing wine and perfumes. Young men on horseback came next. The historian Xenophon, who had ridden in the procession, praised the feisty mounts and the riders who were trying to rein them in. Dignified older men, the city's magistrates, carrying their staffs added a touch of formality to the scene. Young men with large pitchers of water and wine climbed the ascent, and toward the rear other young men led the bulls to the sacrifice. After the religious ceremonies, all the people joined in a feast to honor Athena.

Once the procession began, they first saw the Propylaea, the ceremonial gateway, a building of complicated layout and grand design whose Doric columns seem to uphold the sky. On the right is the small temple of Athena Nike, built to commemorate the victory over

Thucydides on the Great Plague at Athens, 430 B.C.E.

LISTENING TO THE PAST

In 430 B.C.E. many of the people of Attica sought refuge in Athens to escape the Spartan invasion. Overcrowding, the lack of proper sanitation, and the scarcity of clean water exposed the huddled population to virulent disease, and a severe plague attacked the crowded masses. The great historian Thucydides lived in Athens at the time and contracted the disease himself. He was one of the fortunate people who survived the ordeal. For most people, however, the disease proved fatal. Thucydides left a vivid description of the nature of the plague and of people's reaction to it.

" People in perfect health suddenly began to have burning feelings in the head; their eyes became red and inflamed; inside their mouths there was bleeding from the throat and tongue, and the breath became unnatural and unpleasant. The next symptoms were sneezing and hoarseness of voice, and before long the pain settled on the chest and was accompanied by coughing. Next the stomach was affected with stomachaches and with vomitings of every kind of bile that has been given a name by the medical profession, all this being accompanied by great pain and difficulty. In most cases there were attacks of ineffectual retching, producing violent spasms; this sometimes ended with this stage of the disease, but sometimes continued long afterwards. Externally the body was not very hot to the touch, nor was there any pallor: the skin was rather reddish and livid, breaking out into small pustules and ulcers. But inside there was a feeling of burning, so that people could not bear the touch even of the lightest linen clothing, but wanted to be completely naked, and indeed most of all would have liked to plunge into cold water. Many of the sick who were uncared for actually did so, plunging into the water-tanks in an effort to relieve a thirst which was unquenchable; for it was just the same with them whether they drank much or little. Then all the time they were afflicted with insomnia and the desperate feeling of not being able to keep still.

In the period when the disease was at its height, the body, so far from wasting away, showed surprising powers of resistance to all the agony, so that there was still some strength left on the seventh or eighth day, which was the time when, in most cases, death came from the internal fever. But if people survived this critical period, then the disease descended to the bowels, producing violent ulceration and uncontrollable diarrhoea, so that most of them died later as a result of the weakness caused by this. For the disease, first settling in the head, went on to affect every part of the body in turn, and even when people escaped its worst effects, it still left its traces on them by fastening upon the extremities of the body. It affected the genitals, the fingers, and the toes, and many of those who recovered lost the use of these members; some, too, went blind. There were some also who, when they first began to get better, suffered from a total loss of memory, not knowing who they were themselves and being unable to recognize their friends.

Words indeed fail one when one tries to give a general picture of this disease; and as for the suffering of individuals, they seemed almost beyond the capacity of human nature to endure. Here in particular is a point where the plague showed itself to be something quite different from ordinary diseases: though there were many dead bodies lying about unburied, the birds and animals that eat human flesh either did not come near them or, if they did taste the flesh, died of it afterwards. Evidence for this may be found in the fact that there was a complete disappearance of all birds of prey: they were not to be seen either around the bodies or anywhere else. But dogs, being domestic animals, provided the best opportunity of observing this effect of the plague.

These, then, were the general features of the disease, though I have omitted all kinds of peculiarities which occurred in various individual cases. Meanwhile, during all this time there was no serious outbreak of any of the usual kinds of illness; if any such cases did occur, they ended in the plague. Some died in neglect, some in spite of every possible care being taken of them. As for a recognized method of treatment, it

the Persians. The Ionic frieze (a broad band of sculpture) above its columns depicts the struggle between the Greeks and the Persians. Here for all the world to see is a tribute to Athenian and Greek valor—and a reminder of Athens's part in the victory.

To the left of the visitors, as they pass through the Propylaea, stands the Erechtheum, an Ionic temple that housed several ancient shrines. On its southern side is the famous Portico of the Caryatids, a porch whose roof is supported by statues of Athenian maidens. The graceful Ionic columns of the Erechtheum provide a delicate relief from the prevailing Doric order of the massive Propylaea and Parthenon.

As visitors walk on, they obtain a full view of the Parthenon, thought by many to be the perfect temple. The Parthenon is the chief monument to Athena and her city. The sculptures that adorn the temple portray the greatness of Athens and its goddess. The figures on the

The god Asclepius, represented by a snake, putting an end to urban plague. (Bibliothèque nationale de France)

would be true to say that no such thing existed; what did good in some cases did harm in others. Those with naturally strong constitutions were no better able than the weak to resist the disease, which carried away all alike, even those who were treated and dieted with the greatest care. The most terrible thing of all was the despair into which people fell when they realized that they had caught the plague. Terrible, too, was the sight of people dying like sheep through having caught the disease as a result of nursing others. This indeed caused more deaths than anything else. For when people were afraid to visit the sick, then they died with no one to look after them. Indeed, there were many houses in which all the inhabitants perished through lack of attention. When, on the other hand, they did visit the sick, they lost their own lives, and this was particularly true of those who made it a point of honor to act properly. Such people felt ashamed to think of their own safety and went into their friends' houses at times when even the members of the household were so overwhelmed by the weight of their calamities that they had actually given up the usual practice of making laments for the dead. Yet still the ones who felt most pity for the sick and the dying were those who had had the plague themselves and had recovered from it. They knew what it was like and at the same time felt themselves to be safe, for no one caught the disease twice, or, if he did, the second attack was never fatal. . . .

A factor that made matters much worse than they were already was the removal of people from the country into the city, and this particularly affected the newcomers. There were no houses for them, and, living as they did during the hot season in badly ventilated huts,

they died like flies. The bodies of the dying were heaped one on top of the other, and half-dead creatures could be seen staggering about in the streets or flocking around the fountains in their desire for water.

The catastrophe was so overwhelming that people, not knowing what would happen next to them, became indifferent to every rule of religion and law. Athens owed to the plague the beginnings of a state of unprecedented lawlessness. People now began openly to venture on acts of self-indulgence which before then they used to keep in the dark. Thus they resolved to spend their money quickly and to spend it on pleasure, since money and life alike seemed equally ephemeral. As for what is called honor, no one showed himself willing to abide by its laws, so doubtful was it whether one would survive to enjoy the name for it. It was generally agreed that what was both honorable and valuable was the pleasure of the moment and everything that might conceivably contribute to that pleasure. No fear of god or law of man had a restraining influence. As for the gods, it seemed to be the same thing whether one worshiped them or not, when one saw the good and the bad dying indiscriminately. As for offenses against human law, no one expected to be punished. Instead, everyone felt that already a far heavier sentence had been passed on him and was hanging over him, and that before the time for its execution arrived, it was only natural to get some pleasure out of life.

This, then, was the calamity that fell upon Athens, and the times were hard indeed, with people dying inside the city and the land outside being laid waste. 〞

Source: R. Warner, trans., *Thucydides, History of the Peloponnesian War* (Penguin Classics, 1954), pp. 152–156. Translation copyright © Rex Warner, 1954. Introduction and Appendices copyright © M. I. Finley, 1972. Used with permission of Penguin Group (UK) and Curtis Brown Ltd., London, on behalf of the Estate of Rex Warner.

QUESTIONS FOR ANALYSIS

1. What does this account of the plague say about human nature when put in an extreme crisis?
2. Does popular religion offer any solace during such a catastrophe?
3. How did public laws and customs cope with such a disaster?

eastern pediment depict Athena's birth, those on the west the victory of Athena over the god Poseidon in their struggle for the possession of Attica. Inside the Parthenon stood a huge statue of Athena, the masterpiece of the great sculptor Phidias.

On the Acropolis the Athenians had built a magnificent monument to their goddesses and themselves, one that still moves people today. Plutarch in about 47 B.C.E. caught the essence of the sculptures while

they were still intact and undamaged: "In beauty each of them was from the outset antique, and even now in its prime fresh and newly made. Thus each of them is always in bloom, maintaining its appearance as though untouched by time, as though an evergreen breath and undecaying spirit had been mixed in its construction."[5] Even the pollution of modern Athens, while it is destroying these ancient buildings, cannot rob them of their splendor and charm.

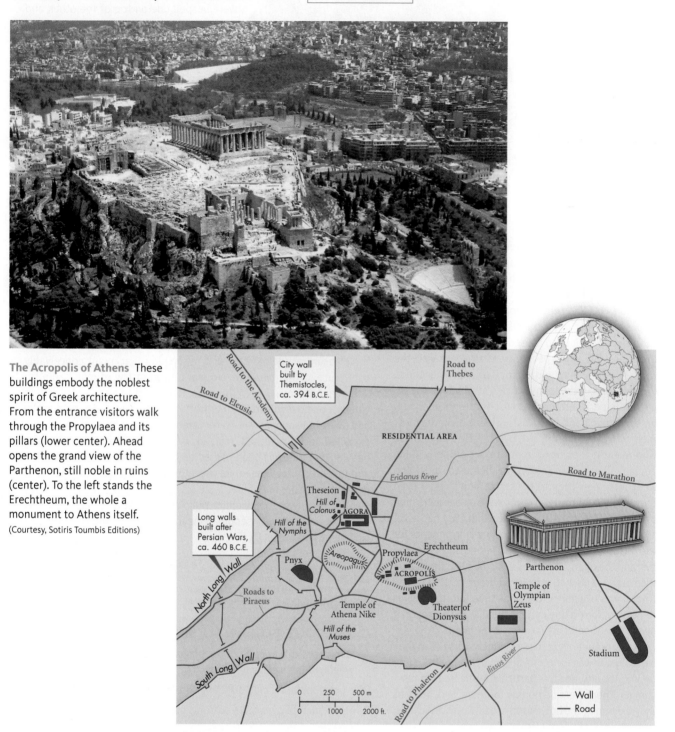

The Acropolis of Athens These buildings embody the noblest spirit of Greek architecture. From the entrance visitors walk through the Propylaea and its pillars (lower center). Ahead opens the grand view of the Parthenon, still noble in ruins (center). To the left stands the Erechtheum, the whole a monument to Athens itself. (Courtesy, Sotiris Toumbis Editions)

City wall built by Themistocles, ca. 394 B.C.E.

Road to the Academy
Road to Eleusis
Road to Thebes
Road to Marathon

RESIDENTIAL AREA

Eridanus River

Theseion
Hill of Colonus
AGORA

Long walls built after Persian Wars, ca. 460 B.C.E.

Hill of the Nymphs

Pnyx

Areopagus

Propylaea
Erechtheum
ACROPOLIS
Parthenon

North Long Wall

Roads to Piraeus

Temple of Athena Nike

Hill of the Muses

Theater of Dionysus

Temple of Olympian Zeus

South Long Wall

Ilissus River

Road to Phaleron

Stadium

0   250   500 m
0   1000   2000 ft.

— Wall
— Road

Map 3.5 **Ancient Athens, ca. 450 B.C.E.** By modern standards, the city of Athens was hardly more than a town, not much larger than one square mile. Yet this small area reflects the concentration of ancient Greek life in the polis.

The development of drama was tied to the religious festivals of the city and was as rooted in the life of the polis as were the architecture and sculpture of the Acropolis. The polis sponsored the production of plays and required wealthy citizens to pay the expenses of their production. At the beginning of the year, dramatists submitted their plays to the archon of the polis. He chose those he considered best and assigned a the-atrical troupe to each playwright. Many plays were highly controversial, but the archons neither suppressed nor censored them.

The Athenian dramatists were the first artists in Western society to examine such basic questions as the rights of the individual, the demands of society on the individual, and the nature of good and evil. Conflict is a constant element in Athenian drama. The dramatists used their art to portray, understand, and resolve life's basic conflicts.

Aeschylus (525–456 B.C.E.), the first of the great Athenian dramatists, was also the first to express the agony of the individual caught in conflict. In his trilogy of plays, *The Oresteia* (ohr-eh-STEE-uh), Aeschylus deals with the themes of betrayal, murder, and reconciliation, urging that reason and justice be applied to reconcile fundamental conflicts. The final play concludes with a prayer that civil dissension never be allowed to destroy the city and that the life of the city be one of harmony and grace.

Sophocles (496–406 B.C.E.) also dealt with matters personal and political. Perhaps his most famous plays are *Oedipus* (EHD-uh-puhs) *the King* and its sequel, *Oedipus at Colonus*. *Oedipus the King* is the tragic story of a man doomed by the gods to kill his father and marry his mother. Try as he might to avoid his fate, his every action brings him closer to its fulfillment. When at last he realizes that he has carried out the decree of the gods, Oedipus blinds himself and flees into exile. In *Oedipus at Colonus* Sophocles dramatizes the last days of the broken king, whose patient suffering and uncomplaining piety win him an exalted position. In the end the gods honor him for his virtue. The interpretation of these two plays has been hotly debated, but Sophocles seems to be saying that human beings should obey the will of the gods, even without fully understanding it, for the gods stand for justice and order.

With Euripides (ca. 480–406 B.C.E.) drama entered a new, and in many ways more personal, phase. To him the gods were far less important than human beings. The essence of Euripides' tragedy is the flawed character— men and women who bring disaster on themselves and their loved ones because their passions overwhelm reason. Although Euripides' plays were less popular in his lifetime than were those of Aeschylus and Sophocles, his work was to have a significant impact on Roman drama.

Writers of comedy treated the affairs of the polis and its politicians bawdily and often coarsely. Even so, their plays also were performed at religious festivals. Best known are the comedies of Aristophanes (eh-ruh-STAH-fuh-neez) (ca. 445–386 B.C.E.), an ardent lover of his city and a merciless critic of cranks and quacks. He lampooned eminent generals, at times depicting them as morons. He commented snidely on Pericles, poked fun at Socrates, and hooted at Euripides. Like Aeschylus, Sophocles, and Euripides, Aristophanes used his art to dramatize his ideas on the right conduct of the citizen and the value of the polis.

Mosaic of the Muses Not found in a great or famous urban center, this mosaic testifies to the wide dissemination of culture and art throughout Greece. The figures of the mosaic represent the nine Muses, goddesses of the arts. The lyre of Apollo occupies the center, and Clio, the goddess of history, is represented by the scroll in the upper left of the lyre. (Professor Nicolas Yalouris, Former General Inspector of Antiquities, Athens)

Daily Life in Periclean Athens

In sharp contrast with the rich intellectual and cultural life of Periclean Athens stands the simplicity of its material life. The Athenians—and in this respect they were typical of Greeks in general—lived very happily with comparatively few material possessions. In the first place, there were very few material goods to own. The thousands of machines, tools, and gadgets considered essential for modern life had no counterparts in Athenian life.

The Athenian house was rather simple. It consisted of a series of rooms opening onto a central courtyard. Many houses had bedrooms on an upper floor. Artisans often set aside a room to use as a shop or work area. Larger houses often had a room at the front where the men of the family ate and entertained guests, and a *gynaikon* (women's quarter) at the back where women worked, ate, and slept. Other rooms included the kitchen and bathroom. By modern standards there was not much furniture. In the men's dining room were couches, a sideboard, and small tables. Cups and other pottery were often hung from pegs on the wall. In the courtyard were the well, a small altar, and a washbasin. If the family lived in the country, the stalls of the animals faced the courtyard. Country dwellers kept oxen for plowing, pigs for slaughtering, sheep for wool, goats for cheese, and mules and donkeys for transportation. Even in the city chickens and perhaps a goat or two roamed the courtyard together with dogs and cats.

Cooking, done over a hearth in the house, provided welcome warmth in the winter. Baking and roasting were done in ovens. Food consisted primarily of various grains, especially wheat and barley, as well as lentils, olives, figs, and grapes. Garlic and onion were popular garnishes, and wine was always on hand. These foods were stored at home in large jars. Women ground wheat into flour, baked it into bread, and on special occasions made honey or sesame cakes. The Greeks used olive oil for cooking, as families still do in modern Greece; they also used it as an ointment and as lamp fuel.

The Greeks did not eat much meat. On special occasions, such as important religious festivals, the family ate the animal sacrificed to the god and gave the god the exquisite delicacy of the thighbone wrapped in fat. The only Greeks who consistently ate meat were the Spartan warriors. They received a small portion of meat each day, together with the infamous Spartan black broth, a ghastly concoction of pork cooked in blood, vinegar, and salt. One Greek, after tasting the broth, commented that he could easily understand why the Spartans were so willing to die.

In the city a man might support himself as a craftsman — a potter, bronzesmith, sailmaker, or tanner — or he could contract with the polis to work on public buildings, such as the Parthenon and Erechtheum. Certain crafts, including spinning and weaving, were generally done by women. Men and women without skills worked as paid laborers but competed with slaves for work. Slaves were usually foreigners and often "barbarians," people whose native language was not Greek. Citizens, slaves, and barbarians were paid the same amount for their work.

Slavery was commonplace in Greece, as it was throughout the ancient world. Greek slavery resembled Mesopotamian slavery. Slaves received some protection under the law and could buy their freedom. On the other hand, masters could mistreat or neglect their slaves, although killing them was illegal. Most slaves in Athens served as domestics and performed light labor around the house. Nurses for children, teachers of reading and writing, and guardians for young men were often slaves.

Picturing the Past

Blacksmith's Shop In the winter the blacksmith's shop, kept warm by a constant fire, was a favorite place for the men to chat and to come in from the cold while the smiths worked. (The Plousios Painter, two-handled jar [amphora]. Greek, Late Archaic Period, about 500–490 B.C. Place of Manufacture: Greece, Attica, Athens. Ceramic, Black Figure. Height: 36.1 cm [14³⁄₁₆ in.]; diameter: 25.9 cm [10³⁄₁₆ in.]. Museum of Fine Arts, Boston. Henry Lillie Pierce Fund, 01.8035. Photograph © 2010 Museum of Fine Arts, Boston)

ANALYZING THE IMAGE What is happening in this scene? What tools and objects are depicted? What are the different men doing?

CONNECTIONS This vase shows the activities of men engaged in a trade. How much do you think the scene shown here differs from the activity of tradespeople today? Consider the people shown, the nature of the work, the clothing, and the objects in use.

To complete this activity online, go to the Online Study Guide at bedfordstmartins.com/mckaywest.

Other slaves were skilled workers who could be found working on public buildings or in small workshops.

Gender and Sexuality

The social condition of Athenian women has been the subject of much debate. Women appear frequently in literature and art, but rarely in historical accounts, which mostly record military and political events in which women seldom played a notable part. Yet that does not mean that women were totally invisible in the life of the polis. In theory, Athenian men believed that the public arena was properly theirs and that women should infrequently appear there. The reality, however, was less limiting.

Citizen women never appeared in court or in the public political assemblies that were the heart of Athenian democracy, though they did attend public festivals, ceremonies, and funerals. They took part in annual processions to honor the goddess Athena and in harvest festivals honoring the goddess Demeter (dih-MEE-tuhr), who protected the city's crops. In a few cases, women were priestesses in the cults of various goddesses. Priestesses prayed in public on behalf of the city and, like priests, were paid for their services. The most prominent priestess was at Delphi (DEHL-figh), near Athens, where the Pythia, a priestess for life, passed on messages about the future from the god Apollo (uh-PAH-loh) to priests for interpretation.

The law protected the status of free women of the citizen class. Only her children, not those of foreigners or slaves, could be citizens. Women in Athens and elsewhere in Greece received a certain amount of social and legal protection from their bridal gift of money or property. Upon marriage the bride's father gave the couple a gift of land or money that the husband administered. It was, however, never his; and in the rare case of divorce, it was returned to the wife. Raping a free woman was a serious offense, severely punished. Yet it was a lesser crime than seduction, because the child of a rape could never inherit the family property. The child of a seduction, if not discovered, could conceivably pass for legitimate. In that case the child would pollute the family line and inherit the family's property. The law was not concerned with the husband's feelings; rather it protected the family by ensuring the legitimacy of its children and the security of its property.

A citizen woman's main functions were to bear and raise children. Childbirth could be dangerous for both mother and infant, so pregnant women usually made sacrifices or visited temples to ask help from the gods. Women relied on their relatives, on friends, and on midwives to assist in the delivery. Greek physicians did not usually concern themselves with obstetrical care.

Existing information shows that women actually lived much freer and more visible lives than Babylonian or Jewish women. Husbands and wives had different duties but shared the goal of building a happy and prosperous home for each other and their children. The wife ran every aspect of the house. She kept the family's accounts and drew up the budget. She saw to the organization of the family's possessions and inspected everything that entered the house. She saw that everything, from clothing and valuables to food, was in good condition and stored in its proper place. The wife supervised the household slaves in their duties, and she taught young maids essential domestic skills, notably spinning cloth and weaving. She thereby made them more proficient in their duties and proud of their accomplishments. She personally cared for slaves who became ill and nursed them back to health, which won their gratitude and respect. The lady of the house praised slaves for good work and disciplined laziness and disobedience. When the crops came in, she directed their storage, just as she had the other goods. As one husband said to his wife: "It would be ridiculous if you were not here at home to take care of everything that I bring in from the outside."[6] He added, "Now we know, dear, what duties have been assigned to us by God. We must try, each of us, to accomplish them as best as we can. The law approves of them, for it joins man and

Young Man and Hetaira Aristocratic young men often received their sexual initiation from hetairai, companions who were often prostitutes. This young man seemingly cannot hold his wine, and his companion kindly sees him through the worst of it. (Martin von Wagner Museum der Universität Würzburg. Photo: Karl Oehrlein)

woman together. And God makes them partners in their children, and law likewise makes them partners in the home. The law also proclaims these duties to be noble."[7] This was a basic, simple, realistic ideal.

Greek sexuality often remains misunderstood today. Some people derive their idea of it from the philosophers Plato and Aristotle, who praised love that was intellectual and nonsexual—platonic love—and were suspicious of the power of sexual passion, warning that it distracted men from reason and the search for knowledge. While they intellectualized sex, the soldier-poet Archilochus (d. 652 B.C.E.) preferred "to light upon the flesh of a maid and ram belly to belly and thigh to thigh."[8] Some few, but revealing, glimpses from the ancient sources indicate that women, too, enjoyed sex for its own sake.

Homosexuality was generally accepted in ancient Greece. In classical Athens, part of an adolescent citizen's training in adulthood was supposed to entail a hierarchical sexual and tutorial relationship with an older man, who most likely was married and may have had other female sexual partners as well. These relationships between adolescents and men were often celebrated in literature and art, in part because Athenians regarded perfection as possible only in the male. The perfect body was that of the young male, and perfect love was that between an adolescent and an older man, not that between a man and an imperfect woman. This love was supposed to become intellectualized and platonic once the adolescent became an adult.

How often actual sexual relations between men or between men and women approached the ideal in Athens is very difficult to say, as most of our sources are prescriptive, idealized, or fictional. A small number of sources refer to female-female sexual desire, the most famous of which are the poems of Sappho, a female poet who lived on the island of Lesbos in the sixth century B.C.E. Today the English word *lesbian* is derived from Sappho's home island of Lesbos. In one of her poems she recalled the words of her lover:

> *Sappho, if you do not come out,*
> *I swear, I will love you no more.*
> *O rise and free your lovely strength*
> *From the bed and shine upon us.*
> *Lifting off your Chian nightgown, and*
> *Like a pure lily by a spring,*
> *Bathe in the water.*[9]

A younger man who was not troubled by these affairs proposed to Sappho, but she refused him because she was past childbearing age. This and the earlier examples indicate that sex was as complicated in ancient Greece as it is now.

Prostitution, both male and female, was another feature of Greek sexuality. It was both common and legal, but was socially tainted. A male prostitute was generally despised, and Athenian men would lose their citizenship if they were convicted of prostitution. Society treated female prostitutes differently. Beautiful, articulate, and accomplished prostitutes were known as *hetairai*, "companions." (See "Individuals in Society: Aspasia," page 81.) Lower-class ordinary prostitutes who only sold sex were called *pornoi*, "whores." Whatever the name, both made their living by selling their favors.

Greek Religion

Greek religion is extremely difficult for modern people to understand, largely because of the great differences between Greek and modern cultures. In the first place, the Greeks had no uniform faith or creed. Although they usually worshiped the same deities—Zeus, Hera, Apollo, Athena, and others—the cults of these gods and goddesses varied from polis to polis. The Greeks had no sacred books such as the Bible, and Greek religion was often more a matter of ritual than of belief. Nor did cults impose an ethical code of conduct. Greeks did not have to follow any particular rule of life, practice certain virtues, or even live decent lives in order to participate. Unlike the Egyptians and Hebrews, the Greeks lacked a priesthood as the modern world understands the term. In Greece priests and priestesses existed to care for temples and sacred property and to conduct the proper rituals, but not to make religious rules or doctrines, much less to enforce them. In short, there existed in Greece no central ecclesiastical authority and no organized creed.

Although temples to the gods were common, they were unlike modern churches or synagogues in that they were not normally places where a congregation met to worship as a spiritual community. Instead, the individual Greek man or woman either visited the temple occasionally on matters of private concern or walked in a procession to a particular temple to celebrate a particular festival. In Greek religion the altar, which stood outside the temple, was important; when the Greeks sought the favor of the gods, they offered sacrifices, usually of goats or chickens. Greek religious observances were generally cheerful. Festivals and sacrifices were frequently times for people to meet together socially, times of high spirits and conviviality rather than of pious gloom. By offering the gods parts of the sacrifice while consuming the rest themselves, worshipers forged a bond with the gods. Some deities were particularly worshiped by men and some by women.

The most important members of the Greek pantheon were Zeus, the king of the gods, and his wife, Hera. Although they were the mightiest and most honored of the deities who lived on Mount Olympus, their divine children were closer to ordinary people. Apollo was especially popular. He represented the epitome of youth, beauty, benevolence, and athletic skill. He was also the

INDIVIDUALS IN SOCIETY

"IF IT IS NECESSARY for me indeed to speak of female virtues, to those of you who have now become widows, I shall explain the entire situation briefly. It is in your hands whether you will not fall below your nature. The greatest glory to you is to be least talked about by men, either for excellence or blame" (Thucydides 2.46.1). These words were reportedly uttered by Pericles to the widows at a public funeral honoring those killed during the first year of the Peloponnesian War. At the same time he was enjoying a long-standing affair with Aspasia, who was very much talked about by men and women. Whether Pericles actually said these words is for the most part irrelevant. Their significance lies in their expression of the Athenian ideal of the proper Athenian lady. In short, she should stay at home and limit her talents to her household. This ideal became the reality for most Athenian women, whose names and actions were not recorded and thus did not become part of history. Aspasia was a notable exception.

Aspasia (as-PAY-zhuh) was born in the Greek city of Miletus and came to Athens in about 445 B.C.E. Little is known about her life, but she played a role in Athenian society that was far more renowned than, and far different from, that allegedly proposed by Pericles. The irony of her life is that she became his mistress and enjoyed a very public career, exactly the opposite of the call for women to stay anonymous attributed to Pericles in the Funeral Oration cited above.

Once in Athens, Aspasia may have become a hetaira (hih-TIGH-ruh), as the comic poet Aristophanes testifies. As such she accompanied men at dinner parties, where their wives would not have been welcome, and also served as a sexual partner. Yet she did more than drink and have sex with her clients. She also provided witty, intellectual conversation and publicly acted with perfect decorum. She thereby filled an intellectual role not usually expected of a proper wife. A successful hetaira could easily become the mistress of a wealthy and prominent man.

Aspasia fits into the category of a lovely and very intelligent companion. Legend reports that she taught rhetoric, an essential tool for Athenian politicians. That meant that her pupils were necessarily men. She thus enjoyed a rare opportunity to influence the men who shaped the political life of Athens. The Roman biographer Plutarch reports that Aspasia enjoyed the company of the foremost men in Athens. Their conversations included philosophy, and she is reputed to have taught Socrates the art of public speaking. While the claim is undoubtedly false, it points to her reputation as a very accomplished woman.

The great change in Aspasia's life came with her introduction to Pericles, who was especially taken with her rare political wisdom. After Pericles divorced his wife, he took Aspasia as his mistress. She and Pericles produced a son, also named Pericles. Aspasia was not an Athenian citizen, and it was illegal for the son of a foreign parent to be granted citizenship. Yet when Pericles' sons by his wife died in the plague, the Athenians made an exception and granted the young Pericles citizenship. That remarkable fact testifies to the respect that many Athenians felt not only for the great statesman but also for Aspasia. Others ridiculed the connection and felt that Pericles was making a fool of himself. The majority thought otherwise, or the son would not have been granted citizenship.

Aspasia's achievements are clear. She lifted herself from a vulnerable to a respected position in Athenian society. It is not enough to ascribe this to her beauty. Her intelligence and her sense of culture were equally, if not more, important. Social mobility in classical Athens was rare, but Aspasia proves that it was possible.

QUESTIONS FOR ANALYSIS

1. What talents enabled Aspasia to rise from the status of companion or courtesan to that of a generally respected person in society?
2. What made Aspasia's position in Athens precarious despite her obvious talents?

Roman portrait of Aspasia based on a Greek statue. (Vatican Museums/ Art Resource, NY)

Sacrificial Scene Much of Greek religion was festive, as this scene demonstrates. The participants include women and boys dressed in their finest clothes and crowned with garlands. Musicians add to the festivities. Only the sheep will not enjoy the ceremony. (National Archaeological Museum, Athens/Archaeological Receipts Fund)

god of music and culture and in many ways symbolized the best of Greek culture. His sister Athena, who patronized women's crafts such as weaving, was also a warrior-goddess. Best known for her cult at Athens, she was highly revered throughout Greece. Other divinities watched over other aspects of human life.

The Greeks also honored some heroes. A hero was born of a union of a god or goddess and a mortal and was considered an intermediate between the divine and the human. A hero displayed his divine origins by performing deeds beyond the ability of human beings. Herakles (or Hercules, as the Romans called him) was the most popular of the Greek heroes. According to belief, he successfully fulfilled twelve labors, all of which pitted him against mythical opponents or tasks. Worshipers believed that he, like other heroes, protected mortals from supernatural dangers and provided an ideal of vigorous masculinity.

Besides the Olympian gods, each polis had its own minor deities, and each deity had his or her own local cult. In many instances Greek religion involved the official gods and goddesses of the polis and their cults. The polis administered the cults and festivals, and everyone was expected to participate in this civic religion. Participating unbelievers, who seem to have been a small minority, were not considered hypocrites. Rather, they were seen as patriotic, loyal citizens who in honoring the gods also honored the polis. Just as Americans stand at the playing of the national anthem whether they are Democrats, Republicans, or neither and whether they agree or disagree with the policies of the current administra-

tion, ancient Greeks honored the polis and demonstrated solidarity with it by participating in the state cults regardless of their views.

Some Greeks turned to mystery cults, the most famous being the Eleusinian mysteries in Attica. These cults promised life after death to those initiated into them. Once people had successfully undergone initiation, they were forbidden to reveal the secrets of the cult. Consequently, modern scholars know comparatively little about them. Furthermore, relatively few people were rich enough to travel to Attica for initiation. Yet mystery cults like Eleusis inspired many similar cults in the Hellenistic period and foreshadowed many aspects of early Christianity.

Much religion was local and domestic. Each village possessed its own cults and rituals, and individual families honored various deities privately in their homes. These native rites often remained unknown beyond their own communities. The celebrations included all elements of society, women and slaves included. Many people also believed that magic rituals and spells were effective and sought the assistance of individuals reputed to have special knowledge or powers to cure disease, drive away ghosts, bring good weather, or influence the actions of others.

Though Greek religion in general was individual or related to the polis, the Greeks also shared some Pan-Hellenic festivals, the chief of which were held at Olympia in honor of Zeus and at Delphi in honor of Apollo. The festivities at Olympia included athletic contests that have inspired the modern Olympic games.

A Greek God Few pieces of Greek art better illustrate the conception of the gods as greatly superior forms of human beings than this magnificent statue, over 6 feet 10 inches in height. Here the god, who may be either Poseidon or Zeus, is portrayed as powerful and perfect but human in form. (National Archaeological Museum, Athens/Archaeological Receipts Fund)

Held every four years, these games were for the glory of Zeus. They attracted visitors from all over the Greek world and lasted well into Christian times. The Pythian (PIH-thee-uhn) games at Delphi were also held every four years, but they included musical and literary contests. Both the Olympic and the Pythian games were unifying factors in Greek life, bringing Greeks together culturally as well as religiously.

The Flowering of Philosophy

The myths and epics of the Mesopotamians are ample testimony that speculation about the origin of the universe and of humans did not begin with the Greeks. The signal achievement of the Greeks was the willingness of some to treat these questions in rational rather than mythological terms. Although Greek philosophy did not fully flower until the classical period, Ionian thinkers in the Archaic period had already begun to ask what the universe was made of. These men are called the Pre-Socratics, for their work preceded the philosophical revolution begun by the Athenian Socrates. Though they were keen observers, the Pre-Socratics rarely undertook deliberate experimentation. Instead, they took individual facts and wove them into general theories. They be-

lieved the universe was simple and was subject to natural laws. Drawing on their observations, they speculated about the basic building blocks of the universe.

The first of the Pre-Socratics, Thales (THAY-leez) (ca. 600 B.C.E.), learned mathematics and astronomy from the Babylonians and geometry from the Egyptians. Yet there was an immense and fundamental difference between Near Eastern thought and the philosophy of Thales. The Near Eastern peoples considered such events as eclipses to be evil omens. Thales viewed them as natural phenomena that could be explained in natural terms. In short, he asked why things happened. He believed the basic element of the universe to be water. Although he was wrong, the way in which he had asked the question was momentous: it was the beginning of the scientific method.

Thales's follower Anaximander (ah-NAK-suh-man-duhr) (d. ca. 547 B.C.E.) continued his work. He theorized that the basic element of the universe was the "boundless" or "endless"—something infinite and indestructible. In his view the earth floats in a void, held in balance by its distance from everything else in the universe. Heraclitus (hehr-uh-KLIGH-tuhs) (ca. 500 B.C.E.), however, declared the primal element to be fire. He also declared that the world had neither beginning nor end. Although the universe was eternal, it changed constantly. An outgrowth of this line of speculation was the theory of Democritus (dih-MAH-kruh-tuhs) (b. ca. 460 B.C.E.) that the universe was made up of invisible, indestructible atoms. The culmination of Pre-Socratic thought was the theory that four simple substances made up the universe: fire, air, earth, and water.

With this impressive heritage behind them, the philosophers of the classical period ventured into new areas of speculation. This development was partly due to the work of Hippocrates (hih-PAH-kruh-teez) (ca. 430 B.C.E.), the father of medicine. Like Thales, Hippocrates sought natural explanations for phenomena. Basing his opinions on empirical knowledge, not on religion or magic, he taught that natural means could be employed to fight disease. The human body, he declared, contained four humors, or fluids: blood, phlegm, black bile, and yellow bile. In a healthy body the four humors were in perfect balance; too much or too little of any particular humor caused illness. But Hippocrates broke away from the mainstream of Ionian speculation by declaring that medicine was a separate craft that had its own set of principles.

The distinction between natural science and philosophy on which Hippocrates insisted was also promoted by the Sophists, who traveled the Greek world teaching young men. Despite differences of opinion on philosophical matters, the Sophists all agreed that human beings were the proper subject of study. They also believed that excellence could be taught, and they used philosophy and rhetoric to prepare young men for life in the polis. The Sophists put great emphasis on logic and the meanings of words. They criticized traditional beliefs, religion, rituals, and myths and even questioned the laws of the polis. In essence, they argued that nothing is absolute, that everything is relative.

Socrates (ca. 470–399 B.C.E.) shared the Sophists' belief that human beings and their environment were the essential subjects of philosophical inquiry. His approach when posing ethical questions and defining concepts was to start with a general topic or problem and to narrow the matter to its essentials. He did so by continuous questioning rather than lecturing, a process known as the Socratic dialogue. Socrates thought that by constantly pursuing excellence, an essential part of which was knowledge, human beings could approach the supreme good and thus find true happiness. Yet in 399 B.C.E. Socrates was brought to trial, convicted, and executed on charges of corrupting the youth of the city and introducing new gods.

Socrates' student Plato (427–347 B.C.E.) carried on his master's search for truth, founding a philosophical school, the Academy. Plato believed that the ideal polis could exist only when its citizens were well educated. From education came the possibility of determining all of the virtues of life and combining them into a system that would lead to an intelligent, moral, and ethical life. He further concluded that only divine providence could guide people to virtue. In short, he equated god with the concept of good. Plato believed that it was the highest duty of true statesmen to educate their people to reach this higher good.

Plato developed the theory that there are two worlds: the impermanent, changing world of appearance that we know through our senses, and the eternal, unchanging realm of "forms" that constitute the essence of true reality. Only the mind can perceive eternal forms. The intellectual journey consists of moving from the realm of appearances to the realm of forms. His perfect polis was utopian and could exist only if its rulers were philosophers.

Aristotle (EH-ruh-STAH-tuhl) (384–322 B.C.E.) carried on the philosophical tradition of Socrates and Plato. A student of Plato, Aristotle founded his own school at the Lyceum, an Athenian gymnasium. Since Aristotle usually discussed topics while walking, his school was called the Peripatetic for those who walk around. The range of Aristotle's thought is staggering. He approached the topic of the ideal polis more realistically than had Plato. He stressed moderation, concluding that the balance of his ideal state depended on people of talent and education who could avoid extremes.

Aristotle tried to understand the changes of nature—what caused them and where they led. His interests embraced logic, ethics, natural science, politics, poetry, and art. His method was the syllogism, whereby he reasoned from a general statement to a particular conclusion. Aristotle also tried to bridge the gap that Plato had created between abstract truth and concrete perception. He argued that the universe is finite, spherical, and eternal. In the process, he discussed an immaterial being that is his conception of god that neither created the universe nor guided it. His god, then, is without purpose. Yet for him scientific endeavor, the highest attainable form of living, reaches the divine.

Aristotle expressed the heart of his philosophy in two works, *Physics* and *Metaphysics*. In them he combined empiricism, or observation, and speculative method. In *Physics* he tried to explain all nature by describing how natural phenomena work on one another and how these actions lead to the results that people see around them daily. He postulated the four principles of matter, form, movement, and goal. A seed, for example, possesses both matter and form. According to Plato, form determines whether the plant will be a rose or poison ivy. Growth represents movement, and the mature plant the goal of the seed. Although Aristotle considered nature impersonal, he also felt that it had its own purposes. In a sense, this is a rudimentary ancestor of the concept of evolution.

In *On the Heaven* Aristotle added ether (the sky) to air, fire, water, and earth as building blocks of the universe. He concluded that the universe revolves and that it is spherical and eternal. He wrongly thought that the earth was the center of the universe, with the stars and planets revolving around it. The Hellenistic scientist Aristarchus of Samos later realized that the earth revolves around the sun, but did not replace Aristotle's view. Not until the sixteenth century C.E. did Nicolaus Copernicus prove that the sun, not the earth, stood at the center of our solar system.

Athenian philosophers thus reflected their own society in their thought, but they also called for a broader examination of the universe and the place of humans in it than had earlier thinkers. Both the breadth of their vision and its limitations are important legacies to Western civilization.

The Final Act

How did the Greek city-states meet political and military challenges, and how did Macedonia become dominant? ■

The turbulent period from 404 to 338 B.C.E. is sometimes mistakenly seen as a time of failure and decline. It was instead a vibrant era in which Plato and Aristotle thought and wrote, one in which architecture, literature, oratory, and historical writing flourished. If the fourth century was a period of decline, this was so only in politics. The Peloponnesian War and its aftermath proved that the polis had reached the limits of its success as an effective political institution. The attempts of various city-states to dominate the others led only to incessant warfare. The polis system was committing suicide.

The Greeks of the fourth century B.C.E. experimented seriously with two political concepts in the hope of preventing war. First was the **Common Peace**, the idea that the states of Greece, whether large or small, should live together in peace and freedom, each enjoying its own laws and customs. In 386 B.C.E. this concept was a vital part of a peace treaty with the Persian Empire in which the Greeks and Persians pledged themselves to live in harmony.

The second concept to become prominent was federalism. The new impetus toward federalism was intended more to gain security through numbers than to prevent war. Greek leagues had usually developed in regions where geography shaped a well-defined area and where people shared a broad kinship. By banding together, the people of these leagues could marshal their resources, both human and material, to defend themselves from outside interference. In the fourth century B.C.E. at least ten other federations of states came into being or were revitalized. Federalism never led to a United States of Greece, but the concept held great importance not only for fourth-century Greeks but also for the Hellenistic period and beyond. In 1787, when the Founding Fathers met in Philadelphia to frame the Constitution of the United States, they studied Greek federalism very seriously in the hope that the Greek past could help guide the American future.

Common Peace A political concept created in the fourth century B.C.E. to prevent war based on the idea that the states of Greece should live together in peace and freedom, each enjoying its own laws and customs.

hegemony Political domination over other states.

The Struggle for Hegemony

The chief states — Sparta, Athens, and Thebes — each tried to create a **hegemony** (hih-JEH-muh-nee), that is, political domination over other states, even though they sometimes paid lip service to the ideals of the Common Peace. In every instance, each major power wanted to be the leader, and the ambition, jealousy, pride, and

Statue of Eirene The Athenians erected this statue of Eirene (Peace) holding Ploutos (Wealth) in her left arm. Athens had seen only war for some fifty-six years, and the statue celebrated the Common Peace of 375 B.C.E. The bitter irony of this poignant scene is that the treaty lasted scarcely a year. (Glyptothek, Munich/Studio Koppermann)

fear of the major powers doomed the effort to achieve genuine peace.

When the Spartan commander Lysander defeated Athens in 404 B.C.E., the Spartans used their victory to build an empire instead of ensuring the freedom of all Greeks. Their decision brought them into conflict with Persia, which now demanded the return of Ionia to its control (see page 68). From 400 to 386 B.C.E. the Spartans fought the Persians for Ionia, a conflict that eventually engulfed Greece itself. After years of stalemate the Spartans made peace with Persia and their Greek enemies. The result was the first formal Common Peace, the King's Peace of 386 B.C.E., which cost Sparta its empire but not its position of dominance in Greece.

Not content with Sparta's hegemony of Greece, the Spartan king Agesilaos (ah-gihs-ihl-A-uhs) betrayed the very concept of the Common Peace to punish cities that had opposed Sparta during the war. He used naked force against old enemies, especially the Thebans, even though they had made peace. Agesilaos's imperialism was soon to lead to Sparta's downfall at the hands of the Thebans, the people he sought to tyrannize.

The first sign of Spartan failure came in 378 B.C.E. after the unprovoked attack on Athens. The enraged Athenians created the Second Athenian Confederacy, a federation of states to guarantee the Greeks their rights under the Common Peace. Thebes joined Athens, and the two fought Sparta until 371 B.C.E. Owing to its growing fear of Theban might, Athens made a separate peace with Sparta. Left alone, Thebes defended itself until later that year, when the brilliant Theban general Epaminondas (ih-pah-muh-NAHN-duhs) routed the Spartan army on the small plain of Leuctra.

The defeat of the once-invincible Spartans stunned the Greeks, who wondered how Thebes would use its victory. Epaminondas, also a gifted statesman, immediately grappled with the problem of how to translate military success into political reality. First, in a series of invasions, he eliminated Sparta as a major power and liberated Messenia. He concluded alliances with many Peloponnesian states but made no effort to dominate them. Steadfastly refusing to create a Theban empire, he instead sponsored federalism in Greece and threw his support behind the Common Peace. Although he made Thebes the leader of Greece from 371 to 362 B.C.E., other city-states and leagues were bound to Thebes only by voluntary alliances. By his insistence on the liberty of the Greeks, Epaminondas, more than any other person in

Greek history, successfully blended the three concepts of hegemony, federalism, and the Common Peace. His premature death at the Battle of Mantinea in 362 B.C.E. put an end to his efforts, but not to these three political ideals. The question was whether anyone or any state could realize them all.

Philip II and Macedonian Supremacy

While the Greek states exhausted themselves in endless conflicts, the new power of Macedonia rose in the north. The land, extensive and generally fertile, nurtured a numerous and hardy people. The Macedonians were Greeks, but their life on the fringe of the Hellenic world made them seem alien and almost non-Greek. Nevertheless, under a strong king Macedonia was a power to be reckoned with, and in 359 B.C.E. such a king ascended to the throne. Philip II was brilliant and cultured, and he fully understood the strengths and needs of the Macedonians, whose devotion he won virtually on the day that he ascended the throne.

The young Philip, already a master of diplomacy and warfare after years spent in Thebes, quickly saw Athens as the principal threat to Macedonia. Once he had secured the borders of Macedonia against barbarian invaders, he launched a series of military operations in the northwestern Aegean. Not only did he win rich territory, but he also slowly pushed the Athenians out of the region. Yet the Greeks themselves opened the road to his ultimate victory in Greece. The opportunity came from still another internal Greek conflict, the Sacred War of 356 to 346 B.C.E. The war broke out when the Phocians, a Greek people in whose land stood the sanctuary of Apollo at Delphi, seized and plundered the sacred temple. Their sacrilege was openly condoned by Athens and Sparta. When the Thebans and other Greeks failed to liberate Delphi, they invited Philip to intervene. He quickly crushed the Phocians in 346 B.C.E., intimidating Athens and Sparta with his fierceness.

Many Greeks feared that Philip wanted not peace but the rule of all of Greece. A comic playwright used graveyard humor to depict one of Philip's ambassadors warning the Athenians:

Do you know that your battle will be with men
Who dine on sharpened swords,
And gulp burning firebrands for wine?

❝ Do you know that your battle will be with men who dine on sharpened swords, and gulp burning firebrands for wine? ❞

—GREEK PLAYWRIGHT MNESIMACHOS

Then immediately after dinner the slave
Brings us dessert— Cretan arrows
Or pieces of broken spears.
We have shields and breastplates for
Cushions and at our feet slings and arrows,
And we are crowned with catapults.[10]

These dire predictions and the progress of Philip's military operations at last had their effect. In 338 B.C.E. the armies of Thebes and Athens met Philip's forces at the Boeotian city of Chaeronea. There Philip's army won a hard-fought victory that gave him command of Greece and put an end to classical Greek freedom. Because the Greeks could not put aside their quarrels, they fell to an invader. Yet Philip was wise enough to retain much of what the fourth-century Greeks had achieved. Not opposed to the concepts of peace and federalism, he sponsored a new Common Peace in which all of Greece except Sparta, which refused to participate, was united in one political body under his leadership. Philip thus used the concepts of hegemony, the Common Peace, and federalism as tools of Macedonian domination. The ironic result was the end of the age of classical Greece.

LOOKING BACK LOOKING AHEAD

ONCE THE PERSIANS had established peace and stability throughout the Near East, they turned to Europe. Cyrus the Great first encountered Greek settlers in Anatolia. His successors unsuccessfully tried to conquer Greece, but by then these Indo-European peoples had turned the peninsula of Greece into one of the most vital beds of culture in Western history. They created governments that relied on popular participation, especially democracy and oligarchy. They also created history in the modern sense of the word and philosophy, and made impressive contributions to art, architecture, and literature. Yet the Greeks nearly destroyed themselves in two centuries of warfare. Nonetheless, they overcame this ordeal to hand their precious heritage on to the West.

The heritage of the Greeks and Macedonians proved essential to the evolution of the Hellenistic period, but the older cultures of the East made the era unique in Western civilization. Although the Greeks failed to establish their beloved polis in the East, they and the Macedonians built monarchies that better governed both themselves and the native peoples with whom they lived. A major aspect of their success was the enormous expansion of trade and commerce, making the Hellenistic period far richer than its predecessor. The wealth of the East combined with the creativity of the Greeks led to new advances in science and medicine. When Alexander conquered much of the East, the Greeks and Macedonians thought themselves superior. Only in time did they appreciate the culture of their neighbors. When they did, they created a sophisticated culture of their own with broader horizons than ever before.

CHAPTER REVIEW

■ **When the Greeks arrived in Hellas, how did they adapt themselves to their new landscape? (p. 58)**

The Greeks entered a land of mountains and small plains, which led them to establish small communities. Sometimes these small communities were joined together in kingdoms, most prominently the Minoan kingdom on the island of Crete and the Mycenaean kingdom on the mainland. Minoans and Mycenaeans used written records, and the fall of these kingdoms led writing to disappear for centuries, a period known as the Greek Dark Age (1100–800 B.C.E.). The poetry of Homer and Hesiod contains scraps of information about earlier Greece.

■ **What was the origin of the polis, and what types of governments were established to rule it? (p. 61)**

Even though kingdoms collapsed in the Dark Age, Greek culture continued to spread, and new independent city-states were formed. Such a community, called a polis, developed social and political institutions. Some poleis were democracies, in which government was shared among all citizens, which meant adult free men. Other Greeks established smaller governing bodies of citizens, called oligarchs, that directed the political affairs of all. Political and social upheaval sometimes led to tyranny, rule by one man who seized power unconstitutionally.

■ **What major developments mark the Archaic Greek period in terms of spread of culture and the growth of cities? (p. 63)**

During the Archaic age (800–500 B.C.E.) Greeks colonized much of the Mediterranean, establishing cities in Asia Minor, southern Italy, Sicily, and southern France. This brought them into contact with many other peoples, and also spread Greek culture widely. During this period Sparta and Athens became the most important poleis.

■ **What were the major developments in literature, philosophy, religion, and art, and how did war affect this intellectual and social process? (p. 67)**

Sparta and Athens joined together to fight the Persian Empire, but later turned against one another in the Peloponnesian War. During this time, Athenian leaders used funds from the Delian League to turn their city into an architectural showplace. Playwrights presented tragedies that examined the rights of the individual and the nature of good and evil and comedies that offered commentary on the leaders and public figures of the day. Although Greeks worshiped the same deities, religion was local, with each polis having its own cult devoted to specific gods and goddesses. Both women and men took part in ceremonies honoring gods and goddesses. Building on the theories of the Pre-Socratic thinkers, philosophers such as Plato and Aristotle developed ideas about the universe and the place of humans in it.

■ **How did the Greek city-states meet political and military challenges, and how did Macedonia become dominant? (p. 85)**

The Greeks destroyed a good deal of their flourishing world in a series of wars. Despite their political advances, they never really learned how to routinely live peacefully with one another, and each tried to create a hegemony over other states. Their disunity allowed for the rise of Macedonia under the leadership of King Philip II, a brilliant military leader.

Suggested Reading

Buckler, John. *Aegean Greece in the Fourth Century B.C.E.* 2003. Treats the history of this very influential century in detail.

Burkert, Walter. *Greek Religion.* 1987. The authoritative study of ancient religious beliefs, with much material from the sources.

Cartledge, Paul. *The Spartans: The World of the Warrior Heroes of Ancient Greece.* 2002. A readable general book on the history and legacy of Sparta.

Cohen, David. *Law, Sexuality, and Society: The Enforcement of Morals in Classical Athens.* 1992. Examines the social and legal context of adultery, same-sex relations, and sexual conduct.

Hansen, Mogens Herman. *Polis: An Introduction to the Ancient Greek City-State.* 2006. The authoritative study of the polis.

Malkin, Irad, ed. *Ancient Perspectives on Greek Ethnicity.* 2001. Deals with how the Greeks and their neighbors defined themselves as a people.

Mikalson, Jon D. *Athenian Popular Religion.* 1987. An invaluable study of religious practices in Athens.

Morgan, Catherine. *Early Greek States Beyond the Polis.* 2003. Demonstrates that Greek states went far beyond the concept of the polis.

Osborne, Robin. *Greece in the Making, 1200–479 B.C.* 2003. Traces the evolution of Greek communities from villages to cities and the development of their civic institutions.

Patterson, Cynthia B. *The Family in Greek History.* 1998. Examines the public and private relations of the family.

Roberts, Jennifer Tolbert. *Athens on Trial: The Antidemocratic Tradition in Western Thought.* 1996. Discusses the antidemocratic tradition in Western thought from its origin in reactions to Athenian democracy to the present.

Skydsgaard, Jens Erik, and Signe Isager. *Ancient Greek Agriculture.* 1995. Examines agriculture as the main source of wealth in Greece.

Thomas, Carol G. *Myth Becomes History.* 1993. An excellent treatment of early Greece and modern historical attitudes toward it.

Tsetskhladze, Gocha R., ed. *Greek Colonization: An Account of Greek Colonies and Other Settlements Overseas.* Vol. 1, 2006; Vol. 2, 2008. The definitive work on the entire span of Greek colonization.

Winkler, John J. *The Constraints of Desire.* 1989. Examines the anthropology of sex and gender in ancient Greece.

Notes

1. J. M. Edmonds, *Greek Elegy and Iambus* (Cambridge, Mass.: Harvard University Press, 1931), I.70, frag. 10.
2. Herodotus 7.226.2.
3. Thucydides, *History of the Peloponnesian War* 1.23.6.
4. Ibid. 7.87.6.
5. Plutarch, *Life of Pericles* 13.5.
6. Xenophon, *Oeconomicus* 7.40.
7. Ibid. 7.29–30.
8. G. Tarditi, *Archilochus Fragmenta* (Rome: Edizioni dell'Ateno, 1968), frag. 112.
9. W. Barnstable, *Sappho* (New York: Garden City, 1965), frag. 24.
10. J. M. Edmonds, *The Fragments of Attic Comedy* (Leiden: E. J. Brill, 1971), 2.366–369, Mnesimachos frag. 7.

Key Terms

Minoan (p. 58)
Mycenaean (p. 58)
polis (p. 61)
acropolis (p.61)
agora (p. 61)
hoplites (p. 62)
monarchy (p. 62)
tyranny (p. 62)
democracy (p. 62)
oligarchy (p. 62)
federalism (p. 63)
helots (p. 65)
Delian League (p. 69)
Common Peace (p. 85)
hegemony (p. 85)

For practice quizzes and other study tools, visit the Online Study Guide at **bedfordstmartins.com/mckaywest**.

For primary sources from this period, see *Sources of Western Society*, Second Edition.

For Web sites, images, and documents related to topics in this chapter, visit Make History at **bedfordstmartins.com/mckaywest**.

4

The Hellenistic World

336–30 B.C.E.

Two years after his conquest of Greece, Philip II of Macedonia fell victim to an assassin's dagger. Philip's twenty-year-old son, historically known as Alexander the Great (r. 336–323 B.C.E.), assumed the Macedonian throne. This young man, one of the most remarkable personalities of Western civilization, was to have a profound impact on history.

In 336 B.C.E. Alexander inherited not only Philip's crown but also his policies. After his victory at Chaeronea (kehr-uh-NEE-uh), Philip had organized the states of Greece into a huge league under his leadership and announced to the Greeks his plan to lead them and his Macedonians against the Persian Empire. After his father's death, Alexander made his father's plan his life's work. By overthrowing the Persian Empire and by spreading Hellenism — Greek culture, language, thought, and way of life — as far as India, Alexander was instrumental in creating a new Hellenistic era. As a result of Alexander's exploits, the individualistic and energetic culture of the Greeks came into intimate contact with the venerable older cultures of the Near East. The Hellenistic period would last until the Roman conquest of Egypt in 30 B.C.E., though Hellenistic thought and culture would endure. ■

Museo Archeologico Nazionale, Naples, Italy/The Bridgeman Art Library

Life in the Hellenistic World. Hellenistic cities were centers of culture and the arts. In this first-century B.C.E. mosaic from Pompeii, masked street musicians perform for passersby.

CHAPTER PREVIEW

Alexander and the Great Crusade

Why did Alexander launch his attack on the Persian Empire, and how extensive were his conquests? ■

Fully intending to carry out Philip's designs to lead the Greeks against the Persians, Alexander proclaimed to the Greek world that the invasion of Persia was to be a great crusade, a mighty act of revenge for the Persian invasion of Greece in 480 B.C.E. (see Chapter 3). It would also be the means by which Alexander would create an empire of his own in the East.

Despite his youth, Alexander was well prepared to invade Persia. Philip had groomed his son to become king and had given him the best education possible. In 334 B.C.E. Alexander led an army of Macedonians and Greeks into Persian territory in Asia Minor. With him went a staff of philosophers and poets, scientists whose job it was to map the country and study strange animals and plants, and a historian to write an account of the campaign. Alexander intended not only a military campaign but also an expedition of discovery.

In the next three years Alexander moved east into the Persian Empire, winning three major battles at the Granicus River, Issus, and Gaugamela (Map 4.1). When he reached Egypt, he seized the land without a battle. After honoring the priestly class, Alexander was proclaimed pharaoh, the legitimate ruler of the country. He next marched to the oasis of Siwah, west of the Nile Valley, to consult the famous oracle of Zeus-Amon (the Greeks believed that Zeus and Amon were the same). No one will ever know what the priest told him, but henceforth Alexander called himself the son of Zeus. Next he marched into western Asia, where at Gaugamela he defeated the Persian army. After this victory the principal Persian capital of Persepolis easily fell to him. There he performed a symbolic act of retribution by burning the buildings of Xerxes, the invader of Greece during the Persian War fifty years earlier. In 330 B.C.E. he took Ecbatana (ehk-BUH-tuh-nuh), the last Persian capital, and pursued the Persian king to his death.

Map 4.1 Alexander's Conquests, 336–324 B.C.E. This map shows the course of Alexander's invasion of the Persian Empire and the speed of his progress. More important than the great success of his military campaigns was his founding of Hellenistic cities in the East.

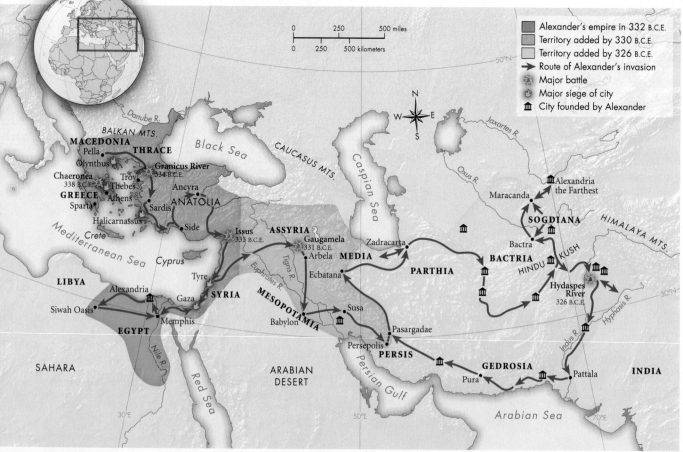

The Persian Empire had fallen, and the war of revenge was over, but Alexander had no intention of stopping. He dismissed his Greek troops but permitted many of them to serve on as mercenaries. Alexander then began his personal odyssey. With his Macedonian soldiers and Greek mercenaries, he set out to conquer the rest of Asia. He plunged deeper into the East, into lands completely unknown to the Greek world. It took his soldiers four additional years to conquer Bactria and the easternmost parts of the now-defunct Persian Empire, but still Alexander was determined to continue his march.

In 326 B.C.E. Alexander crossed the Indus River and entered India. There, too, he saw hard fighting, and finally at the Hyphasis (HIH-fuh-sihs) River his troops refused to go farther. Alexander was enraged by the mutiny, for he believed he was near the end of the world. Nonetheless, the army stood firm, and Alexander relented. Still eager to explore the limits of the world, Alexander turned south to the Arabian Sea. Though the tribes in the area did not oppose him, he waged a bloody, ruthless, and unnecessary war against them. After reaching the Arabian Sea and turning west, he led his army through the grim Gedrosian Desert. The army suffered fearfully, and many soldiers died along the way. Nonetheless, in 324 B.C.E. Alexander returned to his camp at Susa in the Greek-controlled region of Assyria. The great crusade was over, but Alexander never returned to his homeland of Macedonia. He died the next year in Babylon from fever, wounds, and excessive drinking. He was only thirty-two, but in just thirteen years he had created an empire that stretched from his homeland of Macedonia to India.

340–262 B.C.E.	Rise of Epicurean and Stoic philosophies
336 B.C.E.	Alexander becomes king of Macedonia
334–324 B.C.E.	Alexander's Great Crusade
330 B.C.E.	Fall of Persian Empire
ca. 330–200 B.C.E.	Establishment of new Hellenistic cities
326 B.C.E.	Alexander reaches India; troops mutiny
323 B.C.E.	Alexander dies at age thirty-two
323–263 B.C.E.	War of succession leads to the establishment of Antigonid, Ptolemaic, and Seleucid dynasties
ca. 310–212 B.C.E.	Scientific developments in mathematics, astrology, and physics
ca. 200 B.C.E.	Mystery religions start flourishing
30 B.C.E.	Roman conquest of Egypt

Alexander at the Battle of Issus At left, Alexander the Great, bareheaded and wearing a breastplate, charges King Darius, who is standing in a chariot. The moment marks the turning point of the battle, as Darius turns to flee from the attack. (National Museum, Naples/Alinari/Art Resource, NY)

Alexander's Prayer to Establish a "Brotherhood of Man"

LISTENING TO THE PAST

In 324 B.C.E., after returning to Opis, north of Babylon in modern Iraq, Alexander found himself confronted with a huge and unexpected mutiny by his Macedonian veterans. He held a banquet to pacify them, including in the festivities Persians and other Asian followers, some nine thousand in all. During the festivities he offered a public prayer for harmony and partnership in rule between the Macedonians and Persians. Many modern scholars have interpreted this prayer as an expression of his desire to establish a "brotherhood of man." The following passage provides the evidence for this view.

❝ 8. When [Alexander] arrived at Opis, he collected the Macedonians and announced that he intended to discharge from the army those who were useless for military service either from age or from being maimed in the limbs; and he said he would send them back to their own abodes. He also promised to give those who went back as much extra reward as would make them special objects of envy to those at home and arouse in the other Macedonians the wish to share similar dangers and labours. Alexander said this, no doubt, for the purpose of pleasing the Macedonians; but on the contrary they were, not without reason, offended by the speech which he delivered, thinking that now they were despised by him and deemed to be quite useless for military service. Indeed, throughout the whole of this expedition they had been offended at many other things; for his adoption of the Persian dress, thereby exhibiting his contempt for their opinion often caused them grief, as did also his accoutring the foreign soldiers called Epigoni in the Macedonian style, and the mixing of the alien horsemen among the ranks of the Companions. Therefore they could not remain silent and control themselves, but urged him to dismiss all of them from his army; and they advised him to prosecute the war in company with his father, deriding Ammon by this remark. When Alexander heard this . . . , he ordered the most conspicuous of the men who had tried to stir up the multitude to sedition to be arrested. He himself pointed out with his hand to the shield-bearing guards those whom they were to arrest, to the number of thirteen; and he ordered these to be led away to execution. When the rest, stricken with terror, became silent, he mounted the platform again, and spoke as follows:

9. "The speech which I am about to deliver will not be for the purpose of checking your start homeward, for, so far as I am concerned, you may depart wherever you wish; but for the purpose of making you understand when you take yourselves off, what kind of men you have been to us who have conferred such benefits upon you. . . .

10. . . . Most of you have golden crowns, the eternal memorials of your valour and of the honour you receive from me. Whoever has been killed has met with a glorious end and has been honoured with a splendid burial. Brazen statues of most of the slain have been erected at home, and their parents are held in honour, being released from all public service and from taxation. But no one of you has ever been killed in flight under my leadership. And now I was intending to send back those of you who are unfit for service, objects of envy to those at home; but since you all wish to depart, depart all of you! Go back and report at home that your king Alexander, the conqueror of the Persians, Medes, Bactrians, and Sacians; the man who has subjugated the Uxians, Arachotians, and Drangians; who has also acquired the rule of the Parthians, Chorasmians, and Hyrcanians, as far as the Caspian Sea . . . — report that when you returned to Susa you deserted him and went away, handing him over to the protection of conquered foreigners. Perhaps this report of yours will be both glorious to you in the eyes of men and devout I ween in the eyes of the gods. Depart!"

11. Having thus spoken, he leaped down quickly from the platform, and entered the palace, where he paid no attention to the decoration of his person, nor was any of his Companions admitted to see him. Not even on the morrow was any one of them admitted to an audience; but on the third day he summoned the select Persians within, and among them he distributed the commands of the brigades, and made the rule that only those whom he proclaimed his kinsmen should have the honour of saluting him with a kiss. But the Macedonians who heard the speech were thoroughly astonished at the moment, and remained there in silence near the platform; nor when he retired did any of them accompany the king, except his personal Companions and the confidential body-guards. Though they remained most of them had nothing to do or say; and yet they were unwilling to retire. But when the news was reported to them . . . they were no longer able to restrain themselves; but running in a body to the palace, they cast their weapons there in front of the gates as signs of supplication to the king. Standing in front of the gates, they shouted, beseeching to be allowed to enter, and saying that they were willing to surrender the men who had been the instigators of the disturbance on that occasion, and those who had begun the clamour. They also declared they would not retire from the gates either day or night, unless Alexander would take some pity upon them. When he was informed of this, he came out without delay; and seeing them lying on the ground in humble guise, and hearing most of them lamenting with loud voice, tears began to flow also from his own eyes. He made an effort to say something to them, but they continued their importunate entreaties. At length one of them,

Callines by name, a man conspicuous both for his age and because he was a captain of the Companion cavalry, spoke as follows, "O king, what grieves the Macedonians is that you have already made some of the Persians kinsmen to yourself, and that Persians are called Alexander's kinsmen, and have the honour of saluting you with a kiss; whereas none of the Macedonians have as yet enjoyed this honour." Then Alexander, interrupting him, said, "But all of you without exception I consider my kinsmen, and so from this time I shall call you." When he had said this, Callines advanced and saluted him with a kiss, and so did all those who wished to salute him. Then they took up their weapons and returned to the camp, shouting and singing a song of thanksgiving. After this Alexander offered sacrifice to the gods to whom it was his custom to sacrifice, and gave a public banquet, over which he himself presided, with the Macedonians sitting around him; and next to them the Persians; after whom came the men of the other nations, preferred in honour for their personal rank or for some meritorious action. The king and his guests drew wine from the same bowl and poured out the same libations, both the Grecian prophets and the Magians commencing the ceremony. He prayed for other blessings, and especially that harmony and community of rule might exist between the Macedonians and Persians. 〞

Source: Arrian, *Anabasis of Alexander* 7.8.1–11.9 in F. R. B. Goldophin, ed., *The Greek Historians*, vol. 2. Copyright 1942 and renewed 1970 by Random House, Inc. Used by permission of Random House, Inc.

QUESTIONS FOR ANALYSIS

1. What was the purpose of the banquet at Opis?
2. Were all of the guests treated equally?
3. What did Alexander gain from bringing together the Macedonians and Persians?

This bow and arrow case indicates that Alexander's success came at the price of blood. These gilded scenes portray more military conflict than philosophical compassion.
(Archaeological Museum Salonica/Dagli-Orti/The Art Archive)

Alexander's Legacy

What was Alexander's political and cultural legacy? ■

Alexander so quickly became a legend during his lifetime that he still seems superhuman. That alone makes a reasoned interpretation of him very difficult. Some historians have seen him as a high-minded philosopher, and none can deny that he possessed genuine intellectual gifts. Others, however, have portrayed him as a bloody-minded autocrat, more interested in his own ambition than in the common good. Alexander is the perfect example of the need for historians to use care when interpreting known facts. (See "Listening to the Past: Alexander's Prayer to Establish a 'Brotherhood of Man,'" at left.)

What is not disputed is that Alexander was instrumental in changing the face of politics in the eastern Mediterranean. In terms of this, his legacy is clear. His campaign swept away the Persian Empire, which had ruled the East for over two hundred years. In its place he established a Macedonian monarchy. More important in the long run was his founding of new cities and military colonies, which scattered Greeks and Macedonians throughout the East. Thus the practical result of Alexander's campaign was to open the East to the tide of Hellenism.

From Hellenic to Hellenistic

Without intending to do so Alexander changed the face of the world from Greece to India. He created the **Hellenistic** period, thereby ushering in a break with the Greek past. The Hellenic period discussed in Chapter 3 was marked by culture and ethnic unity. Life was primarily Greek, with few significant outside influences. Greeks could travel from Thessaly to Sparta or from Corinth to Syracuse and find the same people speaking the same language. Political institutions were also largely the same, as were religious festivals. Life in the agora was fundamentally alike, as was family life. Greeks ate the same basic foods and enjoyed the same recreation. Nothing was strikingly different from region to region.

Hellenistic The new culture that arose when Alexander overthrew the Persian Empire and began spreading Hellenism, the Greek culture, language, thought, and way of life.

Alexander unknowingly changed that world. The farther eastward he plunged, the more different peoples he encountered. Greeks came into contact with cultures very unlike theirs, many of them with old and venerable traditions. They found cities and kingdoms inhabited by peoples speaking incomprehensible languages. Peoples in the East worshiped their own gods, most of which bore no resemblance to the Olympian gods and goddesses. Easterners ate foods not found at home and lived in vast, open spaces unlike the Greek's small Hellas. Greeks also

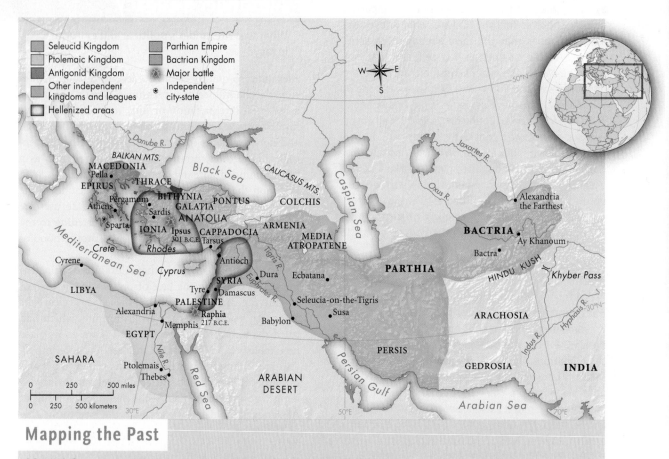

Mapping the Past

Map 4.2 **The Hellenistic World, ca. 263 B.C.E.** This map depicts the Hellenistic world after Alexander's death.
ANALYZING THE MAP Compare this map to Map 4.1 on page 92. After Alexander's death, were the Macedonians and Greeks able to retain control of most of the land he had conquered? What areas were lost?
CONNECTIONS What does this map suggest about the success or failure of Alexander's dreams of conquest?
To complete this activity online, go to the Online Study Guide at bedfordstmartins.com/mckaywest.

did not find the polis. Instead, they confronted monarchy on a scale more pervasive than anything before seen. Alexander did not so much break with the past as offer the Greeks a new, strange, but promising future. Whereas in the Hellenic period similarities largely marked Greek life, now difference became the rule. These were the challenges of the Hellenistic period.

The Political Legacy

The main question at Alexander's death was whether his vast empire could be held together. A major part of his legacy is what he had not done. Although he fathered a successor, the child was too young to assume the duties of kingship and was cruelly murdered by one of Alexander's generals, who viewed him as a future threat. That meant that Alexander's empire was a prize for the taking by the strongest of his generals. Within a week of Alexander's death, a round of fighting began that was to continue for forty years. No single Macedonian general was able

to replace Alexander as emperor of his entire domain. In effect, the strongest divided it among themselves.

By 263 B.C.E. three officers had split the empire into large monarchies (Map 4.2). Antigonus Gonatas became king of Macedonia and established the Antigonid (an-TIH-guh-nuhd) dynasty. Ptolemy (TAH-luh-mee) made himself king of Egypt, and his descendants, the Ptolemies, assumed the powers and position of pharaohs. Seleucus (suh-LOO-kuhs), founder of the Seleucid (SUH-loo-suhd) dynasty, carved out a kingdom that stretched from the coast of Asia Minor to India.

The hold that these new monarchs had over their territories would prove fragile. In 263 B.C.E. Eumenes (yoo-MEHN-eez), the Greek ruler of Pergamum (PUHR-guh-muhm), a city in western Asia Minor, won his independence from the Seleucids and created the Pergamene monarchy. Though the Seleucid kings soon lost control of their easternmost provinces, Greek influence in this area did not wane. In modern Turkestan and Afghanistan another line of Greek kings established the kingdom of

Bactria and even managed to spread their power and culture into northern India.

The political face of Greece itself changed during the Hellenistic period. The day of the polis was over; in its place rose leagues of city-states. The two most powerful and extensive were the Aetolian (ee-TOH-lee-uhn) League in western and central Greece and the Achaean (uh-KEE-uhn) League in the Peloponnesus. Once-powerful city-states like Athens and Sparta sank to the level of third-rate powers.

The political history of the Hellenistic period was dominated by the great monarchies and the Greek leagues. The political fragmentation and incessant warfare that marked the Hellenic period continued on an even wider and larger scale during the Hellenistic period. Never did the Hellenistic world achieve political stability or lasting peace. Hellenistic kings never forgot the vision of Alexander's empire spanning Europe and Asia and secure under the rule of one man. Try though they did, they were never able to re-create it. Just as the Greek states warred against one another until they fell to Macedonia, so the Hellenistic kingdoms repeated their example. After fighting among themselves, they confronted Rome from 146 to 30 B.C.E. They too finally fell to a power that brought the Mediterranean world unity and peace. In this respect Alexander's legacy fell not to his generals but to the Romans of a later era.

The Cultural Legacy

As Alexander waded ever deeper into the East, distance alone presented him with a serious problem: how was he to retain contact with the Greek world behind him? Communications were vital, for he drew supplies and reinforcements from Greece and Macedonia. Alexander had to be sure that he was never cut off and stranded far from the Mediterranean world. His solution was to plant cities and military colonies in strategic places. In these settlements Alexander left Greek mercenaries and Macedonian veterans who were no longer up to active campaigning. Besides keeping the road open to the West, these settlements helped secure the countryside around them.

Alexander's cities and colonies became powerful instruments in the spread of Hellenism throughout the East. The Roman biographer Plutarch described Alexander's achievement in glowing terms: "Having founded over 70 cities among barbarian peoples and having planted Greek magistracies in Asia, Alexander overcame its wild and savage way of life."[1] Alexander opened the East to an enormous wave of immigration,

The Aetolian and Achaean Leagues, ca. 270–200 B.C.E.

and his successors continued his policy by inviting Greek colonists to settle in their realms. For seventy-five years after Alexander's death, Greek immigrants poured into the East. At least 250 new Hellenistic colonies were established. The Mediterranean world had seen no comparable movement of peoples since the Archaic age, when wave after wave of Greeks had turned the Mediterranean basin into a Greek-speaking region (see Chapter 3).

One example of these trends comes from the Hellenistic city of Ay Khanoum. Situated on the modern borders of Russia and Afghanistan and not far from China, the city was predominately Greek. It had the typical Greek trappings of a gymnasium, various temples, and administration buildings. It was not, however, purely Greek. It also contained a temple and artistic remains that prove that the Greeks and the natives had already embraced aspects of each other's religions. One of the most notable discoveries was a long inscription written in Greek verse by a pupil of Aristotle. The inscription, carved in stone, was set up in a public place for all to see. It copied well-known axioms relating to Greek ideals:

> In childhood, learn good manners
> In youth, control your passions
> In middle age, practice justice
> In old age, be of good counsel
> In death, have no regrets.[2]

The inscription provided the Greeks with a link to their faraway homeland. It was also a public way to make at least some of Greek culture available to natives.

The overall result of Alexander's settlements and those of his successors was the spread of Hellenism as far east as India. Throughout the Hellenistic period, Greeks and Easterners became familiar with and adapted themselves to each other's customs, religions, and ways of life. Although Greek culture did not completely conquer the East, it gave the East a vehicle of expression that linked it to the West. Hellenism became a common bond among the East, peninsular Greece, and the western Mediterranean.

❝ In youth, control your passions; in middle age, practice justice; in old age, be of good counsel; in death, have no regrets. ❞

—GREEK INSCRIPTION

The Spread of Hellenism

What effect did Greek migration have on Greek and native peoples? ▪

When the Greeks entered Asia Minor, Egypt, and the more remote East, they encountered civilizations older than their own. In some ways the Eastern cultures were more advanced than the Greek, in other ways less so. Thus this great tide of Greek migration differed from preceding waves, which had spread over land that was uninhabited or inhabited by less-developed peoples.

Hellenistic monarchies offered Greeks economic and social opportunities. To encourage migration, cities were modeled on the polis with all of the familiar trappings of the homeland. In this way Easterners were introduced to Greek language, architecture, culture, and religion. While social mobility was generally greater for Greek men and women, Hellenistic kings ruled their cities tightly, and people had less political power than in classical Greece.

Cities and Kingdoms

One of the major developments of these new kingdoms was the resurgence of monarchy. For most Greeks, monarchs were something out of the heroic past, found in Homer's *Iliad* but not in daily life. Most of the new Hellenistic kingdoms embraced numerous different peoples who had little in common. Hellenistic kings thus needed a new political concept to unite them. One solution was the creation of a ruler cult that linked the king's authority with that of the gods. Thus, royal power had divine approval and was meant to create a political and religious bond between the kings and their subjects. These deified kings were not considered gods as mighty as Zeus or Apollo, and the new ruler cults probably had little religious impact on those ruled. Nonetheless, the ruler cult was an easily understandable symbol of unity within the kingdom.

Hellenistic kingship was hereditary, which gave women who were members of royal families more power than any women in democracies, in which citizenship was limited to men.

sovereign An independent, autonomous state run by its citizens and free of outside interference.

Wives and mothers of kings had influence over their husbands and sons, and a few women ruled in their own right when there was no male heir.

Although Alexander's generals created huge kingdoms, the concept of monarchy, even when combined with the ruler cult, never replaced the ideal of the polis. Consequently, the monarchies never won the deep emotional loyalty that Greeks had once felt for the polis. Hellenistic kings needed large numbers of Greeks to run their kingdoms. Otherwise royal business would grind to a halt, and the conquerors would soon be swallowed up by the far more numerous conquered population. Obviously, then, the kings had to encourage Greeks to immigrate and build new homes. The Hellenistic kings thus confronted the problem of making life in the new monarchies resemble the traditional Greek way of life. Since Greek civilization was urban, the kings continued Alexander's policy of establishing cities throughout their kingdoms in order to entice Greeks to immigrate. From 330 to 200 B.C.E. numerous Hellenistic cities were established. Yet the creation of these cities posed a serious political problem that the Hellenistic kings failed to solve.

To the Greeks civilized life was unthinkable without the polis, which was far more than a mere city. The Greek polis was by definition **sovereign**—an independent, autonomous state run by its citizens, free of any outside power or restraint. Hellenistic kings, however, refused to grant sovereignty to their cities. In effect, the Hellenistic king willingly built a city but refused to build a polis. The Hellenistic monarch gave the city all the external

Royal Couple Cameo This Hellenistic cameo probably portrays King Ptolemy II and his sister Arsinoe II, rulers of the Ptolemaic kingdom of Egypt. During the Hellenistic period portraits of queens became more common because of their increased importance in governing the kingdom. (Erich Lessing/Art Resource, NY)

Street Scene from Ephesus A major paved street in Ephesus runs between houses on the left and the later temple of Hadrian on the right. At the end of the street rises the library of Celsus. Because Hellenistic cities had sound economic bases, people continued to live in them for generations. (ImageState/Alamy)

trappings of a polis. Each had an assembly of citizens, a council to prepare legislation, and a board of magistrates to conduct political business. Yet, however similar to the Greek polis it appeared, such a city could not engage in diplomatic dealings, make treaties, pursue its own foreign policy, or wage its own wars. Nor could it govern its own affairs without interference from the king. In the eyes of the king, the city was an important part of the kingdom, but the welfare of the whole kingdom came first. The city had to follow royal orders, and the king often placed his own officials in it to see that his decrees were followed.

A Hellenistic city differed from a Greek polis in other ways as well. The Greek polis had one body of law and one set of customs. In the Hellenistic city Greeks represented an elite citizen class. Natives and non-Greek foreigners who lived in Hellenistic cities usually possessed lesser rights than Greeks and often had their own laws. In some instances this disparity spurred natives to assimilate Greek culture in order to rise politically and socially. The Hellenistic city was not homogeneous and could not spark the intensity of feeling that marked the polis.

An excellent example of this process comes from the city of Pergamum in northwestern Anatolia. Previously an important strategic site under Alexander, its new Greek rulers turned it into a magnificent city complete with all the typical buildings of the polis, including gymnasia, baths, and one of the finest libraries in all of Hellenistic Greece. They erected temples to the traditional deities, but they also built an imposing temple to the Egyptian gods. Furthermore, Jews established a synagogue in the city. Especially in the agora Greeks and indigenous people met to conduct business and to interact with each other. Greeks felt as though they were at home, and the evolving culture mixed Greek and local elements.

The old Greek cities of Asia Minor actually, if unintentionally, aided this development by maintaining and spreading traditions that went back for centuries. They served as models for the new foundations by providing a rich legacy of culture and tradition. In their very combination of physical beauty, refinement, and sophistication, they inspired imitation of the best in Greek culture.

In many respects the Hellenistic city resembled a modern city. It was a cultural center with theaters, temples, and libraries. It was a seat of learning, a home of poets, writers, teachers, and artists. It was a place where people could find amusement. The Hellenistic city was also an economic center that provided a ready market for grain and produce raised in the surrounding countryside. In short, the Hellenistic city offered cultural and economic opportunities.

Though Hellenistic kings never built a true polis, that does not mean that their urban policy failed. Rather, the Hellenistic city was to remain the basic social and political unit throughout the Hellenistic world until the sixth century C.E. Cities were the chief agents of Hellenization, and their influence spread far beyond their walls. They formed a broader cultural network in which Greek language, customs, and values flourished. Roman

The Great Altar of Pergamum A new Hellenistic city needed splendid art and architecture to prove its worth in Greek eyes. The king of Pergamum ordered the construction of this monumental altar, which is now in Berlin. The scenes depict the mythical victory of the Greek gods over the Giants, who symbolize barbarism. The altar served the propaganda purpose of celebrating the victory of Hellenism over the East. (Bildarchiv Preussischer Kulturbesitz/Art Resource, NY)

rule in the Hellenistic world would later be based on this urban culture, which facilitated the rise and spread of Christianity.

The Lives of the Greeks in the East

If the Hellenistic kings failed to satisfy the Greeks' political yearnings, they nonetheless succeeded in giving them unequaled economic and social opportunities. The ruling dynasties of the Hellenistic world were Macedonian, and Greeks filled all important political, military, and diplomatic positions. They constituted an upper class that sustained Hellenism in the East. Besides building Greek cities, Hellenistic kings offered Greeks land and money as lures to further immigration.

The opening of the East offered ambitious Greeks opportunities for well-paying jobs and economic success. The Hellenistic monarchy, unlike the Greek polis, did not depend solely on its citizens to fulfill its political needs. Talented Greek men had the opportunity to rise quickly in the government bureaucracy. Appointed by the king, these administrators did not have to stand for election each year, as had many officials of a Greek polis. Since they held their jobs year after year, they had ample time to evolve new administrative techniques. Naturally, they became more efficient than the often amateur officials common in Hellenic Greek city-states. The needs of the Hellenistic monarchy and the opportunities it offered thus gave rise to a professional corps of Greek administrators.

Greeks also found ready employment in the armies and navies of the Hellenistic monarchies. Alexander had proved the Greco-Macedonian style of warfare to be far superior to that of other peoples, and Alexander's successors, themselves experienced officers, realized the importance of trained soldiers. Hellenistic kings were reluctant to arm the native populations or to allow them to serve in the army, fearing military rebellions among their conquered subjects. The result was the emergence of professional armies and navies consisting entirely of Greeks.

Greeks were able to dominate other professions as well. Eastern kingdoms and cities recruited Greek writers and artists to create Greek literature, art, and culture. Architects, engineers, and skilled craftsmen found their services in great demand to work on the Greek buildings commissioned by the Hellenistic monarchs. Architects and engineers would sometimes design and build whole cities, which they laid out in checkerboard fashion and filled with typical Greek buildings. An enormous wave of construction took place during the Hellenistic period.

Increased physical and social mobility benefited some women as well as men. More women learned to read than before, and they engaged in occupations in which literacy was beneficial, including care of the sick. During the Hellenistic period some women took part in commercial transactions. They still lived under legal handicaps. In Egypt, for example, a Greek woman needed a male guardian to buy, sell, or lease land; to borrow money; and to represent her in other transactions. Yet often such a guardian was present only to fulfill the letter of the law. The woman was the real agent and handled the business being transacted.

Because real power in the Hellenistic world was held by monarchs, the political benefits of citizenship were much less than they had been in the classical period. The diminished importance of citizenship meant that it was awarded more easily. Even women sometimes received honorary citizenship from foreign cities because of aid given in times of crisis. Few women achieved these honors, however, and those who did were from the upper classes.

Despite the opportunities they offered, the Hellenistic monarchies were hampered by their artificial origins. Their failure to win the political loyalty of their Greek subjects and their policy of wooing Greeks with lucrative positions encouraged feelings of uprootedness and self-serving individualism among Greek immigrants. Once a Greek man had left home to take service with, for instance, the army or the bureaucracy of the Ptolemies, he had no incentive beyond his pay and the comforts of life in Egypt to keep him there. If the Seleucid king offered him more money or a promotion, he might well accept it and take his talents to Asia Minor. Thus professional Greek soldiers and administrators were very mobile and were apt to look to their own interests, not their kingdom's.

One result of these developments was that the nature of warfare changed. Except in the areas of Greece, Hellenistic soldiers were professionals. Unlike the citizen hoplites of classical Greece, these men were trained, full-time soldiers. Hellenistic kings paid them well, often giving them land as an incentive to remain loyal. Only in Macedonia among the kingdoms of Greece was there a national army.

As long as Greeks continued to migrate east, the kingdoms remained stable and strong. In the process

they drew an immense amount of talent from the Greek peninsula, draining the vitality of the Greek homeland. However, the Hellenistic monarchies could not keep recruiting Greeks forever, in spite of their wealth and willingness to spend lavishly. In time the huge surge of immigration slowed greatly. Even then the Hellenistic monarchs were reluctant to recruit Easterners to fill posts normally held by Greeks. The result was at first the stagnation of the Hellenistic world and finally its collapse in the face of the young and vigorous Roman republic.

Greeks and Easterners

Because they understood themselves to be "the West," Greeks generally referred to Egypt and what we now call the Near East collectively as "the East." Many historians have continued that usage, seeing the Hellenistic period as a time when Greek and "Eastern" cultures blended to some degree. Eastern civilizations were older than Greek, and the Greeks were a minority outside of Greece. Hellenistic monarchies were remarkably successful in at least partially Hellenizing Easterners and spreading a uniform culture throughout the East, a culture to which Rome eventually fell heir. The prevailing institutions, laws, and language of the East became Greek. Indeed, the Near East had seen nothing comparable since the days when Mesopotamian culture had spread throughout the area.

Yet the spread of Greek culture was wider than it was deep. Hellenistic kingdoms were never entirely unified in language, customs, and thought. Greek culture took firmest hold along the shores of the Mediterranean, but farther east, in Persia and Bactria, it was less strong. The principal reason for this phenomenon is that Greek culture generally did not extend far beyond the reaches of the cities. Many urban residents adopted the aspects of Hellenism that they found useful, but others in the countryside generally did not embrace it wholly.

The Ptolemies in Egypt provide an excellent example of this situation. They made little effort to spread Greek culture, and unlike other Hellenistic kings they were not city builders, founding only the city of Ptolemais near Thebes. At first native Egyptians retained their traditional language, outlook, religion, and way of life. Initially untouched by Hellenism, the natives were nonetheless the foundation of the kingdom: they fed it by their labor in the fields and financed its operations with their taxes.

Marital Advice This small terra-cotta sculpture is generally seen as a mother advising her daughter, a new bride. Such intimate scenes of ordinary people were popular in the Hellenistic world, in contrast to the idealized statues of gods and goddesses of the classical period. (British Museum/Michael Holford)

The Ptolemaic Kingdom, ca. 200 B.C.E.

Under the pharaohs talented Egyptians had been able to rise to high office, but during the third century B.C.E. the Ptolemies cut off this avenue of advancement. Instead of converting the natives to Hellenism, the Ptolemies tied them to the land even more tightly, making it nearly impossible for them to leave their villages. The bureaucracy of the Ptolemies was ruthlessly efficient, and the native population was viciously and cruelly exploited. Even in times of hardship the king's taxes came first, although payment might mean starvation for the natives. Their desperation was summed up by one Egyptian, who scrawled the warning: "We are worn out; we will run away."[3] To many Egyptians revolt or a life of banditry was preferable to working the land under the harsh Ptolemies.

Throughout the third century B.C.E. the Greek upper class in Egypt had little to do with the native population, but in the second century B.C.E. Greeks and native Egyptians began to intermarry and mingle their cultures. The language of the native population influenced Greek, and many Greeks adopted the Egyptian religion and ways of life. Simultaneously, natives adopted Greek customs and language and began to play a role in the administration of the kingdom and even to serve in the army. While many Greeks and Egyptians remained aloof from each other, the overall result was the evolution of a widespread Greco-Egyptian culture.

The Seleucids meanwhile became the great Hellenizers of this period. Continuing a policy similar to that of the Hittites and Persians before them, they linked western Asia Minor to Central Asia by maintaining a political and economic system that embraced all their subjects. At the same time they established Greek cities and military colonies throughout the region to nurture a vigorous and large Greek population. Especially important to the Seleucids were the military colonies, for they needed Greeks to defend the kingdom from their Persian neighbors.

The Seleucids had no elaborate plan for Hellenizing the native population, but the arrival of so many Greeks had a large impact. Seleucid military colonies were generally founded near native villages, thus exposing rural residents to all aspects of Greek life. Many Easterners found Greek political and cultural forms attractive and imitated them. In Asia Minor and Syria, for instance, numerous native villages and towns developed along Greek lines, and some of them grew into Hellenized cities. The Greek kings who replaced the Seleucids in the third century B.C.E. would spread Greek culture to their neighbors as far east as the Indian subcontinent. While Alexander had opened this vast region by his conquests, the Seleucids made it Greek.

For non-Greeks the prime advantage of Greek culture was its very pervasiveness. The Greek language became the common speech of Egypt and the Near East. Greek became the speech of the royal court, bureaucracy, and army. It was also the speech of commerce: anyone who wanted to compete in business had to learn it. As early as the third century B.C.E. some Greek cities were giving citizenship to Hellenized natives.

The vast majority of Hellenized Easterners, however, took only the externals of Greek culture while retaining the essentials of their own ways of life. Though Greeks

Cultural Blending Ptolemy V, a Macedonian by birth and the Hellenistic king of Egypt, dedicated this stone to the Egyptian sacred bull of the Egyptian god Ptah. Nothing here is Greek or Macedonian, a sign that the conquered had, in some religious and ceremonial ways, won over their conquerors. (Egyptian Museum, Cairo)

ally a ri
try into
The
by stor
puhs) a
tian go
Greek
Asclepi
the judg
people
healing
many H
The
of Serap
have co
who car
dess of t
popular
had bes
founded
riage, c
promise
The r
over the
mysterie
(ee-LO
the Hell
long and
that sens
temples
lived.

Heller

A prime
Greek cu
cities wei
numerou
corporati
of autono
city, obey
ally no re
deed, the
anyone's
(ca. 242–
Jews had
with grea
ify his em
ensured
and Judai
Only t
ca. 164 B
Judaea. H
were a sm
trying to
of Rome.

and Easterners adapted to each other's ways, there was never a true fusion of cultures. Nonetheless, each found useful things in the civilization of the other, and the two fertilized each other. This fertilization, this mingling of Greek and Eastern elements, is what makes Hellenistic culture unique and distinctive.

The Economic Scope of the Hellenistic World

What effects did East-West trade have on ordinary peoples during the Hellenistic period? ■

Alexander's conquest of the Persian Empire not only changed the political face of the ancient world but also brought the East fully into the sphere of Greek economics. Yet the Hellenistic period did not see a revolution in the way people lived and worked. The material demands of Hellenistic society remained as simple as those of Athenian society in the fifth century B.C.E. Clothes and furniture were essentially unchanged, as were household goods, tools, and jewelry. The real achievement of Alexander and his successors was linking East and West in a broad commercial network. The spread of Greeks throughout the Near East and Egypt created new markets and stimulated trade.

Agriculture and Industry

Much of the revenue for the Hellenistic kingdoms was derived from agricultural products, rents paid by the tenants of royal land, and taxation of land. Trying to improve productivity, the rulers sponsored experiments on seed grain, selecting seeds that seemed the most hardy and productive. The Ptolemies made the greatest strides in agriculture, and the reason for their success was largely political. Egypt had a strong tradition of central authority dating back to the pharaohs, which the Ptolemies inherited and tightened. They could decree what crops Egyptian farmers would plant and what animals would be raised, and they had the power to mobilize native labor into the digging and maintenance of canals and ditches. The centralized authority of the Ptolemies explains how agricultural advances occurred at the local level in Egypt. But such progress was not possible in any other Hellenistic monarchy. Despite royal interest in agriculture and a more studied approach to it in the Hellenistic period, there is no evidence that agricultural productivity increased or influenced Eastern practices.

As with agriculture, although demand for goods increased during the Hellenistic period, no new techniques of production appear to have developed. Manual labor, not machinery, continued to turn out the raw materials

and few manufactured goods the Hellenistic world used. Human labor was so cheap and so abundant that kings had no incentive to encourage the invention and manufacture of laborsaving machinery. (See "Living in the Past: Farming in the Hellenistic World," page 104.)

The Ptolemies provide an example of the extremes that could be found. The historian Diodoros, who visited Egypt around 60 B.C.E., gives a grim picture of the miners' lives:

> At the end of Egypt is a region bearing many mines and abundant gold, which is extracted with great pain and expense. . . . For kings of Egypt condemn to the mines criminals and prisoners of war, those who were falsely accused and those who were put into jail because of royal anger, not only them but sometimes also all of their relatives. Rounding them up, they assign them to the gold mines, taking revenge on those who were condemned and through their labors gaining huge revenues. The condemned—and they are very many—all of them are put in chains; and they work persistently and continually, both by day and throughout the night, getting no rest and carefully cut off from escape. For the guards, who are barbarian soldiers and who speak a different language, stand watch over them so that no man can either by conversation or friendly contact corrupt any of them.[4]

Condemned men, women, and children worked until they died.

Apart from gold and silver, which were used primarily for coins and jewelry, iron was the most important metal and saw the most varied use. Even so, the method of its production never became very sophisticated. The Hellenistic Greeks did manage to produce a low-grade steel by adding carbon to iron.

Pottery remained an important commodity, and most of it was made locally. The coarse pottery used in the kitchen did not change at all. Fancier pots and bowls, decorated with a shiny black glaze, came into use during the Hellenistic period. This ware originated in Athens, but potters in other places began to imitate its style, heavily cutting into the Athenian market. In the second century B.C.E. a red-glazed ware, often called Samian, burst on the market and soon dominated it. Athens still

❝ Rounding them up, they assign them to the gold mines, taking revenge on those who were condemned and through their labors gaining huge revenues. ❞

—**DIODOROS**

Archimedes, Scientist and Inventor

INDIVIDUALS IN SOCIETY

ARCHIMEDES (CA. 287–212 B.C.E.) WAS BORN IN THE GREEK CITY OF SYRACUSE in Sicily, an intellectual center in which he pursued scientific interests. He was the most original thinker of his time and a practical inventor. In his book *On Plane Equilibriums* he dealt for the first time with the basic principles of mathematics, including the principle of the lever. He once said that if he were given a lever and a suitable place to stand,

he could move the world. He also demonstrated how easily his compound pulley could move huge weights with little effort:

*A three-masted merchant ship of the royal fleet had been hauled on land by hard work and many hands. Archimedes put aboard her many men and the usual freight. He sat far away from her; and without haste, but gently working a compound pulley with his hand, he drew her towards him smoothly and without faltering, just as though she were running on the surface.**

He likewise invented the Archimedian screw, a pump to bring subterranean water up to irrigate fields, which quickly came into common use. In his treatise *On Floating Bodies* Archimedes founded the science of hydrostatics. He concluded that whenever a solid floats in a liquid, the weight of the solid equals the weight of the liquid displaced. The way he made his discovery has become famous:

When he was devoting his attention to this problem, he happened to go to a public bath. When he climbed down into the bathtub there, he noticed that water in the tub equal to the bulk of his body flowed out. Thus, when he observed this method of solving the problem, he did not wait. Instead, moved with joy, he sprang out of the tub, and rushing home naked he kept indicating in a loud voice that he had indeed discovered what he was seeking. For while running he was shouting repeatedly in Greek, "Eureka, eureka" ("I have found it, I have found it").†

War between Rome and Syracuse unfortunately interrupted Archimedes' scientific life. In 213 B.C.E. during the Second Punic War, the Romans besieged the city. Hiero, its king and Archimedes' friend, asked the scientist for help in repulsing Roman attacks. Archimedes began to build remarkable devices that served as artillery. One shot missiles to break up infantry attacks. Others threw huge masses of stones that fell on the enemy with irresistible speed and noise. They tore gaping holes in the Roman lines and broke up attacks. Against Roman warships he built a machine consisting of huge beams that projected over the targets. Then the artillerymen dropped great weights onto the ships, like bombs. Even more complicated was an apparatus with beams from which

Archimedes' treatises were found on a palimpsest, a manuscript that was erased so that another text could be written over it. In about 1229 C.E. Christian monks erased the manuscript and used it for a prayer book. Scientists were able to read Archimedes' original text using digital processing of infrared light and X-rays. (Image by the Rochester Institute of Technology. Copyright resides with the owner of the Archimedes Palimpsest) large claws dropped onto the hulls of warships, hoisted them into the air, and dropped them back into the sea. In response, the Romans brought up an exceptionally large scaling ladder carried on ships. While it approached, Archimedes' artillery disabled it by hitting it repeatedly with stones weighing 500 pounds. At last the Romans became so fearful that whenever they saw a bit of rope or a stick of timber projecting over the wall they shouted, "There it is. Archimedes is trying some engine on us" and fled. When the Romans finally broke into Syracuse in 212 B.C.E., a Roman soldier came upon Archimedes in his study and killed him.

Much but not all of Archimedes' work survived him. In 1998 a new codex containing many of his treatises, some of them previously lost, turned up at a Christie's auction in New York. Someone had stolen it from a Greek Orthodox library in Constantinople after World War I, and it afterward disappeared into the black market. Although the Greek government tried to prevent its sale, an anonymous buyer generously deposited it at the Walters Art Museum in Baltimore. Using X-rays and other modern techniques, specialists have painstakingly restored the manuscript, which had been painted over in the Middle Ages. Contemporary science is enabling classic scholars to read some of Archimedes' lost works.

QUESTIONS FOR ANALYSIS

1. How useful were Archimedes' inventions?
2. What effect did his weapons have on the Roman attackers?
3. What is the irony of Archimedes' death?

*Plutarch, *Life of Marcellus*.

†Vitruvius, *On Architecture*, 9 Preface, 10.

Rams proved even more effective than catapults in bringing down large portions of walls.

Right from the beginning Macedonian kings showed the way in the practical use of all these machines. There is no better example than Philip II's attack on Perinthos in 340 B.C.E.:

> *Philip launched a siege of Perinthos, advancing engines to the city and assaulting the walls in relays day after day. He built towers 120 feet tall that rose far above the towers of Perinthos. From their superior height he kept wearing down the besieged. He mined under the wall and also rocked it with battering-rams until he threw down a large section of it. The Perinthians fought stoutly and threw up a second wall. Philip rained down great destruction through his many and various arrow-shooting catapults. . . . Philip continually battered the walls with his rams and made breaches in them. With his arrow-firing catapults clearing the ramparts of defenders, he sent his soldiers in through the breaches in tight formation. He attacked with scaling-ladders the parts of the walls that had been cleared.*[5]

❝ With his arrow-firing catapults clearing the ramparts of defenders, he sent his soldiers in through the breaches in tight formation. ❞

—DIODOROS

For the Perinthians this grim story had a happy ending when their allies arrived to lift the siege. Hellenistic generals built larger, more complex, and more effective machines until no city was safe from them.

If these new engines made waging war more efficient, they also added to the misery of the people. War was no longer confined to the battlefield and fought between soldiers. Now the populations of whole cities feared for their lives. Survivors of such a siege as that of Perinthos experienced terror. Many were killed in the slaughter and rape that generally came with the taking of the city. The survivors were often sold into slavery. Ironically, Hellenistic science, dedicated to improving human life, succeeded in making it more dangerous and horrible.

Hellenistic Medicine

The study of medicine flourished during the Hellenistic period. Herophilus, who lived in the first half of the third century B.C.E., worked at Alexandria and studied the writings of Hippocrates (see Chapter 3). He accepted Hippocrates' theory of the four humors and approached the study of medicine in a systematic, scientific fashion: he dissected dead bodies and measured what he observed. He discovered the nervous system and concluded that two types of nerves, motor and sensory, existed. Herophilus also studied the brain, which he considered the center of intelligence, and discerned the cerebrum (suh-REE-bruhm) and cerebellum (ser-uh-BE-luhm). His other work dealt with the liver, lungs, and uterus. His

younger contemporary Erasistratus also conducted research on the brain and nervous system and improved on Herophilus's work. Erasistratus too followed in the tradition of Hippocrates and believed that the best way for the body to heal itself was through diet and air.

Both Herophilus and Erasistratus were members of the Dogmatic school of medicine at Alexandria. In this school speculation played an important part in research, as did the study of anatomy. To learn more about human anatomy, Herophilus and Erasistratus dissected corpses and even vivisected criminals whom King Ptolemy contributed for the purpose. Better knowledge of anatomy led to improvements in surgery. These advances enabled the Dogmatists to invent new surgical instruments and techniques.

In about 280 B.C.E. Philinus and Serapion, pupils of Herophilus, led a reaction against the Dogmatists. Believing that the Dogmatists had become too speculative, they founded the Empiric school of medicine at Alexandria. Claiming that the Dogmatists' emphasis on anatomy and physiology was misplaced, they concentrated instead on the observation and cure of illnesses. They also laid heavier stress on the use of drugs and medicine to treat illnesses. Heraclides of Tarentum (perhaps first century B.C.E.) carried on the Empiric tradition and dedicated himself to the observation and use of medicines. He discovered the benefits of opium and worked with other drugs that relieved pain. He also

Picturing the Past

An Unsuccessful Delivery This funeral monument depicts a mother who has perhaps lost her own life as well as her baby's. Childbirth was the leading cause of death for adult women in antiquity, though monuments showing this are quite rare. Another of the few that do show death in childbirth bears the heartbreaking words attributed to the mother by her grieving family: "All my labor could not bring the child forth; he lies in my womb, among the dead." (National Archaeological Museum, Athens/Archaeological Receipts Fund)

ANALYZING THE IMAGE Who might the various figures in this monument be? What do the expressions and gestures of these people tell us about what happened?

CONNECTIONS What were the main accomplishments of Hellenistic medicine? What did the different schools of Hellenistic medicine have to offer women in childbirth?

To complete this activity online, go to the Online Study Guide at bedfordstmartins.com/mckaywest.

steadfastly rejected the relevance of magic to drugs and medicines.

The Hellenistic world was also plagued by people who claimed to cure illnesses through incantations and magic. Their potions included such concoctions as blood from the ear of an ass mixed with water to cure fever, or the liver of a cat killed when the moon was waning and preserved in salt. Broken bones were treated by applying the ashes of a pig's jawbone to the break. The dung of a goat mixed with old wine was applied to broken ribs. One charlatan claimed that he could cure epilepsy by making the patient drink spring water, drawn at night, from the skull of a man who had been killed but not cremated. These quacks even claimed that they could cure mental illness. The treatment for a person suffering from melancholy was calf dung boiled in wine. No doubt the patient became too sick to be depressed.

Quacks who prescribed such treatments were very popular but did untold harm to the sick and injured. They and greedy physicians also damaged the reputation of dedicated doctors who honestly and intelligently tried to heal and alleviate pain. The medical abuses that arose in the Hellenistic period were so flagrant that the Romans, who later entered the Hellenistic world, developed an intense dislike and distrust of physicians. Nonetheless, the work of men like Herophilus and Serapion made valuable contributions to the knowledge of medicine, and the fruits of their work were preserved and handed on to the West.

 LOOKING BACK LOOKING AHEAD IT CAN SAFELY BE SAID that Philip and Alexander broadened Greek and Macedonian horizons, but not in ways that they had intended. Although Alexander established Macedonian and Greek colonies across western and central Asia for military reasons, they resulted in the spread of Hellenism.

The bond of Hellenism shared among the East, peninsular Greece, and the western Mediterranean was to prove supremely valuable to Rome in its efforts to impose a comparable political unity on the Western world. The economic unity of the Hellenistic world, like its cultural bonds, would likewise prove valuable to the Romans. They would also benefit from the Stoic concept of a universal state governed by natural law. The concept of one law for all people became a valuable tool when the Romans began to deal with many different peoples with different laws. The ideal of the universal state developed in Hellenistic Greece would be a rationale for extending the Roman Empire to the farthest reaches of the world. In the heart of the old Persian Empire, Hellenism was only a new influence that was absorbed by older ways of thought and life. Yet overall, in the exchange of ideas and the opportunity for different cultures to learn about one another, a new cosmopolitan society evolved. That society in turn made possible such diverse advances as a wider extent of trade and agriculture, the creation of religious and philosophical ideas that paved the way for Christianity, greater freedom for women, and remarkable advances in science and medicine.

CHAPTER REVIEW

■ **Why did Alexander launch his attack on the Persian Empire, and how extensive were his conquests? (p. 92)**

Alexander invaded Persia to avenge the Persian invasion of Greece in 480 B.C.E. He also planned to create an empire of his own in the East. In addition to his military objectives, he brought scientists and historians to record his discoveries. By 324 B.C.E. he had succeeded in overturning the Persians and had expanded the empire as far east as the Indus Valley in India.

■ **What was Alexander's political and cultural legacy? (p. 95)**

Alexander's legacy proved of essential importance to the future of the West. He brought the vital civilization of the Greeks into intimate contact with the older cultures of the East. He and his successors established cities and encouraged a third great wave of Greek migration.

■ **What effect did Greek migration have on Greek and native peoples? (p. 98)**

In the Aegean and Near East, Greeks and Easterners adapted to each other's culture, but there was no true fusion of culture. Hellenism influenced the older, well-established ways of thought and life in the East. Yet it also absorbed many aspects of this traditional culture. As both learned more about each other, they developed a new, cosmopolitan society.

■ **What effects did East-West trade have on ordinary peoples during the Hellenistic period? (p. 103)**

For ordinary men and women, the greatest practical boon of the spread of Hellenism was economic. Trade connected the world on a routine basis. Economics brought people together just as surely as it brought them goods. By the end of the Hellenistic period, the ancient world had become far broader and more economically intricate than ever before.

■ **How did Hellenistic religion and intellectual advances affect the lives of men and women? (p. 107)**

Mystery religions, such as the worship of the goddess Isis, provided many people with answers to their questions about the meaning of life and promised life for the soul after death. Jews embraced some aspects of Hellenism but remained attached to their Jewish faith. Others turned to practical philosophies such as Stoicism for ethical guidance. Mathematicians and scientists developed theoretical knowledge and applied this to practical problems in geography, mechanics, and weaponry. Physicians also approached medicine in a systematic fashion, though many people relied on magic and folk cures for treatment of illness.

Suggested Reading

Bar-Kochva, Bezalel. *Judas Maccabaeus*. 1989. Treats the Jewish struggle against the Seleucids and Hellenistic influences.

Bosworth, A. B. *Conquest and Empire: The Reign of Alexander the Great*. 1988. Still the best one-volume treatment of Alexander that sets his career in a broad context.

Burkert, Walter. *Ancient Mystery Cults*. 1987. A brief comparative study written by one of the finest scholars in the field.

Carney, Elizabeth D. *Women and Monarchy in Macedonia*. 2000. Studies the queens of Macedonia and their influence on the exercise of power.

Chaniotis, Angelos. *War in the Hellenistic World*. 2005. Covers the wars of this period, the reasons behind them, and how they were waged.

Errington, R. Malcom. *A History of the Hellenistic World, 323–30 B.C.* 2008. Easily the best coverage of the period: full, scholarly, and readable.

Errington, R. Malcom. *A History of Macedonia*. English trans., 1990. Places Macedonia clearly within a broad Hellenistic context.

Frazer, Peter M. *Cities of Alexander the Great*. 1996. Treats the impact of Greek urbanism in its Eastern setting.

Höbel, Günther. *History of the Ptolemaic Empire*. 2001. Gives a current and sound account of the external affairs and inner workings of the kingdom.

Jaeger, Mary. *Archimedes and the Roman Imagination*. 2008. Puts the discovery of the new codex into the context of Archimedes' other scientific works.

Ma, John. *Antiochus III and the Cities of Western Asia Minor*. 1999. Examines how one of the greatest of the Hellenistic kings dealt successfully with the Greek cities in his kingdom.

Rostovtzeff, Michael. *The Social and Economic History of the Hellenistic World*. 3 vols. 1941. A classic and still valuable introduction to the Hellenistic period.

Sharples, R. W. *Stoics, Epicureans, Sceptics*. 1996. Provides a good synthesis of these three major branches of Hellenistic philosophy.

Sherwin-White, Susan, and Amelie Kuhrt. *From Samarkand to Sardis*. 1992. A study of the Seleucid monarchy from an Asian rather than a Greek perspective.

Shipley, Graham. *The Greek World After Alexander, 323–30 B.C.* 2000. A very thorough discussion of political, socioeconomic, intellectual, and cultural developments.

Notes

1. Plutarch, *Moralia* 328E.
2. Ahmad Hasan Dani et al., *History of Civilizations of Central Asia* (Paris: UNESCO, 1992), p. 107.
3. Quoted in W. W. Tarn and G. T. Griffith, *Hellenistic Civilizations*, 3d ed. (Cleveland and New York: Meridian Books, 1961), p. 199.
4. Diodoros 3.12.1–3.
5. Ibid., 3.12.2–3.

Key Terms

Hellenistic (p. 95)
sovereign (p. 98)
Great Silk Road (p. 107)
Tyche (p. 108)
mystery religions (p. 108)
Epicureanism (p. 109)
Stoicism (p. 110)
natural law (p. 110)
heliocentric theory (p. 111)

For practice quizzes and other study tools, visit the Online Study Guide at **bedfordstmartins.com/mckaywest**.

For primary sources from this period, see *Sources of Western Society*, **Second Edition**.

For Web sites, images, and documents related to topics in this chapter, visit Make History at **bedfordstmartins.com/mckaywest**.

5
The Rise of Rome

ca. 750–31 B.C.E.

"Who is so thoughtless and lazy that he does not want to know in what way and with what kind of government the Romans in less than 53 years conquered nearly the entire inhabited world and brought it under their rule — an achievement previously unheard of?"[1] This question was first asked by Polybius, a Greek historian who lived in the second century B.C.E.

What was that achievement? Was it simply the creation of a huge empire? Hardly. The Persians had done the same thing, and Alexander the Great had conquered vast territories in a shorter time. Was it the creation of a superior culture? Even the Romans admitted that in matters of art, literature, philosophy, and culture they learned from the Greeks. Rome's achievement lay in the ability of the Romans not only to conquer peoples but to incorporate them into the Roman system. Unlike the Greeks, who refused to share citizenship, the Romans extended their citizenship first to the Italians and later to the peoples of the provinces. With that citizenship went Roman government and law. Rome created a world state that embraced the entire Mediterranean area and extended northward.

Nor was Rome's achievement limited to the ancient world. Rome's law, language, and administrative practices shaped later developments in Europe and beyond. London, Paris, Vienna, and many other modern European cities began as Roman colonies or military camps. When the Founding Fathers created the American republic, they looked to Rome as a model. On the darker side, Napoleon and Mussolini paid their own tribute to Rome by aping its forms. Whether Founding Fathers or modern dictators, all were acknowledging admiration for the Roman achievement. ■

Life in the Roman Republic. This fresco from Pompeii shows the wedding of the gods Venus and Mars. Although the event was not real, the dress and finery are typical of that seen at the weddings of Roman nobles.

CHAPTER PREVIEW

The Land and Its Early Settlers
■ How did geography and the Etruscans shape early Roman history?

The Roman Republic
■ What was the nature of the Roman republic?

Roman Expansion
■ How did the Romans take control of the Mediterranean world?

Traditional Life and Greek Influences
■ How did Roman society change during the age of expansion?

The Late Republic
■ What were the main problems and achievements of the late republic?

The Land and Its Early Settlers

How did geography and the Etruscans shape early Roman history? ■

While the Greeks pursued their destiny in the East, other peoples in western Europe developed their own individual societies. The most historically important of them were the Etruscans (ih-TRUS-kuhns) and Romans who entered the peninsula of Italy and came into contact with the older cultures of the Mediterranean. The Etrus-cans were the first significant newcomers, followed by the Romans. Italy gave them a genial homeland with fertile soil capable of supporting a large population, temperate weather, and defensible borders.

The Geography of Italy

West of Greece the boot-shaped peninsula of Italy, with Sicily at its toe, occupies the center of the Mediterranean basin (Map 5.1). To the south lies Africa; the distance between southwestern Sicily and the northern African coast is at one point only about a hundred miles. Italy and Sicily literally divide the Mediterranean into two

Map 5.1 **Italy and the City of Rome, ca. 218 B.C.E.** The geographical configuration of the Italian peninsula shows how Rome stood astride north-south communication routes and how the state that united Italy stood poised to move from Sicily into northern Africa.

basins and form the focal point between the two halves.

Like Greece and other Mediterranean lands, Italy enjoys a genial, almost subtropical climate. The winters are rainy, but the summer months are dry. Because of the climate the rivers of Italy usually carry little water during the summer, and some go entirely dry. The low water level of the Arno, one of the principal rivers in Italy, once led Mark Twain to describe it as "a great historical creek with four feet in the channel that would be a very plausible river if they would pump some water into it."[2] The Arno at least is navigable. Most of Italy's others rivers are unsuitable for regular large-scale shipping. Italian rivers, unlike Twain's beloved Mississippi, never became major thoroughfares for commerce and communications.

Geography discouraged maritime trade as well. Italy lacks the numerous good harbors that are such a feature of the Greek landscape. Only in the south are there good harbors, and Greek colonists had early claimed those ports for themselves. Yet geography gave rise to—and the rivers nourished—a bountiful agriculture that sustained a large population.

Geography encouraged Italy to look to the Mediterranean. In the north Italy is protected by the Apennine Mountains, which break off from the Alps and form a natural barrier. The Apennines retarded but did not prevent peoples from penetrating Italy from the north. Throughout history various invaders have entered Italy by this route. From the north the Apennines run southward for the entire length of the Italian boot, cutting off access to the Adriatic Sea. This barrier induced Italy to look west to Spain and Carthage rather than east to Greece. Even though most of the land is mountainous, the hill country is not as inhospitable as the Greek highlands. The fertility of the soil provided the basis for a large population. Nor did the mountains of Italy so carve up the land as to prevent the development of political unity. Geography proved kinder to Italy than to Greece.

In their southward course the Apennines leave two broad and fertile plains, those of Latium and Campania. These plains attracted settlers and invaders from the time that peoples began to move into Italy. Among these peoples were the Romans, who established their city on the Tiber River in Latium.

This site enjoyed several advantages. The Tiber provided Rome with a constant source of water. Located at an easy crossing point on the Tiber, Rome thus stood astride the main avenue of communications between northern and southern Italy. Positioned amid seven hills,

Chronology

ca. 750 B.C.E.	Arrival of Etruscans in Italy
753 B.C.E.	Founding of Rome
509 B.C.E.	Last of the Etruscan kings expelled from Rome
494–287 B.C.E.	The Struggle of the Orders
390 B.C.E.	Gauls sack Rome
275 B.C.E.	Romans drive Greeks from southern Italy
264–133 B.C.E.	Punic Wars
133–31 B.C.E.	The late republic
101 B.C.E.	Germans conquered in northern Italy
91–88 B.C.E.	The Social War
88–31 B.C.E.	Civil war
44 B.C.E.	Caesar assassinated
31 B.C.E.	Augustus defeats Antony at the Battle of Actium

Rome was defensible and safe from the floods of the Tiber. Rome was in an excellent position to develop the resources of Latium and maintain contact with the rest of Italy.

The Etruscans and the Roman Settlement of Italy

The Etruscans arrived in Italy about 750 B.C.E., establishing permanent settlements that evolved into the first Italian cities. In political organization they resembled the Greek city-states, each governing itself while maintaining contact with its neighbors. The wealth of these cities, along with their political and military institutions, enabled them to form a loosely organized league of cities whose domination extended as far north as the Po Valley and as far south as Latium and Campania (see Map 5.1). Their influence spread over the surrounding countryside, which they regularly cultivated. Having established a strong agricultural base, they mined the rich mineral resources of the land. Secure in their new home, they looked out to the wider world, especially to the East. The Mediterranean has always been a highway, and one of its major routes led to Greece. From an early period the Etruscans began to trade natural products, especially iron, for Greek luxury goods. They developed a rich cultural life that became the foundation of civilization throughout Italy. In the process they came in contact with a small collection of villages subsequently called Rome.

The Romans, to whom the Etruscans introduced the broader world, had settled in Italy by the eighth century B.C.E. According to one legend, Romulus and Remus founded the city in 753 B.C.E. Romulus built his home on the Palatine Hill, while Remus chose the Aventine (see inset of Map 5.1). They built Rome's first walls,

The Etruscans, ca. 500 B.C.E.

reflecting the Etruscan concept of the pomerium, a sacred boundary intended to keep out anything evil or unclean. Under Etruscan influence the Romans prospered, spreading over all of Rome's seven hills.

The Etruscans soon drew the fledgling Rome into their orbit. From 753 to 509 B.C.E. a line of Etruscan kings ruled the city and introduced many customs. The Romans adopted the Etruscan alphabet, which the Etruscans themselves had adopted from the Greeks. The Romans later handed on this alphabet to medieval Europe and thence to the modern Western world. The Romans also adopted symbols of political authority from the Etruscans. The symbol of the Etruscan king's right to execute or scourge his subjects was a bundle of rods and an ax, called the fasces, which the king's retainer carried before him on official occasions. When the Romans expelled the Etruscan kings, they continued using the fasces in this manner. Even the toga, the white woolen robe worn by citizens, came from the Etruscans. In engineering and architecture the Romans adopted the vault and the arch from the Etruscans. Above all, it was thanks to the Etruscans that the Romans truly became urban dwellers.

Under the Etruscans Rome enjoyed contacts with the larger Mediterranean world, while the city continued to grow. In the years 575 to 550 B.C.E. temples and public buildings began to grace the city. The Capitoline Hill became its religious center when the temple of Jupiter Optimus Maximus (Jupiter the Best and Greatest) was built there. Rome's **Forum** ceased to be a cemetery and began its history as a public meeting place, a development parallel to

forum A public meeting place.

that of the Greek agora. Trade in metalwork became common, and wealthier Romans began to import large numbers of fine Greek vases. The Etruscans had found Rome a collection of villages and made it a city.

The Roman Conquest of Italy

Early Roman history is an uneven mixture of fact and legend. Roman traditions often contain an important kernel of truth, but that does not make them history. In many cases legends are significant because they illustrate the ethics, morals, and ideals that Roman society considered valuable. Even the great Roman historian Livy (59 B.C.E.–C.E. 17) admitted that the old tales depicted people not necessarily as they were but as Romans should be.

The Romans expelled the Etruscan king Tarquin the Proud in 509 B.C.E., but, according to legend, not for political reasons. Tarquin had raped the noblewoman Lucretia (loo-KREE-shuh) when she refused his advances. She told her husband and father the whole story the next day. After they promised to avenge her, she committed suicide in shame. In avenging her death, legend has it, the family drove the Etruscans from Rome. In truth the Romans rebelled against Etruscan rule and founded the republic because they desired independence.

In the following years the Romans fought numerous wars with their neighbors on the Italian peninsula. They became soldiers, and the grim fighting bred tenacity, a prominent Roman trait. War also involved diplomacy, at which the Romans became masters. At an early date they learned the value of alliances and how to lead their allies. Alliances with the Latin towns around them pro-

Sarcophagus of Lartie Seianti Although the sarcophagus is this noble Etruscan woman's place of burial, she is portrayed as in life, comfortable and at rest. The influence of Greek art on Etruscan is apparent in almost every feature of the sarcophagus. (Archaeological Museum, Florence/Nimatallah/Art Resource, NY)

Guard Dog The doorways of Roman houses opened directly onto the street. This entrance included a floor mosaic of a dog who was always on guard. The notice warns "CAVE CANEM" (beware of the dog). (Robert Frerck/Odyssey/Chicago)

vided a large reservoir of manpower. Their alliances also involved the Romans in other wars that took them farther afield in the peninsula.

One of the earliest wars involved the neighboring Aequi, who launched a serious invasion. The Romans called on Cincinnatus to assume the office of dictator. In this period the Roman dictator, unlike modern dictators, was a legitimate magistrate given ultimate powers for a specified period of time. The Roman officials found Cincinnatus working his three-acre farm. Wiping his sweat, he listened to the appeal of his countrymen and accepted the office. Fifteen days later, after he had defeated the Aequi, he returned to his farm. Cincinnatus personified the ideal of the Roman citizen—a man of simplicity who put his duty to Rome before any consideration of personal interest or wealth.

Around 390 B.C.E. the Romans suffered a major setback when a new people, the Celts—or **Gauls** (gawls), as the Romans called them—swept aside a Roman army and sacked Rome. More intent on loot than on conquest, the Gauls agreed to abandon Rome in return for a thousand pounds of gold. When the Gauls provided their own scale, the Romans howled in indignation. The Gallic chieftain then threw his sword on the scale, exclaiming "Vae victis" (woe to the conquered). These words, though legendary, became a challenge to the Romans. Thereafter the Romans made it their policy never

to accept peace, much less to surrender, so long as the enemy was still in the field.

From 390 to 290 B.C.E. the Romans rebuilt their city and recouped their losses. They also reorganized their army to create the mobile legion, a flexible unit capable of fighting on either broken or open terrain. The Romans finally brought Latium and their Latin allies fully under their control and conquered Etruria (see Map 5.1). In 343 B.C.E. they grappled with the Samnites in a series of bitter wars for the possession of Campania (kam-PAY-nyuh) and southern Italy. The Samnites were a formidable enemy and inflicted serious losses on the Romans. But the superior organization, institutions, and manpower of the Romans won out in the end. Although Rome had yet to subdue the whole peninsula, for the first time in history the city stood unchallenged in Italy.

The Romans spread their culture by sharing their religious cults, mythology, and drama. They, like the Greeks, liberally shared their religious beliefs with others, which in turn furthered the Romanization of Italy. Yet the spread of Roman culture was not part of a planned ideological onslaught by the Romans. Nor was it different from the ways in which the Romans extended their political, military, and legal systems. Even so, the

Gauls The Roman name for the Celts, a people who swept aside a Roman army and sacked Rome around 390 B.C.E.

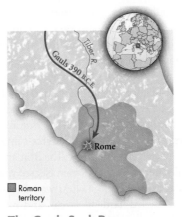

The Gauls Sack Rome, ca. 390 B.C.E.

Roman territory

process eventually created a common ground for all the peoples living in Italy and made Italy Roman. In later years the Romans continued this process until all these influences spread throughout the Mediterranean basin.

With many of their oldest allies, such as the Latin towns, the Romans shared full Roman citizenship. In other instances they granted citizenship without the **franchise**, that is, without the right to vote or hold Roman offices. Allies were subject to Roman taxes and calls for military service but ran their own local affairs. The Latin allies were able to acquire full Roman citizenship by moving to Rome.

A perhaps humble but very efficient means of keeping the Romans and their colonies together were the Roman roads, many of which continued in use as late as the medieval period. These roads provided an easy route of communication between the capital and outlying areas, allowed for the quick movement of armies, and offered an efficient means of trade. They were the tangible sinews of unity.

By their willingness to extend their citizenship, the Romans took Italy into partnership. Here the political genius of Rome triumphed where Greece had failed. Rome proved itself superior to the Greek polis because it both conquered and shared the fruits of conquest with the conquered. The unwillingness of the Greek polis to share its citizenship condemned it to a limited horizon. Not so with Rome. The extension of Roman citizenship strengthened the state, gave it additional manpower and wealth, and laid the foundation of the Roman Empire.

franchise The right to vote or hold Roman office.

patricians The Roman aristocracy; wealthy landowners who held political power.

plebeians The common people of Rome.

senate Originating under the Etruscans as a council of noble elders who advised the king, the Roman senate advised the magistrates; over time its advice came to have the force of law.

The Roman Republic

What was the nature of the Roman republic?

Roman history is usually divided into two periods: the republic, the age in which Rome grew from a small city-state to ruler of an empire, and the empire, the period when the republican constitution gave way to constitutional monarchy.

The Roman republic consisted of a constitution and the people who made it. The Romans' first problem was to create the political institutions needed to govern effectively an ever-expanding and influential state. The second was the sharing of the obligations and privileges that came with that effort. The Romans struggled hard to meet these challenges. In the process they fashioned both a state and a society. The Romans were so successful

that the Roman republic became one of the preeminent institutions of the ancient world—one still admired today.

The Roman State

The Romans summed up their political existence in a single phrase, *senatus populusque Romanum*, "the Roman senate and people," which was often abbreviated as "SPQR." These words were a statement and a proclamation that epitomized the Roman people, their state, and their way of life. SPQR became a shorthand way of saying "Rome," just as "U.S.A." says "the United States of America."

The real genius of the Romans lay in the fields of politics and law. Unlike the Greeks, they did not often speculate on the ideal state or on political forms. Instead, they realistically met actual challenges and created institutions, magistracies, and legal concepts to deal with practical problems. Change was consequently commonplace in Roman political life, and the constitution evolved over time. Moreover, the Roman constitution, unlike the American, was not a single written document. Rather, it was a set of traditional beliefs, customs, and laws.

In the early republic social divisions determined the shape of politics. Political power was in the hands of the aristocracy—the **patricians** (puh-TRIH-shuhns), who were wealthy landowners. Patrician families formed clans, as did aristocrats in early Greece. Patrician men dominated the affairs of state, provided military leadership in time of war, and monopolized knowledge of law and legal procedure. The common people of Rome, the **plebeians** (plih-BEE-uhns), had few of the patricians' political and social advantages. Many plebeian merchants increased their wealth in the course of Roman expansion, and some even formed powerful clans, but most plebeians were poor. They were the artisans, small farmers, and landless urban dwellers. All plebeians, rich and poor alike, were free citizens with a voice in politics. Nonetheless, they were overshadowed by the patricians.

Perhaps the greatest institution of the republic was the **senate**, which had originated under the Etruscans as a council of noble elders who advised the king. During the republic the senate advised the magistrates. Because the senate sat year after year, while magistrates changed annually, it provided stability and continuity. It also served as a reservoir of experience and knowledge. Technically, the senate could not pass legislation; it could only offer advice. But increasingly, because of the senate's prestige, its advice came to have the force of law.

The Romans created several assemblies through which men elected magistrates and passed legislation. The earliest was the comitia curiata, which had religious, political, and military functions. The comitia centuriata (kuh-MI-shee-uh cen-tur-EE-ah-tuh) voted in centuries, or political blocs. The patricians possessed the majority

The Roman Forum The Roman Forum, adorned with stately buildings, formed the center of Roman political and social life. (age fotostock/SuperStock)

of centuries because they shouldered most of the leadership and frontline infantry. Thus they could easily outvote the plebeians. In 471 B.C.E. plebeian men won the right to meet in an assembly of their own, the concilium plebis, and to pass ordinances. Later the bills passed in the concilium plebis were recognized as binding on the entire population.

The chief magistrates of the republic were the two **consuls**, who were elected for one-year terms. At first the consulship was open only to patrician men. The consuls commanded the army in battle, administered state business, convened the comitia centuriata, and supervised financial affairs. In effect, they and the senate ran the state. The consuls appointed quaestors (KWEH-stuhrs) to assist them in their duties, and in 421 B.C.E. the quaestorship became an elective office open to plebeian men. The quaestors took charge of the public treasury and prosecuted criminals in the popular courts.

In 366 B.C.E. the Romans created a new office, that of praetor (PREE-tuhr). When the consuls were away from Rome, the praetors could act in their place. The praetors dealt primarily with the administration of justice. When he took office, a praetor issued a proclamation declaring the principles by which he would interpret the law. These proclamations became very important because they usually covered areas where the law was vague and thus helped clarify the law.

Other officials included the powerful censors who had many responsibilities, the most important being supervision of public morals, the power to determine who lawfully could sit in the senate, the registration of citizens, and the leasing of public contracts. Later officials were the aediles (EE-dihls), who supervised the streets and markets and presided over public festivals.

One of the most important Roman achievements was the development of law. Roman law began as a set of rules that regulated the lives and relations of citizens. This civil law, or *ius civile*, consisted of statutes, customs, and forms of procedure. Roman assemblies added to the body of law, and praetors interpreted it. The spirit of the law aimed at protecting the property, lives, and reputations of citizens, redressing wrongs, and giving satisfaction to victims of injustice.

As the Romans came into more frequent contact with foreigners, they had to devise laws to deal with disputes between Romans and foreigners. In these instances, where there was no precedent to guide the Romans, the legal decisions of the praetors proved of immense importance. The praetors resorted to the law of equity—what they thought was right and just to all parties. Free, in effect, to determine law, the praetors enjoyed a great deal of flexibility. This situation illustrates the practicality and the genius of the Romans. By addressing specific, actual circumstances the praetors developed a body of law, the *ius gentium*, "the law of peoples," that applied to Romans and foreigners and that laid the foundation for a universal conception of law. By the time of the late republic, Roman jurists were reaching decisions on the basis of the Stoic concept of *ius naturale*, "natural law," a universal law that could be applied to all societies.

> **consuls** The two chief Roman magistrates; elected for one-year terms, consuls along with the senate ran the affairs of the state.

The Struggle of the Orders

A vital aspect of early Roman history was a conflict between patricians and plebeians usually known as the **Struggle of the Orders**. The plebeians wanted real political representation and safeguards against patrician domination. They also agitated for social reforms that would give them the right to intermarry with patricians and the ability to climb up the social scale. The plebeian effort to obtain recognition of these rights is the crux of the Struggle of the Orders.

Rome's early wars gave the plebeians the leverage they needed. Rome's survival depended on the army, and the army needed plebeians to fill the ranks of the infantry. The first showdown between plebeians and patricians came in 494 B.C.E. To force the patricians to grant concessions, the plebeians seceded from the state, literally walking out of Rome and refusing to serve in the army. Their general strike worked, and the patricians made important concessions. One of these was social. In 445 B.C.E. the patricians passed a law, the *lex Canuleia*, that for the first time allowed patricians and plebeians to marry one another. Furthermore, the patricians recognized the right of plebeians to elect their own officials, the **tribunes**. The tribunes had the right to protect the plebeians from the arbitrary conduct of patrician magistrates by bringing plebeian grievances to the senate for resolution. The plebeians were not bent on undermining the state. Rather, they used their gains to win full equality under the law.

The law itself was the plebeians' primary target. Only the patricians knew what the law was, and only they could argue cases in court. All too often they used the law for their own benefit. The plebeians wanted the law codified and published. The result of their agitation was the Law of the Twelve Tables, so called because the laws, which covered civil and criminal matters, were inscribed on twelve large bronze plaques. Later still, the plebeians forced the patricians to publish legal procedures as well. The plebeians had broken the patricians' legal monopoly and henceforth enjoyed full protection under the law.

The decisive plebeian victory came with the passage of the Licinian-Sextian laws in 367 B.C.E. Licinius and Sextus were plebeian tribunes who joined the poor to mount a sweeping assault on patrician privilege. Wealthy plebeians wanted the opportunity to provide political leadership for the state. They demanded that the patricians allow them access to all the magistracies. If they could hold the consulship, they could also sit in the senate and advise the senate on policy. The two tribunes won approval from the senate for a law that stipulated that one of the two annual consuls must be a plebeian. Though decisive, the Licinian-Sextian laws did not automatically end the Struggle of the Orders. That happened only in 287 B.C.E. with the passage of a law, the *lex Hortensia*, that gave the resolutions of the concilium plebis the force of law for patricians and plebeians alike.

The results of the compromise between the patricians and the plebeians were far-reaching. Plebeians could now hold the consulship, which brought with it the consular title, places of honor in the senate, and such cosmetic privileges as wearing the purple toga, the symbol of aristocracy. Far more important, the compromise established a new nobility shared by the plebeians and the patricians. This would lead not to major political reform but to an extension of aristocratic rule. Nevertheless, the patricians were wise enough to give the plebeians wider political rights than they had previously enjoyed. The compromise was typically Roman.

The Struggle of the Orders resulted in a Rome stronger and better united than before. It could have led to anarchy, but the values fostered by the social structure predisposed the Romans to compromise, especially in the face of common danger. The Struggle of the Orders ended in 287 B.C.E. with a new concept of Roman citizenship. All male citizens shared equally under the law. Theoretically, all men could aspire to the highest political offices.

Struggle of the Orders A conflict in which the plebeians wanted real political representation and safeguards against patrician domination and the right to intermarry and climb up the social hierarchy.

tribunes Plebeian-elected officials; tribunes brought plebeian grievances to the senate for resolution and protected plebeians from the arbitrary conduct of patrician magistrates.

Roman Expansion

How did the Romans take control of the Mediterranean world? ■

Once the Romans had settled their internal affairs, they turned their attention outward. As seen earlier, they had already come to terms with the Italic peoples in Latium. Only later did Rome achieve primacy over its Latin allies, partly because of successful diplomacy and partly because of overwhelming military power. In 238 B.C.E. Rome expanded even farther in Italy and extended its power across the sea to Sicily, Corsica (KAWR-sih-kuh), and Sardinia.

Italy Becomes Roman

In only twenty years, from 282 to 262 B.C.E., the Romans established a string of colonies throughout Italy, some populated by Romans and others by Latins. The genius of the Romans lay in bringing these various peoples into one political system. First the Romans divided the Italians into two broad classes. Those living closest to Rome were incorporated into the Roman state. They enjoyed the full franchise and citizenship that the

Picturing the Past

Battle Between the Romans and the Gauls Rome's wars with the barbarians of western Europe come to life in this relief from a Roman sarcophagus of 225 B.C.E. Even the bravery and strength of the Gauls were no match for the steadiness and discipline of the Roman legions. (Vanni/Art Resource, NY)

ANALYZING THE IMAGE How would you describe this depiction of war? What does it suggest about the reality of Rome's wars with the barbarians?

CONNECTIONS What was the nature of Rome's overseas conquests? How did the Romans' treatment of the peoples in these unfamiliar territories differ from their conquest of Italy?

To complete this activity online, go to the Online Study Guide at bedfordstmartins.com/mckaywest.

Romans themselves possessed. Italians who lived farther afield were bound by treaty with the Romans and were considered allies. Although they received lesser rights of active citizenship, the allies retained their right of local self-government. The link between the allies and Rome was as much social as political, as both were ruled by aristocrats.

Contacts with their neighbors led the Romans to a better acquaintance with the heritage, customs, and laws of their fellow Italians. Rome and the rest of Italy began to share similar views of their common welfare. By including others in the Roman political and social system, Rome was making Italy Roman.

The Age of Conquest

In 282 B.C.E. the Romans embarked on a series of wars that left them rulers of the Mediterranean world. These wars were often unlike those against the Italians or Etrus-

cans. As they moved south into Italy and later eastward against the Hellenistic kingdoms, the Romans encountered areas largely unknown to them. The wars became fierce and were fought on a larger scale than those in Italy. Yet there was nothing ideological about them. The Romans did not map out grandiose strategies for world conquest. In many instances they did not even initiate action; they simply responded to situations as they arose. Though they sometimes declared war reluctantly, they nonetheless felt the need to dominate, to eliminate any state that could threaten them.

The Samnite wars had drawn the Romans into the political world of southern Italy. In 282 B.C.E., alarmed by the powerful newcomer, the Greek city of Tarentum (tuh-REHN-tuhm) in southern Italy called for help from Pyrrhus (PIHR-uhs), king of Epirus (ih-PIGH-ruhs) in western Greece. A relative of Alexander the Great and an excellent general, Pyrrhus won two furious battles but suffered heavy casualties—thus the phrase "Pyrrhic victory" to describe a victory involving severe losses. Roman bravery and tenacity led Pyrrhus to comment: "If we win one more battle with the Romans, we'll be completely washed up."[3] The Romans threw new legions against Pyrrhus's army, and in the end manpower proved decisive. In 275 B.C.E. the Romans drove Pyrrhus from southern Italy and extended their sway over the area. They then needed to secure the island of Sicily in order to block the expansion northward of Carthage.

> **❝ If we win one more battle with the Romans, we'll be completely washed up. ❞**
>
> —PYRRHUS

The Punic Wars

By 264 B.C.E. Carthage (Map 5.2) was the unrivaled power of the western Mediterranean. Since the second half of the eighth century B.C.E., it had built its wealth on trade in tin and precious metals. It commanded one of the best harbors on the northern African coast and was supported by a fertile hinterland. The Carthaginians were for the most part merchants, not soldiers, and they dominated the commerce of the western Mediterranean. By the fourth century B.C.E. they were fully integrated into the Hellenistic economy, which now spread from Gibraltar to the Parthian empire. Expansion led to war with the Etruscans and Greeks. At the end of a long string of wars, the Carthaginians had created and defended a mercantile empire that stretched from western Sicily to beyond Gibraltar.

The battle for Sicily set the stage for the **First Punic War** between Rome and Carthage, two powers expanding into the same area. The First Punic (PYOO-nihk) War lasted for twenty-three years (264–241 B.C.E.). The Romans quickly learned that they could not conquer Sicily unless they controlled the sea. Although they lacked a fleet and had no seafaring experience, they built a navy. Of the seven major naval battles they fought with the Carthaginians, they won six and finally wore them down. In 241 B.C.E. the Romans took possession of Sicily, which became their first real province. Once again Rome's resources, manpower, and determination proved decisive.

The peace treaty between the two powers brought no peace, in part because in 238 B.C.E. the Romans took advantage of Carthaginian weakness to seize Sardinia and Corsica. The only way Carthage could recoup its fortune was by success in Spain, where the Carthaginians already enjoyed a firm foot-

First Punic War A war between Rome and Carthage in which Rome emerged the victor after twenty-three years of fighting.

hold. In 237 B.C.E. Hamilcar Barca, a Carthaginian commander who had come close to victory in Sicily, led an army to Spain in order to turn it into Carthaginian territory. With him he took his nineteen-year-old son, Hannibal, but not before he led Hannibal to an altar and made him swear to be an enemy to Rome forever. In the following years Hamilcar and his son-in-law Hasdrubal (HAHZ-droo-buhl) subjugated much of southern Spain and in the process rebuilt Carthaginian power. Rome first made a treaty with Hasdrubal setting the boundary between Carthaginian and Roman interests at the Ebro River, and then began to extend its own influence in Spain.

In 221 B.C.E. the young Hannibal became Carthaginian commander in Spain. When Hannibal laid siege to Saguntum (suh-GUHN-tum), which lay within the

Triumphal Column of Caius Duilius This monument celebrates Rome's first naval victory in the First Punic War. In the battle Caius Duilius destroyed fifty Carthaginian ships. He then celebrated his success by erecting this column. The prows of the enemy ships are shown projecting from the column. (Alinari/Art Resource, NY)

North Sea

Baltic Sea

BRITAIN

ATLANTIC
OCEAN

Elbe R.

GERMANY

Vistula R.

BELGICA

Rhine R.

Dnieper R.

Don R.

GAUL

RAETIA

Lugdunum

ALPS

CISALPINE
GAUL

PANNONIA

DACIA

BOSPORAN KINGDOM

Trebia
218 B.C.E.

Po R.

NARBONENSIS

FARTHER
SPAIN

Narbo

Massilia

Ebro R.

Numantia

Arretium

ILLYRICUM

Black Sea

MOESIA

Danube R.

THRACE

Corsica

Lake Trasimene
217 B.C.E.

ITALY

Cannae
216 B.C.E.

Adriatic Sea

MACEDONIA

Byzantium

BITHYNIA AND PONTUS

NEARER
SPAIN

Saguntum

Rome

Capua

Brundisium

Pydna
168 B.C.E.

GALATIA

CAPPADOCIA

Tigris R.

Corduba

Balearic Is.

Sardinia

Tarentum

EPIRUS

Cynoscephalae
197 B.C.E.

Pergamum

ANATOLIA

ASIA

PARTHIA

Gades

New Carthage

Actium

Ephesus

Tarsus

Carrhae
53 B.C.E.

Gibraltar

Drepana
249 B.C.E.

Sicily

Messana

Corinth

Athens

PAMPHYLIA

LYCIA

CILICIA

Antioch

Euphrates R.

MAURETANIA

Carthage

Syracuse

ACHAEA

Rhodes

SYRIA

Zama
202 B.C.E.

Mediterranean Sea

Crete

Cyprus

Damascus

NUMIDIA

AFRICA PROCONSULARIS

JUDAEA

Jerusalem

NORTH AFRICA

Cyrene

Alexandria

Petra

CYRENAICA

SINAI

SAHARA

EGYPT

Nile R.

Red Sea

Roman territory in 264 B.C.E.
Roman territory added by 133 B.C.E.
Roman territory added by 44 B.C.E.
Major battle of the Punic Wars
Other major battle

0   250   500 miles
0   250   500 kilometers

Mapping the Past

Map 5.2 **Roman Expansion During the Republic, ca. 282–44 B.C.E.** Previous maps have shown that the Greeks and Macedonians concentrated their energies on opening the East. This map indicates that Rome for the first time looked to the West.

ANALYZING THE MAP Which years saw the greatest expansion of Roman power? How might the different geographic features have helped or hindered the expansion into certain areas?

CONNECTIONS What does this say about the expansion of Roman power in the Mediterranean? How did the Romans maintain their power across such a wide and diverse area?

To complete this activity online, go to the Online Study Guide at bedfordstmartins.com/mckaywest.

sphere of Carthaginian interest, the Romans declared war, claiming that Carthage had attacked a friendly city. So began the **Second Punic War**, one of the most desperate wars ever fought by Rome. In 218 B.C.E. Hannibal struck first by marching more than a thousand miles over the Alps into Italy. Once there, he defeated one Roman army at the Battle of Trebia and later another at the Battle of Lake Trasimene. The following year Hannibal won his greatest victory at the Battle of Cannae (KAH-nee), in which he inflicted some forty thousand casualties on the Romans. He then spread devastation throughout Italy, and a number of cities in central and southern Italy rebelled against Rome. Syracuse,

Rome's ally during the First Punic War, also went over to the Carthaginians. Yet Hannibal failed to crush Rome's iron circle of Latium, Etruria, and Samnium. The wisdom of Rome's political policy of extending rights and citizenship to its allies showed itself in these dark hours. And Rome fought back.

In 210 B.C.E. Rome found its answer to Hannibal in the young commander Scipio Africanus. Scipio copied Hannibal's methods of mobile warfare, streamlining the legions by making their components capable of independent action and introducing

Second Punic War A war fought between Carthage, led by Hannibal, and Rome; Roman victory meant that the western Mediterranean would henceforth be Roman.

129

new weapons. In the following years Scipio operated in Spain, which in 207 B.C.E. he wrested from the Carthaginians. That same year the Romans sealed Hannibal's fate in Italy. At the Battle of Metaurus the Romans destroyed a major Carthaginian army coming to reinforce Hannibal. Scipio then struck directly at Carthage itself, prompting the Carthaginians to recall Hannibal from Italy to defend the homeland.

In 202 B.C.E., near the town of Zama (see Map 5.2), Scipio defeated Hannibal in one of the world's truly decisive battles. Scipio's victory meant that the world of the western Mediterranean would henceforth be Roman. Roman language, law, and culture, fertilized by Greek influences, would in time permeate this entire region. The victory at Zama meant that Rome's heritage would be passed on to the Western world.

The Second Punic War contained the seeds of still other wars. Unabated fear of Carthage led to the Third Punic War, a needless, unjust, and savage conflict that ended in 146 B.C.E. when Scipio Aemilianus (SIH-pee-oh AY-mil-ee-ah-nus), grandson of Scipio Africanus, destroyed the hated rival. As the Roman conqueror watched the death pangs of that great city, he turned to his friend Polybius with the words "I fear and foresee that someday someone will give the same order about my fatherland."[4] It would, however, be centuries before an invader would stand before the gates of Rome.

During the war with Hannibal, the Romans had invaded Spain, a peninsula rich in material resources and the home of fierce warriors. When the Roman legions tried to reduce the Spanish tribes, they met with bloody and determined resistance. Not until 133 B.C.E., after years of brutal and ruthless warfare, did Scipio Aemilianus finally conquer Spain.

Rome Turns East

During the dark days of the Second Punic War, King Philip V of Macedonia made an alliance with Hannibal against Rome. Despite the mortal struggle in the West, the Romans found the strength to turn eastward to settle accounts. Their first significant victory over the Macedonians came in 197 B.C.E. In defeat the Macedonians agreed to give full liberty to the Greeks. Two years later Rome defeated the Spartans. In 188 B.C.E. the Seleucid kingdom fell to the Romans, but decisive victory came in 146 B.C.E., when the Romans conquered the Achaean League, sacked Corinth, and finally defeated Macedonia, which they made a Roman province. In 133 B.C.E. the king of Pergamum bequeathed his kingdom to the Romans. The Ptolemies of Egypt wisely and safely kept on good terms with the Romans.

The Romans had used the discord and disunity of the Hellenistic world to divide and conquer it. Once they had done so, they faced the formidable challenge of governing it without further warfare, which they met by establishing the first Roman provinces in the East. They ultimately succeeded in fusing the honored culture and civilization of the Hellenistic world, with its blend of Greek and Eastern cultures, with the new and vibrant Roman civilization. Declaring the Mediterranean *mare nostrum*, "our sea," the Romans began to create political and administrative machinery to hold the Mediterranean together under a mutually shared cultural and political system. The Romans were as usual practical as well as somewhat altruistic.

Traditional Life and Greek Influences

How did Roman society change during the age of expansion? ■

Rome had conquered the Mediterranean world, but some Romans considered that victory a misfortune. The historian Sallust (86–34 B.C.E.), writing from hindsight, complained that the acquisition of an empire was the beginning of Rome's troubles:

> But when through labor and justice our Republic grew powerful, great kings defeated in war, fierce nations and mighty peoples subdued by force, when Carthage the rival of the Roman people was wiped out root and branch, all the seas and lands lay open, then fortune began to be harsh and to throw everything into confusion. The Romans had easily borne labor, danger, uncertainty, and hardship. To them leisure, riches—otherwise desirable—proved to be burdens and torments. So at first money, then desire for power grew great. These things were a sort of cause of all evils.[5]

Sallust was not alone in his feelings. In the second century B.C.E. the Romans learned that they could not return to what they fondly considered a simple life. They were the most powerful nation in Europe. They had to change their institutions, social patterns, and way of thinking to meet the new era. It was a daunting challenge, but in the end Rome triumphed here just as it had on the battlefield, for out of the turmoil would come the *pax Romana*—"Roman peace."

How did the Romans of the day meet these challenges? How did they lead their lives and cope with these momentous changes? Obviously there are as many answers to these questions as there were Romans. Yet two men represent the major trends of the second century B.C.E. Cato the Elder shared the mentality of those who longed for the good old days and idealized the traditional agrarian way of life. Scipio Aemilianus led those who embraced the new urban life, with its eager acceptance of Greek culture. Their views exemplify the opposing sets of attitudes that marked Roman society and politics in the age of expansion.

Marcus Cato: The Traditional Ideal

Marcus Cato (234–149 B.C.E.) was born a plebeian, but his talent and energy carried him to Rome's highest offices. He created an image of himself as the bearer of "traditional" Roman virtues. His description of his life is partly invented, but its details reflect the way many Romans actually lived.

Like most Romans, Cato and his family began the day at sunrise. Cato almost certainly started the morning with a light breakfast, usually nothing more than some bread and cheese. After breakfast Cato used the rest of his mornings to plead law cases. Because of his political aspirations, he often walked to the marketplace of the nearby town and defended anyone who wished his help. He received no fees for these services, but in return Cato's clients gave him their political support or their votes in repayment whenever he asked for them. This practice was known as clientage, a Roman custom whereby free men entrusted their lives to a more powerful man in exchange for support in public life and private matters. The bond thus proved reciprocal. Clientage helped men of lower social status to advance themselves and to advance the careers of their patrons.

Cato was the *paterfamilias*, the oldest male head of the family, a part of the patriarchal organization that included several related households (see Chapter 1). The paterfamilias held nearly absolute power over the lives of his wife and children as long as he lived. He could legally kill his wife for adultery or divorce her at will. Until the paterfamilias died, his sons could not legally own property. At his death the wife and children inherited his property. Along with his biological kin, the paterfamilias also had authority over slaves, servants, adopted children, and others who lived in his household. In poor families this group might be very small, but among the wealthy it could include hundreds of slaves and servants.

Cato was married, as were almost all Roman citizens. Grooms were generally somewhat older than their brides, who often married in their early teens. Women could inherit property under Roman law, though they generally received a smaller portion of any family inheritance than their brothers did. A woman's inheritance usually came as a dowry on marriage. In the earliest Roman marriage laws, men could divorce their wives without any grounds while women could not divorce their husbands, but by Cato's time these laws had changed, and both men and women could initiate divorce. By then women also appear to have gained greater control over their dowries, perhaps because Rome's military conquests meant that many husbands were away for long periods of time and women needed some say over family finances.

Both Romans and Greeks felt that children should be raised in the lap by their mother, a woman who kept her house in good order and personally saw to the welfare of her children. In wealthy homes mothers employed slaves as wet nurses. According to Cato, his wife refused to delegate her maternal duties. Like most ordinary Roman women, she nursed her son herself and bathed and swaddled him daily.

Until the age of seven, children were under their mother's care. During this time the mother educated her daughters in the management of the household. After the age of seven, sons — and in many wealthy households daughters too — began to receive formal education. Formal education for wealthy children was generally by tutors, who were often Greek slaves, for parents wanted their children to learn Greek literature and philosophy. By the late republic, there were also a few schools. Most children learned skills from their own parents or through apprenticeships with artisans. Slave boys and girls were occasionally formally apprenticed in trades such as leatherwork, weaving, or metalworking.

In the country Romans like Cato took their main meal at midday. This meal included either coarse bread or porridge; it also included turnips, cabbage, olives, and beans. The family drank ordinary wine mixed with water. (See "Living in the Past: Roman Table Manners," page 132.) Afterward any Roman who could took a nap. This was especially true in the summer, when the

Roman School Seated between two students with scrolls in their hands, the teacher discusses a point with the student on his left. On the far right, a tardy student arrives, lunchbox in hand. Roman education, even in the provinces, lasted well into late antiquity, and was a cultural legacy to the medieval world. (Rheinisches Landesmuseum, Trier)

provided the citizen population with free grain for bread and, later, oil and wine. By feeding the citizenry the emperor prevented bread riots caused by shortages and high prices. For those who did not enjoy the rights of citizenship, the emperor provided grain at low prices. This measure was designed to prevent speculators from forcing up grain prices in times of crisis. By maintaining the grain supply, the emperor kept the favor of the people and ensured that Rome's poor and idle did not starve.

A typical day for the Roman family began with a modest breakfast, as in the days of the republic. Afterward came a trip to the outdoor market for the day's provisions. Seafood was a favorite item, as the Romans normally ate meat only at festivals. While poor people ate salt fish, the more prosperous dined on rare fish, oysters, squid, and eels. Wine was the common drink, and the rich often enjoyed rare vintages imported from abroad. Ordinary men normally worked in small shops attached to their homes, and they sold their goods over the counters. Shoppers strolled along the streets, buying what they wanted or just chatting and enjoying the sights. Street musicians often added an air of festivity. Men frequented barbershops for haircuts and gossip, whereas women usually had their hair done at home by slaves.

gladiators Criminals, slaves, and sometimes free men who fought each other or wild animals to the death in Roman arenas as public entertainment.

Children began their education at home, where parents emphasized moral conduct, especially reverence for the gods and the law and respect for elders. Mothers taught their daughters elementary reading, writing, and arithmetic. Daughters also learned how to manage the house and deport themselves like their mothers. Boys learned the basics of their future calling from their fathers, who also taught them the use of weapons for military service. Boys boxed, learned to ride when possible, and swam, all to increase their strength, while giving them basic skills. Ordinary boys then began plying their fathers' trade. Wealthy boys continued their formal training for a career.

They usually mastered rhetoric and law for a political career. Others entered the army, usually as cadets on the staffs of prominent officers.

Not many Romans pursued a medical career, which was considered beneath their dignity. While many physicians honestly sought to heal their patients and alleviate pain, many other incompetent and greedy practitioners claimed to cure illnesses through incantations and magic. One potion included the liver of a cat killed when the moon was waning, preserved in salt.

Goat dung mixed with old wine was said to be good for healing broken ribs. The learned Pliny the Elder once railed against doctors: "Of all men only a physician can kill a man with total impunity. Oh no, on the contrary, censure goes to him who dies and *he* is guilty of excess, and furthermore *he* is blamed. . . . Let me not accuse their [physicians'] avarice, their greedy deals with those whose fate hangs in the balance, their setting a price on pain and their demands for down payment in case of death, and their secret doctrines."[4] Many Roman doctors did not take the Hippocratic oath seriously.

The emperor and other wealthy citizens also entertained the Roman populace, often at vast expense. The most popular forms of public entertainment were gladiatorial contests and chariot racing. Many **gladiators** were criminals who had been sentenced to death. They were given no defensive weapons and stood little real chance of surviving. Other criminals were sentenced to

Gladiatorial Games Though hardly games, these contests were vastly popular among the Romans. Gladiators were usually slaves, but successful ones could gain their freedom. The fighting was hard but fair, and the gladiators shown here look equally matched.
(Interphoto Press/Alamy)

> ❝ Let me not accuse their [physicians'] avarice, their greedy deals with those whose fate hangs in the balance, their setting a price on pain and their demands for down payment in case of death. ❞

—PLINY THE ELDER

fight in the arena as fully armed gladiators. Some gladiators were the slaves of gladiatorial trainers; others were prisoners of war. Still others were free men who volunteered for the arena. Even women at times engaged in gladiatorial combat. For a criminal condemned to die, the arena was preferable to the imperial mines, where convicts worked digging ore and died under wretched conditions. At least in the arena the gladiator might fight well enough to win freedom. Some Romans protested gladiatorial fighting, but the emperors recognized the political value of such spectacles, and most Romans appear to have enjoyed them. Christian authors generally opposed gladiatorial and animal combat, but this did not lead to immediate bans.

The Romans were even more addicted to chariot racing than to gladiatorial shows. Under the empire four permanent teams competed against one another. Each had its own color—red, white, green, or blue. Two-horse and four-horse chariots ran a course of seven laps, about five miles. One charioteer, Gaius Appuleius Diocles, raced for twenty-four years. During that time he drove 4,257 starts and won 1,462 of them. His admirers honored him with an inscription that proclaimed him champion of all charioteers.

Roman spectacles such as gladiator fights and chariot racing are fascinating subjects for movies and computer games, but they were not everyday activities for Romans. As is evident on tombstone inscriptions, ordinary Romans were proud of their work and accomplishments and affectionate toward their families and friends. An impression of them can be gained from their epitaphs. (See "Living in the Past: Roman Tombstone Epitaphs: Death Remembers Life," page 160.)

Individual inscriptions and public laws testify to the increased manumission of slaves. One law actually restricted the freeing of slaves because this would allow them to receive public grain and gifts of money, both reserved for citizens. Some Romans complained that ex-slaves were debasing pure Roman citizenship. In fact most of those freed were house slaves who had virtually become members of the family. The example of Helene, the slave of Marcus Aurelius Ammonio, is typical: the master "manumitted in the presence of friends his house-born female Helene, about 34 years old, and ordered her to be free."[5] Ammonio then gave her a generous gift of money.

Some household slaves, however, forgot their servile status. That was the case with an educated slave of Plutarch, the famous author. The slave, who had read some of his master's philosophical writings, became insolent, for which Plutarch had him flogged. The slave accused his master of not acting very philosophically. Plutarch told the man with the whip to continue, while he and the slave discussed philosophy. This was an unusual episode. For many slaves, especially those who worked in the mines, life was hard. Those who failed in their escape attempts were returned to their masters and often branded on their foreheads. Others had metal collars fastened around their necks. One collar discovered near Rome read: "I have run away. Capture me. If you take me back to my master Zoninus, you will receive a gold coin."[6] Slavery was declining and manumission increasing, but slavery kept its dark side.

Provincial Life

The rural population throughout the empire left few records, but the inscriptions that remain point to a melding of cultures. This melding can be seen in the evolution of Romance languages, which include Spanish, Italian, French, Portuguese, and Romanian. These languages evolved in the provinces, where people used Latin for legal and state religious purposes, eventually leading to a blending of Latin and their native tongues. The process of cultural exchange was at first more urban than rural, but the importance of cities and towns to the life of the wider countryside ensured that its effects spread far afield.

A brief survey of the provinces illustrates the melding of cultures. For instance, in Gaul country people retained their ancestral gods, and there was not much difference in many parts of the province between the original Celtic villages and their Roman successors. Along the Rhine River, Romans provided the capital for commerce, agricultural development of the land, and large-scale building. Roman merchants also became early bankers, loaning money to the natives and often controlling them financially. The native inhabitants made up the labor force. They normally lived in villages and huts near the villas of successful merchants, whose wives bought Roman household items and clothing. Although Roman ideas spread and there was a good deal of cultural blending, native customs and religions continued to thrive. The Romans

LIVING IN THE PAST

ROMANS USED THEIR TOMBSTONES to commemorate their lives and often to share their personal philosophies. They ordinarily expressed themselves seriously in inscriptions that are also intimate in tone. Typical is the epitaph of Claudia, who proudly described her life as one of an ideal Roman lady: "Stranger, my message is short. Stand by and read it through. Here is the unlovely tomb of a lovely lady. Her parents called her Claudia by name. She loved her husband with all her heart. She bore two sons; of them she leaves one on earth. Under the earth she placed the other. She was charming in conversation and gentle in bearing. She kept house; she worked wool. That's my last word. Go your way."* Particularly touching is the tribute that Paprius Vitalis paid to his deceased wife: "If there is anything good in the lower regions — I, however, finish a poor life without you — be happy there too, sweetest Thelassia . . . married to me for forty years."† Claudia Propontis expressed her devotion more simply in an epitaph inscribed on her patron's tombstone (opposite): "To the spirits of Tiberius Claudius Dionysius. Claudia Propontis made this for her good patron and herself."‡

Others enjoyed their prosperity with wry gratitude. His tombstone shows Lucius Valerianus calmly looking over his very prosperous estates worked by diligent men (below). Yet his epitaph states "I've escaped; got clean away. Good-bye Lady Hope and Fortune. I have nothing more to do with you. Work your worst on other people."§ More than anything, he was glad to escape the worst that Tyche (the goddess of fate or luck) could do. Marcus Antonius Encolpus left a similarly blunt message for the living: "Do not pass by this epitaph, wayfarer, but stop, listen, hear, then go. There is no boat in Hades, no ferryman Charon. No caretaker Aecus, no Cerberus dog. All we dead below have become bones and ashes, nothing more. I have spoken the truth to you. Go now, wayfarer, lest even in death I seem garrulous to you."** All of these people felt that they and their lessons in life were valuable enough to share with others.

*Naphtali Lewis and Meyer Reinhold, *Roman Civilization*, vol. I (New York: Harper Torchbooks, 1951), p. 489.

†Ibid., vol. II, p. 285.

‡David Cherry, ed., *The Roman World: A Sourcebook* (Oxford: Blackwell, 2001), p. 60.

§Mary Johnston, *Roman Life* (Chicago: Scott, Foresman & Co., 1957), p. 405.

**Lewis and Reinhold, vol. II, pp. 284–285.

Tombstone of Lucius Valerianus (Vatican Museums/Alinari/Art Resource, NY)

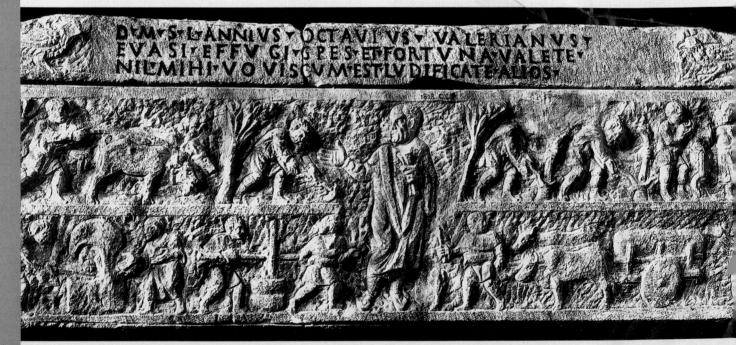

Tombstone of Tiberius Claudius Dionysius (Photo: Vatican Museums)

DIIS·MANIBVS·
TI·CLAVDI·DIONYSI·
FECIT·CLAVDIA·PRE·PONTIS·
PATRONO·BENEMERENTI·
ET·SIBI·

QUESTIONS FOR ANALYSIS

1. Compare the tombstones illustrated here. What do the epitaphs written by Claudia Propontis and Lucius Valerianus tell us about their attitudes toward life and death? Describe the relationship between the funerary images and the inscriptions on these tombstones.

2. Consider all the epitaphs quoted above. How are they alike, and how are they different?

also learned about and began to respect native gods. Worship of them became popular among the Romans and the Greeks, which encouraged local peoples to preserve their religions.

Roman soldiers were important agents in spreading Roman culture. (See "Individuals in Society: Bithus, a Typical Roman Soldier, page 164.") Soldiers had originally been prohibited from marrying, though they often formed permanent relationships with local women. In the late second century the emperor permitted them to marry, and mixed ethnicity couples became common in border areas. Because military units were moved as needed, women often ended up far from their homelands with their soldier husbands.

The situation on the eastern bank of the Rhine was also typical of life on the borders, but it demonstrates the rawer features of frontier life. To this troubled land the Romans brought peace and stability, first by building forts and roads and then by opening the rivers to navigation. Around the forts grew native villages, and peace encouraged more intensive cultivation of the soil. The region became more prosperous than ever before, and prosperity attracted Roman settlers. Roman veterans mingled with the Celtic population and sometimes married into Celtic families. The **villa**, a country estate, was the primary unit of organized political life. This pattern of life differed from that of the Mediterranean, but it prefigured life in the early Middle Ages. In Britain, as well, the normal social and economic structures were farms and agricultural villages. Very few cities were to be found, and many native Britons were largely unacquainted with Greco-Roman culture.

> **villa** A Roman country estate that was the primary unit of organized political life in the provinces.

Across eastern Europe the pattern was much the same. In the Alpine provinces north of Italy, Romans and native Celts came into contact in the cities, but native cultures flourished in the countryside. In Illyria (ih-LIHR-ee-uh) and Dalmatia, regions of modern Albania, Croatia, and Montenegro, the native population never widely embraced either Roman culture or urban life. The Roman soldiers who increasingly settled parts of these lands made little effort to Romanize the natives, and there was less intermarriage than in Celtic areas. To a certain extent, however, Romanization occurred simply because the peoples lived in such close proximity.

In contrast with northern Europe, Asia Minor had long enjoyed the peace and stability of Roman rule. The lives of urban men and women reflected that benefit. In modern Turkey the well-preserved ruins of the ancient city of Aspendos give a full picture of life in this part of the provinces. The city sits among fertile fields, and the resources of the land provided raw materials for industry and trade. Manufactured goods and raw materials passed along a river next to the city that kept it in touch with the rest of the empire and brought in immigrants from elsewhere.

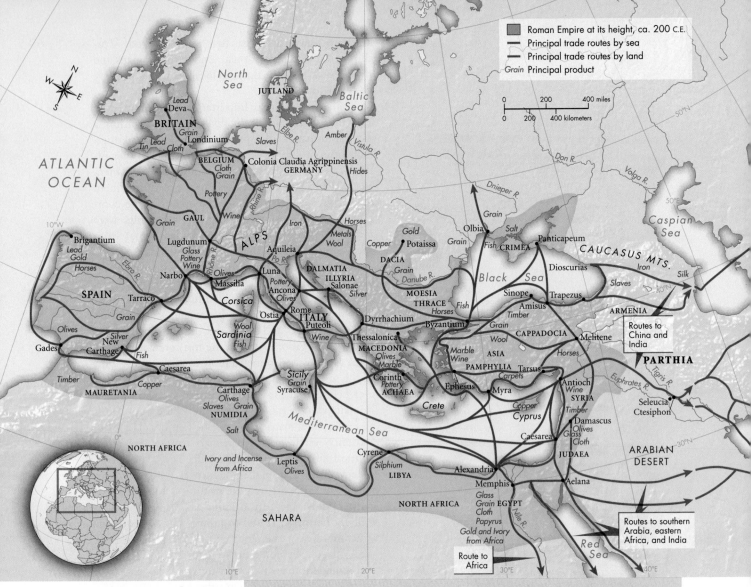

North Sea
JUTLAND
Baltic Sea
BRITAIN
Lead
Deva
Grain
Lead Londinium
Tin Cloth
BELGIUM
Cloth
Grain
Colonia Claudia Agrippinensis
GERMANY
Slaves
Amber
Elbe R.
Vistula R.
Hides
Pottery
ATLANTIC OCEAN
Wine
Rhine R.
Horses
Dnieper R.
Don R.
Volga R.
Grain
GAUL
Iron
Metals
Wool
Copper
Gold
Potaissa
Grain
Olbia
Salt
Fish
CRIMEA
Panticapeum
Caspian Sea
Brigantium
Lead
Gold
Horses
Lugdunum
Glass
Pottery
Wine
ALPS
Aquileia
Po R.
DACIA
Grain
Danube R.
Black Sea
Dioscurias
CAUCASUS MTS.
Iron
Silk
Narbo
Rhône R.
Olives
Luna
Pottery
Massilia
Ancona
Olives
DALMATIA
ILLYRIA
Salonae
Silver
MOESIA
THRACE
Horses
Fish
Sinope
Amisus
Timber
Trapezus
Slaves
ARMENIA
SPAIN
Tarraco
Corsica
Rome
Ostia
ITALY
Puteoli
Dyrrhachium
Byzantium
Grain
Wool
CAPPADOCIA
Melitene
Horses
Routes to China and India
PARTHIA
Grain
Olives
Sardinia
Wool
Fish
Wine
Thessalonica
MACEDONIA
Olives
Marble
Marble
Wine
ASIA
PAMPHYLIA
Tarsus
Carpets
Antioch
Wine
SYRIA
Seleucia
Ctesiphon
Euphrates R.
Tigris R.
Gades
New Carthage
Silver
Fish
Caesarea
Copper
MAURETANIA
Timber
Sicily
Grain
Syracuse
Corinth
Pottery
ACHAEA
Crete
Ephesus
Myra
Copper
Cyprus
Damascus
Olives
Glass
Cloth
Caesarea
JUDAEA
ARABIAN DESERT
Carthage
Olives
Slaves Grain
NUMIDIA
Salt
Mediterranean Sea
NORTH AFRICA
Ivory and Incense from Africa
Leptis
Olives
Cyrene
Silphium
Olives
LIBYA
Alexandria
Memphis
Glass
Grain EGYPT
Cloth
Papyrus
Gold and Ivory from Africa
Aelana
Nile R.
Red Sea
Routes to southern Arabia, eastern Africa, and India
SAHARA
NORTH AFRICA
Route to Africa

Roman Empire at its height, ca. 200 C.E.
Principal trade routes by sea
Principal trade routes by land
Grain Principal product

0   200   400 miles
0 200   400 kilometers

Mapping the Past

Map 6.2 **The Economic Aspect of the Pax Romana, ca. 27–180 C.E.** This map gives a good idea of trade routes and the economic expansion of the Roman Empire at its height. Map 11.2 on page 309 is a similar map that shows trade in roughly the same area nearly a millennium later. Examine both maps and answer the following questions.

ANALYZING THE MAP What similarities and differences do you see in trade in the Mediterranean during these two periods?

CONNECTIONS To what extent did Roman trade routes influence later European trade routes?

To complete this activity online, go to the Online Study Guide at bedfordstmartins.com/mckaywest.

For the people of Aspendos the city was the focus of life. There the men handled their political affairs in the council house, and men and women frequented the ample marketplace for their ordinary needs. Temples and later a Christian basilica gave them ornate buildings in which to worship. In the magnificent theater men and women enjoyed the great plays of the past and those popular in their own day. Absent was a place for gladiatorial games. That too was typical of the eastern Roman Empire, where gladiatorial contests were far less popular than horse racing.

More than just places to live, cities like Aspendos were centers of the intellectual and cultural life that spread abroad. The people here, like those elsewhere in the empire, kept fully in touch with the great thoughts and events of the day. Taken together, the cities of the provinces united in a vibrant economic and cultural life that spanned the entire Mediterranean (Map 6.2). As long as the empire prospered and the revenues reached the imperial coffers, the Romans were willing to let the provinces live and let live. As a result, Europe fully entered into the economic and cultural life of the Mediterranean

Life at a Roman Villa On the European borders of the Roman Empire, the villa was often as important as the town. The villa at Chedworth in Roman Britain, shown here in an archaeological reconstruction (below) and in a reproduction on the site (right), provides an excellent example. The typical villa included a large courtyard with barns, gardens, storehouses, and buildings for processing agricultural products and manufacturing goods. The villa also included the living quarters of the owner and his family and quarters for servants and slaves set apart from the great houses. A small temple or shrine often provided a center for religious devotions. While self-contained, a villa was not necessarily isolated. The villa at Chedworth was connected by roads and rivers to similar neighboring villas. (reconstruction: Courtesy, Professor Albert Schachter; photo: Courtesy, John Buckler)

world. The interconnectedness of the provinces would prove instrumental in facilitating the spread of a small native religion from Judaea.

The Coming of Christianity

Why did Christianity, originally a minor local religion, sweep across the Roman world to change it fundamentally? ■

During the reign of the emperor Tiberius (14–37 C.E.), Jesus preached in Judaea, attracted a following, and was executed on the order of the Roman prefect Pontius

Pilate. At the time a minor event, it has become one of the best known moments in history. How did these two men come to their historic meeting?

The Hellenistic Greeks provided the entire East with a common language, widely shared literary forms, and a pervasive culture that had for years embraced Judaea. Rome contributed political administration to Hellenistic culture. The mixture was not always harmonious. In Judaea, Roman rule aroused hatred and unrest among some Jews. This climate of hostility formed the backdrop of Jesus' life, and it had a fundamental impact on his ministry. These factors also ultimately paved the way for Christianity to spread far from its native land to the broader world of the Roman Empire.

Bithus, a Typical Roman Soldier

INDIVIDUALS IN SOCIETY

FEW PEOPLE THINK OF SOLDIERS as missionaries of culture, but they often are. The culture that they spread is seldom of high intellectual or artistic merit, but they expose others to their own traditions, habits, and ways of thinking. A simple modern example may suffice. In World War II American GIs in Italy taught children there how to play baseball and many other things about the United States. The young Americans themselves learned a great deal about Italian life and values. Even today a stranger can wander around an Italian town and see the results of this meeting of two cultures.

The same was true of the armies of the Roman Empire. The empire was so vast even by modern standards that soldiers were recruited from all parts of it to serve in distant places. A soldier from the province of Syria might find himself keeping watch on Hadrian's Wall in Britain. He brought with him the ideas and habits of his birthplace and through his contact with people in other parts of the empire realized that others lived life differently. Despite their ethnic differences, they were united by many commonly shared beliefs and opinions. Although the Roman Empire never became totally Romanized, soldiers, like officials and merchants, played their part in disseminating Roman ideas of government, religion, and way of life.

One such person was the infantryman Bithus, who was born in Thrace in the northeastern region of modern Greece. His career was eventful but not particularly distinguished. He is, however, typical of many Roman soldiers. Bithus served in the auxiliaries, a secondary force comprised of noncitizens. Bithus's military life took him far from his native Thrace.

His career started with basic training during which he learned to march and to use standard weapons. His training over, Bithus was sent to Syria, where he spent most of his career. There he met others from as far west as Gaul and Spain, from West Africa, and from the modern Middle East. This experience gave him an idea of the size of the empire. It also taught him about life in other areas. Unlike many other cohorts that were shifted periodically, his saw service in one theater. While in the army, he raised a family, much like soldiers today. The children of soldiers like Bithus often themselves joined the army, which thereby became a fruitful source of its own recruitment. After twenty-five years of duty,

This veteran legionary wears body armor made of strips and plates of iron, an outer sheet of leather straps, and a crested helmet. (Courtesy of the Trustees of the British Museum)

Bithus received his diploma on November 7, 88. Upon mustering out of the army he received the grant of Roman citizenship for himself and his family.

In his civilian life the veteran enjoyed a social status that granted him honor and privileges accorded only to Roman citizens. From his military records there is no reason to conclude that Bithus had even seen Rome, but because of his service to it, he became as much a Roman as anyone born there.

The example of Bithus is important because he is typical of thousands of others who voluntarily supported the empire. In the process they learned about the nature of the empire and something about how it worked. They also exchanged experiences with other soldiers and the local population that helped shape a sense that the empire was a human as well as a political unit.

Source: *Corpus Inscriptionum Latinarum*, vol. 16, no. 35 (Berlin: G. Reimer, 1882).

QUESTIONS FOR ANALYSIS

1. What did Bithus gain from his twenty-five years of service in the Roman army?

2. What effect did soldiers such as Bithus have on the various parts of the Roman Empire where they served?

Without an understanding of this age of anxiety in Judaea, one cannot fully appreciate Jesus and his followers.

Unrest in Judaea

The civil wars that destroyed the Roman republic had extended as far as Judaea in the eastern Mediterranean. Jewish leaders took sides in the conflict, and Judaea suffered its share of violence and looting. Although Augustus restored stability, his appointed king for Judaea, Herod (r. 37–4 B.C.E.), was hated by the Jews. At his death the Jews in Judaea broke out in revolt. For the next ten years Herod's successor waged almost constant war against the rebels. Added to the horrors of civil war were famine and plague.

To maintain order Augustus made Judaea a province in 6 C.E., thus putting it fully under Roman administration. Although many prefects tried to perform their duties scrupulously, many others were indifferent to Jewish culture. Often acting from fear rather than cruelty, some prefects fiercely stamped out any signs of popular discontent. Pontius Pilate, prefect from 26 to 36 C.E., is typical of such incompetent officials. Especially hated were the Roman tax collectors, called "publicans," many of whom pitilessly gouged the Jews. Clashes between the Roman troops and Jewish guerrillas inflamed the anger of both sides.

Among the Jews two movements spread. First was the rise of the Zealots (ZEH-luhts), extremists who fought to rid Judaea of the Romans. Resolute in their worship of Yahweh (see Chapter 2), they refused to pay any but the tax levied by the Jewish temple. Their battles with the Roman legionaries were marked by savagery on both sides. As usual, the innocent caught in the middle suffered grievously. As Roman policy grew tougher, even moderate Jews began to hate the conquerors.

The second movement was the growth of militant apocalypticism — the belief that the coming of the **Messiah**, the savior of Israel, was near. This belief was an old one among the Jews. But by the first century C.E. it had become more widespread and

Judaea in the Time of Jesus, ca. 30 C.E.

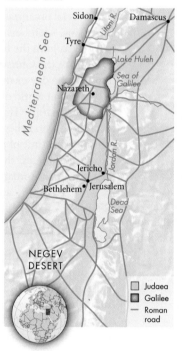

Messiah The savior of Israel, who according to apocalyptic predictions would destroy the Roman Empire and usher in a period of peace and plenty for the Jews; Christians believed that Jesus was the Messiah but that he would establish a spiritual kingdom, not an earthly one.

fervent than ever before. Apocalyptic predictions appeared in many texts, including the anonymous Apocalypse of Baruch, which foretold the destruction of the Roman Empire. First would come a period of great tribulation and misery. At the worst of the suffering, the Messiah would appear and destroy the Roman legions and all the kingdoms that had ruled Israel. Then the Messiah would inaugurate a period of happiness and plenty for the Jews.

As the ravages of war became widespread and conditions worsened, more and more people prophesied the imminent coming of the Messiah. According to Christian Scripture, one such was John the Baptist, "the voice of one crying in the wilderness, Prepare ye the way of the lord" (Matthew 3:3). Many Jews did just that. The sect described in the Dead Sea Scrolls (documents dealing with Jewish religious matters found in 1947 in caves near the Dead Sea) readied itself for the end of the world. Its members were probably Essenes, an ascetic group whose social organization closely resembled that of early Christians. Members of this group shared possessions, precisely as John the Baptist urged people to do. Yet this sect, unlike the Christians, also made military preparations for the day of the Messiah.

The pagan world of Rome is also part of the story of early Christianity. The term **pagans** (PAY-gahns) refers to all those who believed in the Greco-Roman gods. Paganism at the time of Jesus' birth can be broadly divided into three spheres: the official state religion of Rome, the traditional Roman cults of hearth and countryside,

> **pagans** All those who believed in the Greco-Roman gods; non-Christians.

and the new mystery religions that flowed from the Hellenistic East. The official state religion and its cults honored the traditional deities: Jupiter, Juno, Mars, and Vesta (see Chapter 4). Most Romans felt that the official cults had to be maintained for the welfare of the state, and Augustus was careful to link them to him.

For emotional and spiritual satisfaction, many Romans turned to cults of home and countryside. These traditional cults brought the Romans back in touch with nature. Particularly popular was the rustic shrine—often a small building or a sacred tree in an enclosure—honoring the native spirit of the locality. Others found spiritual security and an emotional outlet in the various Hellenistic mystery cults. Mystery religions gave their adherents what neither the traditional cults nor philosophy could—the promise of immortality. Yet the mystery religions were by nature exclusive, and none was truly international, open to everyone.

The Life and Teachings of Jesus

Into this climate of Jewish Messianic hope and Roman religious yearning came Jesus of Nazareth (ca. 3 B.C.E.–

29 C.E.). He was raised in Galilee, stronghold of the Zealots. A Jewish town, Galilee had come under Roman political rule. Roman culture remained a veneer, deeper among those who had political and business dealings with the Greeks and Romans than among ordinary folk. Through Galilee passed major trade routes on which ideas moved as easily as merchandise.

Much contemporary scholarship has attempted to understand who Jesus was and what he meant by his teachings. No agreement on these matters has been reached, and perhaps ultimately no final answers are possible. Historians can only try to understand these events using available sources, knowing that much ultimately remains unknown. Some see Jesus as a visionary and a teacher, others as a magician and a prophet, and still others as a rebel and a revolutionary. The search for the historical Jesus is complicated by many factors. One is the difference between history and faith. History relies on proof for its conclusions; faith depends on belief. Thus whether Jesus is divine is not an issue to be decided by historians. Their role is to understand him in his religious, cultural, social, and historical context.

To sort out the various and often conflicting interpretations, historians must begin with the sources. The principal evidence for the life and deeds of Jesus comes from the four Gospels of the New Testament. The Gospels are records of Jesus' life and teachings. Writing after Jesus' death, the authors sought to use the Gospels to build a community of faith centered on Jesus as the Messiah.

Scholars debate when the Gospels were published, but many historians think that the earliest Gospel, that of Mark, appeared around 70 C.E. and the books of Luke, Matthew, and John early in the second century (ca. 90 C.E.). Biblical scholars have detected a number of discrepancies among the four Gospels. Perhaps the discrepancies came in part from the authors' having heard varying earlier accounts of Jesus' life and mission. Furthermore, the writers gave their own theological interpretations to further their goal of seeking converts. The Gospels were among the most widely circulated early accounts of Jesus' life, and by the fourth century officials in the Christian church decided that they, along with other types of writings such as letters and prophesies, would form Christian Scripture. The four Gospels are called "canonical," from the Greek word that means the "rule" or the "standard."

These canonical writings were not, however, the earliest accounts of Jesus' career. The first followers of Jesus lived by the sayings attributed to him. Their writings about Jesus circulated in slightly different versions before the creation of the Christian church. The early followers were not actually Christian in the strictest sense. They did not see Jesus as the Messiah, nor as the founder of a church. They considered him a teacher whose moral teachings on ethical behavior were appealing in troubled

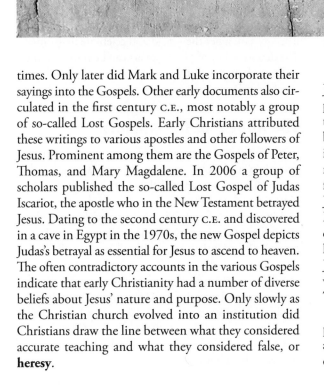

Earliest Known Depiction of Jesus
This mural may be the earliest picture of Jesus. Found in the Roman camp at Dura-Europos on the Euphrates River and dating to 235 C.E., it depicts Jesus healing the paralytic. Early Christians used art to spread the message of the Gospels. (Yale University Art Gallery, Dura-Europos Collection)

times. Only later did Mark and Luke incorporate their sayings into the Gospels. Other early documents also circulated in the first century C.E., most notably a group of so-called Lost Gospels. Early Christians attributed these writings to various apostles and other followers of Jesus. Prominent among them are the Gospels of Peter, Thomas, and Mary Magdalene. In 2006 a group of scholars published the so-called Lost Gospel of Judas Iscariot, the apostle who in the New Testament betrayed Jesus. Dating to the second century C.E. and discovered in a cave in Egypt in the 1970s, the new Gospel depicts Judas's betrayal as essential for Jesus to ascend to heaven. The often contradictory accounts in the various Gospels indicate that early Christianity had a number of diverse beliefs about Jesus' nature and purpose. Only slowly as the Christian church evolved into an institution did Christians draw the line between what they considered accurate teaching and what they considered false, or **heresy**.

Despite this diversity, there were certain things about Jesus' teachings that almost all the sources agree on: he preached of eternal happiness in a life after death. His teachings were essentially Jewish. Jesus was Jewish by birth, and his major deviation from orthodoxy was his insistence that he taught in his own name, not in the name of Yahweh. Was he the Messiah? A small band of followers thought so, and Jesus claimed that he was. Yet Jesus had his own conception of the Messiah. Unlike the Messiah of the Apocalypse of Baruch, Jesus would not destroy the Roman Empire. Jesus believed in a spiritual kingdom, not an earthly one. Shortly before his death, Jesus told the apostles that through his sacrifice he would wipe away all sins. He would save all who came to him. That was his mission.

Of Jesus' life and teachings the prefect Pontius Pilate knew little and cared even less. All that concerned him was the maintenance

heresy Teachings that went against the beliefs of the Christian church.

of peace and order. Some Jews believed that Jesus was the long-awaited Messiah. Others were disappointed because he refused to preach rebellion against Rome. Still others hated and feared Jesus and wanted to be rid of him. The crowds of ordinary, usually poor people following Jesus at the time of the Passover holiday, a highly emotional time in the Jewish year, alarmed Pilate. To avert riot and bloodshed, Pilate condemned Jesus to death. According to Christian Scripture, after being tortured, he was hung from a cross until he died.

On the third day after Jesus' crucifixion, an odd rumor began to circulate in Jerusalem. Some of Jesus' followers said he had risen from the dead, while others accused the followers of having stolen his body. For the earliest Christians and for generations to come, the resurrection of Jesus became a central element of faith—and, more than that, a promise: Jesus had triumphed over death, and his resurrection promised all Christians immortality. In Jerusalem, meanwhile, the tumult subsided and Jesus' followers lived quietly and peacefully.

The Spread of Christianity

The memory of Jesus and his teachings survived and flourished. Believers in his divinity met in small assemblies or congregations, often in one another's homes, to discuss the meaning of his message. These earliest Christians defined their faith to fit the life of Jesus into an orthodox Jewish context. Only later did these congregations evolve into what can be called a church with a formal organization and set of beliefs.

The catalyst in the spread of Jesus' teachings and the formation of the Christian church was Paul of Tarsus, a Hellenized Jew who was comfortable in both the Roman and Jewish worlds. He had begun by persecuting the new sect, but on the road to Damascus he was converted to belief in Jesus. He was the single most important figure responsible for changing Christianity from a Jewish sect into a separate religion. Paul was familiar with Greek philosophy, and one of his seminal ideas may have stemmed from the Stoic concept of the unity of mankind. He proclaimed that the mission of Christianity was "to make one of all the folk of men" (Acts 17:26). He urged the Jews to include **Gentiles** (non-Jews) in the faith. His was the first universal message of Christianity.

Gentiles Non-Jews.

catacombs Huge public underground cemeteries; the Roman catacombs offered refuge in times of persecution and include early pagan and Christian art.

Paul's vision proved both bold and successful. When he traveled abroad, he first met with the leaders of the local synagogue before going out among the people. He said that there was no difference between Jews and Gentiles, which in orthodox Jewish thought was not only revolutionary but also heresy. Paul found a ready audience among the Gentiles, who converted to the new religion with surprising enthusiasm.

Many early Christian converts were women. Paul greeted male and female converts by name in his letters, and he noted that women provided financial support for his activities. Missionaries and others spreading the Christian message worked through families and friendship networks. The growing Christian communities had different ideas about many things, including the proper gender roles for believers. Some communities favored giving women a larger role, while others were more restrictive. Contrary to modern notions, the early Christians were generally tolerated.

Christianity might have remained just another sect had it not reached Rome, the capital of the Western world. Events in Rome proved to be a dramatic step in the spread of Christianity for various reasons. First, Jesus had told his followers to spread his word throughout the world, thus making his teachings universal. The pagan Romans also considered their secular empire universal, and early Christians there combined these two concepts of universalism. Secular Rome provided another advantage to Christianity. If all roads led to Rome, they also led outward to the provinces of central and western Europe. The very stability and extent of the Roman Empire enabled early Christians easily to spread their faith southward to Africa and northward into Europe and across the channel to Britain (see Map 6.2).

Decorations in the **catacombs** of Rome testify to the vitality of the new religion and the pagan toleration of it. The catacombs were huge underground public structures where people were buried. In the early years of persecution, Christians sometimes took refuge in the catacombs. More generally, however, they used them as a meeting place to remember their dead and celebrate their rituals. The development of Christian art can be traced on their walls, with pagan and Christian motifs on early tombs and biblical scenes on later ones.

The Appeal of Christianity

In its doctrine of salvation and forgiveness, Christianity had a powerful ability to give solace and strength to believers. Christians believed that Jesus on the cross had defeated evil and that he would reward his followers with eternal life after death. Christianity also offered the possibility of forgiveness. Human nature was weak, and even the best Christians would fall into sin. But Jesus loved sinners and forgave those who repented.

Christianity was attractive because it gave the Roman world a cause. Instead of passivity, Christianity stressed the ideal of striving for a goal. Christians believed that they should spread the word of God. The Christian was not discouraged by temporary setbacks, believing Christianity to be invincible.

Christianity also gave its devotees a sense of community. Believers met regularly to celebrate the Eucharist, a ritual commemorating the Last Supper, Jesus' last meal with his disciples before his arrest. Each individual community was in turn a member of a greater community. And that community, according to Christian Scripture, was indestructible, for Jesus had promised that "the gates of hell shall not prevail against it" (Matthew 16:18).

> **God wants you to be good citizens. . . . Have respect for everyone and love for your community; fear God and honor the emperor.**
>
> —**PETER**

Christians and Pagans

Early Christians developed their beliefs amid the classical culture of their own past. As Christianity gained converts, several influential Christian thinkers taught Christians to coexist with the pagans around them. The apostle Peter advised:

> *For the sake of the Lord, accept the authority of every social institution: the emperor, as the supreme authority, and the governors as commissioned by him to punish criminals and praise good citizenship. God wants you to be good citizens. . . . Have respect for everyone and love for your community; fear God and honor the emperor.* (Peter 2:11–20)

Peter taught that God sanctioned the emperor as the rightful ruler of the people and his officials who governed them. After all, Jesus had commanded his follower "to render unto Caesar the things that are Caesar's" (Matthew 22:21). That did not prevent them from being good Christians.

Two Christian thinkers taught the early Christians how to combine pagan culture with Christian ethics. Justin Martyr (100–165 C.E.), born in Samaria, established a Christian school in Rome. Originally an adherent of Plato's philosophy, he believed that the pagan philosophers had foreshadowed Christianity. He sought in his works to note the similarities, not the differences, among Christians, pagans, and Jews. He thereby played an important role in creating Christian theology, the rational analysis of religious faith. Despite his efforts to find common ground for Greek philosophy and Christian religion, he never compromised his beliefs. In a local dispute at Rome in 165 C.E. he died defending Christianity, and his fellow believers gave him the name "Martyr" from the Greek word meaning "witness."

The Catacombs of Rome The early Christians used underground crypts and rock chambers to bury their dead. The bodies were placed stacked in these galleries and then sealed up. The catacombs became places of pilgrimage, and in this way the dead continued to be united with the living. (Catacombe di Priscilla, Rome/Scala/Art Resource, NY)

Justin was followed by Tertullian of Carthage (ca. 160–240 C.E.), an even more influential thinker. Tertullian also symbolized some of the contradictions in early Christian beliefs. He called philosophers such as Aristotle "hucksters of eloquence" and asked, "What has Athens to do with Jerusalem?" or "the Academy with the Church?" Yet Tertullian used the teachings of the Stoics to discuss Christian ethical problems. To that extent he combined pagan philosophy with Christian theology. Both Justin and Tertullian gave western Christianity an intellectual as well as a religious foundation.

At first many pagans genuinely misunderstood Christian rites and practices. Many, including people like the historian Tacitus, saw Christianity as a bizarre new sect. Tacitus believed that Christians hated the whole human race. As a rule, early Christians kept to themselves. Romans distrusted and feared their exclusiveness, which seemed unsociable and even subversive. Pagans thought that such secret rites as the Eucharist, at which Christians said that they ate and drank the body and blood of Jesus, were acts of cannibalism. They considered Christianity one of the worst of the mystery cults, for one of the hallmarks of many of those cults was rituals that many Romans found unacceptable.

Christians themselves were partly responsible for the religious misunderstandings. They exaggerated the degree of pagan hostility to them, and most of the gory stories about the martyrs are fictitious. There were indeed some cases of pagan persecution of the Christians, but with few exceptions they were local and sporadic in nature. Overall, pagans and Christians alike enjoyed long periods of tolerance and even friendship. Nonetheless, some pagans thought that Christians were atheists because they denied the existence of pagan gods or called them evil spirits. Christians urged people not to worship pagan gods. In turn,

Christian Oil Lamp When Christianity spread among the Romans, many of them decorated their household goods with Christian symbols. This lamp for an ordinary home includes the cross of Jesus on its neck. **X** (the + when tipped would read "**x**") and **P** are the first two Greek letters of *Christos*, Christ.
(Zev Radovan/www.BibleLandPictures.com)

pagans, who believed in their gods as fervently as the Christians in theirs, feared that the gods would withdraw their favor from the Roman Empire because of Christian blasphemy.

Another source of misunderstanding was that the pagans did not demand that the Christians believe in pagan gods. Official Roman religion was never a matter of belief or ethics but of publicly celebrated rituals linked to the good of the state. All the pagans expected was performance of a ritual sacrifice as a demonstration of patriotism and loyalty. Those Christians who participated were free to worship in peace, no matter what they personally believed.

As time went on, pagan hostility decreased. Pagans realized that Christians were not working to overthrow the state and that Jesus was no rival of Caesar. The emperor Trajan forbade his governors to hunt down Christians. Trajan admitted that he thought Christianity an abomination, but he preferred to leave Christians in peace. After years of suspicion and distrust, Christians took their place as loyal Roman citizens. With fear of persecution disappearing, they freely shared their beliefs. The promise of a happy life after death to all believers increased the popularity of Christianity. By 284 C.E., though still an overall minority, Christianity had become the largest religious group in the empire.

The Empire in Disarray, 235–284 C.E.

What factors led Rome into political and economic chaos? ■

The long years of peace and prosperity abruptly gave way to a period of domestic upheaval and foreign invasion. The last of the five good emperors was followed by a long series of able but ambitious military commanders who used their legions to make themselves emperors. Law yielded to the sword. Yet even during the worst of this ordeal, many people clung to the old Roman ideals. Only the political mechanisms of the empire, its sturdy civil service, its ordinary lower officials, and its loyal soldiers, staved off internal collapse and foreign invasion.

Civil Wars and Foreign Invasions

After the death of Marcus Aurelius, the last of the five good emperors, misrule by his successors led to a long and intense spasm of fighting. More than twenty different emperors ascended the throne in the forty-nine years between 235 and 284. Many rebels, loyal generals and their soldiers, and innocent civilians died in the fighting. At various times parts of the empire were lost to mutinous generals. So many military commanders ruled that the middle of the third century has become known as the age of the **barracks emperors**. The Augustan principate had become a military monarchy, and that monarchy was nakedly autocratic.

While the empire seemed intent on committing suicide, barbarians on the frontiers took full advantage of the chaos to overrun vast areas. When they reached the Rhine and the Danube, they often found gaping holes in the Roman defenses. During much of the third century bands of Goths, a Germanic people, devastated the Balkans as far south as Greece and down into Asia Minor. The Alamanni (ah-luh-MAN-igh), another Germanic people, swept across the Danube. At one point they reached Milan in Italy before being beaten back. Meanwhile, the Franks, still another Germanic folk, hit the Rhine frontier. Once loose, they invaded eastern and central Gaul and northeastern Spain. Saxons from Scandinavia sailed into the English Channel in search of loot. In the east the Sassanids (suh-SAH-nihdz) overran Mesopotamia. If the army had guarded the borders instead of creating and destroying emperors, these onslaughts probably would not have been successful.

Turmoil in Farm and Village Life

This chaos also disrupted areas elsewhere in the empire, even when the local people remained distant from barbarian invaders. Renegade soldiers and corrupt imperial officials together with many greedy local agents preyed on local people. In many places in the countryside, farmers appealed to the government to protect them so that they could cultivate the land. Others encountered officials who requisitioned their livestock and compelled them to do forced labor. Facing ruin, many rural families deserted the land and fled. Although some of those in authority were unsympathetic and even violent to villagers, many others tried to maintain order. Yet even the best of them also suffered. If they could not meet their tax quotas, they had to pay the deficits from their own pockets. Because the local officials were themselves being so hard-pressed, they squeezed what they needed from rural families. By the end of the third century, the entire empire tottered on the brink of ruin.

The Crisis of the Third Century

By 284 C.E. the empire had reached a crisis that threatened its downfall. The position of emperor was no longer gained by lawful succession but rather by victory in civil war. The empire had failed at the top, and the repercussions of the disaster spread throughout the empire with dire effects. The bureaucracy that Claudius and the Flavians had so carefully built was caught up in chaos. Though it still functioned, its efficiency was impaired. The ravages of civil war had greatly damaged the economy. High taxes added enormously to the economic problems. Unable to pay them, many farmers were driven off their land, and those remaining faced ruin. Agricultural productivity accordingly declined. Added to the economic woe was the decline in the value of the currency. Inflation wiped out savings and sent prices soaring. Commerce still flowed, but with reduced efficiency and high costs. These calamities had reduced the empire to a shambles, and many wondered whether it had a future.

> **barracks emperors** The name of the period in the middle of the third century when many military commanders ruled.

Though the picture looked bleak, there were many reasons to hope for better days. The basic organization of the empire remained intact. By their determined efforts, the legions restored order on the frontiers. Despite temporary damage to agriculture, the economic strength of the empire remained essentially sound. Agriculture, however, had problems, with no solutions in sight. Yet some internal developments already promised a brighter future. The Romans still controlled the Mediterranean, which nurtured commerce. Together with the road system, the lines of communication held the empire together. In short, the Roman infrastructure was intact. Other aspects of life also looked promising. If later Latin literature never quite reached the golden age of Augustus, it nonetheless produced gifted writers. Roman artists continued to produce outstanding portraits, paintings, and mosaics. Roman architects built temples and theaters that were as beautiful as those of their predecessors. So the real challenge facing the Romans in 284 was to rebuild their empire on its solid foundation while there was still time.

LOOKING BACK LOOKING AHEAD THE PERIOD OF THE Roman Empire was an amazingly rich era in both economic and cultural terms. Roman emperors developed a system of government that efficiently ruled over vast areas of diverse people. The resulting stability and peace encouraged progress in intellectual matters and writing, leading to a golden age of Latin literature. Religion likewise took an entirely new course with the rise and spread of Christianity. All the while, the Romans incorporated new peoples into their way of life as the empire expanded into northern and western Europe. Yet during a long period of internal crisis and civil war, many barbarians swept over the frontiers to disrupt Roman rule and its life.

Rome saw a new period of transition, late antiquity, during which the old and the new came to terms. People still lived under the authority of the emperors, and the guidance of Roman law and culture continued relatively unchanged. Yet a gentle breeze of change also blew. Government evolved from the SPQR of the past to a new monarchy. Whereas in the past the pagan gods had overseen the welfare of the state, now the Christian God with the earthly aid of the emperor and church officials protected the realm. The empire itself split from the unified principate of Augustus into two tenuously linked empires dividing the Western world. That in the west became the home of barbarians who absorbed much of the prevailing Roman culture while altering it with their own ideas, customs, and even languages.

Through all these changes the lives of ordinary men and women did not change dramatically. They farmed, worked in cities, and hoped for the best for their families. As they took new ideas, blended them with old, and created new cultural forms and ways of meeting life's challenges, they would lay the foundations of the medieval world.

CHAPTER REVIEW

■ **How did Augustus transform the Roman Empire? (p. 146)**

Once Augustus had restored order, he made it endure by remodeling the Roman government. The old constitution of the city-state gave way to the government of an empire. Although Augustus tried to save as much of the old as possible, he necessarily created a virtually new and much expanded system of rule. He created a constitutional monarchy with himself as "first citizen" and made the army a professional force. He would use the army to expand the empire into northern and western Europe.

■ **How did Augustus's successors build on his foundation to enhance Roman power and stability? (p. 154)**

Augustus's success in creating solid political institutions was tested by the dynasty he created, the Julio-Claudians. The fifty years during which they ruled Rome saw emperors and empresses trying to win and hold power through political alliances, murder, and other tactics. In 70 C.E. Vespasian, a military commander, established a new dynasty, the Flavians, who restored some stability in Rome and expanded the empire. The Flavians were followed by a series of effective emperors, later called the five good emperors, who created a more effective bureaucracy and larger army to govern the huge Roman Empire.

■ **What was life like in the city of Rome in the golden age, and what was it like in the provinces? (p. 157)**

For many Romans these were rich and happy years. Much of the population enjoyed sufficient leisure time, which many spent pursuing literature and art. Others preferred watching spectacular games including gladiatorial contests and chariot races. In the ever-expanding provinces, Roman and native cultures combined, and products and peoples moved more easily across huge areas.

■ **Why did Christianity, originally a minor local religion, sweep across the Roman world to change it fundamentally? (p. 163)**

In the early part of the first century a small event with universal repercussions occurred in remote Judaea. There a young Jew named Jesus taught new ideas, promising salvation to all who embraced it. Although Roman officials executed him, his religious vision did not die. Instead it spread across the East, then to Rome, and by the end of the period throughout the empire. Christianity triumphed because it offered morality and a promise of life after death to all people, men and women, regardless of their nationality, race, or social status.

■ What factors led Rome into political and economic chaos? (p. 170)

The good times fell into disarray when a series of weak emperors, many of them backed by soldiers they had commanded, fought for the throne. To worsen matters, barbarians on the frontiers took advantage of these internal troubles to invade, plunder, and destroy. Civil war severely damaged the economy. A rise in taxes drove farmers from their land, leading to a decline in agricultural productivity. Commerce still flowed between the provinces, but inflation and a decline in the value of Roman currency led to higher prices. These factors brought Rome near collapse.

Suggested Reading

Aldrete, Gregory S. *Daily Life in the Roman City*. 2004. Reveals the significance of ordinary Roman life in the cities of Rome, its port Ostia, and Pompeii.

Bradley, Keith R. *Slaves and Masters in the Roman Empire: A Study of Social Control*. 1988. Discusses the social controls in a slaveholding society.

Burns, Thomas S. *Rome and the Barbarians, 100 B.C.–A.D. 400*. 2003. Demonstrates how various barbarian tribes integrated with the Romans to form a new culture.

Campbell, Brian. *War and Society in Imperial Rome, 31 B.C.–A.D. 284*. 2002. Shows how Roman warfare and military life evolved within larger Roman life and how the two influenced each other.

Clark, Gillian. *Christianity and Roman Society*. 2004. Surveys the evolution of Christian life among Christians and with their pagan neighbors.

D'Ambra, Eve. *Roman Women*. 2006. Treats the lives of women of all social ranks.

Ehrman, Bard D. *Lost Scriptures: Books That Did Not Make It into the New Testament*. 2003. A general book written by an eminent scholar on early Christian writings.

Goldsworthy, Adrian. *Roman Warfare*. 2000. Provides a concise treatment of warfare from republican to imperial times.

Kyle, Donald G. *Sport and Spectacle in the Ancient World*. 2007. Deals in grim detail with the ritualized violence of the gladiatorial games.

Levick, Barbara. *Vespasian*. Rev. ed. 2005. Shows how Vespasian used his military success to restore order and initiate economic policies that strengthened the empire.

Moxnes, Halvor, ed. *Constructing Early Christian Families*. 1997. Takes a new approach to early Christianity.

Opper, Thorsten. *Hadrian: Empire and Conflict*. 2008. Examines Hadrian's role in firmly establishing the boundaries of the Roman Empire.

Rostovtzeff, Michael. *The Economic and Social History of the Roman Empire*. 2 vols. 2d ed. Ed. P. M. Fraser. 1957. The classic treatment of the topic that ranges over the entire empire.

Wells, Peter S. *The Barbarians Speak*. 1999. Discusses how indigenous peoples helped shape the face of the Roman Empire.

Notes

1. Virgil, *Aeneid* 6.851–853.
2. Horace, *Odes* 4.15.
3. Virgil, *Georgics* 3.515–519.
4. Pliny, *Natural History* 29.8.18, 21.
5. Napthali Lewis and Meyer Reinhold, *Roman Civilization*, vol. 2 (New York: Harper Torchbooks, 1955), p. 262.
6. Text in Mary Johnston, *Roman Life* (Chicago: Scott, Foresman, and Co., 1957), p. 172.

Key Terms

pax Romana (p. 146)

principate (p. 146)

constitutional monarchy (p. 147)

imperator (p. 147)

barbarians (p. 150)

Praetorians (p. 154)

five good emperors (p. 155)

gladiators (p. 158)

villa (p. 161)

Messiah (p. 165)

pagans (p. 166)

heresy (p. 167)

Gentiles (p. 168)

catacombs (p. 168)

barracks emperors (p. 171)

For practice quizzes and other study tools, visit the Online Study Guide at **bedfordstmartins.com/mckaywest**.

For primary sources from this period, see ***Sources of Western Society***, **Second Edition**.

For Web sites, images, and documents related to topics in this chapter, visit Make History at **bedfordstmartins.com/mckaywest**.

Reconstruction Under Diocletian and Constantine

How did the Roman emperors Diocletian and Constantine attempt to strengthen the Roman Empire, and which of their reforms had long-lasting effects on the empire? ▪

In the middle of the third century, the Roman Empire faced internal turmoil and external attacks. But in the early fourth century, the emperor Diocletian (r. 284–305), who had risen through the ranks of the military to become emperor, restored order, and his successor, Constantine (r. 306–337), continued his work. Economic, social, and religious problems confronted Diocletian and Constantine. They needed additional revenues to support the army and the imperial court, but the wars and invasions had struck a serious blow to Roman agriculture, the primary source of tax revenues. Christianity had become too strong either to ignore or to crush. How Diocletian, Constantine, and their successors responded to these problems influenced later developments.

diocese An administrative unit in the later Roman Empire; adopted by the Christian church as the territory under the authority of a bishop.

tetrarchy Diocletian's four-part division of the Roman Empire.

Map 7.1 The Division of the Roman World, 293 Under Diocletian, the Roman Empire was first divided into a western and an eastern half, a development that foreshadowed the medieval division between the Latin West and the Byzantine East.

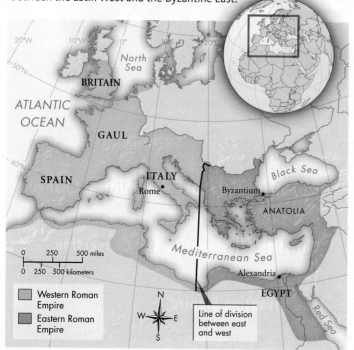

- Western Roman Empire
- Eastern Roman Empire

Line of division between east and west

Political Measures

Under Diocletian, Augustus's polite fiction of the emperor as first among equals gave way to the emperor as absolute autocrat. The princeps became *dominus* (lord). The emperor claimed that he was "the elect of god"— that he ruled because of divine favor. To underline the emperor's exalted position, Diocletian and Constantine adopted the gaudy court ceremonies and trappings of the Persian Empire. People entering the emperor's presence prostrated themselves before him and kissed the hem of his robes.

Diocletian recognized that the empire had become too great for one man to handle and divided it into a western half and an eastern half (Map 7.1). Diocletian assumed direct control of the eastern part; he gave the rule of the western part to a colleague, along with the title *augustus*. Around 293 Diocletian further delegated power by appointing two men to assist the augustus and him, each given the title *caesar*. He further divided each half of the empire into two prefectures and organized the prefectures into administrative units called **dioceses**, which were in turn subdivided into small provinces. Although this system is known as the **tetrarchy** (TEE-trahr-kee) because four men ruled the empire, Diocletian was clearly the senior partner and final source of authority.

Diocletian's political reforms were a momentous step. The reorganization made the empire easier to administer, and placed each of the four central military commands much closer to borders or other trouble spots, so that troops could be sent more quickly when needed. The tetrarchy soon failed because of succession problems, but much of Diocletian's reorganization remained.

Like Diocletian, Constantine came up through the army and ruled from the east, though he had authority over the entire empire. He established a new capital for the empire at Byzantium, an old Greek city on the Bosporus, naming it "New Rome," though it was soon called Constantinople. He sponsored a massive building program of palaces, warehouses, public buildings, and even a hippodrome for horse racing, modeling these on Roman buildings. He built defensive works along the borders of the empire, trying hard to keep it together, as did his successors. Despite their efforts, however, throughout the fourth century, the eastern and the western halves drifted apart.

Economic Issues

Diocletian inherited an empire that was less capable of recovery than in earlier times. Wars and invasions had disrupted normal commerce and the means of production. Mines were exhausted in the attempt to supply much-needed ores, especially gold and silver. In the cities, markets ceased to function, and travel became

Diocletian's Tetrarchy This sculpture represents the possibilities and problems of the tetrarchy established by the emperor Diocletian to rule the Roman Empire. Each of the four men has one hand on another's shoulder, a symbol of solidarity, but the other on his sword, a gesture that proved prophetic when the tetrarchy failed soon after Diocletian's death and another struggle for power began. (Alinari/Art Resource, NY)

ca. 293	Diocletian establishes the tetrarchy
312	Constantine legalizes Christianity in the Roman Empire
325	Council of Nicaea
354–430	Life of Saint Augustine
378	Visigoths defeat the Roman army at Adrianople
380	Theodosius makes Christianity the official religion of the Roman Empire
410	Visigoths sack Rome
476	Odoacer deposes the last Roman emperor in the West
ca. 481–511	Reign of Clovis
493	Theoderic establishes an Ostrogothic state in Italy
527–565	Reign of Justinian
529	*The Rule of Saint Benedict*
597	Pope Gregory I sends missionaries to Britain

dangerous. Merchant and artisan families rapidly left devastated regions. The barracks emperors who preceded Diocletian had dealt with economic hardship by cutting the silver content of coins until money was virtually worthless. The immediate result was crippling inflation throughout the empire.

Diocletian's attempt to curb inflation illustrates the methods of absolute monarchy. In a move unprecedented in Roman history, he issued an edict that fixed maximum prices and wages throughout the empire. He and his assistant emperors dealt with the tax system just as strictly and inflexibly. Taxes became payable in kind, that is, in goods or produce instead of money, which made them difficult to transport to central authorities. Constantine continued these measures and also made

occupations more rigid: all people involved in the growing, preparation, and transportation of food and other essentials were locked into their professions. A baker, for example, could not go into any other business, and his son took up the trade at his death. In this period of severe depression many individuals and communities could not pay their taxes. In such cases local tax collectors, who were also locked into service, had to make up the difference from their own funds. This system soon wiped out a whole class of moderately wealthy people.

The emperors' measures did nothing to address central economic problems. Because of worsening conditions during the third and fourth centuries, many free tenant farmers and their families were killed, fled the land to escape the barbarians, or abandoned farms ravaged in the fighting. Consequently, large tracts of land lay deserted. Great landlords with ample resources began at once to reclaim as much of this land as they could. The huge villas that resulted were self-sufficient. Because they often produced more than they consumed, they successfully competed with the declining cities by selling their surplus in the countryside. They became islands of stability in an unsettled world.

The rural residents who remained on the land were exposed to the raids of barbarians or robbers and to the tyranny of imperial officials. In return for the protection and security landlords could offer, small landholders gave over their lands and their freedom. To guarantee a supply of labor, landlords denied them freedom to move elsewhere. Henceforth they and their families worked their patrons' land, not their own. Free men and women were becoming tenant farmers bound to the land, what would later be called serfs.

The Acceptance of Christianity

The turmoil of the third century seemed to some emperors, including Diocletian, to be the punishment of the gods. They stepped up persecution of Christians who would not sacrifice to Rome's traditional deities and were thus portrayed as disloyal to the empire. These persecutions were never very widespread or long-lived, however, for by the late third century most pagans had become used to Christianity. Constantine made this toleration official, legalizing the practice of Christianity throughout the empire in 312 and later being baptized as a Christian. He supported the church throughout his reign, expecting in return the support of church officials in maintaining order. Constantine freed the clergy from imperial taxation and endowed the building of Christian churches. One of his gifts—the Lateran (LAHT-ur-uhn) Palace in Rome—remained the official residence of the popes until the four-

Arianism A theological belief that originated with Arius, a priest of Alexandria, denying that Christ was divine and co-eternal with God the Father.

heresy The denial of a basic doctrine of faith.

teenth century. He allowed others to make gifts to the church as well, decreeing in 321 that "Every man, when dying, shall have the right to bequeath as much of his property as he desires to the holy and venerable Catholic Church. And such wills are not to be broken."[1] Constantine also declared Sunday a public holiday, a day of rest for the service of God. Because of its favored position in the empire, Christianity slowly became the leading religion (Map 7.2).

In the fourth century theological disputes having to do with the nature of Christ divided the Christian community. For example, **Arianism** (AI-ree-uh-nih-zuhm), developed by Arius (ca. 250–336), a priest of Alexandria, held that Jesus was created by the will of God the Father and thus was not co-eternal with him. Arians reasoned that Jesus the Son must be inferior to God the Father because the Father was incapable of suffering and did not die. Many theologians branded Arius's position a **heresy**, that is, a belief that contradicted what was becoming the more widely accepted position on this issue.

Arianism enjoyed such popularity and provoked such controversy that Constantine, to whom, as he put

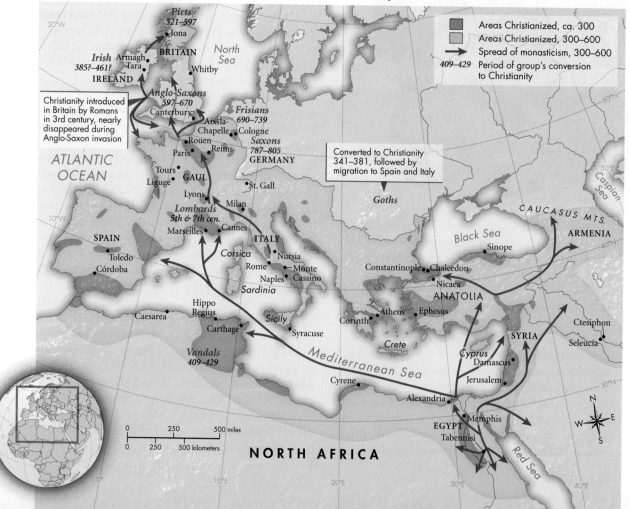

Map 7.2 **The Spread of Christianity to 600** Originating in Judaea, the southern part of modern Israel and Jordan, Christianity first spread throughout the Roman world and then beyond it in all directions.

it, "internal strife within the Church of God is far more evil and dangerous than any kind of war and conflict," interceded. In 325 he summoned church leaders to a council in Nicaea (nigh-SEE-uh) in Asia Minor and presided over it personally "as your fellow servant of our common Lord and Savior."[2] The council produced the Nicene (nigh-SEEN) Creed, which defined the position that Christ is "eternally begotten of the Father" and of the same substance as the Father. Arius and those who refused to accept Nicene Christianity were banished, the first case of civil punishment for heresy. This did not end Arianism, however. Several later emperors were Arian, and Arian missionaries converted many barbarian tribes, who were attracted by the idea that Jesus was God's first-in-command, which fit well with their own warrior hierarchies and was less complicated than the idea of two persons with one substance. The Nicene Creed says little specifically about the Holy Spirit, but in the following centuries the idea that the Father, Son, and Holy Spirit are "one substance in three persons"—the Trinity—became a central doctrine in Christianity, though again there were dissenters.

In 380 the emperor Theodosius (thee-uh-DOH-shee-uhs) made Nicene Christianity the official religion of the empire. Theodosius stripped Roman pagan temples of statues, made the practice of the old Roman state religion a treasonable offense, and persecuted Christians who dissented from orthodox doctrine. Most significant, he allowed the church to establish its own courts and to use its own body of law, called "canon law." The church courts, not the Roman government, had jurisdiction over the clergy and ecclesiastical disputes. At the death of Theodosius, the Christian church was considerably independent of the Roman state. The foundation for later growth in church power had been laid.

Later emperors continued the pattern of active involvement in church affairs. They appointed the highest officials of the church hierarchy; the emperors or their representatives presided at ecumenical councils; and the emperors controlled some of the material resources of the church—land, rents, and dependent peasantry. On the other hand, emperors after Theodosius rarely tried to impose their views in theological disputes.

The Growth of the Christian Church

How did the Christian church develop institutionally and intellectually? ■

As the emperors changed their policies about Christianity from persecution to promotion, the church grew, gradually becoming the most important institution in Europe. The able administrators and highly creative thinkers of the church developed permanent institutions and complex philosophical concepts that drew on the Greco-Roman tradition.

Sarcophagus of Helena This marble sarcophagus was made for Helena, the mother of Emperor Constantine, at her death. Its detailed carvings show victorious Roman horsemen and barbarian prisoners. Like her son, Helena became a Christian. She was sent by Constantine on a journey to bring sacred relics from Jerusalem to Constantinople as part of his efforts to promote Christianity in the empire. (Vanni/Art Resource, NY)

The Church and Its Leaders

The early Christian church benefited from the brilliant administrative abilities of some church leaders. With the empire in decay, educated people joined and worked for the church in the belief that it was the one institution able to provide leadership. Bishop Ambrose of Milan (339–397) is typical of the Roman aristocrats who held high public office, were converted to Christianity, and subsequently became bishops. Like many bishops, Ambrose had a solid education in classical law and rhetoric, which he used to become an eloquent preacher. He had a strong sense of his authority and even stood up to Emperor Theodosius, who had ordered Ambrose to hand over his major church—called a basilica—to the emperor:

apostolic succession The doctrine that all bishops can trace their spiritual ancestry back to Jesus' apostles.

> At length came the command, "Deliver up the Basilica"; I reply, "It is not lawful for us to deliver it up, nor for your Majesty to receive it. By no law can you violate the house of a private man, and do you think that the house of God may be taken away? . . . But do not burden your conscience with the thought that you have any right as Emperor over sacred things. . . . It is written, God's to God and Caesar's to Caesar. The palace is the Emperor's, the churches are the Bishop's. To you is committed jurisdiction over public, not over sacred buildings."[3]

The emperor relented. Ambrose's assertion that the church was supreme in spiritual matters and the state in secular issues was to serve as the cornerstone of the church's position on church-state relations for centuries. Ambrose came to be regarded as one of the fathers of the church, early Christian thinkers whose authority was regarded as second only to the Bible in later centuries.

During the reign of Diocletian, the Roman Empire had been divided for administrative purposes into geographical units called dioceses. Gradually the church adapted this organizational structure. The territory under the authority of a bishop was also called a diocese, with its center a cathedral (from the Latin *cathedra*, meaning "chair"), the church that contained the bishop's official seat of power. A bishop's jurisdiction extended throughout the diocese, and he came

❝ It is written, God's to God and Caesar's to Caesar. The palace is the Emperor's, the churches are the Bishop's. **❞**

—BISHOP AMBROSE OF MILAN

to control a large amount of land that was given to or purchased by the church. Bishops generally came from prominent families and had both spiritual and political power. They claimed to trace their spiritual ancestry back to Jesus' apostles, a doctrine called **apostolic succession**. Because of the special importance of their dioceses, five bishops—those of Antioch, Alexandria, Jerusalem, Constantinople, and Rome—gained the title of patriarch. Their jurisdictions extended over large regions; they consecrated bishops, investigated heresy, and heard judicial appeals.

After the removal of the capital and the emperor to Constantinople, the power of the bishop of Rome grew because he was the only patriarch in the Western Roman Empire. The bishops of Rome stressed that Rome had special significance because of its history as the capital of a worldwide empire. More significantly, they asserted,

Saint Jerome and Saint Ambrose A later woodcarving shows Saint Ambrose and Saint Jerome, two of the most important early church fathers, hard at work writing. Divine inspiration appears in the form of an angel and a dove. (Alinari/Art Resource, NY)

Rome had a special place in Christian history. According to tradition, Saint Peter, chief of Jesus' disciples, had lived in Rome and been its first bishop. His bones and those of disciple Saint Paul were in Rome. Thus as successors of Peter, the bishops of Rome—known as "popes," from the Latin word *papa*, meaning "father"—claimed a privileged position in the church hierarchy, an idea called the **Petrine Doctrine**. They stressed their supremacy over other Christian communities and urged other churches to appeal to Rome for the resolution of disputed doctrinal issues. Not surprisingly, the other patriarchs did not agree. They continued to exercise authority in their own regions, and local churches did as well, but the groundwork had been laid for later Roman predominance on religious matters.

In the fifth century the popes also expanded the church's secular authority. Pope Leo I (pontificate 440–461) made treaties with several barbarian leaders who threatened the city of Rome. Gregory I (pontificate 590–604), later called "the Great," made an agreement with the barbarian groups who had cut off Rome's food supply and reorganized church lands to increase production, which he distributed to the poor. He had been an official for the city of Rome before he became a church official, and his administrative and diplomatic talents helped the church expand. He sent missionaries to the British Isles (see page 196) and wrote letters and guides instructing bishops on practical and spiritual matters. He promoted the ideas of Augustine (see page 184), particularly those that defined church rituals as essential for salvation.

The Development of Christian Monasticism

Christianity began and spread as a city religion. Since the first century, however, some especially pious Christians had felt that the only alternative to the decadence of urban life was complete separation from the world. All-consuming pursuit of material things, sexual promiscuity, and general political corruption disgusted them. They believed that the Christian life as set forth in the Gospel could not be lived in the midst of the immorality of Roman society.

This desire to withdraw from ordinary life led to the development of the monastic life. Some scholars believe that the monastic life of asceticism (extreme material sacrifice, including fasting and the renunciation of sex) appealed to Christians who wanted to make a total response to Christ's teachings; like martyrdom, monasticism involved giving up all for Christ. Saint Anthony of Egypt (251?–356), the earliest monk for whom there is concrete evidence and the man later considered the father of monasticism, went to Alexandria during the persecutions of the emperor Diocletian in the hope of gaining martyrdom. Christians believed that monks,

like the early Christian martyrs executed by Roman authorities before them, could speak to God and that their prayers had special influence.

Monasticism began in Egypt in the third century. At first individuals like Saint Anthony and small groups withdrew from cities and from organized society to seek God through prayer in desert or mountain caves and shelters. Gradually large colonies of monks gathered in the deserts of Upper Egypt. These monks were called hermits, from the Greek word *eremos*, meaning "desert." Many devout women also were attracted to this eremitical (ehr-uh-MIH-tih-uhl) type of monasticism.

> **Petrine Doctrine** A doctrine stating that the popes (the bishops of Rome) were the successors of Saint Peter and therefore heirs to his highest level of authority as chief of the apostles.

The Egyptian ascetic Pachomius (puh-KOH-mee-uhs) (290–346?) drew thousands of men and women to the monastic life at Tabennisi on the Upper Nile. There were too many for them to live as hermits, so Pachomius organized communities of men and women, creating a new type of monasticism, known as coenobitic (seh-nuh-BIH-tik), that emphasized communal living. Saint Basil (329?–379), an influential bishop from Asia Minor and another of the fathers of the church, encouraged coenobitic monasticism. He and much of the church hierarchy thought that communal living provided an environment for training the aspirant in the virtues of charity, poverty, and freedom from self-deception.

Starting in the fourth century, information about Egyptian monasticism came to the West, and both men and women sought the monastic life. Because of the dangers of living alone in the forests of northern Europe, where wild animals, harsh climate, and barbarian tribes posed ongoing threats, the eremitical form of monasticism did not take root. Most of the monasticism that developed in Gaul, Italy, Spain, England, and Ireland was coenobitic.

Monastery Life

In 529 Benedict of Nursia (480–543), who had experimented with both eremitical and communal forms of monastic life, wrote a brief set of regulations for the monks who had gathered around him at Monte Cassino between Rome and Naples. Benedict's guide for monastic life, known as *The Rule of Saint Benedict*, came to influence all forms of organized religious life in the Western Christian church. Men and women in monastic houses all followed sets of rules, first those of Benedict and later those written by other individuals. Because of this, men who lived a communal monastic life came to be called **regular clergy**,

> **regular clergy** Men and women who lived in monastic houses and followed sets of rules, first those of Benedict and later those written by other individuals.

LAS-tih-kuh) (480–543) adapted the *Rule* for use by her community of nuns.

Benedictine monasticism also succeeded partly because it was so materially successful. In the seventh and eighth centuries monasteries pushed back forests and wastelands, drained swamps, and experimented with crop rotation. Benedictine houses made a significant contribution to the agricultural development of Europe. The communal nature of their organization, whereby property was held in common and profits were pooled and reinvested, made this contribution possible.

Finally, monasteries conducted schools for local young people. Some students learned about prescriptions and herbal remedies and went on to provide medical treatment in their localities. A few copied manuscripts and wrote books. Local and royal governments drew on the services of the literate men and able administrators the monasteries produced. This was not what Saint Benedict had intended, but perhaps the effectiveness of the institution he designed made it inevitable.

Christianity and Classical Culture

The growth of Christianity was not simply a matter of institutions such as the papacy and monasteries, but also of ideas. The earliest Christian thinkers sometimes rejected Greco-Roman culture, but as Christianity grew from a tiny persecuted group to the official religion of the Roman Empire, its leaders and thinkers gradually came to terms with classical culture (see Chapter 6). They incorporated elements of Greek and Roman philosophy and learning into Christian teachings, modifying them to fit with Christian notions.

Saint Jerome (340–419), for example, a distinguished theologian and linguist regarded as a father of the church, translated the Old and New Testaments from Hebrew and Greek into vernacular Latin. Called the "Vulgate," his edition of the Bible served as the official translation until the sixteenth century, and scholars rely on it even today. Familiar with the writings of classical authors, Saint Jerome believed that Christians should study the best of ancient thought because it would direct their minds to God. He maintained that the best ancient literature should be interpreted in light of the Christian faith.

from the Latin word *regulus* (rule). Priests and bishops who staffed churches in which people worshiped and who were not cut off from the world were called **secular clergy**. According to official church doctrine, women were not members of the clergy, but this distinction was not clear to most people.

The Rule of Saint Benedict offered a simple code for monks. It outlined a monastic life of regularity, discipline, and moderation in an atmosphere of silence. Each monk had ample food and adequate sleep. The monk spent part of each day in formal prayer, which Benedict called the *Opus Dei* (Work of God). This consisted of chanting psalms and other prayers from the Bible in the part of the monastery church called the "choir." The rest of the day was passed in manual labor, study, and private prayer.

secular clergy Priests and bishops who staffed churches where people worshiped and were not cut off from the world.

Why did the Benedictine form of monasticism eventually replace other forms of Western monasticism? The monastic life as conceived by Saint Benedict struck a balance between asceticism and activity. It thus provided opportunities for men of entirely different abilities and talents — from mechanics to gardeners to literary scholars. The Benedictine form of religious life also proved congenial to women. Five miles from Monte Cassino at Plombariola, Benedict's twin sister Scholastica (skoh-

Christian Notions of Gender and Sexuality

Early Christians both adopted and adapted the then contemporary views of women, marriage, and sexuality. In his plan of salvation, Jesus considered women the equal of men. Women were among the earliest converts to Christianity and took an active role in its spread, preaching, acting as missionaries, being martyred alongside men, and perhaps even baptizing believers. Because early Christians believed that the Second Coming of Christ was imminent, they devoted their energies to their new spiritual family of co-believers. Early Christians often met in people's homes and called one another brother and sister, a metaphorical use of family terms that was new to the Roman Empire. Women and men joyously accepted the ascetic life, renouncing marriage and procreation to use their bodies for a higher calling. Some women, either singly or in monastic communities, declared themselves "virgins in the service of Christ." All this initially made Christianity seem dangerous to many Romans, who viewed marriage as the foundation of society and the proper patriarchal order.

Not all Christian teachings about gender were radical, however. In the first century C.E. male church leaders began to place restrictions on female believers. Women were forbidden to preach and were gradually excluded from holding official positions in Christianity other than in women's monasteries. Women who chose lives of virginity were to be praised; Saint Jerome commented that a woman "who wishes to serve Christ more than the world . . . will cease to be a woman and will be called man," the highest praise he could bestow.[4] Even such women were not to be too independent, however. Both Jewish and classical Mediterranean culture viewed women's subordination as natural and proper, so in limiting the activities of female believers the Christian church was following well-established patterns, just as it modeled its official hierarchy after that of the Roman Empire.

Christian teachings about sexuality built on and challenged classical models. The rejection of sexual activity involved an affirmation of the importance of a spiritual life, but it also incorporated hostility toward the body found in some Hellenistic philosophies. Just as spirit was superior to matter, the mind was superior to the body. Though Christian teachings affirmed that God had created the material world and sanctioned marriage, most Christian thinkers also taught that celibacy was the better life, and that anything that took one's attention from the spiritual world performed an evil function. For most clerical writers (who themselves were male), this temptation came from women, and in some of their writings, women themselves are evil. Thus the writings of the church fathers contain a strong streak of misogyny (hatred of women), which was passed down to later

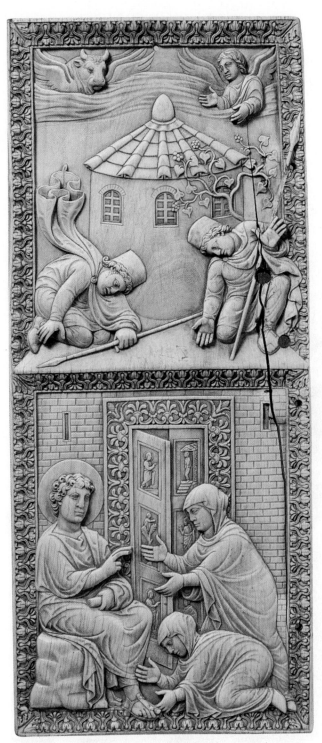

The Marys at Jesus' Tomb This late-fourth-century ivory panel tells the biblical story of Mary Magdalene and another Mary who went to Jesus' tomb to anoint the body (Matthew 28:1–7). At the top guards collapse when an angel descends from Heaven, and at the bottom the Marys listen to the angel telling them that Jesus had risen. Here the artist uses Roman artistic styles to convey Christian subject matter, an example of the assimilation of classical form and Christian teaching.

(Castello Sforzesco/Scala/Art Resource, NY)

Christian thinkers. The church fathers also condemned same-sex relations, which were generally acceptable in the Greco-Roman world, especially if they were between socially unequal individuals.

Saint Augustine on Human Nature, Will, and Sin

The most influential church father in the West was Saint Augustine of Hippo (354–430). Saint Augustine was born into an urban family in what is now Algeria in North Africa. His father, a minor civil servant, was a pa-

gan; his mother, Monica, a devout Christian. Because his family was poor, the only avenue to success in a highly competitive world was a classical education. He excelled at rhetoric and, as was normal for young Roman men, began relations with a concubine, who later had his son.

Augustine took teaching positions first in Rome and then in Milan, where he had frequent conversations with Bishop Ambrose. Through his discussions with Ambrose and his own reading, Augustine became a Christian. He returned to Africa, where his mother and son soon died, and later became bishop of the seacoast city of Hippo Regius. He was a renowned preacher to Christians there, a vigorous defender of orthodox Christianity, and the author of more than ninety-three books and treatises.

Augustine's autobiography, *The Confessions*, is a literary masterpiece and one of the most influential books in the history of Europe. Written in the rhetorical style and language of late Roman antiquity, it marks the synthesis of Greco-Roman forms and Christian thought. *The Confessions* describes Augustine's moral struggle, the conflict between his spiritual and intellectual aspirations and his sensual and material self. Many Greek and Roman philosophers had taught that knowledge and virtue are the same: a person who knows what is right will do what is right. Augustine rejected this idea. People do not always act on the basis of rational knowledge. For example, Augustine considered a life of chastity the best possible life even before he became a Christian. As he notes in *The Confessions*, as a young man he prayed to God for "chastity and continency" and added "but not yet." His education had not made his will strong enough to avoid lust or any other evil; that would come only through God's power and grace.

Augustine's ideas on sin, grace, and redemption became the foundation of all subsequent Western Christian theology, Protestant as well as Catholic. He wrote that the basic force in any individual is the will, which he defined as "the power of the soul to hold on to or to obtain an object without constraint." The end or goal of the will determines the moral character of the individual. When Adam ate the fruit forbidden by God in the Garden of Eden (Genesis 3:6), he committed the "original sin" and corrupted the will. Adam's sin was not simply his own, but was passed on to all later humans through sexual intercourse; even infants were tainted. Original sin thus became a common social stain, in Augustine's opinion, transmitted by concupiscence, or sexual desire. Coitus was theoretically good since it was created by God, but it had been corrupted by sin, so every act of intercourse was evil and every child was conceived through a sinful act. By viewing sexual desire as the result of Adam and Eve's disobedience to divine instructions, Augustine linked sexuality even more clearly with sin than had earlier church fathers. Be-

Heaven in Augustine's *City of God* Augustine's writings were copied and recopied for many centuries in all parts of Europe, and they remained extremely influential. In this copy from a twelfth-century Czech illuminated manuscript of Augustine's *City of God*, the Czech king Wenzeslas and his grandmother are portrayed in the lower right corner; they probably paid for the manuscript. (Erich Lessing/Art Resource, NY)

cause Adam disobeyed God and fell, all human beings have an innate tendency to sin: their will is weak. But according to Augustine, God restores the strength of the will through grace, which is transmitted in certain rituals that the church defined as **sacraments**. Grace results from God's decisions, not from any merit on the part of the individual.

When barbarian forces captured the city of Rome in 410, horrified pagans blamed the disaster on the Christians. In response, Augustine wrote *City of God*. This original work contrasts Christianity with the secular society in which it existed. According to Augustine, history is the account of God acting in time. Human history reveals that there are two kinds of people: those who live the life of the flesh, and those who live the life of the spirit in what Augustine called the City of God. The former will endure eternal hellfire; the latter will enjoy eternal bliss.

Augustine maintained that states came into existence as the result of Adam's fall and people's inclination to sin. He believed that the state was a necessary evil with the power to do good by providing the peace, justice, and order that Christians need in order to pursue their pilgrimage to the City of God. The church is responsible for the salvation of all—including Christian rulers. Church leaders later used Augustine's theory to defend their belief in the ultimate superiority of the spiritual power over the temporal. This remained the dominant political theory until the late thirteenth century.

Whalebone Chest This eighth-century chest made of whalebone, depicting warriors, other human figures, and a horse, tells a story in both pictures and words. The runes along the border are one of the varieties from the British Isles. Contact with the Romans led to the increasing use of the Latin alphabet, though runes and Latin letters were used side-by-side in some parts of northern Europe for centuries. (Erich Lessing/Art Resource, NY)

Barbarian Society

What patterns of social, political, and economic life characterized barbarian society? ■

Augustine's *City of God* was written in response to the conquest of Rome by an army of Visigoths, one of the many peoples the Romans—and later historians—labeled "barbarians." The word *barbarian* comes from the Greek *barbaro*, meaning someone who did not speak Greek. (To the Greeks, others seemed to be speaking nonsense syllables; "barbar" is the Greek equivalent of "blah-blah" or "yada-yada.") The Greeks used this word to include people such as the Egyptians, whom the Greeks respected. As it was used in Latin, however, *barbarian* also came to imply unruly, savage, and primitive, the Romans' judgments of the people who lived beyond the northeastern boundary of Roman territory.

Scholars have long understood the importance of barbarian society, but they have been hampered in investigating it because most barbarian groups did not write and thus kept no written records before Christian missionaries introduced writing. Greek and Roman authors did describe barbarian society, but they were not always objective observers, instead using barbarians to highlight what they thought was right or wrong about their own cultures. Thus written records must be combined with archaeological evidence to gain a more accurate picture.

In addition, historians are increasingly deciphering and using the barbarians' written records that do exist, especially inscriptions carved in stone, bone, and wood and written in the **runic alphabet**. Runic inscriptions come primarily from Scandinavia and the British Isles. Most are short and limited to names, but some describe the actions of kings and other powerful individuals, and a few of them mention the activities of more ordinary people.

Barbarians included many different ethnic groups with social and political structures, languages, laws, and beliefs developed in central and northern Europe over many centuries. Among the largest barbarian groups were Celts (whom the Romans called Gauls) and Germans; Germans were further subdivided into various tribes, such as Ostrogoths, Visigoths, Burgundians, and Franks. *Celt* and *German* are often used as ethnic terms, but they are better understood as linguistic terms, a Celt

sacraments Certain rituals defined by the church in which God bestows benefits on the believer through grace.

runic alphabet Writing system developed in some barbarian groups that helps to give a more accurate picture of barbarian society.

being a person who spoke a Celtic language, an ancestor of the modern Gaelic or Breton language, and a German one who spoke a Germanic language, an ancestor of modern German, Dutch, Danish, Swedish, and Norwegian. Celts, Germans, and other barbarians brought their customs and traditions with them when they moved southward, and these gradually combined with classical and Christian patterns to form a new type of society.

Social and Economic Structures

Barbarian groups usually resided in small villages, and climate and geography determined the basic patterns of how they lived off the land. Many groups lived in small settlements on the edges of clearings where they raised barley, wheat, oats, peas, and beans. Men and women tilled their fields with simple wooden plows and harvested their grains with small iron sickles. The vast majority of people's caloric intake came from grain in some form; the kernels of grain were eaten as porridge, ground up for flour, or fermented into strong, thick beer.

Within the villages, there were great differences in wealth and status. Free men and their families constituted the largest class. The number of cattle a man possessed indicated his wealth and determined his social status. Free men also shared in tribal warfare. Slaves acquired through warfare worked as farm laborers, herdsmen, and household servants.

Ironworking represented the most advanced craft; much of northern Europe had iron deposits, and the dense forests provided wood for charcoal, which was used to provide the clean fire needed to make iron. The typical village had an oven and smiths who produced agricultural tools and instruments of war — one-edged swords, arrowheads, and shields. By the second century C.E. the swords produced by barbarian smiths were superior to the weapons of Roman troops.

In the first two centuries C.E. the quantity and quality of barbarian goods increased dramatically. Goods were used locally and for gift giving, a major social custom. Gift giving conferred status on the giver, whose giving showed his higher (economic) status, cemented friendship, and placed the receiver in his debt. Goods were also traded, though commercial exchange was less important in the barbarian world than in the Roman Empire. Most things that could not be produced in the village were acquired by raiding and warfare rather than by trade.

Barbarian tribes were made up of kin groups comprised of families, the basic social unit in barbarian society. Families were responsible for the debts and actions of their members and for keeping the peace in general. Barbarian law codes set strict rules of inheritance based on position in the family and often set aside a portion of land that could not be sold or given away by any family member so that the family always retained some land.

Visigothic Work and Play
This page comes from one of the very few manuscripts from late antiquity to have survived, a copy of the first five books of the Old Testament — the Pentateuch — made around 600, perhaps in Visigothic Spain or North Africa. The top shows biblical scenes, while the bottom shows people engaged in everyday activities — building a wall, drawing water from a well, and trading punches. (Bibliothèque nationale de France)

Barbarian society was patriarchal: within each household the father had authority over his wife, children, and slaves. Some wealthy and powerful men had more than one wife, a pattern that continued even after they became Christian, but polygamy was not widespread among ordinary people. A woman was considered to be under the legal guardianship of a man, and she had fewer rights to own property than did Roman women. However, once women were widowed (and there must have been many widows in such a violent, warring society), they sometimes assumed their husbands' rights over family property and held the guardianship of their children.

Chiefs and Warriors

Barbarians generally had no notion of the state as we use the term today; they thought in social, not political, terms. The basic social unit was the tribe, a group whose members believed that they were all descended from a common ancestor. Blood united the tribe; kinship protected the members. Every tribe had its customs, and every member knew what they were.

Barbarian tribes were led by tribal chieftains. The chief was the member recognized as the strongest and bravest in battle and was elected from among the male members of the most powerful family. He led the tribe in war, settled disputes among its members, conducted negotiations with outside powers, and offered sacrifices to the gods. The period of migrations and conquests of the Western Roman Empire witnessed the strengthening of the power of chiefs, who often adopted the title of king, though this title implies broader power than they actually had.

Closely associated with the chief in some tribes was the **comitatus**, or "war band." These warriors swore loyalty to the chief, fought with him in battle, and were not supposed to leave the battlefield without him; to do so implied cowardice, disloyalty, and social disgrace. A social egalitarianism existed among members of the war band. The comitatus had importance for the later development of feudalism.

During the migrations and warfare of the third and fourth centuries, the war band was transformed into a system of stratified ranks. Among the Ostrogoths, for example, a warrior nobility evolved. Contact with the Romans stimulated demand for goods such as armbands, which the Romans produced for trade with barbarian groups. Thus armbands, especially the gold ones reserved for elite "royal families," promoted the development of hierarchical ranks within war bands. During the Ostrogothic conquest of Italy, warrior-nobles also began to acquire land as both a mark of prestige and a means to power. As land and wealth came into the hands of a small elite class, social inequalities within the tribe emerged and gradually grew stronger. These inequalities help explain the origins of the European noble class.

Barbarian Law

Early barbarian tribes had no written laws. Law was custom, but certain individuals were often given special training in remembering and retelling laws from generation to generation. Beginning in the late sixth century, however, some tribal chieftains began to collect, write, and publish lists of their customs and laws at the urging of Christian missionaries. The churchmen wanted to understand barbarian ways in order to assimilate the tribes into Christianity. Moreover, by the sixth century many barbarian kings needed written regulations for the Romans under their jurisdiction as well as for their own people.

The law code of the Salian Franks, one of the barbarian tribes, includes a feature common to many barbarian codes. Any crime that involved a personal injury, such as assault, rape, and murder, was given a particular monetary value, called the **wergeld** (WUHR-gehld) (literally "man-money" or "money to buy off the spear"), that was to be paid by the perpetrator to the victim or the family. The Salic law lists many of these:

> If any person strike another on the head so that the brain appears, and the three bones which lie above the brain shall project, he shall be sentenced to 1200 denars, which make 300 shillings. . . .
> If any one have killed a free woman after she has begun bearing children, he shall be sentenced to 2400 denars, which make 600 shillings.[5]

The wergeld varied according to the severity of the crime and also the social status of the victim. The very high fine of 600 shillings for the murder of a woman of childbearing years—the same value attached to military officers of the king, to priests, and to boys preparing to become warriors—suggests the importance of women in Frankish society, at least for their childbearing capacity.

If a person accused of a crime agreed to pay the wergeld and if the victim and his or her family accepted the payment, there was peace. If the accused refused to pay the wergeld or if the victim's family refused to accept it, a blood feud ensued. In this way barbarian law aimed to prevent or reduce violence.

At first, Romans had been subject to Roman law and barbarians to barbarian custom. As barbarian kings accepted Christianity and as Romans and barbarians increasingly intermarried, the distinction between the two sets of law blurred and, in the course of the seventh and eighth centuries, disappeared. The result would be the new feudal law, to which all who lived in certain areas were subject.

comitatus A war band of young men in a barbarian tribe who were closely associated with the king, swore loyalty to him, and fought with him in battle.

wergeld Compensatory payment for death or injury set in many barbarian law codes.

Barbarian Religion

Like Greeks and Romans, barbarians worshiped hundreds of gods and goddesses with specialized functions. They regarded certain mountains, lakes, rivers, or groves of trees as sacred because these were linked to deities. Rituals to honor the gods were held outdoors rather than in temples or churches, often at certain points in the yearly agricultural cycle. Presided over by a priest or priestess understood to have special abilities to call on the gods' powers, rituals sometimes involved animal (and perhaps human) sacrifice. Among the Celts, religious leaders called druids (DROO-ihds) had legal and educational as well as religious functions, orally passing down laws and traditions from generation to generation. Bards singing poems and ballads also passed down myths and stories of heroes and gods, which were written down much later.

The first written records of barbarian religion—as of other aspects of barbarian culture—came from Greeks and Romans who encountered barbarians or spoke with those who had. They understood barbarian traditions through their own belief systems, often equating barbarian gods with Greco-Roman ones and adapting stories and rituals to blend the two. This assimilation appears to have gone both ways, at least judging by the names of the days of the week. In the Roman Empire, the days took their names from Roman deities or astronomical bodies, and they acquired those of corresponding barbarian gods in the Germanic languages of central and northern Europe. Jupiter's day, for example, became Thor's day (Thursday); both of these powerful gods were associated with thunder.

Barbarian Migrations and Political Change

What were some of the causes of the barbarian migrations, and how did they affect the regions of Europe? ■

Migrating groups that the Romans labeled barbarians had pressed along the Rhine-Danube frontier of the Roman Empire off and on since about 100 B.C.E. (see Chapters 5 and 6). As this threat grew in the third and fourth centuries C.E., Roman armies sought to defend the border, but with troop levels low due to illness and a low birthrate, generals were forced to recruit barbarians to fill the ranks of the Roman army. Barbarian refugees and enslaved prisoners of war joined Roman units, and free barbarian units, called *foederati*, allied themselves with Rome. Some barbarian leaders rose to the highest ranks of the Roman army and often assimilated into Roman culture, incorporating their own traditions and intermarrying with Roman families. By the fourth century barbarians made up the majority of those fighting both for and against Rome, and climbed higher and higher in the ranks of the Roman military. Toward the end of the fifth century this barbarian assumption of authority stretched all the way to the top, and the last person with the title of emperor in the Western Roman Empire was deposed by a barbarian general.

Why did the barbarians migrate? In part they were searching for more regular supplies of food, better farmland, and a warmer climate. In part they were pushed by groups living farther eastward, especially by the Huns from Central Asia in the fourth and fifth centuries. Conflicts within and among barbarian groups also led to war and disruption, which motivated groups to move (Map 7.3). Franks fought Alamanni in Gaul; Visigoths fought Vandals in the Iberian Peninsula and across North Africa; and Angles and Saxons fought Britons in England.

Celtic and Germanic People in Gaul and Britain

The Celts present a good example of both assimilation and conflict. Celtic-speaking peoples had lived in central Europe since at least the fifth century B.C.E. and spread out from there to the Iberian Peninsula in the west,

Celtic Brooch This magnificent silver and gold brooch, used to hold a heavy wool cape in place, is decorated with red garnets and complex patterns of interlace. Made in Ireland, its patterns are similar to those found on Irish manuscripts from this era. (National Museum of Ireland, Dublin/ Photo © Boltin Picture Library/The Bridgeman Art Library)

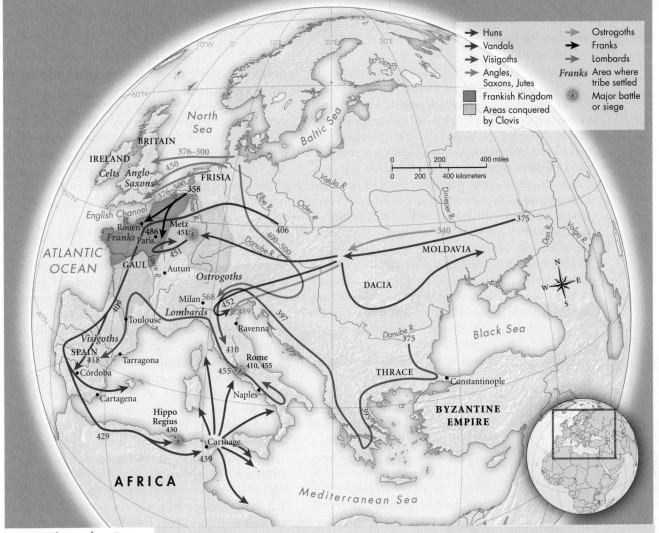

Mapping the Past

Map 7.3 **The Barbarian Migrations, ca. 340–500** This map shows the migrations of various barbarian groups in late antiquity and can be used to answer the following questions.

ANALYZING THE MAP The movements of barbarian peoples used to be labeled "invasions" and are now usually described as "migrations." How do the dates on the map support the newer understanding of these movements?

CONNECTIONS Human migration is caused by a combination of push factors—circumstances that lead people to leave a place—and pull factors—things that attract people to a new location. Based on the information in this and earlier chapters, what push and pull factors might have shaped the migration patterns you see on the map?

To complete this activity online, go to the Online Study Guide at bedfordstmartins.com/mckaywest.

Hungary in the east, and the British Isles in the north. (The Welsh, Britons, and Irish are all peoples of Celtic descent.) As Julius Caesar advanced northward into what he termed Gaul (present-day France) between 58 and 50 B.C.E. (see Chapter 5), he defeated many Celtic tribes. Celtic peoples conquered by the Romans often assimilated Roman ways, adapting the Latin language and other aspects of Roman culture. In Roman Gaul and then in Roman Britain, towns were planned in the Roman fashion, with temples, public baths, theaters, and amphitheaters. In the countryside large manors controlled the surrounding lands. Roman merchants brought Eastern luxury goods and Eastern religions—including Chris-

tianity. The Romans suppressed the Celtic chieftains, and a military aristocracy made up of Romans—some of whom intermarried with Celtic families—governed. In the course of the second and third centuries, many Celts became Roman citizens and joined the Roman army.

By the fourth century C.E. Gaul and Britain were under pressure from Germanic groups moving westward, and Rome itself was threatened (see Map 7.3). Imperial troops withdrew from Britain in order to defend Rome, and the Picts from Scotland and the Scots from Ireland (both Celtic-speaking peoples) invaded territory held by the Britons. According to the eighth-century historian Bede (beed), the Briton king Vortigern invited the Saxons from Denmark to help him against his rivals. Saxons and other Germanic tribes from the area of modern-day Norway, Sweden, and Denmark turned from assistance to conquest, attacking in a hit-and-run fashion. Their goal was plunder, and at first their invasions led to no permanent settlements. As more Germanic peoples arrived, however, they took over the best lands and eventually conquered most of Britain. Some Britons fled to Wales and the westernmost parts of England, north toward Scotland, and across the English Channel to Brittany. Others remained and eventually intermarried with Germanic peoples.

Historians have labeled the years 500 to 1066 (the year of the Norman Conquest) the Anglo-Saxon period of English history, after the two largest Germanic tribes, the Angles and the Saxons. The Germanic tribes destroyed Roman culture in Britain. Christianity disappeared, large urban buildings were allowed to fall apart, and tribal custom superseded Roman law.

Anglo-Saxon England was divided along ethnic and political lines. The Germanic kingdoms in the south, east, and center were opposed by the Britons in the west, who wanted to get rid of the invaders. The Anglo-Saxon kingdoms also fought among themselves, causing boundaries to shift constantly. Finally, in the ninth century, under pressure from the Viking invasions, the Celtic Britons and the Germanic Anglo-Saxons were molded together under the leadership of King Alfred of Wessex (r. 871–899).

The Anglo-Saxon invasion gave rise to a rich body of Celtic mythology, particularly legends about King Arthur, who first appeared in Welsh poetry in the sixth century and later in histories, epics, and saints' lives. Most scholars see Arthur as a composite figure that evolved over the centuries in songs and stories. In their earliest form as Welsh poems, the Arthurian legends may represent Celtic hostility to Anglo-Saxon invaders, but they later came to be more important as representations of the ideal of medieval knightly chivalry and as great stories whose retelling has continued to the present.

Visigoths and Huns

Germanic peoples included a number of groups with very different cultural traditions. The largest Germanic tribe, the Goths, was a polyethnic group consisting of perhaps one hundred thousand people, including fifteen thousand to twenty thousand warriors. The tribe was supplemented by slaves and poor farmers who, because of their desperate situation under Roman rule, joined the Goths during their migrations. Based on their migration patterns, Goths have been further subdivided into Ostrogoths (eastern Goths) and Visigoths (western Goths), both of which played important roles in the political developments of late antiquity.

Pressured by defeat in battle, starvation, and the movement of other groups, the Visigoths moved westward from their homeland north of the Black Sea, and in 376 they petitioned the Roman emperor Valens to admit them to the empire. They offered to fight for Rome in exchange for the province of Thrace in what is now Greece and Bulgaria. Seeing in the hordes of warriors the solution to his manpower problem, Valens agreed. The deal fell apart when crop failures led to famine and Roman authorities exploited the Visigoths' hunger by forcing them to sell their own people as slaves in exchange for dog flesh: "the going rate was one dog for one Goth." The Visigoths revolted, joined with other barbarian enemies of Rome, and defeated the Roman army at the Battle of Adrianople in 378, killing Valens and thousands of Roman soldiers in the process. This left a large barbarian army within the borders of the Roman Empire, and not that far from Constantinople.

Valens's successor made peace with the Visigoths, but relations worsened as the Visigoths continued migrating westward (see Map 7.3). Roman soldiers massacred thousands of their Visigothic allies and their families, and in response the Visigothic king Alaric I invaded Italy and sacked Rome in 410. The Visigoths burned and looted the city for three days, which caused many Romans to wonder whether God had deserted them. Seeking to stabilize the situation at home, the imperial government pulled its troops from the British Isles and many areas north of the Alps, leaving these northern areas vulnerable to other migrating groups. A year later Alaric died, and his successor led his people

Anglo-Saxon Helmet This ceremonial bronze helmet from seventh-century England was found inside a ship buried at Sutton Hoo. The nearly 100-foot-long ship was dragged overland before being buried completely. It held one body and many grave goods, including swords, gold buckles, and silver bowls made in Byzantium. The unidentified person who was buried here was clearly wealthy and powerful. (Courtesy of the Trustees of the British Museum)

" Like unreasoning beasts, they are utterly ignorant of the difference between right and wrong. "

—**AMMIANUS MARCELLINUS**

into southwestern Gaul, where they established the Visigothic kingdom.

One significant factor in the migration of the Visigoths and other Germanic peoples was pressure from nomadic steppe peoples from Central Asia. They included the Alans, Avars, Bulgars, Khazars, and most prominently the Huns, who attacked the Black Sea area and the Eastern Roman Empire beginning in the fourth century. The Roman general and historian Ammianus Marcellinus fought the Huns and later described them with both admiration and scorn:

They are not at all adapted to battles on foot, but they are almost glued to their horses, which are hardy, it is true, but ugly. From their horses by night or day every one of the nation buys and sells, eats and drinks, and bowed over the narrow neck of the animal relaxes into a sleep so deep as to be accompanied by many dreams. . . . They are subject to no royal restraint, but they are content with the disorderly government of important men, and led by them they force their way through every obstacle. No one in their country ever plows a field or touches a plowhandle. They are all without fixed abode, without hearth, or law, or settled mode of life. . . . in wagons their wives weave for them their hideous garments, in wagons they cohabit with their husbands, bear children, and rear them. . . . Like unreasoning beasts, they are utterly ignorant of the difference between right and wrong.[6]

Under the leadership of their warrior-king Attila, the Huns swept into central Europe in 451, attacking Roman settlements in the Balkans and Germanic settlements along the Danube and Rhine Rivers. Several Germanic groups allied with them, as did the sister of the Roman emperor, who hoped to take over power from her brother. Their troops combined with those of the Huns, and a huge army took the city of Metz, now in eastern France. After Attila turned his army southward and crossed the Alps into Italy, a papal delegation, including Pope Leo I himself, asked him not to attack Rome. Though papal diplomacy was later credited with stopping the advance of the Huns, a plague that spread among Hunnic troops and their dwindling food supplies were probably much more important.

The Huns retreated from Italy, and within a year Attila was dead. Later leaders were not as effective, and the Huns were never again an important factor in European history. Their conquests had pushed many Germanic groups together, however, which transformed smaller bands into larger, more unified peoples that could more easily pick the Roman Empire apart.

Barbarian Kingdoms and the End of the Roman Empire

After they conquered an area, barbarians generally established states ruled by kings. The kingdoms did not have definite geographical borders, and their locations shifted as tribes moved. In the fifth century the Burgundians ruled over lands roughly circumscribed by the old Roman army camps in what is now central France and western Switzerland. The Visigoths exercised a weak domination over southern France and much of the Iberian Peninsula (modern Spain) until a Muslim victory at Guadalete in 711 ended Visigothic rule. The Vandals, another Germanic tribe whose destructive ways are commemorated in the word *vandal*, swept across Spain into North Africa in 429, and took over what had been Rome's breadbasket. (See "Living in the Past: The Horses of Spain," page 192.)

Barbarian states eventually came to include Italy itself. The Western Roman emperors were generally chosen by the more powerful successors of Constantine in the East, and they increasingly relied on barbarian commanders and their troops to maintain order. In the 470s a series of these commanders took over authority in name as well as in reality, deposing several Roman emperors. In 476 the barbarian chieftain Odoacer (OH-duh-way-suhr) deposed Romulus Augustus, the last person to have the title of Roman emperor in the West. Odoacer did not take on the title of emperor, calling himself instead the king of Italy, so that this date marks the official end of the Roman Empire in the West. Emperor Zeno, the Roman emperor in the East ruling from Constantinople, worried about Odoacer's growing power, and promised Theoderic (r. 471–526), the leader of the Ostrogoths who had recently settled in the Balkans, the right to rule Italy if he defeated Odoacer. Theoderic's forces were successful, and in 493 Theoderic established an Ostrogothic state in Italy, with his capital at Ravenna.

For centuries, the end of the Roman Empire in the West was seen as a major turning point in history, the fall of the sophisticated and educated classical world to uncouth and illiterate tribes. Over the last several decades, however, many historians have put greater stress on continuities. The Ostrogoths, for example, maintained many Roman ways. Old Roman families continued to run the law courts and the city governments, and well-educated

LIVING IN THE PAST

HORSES WERE FIRST DOMESTICATED about 4000 B.C.E. in Central Asia, probably initially for their meat, but quickly for transportation and warfare. By 2000 B.C.E. warriors' graves in what is now southern Russia contained full-size wood and metal chariots and the skeletons of the horses that pulled them. Paintings from Egypt and Mesopotamia show warriors shooting arrows from horse-drawn chariots. Saddles and stir-

rups, which allow riders to sit securely on a horse's back, were developed much later, probably in India or Central Asia. By 200 C.E. mounted archers were an important part of the barbarian armies, both Germanic and Central Asian, that threatened the Roman Empire. The Romans also used horses, and bred them selectively for speed and sturdiness. Owners of large villas ran horse-breeding operations, supplying the Roman army with horses as they supplied the cities with grain.

All of these uses of the horse came together in the Iberian Peninsula, an area the Romans termed Hispania: the Romans raised horses there, and the Vandals and Suevi — two Germanic tribes — and the Alans — a Central Asian steppe people — conquered the area with horses in the fifth century. Later in that century the Visigoths — another Germanic tribe — took over much of the peninsula in campaigns where their skill with horses proved a decisive factor. This would be true for the next conquest of Spain as well, by Muslims in the eighth century, whose Arabian horses — bred for endurance, speed, and intelligence — had allowed them to sweep swiftly across North Africa.

Horses were a weapon of war, but they were also a place to display artistic skill and cultural values. Metal ornaments for horse harnesses are among the relatively few Visigothic

In this mosaic, a Vandal landowner rides out from his Roman-style house. (Courtesy of the Trustees of the British Museum)

Italians continued to study the Greek classics. Theoderic's adviser Boethius (ca. 480–524) translated Aristotle's works on logic from Greek into Latin. While imprisoned after falling out of royal favor, Boethius wrote *The Consolation of Philosophy*, which argued that philosophical inquiry was valuable for understanding God. This became one of the most widely read books in the Middle Ages, though it did not prevent Boethius from being executed for treason.

In other barbarian states, as well, aspects of classical culture continued. Barbarian kings relied on officials trained in Roman law, and Latin remained the language of scholarly communication. Greco-Roman art

and architecture still adorned the land, and people continued to use Roman roads, aqueducts, and buildings. The Christian church in barbarian states modeled its organization on that of Rome, and many bishops were from upper-class families that had governed the empire.

Very recently some historians and archaeologists have returned to an emphasis on change. They note that people may have traveled on Roman roads, but the roads were rarely maintained, and travel itself was much less secure than during the Roman Empire. Merchants no longer traded over long distances, so people's access to goods produced outside their local area plummeted. Knowledge

Two bronze Visigothic harness pendants from Spain in the sixth century C.E.
(Both images copyright © The Metropolitan Museum of Art/Art Resource, NY)

artifacts that have survived, providing a glimpse of an early version of the horse culture that Spanish conquerors brought to the New World in the sixteenth century and that still remains important in Spain.

Visigothic horse bit from the seventh century C.E., made of iron with silver inlay. Bits allowed riders to control horses more effectively.
(Image copyright © The Metropolitan Museum of Art/Art Resource, NY)

QUESTIONS FOR ANALYSIS

1. Looking at the bit, how might the use of horses have served as a stimulus to the development and improvement of metal technology?

2. What do the decorations of the horse harnesses suggest about Visigothic values and technical abilities?

3. Thinking more speculatively, would you expect the use of horses in war to enhance or lessen social and political hierarchies?

about technological processes such as the making of glass and roof tiles declined or disappeared. There was intermarriage and cultural assimilation among Romans and barbarians, but there was also violence and great physical destruction.

The kingdom established by the Franks is a good example of this combination of peaceful assimilation and violent conflict. The Franks were a confederation of Germanic peoples who originated in the marshy lowlands north and east of the northernmost part of the Roman Empire. In the fourth and fifth centuries they settled within the empire and allied with the Romans, some attaining high military and civil positions. The Franks believed that Merovech, a man of supernatural origins, founded their ruling dynasty, which was thus called Merovingian (mehr-uh-VIHN-jee-uhn).

The reign of Clovis (KLOH-vis) (ca. 481–511) marks the decisive period in the development of the Franks as a unified people. Through military campaigns, Clovis acquired the central provinces of Roman Gaul and began to conquer southern Gaul from the Burgundians and Visigoths. Clovis's conversion to Roman Christianity brought him the crucial support of the bishops of Gaul in his campaigns against tribes that were still pagan or had accepted the Arian version of Christianity. (See "Listening to the Past: Gregory of Tours on the

Gregory of Tours on the Conversion of Clovis

LISTENING TO THE PAST

Modern Christian doctrine holds that conversion is a process, the gradual turning toward Jesus and the teachings of the Christian Gospels. But in the early medieval world, conversion was perceived more as a one-time event determined by the tribal chieftain. If he accepted baptism, the mass conversion of his people followed. This selection about the Frankish king Clovis is from The History of the Franks *by Gregory, bishop of Tours (ca. 504–594), written about a century after the events it describes.*

❝ The first child which Clotild bore for Clovis was a son. She wanted to have her baby baptized, and she kept urging her husband to agree to this. "The gods whom you worship are no good," she would say. "They haven't even been able to help themselves, let alone others. . . . Take your Saturn, for example, who ran away from his own son to avoid being exiled from his kingdom, or so they say; and Jupiter, that obscene perpetrator of all sorts of mucky deeds, who couldn't keep his hands off other men, who had his fun with all his female relatives and couldn't even refrain from intercourse with his own sister. . . .

"You ought instead to worship Him who created at a word and out of nothing heaven, and earth, the sea and all that therein is, who made the sun to shine, who lit the sky with stars, who peopled the water with fish, the earth with beasts, the sky with flying creatures, by whose hand the race of man was made, by whose gift all creation is constrained to serve in deference and devotion the man He made." However often the Queen said this, the King came no nearer to belief. . . . The Queen, who was true to her faith, brought her son to be baptized. . . . The child was baptized; he was given the name Ingomer; but no sooner had he received baptism than he died in his white robes. Clovis was extremely angry. He began immediately to reproach his Queen. "If he had been dedicated in the name of my gods," he said, "he would have lived without question; but now that he has been baptized in the name of your God he has not been able to live a single day!"

Ninth-century ivory carving showing Clovis being baptized by Saint Remi.
(Laurie Platt Winfrey/The Granger Collection, New York)

"I give thanks to Almighty God," replied Clotild, "the Creator of all things who has not found me completely unworthy, for He has deigned to welcome into his Kingdom a child conceived in my womb. . . ."

Some time later Clotild bore a second son. He was baptized Chlodomer. He began to ail and Clovis said, "What else do you expect? It will happen to him as it happened to his brother: no sooner is he baptized in the name of your Christ than he will die!" Clotild prayed to the Lord and at His commands the baby recovered.

Queen Clotild continued to pray that her husband might recognize the true God and give up his idol-worship. Nothing could persuade him to accept Christianity. Finally war broke out against the Alamanni and in this conflict he was forced by necessity to accept what he had refused of his own free will. It so turned out that when the two armies met on the battlefield there was a great slaughter and the troops of Clovis were rapidly being annihilated. He raised his eyes to Heaven when he saw this, felt compunction in his heart and was moved to tears. "Jesus Christ," he said, "you who Clotild maintains to be the Son of the living God, you who deign to give help to those in travail and victory to those who trust in you, in faith I beg the glory of your help. If you will give me victory over my enemies, and if I may have evidence to that miraculous power which the people dedicated to your name say that they have experienced, then I will believe in you and I will be baptized in your name. I have called upon my own gods, but, as I see only too clearly, they have no intention of helping me. I therefore cannot believe that they possess any power for they do not come to the assistance of those who trust them. I now call upon you. I want to believe in you, but I must first be saved from my enemies." Even as he said this the Alamanni turned their backs and began to run away. As soon as they saw that their King was killed, they submitted to Clovis. "We beg you," they said, "to put an end to this slaughter. We are prepared to obey you." Clovis stopped the war. He made a speech in which he called for peace. Then he went home. He told the Queen how he had won a victory by calling on the name of Christ. This happened in the fifteenth year of his reign (496).

The Queen then ordered Saint Remigius, Bishop of the town of Rheims (reemz), to be summoned in secret. She begged him to impart the word of salvation to the King. The Bishop asked Clovis to meet him in private and began to urge him to believe in the true God, Maker of Heaven and earth, and to forsake his idols, which were powerless to help him or anyone else. The King replied: "I have listened to you willingly, holy father. There remains one obstacle. The people under my command will not agree to forsake their gods. I will go and put to them what you have just said to me." He arranged a meeting with his people, but God in his power had preceded him, and before he could say a word all those present shouted in unison: "We will give up worshipping our mortal gods, pious King, and we are prepared to follow the immortal God about whom Remigius preaches." This news was reported to the Bishop. He was greatly pleased and he ordered the baptismal pool to be made ready.... The baptistry was prepared, sticks of incense gave off clouds of perfume, sweet-smelling candles gleamed bright and the holy place of baptism was filled with divine fragrance. God filled the hearts of all present with such grace that they imagined themselves to have been transported to some perfumed paradise. King Clovis asked that he might be baptized first by the Bishop. Like some new Constantine he stepped forward to the baptismal pool, ready to wash away the sores of his old leprosy and to be cleansed in flowing water from the sordid stains which he had borne so long.

King Clovis confessed his belief in God Almighty, three in one. He was baptized in the name of the Father, the Son and the Holy Ghost, and marked in holy chrism [an anointing oil] with the sign of the Cross of Christ. More than three thousand of his army were baptized at the same time. 》

Source: Excerpt from pp. 141–144 in *The History of the Franks* by Gregory of Tours, translated with an Introduction by Lewis Thorpe (Penguin Classics, 1974). Copyright © Lewis Thorpe, 1974. Used with permission of Penguin Group (UK).

QUESTIONS FOR ANALYSIS

1. Who took the initiative in urging Clovis's conversion? What can we deduce from that?
2. According to this account, why did Clovis ultimately accept Christianity?
3. For the Salian Franks, what was the best proof of divine power?
4. On the basis of this selection, do you consider *The History of the Franks* reliable history? Why?

Conversion of Clovis," at left.) Along with brutal violence, however, the next two centuries witnessed the steady assimilation of Franks and Romans, as many Franks adopted the Latin language and Roman ways, and Romans copied Frankish customs and Frankish personal names.

From Constantinople, Eastern Roman emperors worked to hold the empire together and to reconquer at least some of the West from barbarian tribes. The emperor Justinian (r. 527–565) waged long and hard-fought wars against the Ostrogoths and temporarily regained Italy and North Africa, but his conquests had disastrous consequences. Justinian's wars exhausted the resources of the state, destroyed Italy's economy, and killed a large part of Italy's population. The wars also paved the way for the easy conquest of Italy by another Germanic tribe, the Lombards, shortly after Justinian's death. In the late sixth century the territory of the Western Roman Empire came once again under barbarian sway.

Frankish lands, 481
Territory gained under Clovis, 482–511

The Reign of Clovis, ca. 481–511

Christian Missionaries and Conversion

What techniques did missionaries develop to convert barbarian peoples to Christianity? ■

The Mediterranean served as the highway over which Christianity spread to the cities of the Roman Empire. Christian teachings were initially carried by all types of converts, but they were often spread into the countryside and into areas beyond the borders of the empire by those who had decided to dedicate their lives to the church, such as monks. Such missionaries were often sent by popes specifically to convert certain groups. As they preached to barbarian peoples, the missionaries developed new techniques to convert them.

Throughout barbarian Europe, religion was not a private or individual matter; it was a social affair, and the religion of the chieftain or king determined the religion of the people. Thus missionaries concentrated their initial efforts not on ordinary people, but on kings or tribal chieftains and the members of their families, who then ordered their subjects to convert. Queens and other female members of the royal family were often the first converts in an area, and they influenced their husbands and brothers. Germanic kings sometimes accepted Christianity because they came to believe that the Christian God

Staffordshire Hoard Artifact with Biblical Inscription This strip of gold bears a biblical inscription in somewhat misspelled Latin asking God for help against enemies. Made in the seventh century, it was buried sometime later along with hundreds of garnet-inlaid gold and silver weapon parts, and was discovered in 2009 in Staffordshire, England, as part of the largest hoard of Anglo-Saxon gold ever found. Who made it, who owned it, and who buried it will no doubt be a source of debate for decades, as the hoard modifies scholarly opinion about Anglo-Saxon England. (Birmingham Museum and Art Gallery)

was more powerful than pagan gods and that the Christian God—in either its Arian or Roman version—would deliver victory in battle. They also appreciated that Christianity taught obedience to kingly as well as divine authority. Christian missionaries were generally literate, and they taught reading and writing to young men who became priests or officials in the royal household, a service that kings appreciated.

Missionaries' Actions

During the Roman occupation, small Christian communities were scattered throughout Gaul and Britain. The effective beginnings of Christianity in Gaul can be traced to Saint Martin of Tours (ca. 316–397), a Roman soldier who, after giving away half his cloak to a naked beggar, had a vision of Christ and was baptized. Martin founded the monastery of Ligugé, the first in Gaul, which became a center for the evangelization of the region. In 372 he became bishop of Tours and introduced a rudimentary parish system in his diocese.

Martin supported Nicene Christianity (see page 179), but many barbarian groups were converted by Arian missionaries, who also founded dioceses. Bishop Ulfilas (ca. 310–383), an Ostrogoth himself, translated the Bible from the Greek in which it was normally written into the Gothic language, creating a new Gothic script in order to write it down. The Ostrogoths, Visigoths, Lombards, and Vandals were all originally Arians, though over the sixth and seventh centuries most of them converted to Roman Christianity, sometimes peacefully and sometimes as a result of conquest.

Tradition identifies the conversion of Ireland with Saint Patrick (ca. 385–461). Born in England to a Christian family of Roman citizenship, Patrick was captured and enslaved by Irish raiders and taken to Ireland, where he worked as a herdsman for six years. He escaped and

returned to England, where a vision urged him to Christianize Ireland. In preparation, Patrick studied in Gaul and was consecrated a bishop in 432. He returned to Ireland, where he converted the Irish tribe by tribe, first baptizing the king. By the time of Patrick's death, the majority of the Irish people had received Christian baptism.

In his missionary work, Patrick had the strong support of Bridget of Kildare (ca. 450–528), daughter of a wealthy chieftain and his concubine. Bridget defied parental pressure to marry and became a nun. She and the other nuns at Kildare instructed relatives and friends in basic Christian doctrine, made religious vestments (clothing) for churches, copied books, taught children, and above all set a religious example by their lives of prayer. In this way, in Ireland and later in continental Europe, women like the nuns at Kildare shared in the process of conversion.

The Christianization of the English began in earnest in 597, when Pope Gregory I sent a delegation of monks under the Roman Augustine to Britain. Augustine's approach, like Patrick's, was to concentrate on converting the king. When he succeeded in converting Ethelbert, king of Kent, the baptism of Ethelbert's people took place as a matter of course. Augustine established his headquarters, or *see*, at Canterbury, the capital of Kent in southern England.

In the course of the seventh century, two Christian forces competed for the conversion of the pagan Anglo-Saxons: Roman-oriented missionaries traveling north from Canterbury, and Celtic monks from Ireland and northwestern Britain. The Roman and Celtic church organizations, types of monastic life, and methods of arriving at the date of the central feast of the Christian calendar, Easter, differed completely. Through the influence of King Oswiu of Northumbria and the energetic abbess Hilda of Whitby, the Synod (ecclesiastical council) held at Hilda's convent of Whitby in 664 opted to follow the Roman practices. The conversion of the English and the close attachment of the English church to Rome had far-reaching consequences because Britain later served as a base for the Christianization of the continent (see Map 7.2), spreading Roman Christian teachings among both pagans and Arians.

The Process of Conversion

When a ruler marched his people to the waters of baptism, the work of Christianization had only begun. Christian kings could order their subjects to be baptized, married, and buried in Christian ceremonies, which they did increasingly across Europe. Churches could be built, and people could be required to attend services and belong to parishes, but the church could not compel people to accept Christian beliefs, many of which seemed strange or radical, such as "love your enemies."

How did missionaries and priests get masses of pagan and illiterate peoples to understand Christian ideals and teachings? They did so through preaching, assimilation, the ritual of penance, and the veneration of saints. Missionaries preached the basic teachings of Christianity in simplified Latin or translated them into the local language. In monasteries and cathedrals, men — and a few women — wrote hymns, prayers, and stories about the lives of Christ and the saints. People heard these and slowly came to be familiar with Christian notions.

Deeply ingrained pagan customs and practices could not be stamped out by words alone, however, or even by royal edicts. Christian missionaries often pursued a policy of assimilation, easing the conversion of pagan men and women by stressing similarities between their customs and beliefs and those of Christianity. In the same way that classically trained scholars such as Jerome and Augustine blended Greco-Roman and Christian ideas, missionaries and converts mixed pagan ideas and practices with Christian ones. Bogs and lakes sacred to Germanic gods became associated with saints, as did various aspects of ordinary life, such as traveling, planting crops, and worrying about a sick child. Aspects of existing midwinter celebrations, which often centered on the return of the sun as the days became longer, were incorporated into celebrations of Christmas. Spring rituals involving eggs and rabbits (both symbols of fertility) were added to Easter.

The ritual of penance was also instrumental in teaching people Christian ideas. Christianity taught that certain actions and thoughts were sins, that is, against God's commands. Only by confessing these sins and asking forgiveness could a sinning believer be reconciled with God. Confession was initially a public ritual, but by the fifth century individual confession to a parish priest was more common. The person knelt before the priest, who questioned him or her about sins he or she might have committed. The priest then set a penance such as fasting or saying specific prayers to allow the person to atone for the sin. The priest and penitent were guided by manuals known as penitentials (peh-nuh-TEHN-shuhlz), which included lists of sins and the appropriate penance. The seventh-century English penitential of Theodore, for example, stipulated that "if a lay Christian vomits because of drunkenness, he shall do penance for fifteen days," while drunken monks were to do penance for thirty days. Those who "commit fornication with a virgin" were to do penance for a year, as were those who perform "divinations according to the custom of the heathens." Penance for killing someone depended on the circumstances; usually it was seven years, but "in revenge for a brother" it was three years, if by accident, one year, and if "by command of his lord" or in "public war," only forty days.[7] Penance gave new Christians a sense of expected behavior, encouraged the private examination of conscience, and offered relief from the burden of sinful deeds.

> **relics** Bones, articles of clothing, or other objects associated with the life of a saint.

Most religious observances continued to be community matters, as they had been in the ancient world. People joined with family members, friends, and neighbors at their parish church to attend baptisms, weddings, and funerals presided over by a priest. The parish church often housed the **relics** of a saint, that is, bones, articles of clothing, or other objects

Reliquary of Sainte Foy Parish churches often housed relics of patron saints. This reliquary contains the relics of Sainte Foy, a young woman thought to have been martyred in France in the third century. In the ninth century her relics were apparently stolen from one church and placed in another, and this jeweled reliquary was made to house them. The church where they ended up was along a popular pilgrimage route, and her cult was spread by pilgrims throughout Europe. (Erich Lessing/Art Resource, NY)

associated with a person who had lived (or died) in a way that was spiritually heroic or noteworthy. This patron saint was understood to provide protection and assistance for those who came to worship, and the relics served as a link between the material world and the spiritual. Miracle stories about saints and their relics were an important part of Christian preaching and writing. Gregory of Tours, for example, a bishop in the Frankish kingdom, described his father's faith in relics:

> Because my father wished himself to be protected by relics of saints, he asked a cleric to grant him something from these relics, so that with their protection he might be kept safe as he set out on this long journey. He put the sacred ashes in a gold medallion and carried it with him. Although he did not even know the names of the blessed men, he was accustomed to recount that he had been rescued from many dangers. He claimed that often, because of the powers of these relics, he had avoided the violence of bandits, the dangers of floods, the threats of turbulent men, and attacks from swords.[8]

Christians came to venerate the saints as powerful and holy. They prayed to saints or to the Virgin Mary to intercede with God, or they simply asked the saints to assist and bless them. The entire village participated in processions marking saints' days or points in the agricultural year, often carrying images of saints or their relics around the houses and fields. The decision to become Christian was often made first by an emperor or king, but actual conversion was a local matter, as people came to feel that the parish priest and the patron saint pro-

vided them with benefits in this world and the world to come.

The Byzantine Empire

How was the Byzantine Empire able to survive for so long, and what were its most important achievements? ■

Barbarian migrations and Christian conversions occurred throughout all of Europe in late antiquity, but their impact was not the same in the Western and Eastern halves of the Roman Empire. The Western Roman Empire gradually disintegrated, but the Roman Empire continued in the East. The Byzantine or Eastern Roman Empire (see Map 7.1) preserved the forms, institutions, and traditions of the old Roman Empire, and its people even called themselves Romans. Byzantine emperors traced their lines back past Constantine to Augustus, and the senate in Constantinople carried on the traditions of the old Roman senate. Most important, however, is how Byzantium protected the intellectual heritage of Greco-Roman civilization and then passed it on to the rest of Europe.

Sources of Byzantine Strength

While the Western parts of the Roman Empire gradually succumbed to barbarian invaders, the Byzantine Empire

Map 7.4 **The Byzantine Empire, ca. 600** The strategic position of Constantinople on the waterway between the Black Sea and the Mediterranean was clear to Constantine when he chose the city as the capital of the Eastern Roman Empire. Byzantine territories in Italy were acquired in Emperor Justinian's sixth-century wars and were held for several centuries.

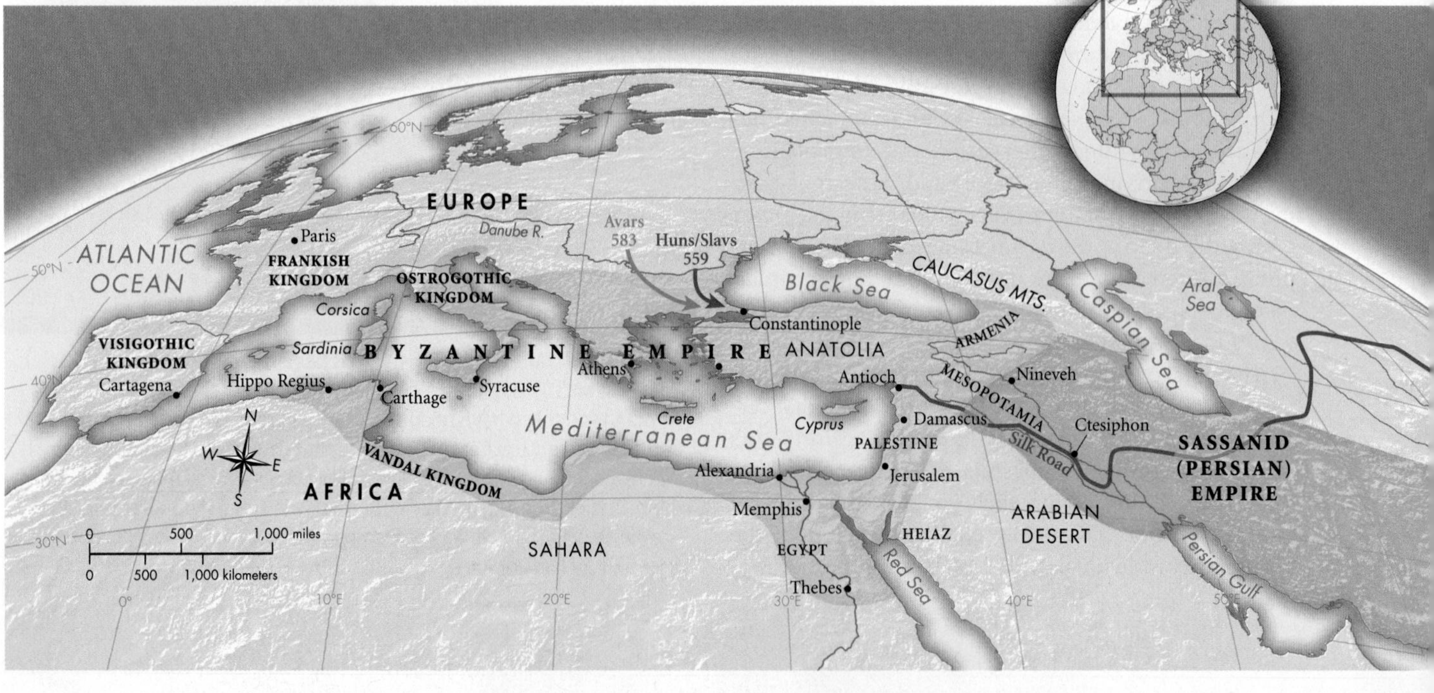

survived Germanic, Persian, and Arab attacks (Map 7.4). In 540 the Huns and Bulgars crossed the Danube and raided as far as southern Greece. In 559 a force of Huns and Slavs reached the gates of Constantinople. In 583 the Avars, a mounted Mongol people who had swept across Russia and southeastern Europe, seized Byzantine forts along the Danube and reached the walls of Constantinople. Between 572 and 630 the Sassanid Persians posed a formidable threat, and the Greeks were repeatedly at war with them. Beginning in 632 Muslim forces pressured the Byzantine Empire (see Chapter 8).

Why didn't one or a combination of these enemies capture Constantinople as the Ostrogoths had taken Rome? The answer lies in strong military leadership and even more in the city's location and its excellent fortifications. Justinian's generals were able to reconquer much of Italy and North Africa from barbarian groups, making them part of the Byzantine Empire. Under the skillful command of General Priskos (d. 612), Byzantine armies inflicted a severe defeat on the Avars in 601, and under Emperor Heraclius I (r. 610–641) they crushed the Persians at Nineveh in Iraq. Massive triple walls, built by the emperors Constantine and Theodosius II (408–450) and kept in good repair, protected Constantinople from sea invasion. Within the walls huge cisterns provided water, and vast gardens and grazing areas supplied vegetables and meat, so the defending people could hold out far longer than the besieging army. Attacking Constantinople by land posed greater geographical and logistical problems than a seventh- or eighth-century government could solve. The site was not absolutely impregnable—as the Venetians demonstrated in 1204 and the Ottoman Turks in 1453—but it was almost so. For centuries, the Byzantine Empire served as a bulwark for the West, protecting it against invasions from the East.

The Law Code of Justinian

One of the most splendid achievements of the Byzantine emperors was the preservation of Roman law for the medieval and modern worlds. Roman law had developed from many sources—decisions by judges, edicts of the emperors, legislation passed by the senate, and the opinions of jurists. By the fourth century it had become a huge, bewildering mass, and its sheer bulk made it almost unusable.

Sweeping and systematic codification took place under the emperor Justinian. He appointed a committee of eminent jurists to sort through and organize the laws. The result was the *Code*, which distilled the legal genius of the Romans into a coherent whole, eliminated outmoded laws and contradictions, and clarified the law itself. Not content with the *Code,* Justinian set about bringing order to the equally huge body of Roman juris-

" Slaves become our property by the Law of Nations when they are either taken from the enemy, or are born of our female slaves. "

—Justinian's *Digest*

prudence (joor-uhs-PROO-duhns), the science or philosophy of law.

During the second and third centuries, the foremost Roman jurists had expressed varied learned opinions on complex legal problems. To harmonize this body of knowledge, Justinian directed his jurists to clear up disputed points and to issue definitive rulings. Accordingly, in 533 his lawyers published the *Digest*, which codified Roman legal thought and contained provisions such as these on slavery:

> *Slaves are brought under our ownership either by the Civil Law or by that of Nations. This is done by the Civil Law where anyone who is over twenty years of age permits himself to be sold for the sake of sharing in his own price [that is, for debt]. Slaves become our property by the Law of Nations when they are either taken from the enemy, or are born of our female slaves. . . .*
>
> *He who conceals a fugitive slave is a thief. . . . And the magistrates are very properly notified to detain fugitive slaves carefully in custody to prevent their escape. . . . Careful custody permits the use of leg irons.*[9]

Finally, Justinian's lawyers compiled a handbook of civil law, the *Institutes*. These three works—the *Code*, the *Digest*, and the *Institutes*—are the backbone of the *corpus juris civilis* (KAWR-puhs JOOR-uhs sih-VIH-luhs), the "body of civil law," which is the foundation of law for nearly every modern European nation.

Byzantine Intellectual Life

The Byzantines prized education; because of them many masterpieces of ancient Greek literature have survived to influence the intellectual life of the modern world. The literature of the Byzantine Empire was predominately Greek, although politicians, scholars, and lawyers also spoke and used Latin. Justinian's *Code* was first written in Latin. More people could read in Byzantium than anywhere else in Christian Europe at the time, and history was a favorite topic.

The most remarkable Byzantine historian was Procopius (ca. 500–562), who left a rousing account praising Justinian's reconquest of North Africa and Italy,

Theodora of Constantinople

INDIVIDUALS IN SOCIETY

THE MOST POWERFUL WOMAN IN BYZANTINE HISTORY was the daughter of a bear trainer for the circus. Theodora (ca. 497–548) grew up in what her contemporaries regarded as an undignified and morally suspect atmosphere, and she worked as a dancer and burlesque actress, both dishonorable occupations in the Roman world. Despite her background, she caught the eye of Justinian, who was then a military leader and whose uncle (and adoptive father) Justin had himself risen from obscurity to become the emperor of the Byzantine Empire. Under Justinian's influence, Justin changed the law to allow an actress who had left her disreputable life to marry whom she liked, and Justinian and Theodora married in 525. When Justinian was proclaimed co-emperor with his uncle Justin on April 1, 527, Theodora received the rare title of *augusta*, empress. Thereafter her name was linked with Justinian's in the exercise of imperial power.

Most of our knowledge of Theodora's early life comes from the *Secret History*, a tell-all description of the vices of Justinian and his court written by Procopius (pruh-KOH-pee-uhs) (ca. 550), who was the official court historian and thus spent his days praising those same people. In the *Secret History* he portrays Theodora and Justinian as demonic, greedy, and vicious, killing courtiers to steal their property. In scene after detailed scene, Procopius portrays Theodora as particularly evil, sexually insatiable, depraved, and cruel, a temptress who used sorcery to attract men, including the hapless Justinian.

In one of his official histories, *The History of the Wars of Justinian*, Procopius presents a very different Theodora. Riots between the supporters of two teams in chariot races — who formed associations somewhat like both street gangs and political parties — had turned deadly, and Justinian wavered in his handling of the perpetrators. Both sides turned against the emperor, besieging the palace while Justinian was inside it. Shouting N-I-K-A (victory), the rioters swept through the city, burning and looting, and destroyed half of Constantinople. Justinian's counselors urged flight, but, according to Procopius, Theodora rose and declared:

> For one who has reigned, it is intolerable to be an exile. . . . If you wish, O Emperor, to save yourself, there is no difficulty: we have ample funds and there are the ships. Yet reflect whether, when you have once escaped to a place of security, you will not prefer death to safety. I agree with an old saying that the purple [that is, the color worn only by emperors] is a fair winding sheet [to be buried in].

Justinian rallied, had the rioters driven into the hippodrome, and ordered between thirty and thirty-five thousand men and women executed. The revolt was crushed and Justinian's authority restored, an outcome approved by Procopius.

Other sources describe or suggest Theodora's influence on imperial policy. Justinian passed a number of laws that improved the legal status of women, such as allowing women to own property the same way that men could and to be guardians over their own children. Justinian is reputed to have consulted her every day about all aspects of state policy, including religious policy regarding the doctrinal disputes that continued throughout his reign. Theodora's influence over her husband and her power in the Byzantine state continued until she died, perhaps of cancer, twenty years before Justinian. Her influence may have even continued after death, for Justinian continued to pass reforms favoring women and, at the end of his life, accepted her interpretation of Christian doctrine. Institutions that she established, including hospitals, orphanages, houses for the rehabilitation of prostitutes, and churches, continued to be reminders of her charity and piety.

Theodora has been viewed as a symbol of the manipulation of beauty and cleverness to attain position and power, and also as a strong and capable co-ruler who held the empire together during riots, revolts, and deadly epidemics. Just as Procopius expressed both views, the debate has continued to today among writers of science fiction and fantasy as well as biographers and historians.

but also wrote the *Secret History*, a vicious and uproarious attack on Justinian and his wife, the empress Theodora. (See "Individuals in Society: Theodora of Constantinople," above.)

Although the Byzantines discovered little that was new in mathematics and geometry, they passed Greco-Roman learning on to the Arabs, who made remarkable advances with it. In science the Byzantines faithfully learned what the ancients had to teach but made advances only in terms of military applications. For example, the best-known Byzantine scientific discovery was an explosive compound known as "Greek fire" that was heated and propelled by a pump through a bronze tube. As the liquid jet left the tube, it was ignited—

The empress Theodora shown with a halo, a symbol of power. Like Justinian, she had power over secular and religious institutions, much to the dismay of many at Justinian's court. (Scala/Art Resource, NY)

QUESTIONS FOR ANALYSIS

1. How would you assess the complex legacy of Theodora?

2. Since the public and private views of Procopius are so different regarding the empress, should he be trusted at all as a historical source?

somewhat like a modern flamethrower. Greek fire saved Constantinople from Arab assault in 678 and was used in both land and sea battles for centuries. In mechanics Byzantine scientists improved and modified artillery and siege machinery.

The Byzantines devoted a great deal of attention to medicine, and the general level of medical competence was far higher in the Byzantine Empire than in western Europe. Yet their physicians could not cope with the terrible disease, often called the "Justinian plague," that swept through the Byzantine Empire and parts of western Europe between 542 and about 560. Probably originating in northwestern India and carried to the Mediterranean region by ships, the disease was similar to that later identified as the bubonic plague. Characterized by high fever, chills, delirium, and enlarged lymph nodes, or by inflammation of the lungs that caused hemorrhages of black blood, the Justinian plague carried off tens of thousands of people. The epidemic had profound political as well as social consequences: it weakened Justinian's military resources, thus hampering his efforts to restore unity to the Mediterranean world.

By the ninth or tenth century, most major Greek cities had hospitals for the care of the sick. The hospitals might be divided into wards for different illnesses, and hospital staff had surgeons, practitioners, and aids with specialized responsibilities. The imperial Byzantine government bore the costs of these medical facilities.

The Orthodox Church

The continuity of the Roman Empire in the East meant that Christianity developed differently there than it did in the West. The emperors in Constantinople were understood to be Christ's representative on earth; their palace was considered holy and was filled with relics and religious images, called icons. Emperors called councils, appointed church officials, and regulated the income of the church. As in Rome, there was a patriarch in Constantinople, but he did not develop the same powers that the pope did in the West because there was never a similar power vacuum into which he needed to step. The **Orthodox church**, the name generally given to the Eastern Christian church, was less independent of secular control than the Western Christian church, although some churchmen did stand up to the emperor. Saint John Chrysostom (ca. 347–407), for example, a bishop and one of the church fathers, thunderously preached against what he saw as the luxury and decadence of the emperor's court and its support of pagan practices, such as erecting statues of rulers. He was banished — twice — but his sermons calling for an ascetic life and support for the poor were copied and recopied for centuries.

> **Orthodox church** Eastern Christian church in the Byzantine Empire.

Monasticism in the Orthodox world differed in fundamental ways from the monasticism that evolved in western Europe. First, while *The Rule of Saint Benedict* gradually became the universal guide for all western European monasteries, each individual house in the Byzantine world developed its own set of rules for organization and behavior. Second, education never became a central feature of Orthodox monasteries. Monks and nuns had

Picturing the Past

Justinian and His Attendants This mosaic indicates the uniting of religious and secular authority in the person of the emperor. It is composed of thousands of tiny cubes of colored glass or stone called *tessarae*, which are set in plaster against a blazing golden background. (Scala/Art Resource, NY)

ANALYZING THE IMAGE Which figure is Justinian, and how did you identify him as such? What types of subjects are shown with him?

CONNECTIONS This representation of Justinian's rule is infused with order and respect. How did Justinian's accomplishments measure up to this depiction?

To complete this activity online, go to the Online Study Guide at bedfordstmartins.com/mckaywest.

to be literate to perform the appropriate rituals, but no Orthodox monastery assumed responsibility for the general training of the local young.

There were also similarities between Western and Eastern monasticism. As in the West, Eastern monasteries became wealthy property owners, with fields, pastures, livestock, and buildings. Since bishops and patriarchs of the Orthodox church were recruited only from the monasteries, these also exercised cultural influence.

Like their counterparts in the West, Byzantine missionaries traveled far beyond the boundaries of the empire seeking converts. In 863 the emperor Michael III sent the brothers Cyril (826–869) and Methodius

(muh-THOH-dee-uhs) (815–885) to preach Christianity in Moravia (the region of modern central Czech Republic). Other missionaries succeeded in converting the Russians in the tenth century. Cyril invented a Slavic alphabet using Greek characters, later termed the "Cyrillic (suh-RIH-lihk) alphabet" in his honor. In the tenth century other missionaries spread Christianity, the Cyrillic alphabet, and Byzantine art and architecture to Russia. The Byzantines were so successful that the Russians would later claim to be the successors of the Byzantine Empire. For a time Moscow was even known as the "Third Rome" (the second Rome being Constantinople).

Greek Fire In this illustration from a twelfth-century manuscript, sailors shoot Greek fire toward an attacking ship from a pressurized tube that looks strikingly similar to a modern flamethrower. The exact formula for Greek fire has been lost, but it was probably made from a petroleum product because it continued burning on water. Greek fire was particularly important in Byzantine defenses of Constantinople from Muslim forces in the late seventh century. (Oronoz)

LOOKING BACK
LOOKING AHEAD

THE CHRISTIAN CHURCH and the barbarian states absorbed many aspects of Roman culture, and the Roman Empire continued to thrive in the East as the Byzantine Empire, but western Europe in 600 was very different than it had been in 250. The Western Roman Empire had slowly disintegrated under pressure from barbarian groups. Barbarian kings ruled small states from Italy to Norway, while churches and monasteries rather than emperors and wealthy individuals took on the role of building new buildings and providing education. The city of Rome no longer attracted a steady stream of aspiring immigrants and had shrunk significantly, as had many other cities, which were no longer centers of innovation. As the vast network of Roman colonies dissolved, economies everywhere became more localized. Commentators such as Augustine advised people to put their faith in the eternal City of God rather than in worldly cities, for human history would always bring great change. People who lived with Augustine in Hippo would have certainly understood such counsel, for they watched the Vandals move swiftly across North Africa and bring an end to Roman rule there. Although Justinian's Byzantine forces retook the area a little over a century later, the culture that survived was as much barbarian as Roman, with smaller cities, less trade, and fewer schools.

Two hundred years after the Vandal attack, the residents of Byzantine North Africa confronted another fast-moving army of conquest, Arabian forces carrying a new religion, Islam. This Arabic expansion dramatically shaped the development of Western civilization. Though the end of the Roman Empire in 476 has long been seen as a dramatic break in European history, the expansion of Islam two centuries later may have been even more significant. Many of the patterns set in late antiquity continued, however. Warrior values such as physical prowess, bravery in battle, and loyalty to one's lord remained central and shaped the development of the political system known as feudalism. The Frankish kingdom established by Clovis continued to expand, becoming the most important state in Europe. The economic and political power of the Christian church expanded as well, with monasteries and convents providing education for their residents. The vast majority of people continued to live in small villages, trying to raise enough grain to feed themselves and their families, and asking the help of the saints to overcome life's difficulties.

CHAPTER REVIEW

■ **How did the Roman emperors Diocletian and Constantine attempt to strengthen the Roman Empire, and which of their reforms had long-lasting effects on the empire? (p. 176)**

In the middle of the third century the Roman Empire faced internal turmoil and external attacks. The emperor Diocletian restored order, dividing the empire into Western and Eastern halves, and introduced a tetrarchy to rule more effectively. The emperor Constantine built on his work, establishing a new capital for the Eastern part of the empire, Constantinople. This political reorganization made the empire more secure, and the division into two parts was long-lasting, but serious economic problems were made worse by the emperors' efforts to increase tax revenues. Many free farmers could not pay the taxes they owed and became tenants of wealthy landholders. Constantine hoped that Christian officials could help him strengthen the empire, and he accepted Christianity. He and later emperors provided economic and political support for the church and intervened in theological and institutional matters. Because of its favored position in the empire, Christianity slowly became the leading religion, and it was the main agent of continuity between the Roman and barbarian worlds.

■ **How did the Christian church develop institutionally and intellectually? (p. 179)**

Christianity gained the support of the fourth-century emperors and gradually adopted the Roman system of hierarchical organization. The church possessed able administrators and leaders who were drawn to it from the chaotic environment of the end of the Roman Empire in the West. Monasteries offered opportunities for individuals to develop deeper spiritual devotion and also provided a model of Christian living, a pattern of agricultural development, and a place for education and learning. Christian thinkers reinterpreted the classics in a Christian sense, incorporating elements of Greek and Roman philosophy and of various pagan religious groups into Christian teachings. Most Christian thinkers accepted Greco-Roman ideas that men were superior to women, though they viewed sexuality and the body with greater suspicion than had ancient pagans and developed a strong sense that chastity and an ascetic life were superior to marriage and family life. Of these early thinkers, called the church fathers, Augustine of Hippo was the most influential. His ideas about sin, free will, sexuality, and the role of government shaped western European thought from the fifth century on.

■ **What patterns of social, political, and economic life characterized barbarian society? (p. 185)**

Many barbarian groups left no written records for much of their history, so historians have to rely on sources produced by outsiders, along with physical evidence. Most barbarian peoples lived in family groups in villages, where men, women, and children shared in the agricultural labor that sustained society. They understood themselves to belong to kin groups and were ruled by tribal chieftains, whose power slowly grew during the period of migration and conquest. Chiefs were supported by bands of warriors, among whom greater social distinctions developed in this era. Barbarian law codes, written down for the first time in the sixth century, set out social and gender distinctions and held the family responsible for the actions of an individual.

■ **What were some of the causes of the barbarian migrations, and how did they affect the regions of Europe? (p. 188)**

The migrations of barbarian groups were caused by many factors, including a search for more regular supplies of food, disputes among groups, and pressure from outside; sometimes they involved military actions, though not always. The migrations of Celtic-speaking peoples and Germanic-speaking peoples proceeded differently, and affected both the regions into which peoples moved and the ones they left behind. Germanic-speaking peoples such as the Visigoths and Ostrogoths defeated Roman armies and established states, eventually pulling apart the Roman Empire in the West. Germanic-speaking Angles and Saxons invaded Celtic-speaking England and established a group of small kingdoms that slowly became more unified. Continental and English barbarian kingdoms adopted some aspects of Roman culture and converted to Christianity, but the end of the Western Roman Empire also meant less trade, poorer material culture, and more disorder.

■ **What techniques did missionaries develop to convert barbarian peoples to Christianity? (p. 195)**

Missionaries often sent by popes traveled throughout Europe and slowly succeeded in converting barbarian peoples. Christian missionaries preached to Germanic, Celtic, and Slavic peoples; instructed them in the basic tenets of the Christian faith; and used the ritual of penance to give them a sense of expected behavior. Seeking to gain more converts, the Christian church incorporated pagan beliefs and holidays, creating new rituals and practices that were meaningful to people, and creating a sense of community through parish churches and the veneration of saints.

■ **How was the Byzantine Empire able to survive for so long, and what were its most important achievements? (p. 198)**

In the East, the Byzantine Empire withstood attacks from barbarian tribes and steppe peoples and remained a state until 1453, a thousand years longer than the Western

Roman Empire. Byzantium preserved the philosophical and scientific texts of the ancient world—which later formed the basis for study in science in both Europe and the Arabic world—and produced a great synthesis of Roman law, the Justinian *Code*, which shapes legal structures in much of Europe and former European colonies to this day. Like the church in the West, the Orthodox church established monasteries and dispatched missionaries, though it remained less independent of secular control than the Western Christian church.

Suggested Reading

Brown, Peter. *Augustine of Hippo*. Rev. ed. 2000. The best biography of Saint Augustine, which treats him as a symbol of change.

Brown, Peter. *The Body and Society: Men, Women, and Sexual Renunciation in Early Christianity*. 1988. Explores early Christian attitudes on sexuality and how they replaced Roman attitudes.

Brown, Peter. *The World of Late Antiquity, A.D. 150–750*. Rev. ed. 1989. A lavishly illustrated survey that stresses social and cultural changes and continuities and has clearly written introductions to the entire period.

Burns, Thomas S. *Rome and the Barbarians, 100 B.C.–400 A.D.* 2003. Argues that Germanic and Roman cultures assimilated more than they conflicted.

Cameron, Averil. *The Mediterranean World in Late Antiquity, A.D. 395–600*. 1993. Focuses especially on political and economic changes.

Clark, Gilian. *Women in Late Antiquity: Pagan and Christian Lifestyles*. 1994. Explores law, marriage, and religious life.

Dunn, Marilyn. *The Emergence of Monasticism: From the Desert Fathers to the Early Middle Ages*. 2003. A thorough study of the beginnings of monasticism.

Evans, James Allan. *The Empress Theodora: Partner of Justinian*. 2003. Provides a brief, yet balanced and thorough treatment of Theodora's life.

Fletcher, Richard. *The Barbarian Conversion: From Paganism to Christianity*. 1998. A superbly written analysis of conversion to Christianity.

Heather, Peter. *The Fall of the Roman Empire: A New History*. 2006. A masterful analysis that asserts the centrality of barbarian military actions in the end of the Roman Empire.

Herrin, Judith. *The Formation of Christendom*. 1987. The best synthesis of the development of the Christian church from the third to the ninth centuries.

Norwich, John Julius. *Byzantium: The Early Centuries*. 1989. An elegantly written brief survey.

Todd, Malcolm. *The Early Germans*. 2d ed. 2004. Uses archaeological and literary sources to analyze Germanic social structure, customs, and religion and to suggest implications for an understanding of migration and ethnicity.

Ward-Perkins, Bryan. *The Fall of Rome and the End of Civilization*. 2006. Uses material evidence to trace the physical destruction and economic dislocation that accompanied the barbarian migrations.

Wells, Peter S. *The Barbarians Speak: How the Conquered Peoples Shaped Roman Europe*. 1999. Presents extensive evidence of Celtic and Germanic social and technical development.

Notes

1. Maude Aline Huttman, ed. and trans., *The Establishment of Christianity and the Proscription of Paganism* (New York: AMS Press, 1967), p. 164.
2. Eusebius, *Life of Constantine the Great*, trans. Ernest Cushing Richardson (Grand Rapids, Mich.: Eerdmans, 1979), p. 534.
3. R. C. Petry, ed., *A History of Christianity: Readings in the History of Early and Medieval Christianity* (Englewood Cliffs, N.J.: Prentice Hall, 1962), p. 70.
4. Saint Jerome, *Commentaries on the Letter to the Ephesians*, book 16, cited in Vern Bulloush, *Sexual Variance in Society and History* (Chicago: University of Chicago Press, 1976), p. 365.
5. E. F. Henderson, ed., *Select Historical Documents of the Middle Ages* (London: G. Bell and Sons, 1912), pp. 176–189.
6. Ammianus Marcellinus, *The History*, vol. I, Loeb Classical Library, trans. John C. Rolfe (Cambridge, Mass.: Harvard University Press, 1935), book 31, pt. 2, pp. 383, 385, 387.
7. John McNeill and Helena M. Gamer, *Medieval Handbooks of Penance: A Translation of the Principle Libri Poenitentiales and Selections from Related Documents* (New York: Columbia University Press, 1938).
8. Gregory of Tours, *The Glory of the Martyrs*, trans. Raymond Van Dam (Liverpool: Liverpool University, 1988), p. 108.
9. S. P. Scott, trans., *Corpus Juris Civilis: The Civil Law* (Cincinnati: The Central Trust, 1932), sections 1.5.5, 11.4.1.

Key Terms

diocese (p. 176)
tetrarchy (p. 176)
Arianism (p. 178)
heresy (p. 178)
apostolic succession (p. 180)
Petrine Doctrine (p. 181)
regular clergy (p. 181)
secular clergy (p. 182)
sacraments (p. 185)
runic alphabet (p. 185)
comitatus (p. 187)
wergeld (p. 187)
relics (p. 197)
Orthodox church (p. 201)

For practice quizzes and other study tools, visit the Online Study Guide at **bedfordstmartins.com/mckaywest**.

For primary sources from this period, see ***Sources of Western Society*, Second Edition**.

For Web sites, images, and documents related to topics in this chapter, visit Make History at **bedfordstmartins.com/mckaywest**.

8
Europe in the Early Middle Ages

600–1000

By the fifteenth century scholars in the growing cities of northern Italy began to think that they were living in a new era, one in which the glories of ancient Greece and Rome were being reborn. What separated their time from classical antiquity, in their opinion, was a long period of darkness, to which a seventeenth-century professor gave the name "Middle Ages." In this conceptualization, Western history was divided into three periods — ancient, medieval, and modern — an organization that is still in use today.

For a long time the end of the Roman Empire in the West was seen as the division between the ancient period and the Middle Ages, but, as we saw in the last chapter, there was continuity as well as change, and the transition from ancient to medieval was a slow process, not a single event. The agents in this process included not only the barbarian migrations that broke the Roman Empire apart but also the new religion of Islam, Slavic and steppe peoples in eastern Europe, and Christian officials and missionaries. The period from the end of antiquity (ca. 600–1000), conventionally known as the "early Middle Ages," was a time of disorder and destruction, but it also marked the creation of a new type of society. While agrarian life continued to dominate Europe, political structures that would influence later European history began to form, and Christianity continued to spread. People at the time did not know that they were living in an era that would later be labeled "middle" or sometimes even "dark," and we can wonder whether they would have shared this negative view of their own times. ■

Life in the Early Middle Ages. In this manuscript illumination from Spain, Muslim fishermen take a rich harvest from the sea. Fish were an important part of the diet of all coastal peoples in medieval Europe and were often salted and dried to preserve them for later use.

CHAPTER PREVIEW

The Spread of Islam
■ How did Islam take root in the Middle East and the Iberian Peninsula, and how did this influence life in Spain?

Frankish Rulers and Their Territories
■ How did Frankish rulers govern their kingdoms?

Early Medieval Culture
■ What were the significant intellectual and cultural changes in Charlemagne's era?

Invasions and Migrations
■ How did the invasions and migrations of the Vikings, Magyars, and Muslims shape Europe?

Political and Economic Decentralization
■ What political and economic structures developed in Europe after the invasions?

The Spread of Islam

How did Islam take root in the Middle East and the Iberian Peninsula, and how did this influence life in Spain? ■

In the seventh century C.E. two empires dominated the area today called the Middle East: the Byzantine-Greek-Christian empire and the Sassanid-Persian-Zoroastrian empire. Between the two lay the Arabian peninsula, where a merchant called Muhammad began to have religious visions around 610. By the time he died in 632, all Arabia had accepted his creed of Islam. A century later his followers controlled what is now Syria, Palestine, Egypt, North Africa, Spain, and part of France. This Arabic expansion profoundly affected the development of Western civilization as well as the history of Africa and Asia.

The Arabs

In Muhammad's time Arabia was inhabited by various tribes, many of them Bedouins (BEH-duh-uhnz). These nomadic peoples grazed goats and sheep on the sparse patches of grass that dotted the vast semiarid peninsula.

The power of the Bedouins came from their fighting skills, and they used horses and camels to travel long distances. Other Arabs lived more settled lives in the southern valleys and coastal towns along the Red Sea, such as Yemen, Mecca, and Medina, supporting themselves by agriculture and trade. Caravan routes crisscrossed Arabia and carried goods to Byzantium, Persia, and Syria. The wealth produced by business transactions led to luxurious living for many residents in the towns.

For all Arabs, the basic social unit was the clan—a group of blood relations connected through the male line. Clans expected loyalty from their members and in turn provided support and protection. Although the nomadic Bedouins condemned the urbanized lifestyle of the cities as immoral and corrupt, Arabs of all types respected one another's customs, which included observance of family obligations and avoidance of socially unacceptable behavior. In addition, they had certain religious rules and rituals in common. For example, all Arabs kept three months of the year as sacred; during that time fighting stopped so that everyone could attend holy ceremonies in peace. The city of Mecca was the religious center of the Arab world, and fighting was never tolerated there. All Arabs prayed at the Ka'ba (KAH-buh), the sanctuary in Mecca. Within the Ka'ba was a sacred black stone that Arabs believed had fallen from

Muhammad and the Earlier Prophets Muhammad (center), with his head surrounded by fire representing religious fervor, leads Abraham, Moses, and Jesus in prayer (left). Islamic tradition holds that Judaism, Christianity, and Islam all derive from the religion of Abraham, but humankind has strayed from that faith. Therefore, Muhammad, as "the seal [last] of the prophets," had to transmit God's revelations to humankind. (Bibliothèque nationale de France)

Heaven and was thus the dwelling place of a god. Strong economic links connected all Arab peoples, but what eventually molded the diverse Arab tribes into a powerful political and social unity was the religion based on the teachings of Muhammad.

The Prophet Muhammad

Except for a few vague remarks in the **Qur'an** (kuh-RAHN), the sacred book of Islam, Muhammad (ca. 571–632) left no account of his life. Arab tradition accepts some of the sacred stories that developed about him as historically true, but those accounts were not written down until about a century after his death. (Similarly, the earliest accounts of the life of Jesus, the Christian Gospels, were not written until forty to sixty years after his death.) Orphaned at the age of six, Muhammad was raised by his grandfather. As a young man he became a merchant in the caravan trade. Later he entered the service of a wealthy widow, and their subsequent marriage brought him financial independence.

The Qur'an reveals Muhammad to be an extremely devout man, ascetic, self-disciplined, and literate, but not formally educated. He prayed regularly, and when he was about forty he began to experience religious visions. Unsure for a time about what he should do, Muhammad discovered his mission after a vision in which the angel Gabriel instructed him to preach. Muhammad described his visions in a stylized and often rhyming prose and used this literary medium as his *Qur'an*, or "prayer recitation."

Muhammad's revelations were written down by his followers during his lifetime and organized into chapters, called *sura*, shortly after his death. In 651 Muhammad's third successor arranged to have an official version published. The Qur'an is regarded by Muslims as the direct words of God to his Prophet Muhammad and is therefore especially revered. (When Muslims use translations of the Qur'an, they do so alongside the original Arabic, the language of Muhammad's revelations.) At the same time, other sayings and accounts of Muhammad, which gave advice on matters that went beyond the Qur'an, were collected into books termed *hadith* (huh-DEETH). Muslim tradition (*Sunna*) consists of both the Qur'an and the hadith.

Muhammad's visions ordered him to preach a message of a single God and to become God's prophet, which he began to do in his hometown of Mecca. He gathered followers slowly, but also provoked a great deal of resistance, and in 622 he migrated with his followers to

ca. 571–632	Life of the Prophet Muhammad
651	Official version of the Qur'an published
711	Muslim forces defeat Visigothic kingdom
711–720	Muslim conquest of Spain
ca. 760–840	Carolingian Renaissance
768–814	Reign of Charlemagne
800	Imperial coronation of Charlemagne
800–900	Free peasants in western Europe increasingly tied to the land as serfs
843	Treaty of Verdun divides Carolingian kingdom
850–1000	Most extensive Viking voyages and conquests
ca. 900	Establishment of Kievan Rus
911	Vikings establish Normandy
950	Muslim Córdoba is Europe's largest and most prosperous city
1000	Stephen crowned first king of Hungary

Medina, an event termed the *hijra* (hih-JIGH-ruh) that marks the beginning of the Muslim calendar. At Medina Muhammad was much more successful, gaining converts and working out the basic principles of the faith. That same year, through the Charter of Medina, the first *umma*, or religious and political community, was formed, and it included the local Jewish community. This umma established a precedent for the later protection of Jews under Islam.

Qur'an The sacred book of Islam.

In 630 Muhammad returned to Mecca at the head of a large army, and he soon united the nomads of the desert and the merchants of the cities into an umma of *Muslims*, a word meaning those who comply with God's will. The religion itself came to be called Islam, which means "submission to God." The Ka'ba was rededicated as a Muslim holy place, and Mecca became the most holy city in Islam. According to Muslim tradition, the Ka'ba predates the creation of the world and represents the earthly counterpart of God's heavenly throne, to which "pilgrims come dishevelled and dusty on every kind of camel."[1]

By the time Muhammad died in 632 the crescent of Islam, the Muslim symbol, prevailed throughout the Arabian peninsula. During the next century one rich province of the old Roman Empire after another came under Muslim domination—first Syria, then Egypt, and then all of North Africa (Map 8.1). Long and bitter wars (572–591, 606–630) between the Byzantine and Persian Empires left both so weak and exhausted that they easily fell to Muslim attack.

209

The Teachings and Expansion of Islam

Muhammad's religion eventually attracted great numbers of people, partly because of the straightforward nature of its doctrines. The strictly monotheistic theology outlined in the Qur'an has only a few central tenets: Allah, the Arabic word for God, is all-powerful and all-knowing. Muhammad, Allah's prophet, preached his word and carried his message. Muhammad described himself as the successor both of the Jewish patriarch Abraham and of Christ, and he claimed that his teachings replaced theirs. He invited and won converts from Judaism and Christianity.

Five Pillars of Islam The five practices Muslims must fulfill according to the shari'a, or sacred law, including the profession of faith, prayer, fasting, giving alms to the poor, and pilgrimage to Mecca.

Because Allah is all-powerful, believers must submit themselves to him. All Muslims have the obligation of the jihad (literally, "self-exertion") to strive or struggle to lead a virtuous life and to spread God's rule and law. In some cases striving is individual against sin; in others it is social and communal and could involve armed conflict, though this is not an essential part of jihad (jee-HAHD). The Islamic belief of "striving in the path of God" is closely related to the central feature of Muslim doctrine, the coming Day of Judgment. Muslims believe with conviction that the Day of Judgment will come; consequently, all of a Muslim's thoughts and actions should be oriented toward the Last Judgment and the rewards of Heaven.

To merit the rewards of Heaven, a person must follow the strict code of moral behavior that Muhammad prescribed. The Muslim must recite a profession of faith in God and in Muhammad as God's prophet: "There is no god but God and Muhammad is his prophet." The believer must pray five times a day, fast and pray during the sacred month of Ramadan, and contribute alms to the poor and needy. If possible, the believer must make a pilgrimage to Mecca once during his or her lifetime. According to the Muslim shari'a (shuh-REE-uh), or sacred law, these five practices—the profession of faith, prayer, fasting, giving alms to the poor, and pilgrimage to Mecca—constitute the **Five Pillars of Islam**. The Muslim who faithfully observes the laws of the Qur'an can hope for salvation.

The Qur'an forbids alcoholic beverages and gambling. It condemns business usury—that is, lending money at interest rates or taking advantage of market demand for products by charging high prices for them. A number of foods, such as pork, are also forbidden, a dietary regulation adopted from the Mosaic law of the Hebrews.

Polygyny, the practice of men having more than one wife, was common in Arab society before Muhammad, though for economic reasons the custom was limited to the well-to-do. The Qur'an limited the number of wives a man could have, however: "[Of] women who seem good in your eyes, marry but two, three, or four;

Map 8.1 The Spread of Islam, 622–900 The rapid expansion of Islam in a relatively short span of time testifies to the Arabs' superior fighting skills, religious zeal, and economic organization as well as to their enemies' weakness.

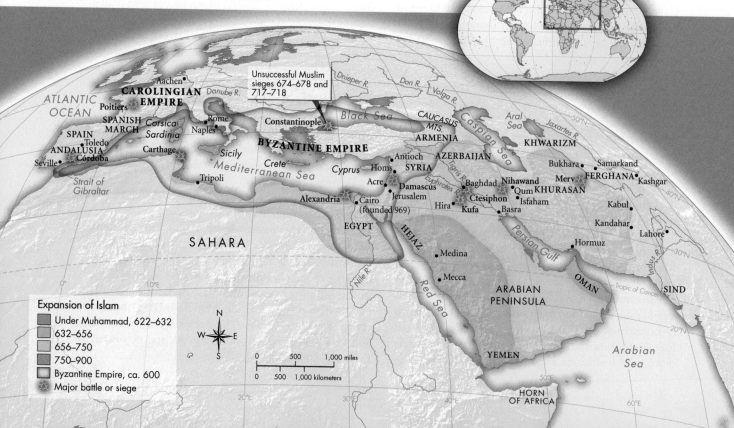

Expansion of Islam
- Under Muhammad, 622–632
- 632–656
- 656–750
- 750–900
- Byzantine Empire, ca. 600
- ✳ Major battle or siege

and if ye still fear that ye shall not act equitably then only one" (Sura 4:3).

The Qur'an sets forth a strict sexual morality and condemns immoral behavior on the part of men as well as women: "The whore and the fornicator: whip each of them a hundred times. . . . The fornicator shall not marry other than a whore; and the whore shall not marry other than a fornicator" (Sura 24:2–3).

The Qur'an also set out rules for inheritance:

> Men who die and leave wives behind shall bequeath to them a year's maintenance. . . . And your wives shall have a fourth part of what you leave, if you have no issue [offspring]; but if you have issue, then they shall have an eighth part. . . . With regard to your children, God commands you to give the male the portion of two females. (Sura 4:11–12)

With respect to matters of property, Muslim women of the early Middle Ages had more rights than Western women. For example, a Muslim woman retained complete jurisdiction over one-third of her property when she married and could dispose of it in any way she wished. Women in most European countries and the United States did not gain these rights until the nineteenth century.

Every Muslim hoped that by observing the laws of the Qur'an, he or she could achieve salvation, and it was the tenets of Islam preached by Muhammad that bound all Arabs together. Despite the clarity and unifying force of Muslim doctrine, however, divisions developed within the Islamic faith within decades of Muhammad's death. Neither the Qur'an nor the hadith gave clear guidance about how successors to Muhammad were to be chosen, but a group of Muhammad's closest followers chose Abu Bakr (uh-BOO BAH-kuhr), who was a close friend of the Prophet's and a member of a clan affiliated with the Prophet's clan, as **caliph** (KAY-luhf), a word meaning "successor." Another faction backed Ali, Muhammad's cousin and son-in-law, who, they stated, the Prophet had designated as imam, or leader. Ali was chosen as the fourth caliph in 656, but was assassinated only five years later. His supporters began to assert that he should rightly have been the first caliph and that any caliph who was not a descendant of Ali was a usurper. These supporters of Ali—termed Shi'ites (SHEE-ights) or Shi'a (SHEE-ah) from Arabic terms meaning "supporters" or "partisans" of Ali—saw Ali and subsequent imams as the divinely inspired leaders of the community. The larger body of Muslims who accepted the first elections—termed Sunnis, a word derived from *Sunna*, the traditional beliefs and practices of the community—saw the caliphs as political leaders. Since Islam did not have an organized church and priesthood, the caliphs had an additional function of safeguarding and enforcing the religious law (*shari'a*) with the advice of scholars (*ulama*), particularly the jurists, judges, and scholastics who were knowledgeable about the Qur'an

" Men who die and leave wives behind shall bequeath to them a year's maintenance. "

—THE QUR'AN

and hadith. Over the centuries enmity between Sunni and Shi'a Muslims has sometimes erupted into violence.

After the assassination of Ali, the caliphate passed to members of the Umayyad (oo-MIGH-uhd) clan, who asserted control and brought stability to the growing Muslim empire. They established their capital at Damascus in Syria, and the Muslim faith continued to expand eastward to India and westward across North Africa. By the early tenth century a Muslim proverb spoke of the Mediterranean Sea as a Muslim lake, though the Greeks at Constantinople contested that notion.

Life in Muslim Spain

In Europe, Muslim political and cultural influence was felt most strongly in the Iberian Peninsula. In 711 a Muslim force crossed the Strait of Gibraltar and easily defeated the weak Visigothic kingdom. A few Christian princes supported by the Frankish rulers held out in northern mountain fortresses, but by 720 the Muslims controlled most of Spain. A member of the Umayyad Dynasty, Abd al-Rahman (AHB-dal-ruh-MAHN) (r. 756–788) established a kingdom in Spain with its capital at Córdoba (KAWR-doh-buh).

Throughout the Islamic world, Muslims used the term **al-Andalus** to describe the part of the Iberian Peninsula under Muslim control. The name probably derives from the Arabic for "land of the Vandals," the Germanic people who swept across Spain in the fifth century (see Chapter 7). In the eighth century al-Andalus included the entire peninsula from Gibraltar in the south to the Cantabrian Mountains in the north (see Map 8.1). Today we often use the word *Andalusia* (an-duh-LOO-zhuh) to refer especially to southern Spain, but eighth-century Christians throughout Europe called the peninsula "Moorish Spain" because the Muslims who invaded and conquered it were Moors—Berbers from northwest Africa.

The ethnic term *Moorish* can be misleading, however, because the peninsula was home to sizable numbers of Jews and Christians as well as Muslim Moors. In business transactions and in much of daily life, all peoples used the Arabic language. With Muslims, Christians,

> **caliph** A successor, as chosen by a group of Muhammad's closest followers.
>
> **al-Andalus** The part of the Iberian Peninsula under Muslim control in the eighth century, encompassing most of modern-day Spain.

and Jews trading with and learning from one another and occasionally intermarrying, Moorish Spain and Norman Sicily (see Chapter 9) were the only distinctly pluralistic societies in medieval Europe.

Some scholars believe that the eighth and ninth centuries in Andalusia were an era of remarkable interfaith harmony. Jews in Muslim Spain were generally treated well, and Córdoba became a center of Jewish as well as Muslim learning. Many Christians adopted Arabic patterns of speech and dress, gave up the practice of

Muslim Garden in Spain Tranquil gardens such as this one built by Muslim rulers in Granada represented paradise in Islamic culture, perhaps because of the religion's desert origins. Muslim architectural styles shaped those of Christian Spain and were later taken to the New World by Spanish conquerors. (Ric Ergenbright/Corbis)

eating pork, and developed an appreciation for Arabic music and poetry. Some Christian women of elite status chose the Muslim practice of veiling their faces in public. Records describe Muslim and Christian youths joining in celebrations and merrymaking.

From the sophisticated centers of Muslim culture in Baghdad, Damascus, and Cairo, al-Andalus seemed a provincial backwater, a frontier outpost with little significance in the wider context of Islamic civilization. On the other hand, "northern barbarians," as Muslims called the European peoples, acknowledged the splendor of Spanish culture. The Saxon nun and writer Hroswitha of Gandersheim (roz-WEETH-uh of GAHN-duhr-shighm) called the city of Córdoba "the ornament of the world." By 950 the city had a population of about a half million, making it Europe's largest and most prosperous city. Many residents lived in large houses and easily purchased the silks and brocades made by the city's thousands of weavers. The streets were well-paved and well-lighted—a sharp contrast to the dark and muddy streets of other cities in Europe—and there was an abundance of fresh water for drinking and bathing. The largest library contained 400,000 volumes, a vast collection, particularly when compared with the largest library in northern Europe at the Benedictine abbey of St. Gall in Switzerland, which had only 600 books.

In Spain, as elsewhere in the Arab world, the Muslims had an enormous impact on agricultural development. They began the cultivation of rice, sugar cane, citrus fruits, dates, figs, eggplants, carrots, and, after the eleventh century, cotton. These crops, together with new methods of field irrigation, provided the population with food products unknown in the rest of Europe. Muslims also brought technological innovations westward, including new kinds of sails and navigational instruments, as well as paper. (See "Living in the Past: Muslim Technology: Advances in Papermaking," page 214.)

Muslim-Christian Relations

What did early Muslims think of Jesus? Jesus is mentioned many times in the Qur'an, which affirms that he was born of Mary the Virgin. He is described as a righteous prophet chosen by God who performed miracles and continued the work of Abraham and Moses, and he was a sign of the coming Day of Judgment. But Muslims held that Jesus was an apostle only, not God, and that people (that is, Christians) who called Jesus divine committed blasphemy (showing contempt for God). The Christian doctrine of the Trinity—that there is one God in three persons (Father, Son, and Holy Spirit)—posed a powerful obstacle to Muslim-Christian understanding because of Islam's emphasis on the absolute oneness of God. Muslims esteemed the Judeo-Christian Scriptures as part of God's revelation, although they believed that the Qur'an superseded them.

Harvesting Dates This detail from an ivory casket given to a Córdoban prince reflects the importance of fruit cultivation in the Muslim-inspired agricultural expansion in southern Europe in the ninth and tenth centuries. (Louvre/Réunion des Musées Nationaux/Art Resource, NY)

Muslims call Jews and Christians *dhimmis*, or "protected people," because they were "people of the book," that is, the Hebrew Scriptures. Christians and Jews in the areas Muslims conquered were allowed to continue practicing their faith, although they did have to pay a special tax. This toleration was sometimes accompanied by suspicion, however. In Spain, Muslim teachers increasingly feared that close contact with Christians and Jews would lead to Muslim contamination and threaten the Islamic faith. Thus, beginning in the late tenth century, Muslim regulations began to officially prescribe what Christians, Jews, and Muslims could do. A Christian, however much assimilated, remained an **infidel**. An infidel was an unbeliever, and the word carried a pejorative or disparaging connotation.

By about 950 Caliph Abd al-Rahman III (912–961) of the Umayyad Dynasty of Córdoba ruled most of the Iberian Peninsula from the Mediterranean in the south to the Ebro River in the north. Christian Spain consisted of the tiny kingdoms of Castile, León, Catalonia, Aragon, Navarre, and Portugal. Civil wars among al-Rahman's descendants weakened the caliphate, and the small northern Christian kingdoms began to expand southward, sometimes working together. When Christian forces conquered Muslim territory, Christian rulers regarded their Muslim and Jewish subjects as infidels and enacted restrictive measures similar to those in Muslim lands. Christian bishops worried that even a knowledge of Islam would lead to ignorance of essential Christian doctrines, and interfaith contacts declined. Christians' perception of Islam as a menace would help inspire the Crusades of the eleventh through thirteenth centuries.

Science and Medicine

Despite growing suspicions on both sides, the Islamic world profoundly shaped Christian European culture in Spain and elsewhere. Toledo, for example, became an important center of learning through which Arab intellectual achievements entered and influenced western Europe. Arabic knowledge of science and mathematics, derived from the Chinese, Greeks, and Hindus, was highly sophisticated. The Muslim mathematician al-Khwarizmi (al-KHWAHR-uhz-mee) (d. 830) wrote the important treatise *Algebra*, the first work in which the word *algebra* is used mathematically. Al-Khwarizmi adopted the Hindu system of numbers (1, 2, 3, 4), used it in his *Algebra*, and applied mathematics to problems of physics and astronomy. (Since our system of numbers is actually Hindu in origin, the term *Arabic numerals*, coined about 1847, is a misnomer.) Scholars in Baghdad translated Euclid's *Elements*, the basic text for plane and solid geometry (see Chapter 5). Muslims also instructed Westerners in the use of the zero, which permitted the execution of complicated problems of multiplication and long division. Use of the zero represented an enormous advance over clumsy Roman numerals.

infidel A disparaging term used for a person who does not believe in a particular religion.

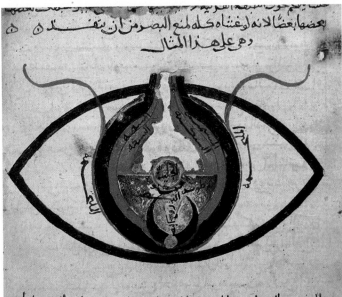

Eye in Muslim Medical Text This illustration of the eye comes from a book on eye diseases written about 1200 in Arabic. The author draws on a long tradition of research into eye diseases in the Muslim world to provide advice to physicians about treatment, including the removal of cataracts. Muslim and Jewish medical practitioners were particularly known for their skills in healing ailments of the eyes, which were common in medieval Europe. (Egyptian Museum Cairo/Gianni Dagli Orti/The Art Archive)

Muslim Technology: Advances in Papermaking

LIVING IN THE PAST

ALONG WITH SCIENTIFIC AND MEDICAL KNOWLEDGE, technological advances often entered Europe through Muslim Spain. One of these was papermaking. Ancient Egyptians had made a writing surface by weaving pounded papyrus stalks (the origin of the word *paper*), and sometime before 100 B.C.E. the Chinese invented paper that could be made from many different materials. They shredded and mashed rags and woody plant fibers in water to make a pulp, dipped a large, flat wire screen into this pulp to form a mat of fibers, and pressed the resulting sheet between layers of felt to dry. The Chinese used paper for wrapping and writing, and merchants and Buddhist missionaries carried the skills of papermaking to Samarkand in Central Asia (see Map 8.1). When this area was conquered by Arab armies, papermaking techniques spread into Muslim areas. Muslim papermakers improved on Chinese techniques, producing thicker and smoother sheets by using starch to fill the pores in the surfaces of the sheets. They carried this new method to Iraq, Syria, Egypt, and the Maghrib (North Africa), from where it entered Spain. Paper mills that produced large quantities were opened in Baghdad around 800 and in Muslim Spain around 1100.

By that point, paper was the most common writing surface in the Muslim world, though Christian Europeans were still largely using parchment or vellum, both made in a time-consuming process from stretched animal skins. The oldest surviving Christian text on paper is the *Missal of Silos*, a prayer book written in the eleventh century by Christian monks at the abbey of Santo Domingos de Silos in North Spain on paper made in Muslim mills. The first paper mill in Christian Europe was opened in Fabriano, Italy, about 1200, and other cities quickly followed. Paper allowed the expansion of business and government record keeping, providing an important tool for bureaucrats as well as scholars.

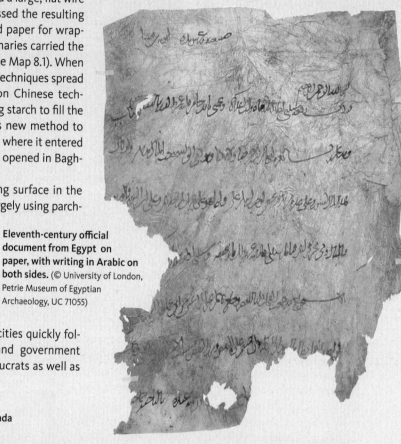

Eleventh-century official document from Egypt on paper, with writing in Arabic on both sides. (© University of London, Petrie Museum of Egyptian Archaeology, UC 71055)

Thirteenth-century Qur'an written on paper in Granada in southern Spain. (© British Library Board)

Late medieval engraving of a paper mill, using the process developed by Muslim papermakers. At the right rear a cogged wooden wheel (probably driven by water) drives large wooden hammers that break up fibers, while workers dip the screen of fibers in water and stack finished sheets. (From Dard Hunter, *Papermaking: The History and Technique of an Ancient Craft*, 2d ed. [New York: Knopf, 1967])

QUESTIONS FOR ANALYSIS

1. What advantages did paper offer over other writing materials?

2. Consider the traditions and rapid expansion of Islam. How might these factors have contributed to the use and spread of paper technology?

3. From the description and illustration of the process, why were paper mills generally located along streams?

Middle Eastern Arabs translated and codified the scientific and philosophical learning of Greek and Persian antiquity. In the ninth and tenth centuries that knowledge was brought to Spain, where between 1150 and 1250 it was translated into Latin. Europeans' knowledge of Aristotle changed the entire direction of European philosophy and theology (see Chapter 11). Isaac Newton's discoveries in mathematics in the seventeenth century rested on ancient Greek theories that had been translated in Spain.

Muslim medical knowledge far surpassed that of the West. By the ninth century Arab physicians had translated most of the treatises of Hippocrates. The Baghdad physician al-Razi (865–925) produced an encyclopedic treatise on medicine that was translated into Latin and circulated widely in the West. Al-Razi was the first physician to make the clinical distinction between measles and smallpox. The great surgeon of Córdoba, al-Zahrawi (d. 1013), produced an important work in which he discussed the cauterization of wounds (searing with a branding iron) and the crushing of stones in the bladder. Arabic science reached its peak in the physician, philologist, philosopher, poet, and scientist ibn-Sina of Bukhara (980–1037), known in the West as Avicenna (ah-vuh-SEH-nuh). His *Canon of Medicine* codified all Greco-Arabic medical thought, described the contagious nature of tuberculosis and the spreading of diseases, and listed 760 pharmaceutical drugs.

Unfortunately, many of these treatises came to the West as translations from Greek to Arabic and then to Latin and inevitably lost a great deal in translation. Nevertheless, in the ninth and tenth centuries Arabic knowledge and experience in anatomy and pharmaceutical prescriptions much enriched Western knowledge.

Frankish Rulers and Their Territories

How did Frankish rulers govern their kingdoms? ■

Several centuries before the Muslim conquest of Spain, the Frankish king Clovis converted to Roman Christianity and established a large kingdom in what had been Roman Gaul (see Chapter 7). Though at that time the Frankish kingdom was simply one barbarian kingdom among many, it grew to become the most important state in Europe, expanding to become an empire. Rulers after Clovis used a variety of tactics to enhance their authority and create a stable system. Charles the Great (r. 768–814), generally known by the French version of his name, Charlemagne (SHAHR-luh-mayne), built on the military and diplomatic foundations of his ancestors and on the administrative machinery of the Merovingian kings. He expanded the Frankish kingdom into what is now Germany and Italy and, late in his long reign, was crowned emperor by the pope.

The Merovingians

Clovis established the Merovingian dynasty in the late fifth century (see Chapter 7), and under Clovis the Frankish kingdom included much of what is now France and a large section of southwestern Germany. At his death, the kingdom was divided among his four sons, not according to strict acreage but in portions yielding roughly equal revenues. Historians have long described Merovingian Gaul in the sixth and seventh centuries as wracked by civil wars, chronic violence, and political instability as Clovis's descendants fought among themselves. So brutal and destructive were these wars and so violent the ordinary conditions of life that the term *Dark Ages* was at one time used to designate the entire Merovingian period. Now historians point to creativity in this era as well as violence, and note that even the civil wars did not threaten the Merovingian royal family, as the conflicts were led by family members rather than outsiders trying to gain the throne.

Merovingian rulers had multiple sources of income. These included revenues from the royal estates and the "gifts" of subject peoples, such as plunder and tribute paid by peoples east of the Rhine River. New lands might be conquered and confiscated, and served to replace lands donated as monastic or religious endowments. All free landowners paid a land tax, although some landowners gradually gained immunity from doing so. Fines imposed for criminal offenses and tolls and customs duties on roads, bridges, and waterways (and the goods transported over them) also yielded income. As with the Romans, the minting of coins was a royal monopoly, with drastic penalties for counterfeiting.

The Franks also adapted some of their offices and units of government from the Romans. For example, the basis of the administrative system in the Frankish kingdom was the **civitas** (SIH-vih-tahs)—Latin for a city and surrounding territory—similar to the political organization of the Roman Empire. A **comites** (KOH-meh-tehs)—senior official or royal companion, later called a count—presided over the civitas, as had governors in Rome. He collected royal revenue, heard lawsuits, enforced justice, and raised troops. Many comites came from families that had been administrators in Roman Gaul and were usually native to the regions they administered and knew their areas well. Frankish royal administration involved another official, the *dux* (dooks) or duke. He was a military leader, commanding troops in the territory of several civitas, and thus responsible for all defensive and offensive strategies. Clovis and his descendants also issued capitularies—Roman-style administrative and legislative orders—in an attempt to maintain order in Merovingian society. Some of these laws were designed to protect the clergy and church property from violence,

civitas The city and surrounding territory that served as a basis of the administrative system in the Frankish kingdoms, based on Roman models.

comites A senior official or royal companion, later called a count, who presided over the civitas.

Merovingian Army and Sword This sixth- or seventh-century ivory depicts a nobleman in civilian dress followed by seven warriors. The power of the Frankish aristocracy rested on such private armies. Here the soldiers carry spears and bows and arrows, but iron swords like the one shown here were also common weapons. (ivory: Rheinisches Landesmuseum, Trier; sword: Musée des Beaux-Arts Troyes/Gianni Dagli Orti/The Art Archive)

others were meant to define ownership and inheritance, and still others set out to punish crimes such as drunkenness, robbery, arson, rape, and murder.

Within the royal household, Merovingian politics provided women with opportunities, and some queens not only influenced but occasionally also dominated events. Because the finances of the kingdom were merged with those of the royal family, queens often had control of the royal treasury just as more ordinary women controlled household expenditures. The status of a princess or queen also rested on her diplomatic importance, with her marriage sealing or divorce breaking an alliance; on her personal relationship with her husband and her ability to give him sons and heirs; and on her role as the mother and guardian of princes who had not reached legal adulthood.

Queen Brunhilda (543?–613), for example, married first one Frankish king and at his death another. When her second husband died, Brunhilda overcame the objections of the nobles and became regent for her son until he came of age. Later she governed as regent for her grandsons and, when she was nearly seventy, for her great-grandson. Stories of her ruthlessness spread during her lifetime and were later much embellished by Frankish historians uncomfortable with such a powerful woman. The evil Brunhilda, they alleged, killed ten kings of the Franks in pursuit of her political goals, and was finally executed by being torn apart by horses while cheering crowds looked on. How much of this actually happened is impossible to say, but Brunhilda's legend became a model for the wicked queen in European folklore.

Merovingian rulers and their successors led peripatetic lives, traveling constantly to check up on local administrators and peoples. Merovingian kings also relied on the comites and bishops to gather and send local information to them. The court or household of Merovingian kings included scribes who kept records, legal officials who advised the king on matters of law, and treasury agents responsible for aspects of royal finance. These officials could all read and write Latin. Over them all presided the mayor of the palace, the most important secular figure after the king, who governed the palace and the kingdom in the king's absence. Mayors were usually from one of the great aristocratic families, which increasingly through intermarriage blended Frankish and Roman elites. These families possessed landed wealth—villas over which they exercised lordship, dispensing local customary, not royal, law—and they often had rich and lavish lifestyles.

The Rise of the Carolingians

From this aristocracy one family gradually emerged to replace the Merovingian dynasty. The rise of the Carolingians—whose name comes from the Latin *Carolus*, or Charles, the name of several important members of the family—rests on several factors. First, the Carolingian Pippin I (d. 640) acquired the powerful position of mayor of the palace and passed the title on to his heirs. As mayors of the palace and heads of the Frankish bureaucracy, Pippin I and his descendants were entrusted with extraordinary amounts of power and privilege by the Merovingian kings. Although the mayor of the palace was technically employed by the ruling family, the Carolingians would use their influential position to win support for themselves and eventually subvert Merovingian authority. Second, a series of advantageous marriage alliances brought the family estates and influence in different parts of the Frankish world, and provided the Carolingians with landed wealth and treasure with which to reward their allies and followers. Third, military victories over supporters of the Merovingians gave the Carolingians a reputation for strength and ensured their dominance. Pippin I's great-grandson, Charles Martel (r. 714–741), waged war successfully against the Saxons, Frisians, Alamanni, and Bavarians, which further enhanced the family's prestige. In 732 Charles Martel defeated a Muslim force near Poitiers (pwah-ty-AY) in central France. Muslims and Christians have interpreted the battle differently. To the Muslims it was a minor skirmish won by the Franks because of Muslim difficulties in maintaining supply lines over long distances and the distraction of ethnic conflicts and unrest in Islamic Spain. For Christians the Frankish victory was one of the great battles of history, halting Muslim expansion in Europe. Charles Martel and later Carolingians used it to enhance their reputation, portraying themselves as defenders of Christendom against the Muslims.

The Battle of Poitiers helped the Carolingians acquire the support of the church, perhaps their most important asset. Charles Martel and his son Pippin III (r. 751–768) further strengthened their ties to the church by supporting the work of Christian missionaries. The most important of these missionaries was the Englishman Boniface (BAH-nuh-fays) (680–754), who had close ties to the Roman pope. Boniface ordered the oak of Thor, a tree sacred to many pagans, cut down and used the wood to build a church. When the god Thor did not respond by killing him with his lightning bolts, Boniface won many converts. As they preached, baptized, and established churches, missionaries included the Christian duty to obey secular authorities as part of their message, thus extending to Frankish rulers the church's support of secular power that had begun with Constantine (see Chapter 7).

As mayor of the palace, Charles Martel had exercised the power of king of the Franks. His son Pippin III aspired to the title as well as the powers. Pippin's diplomats were able to convince an embattled Pope Zacharias to rule in his favor in exchange for military support against the Lombards, who were threatening the papacy. Zacharias invoked his apostolic authority

Saint Boniface The top of this illustration from an early eleventh-century Fulda Mass book shows Saint Boniface baptizing. The bottom panel shows his death scene, with the saint protecting himself with a Gospel book. The fluttering robes are similar to those in earlier Anglo-Saxon books, probably modeled on illustrations in books that Boniface brought to Fulda Abbey from England. (Stadtsbibliothek Bamberg, Ms. Lit. I, fol. 126v)

as pope, and declared that Pippin should be king "in order to prevent provoking civil war [between the Merovingians and Carolingians] in Francia."[2] Chilperic, the last Merovingian ruler, was consigned to a monastery. An assembly of Frankish magnates elected Pippin king, and Boniface anointed him. When in 754 Lombard expansion again threatened the papacy, Pope Stephen II journeyed to the Frankish kingdom seeking help. On this occasion, he personally anointed Pippin with the sacred oils and gave him the title "Patrician of the Romans." Pippin promised restitution of the papal lands and later made a gift of estates in central Italy.

Because of his anointment, Pippin's kingship took on a special spiritual and moral character. Prior to Pippin only priests and bishops had received anointment. Pippin became the first to be anointed with the sacred oils and acknowledged as *rex et sacerdos* (reks et SAHK-ehr-dohse), meaning king and priest. Anointment, not royal blood, set the Christian king apart. By having himself anointed, Pippin cleverly eliminated possible threats to the Frankish throne by other claimants, and the pope promised him support in the future. An important alliance had been struck between the papacy and the Frankish monarchs. When Pippin died, his son Charles, generally known as Charlemagne, succeeded him.

The Warrior-Ruler Charlemagne

Charlemagne's adviser and friend Alcuin (ca. 735–804; see page 223) wrote that "a king should be strong against his enemies, humble to Christians, feared by pagans, loved by the poor and judicious in counsel and maintaining justice."[3] Charlemagne worked to realize that ideal in all its aspects. Through brutal military expeditions that brought wealth—lands, booty, slaves, and tribute—and by peaceful travel, personal appearances, and the sheer force of his personality, Charlemagne sought to awe newly conquered peoples and rebellious domestic enemies.

Charlemagne's accomplishments were made possible in part by the administrative, military, and diplomatic foundations of the Merovingian kings and his Carolingian ancestors, but much of his success can be attributed to his personal qualities. Charlemagne's secretary Einhard described many of these qualities in his biography of the ruler:

Charles was large and strong, and of lofty stature, though not disproportionately tall . . . the upper part of his head was round, his eyes very large and animated, nose a little long, hair fair, and face laughing and merry. Thus his appearance was always stately and dignified . . . although his neck was thick and somewhat short, and his belly rather prominent; but the symmetry of the rest of his body concealed these defects. His gait was firm, his whole carriage manly and his voice clear, but not so strong as his size led one to expect. His health was excellent, except during the four years preceding his death. . . . In accordance with the national custom, he took frequent exercise on horseback and in the chase. . . . He . . . often practiced swimming, in which he was such an adept that none could surpass him.[4]

In this section, Einhard tempers his idealization of the warrior-ruler with less-than-flattering details about his thick neck and potbelly, a balanced portrayal that continues throughout the biography, which is why historians consider it generally accurate. In fact, on some details Einhard may have been overly negative; he claims that Charlemagne could not write, but recent scholarship suggests that he could. Although Charlemagne was a man of action and not an intellectual, he certainly appreciated good literature, such as Saint Augustine's *City of God*, and Einhard considered him an unusually effective speaker.

Speeches were not Charlemagne's usual tactic against those who opposed him; force was. If an ideal king was "strong against his enemies" and "feared by pagans," Charlemagne more than met the standard. His reign was characterized by constant warfare; according to the chroniclers of the time, only seven years between 714 and 814 were peaceful. In continuing the expansionist policies of his ancestors, Charlemagne fought more than fifty campaigns and became the greatest warrior of the early Middle Ages. He subdued all of the north of modern France, but his greatest successes were in today's Germany, battles he justified as spreading Christianity to pagan peoples. In the course of a bloody thirty-year war against the Saxons, he added most of the northwestern German peoples to the Frankish kingdom. Einhard reported that Charlemagne ordered more than four thousand Saxons killed on one day and deported thousands more. Those who surrendered were forced to become Christian, often in mass baptisms. He established bishoprics in areas he had conquered so that church officials and church institutions became important means of imposing Frankish rule.

Charlemagne also achieved spectacular results in the south, incorporating Lombardy into the Frankish kingdom. He ended Bavarian independence and defeated the nomadic Avars, opening eastern Germany for later settlement by Franks. He successfully fought the Byzantine Empire for Venetia, Istria, and Dalmatia and temporarily annexed those areas to his kingdom. Charlemagne's only defeat came at the hands of the Basques of northwestern Spain.

Although it was a forbidden topic during Charlemagne's lifetime, the ill-fated Spanish expedition inspired the great medieval epic, *The Song of Roland*. Based on legend and written in about 1100 at the beginning of the European crusading movement, the poem differs in many of its details from the historical evidence. *The Song of Roland* remains an important document, however, because it helped create the ideals of knightly chivalry and because it reveals the popular image of Charlemagne as a sacred king that emerged in the centuries after his death.

By around 805 the Frankish kingdom included all of northwestern Europe except Scandinavia and Britain (Map 8.2). Not since the Roman emperors of the third century c.e. had any ruler controlled so much of the Western world. Other than brief periods under Napoleon and Hitler, Europe would never again see as large a unified state as it had under Charlemagne, which is one reason he has become an important symbol of European unity in the twenty-first century.

Carolingian Government and Society

Charlemagne's empire was not a state as people today understand that term; it was a collection of peoples and clans. For administrative purposes, Charlemagne divided his entire kingdom into counties based closely on the old Merovingian civitas. Each of the approximately six hundred counties was governed by a count (or in his absence by a viscount), who published royal orders, held courts and resolved legal cases, collected taxes and tolls, raised troops for the army, and supervised maintenance of roads and bridges. Counts were originally sent out from the royal court; later a person native to the region was appointed. As a link between local authorities and the central government, Charlemagne appointed officials called *missi dominici* (mih-see doh-MEH-nee-chee), "agents of the lord king," who checked up on the counts and held courts to handle judicial and financial issues.

Map 8.2 Charlemagne's Conquests, ca. 768–814

Though Charlemagne's hold on much of his territory was relatively weak, the size of his empire was not equaled again until the nineteenth-century conquests of Napoleon.

Considering the size of Charlemagne's empire, the counts and royal agents were few and far between, and the authority of the central government was weak. The abbots and bishops who served as Charlemagne's advisers envisioned a unified Christian society presided over by a king who was responsible for maintaining peace, law, and order and doing justice. This remained a vision, however, not reality. Instead, society was held together by alliances among powerful families, along with dependent relationships cemented by oaths promising faith and loyalty. These were the seeds from which medieval feudalism was to develop.

Family alliances were often cemented by sexual relations, including those of Charlemagne himself. Charlemagne had a total of four legal wives, most from other Frankish tribes, and six concubines. Charlemagne's personal desires certainly shaped his complicated relationships—even after the age of sixty-five he continued to sire children—but the security and continuation of his dynasty and the need for diplomatic alliances were also important motives. Despite all the women, only three of Charlemagne's sons reached adulthood, and only one outlived him. Four surviving grandsons did ensure perpetuation of the family, however, and the marriages themselves linked Charlemagne with other powerful families even in the absence of sons.

In terms of social changes, the Carolingian period witnessed moderate population growth. The highest aristocrats and church officials lived well, with fine clothing and at least a few rooms heated by firewood. Male nobles hunted and managed their estates, while female nobles generally oversaw the education of their children and sometimes inherited and controlled land on their own. Craftsmen and craftswomen on manorial estates manufactured textiles, weapons, glass, and pottery, primarily for local consumption. Sometimes abbeys and

Picturing the Past

Charlemagne and His Wife This illumination from a ninth-century manuscript portrays Charlemagne with one of his wives. Marriage was an important tool of diplomacy for Charlemagne, and he had a number of wives and concubines. (Erich Lessing/Art Resource, NY)

ANALYZING THE IMAGE What does Charlemagne appear to be doing? How would you characterize his wife's reaction?

CONNECTIONS Does this depiction of a Frankish queen match what you've read about Frankish queens? On what accomplishments did a queen's status rest?

To complete this activity online, go to the Online Study Guide at bedfordstmartins.com/mckaywest.

Medieval Plowing Peasants work heavy soil with a hoe and a simple wooden plow pulled by two oxen, from an illustrated encyclopedia written by a Carolingian scholar who had studied under Alcuin at Charlemagne's palace school. Some medieval manuscripts present idealized depictions of rural life, but here the artist captures the hard physical labor involved. (Bildarchiv Preussischer Kulturbesitz/Art Resource, NY)

manors served as markets; goods were shipped away to towns and fairs for sale; and a good deal of interregional commerce existed. In the towns, artisans and merchants produced and traded luxury goods for noble and clerical patrons. When compared with earlier Roman cities or with Muslim cities of the time, such as Córdoba and Baghdad, however, Carolingian cities were small; few north of the Alps had more than seven thousand people. Even in Charlemagne's main political center at Aachen, most buildings were made of wood and earth, streets were narrow and muddy, and beggars were a common sight.

The modest economic expansion benefited townspeople and nobles, but it did not significantly alter the lives of most people, who continued to live in a vast rural world dotted with isolated estates and small villages. Here life was precarious. Crops could easily be wiped out by hail, cold, or rain, and transporting food from other areas was impossible. People's diets centered on grain, which was baked into bread, brewed into beer, and especially cooked into gruel. To this were added seasonal vegetables such as peas, cabbage, and onions, and tiny amounts of animal protein, mostly cheese. Clothing and household goods were just as simple, and houses were drafty, smoky, and often shared with animals. Lice, fleas, and other vermin spread disease, and the poor diet led to frequent stomach disorders. Work varied by the season, but at all times of the year it was physically demanding and yielded relatively little. What little there was had to be shared with landowners, who demanded their taxes and rents in the form of crops, animals, or labor.

The Imperial Coronation of Charlemagne

In autumn of the year 800, Charlemagne paid a momentous visit to Rome. Einhard gives this account of what happened:

> His last journey there [to Rome] was due to another factor, namely that the Romans, having inflicted many injuries on Pope Leo—plucking out his eyes and tearing out his tongue, he had been compelled to beg the assistance of the

king. Accordingly, coming to Rome in order that he might set in order those things which had exceedingly disturbed the condition of the Church, he remained there the whole winter. It was at the time that he accepted the name of Emperor and Augustus. At first he was so much opposed to this that he insisted that although that day was a great [Christian] feast, he would not have entered the Church if he had known beforehand the pope's intention. But he bore very patiently the jealousy of the Roman Emperors [that is, the Byzantine rulers] who were indignant when he received these titles. He overcame their arrogant haughtiness with magnanimity, . . . by sending frequent ambassadors to them and in his letters addressing them as brothers.[5]

For centuries scholars have debated the reasons for the imperial coronation of Charlemagne. Did Charlemagne plan the ceremony in Saint Peter's on Christmas Day, or did he merely accept the title of emperor? What did he have to gain from it? If, as Einhard implies, the coronation displeased Charlemagne, was that because it put the pope in the superior position of conferring power on the emperor? What were Pope Leo's motives in arranging the coronation?

Though final answers will probably never be found, several things seem certain. First, after the coronation Charlemagne considered himself an emperor ruling a Christian people. Through his motto, *Renovatio romani*

> ❝ He overcame their arrogant haughtiness with magnanimity, . . . by sending frequent ambassadors to them and in his letters addressing them as brothers. ❞
>
> **—EINHARD**

imperi (Revival of the Roman Empire), Charlemagne was consciously perpetuating old Roman imperial notions while at the same time identifying with the new Rome of the Christian church. In this sense, Charlemagne might be considered a precursor to the eventual Holy Roman emperor, although that term didn't come into use for two more centuries. Second, Leo's ideas about gender and rule undoubtedly influenced his decision to crown Charlemagne. In 800 the ruler of the Byzantine Empire was the empress Irene, the first woman to rule Byzantium in her own name, but Leo did not regard her authority as legitimate because she was female. He thus claimed to be placing Charlemagne on a vacant throne. Third, both parties gained: the Carolingian family received official recognition from the leading spiritual power in Europe, and the papacy gained a military protector.

Not surprisingly, the Byzantines regarded the papal acts as rebellious and Charlemagne as a usurper. The imperial coronation thus marks a decisive break between Rome and Constantinople. From Baghdad, however, Harun-al-Rashid (hah-ROON-ahl-rah-SHEED), caliph of the Abbasid (uh-BAH-suhd) Empire (786–809), congratulated the Frankish ruler with the gift of an elephant. It was named Abu'l Abbas after the founder of the Abbasid Dynasty and may have served as a symbol of the diplomatic link Harun-al-Rashid hoped to forge with the Franks against Byzantium. Having plodded its way to Charlemagne's court at Aachen, the elephant survived for nine years, and its death was considered important enough to be mentioned in the Frankish *Royal Annals* for the year 810. Like everyone else at Aachen, the elephant lived in a city that was far less sophisticated, healthy, and beautiful than the Baghdad of Harun-al-Rashid.

The coronation of Charlemagne, whether planned by the Carolingian court or by the papacy, was to have a profound effect on the course of German history and on the later history of Europe. In the centuries that followed, German rulers were eager to gain the imperial title and to associate themselves with the legends of Charlemagne and ancient Rome. Ecclesiastical authorities, on the other hand, continually cited the event as proof that the dignity of the imperial crown could be granted only by the pope.

Early Medieval Culture

What were the significant intellectual and cultural changes in Charlemagne's era? ◼

As he built an empire through conquest and strategic alliances, Charlemagne also set in motion a cultural revival that had long-lasting consequences. The stimulus he gave to scholarship and learning may, in fact, be his most enduring legacy, although at the time most people continued to live in a world where knowledge was transmitted orally.

The Carolingian Renaissance

In Roman Gaul through the fifth century, the general culture rested on an education that stressed grammar, Greco-Roman works of literature and history, and the legal and medical treatises of the Roman world. Beginning in the seventh and eighth centuries, a new cultural tradition common to Gaul, Italy, the British Isles, and to some extent Spain emerged. This culture was based primarily on Christian sources. Scholars have called the new Christian and ecclesiastical culture of the period from about 760 to 840, and the educational foundation on which it was based, the "Carolingian Renaissance" because Charlemagne was its major patron.

Charlemagne directed that every monastery in his kingdom should cultivate learning and educate the monks and secular clergy so that they would have a better understanding of the Christian writings. He also urged the establishment of cathedral and monastic schools where boys might learn to read and to pray properly. Thus the main purpose of this rebirth of learning was to promote an understanding of the Scriptures and of Christian writers and to instruct people to pray and praise God in the correct manner.

Women shared with men the work of evangelization and the new Christian learning. Rulers, noblemen, and

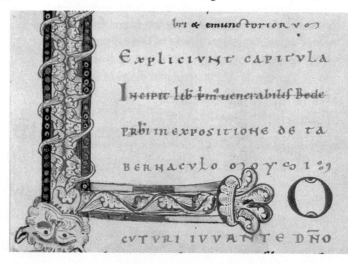

Carolingian Minuscule In the Carolingian period books played a large role in the spread of Christianity and in the promotion of learning. The development of the clearer script known as Carolingian minuscule shown here made books more legible and copying more efficient because more words could fit on the page. (The Schoyen Collection MS 076, Schoyen Bede de Tabernaculo, Oslo and London)

Saint Matthew This manuscript illumination shows Saint Matthew hard at work writing the Gospel that bears his name. He is holding a horn with ink in one hand and a quill in the other. Produced around 800 for Ebbo, the archbishop of the Frankish city of Reims, the illustrations in these Gospels seem strikingly modern in their portrayal of human emotion. (Erich Lessing/Art Resource, NY)

noblewomen founded monasteries for nuns, each governed by an abbess. The abbess oversaw all aspects of life in the monastery. She handled the business affairs, supervised the copying of manuscripts, and directed the daily round of prayer and worship. Women's monasteries housed women who were unmarried, and also often widows, children being taught to read and recite prayers and chants, elderly people seeking a safe place to live, and travelers needing hospitality. Some female houses were, in fact, double monasteries in which the abbess governed two adjoining establishments, one for women and one for men. Monks provided protection from attack and did the heavy work on the land in double monasteries, but nuns did everything else.

In monasteries and cathedral schools, monks, nuns, and scribes copied books and manuscripts and built up libraries. They developed the beautifully clear handwriting known as "Carolingian minuscule," with both uppercase and lowercase letters, from which modern Roman type is derived. Carolingian minuscule improved the legibility of texts and allowed more words to fit on a sheet of vellum — calfskin or lambskin specially prepared for writing. Scribes primarily copied Christian works, but also ancient secular literature. In this era before printed books, works could survive only if they were copied. Almost all of the works of Roman authors that we are now

able to read were preserved by the efforts of Carolingian scribes. Some scholars went beyond copying to develop their own ideas, and by the middle years of the ninth century there was a great outpouring of more sophisticated original works. Ecclesiastical writers imbued with the legal ideas of ancient Rome and the theocratic ideals of Saint Augustine instructed the semibarbaric rulers of the West.

The most important scholar at Charlemagne's court was Alcuin, who came from Northumbria, one of the kingdoms in England. He was the leader of a palace school at Aachen, where Charlemagne assembled learned men from all over Europe. From 781 until his death, Alcuin was the emperor's chief adviser on religious and educational matters. An unusually prolific writer, he prepared some of the emperor's official documents and wrote many moral *exempla*, or "models," that set high standards for royal behavior and constitute a treatise on kingship. Alcuin's letters to Charlemagne set forth political theories on the authority, power, and responsibilities of a Christian ruler.

Through monastic and cathedral schools, basic literacy in Latin was established among some of the clergy and even among some of the nobility, a change from Merovingian times. By the tenth century the patterns of thought and the lifestyles of educated western Europeans were those of Rome and Latin Christianity. Most people, however, continued to live in an oral and visual world. They spoke local languages, which did not have a written form. Christian services continued to be conducted in Latin, but not all village priests were able to attend a school, and many simply learned the service by rote. Some Latin words and phrases gradually penetrated the various vernacular languages, but the Carolingian Renaissance did not trickle down to ordinary people.

This division between a learned culture of Latin that built on the knowledge of the ancient world and a vernacular culture of local traditions can also be seen in medicine. Christian teaching supported concern for the poor, sick, and downtrodden. Churchmen taught that all knowledge came from God, who had supplied it for people to use for their own benefit. The foundation of a school at Salerno in southern Italy in the ninth century gave a tremendous impetus to medical study. The school's location attracted Arabic, Greek, and Jewish physicians from all over the Mediterranean region. Students flocked there even from northern Europe.

Despite the advances at Salerno, however, physicians were few in the early Middle Ages, and only the rich could afford them. Local folk medicine practiced by nonprofessionals provided help for commoners, with treatments made from herbs, bark, and other natural ingredients. Infants and children were especially susceptible to a range of illnesses, and about half of the children born died before age five. Although a few people, such as Queen Brunhilda, lived into their seventies, most did not, and a forty-year-old was considered old.

Scholarship and Religious Life in Northumbria

Charlemagne's court at Aachen was not the only center of learning in early medieval Christian Europe. Another was the Anglo-Saxon kingdom of Northumbria, situated at the northernmost tip of the old Roman world. Northumbrian creativity owes a great deal to the intellectual curiosity and collecting zeal of Saint Benet Biscop (ca. 628–689), who brought manuscripts and other treasures back from Italy. These formed the library on which much later study rested.

Northumbrian monasteries produced scores of books: missals (used for the celebration of the Mass); psalters (SAL-tuhrs), which contained the 150 psalms and other prayers used by the monks in their devotions; commentaries on the Scriptures; illuminated manuscripts; law codes; and collections of letters and sermons. (See "Individuals in Society: The Venerable Bede," at right.) The finest product of Northumbrian art is probably the Gospel book produced at Lindisfarne monastery around 700. The book was produced by a single scribe working steadily over a period of several years, with the expenses involved in the production of such a book—for vellum, coloring, and gold leaf—probably supplied by the monastery's aristocratic patrons.

As in Charlemagne's empire, women were important participants in Northumbrian Christian culture. Perhaps the most important abbess of the early medieval period anywhere in Europe was Saint Hilda (d. 680). A noblewoman of considerable learning and administrative ability, she ruled the double monastery of Whitby on the Northumbrian coast, advised kings and princes, and encouraged scholars and poets. In the seventh century two Christian forces were competing for the conversion of the pagan Anglo-Saxons in England: Roman-oriented missionaries traveling north from Canterbury, and Celtic monks from Ireland and northwestern Britain. The Roman and Celtic churches differed completely in their organization, types of monastic life, and methods of arriving at the date of the central feast of the Christian calendar, Easter. Through the influence of Abbess Hilda and the rulers of Northumbria, the Synod of Whitby (ecclesiastical council) held at Hilda's convent in 664 opted to follow the Roman practices. The missionaries who traveled from England to convert people on the continent, including Saint Boniface, thus viewed loyalty to Rome as a central part of Christian teachings. Several generations after Hilda, Boniface wrote many letters pleading for copies of books to send to Whitby and other houses of nuns; these letters attest to the nuns' intellectual reputations.

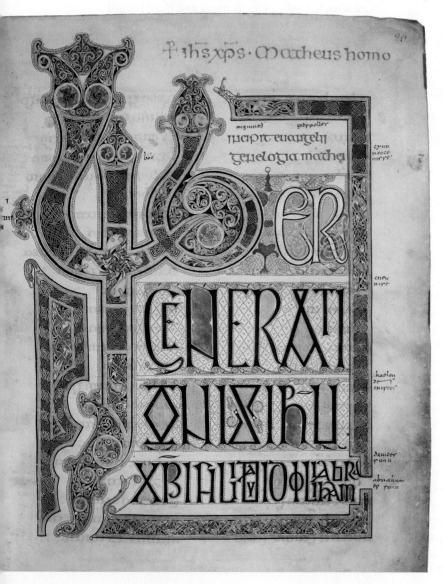

Lindisfarne Gospels The opening page of the Lindisfarne Gospels, produced around 700 by a monk at Lindisfarne Abbey in Northumbria. The style combines Celtic and Anglo-Saxon elements, with swirling geometric patterns that often look like animals or fill a whole page with vibrant color. (© British Library Board)

INDIVIDUALS IN SOCIETY

THE FINEST REPRESENTATIVE OF NORTHUMBRIAN, and indeed all Anglo-Saxon, scholarship is Bede (ca. 673–735). He was born into a noble family, and when he was seven his parents gave him as an oblate to Benet Biscop's monastery at Wearmouth. Later he was sent to the new monastery at Jarrow five miles away. Surrounded by the hundreds of pagan and Christian books Benet Biscop had brought from Italy, Bede spent the rest of his life there, studying and writing. He wrote textbooks on grammar and writing designed to help students master the intricacies of Latin, commentaries on the Old and New Testaments, historical works relating the lives of abbots and the development of the church, and scientific works on time. His biblical commentaries survive in hundreds of manuscripts, indicating that they were widely studied throughout the Middle Ages. His doctrinal works led him to be honored after his death with the title "Venerable," and centuries after his death to be named a "doctor of the church" by the pope.

Bede's religious writings were actually not that innovative, but his historical writings were, particularly his best-known work, the *Ecclesiastical History of the English People*, written about 720. The book is just what its title says it is: an *ecclesiastical* history, in which Bede's main topic is the growth of Christianity in England. It begins with a short discussion of Christianity in Roman Britain, then skips to Augustine of Canterbury's mission to the Anglo-Saxons (see page 196). Most of the book tells the story of Christianity's spread from one small kingdom in England to another, with missionaries and the kings who converted as its heroes, and ends with Bede's own day. Bede searched far and wide for his information, discussed the validity of his evidence, compared various sources, and exercised critical judgment. He includes accounts of miracles, but, like the stories of valiant missionaries, these are primarily related to provide moral lessons, which all medieval writers thought was the chief purpose of history.

One of the lessons that Bede sought to tell with history is that Christianity should be unified, and one feature of the *Ecclesiastical History of the English People* inadvertently provided a powerful model for this. In his history, Bede adopted a way of reckoning time proposed by an earlier monk that would eventually provide a uniform chronology for all Christians. He dated events from the incarnation of Christ, rather than from the foundation of the city of Rome, as the Romans had done, or from the regnal years of kings, as the Germans did. His history was recopied by monks in many parts of Europe, who used this dating method, *anno Domini*, "in the year of the Lord" (later abbreviated A.D.), for their own histories as well. (Though Bede does talk about "before the time of the incarnation of our Lord," the reverse dating system of B.C., "before Christ," does not seem to have been widely used before 1700.) Disputes about whether the year began with the incarnation (that is, the conception) of Christ or his birth, and whether these occurred in 1 B.C. or 1 A.D. (the Christian calendar does not have a year zero), continued after Bede, but his method triumphed.

A manuscript portrait of Bede, set within the first letter of a copy of his *Life of St. Cuthbert*. This is the letter "d," with the monster's head forming the upward line and Bede's foot the short downward line. There are no contemporary descriptions of Bede, so the later manuscript illuminator was free to imagine what he looked like. (Bodleian Library, University of Oxford, Ms Digby 20, folio 194r)

QUESTIONS FOR ANALYSIS

1. How do the career and accomplishments of Bede fit with the notion of an early medieval "renaissance" of learning?

2. Does Bede's notion that history has a moral purpose still shape the writing of history? Do you agree with him?

3. The Christian calendar dates from a midpoint rather than from a starting point, the way many of the world's calendars do. What advantages does this create in reckoning time? What would you see as the primary reason the Christian calendar has now been widely adopted worldwide?

Nuns and Learning In this tenth-century manuscript, the scholar Saint Aldhelm offers his book *In Praise of Holy Virgins* to a group of nuns, one of whom already holds a book. Early medieval nuns and monks spent much of their time copying manuscripts, preserving much of the learning of the classical world as well as Christian texts. (His Grace the Archbishop of Canterbury and the Trustees of Lambeth Palace Library. MS 200, fol. 68v)

Treaty of Verdun Treaty signed in 843 by Charlemagne's grandsons dividing the Carolingian Empire into three parts and setting the pattern for political boundaries in Europe still in use today.

At about the time the monks at Lindisfarne were producing their Gospel book, another author was probably at work on a nonreligious epic poem, *Beowulf* (BAY-uh-woolf). The poem tells the story of the hero Beowulf's progress from valiant warrior to wise ruler: first he fights and kills the monster Grendel and Grendel's mother, and later in life he slays a dragon that was threatening his people, dying in the process. In contrast to most writings of this era, which were in Latin, *Beowulf* was written in the vernacular Anglo-Saxon. The identity of its author (or authors) is unknown, but it was written in Christian England, and the author might have been a Northumbrian monk. All the events of the tale take place in (an imagined) pagan Denmark and Sweden, however, suggesting the close relationship between England and the northern European continent in the early Middle Ages. Given the challenges that would face them in the ninth century, actual residents of Europe may have wished they had more warriors like the fictional Beowulf.

The Treaty of Verdun, 843

Invasions and Migrations

How did the invasions and migrations of the Vikings, Magyars, and Muslims shape Europe? ■

Charlemagne left his vast empire to his sole surviving son, Louis the Pious (r. 814–840), who attempted to keep the empire intact. This proved to be impossible. Members of the nobility engaged in plots and open warfare against the emperor, often allying themselves with one of Louis's three sons. In 843, shortly after Louis's death, those sons agreed to the **Treaty of Verdun** (vehr-DUHN), which divided the empire into three parts: Charles the Bald received the western part; Lothar the middle and the title of emperor; and Louis the eastern part, from which he acquired the title "the German." Though no one knew it at the time, this treaty set the pattern for political boundaries in Europe that has been maintained until today.

After the Treaty of Verdun, continental Europe was fractured politically. All three kingdoms controlled by the sons of Louis the Pious were torn by domestic dissension and disorder. The frontier and coastal defenses erected by Charlemagne and maintained by Louis the Pious

Map 8.3 **Invasions and Migrations of the Ninth Century** This map shows the Viking, Magyar, and Arab invasions and migrations in the ninth century. Compare it with Map 7.3 (page 189) on the barbarian migrations of late antiquity to answer the following questions.

ANALYZING THE MAP What similarities do you see in the patterns of migration in these two periods? What significant differences?

CONNECTIONS How did Viking expertise in shipbuilding and sailing make their migrations different from those of earlier Germanic tribes? How did this set them apart from the Magyar and Muslim invaders of the ninth century?

To complete this activity online, go to the Online Study Guide at bedfordstmartins.com/mckaywest.

were neglected. No European political power was strong enough to put up effective resistance to external attacks. Beginning around 850 three main groups began relentless attacks on Europe: Vikings from Scandinavia, representing the final wave of Germanic migrants; Muslims from the Mediterranean; and Magyars forced westward by other peoples (Map 8.3).

Vikings in Western Europe

From the moors of Scotland to the mountains of Sicily, there arose in the ninth century the prayer, "Save us,

O God, from the violence of the Northmen." The Northmen, also known as Vikings, were Germanic peoples from the area of modern-day Norway, Sweden, and Denmark who had remained beyond the sway of the Christianizing influences of the Carolingian Empire. The Vikings retained most aspects of Germanic society (see Chapter 7): they had strong clan loyalties and responsibilities, many gods and goddesses, and oral traditions of law and poetry.

Some scholars believe that the name *Viking* derives from the old Norse word *vik*, meaning "creek." A Viking, then, was someone who waited in a creek or bay to attack

" Save us, O God, from the violence of the Northmen. "

—NINTH-CENTURY PRAYER

passing vessels, which accurately captures the great speed and maneuverability of their boats. Propelled either by oars or by sails, deckless, and about sixty-five-feet long, a Viking ship could carry between forty and sixty men—enough to harass an isolated monastery or village. These ships, navigated by experienced and fearless sailors, moved through complicated rivers, estuaries, and waterways in Europe. The Carolingian Empire, with no navy, was helpless. The Vikings moved swiftly, attacked, and escaped to return again.

Scholars disagree about the reasons for Viking attacks and migrations. A very unstable Danish kingship and disputes over the succession led to civil war and disorder, which may have driven warriors abroad in search of booty and supporters. The population of Scandinavia may have grown too large for the available land to support. Cities on the coasts of northern Europe offered targets for plunder. Goods plundered could then be sold, and looting raids turned into trading ventures. Some scholars assert that the Vikings were looking for trade and new commercial contacts from the beginning.

Whatever the motivations, Viking attacks were savage. The Vikings burned, looted, and did extensive property damage, although there is little evidence that they caused long-term physical destruction—perhaps because, arriving in small bands, they lacked the manpower to do so. They seized magnates and high churchmen and held them for ransom; they also demanded tribute from kings. In 844–845 Charles the Bald had to raise seven thousand pounds of silver, and across the English Channel Anglo-Saxon rulers collected a land tax, the Danegeld, to buy off the Vikings. In the Seine and Loire Valleys the frequent presence of Viking war bands seems to have had economic consequences, stimulating the production of food and wine and possibly the manufacture (for sale) of weapons and the breeding of horses.

The slave trade represented an important part of Viking plunder and commerce. Slaves, known as *thralls*, were common in Scandinavian society, and Vikings took people from the British Isles and territories along the Baltic Sea as part of their booty. They sold them as slaves in the markets of Magdeburg and Regensburg, at the fairs of Lyons, and in seaports of the Muslim world. Dublin became a center of the Viking slave trade, with hundreds and sometimes thousands of young men and women bought and sold there in any one year.

In the early tenth century Danish Vikings besieged Paris with fleets of more than a hundred highly maneuverable ships, and the Frankish king Charles the Simple bought them off in 911 by giving them a large part of northern France. There the Vikings established the province of "Northmanland," or Normandy as it was later known, intermarrying with the local population and creating a distinctive Norman culture. From there they sailed around Spain and into the Mediterranean, eventually conquering Sicily from the Muslim Arabs in 1060–1090, while other Normans crossed the English Channel, defeating Anglo-Saxon forces in 1066. Between 850 and 1000 Viking control of northern Europe reached its zenith. Norwegian Vikings moved farther west than any Europeans had before, establishing permanent settlements on Iceland and short-lived settlements in Greenland and Newfoundland in what is now Canada. (See "Listening to the Past: Eirik's Saga," page 230.)

The Vikings made positive contributions to the areas they settled. They carried their unrivaled knowledge of shipbuilding and seamanship everywhere. The northeastern and central parts of England where the Vikings settled became known as the *Danelaw* because Danish, not English, law and customs prevailed there. Scholars believe that some legal institutions, such as the ancestor of the modern grand jury, originated in the Danelaw. Exports from Ireland included iron tools and weapons manufactured there by Viking metal-smiths.

Slavs and Vikings in Eastern Europe

Vikings also brought change in eastern Europe, which was largely populated by Slavs. In antiquity the Slavs lived in central Europe, farming with iron technology, building fortified towns, and worshiping a variety of deities. With the start of the mass migrations of the late Roman Empire, the Slavs moved in different directions and split into what later historians identified as three groups: West, South, and East Slavs.

The group labeled the West Slavs included the Poles, Czechs, Slovaks, and Wends. The South Slavs, comprising peoples who became the Serbs, Croats, Slovenes, Macedonians, and Bosnians, migrated southward into the Balkans. In the seventh century Slavic peoples of the west and south created the state of Moravia along the banks of the Danube River. By the tenth century Moravia's residents were Roman Christian, along with most of the other West and South Slavs. The pattern was similar to that of the Germanic tribes: first the ruler was baptized, and then missionaries preached, built churches, and spread Christian teachings among the common people. The ruler of Poland was able to convince the pope to establish an independent archbishopric there in 1000, the beginning of a long-lasting connection between Poland and the Roman church. In the Balkans the Serbs accepted Orthodox Christianity, while the Croats became Roman Christian, a division with a long impact; it was one of the factors in the civil war in this area in the late twentieth century.

Between the fifth and ninth centuries the eastern Slavs moved into the vast areas of present-day European Russia and Ukraine. This enormous area consisted of an immense virgin forest to the north, where most of the eastern Slavs settled, and an endless prairie grassland to the south. In the tenth century Ibrahim Ibn Jakob, a learned Jew from the Muslim caliphate in Córdoba in Spain, traveled in Slavic areas. He found the Slavs to be "violent and inclined to aggression," but far cleaner than Christians in other parts of Europe in which he had traveled, "who wash only once or twice a year." Such filthy habits were unacceptable to someone raised in Muslim Spain, but the Slavs had an ingenious way of both getting clean and staying healthy: "They have no bathhouses as such, but they do make use of wooden huts (for bathing). They build a stone stove, on which, when it is heated, they pour water. . . . They hold a bunch of grass in their hands, and waft the stream around. Then their pores open, and all excess matter escapes from their bodies."[6]

In the ninth century the Vikings appeared in the lands of the eastern Slavs. Called "Varangians" in the old Russian chronicles, the Vikings were interested primarily in gaining wealth through plunder and trade, and the opportunities were good. Moving up and down the rivers, they soon linked Scandinavia and northern Europe to the Black Sea and to the Byzantine Empire's capital at Constantinople. They raided and looted the cities along the Caspian Sea several times in the tenth century, taking booty and slaves, which they then sold elsewhere; thus raiding turned into trading, and the Scandinavians later established settlements, intermarried, and assimilated with Slavic peoples.

In order to increase and protect their international commerce and growing wealth, the Vikings declared themselves the rulers of the eastern Slavs. According to tradition, the semi-legendary chieftain Ruirik founded a princely dynasty about 860. In any event, the Varangian ruler Oleg (r. 878–912) established his residence at Kiev in modern-day Ukraine. He and his successors ruled over a loosely united confederation of Slavic territories known as Rus, with its capital at Kiev, until 1054. (The word *Russia* comes from *Rus*, though the origins of *Rus* are hotly debated, with some historians linking it with Swedish words and others with Slavic words.)

Oleg and his clansmen quickly became assimilated into the Slavic population, taking local wives and emerging as the noble class. Missionaries of the Byzantine Empire converted the Vikings and local Slavs to Eastern Orthodox Christianity, accelerating the unification of the two groups. Thus the rapidly Slavified Vikings left two important legacies for the future: in about 900 they created a loose unification of Slavic territories, **Kievan Rus**, under a single ruling prince and dynasty, and they imposed a basic religious unity by accepting Orthodox Christianity, as opposed to Roman Catholicism, for themselves and the eastern Slavs.

Even at its height under Great Prince Iaroslav (YAHR-uh-slahv) the Wise (r. 1019–1054), the unity of Kievan Rus was extremely tenuous. Trade, not government, was

Kievan Rus, ca. 1050

- Area settled by Varangians, ca. 880
- Kievan Rus, 1054

Kievan Rus A confederation of Slavic territories, with its capital at Kiev, ruled by descendants of the Vikings.

Animal Headpost from Viking Ship Skilled woodcarvers produced ornamental headposts for ships, sledges, wagons, and bedsteads. The fearsome quality of many carvings suggests that they were intended to ward off evil spirits and to terrify. (© University Museum of Cultural Heritage, Oslo. Photographer: Eirik Irgens Johnsen)

Political Revival and the Origins of the Modern State

How did medieval rulers create larger and more stable territories? ■

The modern state is an organized territory with definite geographical boundaries, a body of law, and institutions of government. The modern national state counts on the loyalty of the majority of its citizens; in return it provides citizens with order and protection. It supplies a currency or medium of exchange that permits financial and commercial transactions, and it conducts relations with foreign governments. To accomplish these minimal functions, the state must have officials, bureaucracies, laws, courts of law, soldiers, information, and money. This modern concept of state could not exist during the political instability of the early Middle Ages. Boundaries and loyalties were in constant flux. Civil unrest was rampant. Rulers did not have jurisdiction over many people or the income to support a bureaucracy, and their laws affected a relative few. There existed many, frequently overlapping layers of authority — earls, counts, barons, knights — between a king and the ordinary people.

Beginning in the eleventh century medieval rulers worked to promote domestic order, reducing private warfare and civil anarchy. In some parts of Europe lords in control of large territories began to manipulate feudal institutions to build up their power even further, becoming kings over growing and slowly centralizing states. As rulers expanded their territories and extended their authority, they developed larger bureaucracies, armies, judicial systems, and other institutions of state to maintain control. Because these institutions cost money, rulers in various countries initiated systems for generating revenue and handling financial matters. Although some rulers were more successful than others, the solutions they found to these problems laid the foundations for modern national states.

England

Throughout the ninth century the Vikings had made a concerted effort to conquer and rule all of Anglo-Saxon England. Because of its proximity to Scandinavia and its lack of unity under a single ruler, England probably suffered more from Viking invasions than any other part of Europe. In 878 the remarkable Alfred, king of the West Saxons (or Wessex), defeated the Vikings, inaugurating a period of recovery and stability in England. Alfred and his immediate successors built a system of local defenses and slowly extended royal rule beyond Wessex to other Anglo-Saxon peoples until one law, royal law, took precedence over local custom. England was divided into local units called "shires," or counties, each under the jurisdiction of a shire-reeve (a word that soon evolved into "sheriff") appointed by the king. Sheriffs were unpaid officials from well-off families responsible for collecting taxes, catching and trying criminals, and raising infantry.

The Viking invasions of England did not end, however, and the island eventually came under Viking rule. The Viking Canute (r. 1016–1035) made England

The Bayeux Tapestry William's conquest of England was recorded in an embroidery panel measuring 231 feet by 19 inches. In this scene, two nobles (center left) and a bishop (center right) acclaim Harold Godwinson as king of England (center). Harold holds a scepter and an orb with a cross on top, symbolizing his secular and religious authority. The embroidery provides an important historical source for the clothing, armor, and lifestyles of the Norman and Anglo-Saxon warrior classes. It is now on display in Bayeux (bay-YUH), France, and is incorrectly called a "tapestry," a different kind of needlework. (Tapisserie de Bayeux et avec autorisation spéciale de la Ville de Bayeux)

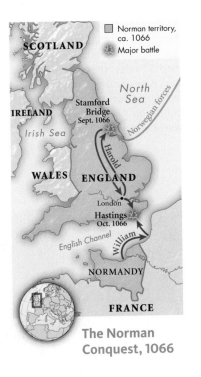

Norman territory, ca. 1066

Major battle

The Norman Conquest, 1066

936–973	Reign of Otto I in Germany; facilitates spread of Christianity in the Baltics and eastern Europe
ca. 1000s	"Holy Roman Empire" increasingly used to describe central European territories
1059	Lateran Council restricts election of the pope to the college of cardinals
1061–1091	Normans defeat Muslims and Byzantines in Sicily
1066	Norman conquest of England
1075	Pope Gregory VII decrees that clerics who accept lay investiture will be deposed and involved laymen excommunicated
1095–1291	Crusades
1100–1135	Reign of Henry I of England; establishment of the Exchequer, England's bureau of finance
1100–1200	Establishment of canon law
1154–1189	Reign of Henry II of England; revision of legal procedure; beginnings of common law
1162	Thomas Becket named archbishop of Canterbury
1170	Thomas Becket assassinated
1180–1223	Reign of Philip II (Philip Augustus) in France; territory of France greatly expanded
1198–1216	Innocent III; height of the medieval papacy
1208	Crusade against the Albigensians begins
1215	Magna Carta
1230s	Papacy creates the Inquisition
1290	Jews expelled from England
1298	Pope Boniface VIII orders all nuns to be cloistered
1306	Jews expelled from France
1397	Queen Margrete establishes Union of Kalmar

the center of his empire while promoting a policy of assimilation and reconciliation between Anglo-Saxons and Vikings. When Canute's heir Edward died childless, there were a number of claimants to the throne of England—the Anglo-Saxon noble Harold Godwinson (ca. 1022–1066), who had been crowned by English nobles; the Norwegian king Harald III (r. 1045–1066), grandson of Canute; and Duke William of Normandy, who was the illegitimate son of Edward's cousin.

In 1066 the forces of Harold Godwinson crushed an invading Norwegian army in northern England, then quickly marched south when they heard that William had invaded England with his Norman vassals. Harold's soldiers were exhausted, and they were decisively defeated by William's at the Battle of Hastings—an event now known as the Norman conquest. In both England and Normandy, William the Conqueror limited the power of his noble vassals and church officials and transformed the feudal system into a unified monarchy. In England he replaced Anglo-Saxon sheriffs with Normans. He retained another Anglo-Saxon device, the writ, through which the central government communicated with people at the local level, using the local tongue.

In addition to retaining Anglo-Saxon institutions that served his purposes, William also introduced a major innovation, the Norman inquest or general in-

quiry. William wanted to determine how much wealth there was in his new kingdom, who held what land, and what land had been disputed among his vassals since the conquest of 1066. Groups of royal officials were sent to every part of the country, and in every village groups of local men were put under oath to answer the questions of the king's officials. In the words of a contemporary chronicler:

He sent his men over all England into every shire and had them find out how many hundred hides there were in the shire [a hide was a measure of land large enough to support one family], or what land and cattle the king himself had, or what dues he ought to have in twelve months from the shire. Also . . . what or how

241

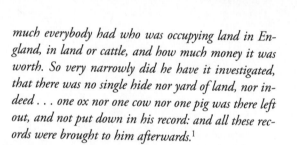

much everybody had who was occupying land in England, in land or cattle, and how much money it was worth. So very narrowly did he have it investigated, that there was no single hide nor yard of land, nor indeed . . . one ox nor one cow nor one pig was there left out, and not put down in his record: and all these records were brought to him afterwards.[1]

The resulting record, called the **Domesday Book** (DOOMZ-day) from the Anglo-Saxon word *doom*, meaning "judgment," still survives. It is an invaluable source of social and economic information about medieval England.

The *Domesday Book* provided William and his descendants with information vital for the exploitation and government of the country. Knowing the amount of wealth every area possessed, the king could tax accordingly. Knowing the amount of land his vassals had, he could allot knight service fairly. The book helped William and future English kings regard their country as one unit.

William's son Henry I (r. 1100–1135) established a bureau of finance called the **Exchequer** (named for the checkered tablecloth on which officials placed markers representing money as they figured out what was owed and paid), which became the first institution of the government bureaucracy of England. In addition to various taxes and annual gifts, Henry's income came from money paid to the Crown for settling disputes and as penalties for crimes, as well as money due to him in his private position as feudal lord. The latter would include the fee paid by a vassal's son in order to inherit the father's properties and the fee paid by a knight who wished to avoid military service. Henry, like other medieval kings, made no distinction between his private income and state revenues, though the officials of the Exchequer began to keep careful records of the monies paid into and out of the royal treasury.

In 1128 Henry's daughter Matilda was married to Geoffrey of Anjou; their son became Henry II of England and inaugurated the Angevin (AN-juh-vuhn; from Anjou, his father's county) dynasty. Henry II inherited the French provinces of Anjou, Normandy, Maine, and Touraine in northwestern France, and then in 1152 he claimed lordship over Aquitaine, Poitou (pwah-TOO), and Gascony in southwestern France through his marriage to the great heiress Eleanor of Aquitaine (Map 9.1). Each of the provinces in Henry's Angevin empire was separate and was only loosely linked to the others by dynastic law and personal oaths. The histories of England and France became closely inter-

Domesday Book A general inquiry about the wealth of his lands ordered by William of Normandy; it is a valuable source of social and economic information about medieval England.

Exchequer The bureau of finance established by Henry I; the first institution of the governmental bureaucracy of England.

twined, however, leading to disputes and conflicts down to the fifteenth century.

France

France also became increasingly unified in this era. Following the death of the last Carolingian ruler in 987, an assembly of nobles selected Hugh Capet (kah-PAY) as his successor. Soon after his own coronation, Hugh crowned his oldest surviving son Robert as king to ensure the succession and prevent disputes after his death. This broke with the earlier practices of elective kingship or dividing a kingdom among one's sons, establishing instead the principle of **primogeniture** (prigh-muh-JEH-nuh-choor), in which the king's eldest son received the Crown as his rightful inheritance. Primogeniture became the standard pattern of succession in medieval western Europe, and also became an increasingly common pattern of inheritance for noble titles as well as land and other forms of wealth among all social classes.

The Capetian (kuh-PEE-shuhn) kings were weak, but they laid the foundation for later political stability. This stability came slowly. In the early twelfth century France still consisted of a number of virtually independent provinces. Each was governed by a local ruler; each had its own laws, customs, coinage, and dialect. Unlike the king of England, who reigned supreme over a unified kingdom, the king of France maintained clear jurisdiction over a relatively small area. Chroniclers called King Louis VI (r. 1108–1137) king of Saint-Denis because the territory he controlled was limited to Paris and the Saint-Denis area surrounding the city (see Map 9.1). This region, called the Île-de-France (IHL-duh-frahnz), or royal domain, became the nucleus of the French state. Over time medieval French kings worked to increase the royal domain and extend their authority over the provinces.

The work of unifying France began under Louis VI's grandson Philip II (r. 1180–1223). Rigord, Philip's biographer, gave him the Roman title "Augustus" (from a Latin word meaning "to increase") because he vastly enlarged the territory of the kingdom of France. When King John of England, who was Philip's vassal for the rich province of Normandy, defaulted on his feudal obligation to come to the French court, Philip declared that Normandy forfeit to the French crown. He enforced his declaration militarily, and in 1204 Normandy fell to the French. He gained other northern provinces as well, and by the end of his reign Philip was effectively master of northern France. In the thirteenth century Philip Augustus's descendants acquired important holdings in the south. By the end of the thirteenth century most of the provinces of modern France had been added to the royal domain through diplomacy, marriage, war, and inheritance.

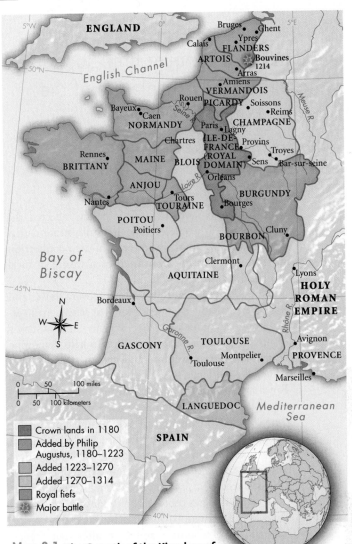

Map 9.1 The Growth of the Kingdom of France, 1180–1314 Some scholars believe that Philip II received the title "Augustus" (from a Latin word meaning "to increase") because he vastly expanded the territories of the kingdom of France. The province of Toulouse in the south became part of France as a result of the crusade against the Albigensians (see page 265).

In addition to expanding the royal territory, Philip Augustus devised a method of governing the provinces and providing for communication between the central government in Paris and local communities. Each province retained its own institutions and laws, but royal agents were sent from Paris into the provinces as the king's official representatives with authority to act for him. These agents were often middle-class lawyers who possessed full judicial, financial, and military jurisdiction in their districts. They were never natives of the provinces to which they were assigned, and they

primogeniture An inheritance system in which the oldest son inherits all land and noble titles.

❝ There was not a people . . . that could harm or conquer him, supported as he was by the consolation of the heavenly King. ❞

— **HROSWITHA OF GANDERSHEIM**

could not own land there. This policy reflected the fundamental principle of French administration that officials should gain their power from their connection to the monarchy, not from their own wealth or local alliances.

Philip Augustus and his successors were slower and less effective than were English kings at setting up an efficient bureau of finance. There was no national survey of property like the *Domesday Book* to help determine equitable levels of taxation, and French nobles—who owned the most land—resisted paying any taxes or fees. Royal agents sent from Paris had the official authority to collect revenue, but in many areas they did not have the power to actually do so if a local noble or provincial governing body refused. Because, by design, agents had no connections to the communities to which they were sent, they did not have local networks of power on which to rely for assistance, as did English sheriffs. Not until the fourteenth century, as a result of the Hundred Years' War, did a national financial bureau emerge—the Chamber of Accounts—and even after that French nobles continued to pay little or no taxes, a problem that would help spark the French Revolution.

Central Europe

In central Europe the German king Otto I (r. 936–973) defeated many other lords to build his power from his original base in Saxony. Some of our knowledge of Otto derives from *The Deeds of Otto*, a history of his reign in heroic verse written by a nun, Hroswitha of Gandersheim (ca. 935–ca. 1003). Hroswitha viewed the decline of the Carolingians and the rise of the Ottonians as God's will:

> *After the King of Kings, Who alone rules forever, by His own power changing the fortunes of all kings, decreed that the distinguished realm of the Franks be transferred to the famous race of the Saxons, a race which because of its steadfast rigor of spirit fittingly derived its name from rock [saxum was "rock" in Latin], the son of the great and revered Duke Otto, namely Henry, was the first to receive the kingly authority to be administered with moderation in behalf of a righteous nation.*

Otto's victories were also part of God's plan: "As often as he set out for war, there was not a people, though haughty because of its strength, that could harm or conquer him, supported as he was by the consolation of the heavenly King."[2]

Otto had God's money as well as God's favor, garnering financial support from church leaders and the bulk of his army from ecclesiastical lands. He also asserted the right to control ecclesiastical appointments. Before receiving religious consecration and being invested with the staff and ring symbolic of their offices, bishops and abbots had to perform feudal homage for the lands that accompanied the church office. This practice, later known as "lay investiture," created a grave crisis between

Seal of Frederick Barbarossa Rulers and other figures of authority signed proclamations, laws, and documents to make them official, but they also attached wax seals that often bore their likenesses. Like the portrait of William the Conqueror on the Bayeux tapestry, this seal of Frederick Barbarossa shows him seated on a throne, wearing a crown, and holding an orb and a scepter, all of which were symbols of power. (Bildarchiv Preussischer Kulturbesitz/Art Resource, NY)

the church and the monarchy in the eleventh century (see page 253). Hroswitha might not have been so lavish with her praise of Otto had she known the troubles his policies would bring to the church.

In 955 Otto I inflicted a crushing defeat on the Magyars in the Battle of Lechfeld (see Chapter 8), which made Otto a great hero to the Germans. In 962 he used this victory to have himself crowned emperor by the pope in Aachen, which had been the capital of the Carolingian Empire. He chose this site to symbolize his intention to continue the tradition of Charlemagne and to demonstrate papal support for his rule. It was not exactly clear what Otto was the emperor of, however, though by the eleventh century people were increasingly using the term **Holy Roman Empire** to refer to a loose confederation of principalities, duchies, cities, bishoprics, and other types of regional governments stretching from Denmark to Rome and from Burgundy to Poland (Map 9.2).

In this large area of central Europe, unified nation-states did not come into existence until the nineteenth century. Before that time the Holy Roman emperors shared power with princes, dukes, archbishops, counts, bishops, abbots, and cities. The office of emperor remained an elected one, though the electors included only seven men—four secular rulers of large territories within the empire and three archbishops.

Through most of the first half of the twelfth century, civil war wracked Germany. When Conrad III died in 1152, the resulting anarchy was so terrible that the electors decided the only alternative to continued chaos was the selection of a strong ruler. They chose Frederick Barbarossa of the house of Hohenstaufen (HOH-uhn-shtow-fuhn) (r. 1152–1190).

Like William the Conqueror in England and Philip in France, Frederick required vassals to take an oath of allegiance to him as emperor and appointed officials to exercise full imperial authority over local communities. He forbade private warfare and established sworn peace associations with the princes of various regions. These peace associations punished criminals and those who breached the peace, with penalties ranging from maiming to execution.

Frederick Barbarossa surrounded himself with men trained in the Roman law that had been codified during the rule of the emperor Justinian (see Chapter 7). Justinian's *Code* stated that "what pleases the prince has the force of law," an idea Frederick used to justify his assertion of imperial rights over the increasingly wealthy towns of northern Italy. Soldiers backed up his legal claims; between 1154 and 1188 Frederick made six expeditions into Italy. While he initially made significant conquests in the north, the Italian cities formed leagues to oppose him, and also allied with the papacy. In 1176 Frederick suffered a crushing defeat at Legnano, where

the league armies took massive amounts of booty and many prisoners (see Map 9.2). This battle marked the first time a feudal cavalry of armed knights was decisively defeated by an army largely made of infantrymen from the cities. Frederick was forced to recognize the municipal autonomy of the northern Italian cities and the pope's sovereignty in central Italy.

Holy Roman Empire
The loose confederation of principalities, duchies, cities, bishoprics, and other types of regional governments stretching from Denmark to Rome and from Burgundy to Poland.

Map 9.2 **The Holy Roman Empire, ca. 1200** Frederick Barbarossa greatly expanded the size of the Holy Roman Empire, but it remained a loose collection of various types of governments.

Sicily

The kingdom of Sicily is a good example of how a strong government could be built on a feudal base by determined rulers. Between 1061 and 1091 a bold Norman knight, Roger de Hauteville, with papal support and a small band of mercenaries, defeated the Muslims and Byzantines who controlled Sicily. Roger then faced the problem of governing Sicily's heterogeneous population of native Sicilians, Italians, Greeks, Jews, Arabs, and Normans. Roger distributed scattered fiefs to his followers so no vassal would have a centralized power base. He took an inquest of royal property and rights and forbade private warfare. To these Norman practices, Roger fused Arabic and Greek governmental devices. For example, he retained the main financial agency of the previous Muslim rulers, the diwān (dee-WAHN), a sophisticated bureau for record keeping and administration.

In the multicultural society of medieval Sicily, Muslims and Greeks, as well as Normans, staffed the diwān

Kingdom of Sicily, 1137

PAPAL STATES

Adriatic Sea

Rome

Capua

Naples   Salerno

KINGDOM OF SICILY

Palermo   Messina

Sicily

as well as the army and judiciary. The diwān kept official documents in Greek, Latin, and Arabic. It supervised the royal estates in Sicily, collected revenues, managed the state monopoly of the sale of salt and lumber, and registered all income to the treasury. With revenues derived from those products, Roger hired mercenaries. He encouraged appeals from local courts to his royal court because such appeals implied respect for his authority.

In 1137 Roger's son and heir, Count Roger II, took the city of Naples and much of the surrounding territory in southern Italy. The entire area came to be known as the kingdom of Sicily (or sometimes the kingdom of the Two Sicilies), and was often caught up in conflicts between the pope, the Holy Roman emperor, and the kings of France and Spain over control of Italy.

Roger II's grandson Frederick II (r. 1212–1250), who was also the grandson of Frederick Barbarossa of Germany, was crowned king of the Germans at Aachen (1216) and Holy Roman emperor at Rome (1220). He concentrated his attention on Sicily, however, and showed little interest in the northern part of the Holy Roman Empire. Frederick repeated Roger's ban on private warfare and placed all castles and towers under royal administration. He also replaced town officials with royal governors and subordinated feudal and ecclesiastical courts to the king's courts. Royal control of the nobility, of the towns, and of the judicial system added up to great centralization, which required a professional bureaucracy and sound state financing.

Frederick had grown up in multicultural Sicily, knew six languages, wrote poetry, and supported scientists, scholars, and artists, whatever their religion or background. In 1224 he founded the University of Naples to train officials for his bureaucracy. He too continued the use of Muslim institutions such as the diwān, and he tried to administer justice fairly to all his subjects, declaring, "We cannot in the least permit Jews and Saracens [Muslims] to be defrauded of the power of our protection and to be deprived of all other help, just because the difference of their religious practices makes them hate-

Palatine Chapel at Palermo Muslim craftsmen from Egypt painted the wooden ceiling of the royal chapel for King Roger of Sicily. This section shows the diverse peoples—Jews, Christians, and Muslims—who lived in Palermo. (Burgerbibliothek Bern Cod. 120 II, fol. 98r)

66 We cannot in the least permit Jews and Saracens [Muslims] to be defrauded of the power of our protection. 99

— KING FREDERICK II

ful to Christians," implying a degree of toleration exceedingly rare at the time.[3]

Because of his broad interests and abilities, Frederick's contemporaries called him the "Wonder of the World." He certainly transformed the kingdom of Sicily. But Sicily required constant attention, and Frederick's absences on crusades and on campaigns in mainland Italy took their toll. Shortly after he died, the unsupervised bureaucracy fell to pieces. The pope, as feudal overlord of Sicily, called in a French prince to rule. Frederick's reign had also weakened imperial power in the German parts of the empire, and in the later Middle Ages lay and ecclesiastical princes held sway in the Holy Roman Empire. This was one of the reasons that Germany and Italy did not become unified states until the nineteenth century.

The Iberian Peninsula

From the eleventh to the thirteenth centuries, power in the Iberian Peninsula shifted from Muslim to Christian rulers. In the eleventh century divisions and civil war in the caliphate of Córdoba allowed Christian armies to conquer an increasingly large part of the Iberian Peninsula. Castile, in the north-central part of the peninsula, became the strongest of the growing Christian kingdoms, and Aragon, in the northeast, the second most powerful. In 1085 King Alfonso VI of Castile and León captured Toledo in central Spain. The following year forces of the Almoravid dynasty that ruled much of northwestern Africa defeated Christian armies, and halted Christian advances southward, though they did not retake Toledo. The Almoravids reunified the Muslim state for several generations, but the Christians regrouped, and in their North African homeland the Almoravids were overthrown by a rival dynasty, the Almohads, who then lay claim to the remaining Muslim territories in southern Spain.

Alfonso VIII (1158–1214), aided by the kings of Aragon, Navarre, and Portugal, crushed the Almohad-led Muslims at Las Navas de Tolosa in 1212, accelerating the Christian push southward. James the Conqueror of Aragon (r. 1213–1276) captured Valencia on the

Córdoba Mosque and Cathedral The huge arches of the Great Mosque at Cordóba dwarf the cathedral built in the center after the city was conquered by Christian armies in 1236. During the reconquista, Christian kings often transformed mosques into churches, often by simply adding Christian elements such as crosses and altars to the existing structures. (dbimages/Alamy)

The Magna Carta

Henry II's sons Richard I, known as the Lion-Hearted (r. 1189–1199), and John (r. 1199–1216) lacked their father's interest in the work of government. Richard looked on England as a source of revenue for his military enterprises. Soon after his accession, he departed on a crusade to the Holy Land. During his reign he spent only six months in England, and the government was run by ministers trained under Henry II.

John's basic problems were financial. King John inherited a heavy debt from his father and brother, and his efforts to squeeze money from knights, widows, and merchants created an atmosphere of resentment. In July 1214 John's cavalry suffered a severe defeat at the hands of Philip Augustus of France at Bouvines in Flanders. This battle ended English hopes for the recovery of territories from France and also strengthened the opposition to John. His ineptitude as a soldier in a society that idealized military glory was the final straw. Rebellion begun by northern barons eventually grew to involve many key members of the English nobility. After lengthy negotiations, John met the barons in 1215 at Runnymede and was forced to approve the peace treaty called **Magna Carta**. The document name comes from the Latin words *magna*, meaning "great or large" (because it was so long and detailed), and *carta*, for "charter."

Magna Carta A peace treaty intended to redress the grievances that particular groups had against King John, later viewed as the source of English rights and liberty more generally.

To contemporaries, Magna Carta was intended to redress the grievances that particular groups—the barons, the clergy, the merchants of London—had against King John. Charters were not unusual: many kings and lords at the time issued them and then sometimes revoked them, as John did almost immediately. This revocation was largely ignored, however, and every English king until 1485 reissued Magna Carta as evidence of his promise to observe the law. Thus, this charter alone acquired enduring importance. It came to signify the principle that everyone, including the king and the government, must obey the law.

In the later Middle Ages references to Magna Carta underlined the old Augustinian theory that a government, to be legitimate, must promote law, order, and justice (see Chapter 6). An English king may not disregard or arbitrarily suspend the law to suit his convenience. The Magna Carta also contains the germ of the idea of "due process of law," meaning that a person has the right to be heard and defended in court and is entitled to the protection of the law. Because later generations referred to Magna Carta as a written statement of English liberties, it gradually came to have an almost sacred importance as a guarantee of law and justice.

Law in Everyday Life

Statements of legal principles such as the Magna Carta were not how most people experienced the law in medieval Europe. Instead they were involved in or witnessed something judged to be a crime, and then experienced or watched the determination of guilt and the punishment. Judges determined guilt or innocence in a number of ways. In some cases, particularly those in which there was little clear evidence, they ordered a trial by ordeal. An accused person could be tried by fire or water. In the latter case, the accused was tied hand and foot and dropped in a lake or river. People believed that water was a pure substance and would reject anything foul or unclean. Thus a person who sank was considered innocent; a person who floated was found guilty. Trial by ordeal was a ritual that appealed to the supernatural for judgment. God determined guilt or innocence, and thus a priest had to be present to bless the water.

Trials by ordeal are fascinating to modern audiences, but they were relatively rare, and their use declined over the High Middle Ages as judges and courts increasingly favored more rational procedures. Instead judges heard testimony, sought witnesses, and read written evidence if it was available. A London case in 1277 provides a good example of how law worked on the ground. Around Easter, the owner of a house in the city in which the tenant had disappeared sent a man to clean it, "but when he came to a dark and narrow place where coals were usually kept, he there found [a] headless body; upon seeing which, he sent word to the chamberlain and sheriffs." These officials went to the house "and calling together the good men of that ward . . . diligent inquisition was made as to how this had happened." The men who lived nearby said that the headless body belonged to Symon de Winten, a tavern owner, whom they had seen quarreling with his servant Roger in early December. That night Roger "seized a knife, and with it cut the throat of Symon quite through, so that the head was entirely severed from the body." He had stuffed the body in the coal room, stolen clothes and a silver cup, and disappeared. "Being asked what became of the head so cut off, they say they know not," and Roger "has not been seen since."[5] The surviving records don't indicate whether Roger was ever caught, but they do indicate that the sheriffs took something as "surety" from the neighbors who testified, that is, cash or goods as a pledge that their testimony was true. Taking sureties from witnesses was a common practice, which may be why the neighbors had not come forward on their own even though they seemed to have very intimate knowledge of the murder, which had happened months earlier. People were supposed to report crimes, and because towns and villages had no police as we know them, they were expected to chase the perpetrator and yell to others to join what was

Punishment of Adulterers A man and a woman found guilty of adultery are led naked through the streets in this thirteenth-century French manuscript, preceded by heralds blowing horns and followed by men carrying sticks. This procession may be driving the couple out of town; banishment was a very common punishment for a number of crimes, including theft and assault. (Visual Arts Library/Art Resource, NY)

termed "raising the hue and cry." They could be fined for not doing so, but it is clear from this case that such community involvement in crime fighting did not always happen.

Had Roger been caught and found guilty, his punishment would have been as public as the investigation. Murder was a capital crime, as were a number of other violent acts, and executions took place outdoors on a scaffold. Hanging was the most common method of execution, although nobles might be beheaded because hanging was seen as demeaning. More serious crimes, such as treason or rebellion, were sometimes punished by quartering, that is, pulling the person apart by ropes attached to horses. Execution for heresy and other religious crimes was often by burning (see page 266). Executioners were feared figures, but they were also well-paid public officials and were a necessary part of the legal structure.

The Papacy

How did the papacy attempt to reform the church, and what were the results of the efforts? ■

Kings and emperors were not the only rulers consolidating their power in the High Middle Ages; the papacy did as well, through a series of measures that made the church more independent of secular control. In the ninth and tenth centuries factions in Rome had sought to control the papacy for their own material gain, and feudal lords everywhere controlled the appointment of church officials. Popes and bishops were appointed to advance the political ambitions of their own families rather than for special spiritual qualifications. A combination of political machinations and sexual immorality ensued, damaging the church's moral prestige. Under the leadership of a series of reforming popes in the eleventh century, the church tried to correct some of these problems, but the popes' efforts were sometimes challenged by medieval kings and emperors.

The Gregorian Reforms

During the ninth and tenth centuries the church had come under the control of kings and feudal lords, who chose priests and bishops in their territories, granting them fiefs and expecting loyalty and service in return. Church offices from village priest to pope were sources of income as well as positions of authority. Officeholders had the right to collect taxes and fees and often the profits from the land under their control. Church offices were thus sometimes sold outright—a practice called **simony** (SIGH-muh-nee), after Simon Magus, a wealthy man mentioned in the New Testament who wanted to buy his way into Heaven. Not surprisingly, clergy at all levels who had bought their positions or had been granted them for political reasons provided

> **simony** The buying and selling of church offices, officially prohibited but often practiced.

little spiritual guidance, and their personal lives were rarely models of high moral standards.

Popes were chosen by wealthy Roman families from among their members, and after gaining the papal office they paid more attention to their families' political fortunes than to the institutional or spiritual health of the church. For example, Pope John XII (pontificate 955–963) was appointed pope by his powerful father when he was only eighteen, and lacking interest in spiritual matters he concentrated on expanding papal territories.

At the local parish level, there were many married priests. Taking Christ as the model for the priestly life, the Roman church had always encouraged clerical celibacy, and celibacy had been an obligation for ordination since the fourth century. But in the tenth and eleventh centuries probably a majority of European priests were married or living with women, and in some cases they were handing down church positions and property to their children.

Serious efforts to change all this began under Pope Leo IX (pontificate 1049–1054). Leo ordered clergy in Rome to dismiss their wives and invalidated the ordination of church officials who had purchased their offices. Pope Leo and his successors believed that secular or lay control over the church was largely responsible for its lack of moral leadership, so they proclaimed the church independent from secular rulers. The Lateran Council of 1059 decreed that the authority and power to elect the pope rested solely in the **college of cardinals**, a special group of priests from the major churches in and around Rome. The college retains that power today. In the Middle Ages the college of cardinals numbered around twenty-five or thirty, most of them from Italy. In 1586 the figure was set at seventy, though today it is much larger, with cardinals from around the world. When the office of pope was vacant, the cardinals were responsible for governing the church.

Leo's successor Pope Gregory VII (pontificate 1073–1085) was even more vigorous in his championing of reform and expansion of papal power; for that reason, the eleventh-century movement is frequently called the "Gregorian reform movement." He denounced clerical marriage and simony in harsh language and ordered those who disagreed excommunicated (cut off from the sacraments and all Christian worship). He believed

college of cardinals A special group of high clergy with the authority and power to elect the pope and the responsibility to govern the church when the office of the pope is vacant.

Emperor Otto III Handing a Staff to Archbishop Adalbert of Prague In this panel from a massive bronze door commemorating an event from the late tenth century, the emperor gives the bishop his staff, the symbol of the bishop's spiritual authority. Receiving the staff from the emperor gave the appearance that the bishop gained his spiritual rights from the secular power. Pope Gregory VII vigorously objected to this practice. (Bildarchiv Preussischer Kulturbesitz/Art Resource, NY)

that the pope, as the successor of Saint Peter, was the vicar of God on earth and that papal orders were the orders of God. Thus he was the first pope to emphasize the political authority of the papacy. Gregory was particularly opposed to **lay investiture**—the selection and appointment of church officials by secular authority, often symbolized by laymen giving bishops and abbots their symbols of office, such as a staff and ring. In February 1075 Pope Gregory held a council at Rome that decreed that clerics who accepted investiture from laymen were to be deposed, and laymen who invested clerics were to be excommunicated.

The church's penalty of **excommunication** relied for its effectiveness on public opinion. Gregory believed that the strong support he enjoyed for his moral reforms would carry over to his political ones; he thought that excommunication would compel rulers to abide by his changes. Immediately, however, Henry IV in the Holy Roman Empire, William the Conqueror in England, and Philip I in France protested. Gregory's reforms would deprive them not only of church income but also of the right to choose which monks and clerics would help them administer their kingdoms. The tension between the papacy and the monarchy would have a major impact on both institutions and society.

Meanwhile, the Gregorian reform movement built a strict hierarchical church structure with bishops and ordained priests higher in status than nuns, who could not be ordained. The double monasteries of the early Middle Ages were placed under the authority of male abbots. Church councils in the eleventh and twelfth centuries forbade monks and nuns to sing church services together and ordered priests to limit their visits to convents, heightening the sense that contact with nuns should be viewed with suspicion and avoided when possible. The reformers' emphasis on clerical celibacy and chastity led them to portray women as impure and lustful, judgments they extended not only to the (in their words) "she-wolves" and "harlots" married to priests, but also to nuns. Thus in 1298 in the papal decree *Periculoso* Pope Boniface VIII ordered all nuns to be strictly cloistered, that is, to remain permanently inside the walls of the convent, and for visits with those from outside the house, including family members, to be limited. *Periculoso* was not enforced everywhere, but it did mean that convents became more cut off from medieval society. People also gave more donations to male monastic houses where monks who had been ordained as priests could say memorial masses, and fewer to women's houses, many of which became impoverished.

Emperor Versus Pope

The strongest reaction to Gregory's moves came from the Holy Roman Empire. Pope Gregory accused Henry of lack of respect for the papacy and insisted that dis-

obedience to the pope was disobedience to God. Henry argued that Gregory's type of reform undermined royal authority and that the pope was a "false monk" who instead of respecting rulers and bishops "hast trodden them under foot like slaves ignorant of what their master is doing." Within the empire, those who had the most to gain from the dispute quickly took advantage of it. In January 1076 many of the German bishops who had been invested by Henry withdrew their allegiance from the pope. Gregory replied by excommunicating them and suspending Henry, "who has risen against the church with unheard of insolence." The pope "absolve[d] all Christians from the oath which they have made to [Henry]," which delighted the lay nobility, for they could now advance their own interests without interference from the king. Powerful nobles invited the pope to come to Germany to settle their dispute with Henry, and Gregory hastened to support them. The Christmas season of 1076 witnessed an ironic situation in Germany: the clergy supported the emperor, while the great nobility favored the pope.

lay investiture The selection and appointment of church officials by secular authority.

excommunication A penalty used by the Christian church that meant being cut off from the sacraments and all Christian worship.

Henry managed to outwit the pope temporarily. Crossing the Alps in January 1077, he approached the castle of Countess Matilda of Tuscany (ca. 1046–1115) at Canossa in the Apennines (AH-puh-nighnz), where the pope was staying. According to a letter later sent by the pope to his German noble allies, Henry stood for three days in the snow "with bare feet and clad in wool . . . imploring with many tears" that the pope lift the excommunication. Henry's pleas for forgiveness "moved all those who were present there to such pity and depth of compassion" that they interceded for Henry, and the pope readmitted the emperor to the Christian community, though he warned "that the whole question at issue is as yet little cleared up."[6]

Gregory was right. When the sentence of excommunication was lifted, Henry regained the emperorship and authority over his rebellious subjects, but continued his moves against papal power. In 1080 Gregory again excommunicated and deposed the emperor. In return, when Gregory died in 1085, Henry invaded Italy, captured Rome, and controlled the city. But Henry won no lasting victory. Gregory's successors encouraged Henry's sons to revolt against their father.

Finally, in 1122 at a conference held at Worms, the issue was settled by compromise. Bishops were to be chosen according to canon law—that is, by the clergy—in the presence of the emperor or his delegate. The emperor surrendered the right of investing bishops with the ring and staff. But since lay rulers were permitted to be present at ecclesiastical elections and to accept

Countess Matilda A staunch supporter of the reforming ideals of the papacy, Countess Matilda planned this dramatic meeting at her castle. The arrangement of the figures—King Henry kneeling, Abbot Hugh of Cluny lecturing, and Matilda persuading—suggests contemporary understanding of the scene in which Henry received absolution. Matilda's vast estates in northern Italy and her political contacts in Rome made her a person of considerable influence in the late eleventh century. (Biblioteca Apostolica Vaticana)

or refuse feudal homage from the new prelates, they still possessed an effective veto over ecclesiastical appointments. Papal power was enhanced, but neither side won a clear victory.

The long controversy over lay investiture had tremendous social and political consequences in Germany. The lengthy struggle between papacy and emperor allowed emerging noble dynasties to enhance their position. To control their lands, the great lords built castles, symbolizing their increased power and growing independence. (See "Living in the Past: Life in an English Castle," page 256.) The German high aristocracy subordinated the knights, enhanced restrictions on peasants, and compelled Henry IV and Henry V to surrender certain rights and privileges. When the papal-imperial conflict ended in 1122, the nobility held the balance of power in Germany, and later German kings, such as Frederick Barbarossa, would fail in their efforts to strengthen the monarchy against the princely families. For these reasons, particularism, localism, and feudal independence characterized the Holy Roman Empire in the High Middle Ages.

The Popes and Church Law

In the late eleventh century and throughout the twelfth and thirteenth, the papacy pressed Gregory's campaign for reform of the church. The popes held a series of councils that met in the papal palace of the Lateran in Rome. These Lateran councils ratified decisions ending lay investiture, ordered bishops to live less extravagantly, and passed other measures designed to make procedures more uniform. They passed a series of measures against clerical marriage and concubinage, ordering married priests to give up their wives and children or face dismissal. Most apparently obeyed, though we have little information on what happened to the families. Marriage was defined as a sacrament, a ceremony that provided visible evidence of God's grace, and as the expected norm for all lay Christians. As such, it was indissoluble, though there was the possibility of annulment. The councils also ruled on consanguinity, or the degree to which blood or marital kinship would prohibit people from marrying each other.

Pope Urban II laid the foundations for the papal monarchy by reorganizing the central government of the Roman church, the papal writing office (the chancery), and papal finances. He recognized the college of cardinals as a definite consultative body. These agencies, together with the papal chapel, constituted the *curia Romana* (Roman curia) — the papacy's administrative bureaucracy and its court of law. The papal curia, although not fully developed until the mid-twelfth century, was the first well-organized institution of monarchical authority in medieval Europe.

The Roman curia had its greatest impact as a court of law. As the highest ecclesiastical tribunal, it formulated church law, termed **canon law**. The church developed a system of courts separate from those of secular rulers that handled disputes over church property and ecclesiastical elections, and especially questions of marriage and annulment. Cases went first to a local church court, but could be appealed to Rome if individuals were unhappy about the decision. Most of the popes in the twelfth and thirteenth centuries were canon lawyers who expanded the authority of church courts.

The most famous of the lawyer-popes was Innocent III (ponticiate 1198–1216), who became the most powerful pope in history. During his pontificate the church in Rome declared itself to be supreme, united, and "catholic" (worldwide), responsible for the earthly well-being as well as the eternal salvation of Christians everywhere. Innocent pushed the kings of France, Portugal, and England to do his will, compelling King Philip Augustus of France to take back his wife, Ingeborg of Denmark. He forced King John of England to accept as archbishop of Canterbury a man John did not want.

Innocent called the fourth Lateran Council in 1215, which affirmed the idea that ordained priests had the power to transform bread and wine during church ceremonies into the body and blood of Christ (a change termed "transubstantiation"). This power was possessed by no other group in society, not even kings. According to papal doctrine, priests now had the power to mediate for everyone with God, which set the spiritual hierarchy of the church above the secular hierarchies of kings and other rulers. The council also affirmed that Christians should confess their sins to a priest at least once a year and ordered Jews and Muslims to wear special clothing that set them apart from Christians.

By the early thirteenth century papal efforts at reform begun more than a century earlier had attained phenomenal success. Some of Innocent III's successors, however, abused their prerogatives, even using secular weapons, including military force, to maintain their leadership. The conflict between the papacy and secular powers was not over, and it emerged again in the late thirteenth century (see Chapter 11).

The Crusades

How did the motives, course, and consequences of the Crusades reflect and shape developments in Europe? ■

The Crusades of the eleventh and twelfth centuries were the most obvious manifestation of the papal claim to the leadership of Christian society. The **Crusades** were wars sponsored by the papacy for the recovery of the holy city of Jerusalem from the Muslims. The enormous popular response to papal calls for crusading reveals the influence of the reformed papacy and the depth of religious fervor among many different types of people. The Crusades also reflected the church's new understanding of the noble warrior class, for whom war against the church's enemies was understood as a religious duty. The word *crusade* was not actually used at the time and did not appear in English until the late sixteenth century. It means literally "taking the cross," from the cross that soldiers sewed on their garments as a Christian symbol. At the time people going off to fight simply said they were taking "the way of the cross" or "the road to Jerusalem."

> **canon law** Church law, which had its own courts and procedures.
>
> **Crusades** Holy wars sponsored by the papacy for the recovery of the Holy Land from the Muslims from the late eleventh to the late thirteenth centuries.

Background and Motives

The medieval church's attitude toward violence was contradictory. On the one hand, church councils threatened excommunication for anyone who attacked peasants, clerics, or merchants or destroyed crops and unfortified places, a movement termed the Peace of God. They tried to limit the number of days on which fighting was permitted, prohibiting it on Sundays, on special feast days, and in the seasons of Lent and Advent. On the other hand, popes supported armed conflict against kings and emperors if this worked to their advantage, thus encouraging warfare among Christians. After a serious theological disagreement in 1054 split the Orthodox church of Byzantium and the Roman church of the West, the pope also contemplated invading the Byzantine Empire. As a result of the dispute, the pope and the patriarch of Constantinople excommunicated each other and declared the beliefs of the other to be "anathema" (uh-NAH-thuh-muh), that is, totally unacceptable for Christians. In the years that followed, the pope believed that a military campaign might increase Roman influence in Byzantine territories and eventually lead to the reunion of the two churches, with himself at the head.

Although conflicts in which Christians fought Christians were troubling to many thinkers, war against

LIVING IN THE PAST

CASTLES SERVED NOBLES as places from which they could oppose the expansion of royal authority, but they also served kings seeking to build up and maintain their power. Recognizing their value, William the Conqueror and his successors ordered the building of castles at strategic points around England. Edward I, for example, built Harlech Castle on a cliff overlooking the sea on the west coast of Wales as part of his campaign to conquer Wales and destroy the power of the Welsh nobility. The inner buildings of the castle were often built in wood originally, and then in stone, and the towers and outer walls were built in stone as well, all of which required extensive quarrying and hauling, part of the labor obligations of the peasants who lived in the surrounding area.

Castles were built for military purposes, but they were also places of residence. The lord and his family lived in the inner halls and towers, and their servants and supporters often lived there as well. During times of unrest or attack, peasants from nearby villages sometimes moved within the walls, living in the open or in hastily erected cloth and wood shelters with their animals. No one was very comfortable. Stone castle walls were cold and damp, and the small windows, designed for security, let in little light, augmented only by torches, oil lamps, and candles. While "medieval banquets" today offer exotic food and sumptuous settings, most meals in a castle such as Harlech—for those in the hall or in the yard—were simple, and were served in ceramic or wooden dishes and pitchers, not elegant plates and silver flagons.

Pottery pitcher for wine or ale made in Lincolnshire, 1000–1200 (Courtesy of the Trustees of the British Museum)

Pottery baking dish from Norman England, ca. 1000 (Ashmolean Museum, University of Oxford)

QUESTIONS FOR ANALYSIS

1. What strategic value is gained by placing a castle on a hill or cliff? What other features of Harlech Castle increase its military functions? Looking at the picture and the floor plan, what features of a castle, other than those mentioned above, might make life difficult for residents?

2. The dishes shown were for everyday use and were quite common, but few have survived. Why might this be? Even more often, medieval dishes were made out of wood, but almost none of these have survived. Why might this be?

3. How do these illustrations and objects fit with the view of life in a medieval castle presented in contemporary movies and other media?

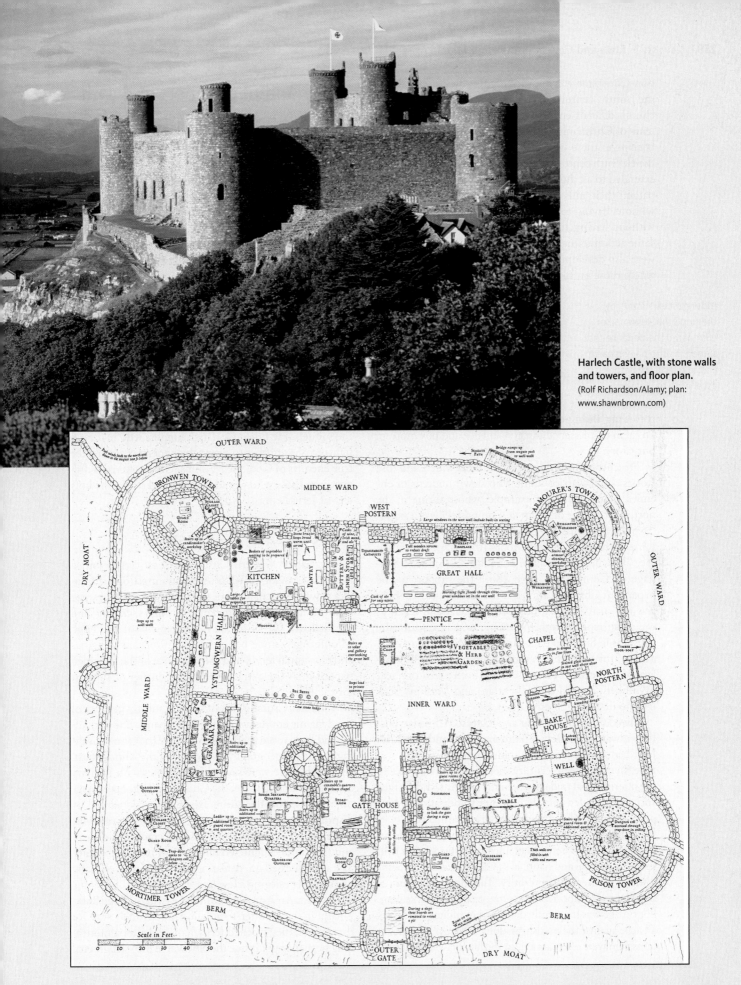

Harlech Castle, with stone walls and towers, and floor plan.
(Rolf Richardson/Alamy; plan: www.shawnbrown.com)

257

non-Christians was another matter. By the ninth century popes and other church officials encouraged war in defense of Christianity, promising spiritual benefits to those who died fighting. By the eleventh century these benefits were extended to all those who joined a campaign: their sins would be remitted without having to do penance, that is, without having to confess to a priest and carry out some action to make up for the sins. Christian thinkers were also developing the concept of purgatory, a place where those on their way to Heaven stayed for a while to do any penance they had not completed while alive. (Those on their way to Hell went straight there.) Engaging in holy war could shorten one's time in purgatory, or, as many people understood the promise, allow one to head straight to paradise. Popes signified this by providing **indulgences**, grants with the pope's name on them that lessened earthly penance and postmortem purgatory.

indulgences Grants by the pope that lessened or eliminated the penance that sinners had to pay on earth and in purgatory before ascending to Heaven.

Preachers communicated these ideas widely and told stories about warrior-saints who slew hundreds of enemies. Saint James, for example, whose shrine in the northwest corner of Spain at Compostela was a popular place for Christian pilgrims to visit, was known as *Matamoros*, the Killer of Moors (that is, of Muslims). (See "Listening to the Past: The Pilgrim's Guide to Santiago de Compostela" page 286.) The support of the papacy for Christian armies in the reconquista in Spain was not just spiritual, but also financial and legal, as was papal support in the Norman campaign against the Muslims in Sicily. In both campaigns Pope Gregory VII asserted that any land conquered from the Muslims belonged to the papacy because it had been a territory held by infidels, a word that Christians and Muslims both used to describe the other.

The ideology of holy war also increased Christian hostility toward Jews. Between the sixth and tenth centuries Jews had settled along the trade routes of western Europe. In the eleventh century they played a major role in the international trade between the Muslim Middle East and the West. Jews also lent money to peasants, townspeople, and nobles, and debt bred resentment.

Religious zeal led increasing numbers of people to go on pilgrimages to holy places, including shrines that held the relics of local and national saints, such as that of Saint Thomas Becket in Canterbury. The more adventurous traveled to Compostela or Rome, or even to Jerusalem. Pilgrimage was frequently described in military terms, as a battle against the hardships along the way. Pilgrims to Jerusalem were often armed, so the line between pilgrim-

❝ Amid the sound of trumpets and with everything in an uproar they attacked boldly, shouting 'God help us!' ❞

— FULCHER OF CHARTRES

age and holy war on this particular route was increasingly blurred.

The Arabic Muslims who had ruled Jerusalem and the surrounding territory for centuries allowed Christian pilgrims to travel freely, but in the late eleventh century the Seljuk (SEHL-jook) Turks took over Palestine, defeating both Arabic and Byzantine armies (Map 9.4). The emperor at Constantinople appealed to the West for support, asserting that the Turks would make pilgrimages to holy places more dangerous, and that the holy city of Jerusalem should be in Christian hands. The emperor's appeal fit well with papal aims, and in 1095 Pope Urban II called for a great Christian holy war against the infidels. He urged Christian knights who had been fighting one another to direct their energies against the true enemies of God, the Muslims. Urban offered indulgences to those who would fight for and regain the holy city of Jerusalem.

The Course of the Crusades

Thousands of Western Christians of all classes joined the First Crusade in 1096. Although most of the Crusaders were French, pilgrims from many regions streamed southward from the Rhineland, through Germany and the Balkans. Of all of the developments of the High Middle Ages, none better reveals Europeans' religious and emotional fervor and the influence of the reformed papacy than the extraordinary outpouring of support for the First Crusade.

The First Crusade was successful, mostly because of the dynamic enthusiasm of the participants. The Crusaders had little more than religious zeal. They knew nothing about the geography or climate of the Middle East. Although there were several high nobles with military experience among them, the Crusaders could never agree on a leader, and the entire expedition was marked by disputes among the great lords. Lines of supply were never set up. Starvation and disease wracked the army, and the Turks slaughtered hundreds of noncombatants. The army pressed on, defeating the Turks in several land battles and besieging a few larger towns. (See "Listening to the Past: An Arab View of the Crusades," page 260.) Finally in 1099, after they had been on their way for three years, they reached Jerusalem, and after a month-long siege they got inside the city, where they slaughtered

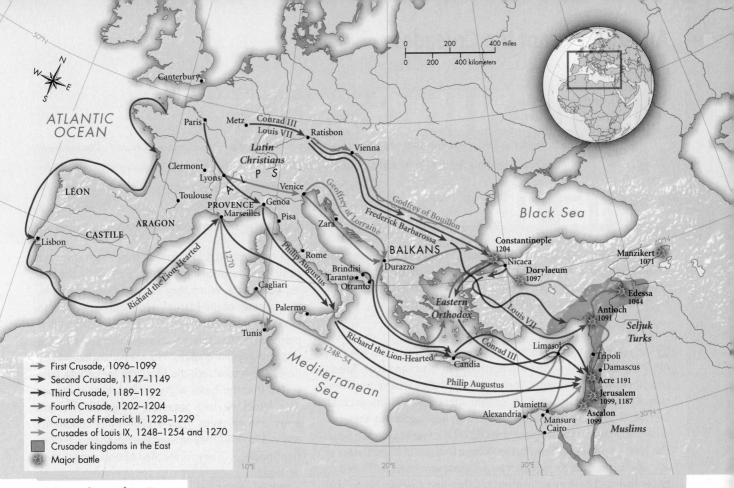

Map labels:
- Canterbury
- ATLANTIC OCEAN
- Paris
- Metz
- Conrad III
- Louis VII
- Ratisbon
- Vienna
- Latin Christians
- Clermont
- Lyons
- LÉON
- Toulouse
- PROVENCE
- Marseilles
- Venice
- Genoa
- Pisa
- Zara
- Geoffrey of Lorraine
- Frederick Barbarossa
- Godfrey of Bouillon
- Black Sea
- Constantinople 1204
- Nicaea
- Dorylaeum 1097
- Manzikert 1071
- Edessa 1044
- Antioch 1091
- Seljuk Turks
- LISBON
- CASTILE
- ARAGON
- 1270
- Richard the Lion-Hearted
- Rome
- BALKANS
- Durazzo
- Brindisi
- Taranto
- Otranto
- Philip Augustus
- Cagliari
- Palermo
- Tunis
- Eastern Orthodox
- Louis VII
- Candia
- Conrad III
- Limasol
- Tripoli
- Damascus
- Acre 1191
- Jerusalem 1099, 1187
- Ascalon 1099
- Damietta
- Alexandria
- Mansura
- Cairo
- Muslims
- Mediterranean Sea
- 1248-54
- Richard the Lion-Hearted
- Philip Augustus

Scale: 0 200 400 miles / 0 200 400 kilometers

Legend:
→ First Crusade, 1096–1099
→ Second Crusade, 1147–1149
→ Third Crusade, 1189–1192
→ Fourth Crusade, 1202–1204
→ Crusade of Frederick II, 1228–1229
→ Crusades of Louis IX, 1248–1254 and 1270
▪ Crusader kingdoms in the East
✸ Major battle

Mapping the Past

Map 9.4 **The Crusades** This map shows the many different routes that Western Christians took over the centuries to reach Jerusalem.

ANALYZING THE MAP How were the results of the various Crusades shaped by the routes that the Crusaders took?

CONNECTIONS How did the routes and Crusader kingdoms offer opportunities for profit?

To complete this activity online, go to the Online Study Guide at bedfordstmartins.com/mckaywest.

the Muslim defenders. Fulcher of Chartres, a chaplain on the First Crusade, described the scene:

> Amid the sound of trumpets and with everything in an uproar they attacked boldly, shouting "God help us!" . . . They ran with the greatest exultation as fast as they could into the city and joined their companions in pursuing and slaying their wicked enemies without cessation. . . . Many of the Saracens who had climbed to the top of the Temple of Solomon in their flight were shot to death with arrows and fell headlong from the roof. Nearly ten thousand were beheaded in this Temple. If you had been there your feet would have been stained to the ankles in the blood of the slain. What shall I say? None of them were left alive. Neither women nor children were spared.[7]

With Jerusalem taken, some Crusaders proclaimed the area they had conquered as a Christian kingdom, but many regarded their mission as accomplished and set off for home. Only the appearance of Egyptian troops in 1101 convinced the Crusaders that they needed to stay, and slowly institutions were set up to rule territories and the Muslim population. Four small "Crusader states" — Jerusalem, Edessa, Tripoli, and Antioch — were established, and castles and fortified towns were built to defend against Muslim reconquest (see Map 9.4). Reinforcements arrived in the form of pilgrims and fighters from Europe, so that there was constant coming and going by land and more often by sea after the Crusaders conquered port cities such as Acre. Between 1096 and 1270 the crusading ideal was expressed in eight papally approved expeditions, though none after the First Crusade accomplished very much. Despite this lack of success, for roughly two hundred years members of noble families in Europe went nearly every generation.

The Crusades inspired the establishment of new religious orders, particularly military orders dedicated to protecting the Christian kingdoms. The most important

259

Picturing the Past

The Capture of Jerusalem in 1099 As engines hurl stones to breach the walls, Crusaders enter on scaling ladders. Scenes from Christ's Passion in the top half of the piece identify the city as Jerusalem. (Bibliothèque nationale de France)

ANALYZING THE IMAGE What do you think the author's point of view is about the events shown? Would you characterize the painting as a positive or negative depiction of war? What does this suggest about the artist's motives in creating this work?

CONNECTIONS How might the images shown be different if this had been drawn by a Muslim artist living in Jerusalem?

To complete this activity online, go to the Online Study Guide at bedfordstmartins.com/mckaywest.

was the Knights Templars, founded in 1119 with the strong backing of Saint Bernard of Clairvaux (klehr-VOH) (see page 295), who described the ideal Templar as a man "without doubt, fortified by both arms [armor and faith], he fears neither demon nor man. Nor, indeed, is he afraid of death." Speaking of both the Templars and the Crusades in general, Saint Bernard commented, "If the cause of the fighting is good, the consequence of the fighting cannot be evil."[8] Many people going off to the Holy Land put their property in Europe under Templar protection, and by the end of the thirteenth century the order was extremely wealthy, with secret rituals in which members pledged obedience to their leaders. The Templars began serving as moneylenders and bankers, which further increased their wealth. In 1307 King Philip IV of France sought to grab that wealth for himself; he arrested many Templars, accusing them of heresy, blasphemy, and sodomy. They were tortured, and a number were burned at the stake.

Women from all walks of life participated in the Crusades. Because of the chroniclers' belief that the *fragilitas sexus* (weaker sex) was unfit for arms, the chronicles tended to focus on male Crusaders. In addition, because of the chroniclers' aristocratic bias, most of the women Crusaders we do know of are either royalty or nobility. After her husband, King Fulk, died, Queen Melisande ruled the Latin kingdom of Jerusalem. When King Louis IX of France was captured on the Seventh Crusade (1248–1254), his wife Queen Marguerite negotiated the surrender of the Egyptian city of Damietta to the Muslims. In war zones some women concealed their sex by donning chain mail and helmets and fought with the knights. Others joined in the besieging of towns and castles. They assisted in filling the moats surrounding fortified places with earth so that ladders and war engines could be brought close. More typically, women provided water to fighting men, a service not to be underestimated in the hot, dry climate of the Middle East. They worked as washerwomen, foraged for food, and provided sexual services. There were many more European men than women, however, so marriage and sexual relations between Christian men and Muslim women were not unheard of, although marriages between Western Christian men and Orthodox Christian women who lived in the area were more common.

The Muslim states in the Middle East were politically fragmented when the Crusaders first came, and it took about a century for them to reorganize. They did so dramatically under Saladin (Salah al-Din), who unified Egypt and Syria, and in 1187 the Muslims retook Jerusalem. Christians immediately attempted to take it back in what was later called the Third Crusade (1189–1192). Frederick Barbarossa of the Holy Roman Empire, Richard the Lion-Hearted of England, and Philip Augustus of France participated, and the Third Crusade

was better financed than previous ones. But disputes among the leaders and strategic problems prevented any lasting results. The Crusaders were not successful in retaking Jerusalem, but they did keep their hold on port towns, and Saladin allowed pilgrims safe passage to Jerusalem. He also made an agreement with Christian rulers for keeping the peace. From that point on, the Crusader states were more important economically than politically or religiously, giving Italian and French merchants direct access to Eastern products such as perfumes and silk.

In 1202 Innocent III sent out preachers who called on Christian knights to retake Jerusalem. Those who responded—in what would become the Fourth Crusade—negotiated with the Venetians to take them by boat to Cairo, but Venetian interests combined with a succession struggle over the Byzantine throne led the fleet to instead go to Constantinople. The Crusaders expected to be welcomed, and when they were not, they decided to capture and sack Constantinople, destroying its magnificent library and shipping gold, silver, and relics home. The Crusaders installed one of their own as emperor, but in reality the Byzantine Empire was divided among the Crusaders, the Venetians, and the Byzantine imperial family. The Byzantines reasserted their control over the empire in 1261, but it was much smaller and weaker and soon consisted of little more than the city of Constantinople. Moreover, the assault by one Christian people on another—even though one of the original goals of the Crusades had been to reunite the Greek and Latin churches—made the split between the churches permanent. It also helped discredit the entire crusading movement and obviously had no effect on Muslim control of Jerusalem and other areas.

During the thirteenth century criticism of the Crusades increased. Military orders such as the Templars were criticized for their wealth rather than being admired for their dedication and bravery. Fewer people were inspired to go, so crusading armies included more mercenaries, who had to be paid, and many at home regarded the whole enterprise as a way for the church to expand its bureaucracy and tax levies.

There were a few more efforts. The Seventh Crusade in 1248, led by King Louis IX of France (r. 1223–1270), tried to come in through Egypt. Louis also sent monks to the court of the Mongols in Central Asia, who were at this point led by Chinggis Khan, to make a treaty that would encircle the Muslims. The monks were unsuccessful, but they brought back geographical knowledge of Asia and the peoples they had encountered. Louis himself was captured in the crusade, but ransomed himself and then led another, on which he was killed. Though Louis was made a saint shortly after his death, his crusades had accomplished nothing. In the end, it was the Mamluk rulers of Egypt who conquered the Crusader

INDIVIDUALS IN SOCIETY

IN THE WINTER OF 1095–1096 news of Pope Urban II's call for a crusade spread. In spring 1096 the Jews of northern France, fearing that a crusade would arouse anti-Semitic hostility, sent a circular letter to the Rhineland's Jewish community seeking its prayers. Jewish leaders in Mainz responded, "All the [Jewish] communities have decreed a fast. . . . May God save us and save you from all distress and hardship. We are deeply fearful for you. We,

however, have less reason to fear (for ourselves), for we have heard not even a rumor of the crusade."* Ironically, French Jewry survived almost unscathed, while the Rhenish Jewry suffered frightfully.

Beginning in the late tenth century Jews trickled into Speyer — partly through Jewish perception of opportunity and partly because of the direct invitation of the bishop of Speyer. The bishop's charter meant that Jews could openly practice their religion, could not be assaulted, and could buy and sell goods. But they could not proselytize their faith, as Christians could. Jews also extended credit on a small scale and, in an expanding economy with many coins circulating, determined the relative value of currencies. Unlike their Christian counterparts, many Jewish women were literate and acted as moneylenders. Jews also worked as skilled masons, carpenters, and jewelers. As the bishop had promised, the Jews of Speyer lived apart from Christians in a walled enclave where they exercised autonomy: they maintained law and order, raised taxes, and provided religious, social, and educational services for their community. (This organization lasted in Germany until the nineteenth century.) Jewish immigration to Speyer accelerated; everyday relations between Jews and Christians were peaceful.

But Christians resented Jews as newcomers, outsiders, and aliens; for enjoying the special protection of the bishop; and for providing economic competition. Anti-Semitic ideology had received enormous impetus from the virulent anti-Semitic writings of Christian apologists in the first six centuries C.E. Jews, they argued, were *deicides* (DEE-uh-sighdz) (Christ killers). Worse, Jews could understand the truth of Christianity but deliberately rejected it; thus they were inhuman. By the late eleventh century anti-Semitism was an old and deeply rooted element in Western society.

Late in April 1096 Emich of Leisingen, a petty lord from the Rhineland who had the reputation of being a lawless thug, approached Speyer with a large band of Crusaders. Joined by a mob of burghers, they planned to surprise the Jews in their synagogue on Saturday morning, May 3, but the Jews prayed early and left before the attackers arrived. Furious, the

This illustration from the margins of a thirteenth-century chronicle written by an English monk shows Jews — identified by the tablets they were required to wear on their clothing — being beaten. Such violence sometimes escalated into mass murder. (© British Library Board)

mob randomly murdered eleven Jews. The bishop took the entire Jewish community into his castle, arrested some of the burghers, and cut off their hands. News of these events raced up the Rhine to Worms, creating confusion in the Jewish community. Some took refuge with Christian friends; others sought the bishop's protection.

A combination of Crusaders and burghers killed a large number of Jews, looted and burned synagogues, and desecrated the Torah (see Chapter 2) and other books in Speyer. Proceeding to the old and prosperous city of Mainz, Crusaders continued attacking Jews. Facing overwhelming odds, eleven hundred Jews killed their families and themselves. Crusaders and burghers vented their hatred by inflicting barbaric tortures on the wounded and dying. The Jews were never passive; everywhere they resisted.

If the Crusades had begun as opposition to Islam, after 1096 that hostility extended to all those whom Christians saw as enemies of society, including heretics such as the Albigensians and Jews. But Jews continued to move to the Rhineland and to make important economic and intellectual contributions. Crusader-burgher attacks served as harbingers of events to come in the later Middle Ages and well into modern times.

QUESTIONS FOR ANALYSIS

1. What were the roots of the anti-Semitic ideology of the Middle Ages, and how did the ideology contribute to the attacks on the Jews of Speyer?

2. Modern scholars would agree that the attackers had "dehumanized" the Jews of Speyer. What is meant by this term, and can you give other examples?

*Quoted in R. Chazan, *In the Year 1096: The First Crusade and the Jews* (Philadelphia: Jewish Publication Society, 1996), p. 28.

states, and in 1291 their last stronghold, the port of Acre, fell in a battle that was just as bloody as the first battle for Jerusalem two centuries earlier. Some knights continued their crusading efforts in Spain, where the rulers of Aragon and Castile continued fighting Muslims until 1492.

Crusades Within Europe

Crusades were also mounted against groups within Europe that were perceived as threats. The Teutonic Knights, a military order, waged a crusade against pagans in the Baltic region and eventually formed a state there. The popes declared several campaigns against German emperors to be crusades, offering indulgences to those who fought in them. In 1208 Pope Innocent III proclaimed a crusade against a group from the city of Albi in southern France known as the Albigensians (al-buh-JEHN-see-uhns). The Albigensians asserted that the material world was created not by the good God of the New Testament, but by a different evil God of the Old Testament. The good God had created spiritual things, and the evil God had created material things. In this dualistic understanding, the soul was good and the body evil. Forces of good and evil battled constantly, and the best life was one of extreme asceticism with as few physical and material things as possible. Albigensians were divided into the "perfect," who followed the principles strictly, and the "believers," who led ordinary lives until their deaths, when they repented and were saved. They used the teachings of Jesus about the evils of material goods to call for the church to give up its property, rejected the authority of the pope and the sacraments of the church, and began setting up their own bishoprics.

The Albigensians won many adherents in southern France, especially in the towns and cities of this densely populated area. Faced with widespread defection, Pope Innocent III proclaimed a crusade against them, and fearing that religious division would lead to civil disorder, the French monarchy joined the crusade. The French inflicted a savage defeat on the Albigensians in 1213. After more years of fighting, the leaders agreed to terms of peace, which left the French monarchy the primary beneficiary.

The end of the war did not mean an end to Albigensianism, but henceforth the papacy decided to combat heresy through education and individual punishment. The pope founded the University of Toulouse, which he hoped would promote knowledge of correct belief. In the 1230s the papacy established the papal **Inquisition**, sending out inquisitors with the power to seek suspected heretics, question them in private without revealing who had

Inquisition Court established in the 1230s by the papacy with power to investigate and try individuals for heresy and other religious crimes.

denounced them, and sentence them to punishments ranging from penance to life imprisonment. (For more on the Inquisition, see Chapter 11.) Heretics who did not repent were handed over to the secular government to be burned, and their property was confiscated. These measures were very successful, and the last Albigensian leaders were burned in the 1320s, though their beliefs did not die out completely.

Consequences of the Crusades

The Crusades testified to the religious enthusiasm of the High Middle Ages and gave kings and the pope opportunities to expand their bureaucracies. They also provided kings with the perfect opportunity to get rid of troublemaking knights, particularly restless younger sons for whom the practice of primogeniture meant few prospects. Some of them were able to carve out lordships in Palestine, Syria, and Greece. Even some members of the middle class who stayed at home profited from the Crusades. Nobles often had to borrow money from burghers to pay for their expeditions, and they put up part of their land as security. If a noble did not return home or could not pay the interest on the loan, the middle-class creditor took over the land.

The Crusades introduced some Europeans to Eastern luxury goods, but their immediate cultural impact on the West remains debatable. Strong economic and intellectual ties with the East had already been developed by the late eleventh century. The Crusades did provide great commercial profits for Italian merchants, who profited from outfitting military expeditions, the opening of new trade routes, and the establishment of trading communities in the Crusader states. After those kingdoms collapsed, Muslim rulers still encouraged trade with European businessmen. Commerce with the West benefited both Muslims and Europeans, and it continued to flourish.

The Crusades proved to be a disaster for Jewish-Christian relations. Inspired by the ideology of holy war and resentment of Jewish economic activities, Christian armies on their way to Jerusalem on the First Crusade joined with local mobs to attack Jewish families and sometimes entire Jewish communities. (See "Individuals in Society: The Jews of Speyer," page 264.) Later Crusades brought similar violence, enhanced by accusations that Jews engaged in the ritual murder of Christians to use their blood in religious rites. These accusations, termed the "blood libel," were condemned by Christian rulers and higher church officials, but were often spread through sermons preached by local priests. Legal restrictions on Jews gradually increased throughout Europe. Jews were forbidden to have Christian servants or employees, to hold public office, to appear in public on Christian holy days, and to enter Christian parts of town without badges marking them as Jews.

They were prohibited from engaging in any trade with Christians except money-lending—which only fueled popular resentment—and in 1275 King Edward I of England prohibited that as well. In 1290 he expelled the Jews from England in return for a large parliamentary grant; it would be four centuries before they would be allowed back in. King Philip the Fair of France followed Edward's example in 1306, and many Jews went to the area of southern France known as Provence, which was not yet part of the French kingdom. In July 1315 the king's need for revenue led him to readmit the Jews to France in return for a huge lump sum and for an annual financial subsidy, but the returning Jews faced hostility and increasing pressure to convert, as did Jews in Aragon and Castile.

The Crusades also left an inheritance of deep bitterness in Christian-Muslim relations. Each side dehumanized the other, viewing those who followed the other religion as infidels. Whereas Europeans perceived the Crusades as sacred religious movements, Muslims saw them as expansionist and imperialistic. Even today some Muslims see the conflict between Arab and Jew as just another manifestation of the medieval Crusades and view the leaders of the state of Israel as new Crusaders or as tools of Western imperialism.

The European Crusades shaped the identity of the West. They represent the first great colonizing movement beyond the geographical boundaries of the European continent. The ideal of a sacred mission to conquer or convert Muslim peoples entered Europeans' consciousness and became a continuing goal. When in 1492 Christopher Columbus sailed west, hoping to reach India, he used the language of the Crusades in his diaries, which show that he was preoccupied with the conquest of Jerusalem (see Chapter 15). Columbus wanted to establish a Christian base in India from which a new crusade against Islam could be launched.

The Expansion of Christianity

How did Christianity expand in northern and eastern Europe? ■

The Crusades had a profound impact on both Europe and the Middle East, but they were not the only example of Christian expansion in the High Middle Ages. As we saw earlier, Christian kingdoms were established in the Iberian Peninsula through the reconquista, reducing Muslim holdings to the small state of Granada in the south. The reconquista brought the establishment of a Roman ecclesiastical structure, and by the end of the thirteenth century Spain had fifty-one bishoprics. These

Map 9.5 **The Baltic Region, ca. 1300** By 1300 most of the Baltic area had been Christianized through the efforts of bishops, monks, the military order of the Teutonic Knights, and German settlers.

bishoprics, along with new monasteries, aided the growth of Christian culture. Both also enhanced royal power, for church officials provided financial, political, and ideological support for the monarchs who had endowed their institutions.

The pattern in Spain was replicated in northern and eastern Europe in the centuries after 1000. People and ideas moved from western France and western Germany into Ireland, Scandinavia, the Baltic lands, and eastern Europe, with significant cultural consequences for those territories. Wars of expansion, the establishment of new Christian bishoprics, and the vast migration of colonists, together with the papal emphasis on a unified Christian world, brought about the gradual Christianization of a larger area (Map 9.5).

Northern Europe

Ireland had been Christian since the days of Saint Patrick (see Chapter 7), but in the twelfth century Norman knights crossed from England, defeated Irish lords, and established fiefs with the kings of England as the ultimate authority. They also established bishoprics with defined territorial dioceses. Similarly, Anglo-Norman knights poured into Scotland in the twelfth century, bringing the fief and the diocese.

Latin Christian influences entered the Scandinavian and Baltic regions also primarily through the erection of dioceses. As an easily identifiable religious figure, as judge, and as the only person who could ordain priests, the bishop was the essential instrument in the spread of Christianity. Otto I established the first Scandinavian dioceses in Denmark. In Norway Christianity spread in coastal areas beginning in the tenth century, and King Olaf II (r. 1015–1028) brought in clergy and bishops from England and Germany to establish the church more firmly. From Norway Christianity spread to Iceland. In all of these areas, royal power advanced institutional Christianity; the traditional Norse religions practiced by the Vikings were outlawed and their adherents sometimes executed.

Christianity progressed more slowly in Sweden and Finland, in part because royal power was weaker. In 1164, however, Uppsala in Sweden, long a center of the pagan cults of Thor and Odin, became a diocese. Sweden took over much of modern-day Finland in the thirteen' century, and Swedish-speaking settlers moved into i' lands and coastal areas. Christian missionaries preached

Hedwig of Bavaria Married to the duke of Silesia, Hedwig (1174–1243) worked to expand both Christianity and German influence in eastern Europe, inviting German clergy into her duchy and founding several monasteries. In this manuscript commissioned by her fourteenth-century descendants (shown kneeling), Hedwig carries a book, a rosary, and a tiny statue of the Virgin Mary, references to her devout character. (The John Paul Getty Museum, Los Angeles, Court Atelier of Duke Ludwig I of Liegnitz and Brieg [illuminator], *Vita beatae Hedwigis*, 1353. Tempera colors, colored washes and ink bound between wood boards covered with red-stained pigskin, 34.1 × 24.8 cm)

baptized, and built churches, working among both the Swedish-speaking and Finnish-speaking populations, though pagan and Christian practices existed side-by-side for centuries. The Sami people of the far north in Scandinavia (formerly known as Lapps), who lived by fishing, hunting, and herding reindeer, remained pagan until the eighteenth century.

Centralized monarchy came to Scandinavia somewhat later than it did to western Europe. There was little feudalism in the classic sense of fiefs and oaths of loyalty, and during the High Middle Ages higher nobles frequently came into conflict with monarchs. In 1397 Queen Margrete I (1353–1412) united the crowns of Denmark, Sweden-Finland, and Norway in the Union of Kalmar. She built up royal power and worked toward creating a stronger state, checking the power of the nobility and creating a stronger financial base for the monarchy. The union gradually disintegrated in the fifteenth century, though Denmark continued to rule Norway until 1814.

Eastern Europe

The German emperor Otto I planted a string of dioceses along his northern and eastern frontiers, hoping to pacify the newly conquered Slavs in eastern Europe. Frequent Slavic revolts illustrate the people's resentment of German lords and clerics and indicate that the church did not easily penetrate the region. In the same way that French knights had been used to crush the Albigensians, German nobles built castles and ruthlessly crushed revolts. Albert the Bear, for example, a German noble, proclaimed a crusade against the Slavs and invited German knights to colonize conquered territories. A military order of German knights founded in Palestine, the Teutonic (too-TAH-nihk) Knights, moved their operations to eastern Europe and waged wars against the pagan Prussians in the Baltic region. After 1230, from a base in Poland, they established a new territory, Christian Prussia, and gradually the entire eastern shore of the Baltic came under their hegemony.

The church also moved into central Europe, first in Bohemia in the tenth century and from there into Poland and Hungary in the eleventh. In the twelfth and thirteenth centuries, thousands of settlers poured into eastern Europe. New immigrants were German in descent, name, language, and law. Hundreds of small market towns populated by these newcomers supplied the needs of the rural countryside. Larger towns such as Kraków and Riga engaged in long-distance trade and gradually grew into large urban centers.

Christendom

Through the actions of the Roman emperors Constantine and Theodosius (see Chapter 7), Christianity became in some ways a state as well as a religion. Early medieval writers began to use the word **Christendom** to refer to this realm of Christianity. Sometimes notions of Christendom were linked directly to specific states, such as Charlemagne's empire and the Holy Roman Empire. More often Christendom was vague, a sort of loose sense of the body of all people who were Christian. When the pope called for Crusades, for example, he spoke not only of the retaking of Jerusalem, but also of the defense of Christendom. When missionaries, officials, and soldiers took Christianity into the Iberian Peninsula, Scandinavia, or the Baltic region, they understood what they were doing as the expansion of Christendom.

From the point of view of popes such as Gregory VII and Innocent III, Christendom was a unified hierarchy with the papacy at the top. They pushed for uniformity of religious worship and campaigned continually for the same pattern of religious service, the Roman liturgy in Latin, in all countries and places. They forbade vernacular Christian rituals or those that differed in their pattern of worship. Under Innocent III papal directives and papal legates flowed to all parts of Europe; twelve hundred church officials obediently came to Rome from the borderlands as well as the heartland for the Fourth Lateran Council of 1215; and the same religious service was celebrated everywhere.

As we have seen in this chapter, however, not everyone had the same view. Kings and emperors may have accepted the Roman liturgy in the areas under their control, but they had their own ideas of the way power should operate in Christendom, even if this brought them into conflict with the papacy. This did not mean that they had any less loyalty to Christendom as a concept, however, but simply a different idea about how it should be structured and who could best defend it. The battles in the High Middle Ages between popes and kings and between Christians and Muslims were signs of how deeply religion had replaced tribal, political, and ethnic structures as the essence of Western culture.

> **Christendom** The term used by early medieval writers to refer to the realm of Christianity.

 LOOKING BACK LOOKING AHEAD

THE HIGH MIDDLE AGES were a time when kings, emperors, and popes expanded their powers and created financial and legal bureaucracies to support those powers. As monarchs developed these new institutions, their kingdoms began to function more like modern states than disorganized territories. With political expansion and stability came better communication of information, more uniform legal systems, and early financial institutions. Popes made the church more independent of lay control, established the papal curia and a separate system of canon law, and developed new ways of raising revenue. They supported the expansion of Christianity in southern, northern, and eastern Europe and proclaimed a series of Crusades against Muslims to extend still further the boundaries of a Christendom under their control.

Many of the systems of the High Middle Ages expanded in later centuries and are still in existence today: the financial department of the British government remains the Exchequer; the pope is still elected by the college of cardinals and is assisted by the papal curia; the legal systems of Britain and many former British colonies (including the United States) are based on common law; the Roman Catholic, Eastern Orthodox, and Anglican Churches still operate law courts that make rulings based on canon law. These systems also contained the seeds of future problems, however, for wealthier nations could sustain longer wars, independent popes more easily abuse their power, and crusading ideology justify the enslavement or extermination of whole peoples.

Despite the long-lived impact of the growth of centralized political and ecclesiastical power—for good or ill—most people who lived during the high medieval period witnessed changes much closer to home that had a far greater impact on their own lives, families, and local communities. Kings and popes sent tax collectors, judges, and sometimes soldiers, but they were far away. For most people, what went on in their families and local communities was far more important.

CHAPTER REVIEW

■ **How did medieval rulers create larger and more stable territories? (page 240)**

Feudal rulers in the High Middle Ages began to develop new institutions of government that enabled them to assert their power over lesser lords and the general population. As they expanded territories and extended authority, medieval rulers required more officials, larger armies, and more money with which to pay for them. Rulers manipulated feudal institutions to build up their wealth and power. The most effective financial bureaucracies were those developed under William the Conqueror in England, including a bureau of finance called the Exchequer, and those in Sicily, where Norman rulers retained the main financial agency that had been created by their Muslim predecessors, the diwān. In central Europe the German king Otto had himself declared emperor and tried to follow a similar path, but the many layers of power in the empire forced Otto and his successors to share power with lesser rulers such as dukes and counts. As a result unified nation-states would not develop there until the nineteenth century. In the Iberian Peninsula Christian rulers of small states slowly expanded their territories, taking over land from Muslim rulers in the reconquista.

■ **How did the administration of law evolve in the High Middle Ages? (page 248)**

In the twelfth and thirteenth centuries rulers in Europe sought to transform a hodgepodge of oral and written customs and rules into a uniform system of laws acceptable and applicable to all their peoples. In France local laws and procedures were maintained, but, for the first time, Louis IX established a royal, or supreme, court that published laws and heard appeals. In the Holy Roman Empire law was codified at two levels: manorial courts for minor matters such as debt and trespass, and regional courts for more serious crimes such as arson and murder. In England the king's court regularized procedures, and the idea of a common law that applied to the whole country developed. A dispute over the legal authority of the clergy led King Henry II to have Thomas Becket, the archbishop of Canterbury, assassinated. In the aftermath, Becket became a martyr and a saint, and his desire to keep church law separate from English common law won out. Fiscal and legal measures by Henry's son John led to opposition from the high nobles of England, who forced him to sign the Magna Carta, agreeing to observe the law. Most people's experience with the law was not at the national level, but in their own neighborhoods, as they witnessed crimes, helped or hindered in the pursuit of perpetrators, and watched punishments.

■ **How did the papacy attempt to reform the church, and what were the results of the efforts? (page 251)**

Beginning in the eleventh century, a series of reforming popes attempted to re-establish the church's moral leadership by prohibiting the buying and selling of church offices, ending clerical marriage, and eliminating secular control of the church. They decreed that the power to elect the pope rested solely in the college of cardinals, and that lay rulers should not even play a role in handing over the symbols of office to church officials. The dispute over lay investiture led to a grave conflict with the kings of England and France and with the Holy Roman emperors. The papacy achieved a technical success on the religious issue, but in Germany this conflict greatly increased the power of the nobility at the expense of the emperor. Popes and church councils also created an expanded system of church law, ordered women's convents to be enclosed, and made marriage indissoluble.

■ **How did the motives, course, and consequences of the Crusades reflect and shape developments in Europe? (page 255)**

A papal call to retake the holy city of Jerusalem led to the Crusades, nearly two centuries of warfare between Christians and Muslims. The enormous popular response to the Crusades reveals the influence of the reformed papacy and a new sense that war against the church's enemies was a duty of nobles and a sacred cause. The desires for adventure, booty, and land were also significant motives. The Crusades were initially successful, and small Christian states were established in the Middle East. They did not last very long, however, and other effects of the Crusades were disastrous. Jewish communities in Europe were regularly attacked; the papacy's reputation was damaged; relations between the Western and Eastern Christian churches were poisoned by the Crusaders' attack on Constantinople; and Christian-Muslim relations became more uniformly hostile than they had been earlier.

■ **How did Christianity expand in northern and eastern Europe? (page 266)**

The Middle Ages saw the penetration of Christianity into northern and eastern Europe. Christian warriors, clergy, and settlers moved out in all directions from western and central Europe, bringing Christianity through conquest and colonization. The movement of people was particularly evident in eastern Europe, where German-speaking settlers moved into areas populated by Slavs, establishing towns and bishoprics. The bishop, who served as a central figure and had the power to ordain priests, was the essential instrument in the spread of Christianity. Papal emphasis on a unified Catholic Church, the Crusades in the Middle East, and the expansion of Christianity in Iberia, Scandinavia, and the Baltic region created a stronger sense of loyalty to Christendom among many people living in Europe.

Suggested Reading

Abulafia, David. *Frederick II: A Medieval Emperor.* 1992. A beautifully written biography that sets Frederick's life in a broad context.

Bartlett, Robert. *England Under the Norman and Angevin Kings, 1075–1225.* 2000. An excellent synthesis of social, cultural, and political history in highly readable prose.

Bartlett, Robert. *The Making of Europe: Conquest, Colonization and Cultural Change, 950–1350.* 1993. A broad survey of many of the developments traced in this chapter.

Chazan, Robert. *In the Year 1096: The First Crusade and the Jews.* 1996. A thorough discussion of the Rhineland Jews and many issues related to the Jews and the Crusades.

Edgington, Susan B., and Sarah Lambert, eds. *Gendering the Crusades.* 2002. Articles that look at the roles of men and women.

Fletcher, Richard. *The Cross and the Crescent: Christianity and Islam from Muhammad to the Reformation.* 2003. A highly readable introduction to the intricate and controversial relationships between Christianity and Islam down to the sixteenth century.

Holt, J. C. *Magna Carta,* 2d ed. 1992. The authoritative study of the Magna Carta.

Johns, Jeremy. *Arabic Administration in Norman Sicily.* 2002. A comprehensive account of Arabic influences on the politics of Norman Sicily.

Lowney, Chris. *A Vanished World: Medieval Spain's Golden Age of Enlightenment.* 2006. Explores the complex interactions among Jews, Muslims, and Christians in the era of practical coexistence, and traces growing intolerance.

Madden, Thomas. *The New Concise History of the Crusades.* 2005. A highly readable brief survey by the preeminent American scholar of the Crusades.

O'Shea, Stephen. *The Perfect Heresy: The Revolutionary Life and Death of the Medieval Cathars.* 2000. A stimulating journalistic account of this Christian heresy.

Prestwich, Michael. *Armies and Warfare in the Middle Ages: The English Experience.* 1996. An exciting and readable survey of many aspects of English warfare.

Rubin, Miri. *Gentile Tales: The Narrative Assault on Late Medieval Jews.* 2004. Explores the way that stories that were spread about Jews contributed to violence against them.

Tellenbach, Gerd. *The Church in Western Europe from the Tenth to the Twelfth Century.* 1993. A very good survey by an expert on the investiture controversy.

Tyerman, Christopher. *Fighting for Christendom: Holy War and the Crusades.* 2005. Assesses the impact of the Crusades on modern times.

Notes

1. D. C. Douglas and G. E. Greenaway, eds., *English Historical Documents,* vol. 2 (London: Eyre & Spottiswoode, 1961), p. 853.
2. *Hrosvithae Liber Tertius, a Text with Translation,* ed. and trans. Mary Bernardine Bergman (Covington, Ky.: The Sisters of Saint Benedict, 1943), pp. 45 and 53.
3. J. Johns, *Arabic Administration in Norman Sicily: The Royal Dīwān* (New York: Cambridge University Press, 2002), p. 293.
4. Robert Bartlett, *The Making of Europe: Conquest, Colonization and Cultural Change, 950–1350* (Princeton, N.J.: Princeton University Press, 1993), p. 178.
5. H. T. Riley, ed., *Memorials of London* (London: Longmans Green, 1868).
6. Quotations related to the dispute between Henry and Gregory are all from E. F. Henderson, ed., *Select Historical Documents of the Middle Ages* (London: George Bell and Sons, 1892), pp. 372–373, 376–377, 385–387.
7. Fulcher of Chartres, *A History of the Expedition to Jerusalem, 1095–1127,* trans. Frances Rita Ryan, ed. Harold S. Fink (Knoxville: University of Tennessee Press, 1969), pp. 121–123.
8. Quoted in Jo Ann H. Moran Cruz and Richard Gerberding, *Medieval Worlds: An Introduction to European History 300–1492* (Boston: Houghton Mifflin, 2004), p. 305.

Key Terms

Domesday Book (p. 242)
Exchequer (p. 242)
primogeniture (p. 243)
Holy Roman Empire (p. 245)
reconquista (p. 248)
common law (p. 249)
Magna Carta (p. 250)
simony (p. 251)
college of cardinals (p. 252)
lay investiture (p. 253)
excommunication (p. 253)
canon law (p. 255)
Crusades (p. 255)
indulgences (p. 258)
Inquisition (p. 265)
Christendom (p. 269)

For practice quizzes and other study tools, visit the Online Study Guide at **bedfordstmartins.com/mckaywest**.

For primary sources from this period, see *Sources of Western Society*, **Second Edition**.

For Web sites, images, and documents related to topics in this chapter, visit Make History at **bedfordstmartins.com/mckaywest**.

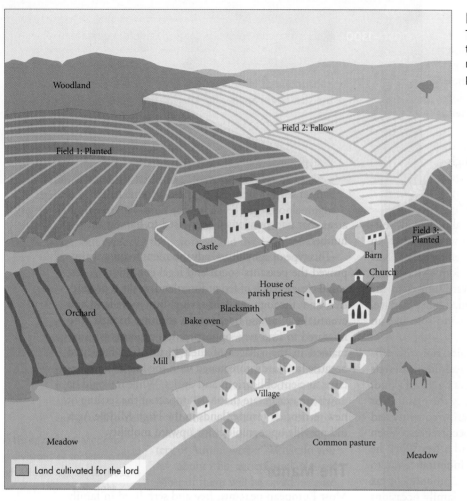

Figure 10.1 **A Medieval Manor**
The basic unit of rural organization and the center of life for most people, the manor constituted the medieval peasants' world.

and all sorts of sterilizing products, and bark for the manufacture of rope. From the forests came wood for the construction of barrels, vats, and other storage containers. Last but hardly least, the forests were used for feeding pigs, cattle, and domestic animals on nuts, roots, and wild berries. If the manor was intersected by a river, it had a welcome source of fish and eels.

Lords generally appointed officials—termed "bailiffs" in England—from outside the village to oversee the legal and business operations of their manors, collect taxes and fees, and handle disputes. Villages in many parts of Europe also developed institutions of self-government to handle issues such as crop rotation, and they chose additional officials such as constables and ale-tasters without the lord's interference. We do not know how these officials were chosen or elected in many cases, but we do know that they were always adult men and were generally heads of households. Women had no official voice in running the village, nor did slaves or servants (female or male), who often worked for and lived with wealthier village families or the lord. Women did buy, sell, and hold land independently and, especially as widows, head households. In areas of Europe where men were gone fishing or foresting for long periods of time, or where men left seasonally or more permanently in search of

work elsewhere, women made decisions about the way village affairs were to be run, though they did not set up formal institutions to do this.

Manors do not represent the only form of medieval rural economy. In parts of Germany and the Netherlands and in much of southern France, free independent farmers owned land outright, free of rents and services. Their farms tended to be small and were surrounded by large estates that gradually swallowed them up. In Scandinavia the soil was so poor and the climate so harsh that people tended to live on widely scattered farms rather than in villages, but they still lived in relatively small family groups.

Work

The peasants' work was typically divided according to gender. Men were responsible for clearing new land, plowing, and caring for large animals, and women were responsible for caring for small animals, spinning, and preparing food. Both sexes planted and harvested, though often there were gender-specific tasks within each of these major undertakings. Women and men worked in the vineyards and in the preparation of crops needed by the textile industry—flax and plants used for dyeing cloth. In fishing communities wives and daughters dried and salted fish for later use, while husbands and sons went out in boats.

Once children were able to walk, they helped their parents in the hundreds of chores that had to be done. Small children were set to collecting eggs if the family had chickens, or gathering twigs and sticks for firewood. As they grew older, children had more responsible tasks, such as weeding the family's vegetable garden, milking the cows, shearing the sheep, cutting wood for fires, and helping with the planting or harvesting. (For more on children, see "Living in the Past: Child's Play," page 292.)

Medieval farmers employed what historians term the **open-field system**, a pattern that differs sharply from modern farming practices. In the open-field system, the arable land of a manor was divided into two or three fields without hedges or fences to mark the individual holdings of the lord, serfs, and freemen. The village as a whole decided what would be planted in each field, rotating the crops according to tradition and need. Some fields would be planted in crops such as wheat, rye, peas, or barley for human consumption, some in oats or other crops for both animals and humans, and some would be left unworked or fallow to allow the soil to rejuvenate. The exact pattern of this rotation varied by location, but in most areas with open-field agriculture the holdings farmed by any one family did not consist of a whole field but, instead, of strips in many fields. If one strip held by a family yielded little, strips in a different field might be more bountiful. Families worked their own land and the lord's, but also cooperated with other families if they needed help, particularly during harvest time. This meant that all shared in any disaster as well as in any large harvest.

The milder climate of the Mediterranean area allowed for more frequent planting and a greater range of agricultural products; families tended to farm individual square plots rather than long strips. Milder climate also meant that more work (and play) could take place outdoors, which may have somewhat alleviated crowding in households with many family members.

open-field system System in which the arable land of a manor was divided into two or three fields without hedges or fences to mark individual holdings.

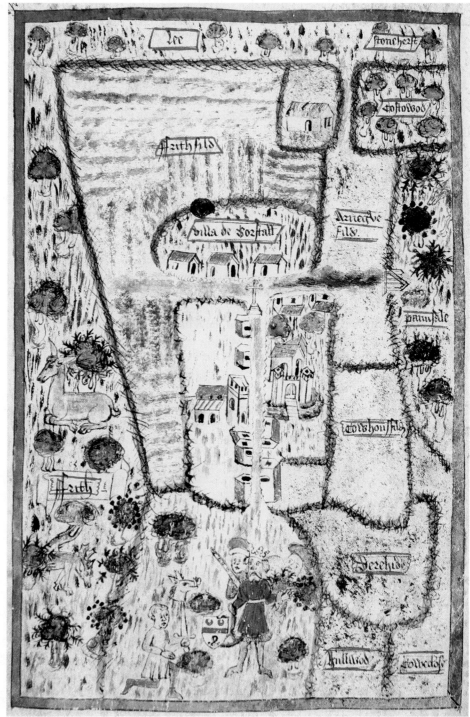

Boarstall Manor, Buckinghamshire
In 1440 Edmund Rede, lord of this estate, had a map made showing his ancestor receiving the title from King Edward I (bottom). Note the manor house, church, and peasants' cottages along the central road. In the common fields, divided by hedges, peasants cultivated on a three-year rotation cycle: winter wheat, spring oats, a year fallow. We don't know whether peasants were allowed to hunt the deer shown in the forest. (Buckinghamshire Record Office, Aylesbury)

Meteorologists think that a slow but steady retreat of polar ice occurred between the ninth and eleventh centuries, and Europe experienced a significant warming trend during the tenth and eleventh centuries. While not approaching the temperatures of the Mediterranean area, England, France, and Germany experienced exceptionally clement weather at this time. The mild winters and dry summers associated with this warming trend helped to increase agricultural output throughout Europe.

The tenth and eleventh centuries also witnessed a number of agricultural improvements, especially in the development of mechanisms that replaced or aided human labor. Mills driven by wind and water power represented significant engineering advancements. A water mill unearthed near Monte Cassino in Italy could grind about 1.5 tons of grain in ten hours, a quantity that would formerly have required the exertions of forty people. Water mills were also well suited to the process known as fulling—cleansing and beating woven cloth so that tiny fibers filled in the holes between the threads, making the cloth more wind- and water-proof—enabling men and women to full cloth at a much faster rate. In the flat areas of northern Europe, such as Holland, where fast-flowing streams were rare, windmills were more common than water mills.

Women's productivity in medieval Europe grew because of water and wind power. In the ancient world, slaves had been responsible for grinding the grain for bread; as slavery was replaced by serfdom, grinding became a woman's task. When water- and wind-driven mills were introduced into an area, women were freed from the task of grinding grain and could turn to other tasks, such as raising animals, working in gardens or vineyards, and raising and preparing flax to make linen.

Women could also devote more time to spinning yarn, which was the bottleneck in cloth production, as each weaver needed at least six spinners. Thus wind and water power contributed to the increase in cloth production in medieval Europe.

In the early twelfth century the production of iron increased significantly. Much of this was used for weapons and armor, but it also filled a growing demand in agriculture. Iron was first used for plowshares (the part of the plow that cuts the furrow and grinds up the earth), and then for pitchforks, spades, and axes. Harrows—cultivating instruments with heavy teeth that broke up and smoothed the soil—began to have iron instead of wooden teeth, making them more effective and less likely to break.

Plows and harrows were increasingly drawn by horses rather than oxen. The development of the padded horse collar that rested on the horse's shoulders and was attached to the load by shafts led to dramatic improvements. The horse collar meant that the animal could put its entire weight into the task of pulling. The use of horses spread in the twelfth century because their greater speed brought greater efficiency to farming and reduced the amount of human labor involved. Oxen were still used in areas where the soil was heavy and muddy, or where people could not afford the more expensive horses.

The thirteenth century witnessed a tremendous spurt in the use of horses to haul carts to market. Consequently, goods reached market faster, and peasants had access to more markets. Peasants not only sold vegetables, grain, and animals, but also bought metal tools, leather shoes, and other goods. Their opportunities for spending on at least a few nonagricultural goods multiplied.

Ox Team Plowing From an eleventh-century calendar showing manorial occupations, this illustration for January—the time for sowing winter wheat—shows two pair of oxen pulling a wheeled plow. Wheeled plows allowed for faster work and deeper tillage, but still required large inputs of human labor. Here one man prods the animals, a second directs the plow blade, and a third drops seed in the ground. (© British Library Board, Cott. Tib. B.V.3, Min. Pt 1)

people could
person if no p
believed that t
the divine assi
tian life and t
enhanced the
did not repla

Muslims

The centrality
most Europea
pate were clear
lims in the Iber
establishing ki
conquista (see
territories, and
forced out, lea
in Christian E
isolated village
lim rituals and
reciting verses f
of the day, and
might hide thi
or government

Islam was ge
but by the late
many areas, oft
as clients of ru
There were Jev
cities and in th
Worms, Speyer
meat to be har
own butchers;
trades as well. J
urday, the Sabl
annual cycle of
Rosh Hashana
over in the spir
prayers, service
commemorated
cluding various
captivity.

Jews could su
but rulers and
trade with Chr
This enhanced C
of holy war tha
ter 9). Violence
tivities increase
expelled from E
of them went
Iberian Peninsu
comed them, th
ally became mor
to live in the ind

Making Cloth In this household scene women in the foreground prepare cloth while men in the background eat a meal. The woman on the left is trimming small threads off with a one-bladed shear, and the one on the right is boiling the cloth to clean and bleach it. Women usually made the clothing for themselves and their families, although the more elaborate clothing worn by nobles was made by professional tailors and seamstresses. (Austrian National Library, Vienna/The Bridgeman Art Library)

By twenty-first-century standards, medieval agricultural yields were very low, but there was striking improvement between the fifth and the thirteenth centuries. Increased agricultural output had a profound impact on society, improving Europeans' health, commerce, industry, and general lifestyle. More food meant that fewer people suffered from hunger and malnourishment on a daily basis, and that devastating famines were rarer. Higher yields brought more food for animals as well as people, and the amount of meat that people ate increased slightly. A better diet had an enormous impact on women's lives in particular. More food meant increased body fat, which increased fertility, and more meat—which provided iron—meant that women were less anemic and less subject to opportunistic diseases. Some researchers believe that it was during the High Middle Ages that Western women began to outlive men. Improved opportunities also encouraged people to marry somewhat earlier, which meant larger families and further population growth.

Home Life and Diet

Life for most people in medieval Europe meant country life. Most people rarely traveled more than twenty-five miles beyond their villages. Everyone's world was small, narrow, and provincial in the original sense of the word: limited by the boundaries of the province. This way of life did not have entirely unfortunate results. People were closely connected with their family, certain of its support and help in time of trouble. The relative peace and political stabilization allowed people to develop a strong sense of place and a pride in their community.

In western and central Europe, villages were generally made up of small houses for individual families. Households consisted of one married couple, their children (including stepchildren), and perhaps one or two other relatives—a grandmother, a cousin whose parents had died, an unmarried sister or brother of one of the spouses. The household thus contained primarily a nuclear family, although some homes contained only an unmarried person, a widow, or several unmarried people living together. In southern and eastern Europe, extended families were more likely to live in the same household or very near one another. Father and son, or two married brothers, and the families of both might share a house, forming what demographers call a stem or complex household.

The size and quality of peasants' houses varied according to their relative prosperity, and that prosperity usually depended on the amount of land held. Poorer peasants lived in windowless cottages built of wood and clay or wattle (poles interwoven with branches or reeds) and thatched with straw. Such a cottage consisted of one large room that served as the kitchen and living quarters for all. The house had an earthen floor and a

The Lady and the Unicorn Tapestry This tapestry, woven in Flanders for a nobleman at the French court, expresses many of the ideals of noble life. A beautiful young woman stands in front of a tent with battle flags. On her right is a lion, symbol of earthly power. On her left is a unicorn, a beast that could only be captured by a virgin. Medieval people viewed the unicorn both as an allegory of Christ (who was "captured" by the Virgin Mary when he was born) and of an earthly lover tamed by his beloved. The enigmatic words "to my only desire" on the top of the tent may refer to either spiritual or romantic love, for both were viewed as appropriate motivations for noble action. (Erich Lessing/Art Resource, NY)

and defended society with the sword and the peasants provided sustenance through their toil, so the monks and nuns worked to secure God's blessing for society with their prayers and chants.

Monastic Revival

In the early Middle Ages many religious houses followed the Benedictine *Rule*, while others developed their own patterns (see Chapter 7). In the High Middle Ages this diversity became more formalized, and **religious orders**, groups of monastic houses following a particular rule, were established. Historians term the foundation, strengthening, and reform of religious orders in the High Middle Ages the "monastic revival." They link it with the simultaneous ex-

religious orders Groups of monastic houses following a particular rule.

pansion of papal power (see Chapter 9) because many of the same individuals were important in both.

The best Benedictine monasteries had been centers of learning, copying and preserving manuscripts, maintaining schools, and setting high standards of monastic observance. Charlemagne had encouraged and supported these monastic activities, and the collapse of the Carolingian Empire had disastrous effects.

The Viking, Magyar, and Muslim invaders attacked and ransacked many monasteries across Europe, causing some religious communities to flee and disperse. In the period of political disorder that followed the disintegration of the Carolingian Empire, many religious houses fell under the control and domination of local lords. Powerful laymen appointed themselves or their relatives as abbots, took the lands and goods of monasteries, and spent monastic revenues. The level of spiritual observance and intellectual activity in monasteries and convents declined.

The secular powers who selected church officials compelled them to become vassals. Abbots, bishops, and archbishops thus had military responsibilities that required them to fight alongside their lords, or at least to send contingents of soldiers when called on to do so. As feudal lords themselves, ecclesiastical officials also had judicial authority over knights and peasants on their lands. The conflict between a church official's religious duties on the one hand and his judicial and military obligations on the other posed a serious dilemma.

The first sign of reform came in 909, when William the Pious, duke of Aquitaine, established the abbey of Cluny in Burgundy. Duke William declared that the monastery was to be free from any feudal responsibilities to him or any other lord, its members subordinate only to the pope. The monastery at Cluny came to exert vast religious influence and initially held high standards of religious behavior. Cluny gradually came to stand for clerical celibacy and the suppression of simony (the sale of church offices). In the eleventh century Cluny was fortunate in having a series of highly able abbots who ruled for a long time. In a disorderly world, Cluny gradually came to represent stability. Therefore, laypersons placed lands under its custody and monastic priories under its jurisdiction for reform (a priory is a religious house, with generally a smaller number of residents than an abbey, governed by a prior or prioress). Benefactors wanted to be associated with Cluniac piety, and monasteries under Cluny's jurisdiction enjoyed special protection, at least theoretically, from violence. In this way, hundreds of monasteries, primarily in France and Spain, came under Cluny's authority.

Deeply impressed laypeople showered gifts on monasteries with good reputations, such as Cluny and its many daughter houses. But as the monasteries became richer, the lifestyle of the monks grew increasingly luxurious. Monastic observance and spiritual fervor declined. Soon fresh demands for reform were heard, and the result was the founding of new religious orders in the late eleventh and early twelfth centuries.

The **Cistercians** (sihs-TUHR-shuhnz), because of their phenomenal expansion and the great economic, political, and spiritual influence they exerted, are the best representatives of the new reforming spirit. In 1098 a group of monks left the rich abbey of Molesmes in Burgundy because, in the words of the twelfth-century chronicler-monk William of Malmesbury, "purity could not be preserved in a place where riches and gluttony warred against even the heart that was well inclined." They founded a new house in the swampy forest of Cîteaux (si-TOH), planned to avoid all involvement with secular feudal society, and decided to accept only uncultivated lands far from regular habitation. The early Cistercians (the word is derived from *Cîteaux*) determined to keep their services simple and their lives austere. "They wear nothing made with furs or linen," wrote William, never "eat lard or meat . . . nor do they ever speak, save only to the abbot. . . . While they bestow care on the stranger and the sick, they inflict intolerable mortifications on their own bodies, for the health of their souls."

The first monks at Cîteaux experienced sickness, a dearth of recruits, and terrible privations. But their high ideals made them, in William's words, "a model for all monks, a mirror for the diligent, and a spur for the indolent."[7] In 1112 a twenty-three-year-old nobleman called Bernard joined the community at Cîteaux, together with some of his brothers and other noblemen. Three years later Bernard was appointed founding abbot of Clairvaux (klahr-VOH) in Champagne. From this position he conducted a vast correspondence, attacked the theological views of Peter Abelard (see Chapter 11), intervened in the disputed papal election of 1130, drafted a constitution for the Knights Templars, and preached the Second Crusade. This reforming movement gained impetus. Cîteaux founded 525 new monasteries in the course of the twelfth century, and its influence on European society was profound (Map 10.2). In England the very long-lived Saint Gilbert (1085?–1189) organized a community of nuns at Sempringham that followed the more rigorous Cistercian rule "as far as the weakness of their sex allowed," as Gilbert put it. This convent established several daughter houses, and Gilbert asked the Cistercians to take them all on as official female branches. They refused, saying that they did not want the burden of overseeing women, setting a pattern for other men's religious orders.

> **Cistercians** Religious order founded in the late eleventh century that adopted an austere lifestyle and tried to separate from feudal power structures.

Unavoidably, Cistercian success brought wealth, and wealth brought power. By the later twelfth century economic prosperity and political power had begun to compromise the original Cistercian ideals.

Life in Convents and Monasteries

Medieval monasteries were religious institutions whose organization and structure fulfilled the social needs of the feudal nobility. The monasteries provided noble boys with education and opportunities for ecclesiastical careers. Although a few men who rose in the ranks of church officials were of humble origins, most were from high-status families. Many had been given as child oblates by their parents. Some men did become monks as adults, apparently for a wide variety of reasons: belief in a direct call from God, disgust with the materialism and violence of the secular world, the encouragement and inspiration of others, economic failure or lack of opportunity, poverty, sickness, and fear of Hell. Beginning in the thirteenth century more boys and men from

LOOKING BACK LOOKING AHEAD THE IMAGE OF EUROPEAN society as divided into three orders—those who fight, those who pray, those who work— was overly simplistic when it was first developed in the ninth century, but it did encompass most of the European population. Movement between those groups was possible: both noble and peasant children given as oblates could become monks and nuns; members of noble families became abbots and abbesses; through service to a lord a few peasants rose to the rank of knight; younger sons of knights could sink to the peasantry if they had too many brothers and were unlucky in war or marriage.

By the eleventh century, though the three-part social model still encompassed most people, growing towns housed increasing numbers of men and women who fit into none of the groups. Townspeople were recruited from all three orders, and the opportunities offered by towns eventually speeded up social and economic change. As they grew, towns replaced monasteries as the primary centers of culture in medieval Europe, with their walls and cathedrals dominating the landscape.

CHAPTER REVIEW

■ What was life like for the rural common people of medieval Europe? (p. 274)

Generalizations about peasant life in the High Middle Ages must always be qualified according to manorial customs, geography, and the leadership of local lords. Everywhere, however, the success of crops and the payment of rents preoccupied peasants, with men, women, and children all working the land. Peasants lived in villages in crowded one-room houses. Although peasants led hard lives, the reclamation of wastelands and forestlands, migration to frontier territory, or manumission offered means of social mobility. The warmer climate of the High Middle Ages and technological improvements such as water mills and horse-drawn plows increased the available food supply, though the mainstay of the peasant diet was still coarse bread. Death in childbirth of both infant and mother was a common occurrence, though there were some improvements in health care through the opening of hospitals.

■ How did religious practices and attitudes permeate everyday life? (p. 283)

Among Christians the village church was the center of community life, where people attended services, honored the saints, and experienced the sacraments. People also carried out rituals full of religious meaning in their daily lives, and every major life transition—childbirth, marriage, death—was marked by a ceremony that included religious elements. This was true for Muslims and Jews as well as for Christians, but the centrality of Christian ceremonies for most people meant that Muslims and Jews were increasingly marked as outsiders.

■ What were the lives of nobles like in medieval Europe? (p. 290)

Nobles were a tiny fraction of the total population, but they exerted great power over all aspects of life. Aristocratic values and attitudes, often described as chivalry, transformed the knightly class and set an ideal for the nobility. Around 1100 the knightly class began to unite in its ability to fight on horseback, in its insistence that each member was descended from a valorous ancestor, and in its position at the top of the social hierarchy. Noble children were trained for their later roles in life, with boys trained for war and women for marriage and running estates. Noblemen often devoted considerable time to fighting, and intergenerational squabbles were common. Yet noblemen, and sometimes noblewomen, also had heavy judicial, political, and economic responsibilities.

■ What roles did the men and women affiliated with religious orders play in medieval society? (p. 293)

Monks and nuns were thought of as a crucial part of medieval society, their prayers interceding between God and the people. The monastic revival of the High Middle Ages witnessed the growth and reform of monastic life. Monasteries owned large amounts of land and served as centers of learning, where manuscripts were copied and original works written. Monks and nuns offered social services, feeding the poor and educating children.

Suggested Reading

Arnold, John H. *What Is Medieval History?* 2008. A very brief guide to the study of medieval history, with many examples of sources and methods taken from everyday life.

Bennett, Judith M. *A Medieval Life: Cecelia Penifader of Brigstock, c. 1297–1344.* 1998. An excellent brief introduction to all aspects of village life from the perspective of one woman; designed for students.

Bouchard, Constance Brittain. *Strong of Body, Brave and Noble: Chivalry and Society in Medieval France.* 1996. Contrasts the literary ideal with real noble life, and includes a discussion of noble families as well as the relations between nobles and other groups in society.

Brooke, Rosalind, and Christopher Brooke. *Popular Religion in the Middle Ages.* 1984. A readable synthesis of material on the beliefs and practices of ordinary Christians.

Duby, Georges. *The Chivalrous Society.* Trans. C. Postan. 1977. A classic study of the three orders as a model of medieval society.

Glick, Leonard B. *Abraham's Heirs: Jews and Christians in Medieval Europe.* 1999. Provides information on many aspects of Jewish life and Jewish-Christian relations.

Hanawalt, Barbara A. *The Ties That Bound: Peasant Families in Medieval England.* 1986. A very readable study of gender and family relations in the countryside.

Herlihy, David. *Medieval Households.* 1985. Treats marriage patterns, family size, sexual relations, and emotional life.

Kaeuper, Richard W. *Chivalry and Violence in Medieval Europe.* 2006. Examines the role chivalry played in promoting violent disorder.

Karras, Ruth M. *From Boys to Men: Formations of Masculinity in Late Medieval Europe.* 2002. Explores the way boys of different social groups were trained in what it meant to be a man; designed for students.

Lawrence, C. H. *Medieval Monasticism: Forms of Religious Life in Western Europe in the Middle Ages.* 1988. Provides a solid introduction to monastic life as it was practiced.

Newman, Barbara. *Voice of the Living Light: Hildegard of Bingen and Her World.* 1998. A book designed for general readers that places the medieval mystic within her social, intellectual, and political contexts.

Shahar, Shulamit. *Childhood in the Middle Ages.* 1990. Surveys ideas about childhood and examines children's actual experiences.

Shahar, Shulamit. *The Fourth Estate: A History of Women in the Middle Ages.* 2d ed. 2003. Analyzes attitudes toward women and provides information on the lives of women, including nuns, peasants, noblewomen, and townswomen, in western Europe between the twelfth and the fifteenth centuries.

Shinners, John. *Medieval Popular Religion, 1000–1500.* 2d ed. 2006. An excellent collection of a wide variety of sources that provide evidence about the beliefs and practices of ordinary Christians.

Webb, Diana. *Medieval European Pilgrimage, c. 700–c. 1500.* 2002. Examines the role of pilgrimage in Christianity.

Notes

1. Honorius of Autun, "Elucidarium sive Dialogus de Summa Totius Christianae Theologiae," in *Patrologia Latina*, ed. J. P. Migne (Paris: Garnier Brothers, 1854), vol. 172, col. 1149.

2. M. Chibnall, ed. and trans., *The Ecclesiastical History of Ordericus Vitalis* (Oxford: Oxford University Press, 1972), 2.xiii.

3. J. Boswell, *The Kindness of Strangers: The Abandonment of Children in Western Europe from Late Antiquity to the Renaissance* (New York: Pantheon Books, 1989), pp. 297, 299, and Conclusion.

4. Thirteenth-century sermon story, in David Herlihy, ed., *Medieval Culture and Society* (New York: Harper and Row, 1968), pp. 295, 298.

5. Translated and quoted in Susan C. Karant-Nunn, *The Reformation of Ritual: An Interpretation of Early Modern Germany* (London: Routledge, 1997), p. 77.

6. Honorius of Autun, "Elucidarium sive Dialogus," vol. 172, col. 1148.

7. William of Malmesbury, *Chronicle*, in James Bruce Ross and Mary Martin McLaughlin, eds., *The Portable Medieval Reader* (New York: Viking, 1949), pp. 57–58.

8. *Dulcitius* in Herlihy, *Medieval Culture and Society*, pp. 112–113, 115.

Key Terms

the three orders (p. 274)
open-field system (p. 277)
oblates (p. 281)
nobility (p. 290)
chivalry (p. 290)
tournament (p. 291)
religious orders (p. 294)
Cistercians (p. 295)
abbess/prioress (p. 297)
abbot/prior (p. 298)

For practice quizzes and other study tools, visit the Online Study Guide at **bedfordstmartins.com/mckaywest**.

For primary sources from this period, see *Sources of Western Society*, **Second Edition**.

For Web sites, images, and documents related to topics in this chapter, visit Make History at **bedfordstmartins.com/mckaywest**.

11

The Creativity and Challenges of Medieval Cities

1100–1300

The High Middle Ages witnessed some of the most remarkable achievements in the entire history of Western society. Europeans displayed tremendous creativity and vitality in many facets of culture. Relative security and an increasing food supply allowed for the growth and development of towns and a revival of long-distance trade. City dwellers thus had a greater variety of material goods than did villagers, and they also interacted with a greater variety of people. Some urban merchants and bankers became as wealthy as great nobles, though cities were also home to large numbers of poor people. Trade brought in new ideas as well as merchandise, and cities developed into intellectual and cultural centers. The university, a new — and very long-lasting — type of educational institution, came into being, providing advanced training in theology, medicine, and law. Traditions and values were spread orally through stories and songs, as people gathered to hear about the exploits of great kings or the affairs of great lovers. Some of these stories were written down as part of the development of vernacular literature, for more people could read in cities than in rural areas. Gothic cathedrals, where people saw beautiful stained-glass windows and listened to complex music, manifested medieval people's deep Christian faith and their pride in their own cities. Many urban residents were increasingly dissatisfied with the Christian church, however, and turned to heretical movements that challenged church power. ∎

Snark/Art Resource, NY

Life in a Medieval City. This detail from a manuscript illumination shows a street scene of a medieval town, with a barber, cloth merchants, and an apothecary all offering their wares and services on the ground floors of their household-workshops.

CHAPTER PREVIEW

Towns and Economic Revival
■ How did medieval cities originate, and what impact did they have on the economy and on culture?

Urban Life
■ What was life like in the cities, and how did it differ for the members of different social classes?

Medieval Universities
■ How did universities evolve, and what needs of medieval society did they serve?

Literature and Architecture
■ How did literature and architecture express the ideals, attitudes, and interests of medieval people?

Cities and the Church
■ How did the growth of the cities affect attitudes toward the church, and what was the church's response?

Towns and Economic Revival

How did medieval cities originate, and what impact did they have on the economy and on culture? ■

The rise of towns and the growth of a new business and commercial class was a central part of Europe's recovery after the disorders of the tenth century. The growth of towns was made possible by some of the changes we have already traced: a rise in population; increased agricultural output, which provided an adequate food supply for new town dwellers; and a small amount of peace and political stability, which allowed merchants to transport and sell goods. As towns gained legal and political rights, merchant and craft guilds grew more powerful, and towns became centers of production as well as trading centers. The development of towns was to lay the foundations for Europe's transformation, centuries later, from a rural agricultural society into an urban industrial society—a change with global implications.

The Rise of Towns

Early medieval society was agricultural and rural. The emergence of a new class that was neither of these constituted a social revolution. Most of the members of the new class—artisans and merchants—came from the peasantry. The landless younger sons of large families were driven away by land shortage. Some were forced by war and famine to seek new possibilities. Others were immigrants colonizing newly conquered lands, as in central Europe and Spain after the reconquista (see Chapter 9). And some were unusually enterprising, adventurous, and curious; they were simply willing to take a chance.

Medieval towns began in many different ways. Some were fortifications erected as a response to the ninth-century Viking invasions, into which farmers from the surrounding countryside moved when their area was attacked. Later, merchants were attracted to the fortifications because they had something to sell and wanted to be where the customers were. Merchants and foreign traders settled just outside the

Emperor Frederick II Granting Privileges A young and handsome Frederick II, with a laurel wreath symbolizing his position as emperor, signs a grant of privileges for a merchant of the Italian city of Asti in this thirteenth-century manuscript. Frederick wears the flamboyant and fashionable clothing of a high noble—long-toed shoes, slit sleeves, and a cape of ermine tails—while the merchant seeking his favor is dressed in more sober and less expensive garb. (Scala/Art Resource, NY)

walls in the faubourgs (foh-BUHRZ) or suburbs—both of which mean "outside" or "in the shelter of the walls." Other towns grew up around great cathedrals (see page 326) and monasteries whose schools drew students—potential customers—from far and wide. Many other towns grew from the sites of earlier Roman army camps. The restoration of order and political stability promoted rebirth and new development in these locations.

Whether evolving from a newly fortified place, an old Roman army camp, or a cathedral site, medieval towns had a few common characteristics. Each town had a marketplace, and most had a mint for the coining of money. The town also had a court to settle disputes. In addition, medieval towns were enclosed by walls. The terms *burgher* (BUR-guhr) and *bourgeois* derive from the Old English and Old German words *burg*, *burgh*, *borg*, and *borough* for "a walled or fortified place." Thus a burgher or bourgeois originally was a person who lived or worked inside the walls.

No matter where groups of traders congregated, they settled on someone's land and had to secure permission to live and trade from the king, count, abbot, or bishop. Aristocratic nobles and churchmen were initially hostile to the new middle class. They soon realized, however, that profits and benefits flowed to them and their territories from the towns set up on their land.

The growing towns of medieval Europe slowly gained legal and political rights, including the right to hold municipal courts that alone could judge members of the town, the right to select the mayor and other municipal officials, and the right to tax residents. Feudal lords were often reluctant to grant towns self-government, fearing loss of authority and revenue if they gave the merchants full independence. When burghers bargained for a town's political independence, however, they offered sizable amounts of ready cash and sometimes promised payments for years to come. Consequently, feudal lords ultimately agreed to self-government.

In addition to working for the political independence of the towns, merchants and townspeople tried to acquire liberties for themselves. In the Middle Ages *liberties* meant special privileges. Town liberties included the privilege of living and trading on the lord's land. The most important privilege a medieval townsperson could gain was personal freedom. It gradually developed that an individual who lived in a town for a year and a day was free of servile obligations and status. Serfs who fled their manors for towns and were able to find work and avoid recapture became free of personal labor obligations. Thus the growth of towns contributed to a slow

decline of serfdom in western Europe, although this would take centuries.

As population increased, towns rebuilt their walls, expanding the living space to accommodate growing numbers. Through an archaeological investigation of the amount of land gradually enclosed by walls, historians have extrapolated rough estimates of medieval towns' populations. For example, the walled area of the German city of Cologne equaled roughly 250 acres in the tenth century. In the fourteenth century it had expanded to about 1,000 acres and had a population of probably 40,000. The concentration of the textile industry in the Low Countries (present-day Holland, Belgium, and French Flanders) brought into being the most populous cluster of cities in western Europe: Ghent with about 56,000 people, Bruges (broozh) with 27,000, and Tournai and Brussels with perhaps 20,000 each. Venice, Florence, and Paris, each with about 110,000 people, and Milan with possibly 200,000 led all Europe in population (Map 11.1).

Merchant and Craft Guilds

The merchants, who were influential in winning towns' independence from feudal lords, also used their power and wealth to control life within the city walls. The merchants of a town joined together to form a **merchant guild** that prohibited nonmembers from trading in the town. Guild members often made up the earliest town government, serving as mayors and members of the city council, so that a town's economic policies were determined by its merchants' self-interest. By the late eleventh century, especially in the towns

merchant guild A band of merchants that prohibited nonmembers from trading in the town.

ca. 1100	Merchant guilds become rich and powerful in many cities; artisans begin to found craft guilds
1100–1300	Height of construction of cathedrals in Europe
1143	Founding of Lübeck, first city in the Hanseatic League
ca. 1200	Founding of first universities
1216	Papal recognition of Dominican order
1221	Papal recognition of Franciscan order
1225–1274	Life of Thomas Aquinas; *Summa Theologica*
1233	Papacy begins to use friars to staff the Inquisition
ca. 1300	Bill of exchange becomes most common method of commercial payment in western Europe
1300s	Clocks in general use throughout Europe
1302	Pope Boniface VIII declares all Christians subject to the pope in *Unam Sanctam*

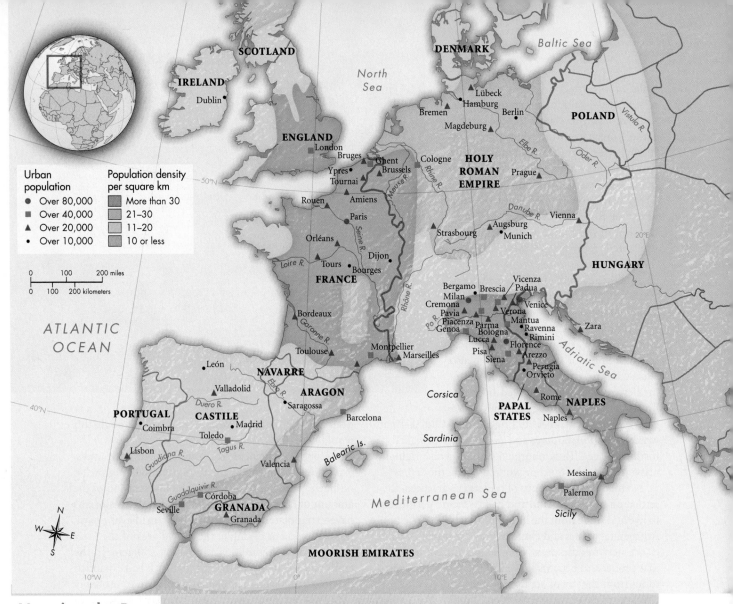

Urban population
- ● Over 80,000
- ■ Over 40,000
- ▲ Over 20,000
- • Over 10,000

Population density per square km
- More than 30
- 21–30
- 11–20
- 10 or less

0   100   200 miles
0   100   200 kilometers

Mapping the Past

Map 11.1 **European Population Density, ca. 1300** The development of towns and the reinvigoration of trade were directly related in medieval Europe. Using all three maps in this chapter and the information in your text, answer the following questions.

ANALYZING THE MAP What were the four largest cities in Europe? What part of Europe had the highest density of towns?

CONNECTIONS What role did textile and other sorts of manufacturing play in the growth of towns? How was the development of towns related to that of universities, monastery schools, and cathedral schools?

To complete this activity online, go to the **Online Study Guide** at bedfordstmartins.com/mckaywest.

---

of the Low Countries and northern Italy, the leaders of the merchant guilds were rich and powerful. They constituted an oligarchy in their towns, controlling economic life and bargaining with kings and lords for political independence.

While most towns were initially established as trading centers, they quickly became centers of production as well. Peasants looking for better opportunities left their villages — either with their lord's approval or without it — and moved to towns, providing both

workers and mouths to feed. Some began to specialize in certain types of food and clothing production: some made and sold bread, and others bought cloth and sewed it into clothing. Others purchased and butchered cattle, and then sold the meat to people who made small meat pies and sold the leather to those who made shoes or bags. Merchants often imported raw materials such as iron or silver, which they sold to people who made armaments and tableware. Wealthy merchants then bought these products for their own use, or they

Spanish Apothecary A Spanish pharmacist, seated outside his shop located within the town walls, describes the merits of his goods to a crowd of Christians and Muslims. This thirteenth-century painting captures the variety of people and products that could be found in cities, particularly those in Spain, where urban residents included Christians, Muslims, and Jews. (Laurie Platt Winfrey/The Granger Collection, New York)

exported the finished products to other areas. Over time certain cities became known for their fine fabrics, their reliable arms and armor, or their elegant gold and silver work.

Like merchants, producers recognized that organizing would bring benefits, and beginning in the twelfth century in many cities they developed **craft guilds** that regulated most aspects of production. They set quality standards for their particular product, and they regulated the size of workshops, the training period, and the conduct of members. In most cities individual guilds, such as those of shoemakers or blacksmiths, achieved a monopoly in the production of one particular product, forbidding nonmembers to work. The craft guild then chose some of its members to act as inspectors and set up a court to hear disputes between members, though the city court remained the final arbiter.

Each guild set the pattern by which members were trained. A boy who wanted to become a weaver, for instance, or whose parents wanted him to, spent four to seven years as an apprentice, often bound by a contract such as the following from thirteenth-century Marseilles in southern France:

April the ninth. I, Peter Borre, in good faith and without guile, place with you, Peter Feissac, weaver, my son Stephen, for the purpose of learning the trade and craft of weaving, to live at your house, and to do work for you from the feast of Easter next for four continuous years, promising you by this agreement to take care that my son does the said work, and that he will be faithful and trustworthy in all that he does, and that he will neither steal nor take anything away from you, nor flee nor depart from you for any reason, until he had completed his apprenticeship.[1]

When the apprenticeship was finished, a young artisan spent several years as journeyman, working in the shop of a master artisan. He then could make his "masterpiece"—in the case of weavers, a long piece of cloth. If the other masters judged the cloth acceptable, and if they thought the market in their town was large enough to support another weaver, the journeyman could then become a master and start a shop. Though the time required as an apprentice and as a journeyman varied slightly from guild to guild, all guilds followed this three-stage process. Guilds limited the amount of raw materials each master could have and the size of the workshop, thus assuring each master that his household-workshop would be able to support itself.

Many guilds required masters to be married, as they recognized the vital role of the master's wife. She assisted in running the shop, often selling the goods her husband had produced. Their children, both male and female, also worked alongside the apprentices and journeymen. The

craft guild A band of producers that regulated most aspects of production.

sons were sometimes formally apprenticed, but the daughters were generally not because many guilds limited formal membership to males. Most guilds did allow a master's widow to continue operating a shop for a set period of time after her husband's death, for they recognized that she had the necessary skills and experience. Such widows paid all guild dues, but they were not considered full members and could not vote or hold office in the guild. The fact that women were not formally guild members did not mean that they did not work in guild shops, however, for alongside the master's wife and daughters female domestic servants often performed such less-skilled tasks as preparing raw materials and cleaning finished products. In addition, there were a few all-female guilds in several European cities, particularly in Cologne and Paris, in which girls were formally apprenticed in the same way boys were in regular craft guilds.

Both craft and merchant guilds were not only economic organizations, but also systems of social support. Though they were harsh against outsiders, they were protective and supportive of their members. They took care of elderly masters who could no longer work, and they often supported masters' widows and orphans. They maintained an altar at a city church and provided for the funerals of members and baptisms of their children. Guild members marched together in city parades and reinforced their feelings of solidarity with one another by special ceremonies and distinctive dress. Merchant guilds in some parts of Europe, such as the Hansa cities of Hamburg, Lübeck, and Bremen, had special buildings for celebrations and ceremonies.

The Revival of Long-Distance Trade

The growth of towns went hand in hand with a remarkable revival of trade as artisans and craftsmen manufactured goods for both local and foreign consumption (Map 11.2). Most trade centered in towns and was controlled by professional traders. Long-distance trade was risky and required large investments of capital. Robbers and thieves roamed virtually all of the overland trade routes. Pirates infested the sea-lanes, and shipwrecks were common. Since the risks were so great, merchants preferred to share them. A group of people would thus pool their capital to finance an expedition to a distant place. When the ship or caravan returned and the goods brought back were sold, the investors would share the profits. If disaster struck the caravan, an investor's loss was limited to the amount of that individual's investment.

Which towns took the lead in medieval international trade? In the late eleventh century the Italian cities, especially Venice, led the West in trade in general and completely dominated trade with the East. Ships carried salt from the Venetian lagoon, pepper and other spices from India and North Africa, and silks and purple textiles from the East to northern and western Europe. In the thirteenth century Venetian caravans brought slaves from the Crimea and Chinese silks from Mongolia to the West. The towns of Bruges, Ghent, and Ypres (EE-pruh) in Flanders built a vast industry in the manufacture of cloth, becoming leaders in the trade of textiles.

Two circumstances help explain the lead Venice and the Flemish towns gained in long-distance trade. Both areas enjoyed a high degree of peace and political stability. Geographical factors were equally, if not more, important. Venice was ideally located at the northwestern end of the Adriatic Sea, with easy access to the transalpine land routes as well as the Adriatic and Mediterranean sea-lanes. The markets of North Africa, Byzantium, and Russia and the great fairs (large periodic gatherings that attracted buyers, sellers, and goods) of Ghent in Flanders and Champagne in France provided commercial opportunities that Venetian merchants quickly seized. The geographical situation of Flanders also offered unusual possibilities: just across the Channel from England, Flanders had easy access to English wool. Because the weather in England was colder than in most of Europe, English sheep grew longer and denser wool than sheep elsewhere. With this wool, cloth makers could produce high-quality cloth, which was the most valuable manufactured product handled by merchants and one of the few European products for which there was a market in the East.

From the late eleventh through the thirteenth centuries, Europe enjoyed a steadily expanding volume of international trade. Demand for sugar (to replace honey), pepper, cloves, and Asian spices to season a bland diet; for fine wines from the Rhineland, Burgundy, and Bordeaux; for luxury woolens from Flanders and Tuscany; for furs from Ireland and Russia; for brocades and tapestries from Flanders and silks from Constantinople and even China; for household furnishings such as silver plate—not to mention the desire for products associated with a military aristocracy such as swords and armor—surged markedly. As the trade volume expanded, the use of cash became more widespread. Beginning in the 1160s the opening of new silver mines in Germany, Bohemia, northern Italy, northern France, and western England led to the minting and circulation of vast quantities of silver coins.

Increased trade also led to a higher standard of living. Contact with Eastern civilizations introduced Europeans to eating utensils, and table manners improved. Nobles learned to eat with forks and knives instead of tearing the meat from a roast with their hands. They began to use napkins instead of wiping their greasy fingers on their clothes or on the dogs lying under the table.

Business Procedures

The economic surge of the High Middle Ages caused business procedures to change radically. To meet the greater volume of goods being exchanged, the work of merchants became specialized. Three separate types of merchants emerged: the sedentary merchant who ran the "home office," financing and organizing the firm's entire export-import trade; the carriers who transported goods by land and sea; and the company agents living abroad who, on the advice of the home office, looked after sales and procurements.

Commercial correspondence, unnecessary when one businessperson oversaw everything and made direct bargains with buyers and sellers, proliferated, and regular courier service among commercial cities began.

Commercial accounting became more complex when firms had to deal with shareholders, manufacturers, customers, branch offices, employees, and competing firms. Tolls on roads became high enough to finance what has been called a "road revolution" involving new surfaces, bridges, new passes through the Alps, and new inns and hospices for travelers. The growth of mutual confidence among merchants facilitated the growth of sales on credit.

In all these business transformations, merchants of the Italian cities led the way. (See "Individuals in Society: Francesco Datini," page 310.) They formalized their agreements with new types of contracts, including permanent partnerships termed *compagnie* (kahm-pah-NYEE) (literally "bread together," that is, sharing bread; the root of the word *company*). Many of these

Map 11.2 **Trade and Manufacturing in Thirteenth-Century Europe** Note the overland and ocean lines of trade and the sources of silver, iron, copper, lead, paper, wool, carpets and rugs, and slaves.

Francesco Datini

INDIVIDUALS IN SOCIETY

IN 1348, WHEN HE WAS A YOUNG TEENAGER, Francesco Datini (1335–1410) lost his father, his mother, a brother, and a sister to the Black Death epidemic that swept through Europe (see Chapter 12). Leaving his hometown of Prato in northern Italy, he apprenticed himself to merchants in nearby Florence for several years to learn accounting and other business skills. At fifteen, he moved to the city of Avignon (ah-veen-YOHN) in southern France. The popes were at this point living in Avignon instead of Rome, and the city offered many opportunities for an energetic and enterprising young man. Datini first became involved in the weapons trade, which offered steady profits, and then became a merchant of spices, wool and silk cloth, and jewels. He was very successful, and when he was thirty-one he married the young daughter of another merchant in an elaborate wedding that was the talk of Avignon.

In 1378 the papacy returned to Italy, and Datini soon followed, setting up trading companies in Prato, Pisa, Florence, and eventually other cities as well. He focused on cloth and leather and sought to control the trade in products used for preparation as well, especially the rare dyes that created the brilliant colors favored by wealthy noblemen and townspeople. He eventually had offices all over Europe and became one of the richest men of his day, opening a mercantile bank and a company that produced cloth as well as many branch offices.

Datini was more successful than most, but what makes him particularly stand out was his record keeping. He kept careful account books and ledgers, all of them headed by the phrase "in the name of God and profit." He wrote to the managers of each of his offices every week, providing them with careful advice and blunt criticism: "You cannot see a crow in a bowl of milk." Taking on the son of a friend as an employee,

Statue of Francesco Datini located outside the city hall in Prato. (Peter Horree/Alamy)

he wrote to the young man: "Do your duty well, and you will acquire honor and profit, and you can count on me as if I were your own father. But if you do not, then do not count on me; it will be as if I had never known you."

When Datini was away from home, which was often, he wrote to his wife every day, and she sometimes responded in ways that were less deferential than we might expect of a woman who was many years younger. "I think it is not necessary," she wrote at one point, "to send me a message every Wednesday to say that you will be here on Sunday, for it seems to me that on every Friday you change your mind."

Datini's obsessive record keeping lasted beyond his death, for someone saved all of his records — hundreds of ledgers and contracts, eleven thousand business letters, and over a hundred thousand personal letters — in sacks in his opulent house in Prato, where they were found in the nineteenth century. They provide a detailed picture of medieval business practices and also reveal much about Datini as a person. Ambitious, calculating, luxury-loving, and a workaholic, Datini seems similar to a modern CEO. Like many of today's self-made billionaires, at the end of his life Datini began to think a bit more about God and less about profit. In his will, he set up a foundation for the poor in Prato and a home for orphans in Florence, both of which are still in operation. In 1967 scholars established an institute for economic history in Prato, naming it in Datini's honor; the institute now manages the collection of Datini's documents and gathers other relevant materials in its archives.

Source: Iris Origo, *The Merchant of Prato: Francesco di Marco Datini, 1335–1410* (New York: Alfred A. Knopf, Inc., 1957).

QUESTIONS FOR ANALYSIS

1. How would you evaluate Datini's motto, "In the name of God and profit"? Is it an honest statement of his aims, a hypocritical justification of greed, a blend of both, or something else?

2. Changes in business procedures in the Middle Ages have been described as a "commercial revolution." Do Datini's business ventures support this assessment? How?

compagnies began as agreements between brothers or other relatives and in-laws, but they quickly grew to include people who were not family members. In addition, they began to involve individuals—including a few women—who invested only their money, leaving the actual running of the business to the active partners.

The ventures of the German Hanseatic League also illustrate these new business procedures. The **Hanseatic League** was a mercantile association of towns. Initially the towns of Lübeck and Hamburg wanted mutual security, exclusive trading rights, and, where possible, a monopoly. During the next century, perhaps two hundred cities from Holland to Poland joined the league, but Lübeck (founded in 1143) always remained the dominant member. From the thirteenth to the sixteenth centuries, the Hanseatic League controlled the trade of northern Europe. In the fourteenth century the league branched out into southern Germany and Italy by land and into French, Spanish, and Portuguese ports by sea.

At cities such as Bruges and London, Hansa merchants secured special trading concessions, exempting them from all tolls and allowing them to trade at local fairs. Hansa merchants established foreign trading centers, called "factories" because the commercial agents in them were called "factors." (Later this word, or "manufactory," would be applied to centers of production as well.) The most famous factory was the London Steelyard, a walled community with warehouses, offices, a church, and residential quarters for company representatives. By the late thirteenth century Hansa merchants had developed an important business technique, the business register. Merchants publicly recorded their debts and contracts and received a league guarantee for them.

The dramatic increase in trade ran into two serious difficulties in medieval Europe. One was the problem of minting money. Despite investment in mining operations to increase the production of metals, the amount of gold, silver, and copper available for coins was not adequate for the increased flow of commerce. Merchants developed paper letters of exchange, in which coins or goods in one location were exchanged for a sealed letter (much like a modern deposit statement), which could be used in place of metal coinage elsewhere. This made the long, slow, and very dangerous shipment of coins unnecessary. Begun in the late twelfth century, the bill of

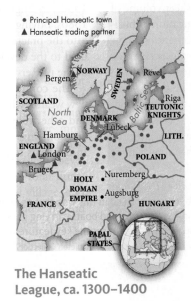

• Principal Hanseatic town
▲ Hanseatic trading partner

The Hanseatic League, ca. 1300–1400

exchange was the normal method of making commercial payments by the early fourteenth century among the cities of western Europe, and it proved to be a decisive factor in the later development of credit and commerce in northern Europe.

The second problem was a moral and theological one. Church doctrine frowned on lending money at interest, termed *usury* (YOO-zhuh-ree). This doctrine was developed in the early Middle Ages when loans were mainly for consumption, to tide someone over, for instance, until the next harvest. Theologians reasoned that it was wrong for a Christian to take advantage of the bad luck or need of another Christian. This restriction on Christians is one reason why Jews were frequently the moneylenders in early medieval society; it was one of the few occupations not forbidden them by Christian authorities.

> **Hanseatic League** A mercantile association of towns begun in northern Europe that allowed for mutual protection and security.

As money-lending became more important to commercial ventures, the church relaxed its position. It declared that some interest was legitimate as a payment for the risk the investor was taking, and that only interest above a certain level would be considered usury. (This definition of usury has continued; modern governments generally set limits on the rate legitimate businesses may charge for loaning money.) The church itself then got into the money-lending business, opening pawnshops in cities and declaring that the shops were benefiting the poor by charging a lower rate of interest than was available from secular moneylenders. In rural areas, Cistercian monasteries loaned money at interest.

The stigma attached to lending money was in many ways attached to all the activities of a medieval merchant. Medieval people were uneasy about a person making a profit merely from the investment of money rather than labor, skill, and time. Merchants themselves shared these ideas to some degree, so they gave generous donations to the church and to charities. They also took pains not to flaunt their wealth through flashy dress and homes. By the end of the Middle Ages, society had begun to accept the role of the merchant, with preachers in Italian cities sometimes comparing merchants, who redeemed loans and merchandise, to Christ, who had redeemed the human race from the snares of the Devil.

Mirrors The commercial revolution brought new consumer goods into Europe, including exotic materials such as African ivory, here made into an intricately carved mirror case showing a chivalric hunting scene for a wealthy customer (right). More ordinary people used mirrors as well, as seen in this wooden carving of a woman admiring herself in a mirror (left). The carving, called a *misericord*, decorated the underside of the seat in a choir stall in a church in Beauvais, France. Secular scenes of everyday life were often shown in misericords, but the carving may also represent the sin of vanity, often symbolized by a woman holding a mirror. (woman: Réunion des Musées Nationaux/Art Resource, NY; ivory: V&A Images, London/Art Resource, NY)

had gathered, and pawnbrokers selling used clothing and household goods. Because there was no way to preserve food easily, people—usually female family members or servants—had to shop every day, and the market was where they met their neighbors, exchanged information, and talked over recent events.

In some respects the entire city was a marketplace. A window or door in a craftsman's home opened onto the street and displayed the finished product made within to attract passersby. The family lived above the business on the second or third floor. As the business and the family expanded, additional stories were added. Second and third stories were built jutting out over the ground floor and thus over the street. Since the streets were narrow to begin with, houses lacked fresh air and light. Initially, houses were made of wood and thatched with straw. Fire was a constant danger; because houses were built so close to one another, fires spread rapidly. Municipal governments consequently urged construction in stone or brick.

Most medieval cities developed with little town planning. As the population increased, space became more and more limited. Air and water pollution presented serious problems. Many families raised pigs for household consumption in sties next to the house. Horses and oxen, the chief means of transportation and power, dropped tons of dung on the streets every year. It was universal practice in the early towns to dump household waste, both animal and human, into the road in front of one's house. The stench must have been abominable. In 1298 the burgesses of the town of Boutham in Yorkshire, England, received the following order:

To the bailiffs of the abbot of St. Mary's York, at Boutham. Whereas it is sufficiently evident that the pavement of the said town of Boutham is so very greatly broken up . . . , and in addition the air is so corrupted and infected by the pigsties situated in the king's highways and in the lanes of that town and by the swine feeding and frequently wandering about . . . and by dung and dunghills and many other foul things placed in the streets and lanes, that great repugnance overtakes the king's ministers staying in that town and also others there dwelling and passing through, the advantage of more wholesome air is impeded, the state of men is grievously injured, and other unbearable inconveniences . . . , to the nuisance of the king's ministers aforesaid and of others there dwelling . . . : the king, being unwilling longer to tolerate such great and unbearable defects there, orders the bailiffs to cause the pavement to be suitably repaired within their liberty before All Saints next, and to cause the pigsties, aforesaid streets and lanes to be cleansed from all dung . . . and to cause them to be kept thus cleansed hereafter.[2]

❝ The air is so corrupted . . . by dung and dunghills and many other foul things placed in the streets and lanes, that great repugnance overtakes the king's ministers staying in that town. ❞

—ROYAL ORDER TO THE CITIZENS OF BOUTHAM, ENGLAND

People of all sorts, from beggars to fabulously wealthy merchants, regularly rubbed shoulders in the narrow streets and alleys of crowded medieval cities. This interaction did not mean that people were unaware of social differences, however, for clothing was a clear marker of social standing and sometimes of occupation. Monks, nuns, and friars wore black, white, or grey woolen clothing that marked them as members of a particular religious order, while priests and bishops wore layers of specialized clothing, especially when they were officiating at religious services. Military men and servants who lived in noble households dressed in distinctive colors known as livery (LIH-vuh-ree). Wealthier urban residents wore bright colors, imported silk or fine woolen fabrics, and fancy headgear, while poorer ones wore darker clothing made of rough linen or linen and wool blends. When universities developed in European cities, students wore clothing and headgear that marked their status. University graduates—lawyers, physicians, and professors—often wore dark robes, trimmed with fur if they could afford it; the robes worn in contemporary academic ceremonies are descended from medieval dress.

In the later Middle Ages many cities attempted to make clothing distinctions a matter of law as well as of habit. City councils passed **sumptuary laws** that regulated the value of clothing and jewelry that people of different social groups could wear; only members of high social groups could wear velvet, satin, pearls, or fur, for example, or have clothing embroidered with gold thread or dyed in colors that were especially expensive to produce, such as the purple dye that came from mollusk shells. Along with enforcing social differences, sumptuary laws also attempted to impose moral standards by prohibiting plunging necklines on women or doublets (fitted buttoned jackets) that were too short on men and to protect local industries by restricting the use of imported fabrics or other materials.

Some of these laws marked certain individuals as members of groups not fully acceptable in urban society.

> **sumptuary laws** Laws that regulated the value and style of clothing and jewelry that various social groups could wear, as well as the amount they could spend on celebrations.

Poor Man at Work In this Italian fresco, a poor man grinds ingredients for medicine outside an apothecary's shop. The urban poor often survived by a combination of begging, picking up odd jobs when they could, and illegal activities. (Scala/Art Resource, NY)

Prostitutes might be required to wear red or yellow bands on their clothes that were supposed to represent the flames of Hell, and Jews yellow circles or stars to distinguish them from their Christian neighbors. (Many Jewish communities also developed their own sumptuary laws prohibiting extravagant or ostentatious dress.) In some cities, sumptuary laws were expanded to include restrictions on expenditures for parties and family celebrations, again set by social class. Weddings for members of the nobility or the urban elite could include imported wine, fancy food, musicians, and hundreds of guests, while those for the children of artisans could serve only local beer to several dozen guests. Sumptuary laws were frequently broken and were difficult to enforce, but they provide evidence of the many material goods available to urban dwellers as well as the concern of city leaders about the social mobility and extravagance they saw all around them.

Servants and the Poor

Many urban houses were larger than the tiny village dwellings, so families took in domestic servants. A less wealthy household employed one woman who assisted in all aspects of running the household, and a wealthier one employed a large staff of male and female servants with specific duties. When there was only one servant, she generally lived and ate with the family, for there was rarely enough space for separate quarters. Even in wealthier households that had many rooms, servants were rarely separated from their employers the way they would be in the nineteenth century, but instead lived on intimate terms with them. In Italian cities, household servants included slaves, usually young women brought in from areas outside of Western Christianity, such as the Balkans.

Along with live-in servants, many households hired outside workers to do specific tasks. Urban workers laundered clothing and household linens, cared for children or invalids, repaired houses and walls, and carried messages or packages around the city or the surrounding countryside. In contrast to rural peasants who raised most of their own food, urban workers bought all their food, so they felt any increase in the price of ale or bread immediately. Their wages were generally low, and children from such families sought work at very young ages.

In cities with extensive cloth production, such as Florence or the towns of Flanders, the urban poor included workers who were paid by the piece. If prices dipped and merchants opted not to put finished goods up for sale at the lower rate, they did not purchase the finished pieces or pay the workers for their labor. The workers were left with thread or unfinished cloth that they technically did not own, and they had no wages with which to buy food.

The possibilities for legitimate employment were often very limited, and illegal activities offered another way for people to support themselves. They stole merchandise from houses, wagons, and storage facilities, fencing it to local pawnbrokers or taking it to the next town to sell. They stole goods or money directly from people, cutting the strings of their bags or purses. They sold sex for money—what later came to be called prostitution—standing on street corners or moving into houses that by the fifteenth century became official city brothels. They made and sold mixtures of herbs and drugs claiming to heal all sorts of ailments, perhaps combining this with a puppet show, trained animals, magic tricks, or music to draw customers. Or they did all these things and also worked as laundresses, day laborers, porters, peddlers, or street vendors when they could. Cities also drew in orphans, blind people, and the elderly, who resorted to begging for food and money.

Popular Entertainment

Games and sports were common forms of entertainment and relaxation. There were games akin to modern football, rugby, stickball, and soccer in which balls were kicked, hit, and thrown; wrestling matches; and dog fights. People played card and board games of all types, with paper providing the material for the cards themselves and for writing down rules. They played with dice carved from stone or bone, or with the knucklebones of animals or wood carved in knucklebone shape, somewhat like modern jacks. They trained dogs to fight each other or put them in an enclosure to fight a captured bear. In Spain, Muslim knights confronted and killed bulls from horseback as part of religious feast days, developing a highly ritualized ceremony that would later be further adapted by Spain's Christian conquerors. All these sports and games were occasions for wagering and gambling, which preachers sometimes condemned (especially when the games were attached to a holiday or saint's day celebration) but had little power to control.

Religious and family celebrations also meant dancing, which the church also attempted to ban or at least regulate, again with little success. Men and women danced in lines toward a specific object, such as a tree or a maypole, or in circles, groups, or pairs with specific step patterns. They were accompanied by a variety of instruments: reed pipes such as the chalumeau (an ancestor of the clarinet) and shawm (predecessor to the oboe); woodwinds such as flutes, panpipes, and recorders; stringed instruments including dulcimers, harps, lyres, lutes, zithers, and mandolins; brass instruments such as horns and trumpets; and percussion instruments like drums and tambourines. Many of these instruments were simple and were made by their players. Musicians

Young Men Playing Stickball With their tunics hitched up in their belts so that they could move around more easily, young men play a game involving hitting a ball with a stick. Games involving bats and balls were popular, for the equipment needed was made from simple, inexpensive materials. (The Granger Collection/The Art Archive)

playing string or percussion instruments often sang as well, and people sang without instrumental accompaniment on festive occasions or while working.

Medieval Universities

How did universities evolve, and what needs of medieval society did they serve? ■

Just as the first strong secular states emerged in the thirteenth century, so did the first universities. This was no coincidence. The new bureaucratic states and the church needed educated administrators, and universities were a response to this need. Medieval universities were educational guilds that produced educated and trained individuals, and their influence on institutionalized learning in the Western world continues today.

Origins

In the early Middle Ages, outside of the aristocratic court or the monastery, anyone who received an education got it from a priest. Priests instructed boys on the manor in the Latin words of the Mass and taught them the rudiments of reading and writing. Few boys acquired elementary literacy, however, and peasant girls did not obtain even that. The peasant father who wished to send his son to school had to secure the permission of his lord because the result of formal schooling tended to be a career in the church or some trade. Because the lord stood to lose the services of educated peasants, he limited the number of serfs sent to school.

Since the time of the Carolingian Empire, monasteries and cathedral schools had offered most of the available formal instruction. The monasteries were geared to religious concerns and wished to maintain an atmosphere of seclusion and silence, so they were unwilling to accept large numbers of noisy lay students. In contrast, schools attached to cathedrals and run by the bishop and his clergy were frequently situated in bustling cities, and in the eleventh century in Italian cities like Bologna (boh-LOH-nyuh), wealthy businessmen established municipal schools. In the course of the twelfth century, cathedral schools in France and municipal schools in Italy developed into educational institutions that attracted students from a wide area (Map 11.3). These schools were called *studium generale* (general center of study) or *universitas magistrorum et scholarium* (universal society of teachers and students),

Map 11.3 **Intellectual Centers of Medieval Europe** Universities provided more sophisticated instruction than did monastery and cathedral schools, but all served to educate European males who had the money to attend.

the origin of the English word *university*. The first European universities appeared in Italy in Bologna, where the specialty was law, and Salerno, where the specialty was medicine.

Legal Curriculum

The growth of the University of Bologna coincided with a revival of interest in Roman law during the investiture controversy. The study of Roman law as embodied in the Justinian *Code* had never completely died out in the West, but in the late eleventh century a complete manuscript of the *Code* was discovered in a library in Pisa. This discovery led scholars in nearby Bologna, beginning with Irnerius (ehr-NEH-ree-uhs) (ca. 1055–ca. 1130), to study and teach Roman law intently. Irnerius's fame attracted students from all over Europe.

Irnerius and other teachers at Bologna taught law not as a group of discrete bits of legislation, but as an organic whole related to the society it regulated, an all-inclusive system based on logical principles that could be applied to difficult practical situations. Thus, as social and economic structures changed, law would change with them. Jurists educated at

Bologna and later at other universities—such as Montpellier in France, where Roman law formed an increasingly large part of the legal curriculum—were hired by rulers and city councils to systematize their law codes and write legal treatises. In the 1260s the English jurist Henry Bracton wrote a comprehensive treatise bringing together the laws and customs of England, and King Alfonso X of Castile issued the *Siete Partidas* (Book in Seven Parts) that set out a detailed plan for administering his whole kingdom according to Roman legal principles.

Canon law (see Chapter 9) was also shaped by the re-invigoration of Roman law, and canon lawyers in ever greater numbers were hired by church officials or became prominent church officials themselves. In about 1140 the Benedictine monk Gratian put together a collection of nearly 3,800 texts covering all areas of canon law. His collection, known as the *Decretum*, became the standard text on which teachers of canon law lectured and commented.

Jewish scholars as well as Christian ones produced elaborate commentaries on law and religious tradition. Medieval universities were closed to Jews, but in some cities in the eleventh century special rabbinic academies opened that concentrated on the study of the Talmud, a compilation of legal arguments, proverbs, sayings, and folklore that had been produced in the fifth century in Babylon (present-day Iraq). The Talmud was written in Aramaic, so that learning to read it required years of study, and medieval scholars began to produce commentaries on the Talmud to help facilitate this. Men seeking to become rabbis—highly respected figures within the Jewish community, with authority over economic and social as well as religious matters—spent long periods of time studying the Talmud, which served as the basis for their legal decisions in all areas of life.

Picturing the Past

Law Lecture at Bologna This beautifully carved marble sculpture, with the fluid lines of clothing characteristic of late Gothic style, suggests the students' intellectual intensity. (Museo Civico, Bologna/ Scala/Art Resource, NY)

ANALYZING THE IMAGE Medieval students often varied widely in age. Does this image reflect that reality? Can the students pictured be classified in other ways, such as by class, sex, or race?
CONNECTIONS In what ways does this image resemble a typical university classroom today? In what ways does it differ?

To complete this activity online, go to the Online Study Guide at bedfordstmartins.com/mckaywest.

Medical Training

At Salerno in southern Italy interest in medicine had persisted for centuries. Medical practitioners—mostly men, but apparently also a few women—received training first through apprenticeship and then in an organized medical school. Individuals associated with Salerno, such as Constantine the African (1020?–1087)—who was a convert from Islam and later a Benedictine monk—began to translate medical works out of Arabic. These translations included writings by the ancient Greek physicians and Muslim medical writers. Students of medicine poured into Salerno.

Medical studies at Salerno were based on classical ideas, particularly those of Hippocrates and Aristotle (see Chapter 3). For the ancient Greeks, ideas about the human body were very closely linked to philosophy and to ideas about the natural world in general. Prime among these was the notion of the four bodily humors—blood, phlegm, black bile, and yellow bile—fluids contained in the body that influenced bodily health. Each individual was thought to have a characteristic temperament or complexion determined by the balance of the four humors, in the same way that we might describe a person today as having a "positive outlook" or a "type-A" personality. Disease was generally regarded as an imbalance of bodily humors, which could be diagnosed by taking a patient's pulse or examining his or her urine. Treatment was thus an attempt to bring the humors back into balance, which might be accomplished through diet or drugs—mixtures of herbal or mineral substances—or more directly by vomiting, emptying one's bowels, or bloodletting. The bodily humors were somewhat gender-related—women were regarded as tending toward cold and wet humors and men toward hot and dry—so therapies were also gender-distinctive. The exact balance of humors was different for each individual, however, and heat could cause one fluid to transform into another.

Heat was also viewed as important in reproduction. The sex of an infant, for example, was believed to be determined largely by the amount of heat present during intercourse and gestation; males resulted when there was the proper amount of heat, which caused their sexual organs to be pushed outside the body, and females when there was too little heat, which caused their sexual organs to remain internal. Men's greater heat continued throughout their lives, causing them to burn up their hair and go bald and to develop broader shoulders and bigger brains (because heat rises and causes things to expand).

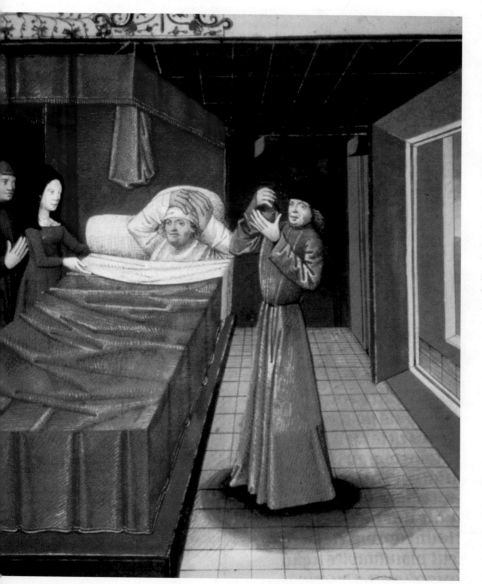

Physician's Diagnosis University-trained physicians rarely touched patients, but instead diagnosed illness by looking at patients' urine. This illustration appeared in a French translation of *De Proprietatibus Rerum* (The Properties of Things), a medieval encyclopedia by Bartholomaeus Anglicus, an English Franciscan who taught at the universities of Paris and Magdeburg in Germany. This encyclopedia, which was widely copied, includes material from Greek, Arabic, and Jewish medical writers. (Snark/Art Resource, NY)

The ideas of this medical literature spread throughout Europe from Salerno and became the basis of training for physicians at other medieval universities. University training gave physicians high social status and allowed them to charge high fees. They were generally hired directly by patients as needed, though some had more permanent positions as members of the household staffs of especially wealthy nobles or rulers.

> ❝ By doubting we come to questioning, and by questioning we perceive the truth. ❞
> —PETER ABELARD

Theology and Philosophy

Law and medicine were important academic disciplines in the Middle Ages, but theology was "the queen of sciences," so termed because it involved the study of God, who made all knowledge possible. Paris became the place to study theology. In the first decades of the twelfth century, students from all over Europe crowded into the cathedral school of Notre Dame (NOH-truh DAHM) in Paris.

University professors (a term first used in the fourteenth century) were known as "schoolmen" or **Scholastics**. They developed a method of thinking, reasoning, and writing in which questions were raised and authorities cited on both sides of a question. The goal of the Scholastic method was to arrive at definitive answers and to provide rational explanations for what was believed on faith. Schoolmen held that reason and faith constituted two harmonious realms whose truths complemented each other.

The Scholastic approach rested on the recovery of classical philosophical texts. Ancient Greek and Arabic texts entered Europe in the early twelfth century by way of Islamic intellectual centers at Baghdad, Córdoba, and Toledo (see Chapter 8). The major contribution of Arabic culture to the new currents of Western thought rested in the stimulus Arabic philosophers and commentators gave to Europeans' reflection on ancient Greek texts and the ways these texts fit with Christian teachings.

Abelard and Heloise

One of the young men drawn to Paris was Peter Abelard (A-buh-lahrd) (1079–1142), the son of a minor Breton knight. Abelard studied in Paris, quickly absorbed a large amount of material, and set himself up as a teacher. He was fascinated by logic, which he believed could be used to solve most problems. He had a brilliant mind and, though orthodox in his philosophical teaching, appeared to challenge ecclesiastical authorities. His book *Sic et Non* (seek eht nohn) (Yes and No) was a list of apparently contradictory propositions drawn from the Bible and the writings of the church fathers. One such proposition, for example, stated that sin is pleasing to God and is not pleasing to God. Abelard used a method of systematic doubting in his writing and teaching. As he put it in the preface to *Sic et Non*, "By doubting we come to questioning, and by questioning we perceive the truth." While other scholars merely asserted theological principles, Abelard discussed and analyzed them. Through reasoning he even tried to describe the attributes of the three persons of the Trinity, the central mystery of the Christian faith. Abelard was severely censured by a church council, but his cleverness, boldness, and imagination made him a highly popular figure among students.

Abelard's reputation for brilliance drew the attention of one of the cathedral canons, Fulbert, who hired Abelard to tutor his intelligent niece Heloise. The relationship between teacher and pupil passed beyond the intellectual. Heloise became pregnant, and Canon Fulbert pressured the couple to marry. The couple agreed, but wanted the marriage kept secret for the sake of Abelard's career. Distrusting Abelard, Canon Fulbert hired men to castrate him. Wounded in spirit as well as body, Abelard persuaded Heloise to enter a convent. He became a monk of Saint-Denis, and their baby, baptized Astrolabe for a recent Muslim navigational invention, was given to Heloise's family for adoption. Abelard spent his later years as abbot of an obscure monastery in Brittany, where he supposedly wrote an autobiographical statement, *A History of My Calamities*, describing his rise and fall.

Heloise secured a copy of Abelard's *History* and took great exception to his statement that their relationship had been based solely on physical desire. She felt that she gained no spiritual reward from her life in the convent, because she had not entered out of religious convictions, and she even railed against God in letters: "O God— if I dare say it—cruel to me in everything! . . . Of all wretched women I am the most wretched, and amongst the unhappy I am unhappiest. The higher I was exalted when you preferred me to all other women, the greater my suffering over my fall and yours."[3] Despite her unhappiness, she became a competent prioress who looked after the nuns in her care, and she succeeded in convincing Abelard to provide letters of spiritual direction

Scholastics University professors who developed a method of thinking, reasoning, and writing in which questions were raised and authorities cited on both sides of a question.

> ❝ The higher I was exalted when you preferred me to all other women, the greater my suffering over my fall and yours. ❞

—HELOISE

for her community. The two unfortunate lovers were united in death and later buried together in a cemetery in Paris. Both *A History of My Calamities* and the letters of Abelard and Heloise are examples of the new self-awareness of the period, grounded in the rebirth of learning of which the development of universities was an important part.

Thomas Aquinas

Thirteenth-century Scholastics devoted an enormous amount of time to collecting and organizing knowledge on all topics. Such a collection was published as a *summa* (SOO-muh), or reference book. There were *summae* on law, philosophy, vegetation, animal life, and theology. Saint Thomas Aquinas (1225–1274), a professor at Paris, produced the most famous collection, the *Summa Theologica*, which deals with a vast number of theological questions.

Prime among these questions was the relationship between reason and faith, a central issue for all Scholastic philosophers. Aquinas drew an important distinction between them. He maintained that, although reason can demonstrate many basic Christian principles such as the existence of God, other fundamental teachings such as the Trinity and original sin cannot be proved by logic. That reason cannot establish them does not mean they are contrary to reason. Rather, people understand such doctrines through revelation embodied in Scripture. Scripture cannot contradict reason, nor reason Scripture:

> *The light of faith that is freely infused into us does not destroy the light of natural knowledge [reason] implanted in us naturally. For although the natural light of the human mind is insufficient to show us these things made manifest by faith, it is nevertheless impossible that these things which the divine principle gives us by faith are contrary to these implanted in us by nature [reason]. Indeed, were that the case, one or the other would have to be false, and, since both are given to us by God, God would have to be the author of untruth, which is impossible. . . . [I]t is impossible that those things which are of philosophy can be contrary to those things which are of faith.*[4]

Aquinas also investigated the branch of philosophy called *epistemology* (ih-pihs-tuh-MAH-luh-jee), which is concerned with how a person knows something. Aquinas stated that one knows, first, through sensory perception of the physical world—seeing, hearing, touching, and so on. He maintained that there can be nothing in the mind that is not first in the senses. Second, knowledge comes through reason, the mind exercising its natural abilities. Aquinas stressed the power of human reason to know, even to know God. His five proofs for God's existence exemplify the Scholastic method of knowing. His work later became the fundamental text of Roman Catholic doctrine.

Life at a University

The influx of students eager for learning, together with dedicated and imaginative teachers, created the atmosphere in which universities grew. In northern Europe—at Paris and later at Oxford and Cambridge in England—associations or guilds of professors organized universities. They established the curriculum, set the length of time for study, and determined the form and content of examinations. By the end of the fifteenth century there were at least eighty universities in Europe. Some universities also offered younger students training in the liberal arts that could serve as a foundation for more specialized study in all areas.

Students at universities were generally considered to be lower-level members of the clergy—this was termed being in "minor orders"—so that any students accused of legal infractions were tried in church, rather than in city, courts. This clerical status, along with widely held ideas about women's lesser intellectual capabilities, meant that university education was restricted to men. Even more than feudal armies—which were often accompanied by women who did laundry, found provisions, cooked meals, and engaged in sex for money—universities were all-male communities. (Most European universities did not admit women or grant degrees to them until after World War I.)

Though university classes were not especially expensive, the many years that university required meant that the sons of peasants or artisans could rarely attend, unless they could find wealthy patrons who would pay their expenses while they studied. Most students were the sons of urban merchants or lower-level nobles, especially the younger sons who would not inherit family lands.

At all universities the standard method of teaching was the lecture—that is, a reading. The professor read a passage from the Bible, the Justinian *Code*, or one of Aristotle's treatises. He then explained and interpreted the passage; his interpretation was called a *gloss*. Texts and glosses were sometimes collected and reproduced as textbooks. For example, the Italian Peter Lombard

(d. 1160), a professor at Paris, wrote what became the standard textbook in theology, *Sententiae* (The Sentences), a compilation of basic theological principles. Because books had to be copied by hand, they were extremely expensive, and few students could afford them. Students therefore depended on their own or friends' notes accumulated over a period of years. The choice of subjects was narrow. The syllabus at all universities consisted of a core of ancient texts that all students studied and, if they wanted to get ahead, mastered.

Examinations were given after three, four, or five years of study, when the student applied for a degree. The professors determined the amount of material students had to know for each degree, and students frequently insisted that the professors specify precisely what that material was. Examinations were oral and very difficult. If the candidate passed, he was awarded a license to teach, which was the earliest form of academic degree. Initially these licenses granted the title of *master* or *doctor*, still in use today and both derived from Latin words meaning "teach." Bachelor's degrees came later. Most students, however, did not become teachers. They staffed the expanding diocesan, royal, and papal administrations.

Students did not spend all their time listening to lectures or debating. Much information about medieval students concerns what we might call "extracurricular" activities: university regulations forbidding them to throw rocks at professors; sermons about breaking and entering, raping local women, attacking town residents, and disturbing church services; and court records discussing their drunken brawls, riots, and fights and duels. Students lived in rented rooms or by the late thirteenth century in residential colleges, both of which could be costly. The money sent by parents or patrons was often not sufficient for all expenses, so students augmented it by begging, thieving, or doing odd jobs. They also delayed finishing their studies because life as a student could be pleasant, without the responsibilities that came with becoming fully adult.

Student life was described by those who knew it best—students themselves—in poems, usually anonymous, that celebrated the joys of Venus (the goddess of love) and other gods:

> *When we are in the tavern,*
> *we do not think how we will go to dust,*
> *but we hurry to gamble,*
> *which always makes us sweat. . . .*
> *Here no-one fears death,*
> *but they throw the dice in the name of Bacchus. . . .*
> *To the Pope as to the king*
> *they all drink without restraint.*[5]

Literature and Architecture

How did literature and architecture express the ideals, attitudes, and interests of medieval people? ■

The High Middle Ages saw the creation of new types of literature, architecture, and music. Technological advances in such areas as papermaking and stone masonry made innovations possible, as did the growing wealth and sophistication of patrons. Artists and artisans flourished in the more secure environment of the High Middle Ages, producing works that celebrated the glories of love, war, and God.

Vernacular Literature and Drama

Latin was the language used in university education, scholarly writing, and works of literature; in short, it was the language of high culture. In contrast to Roman times, however, by the High Middle Ages no one spoke Latin as his or her original mother tongue. The barbarian invasions, the mixture of peoples, and evolution over time had resulted in a variety of local dialects that blended words and linguistic forms in various ways. These dialects were regionally specific, and as kings increased the size of their holdings they often ruled people who spoke many different dialects.

In the early Middle Ages almost all written works continued to be in Latin, but in the High Middle Ages some authors began to write in their local dialect, that is, in the everyday language of their region, which linguistic historians call the vernacular. This new **vernacular literature** gradually transformed some local dialects into literary languages, such as French, German, Italian, and English, while other dialects, such as Breton and Bavarian, remained (and remain to this day) largely means of oral communication. Most people in the High Middle Ages could no more read vernacular literature than they could read Latin, however, so oral transmission continued to be the most important way information was conveyed and traditions were passed down.

vernacular literature
Writings in the author's local dialect, that is, in the everyday language of the region.

By the thirteenth century techniques of making paper from old linen cloth and rags began to spread from Spain, where they had been developed by the Arabs, providing a much cheaper material on which to write (see Chapter 8). People started to write down things that were more mundane and less serious—personal letters, lists, poems, songs, recipes, rules, instructions—in various vernacular dialects, using spellings that were often

LISTENING TO THE PAST

Whether female or male, the troubadour poets celebrated fin'amor, a Provençal word for the pure or perfect love a knight was supposed to feel for his lady, which has in English come to be called "courtly love." In courtly love poetry, the writer praises his or her love object, idealizing the beloved and promising loyalty and great deeds. Most of these songs are written by, or from the perspective of, a male lover who is socially beneath his

female beloved; her higher status makes her unattainable, so the lover's devotion can remain chaste and pure, rewarded by her handkerchief, or perhaps a kiss, but nothing more. The noblemen and noblewomen who listened to these songs viewed such love as ennobling, and some authors even wrote courtly love poetry directed to the Virgin Mary, the ultimate unattainable woman.

Scholars generally agree that poetry praising pure and perfect love originated in the Muslim culture of the Iberian Peninsula, where hetero-sexual romantic love had long been the subject of poems and songs. Southern France was a border area where Christian and Muslim cultures mixed; Spanish Muslim poets sang at the courts of Christian nobles, and Provençal poets picked up their romantic themes.

Other aspects of courtly love are hotly debated. Was it simply a liter-ary convention, or did it shape actual behavior? Did it celebrate adultery, or was true courtly love pure (and unrequited)? How should we interpret medieval physicians' reports of people (mostly young men) becoming gravely ill from "lovesickness"? Did the doctors really believe in the phys-ical power of love? Were there actually "courts of love" in which women judged lovers based on a system of rules? Did courtly love lead to greater respect for women or toward greater misogyny, as desire for a beloved so often ended in frustration?

It is very difficult to know whether courtly love literature influenced the treatment of real women to any great extent — peasant women were certainly no less in danger of rape from knightly armies in the thirteenth century than they had been in the tenth — but it did introduce an ideal of heterosexual romance into Western literature that had not been there in the classical or early medieval period. People who study contemporary popular culture note how much courtly love ideals still shape romantic conventions. Countless movies, songs, and novels explore love between people of different social groups, though now the love generally remains pure by having either the lover or the beloved tragically die young.

The following poem was written by Arnaut Daniel, a thirteenth-century troubadour praised by writers from Dante in the thirteenth cen-tury to Ezra Pound in the twentieth. Not much is known about him, but the songs that have survived capture courtly love conventions perfectly.

❝ I only know the grief that comes to me,
to my love-ridden heart, out of over-loving,
since my will is so firm and whole
that it never parted or grew distant from her
whom I craved at first sight, and afterwards:
and now, in her absence, I tell her burning words;
then, when I see her, I don't know, so much I have to, what to say.

To the sight of other women I am blind, deaf to
    hearing them
since her only I see, and hear and heed,
and in that I am surely not a false slanderer,
since heart desires her more than mouth may say;
wherever I may roam through fields and valleys,
    plains and mountains
I shan't find in a single person all those qualities
which God wanted to select and place in her.

I have been in many a good court,
but here by her I find much more to praise:
measure and wit and other good virtues,
beauty and youth, worthy deeds and fair disport;
so well kindness taught and instructed her
that it has rooted every ill manner out of her:
I don't think she lacks anything good.

No joy would be brief or short
coming from her whom I endear to guess [my
    intentions],
otherwise she won't know them from me,
if my heart cannot reveal itself without words,
since even the Rhone [River], when rain swells it,
has no such rush that my heart doesn't stir
a stronger one, weary of love, when I behold her.

Joy and merriment from another woman seems false
    and ill to me,
since no worthy one can compare with her,
and her company is above the others'.
Ah me, if I don't have her, alas, so badly she has
    taken me!
But this grief is amusement, laughter and joy,
since in thinking of her, of her am I gluttonous and
    greedy:
ah me, God, could I ever enjoy her otherwise!

And never, I swear, I have liked game or ball so
    much,
or anything has given my heart so much joy
as did the one thing that no false slanderer
made public, which is a treasure for me only.

Do I tell too much? Not I, unless she is
   displeased:
beautiful one, by God, speech and voice
I'd lose ere I say something to annoy you.

And I pray my song does not displease you
since, if you like the music and lyrics,
little cares Arnaut whether the unpleasant
   ones like them as well. 🔊

*Far fewer poems by female troubadours
(trobairitz) have survived than by male, but those
that have express strong physical and emotional
feelings. The following song was written in the
twelfth century by Countess of Dia. She was
purportedly the wife of a Provençal nobleman,
though biographies of both troubadours and
trobairitz were often made up to fit the conventions of courtly love, so we don't know for sure.
The words to at least four of her songs have survived, one of them with the melody, which is
very rare.*

🔊 I've suffered great distress
From a knight whom I once owned.
Now, for all time, be it known:
I loved him — yes, to excess. His jilting I've
   regretted,
Yet his love I never really returned. Now for
   my sin I can only burn:
Dressed, or in my bed.

O if I had that knight to caress
Naked all night in my arms,
He'd be ravished by the charm
Of using, for cushion, my breast. His love
   I more deeply prize
Than Floris did Blancheor's
Take that love, my core, My sense, my life,
   my eyes!

Lovely lover, gracious, kind,
When will I overcome your fight?
O if I could lie with you one night!
Feel those loving lips on mine! Listen, one
   thing sets me afire:
Here in my husband's place I want you,
If you'll just keep your promise true: Give me
   everything I desire. 🔊

In this fourteenth-century painting, a lady puts the helmet on her
beloved knight. (akg-images)

QUESTIONS FOR ANALYSIS

1. Both of these songs focus on a beloved who does not return the
   lover's affection. What similarities and differences do you see in
   them?

2. How does courtly love reinforce other aspects of medieval society?
   Are there aspects of medieval society it contradicts?

3. Can you find examples from current popular music that parallel
   the sentiments expressed in these two songs?

Source: First poem: Used by permission of Leonardo Malcovati, editor and translator of
Prosody in England and Elsewhere: A Comparative Approach (London: Gival Press, 2006) and
online at www.trobar.org; second poem: Three verses from lyrics by the Countess of Dia,
often called Beatritz, the Sappho of the Rhone, in *Lyrics of the Middle Ages: An Anthology*,
edited and translated by James J. Wilhelm. © 1990 James J. Wilhelm. Reprinted with
permission. All rights reserved.

personal and idiosyncratic. The writings included fables, legends, stories, and myths that had circulated orally for generations, and slowly a body of written vernacular literature developed.

Stories and songs in the vernacular were performed and composed at the courts of nobles and rulers. In Germany and most of northern Europe, the audiences favored stories and songs recounting the great deeds of warrior heroes, such as the knight Roland who fought against the Muslims and Hildebrand who fought the Huns. These epics, known as *chansons de geste* (SHAN-suhn duh JEHST; songs of great deeds), celebrate violence, slaughter, revenge, and physical power. In southern Europe, especially in the area of southern France known as Provence, poets who called themselves **troubadours** (TROO-buh-dorz) wrote and sang lyric verses celebrating love, desire, beauty, and gallantry. (See "Listening to the Past: Courtly Love Poetry," page 324.) A troubadour was a poet who wrote lyric verse in Provençal (proh-vahn-SAHL), the regional spoken language of southern France, and sang it at one of the noble courts. Troubadours included a few women, called *trobairitz*, most of whose exact identities are not known.

Eleanor of Aquitaine may have taken troubadour poetry from France to England when she married Henry II. Since the songs of the troubadours were widely imitated in Italy, England, and Germany, they spurred the development of vernacular literature there as well. The romantic motifs of the troubadours also influenced the northern French *trouvères* (troo-VEHRZ), who wrote adventure-romances in the form of epic poems in a language we call Old French, the ancestor of modern French. At the court of his patron, Marie of Champagne, Chrétien de Troyes (ca. 1135–ca. 1190) used the legends of the fifth-century British king Arthur (see Chapter 7) as the basis for innovative tales of battle and forbidden love. His most popular story is that of the noble Lancelot, whose love for Guinevere, the wife of King Arthur, his lord, became physical as well as spiritual. Most of the troubadours and trouvères came from and wrote for the aristocratic classes, and their poetry suggests the interests and values of noble culture. Their influence eventually extended to all social groups, however, for people who could not read heard the poems and stories from people who could, so that what had originally come from oral culture was recycled back into it every generation.

Drama, derived from the church's liturgy, emerged as a distinct art form during the High Middle Ages. Plays based on biblical themes and on the lives of the saints were performed in the towns, first in churches and then at the town marketplace. Mystery plays were financed and performed by "misteries," members of the craft guilds, and miracle plays were acted by amateurs or professional actors, not guild members. By combining comical farce based on ordinary life with serious religious scenes, plays gave ordinary people an opportunity to identify with religious figures and think about the mysteries of their faith.

Churches and Cathedrals

The development of secular vernacular literature focusing on human concerns did not mean any lessening of the importance of religion in medieval people's lives. As we have seen, religious devotion was expressed through daily rituals, holiday ceremonies, and the creation of new institutions such as universities and religious orders. People also wanted permanent visible representations of their piety, and both church and city leaders wanted physical symbols of their wealth and power. These aims found their outlet in the building of tens of thousands of churches, chapels, abbeys, and, most spectacularly, **cathedrals** in the twelfth and thirteenth centuries. A cathedral is the church of a bishop and the administrative headquarters of a diocese. The word comes from the Greek word *kathedra*, meaning seat, because the bishop's throne, a symbol of the office, is located in the cathedral.

Most of the churches in the early Middle Ages had been built primarily of wood, which meant they were susceptible to fire. They were often small, with a flat roof, in a rectangular or slightly cross-shaped form called a *basilica*, based on earlier Roman public buildings. With the end of the Viking and Magyar invasions and the increasing political stability of the eleventh century, bishops and abbots supported the construction of larger and more fire-resistant churches made almost completely out of stone. These were based on the basilican style, but features were added that made the cross shape more pronounced. As the size of the church grew horizontally, it also grew vertically. Builders adapted Roman-style rounded barrel vaults made of stone for the ceiling; this use of Roman forms led the style to be labeled **Romanesque**.

The next architectural style was **Gothic**, so named by later Renaissance architects who thought that only the uncouth Goths could have invented such a disunified style. In Gothic churches the solid stone barrel-vaulted roof was replaced by a roof made of stone ribs with plaster in between. This made the ceiling much lighter, so that the side pillars and walls did not need to carry so much weight. Exterior arched stone supports called *flying buttresses* also carried some of the weight of

troubadours Poets who wrote and sang lyric verses celebrating love, desire, beauty, and gallantry.

cathedral The church of a bishop and the administrative headquarters of a diocese.

Romanesque An architectural style with rounded arches and small windows.

Gothic An architectural style typified by pointed arches and large stained-glass windows.

the roof, so solid walls could be replaced by windows, which let in great amounts of light. (See "Living in the Past: Medieval Churches, from Romanesque to Gothic," page 328.)

Begun in the Île-de-France in the twelfth century, Gothic architecture spread throughout France with the expansion of royal power. From France the new style spread to England, Germany, Italy, Spain, and eastern Europe. In those countries, the Gothic style competed with strong indigenous architectural traditions and thus underwent transformations that changed it to fit local usage. French master masons were soon invited to design and supervise the construction of churches in other parts of Europe.

The economic growth of the period meant that merchants, nobles, and the church could afford the costs of this unparalleled building boom. Extraordinary amounts of money were needed to build these houses of worship. Consider, for example, the expense and labor involved in quarrying and transporting the stone alone. More stone was quarried for churches in medieval France than had been mined in ancient Egypt, where the Great Pyramid alone consumed 40.5 million cubic feet of stone.

Money was not the only need. A great number of artisans had to be assembled: quarrymen, sculptors, stonecutters, masons, mortar makers, carpenters, blacksmiths, glassmakers, roofers. Each master craftsman had apprentices, and unskilled laborers had to be recruited for the heavy work. Bishops and abbots sketched out what they wanted and set general guidelines, but they left practical needs and aesthetic considerations to the master mason. He held overall responsibility for supervision of the project. (Medieval chroniclers applied the term *architect* to the abbots and bishops who commissioned the projects or the lay patrons who financed them, not to the draftsmen who designed them.) Master masons were paid higher wages than other masons; their contracts usually ran for several years, and great care was taken in their selection.

Since cathedrals were symbols of civic pride, towns competed to build the largest and most splendid church. In northern France in the late twelfth and early thirteenth centuries, cathedrals grew progressively taller.

Notre Dame Cathedral, Paris This view offers a fine example of the twin towers (left), the spire and great rose window over the south portal (center), and the flying buttresses that support the walls and the vaults. Like hundreds of other churches in medieval Europe, it was dedicated to the Virgin Mary. With a spire rising more than 300 feet, Notre Dame was the tallest building in Europe. (David R. Frazier/Photo Researchers)

Aftermath

In France thousands of soldiers and civilians had been slaughtered and hundreds of thousands of acres of rich farmland were ruined, leaving the rural economy of many parts of France a shambles. The war had disrupted trade and the great fairs, resulting in the drastic reduction of French participation in international commerce. Defeat in battle and heavy taxation contributed to widespread dissatisfaction and aggravated peasant grievances.

The war had wreaked havoc in England as well, even though only the southern coastal ports saw battle. England spent the huge sum of over £5 million on the war effort, and despite the money raised by some victories, the net result was an enormous financial loss. The government attempted to finance the war by raising taxes on the wool crop, which priced wool out of the export market.

In both England and France, men of all social classes had volunteered to serve in the war in the hope of acquiring booty and becoming rich. Some were successful in the early years of the war, as one chronicler reported: "For the woman was of no account who did not possess something from the spoils of . . . cities overseas in clothing, furs, quilts, and utensils . . . tablecloths and jewels, bowls of murra [semiprecious stone] and silver, linen and linen cloths."[8] As time went on, however, most fortunes seem to have been squandered as fast as they were made. In addition, the social order was disrupted as the knights who ordinarily served as sheriffs, coroners, jurymen, and justices of the peace were abroad.

The war stimulated technological experimentation, especially with artillery. Cannon revolutionized warfare, making the stone castle no longer impregnable. Because only central governments, not private nobles, could afford cannon, they strengthened the military power of national states.

The long war also had a profound impact on the political and cultural lives of the two countries. Most notably, it stimulated the development of the English Parliament. Between 1250 and 1450, **representative assemblies** flourished in many European countries. In the English Parliament, German diets, and Spanish cortes, deliberative practices developed that laid the foundations for the representative institutions of modern democratic nations. While representative assemblies declined in most countries after the fifteenth century, the English Parliament endured. Edward III's constant need for money to pay for the war compelled him to summon not only the great barons and bishops, but knights of the shires and burgesses from the towns as well. Parliament met in thirty-seven of the fifty years of Edward's reign.

representative assemblies
Deliberative meetings of lords and wealthy urban residents that flourished in many European countries between 1250 and 1450 and were the precursors to the English Parliament, German diets, and Spanish cortes.

The frequency of the meetings is significant. Representative assemblies were becoming a habit. Knights and wealthy urban residents—or the "Commons," as they came to be called—recognized their mutual interests and began to meet apart from the great lords. The Commons gradually realized that they held the country's purse strings, and a parliamentary statute of 1341 required parliamentary approval of all nonfeudal levies. By signing the law, Edward III acknowledged that the king of England could not tax without Parliament's consent. During the course of the war, money grants were increasingly tied to royal redress of grievances: to raise money, the government had to correct the wrongs its subjects protested.

In England, theoretical consent to taxation and legislation was given in one assembly for the entire country. France had no such single assembly; instead, there were many regional or provincial assemblies. Why did a national representative assembly fail to develop in France? Linguistic, geographical, economic, legal, and political differences were very strong. People tended to think of themselves as Breton, Norman, Burgundian, and so on, rather than French. Provincial assemblies, highly jealous of their independence, did not want a national assembly. The costs of sending delegates to it would be high, and the result was likely to be increased taxation. In addition, the initiative for convening assemblies rested with the king. But some monarchs lacked the power to call such assemblies, and others, including Charles VI, found the idea of representative assemblies thoroughly distasteful.

In both countries, however, the war did promote the growth of nationalism—the feeling of unity and identity that binds together a people. After victories, each country experienced a surge of pride in its military strength. Just as English patriotism ran strong after Crécy and Poitiers, so French national confidence rose after Orléans. French national feeling demanded the expulsion of the enemy not merely from Normandy and Aquitaine but from all French soil. Perhaps no one expressed this national consciousness better than Joan when she exulted that the enemy had been "driven out of *France*."

Challenges to the Church

What challenges faced the Christian church in the fourteenth century, and how did church leaders, intellectuals, and ordinary people respond? ∎

In times of crisis or disaster, people of all faiths have sought the consolation of religion. In the fourteenth century, however, the official Christian church offered little solace. In fact, although many monks, nuns, and friars had committed their lives to helping the sick and the hungry, the leaders of the church added to the sorrow and misery of the times. In response to this lack of leadership, members of the clergy challenged the power of the pope, and laypeople challenged the authority of the church itself. Women and men increasingly relied on direct approaches to God, often through mystical encounters, rather than on the institutional church.

The Babylonian Captivity and Great Schism

Conflicts between the secular rulers of Europe and the popes were common throughout the High Middle Ages, and in the early fourteenth century the dispute between King Philip the Fair of France and Pope Boniface VIII became particularly bitter (see Chapter 11). With Boniface's death, in order to control the church and its policies, Philip pressured the new pope, Clement V, to settle permanently in Avignon in southeastern France, where the popes already had their summer residence. Clement, critically ill with cancer, lacked the will to resist Philip. The popes lived in Avignon from 1309 to 1376, a period in church history often called the **Babylonian Captivity** (referring to the seventy years the ancient Hebrews were held captive in Mesopotamian Babylon; see Chapter 3).

The Babylonian Captivity badly damaged papal prestige. The Avignon papacy reformed its financial administration and centralized its government. But the seven popes at Avignon concentrated on bureaucratic matters to the exclusion of spiritual objectives. Though some of the popes led austere lives, the general atmosphere was one of luxury and extravagance. The leadership of the church was cut off from its historic roots and the source of its ancient authority, the city of Rome. In 1377 Pope Gregory XI brought the papal court back to Rome. Unfortunately, he died shortly after the return. Between the time of Gregory's death and the opening of the conclave, Roman citizens put great pressure on the cardinals to elect an Italian. At the time, none of the cardinals protested this pressure, and they chose a distinguished administrator, the archbishop of Bari, Bartolomeo Prignano, who took the name Urban VI.

Urban VI (pontificate 1378–1389) had excellent intentions for church reform, but he went about it in a tactless and bullheaded manner. He attacked clerical luxury, denouncing individual cardinals by name, and even threatened to excommunicate certain of them. The cardinals slipped away from Rome and met at Anagni. They declared Urban's election invalid because it had come about under threats from the Roman mob, and they asserted that Urban himself was excommunicated. The cardinals then elected Cardinal Robert of Geneva, the cousin of King Charles V of France, as pope. Cardinal Robert took the name Clement VII. There were thus two popes in 1378 — Urban at Rome and Clement VII

(pontificate 1378–1394), who set himself up at Avignon in opposition to Urban. So began the **Great Schism**, which divided Western Christendom until 1417.

The powers of Europe aligned themselves with Urban or Clement along strictly political lines. France naturally recognized the French pope, Clement. England, France's long-time enemy, recognized the Italian pope, Urban. Scotland, whose attacks on England were subsidized by France, followed the French and supported Clement. Aragon, Castile, and Portugal hesitated before deciding for Clement at Avignon. The German emperor, who bore ancient hostility to France, recognized Urban. At first the Italian city-states recognized Urban; when he alienated them with his attacks on luxury, they opted for Clement.

John of Spoleto, a professor at the law school at Bologna, eloquently summed up intellectual opinion of the schism: "The longer this schism lasts, the more it appears to be costing, and the more harm it does; scandal, massacres, ruination, agitations, troubles and disturbances."[9] The common people, wracked by inflation, wars, and plague, were thoroughly confused about which pope was legitimate. The schism weakened the religious faith of many Christians and brought church leadership into serious disrepute.

Allegiance to Rome
Allegiance to Avignon
Official allegiance to Rome but with shifting local allegiances

The Great Schism, 1378–1417

Critiques, Divisions, and Councils

Criticism of the church during the Avignon papacy and the Great Schism often came from the ranks of highly learned clergy and lay professionals. One of these was William of Occam (1289?–1347?), a Franciscan friar and philosopher. Occam saw the papal court at Avignon firsthand and became convinced that the Avignon popes were heretics. He argued vigorously against the papacy and also wrote philosophical works in which he questioned the connection between reason and faith that had been developed by Thomas Aquinas (see Chapter 11). All governments should have limited powers and be accountable to those they govern, according to Occam, and church and state should be separate.

The Italian lawyer and university official Marsiglio of Padua (ca. 1275–1342)

Babylonian Captivity The period from 1309 to 1376 when the popes resided in Avignon rather than in Rome. The phrase refers to the seventy years when the Hebrews were held captive in Babylon.

Great Schism The division, or split, in church leadership from 1378 to 1417 when there were two, then three, popes.

Decorative Spoon Taking as his text a contemporary proverb, "When the fox preaches, beware your geese," the artist shows, in the bowl of this spoon from the southern Netherlands, a fox dressed as a monk or friar, preaching with three dead geese in his hood, while another fox grabs one of the congregation. The preaching fox reads from a scroll bearing the word *pax* (peace), implying the perceived hypocrisy of the clergy. The object from about 1430 suggests the widespread criticism of churchmen in the later Middle Ages. (Painted enamel and gilding on silver; 17.6 cm [6-⅞ in]. Museum of Fine Arts, Boston, Helen and Alice Coburn Fund, 51.2472)

lieved that an elected council should be supreme and should even have the power to depose popes.

The English scholar and theologian John Wyclif (WIH-klihf) (ca. 1330–1384) went further than the conciliarists in his argument against medieval church structure. Wyclif wrote that Scripture alone should be the standard of Christian belief and practice, and papal claims of secular power had no foundation in the Scriptures. He urged that the church be stripped of its property. He wanted Christians to read the Bible for themselves and produced the first complete translation of the Bible into English. Although his ideas were condemned by church leaders, they were spread by humble clerics and enjoyed great popularity in the early fifteenth century.

Wyclif's followers, called Lollards by those who ridiculed them, from a Dutch word for "mumble," spread his ideas and made many copies of his Bible. Lollard teaching allowed women to preach, and women played a significant role in the movement. Lollards were persecuted in the fifteenth century; some were executed, some recanted, and others continued to meet secretly in houses, barns, and fields to read and discuss the Bible and other religious texts in English. Historians differ in their views on how widespread their beliefs were by the time Protestant ideas came into England in the sixteenth century, for Lollard records were intentionally hidden and thus are difficult to trace; however, the Lollard emphasis on biblical literacy certainly created groups of individuals who were open to Protestant views and practices.

Students returning from study at the University of Oxford around 1400 brought Wyclif's ideas with them to Prague, the capital of what was then Bohemia and is now the Czech Republic. There another university theologian, Jan Hus (ca. 1372–1415), built on them; he also denied papal authority, called for translations of the Bible into the local Czech language, and declared indulgences—papal offers of remission of penance—useless. Hus preached in Czech, first in Prague and, when he was forced to leave the city, throughout the countryside. He gained many followers, who linked his theological ideas with their opposition to the church's wealth and power and with a growing sense of Czech nationalism in opposition to the international power of the pope. Hus's followers were successful at defeating the combined armies of the pope and the emperor many times. In the 1430s the emperor finally agreed to recognize the Hussite church in Bohemia, which later merged with other Protestant churches.

Division of any type threatened the church, and in response to continued calls throughout Europe for a council, the cardinals of Rome and Avignon summoned a council at Pisa in 1409. That gathering of prelates and theologians deposed both popes and selected another. Neither the Avignon pope nor the Roman pope would

agreed with Occam. In his *Defensor Pacis* (The Defender of the Peace), Marsiglio argued against the medieval idea of a society governed by both church and state, with church supreme. Instead, Marsiglio claimed, the state was the great unifying power in society, and the church should be subordinate to it. Church leadership should rest in a general council made up of laymen as well as priests, and superior to the pope. Marsiglio was excommunicated for these radical ideas, and his work was condemned as heresy—as was Occam's—but in the later fourteenth century many thinkers agreed with these two critics of the papacy. They believed that reform of the church could best be achieved through periodic assemblies, or councils, representing all the Christian people. Those who argued this position were called **conciliarists**. Some believed a council of clergy should share power with the papacy, while others be-

conciliarists People who believed that the authority in the Roman church should rest in a general council composed of clergy, theologians, and laypeople, rather than in the pope alone.

resign, however, and the appalling result was the creation of a threefold schism.

Finally, under pressure from the German emperor Sigismund (SIH-guhs-muhnd), a great council met at the imperial city of Constance (1414–1418). It had three objectives: to end the schism, to reform the church "in head and members" (from top to bottom), and to wipe out heresy. The council moved first on the last point: despite being granted a safe-conduct to go to Constance by the emperor, Jan Hus was tried, condemned, and burned at the stake as a heretic in 1415. The council also eventually healed the schism. It deposed both the Roman pope and the successor of the pope chosen at Pisa, and it isolated the Avignon antipope. A conclave elected a new leader, the Roman cardinal Colonna, who took the name Martin V (pontificate 1417–1431).

Martin proceeded to dissolve the council. Nothing was done about reform, the third objective of the council. In the later fifteenth century the papacy concentrated on Italian problems to the exclusion of universal Christian interests. But the schism and the conciliar movement had exposed the crying need for ecclesiastical reform, thus laying the foundation for the great reform efforts of the sixteenth century.

The Hussite Revolution, 1415–1436

Lay Piety and Mysticism

The moral failings of the monks and parish clergy and the scandal of the Great Schism did much to weaken the spiritual mystique of the clergy in the popular mind. Thus during the fourteenth and fifteenth centuries laypeople began to develop their own forms of piety. They also exercised increasing control over parish affairs, taking responsibility for the management of parish lands and securing jurisdiction over the structure of the church building and its vestments, books, and furnishings.

Lay Christian men and women often formed **confraternities**, voluntary lay groups organized by occupation, devotional preference, neighborhood, or charitable activity. Confraternities expanded rapidly in larger cities and many villages with the growth of the mendicant orders in the thirteenth century. Some confraternities specialized in praying for souls in purgatory, either for specific individuals or for the anonymous mass of all souls. In England confraternities were generally associated with a parish and are called parish guilds, parish fraternities, or lights; by the late Middle Ages they held dances, church

confraternities Voluntary lay groups organized by occupation, devotional preference, neighborhood, or charitable activity.

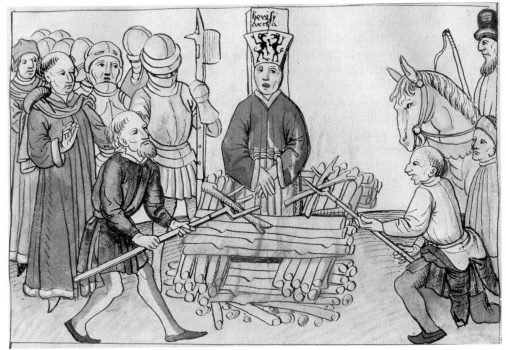

The Execution of Jan Hus This fifteenth-century manuscript illustration shows workers placing logs on Hus's funeral pyre at the Council of Constance, while soldiers, officials, a priest, and a cardinal look on. Hus became an important symbol of Czech independence, and in 1990 the Czech Republic declared July 6, the date of his execution in 1415, a national holiday. (University Library, Prague/Gianni Dagli Orti/The Art Archive)

festivals, and collections to raise money to clean and repair church buildings and to supply churches with candles and other liturgical objects. Like craft guilds, most confraternities were groups of men, but separate women's confraternities were formed in some towns, often to oversee the production of vestments, altar cloths, and other items made of fabric. All confraternities carried out special devotional practices such as prayers or processions, often without the leadership of a priest.

In Holland beginning in the late fourteenth century, a group of pious laypeople called the Brethren and Sisters of the Common Life lived in stark simplicity while daily carrying out the Gospel teaching of feeding the hungry, clothing the naked, and visiting the sick. The Brethren also taught in local schools with the goal of preparing devout candidates for the priesthood. They sought to make religion a personal inner experience. The spirituality of the Brethren and Sisters of the Common Life found its finest expression in the classic *The Imitation of Christ* by the Dutch monk Thomas à Kempis (1380?–1471), which gained wide appeal among laypeople. It urges Christians to take Christ as their model, seek perfection in a simple way of life, and look to the Scriptures for guidance in living a spiritual life. In the mid-fifteenth century the movement had founded houses in the Netherlands, in central Germany, and in the Rhineland.

Most of this piety centered on prayer, pious actions, and charitable giving, but for some individuals, both laypeople and clerics, religious devotion included mystical experiences. (See "Individuals in Society: Meister Eckhart," at right.) Bridget of Sweden (1303–1373) was a noblewoman who journeyed to Rome after her husband's death. She began to see visions and gave advice based on these visions to both laypeople and church officials. Because she could not speak Latin, she dictated her visions in Swedish; these were later translated and eventually published in Latin. At the end of her life Bridget made a pilgrimage to Jerusalem, where she saw visions of the Virgin Mary, who described to her exactly how she was standing "with my knees bent" when she gave birth to Jesus, and how she "showed to the shepherds the nature and male sex of the child."[10] Bridget's visions convey her deep familiarity with biblical texts taught to her through sermons or stories, as there was no Bible available in Swedish. They also provide evidence of the ways in which laypeople used their own experiences to enhance their religious understanding; Bridget's own experiences of childbirth shaped the way she viewed the birth of Jesus, and she related to the Virgin Mary in part as one mother to another.

The confraternities and mystics were generally not considered heretical unless they began to challenge the authority of the papacy the way some conciliarists and Wyclif and Hus did. However, the movement of lay piety did alter many people's perceptions of their own spiritual power.

Social Unrest in a Changing Society

How did economic and social tensions contribute to revolts, crime, violence, and a growing sense of ethnic and national distinctions? ▪

At the beginning of the fourteenth century famine and disease profoundly affected the lives of European peoples. As the century wore on, decades of slaughter and destruction, punctuated by the decimating visits of the Black Death, added further woes. In many parts of France and the Low Countries, fields lay in ruin or untilled for lack of labor power. In England, as taxes increased, criticisms of government policy and mismanagement multiplied. Crime and new forms of business organization aggravated economic troubles, and throughout Europe the frustrations of the common people erupted into widespread revolts.

Peasant Revolts

Nobles and clergy lived on the produce of peasant labor, thinking little of adding taxes to the burden of peasant life. While peasants had endured centuries of exploitation, the difficult conditions of the fourteenth and fifteenth centuries spurred a wave of peasant revolts across Europe. Peasants were sometimes joined by their urban counterparts on the social ladder, resulting in a wider revolution of poor against rich.

The first large-scale rebellion was in Flanders in the 1320s (Map 12.3). In order to satisfy peace agreements, Flemish peasants were forced to pay taxes to the French, who claimed fiscal rights over the county of Flanders. Monasteries also pressed peasants for additional money above their customary tithes. In retaliation, peasants burned and pillaged castles and aristocratic country houses. A French army crushed peasant forces, and savage repression and the confiscation of peasant property followed in the 1330s.

In 1358, when French taxation for the Hundred Years' War fell heavily on the poor, the frustrations of the French peasantry exploded in a massive uprising called the **Jacquerie** (zhah-kuh-REE), after a mythical agricultural laborer, Jacques Bonhomme (Good Fellow). Peasants blamed the nobility for oppressive taxes, for the criminal banditry of the countryside, for losses on the battlefield, and for the general misery. Crowds swept through the countryside, slashing the throats of nobles,

Jacquerie A massive uprising by French peasants in 1358 protesting heavy taxation.

INDIVIDUALS IN SOCIETY

MYSTICISM — THE DIRECT EXPERIENCE OF THE DIVINE through sudden insight or intuition — is an aspect of many world religions and has been part of Christianity throughout its history. During the late Middle Ages, however, mysticism became an important part of the piety of many laypeople, especially in the Rhineland area of Germany, rather than a rare experience of only a few. In this they were guided by the sermons of the churchman generally known as Meister Eckhart. Born into a German noble family, Eckhart (1260–1329?) joined the Dominican order and studied theology at Paris and Cologne, attaining the academic title of "master" (*Meister* in German). The leaders of the Dominican order appointed him to a series of administrative and teaching positions, and he wrote learned treatises in Latin that reflected his scholastic training and deep understanding of classical philosophy.

He also began to preach in German, attracting many listeners through his beautiful language and mystical insights. God, he said, was "an oversoaring being and an overbeing nothingness," whose essence was beyond the ability of humans to express: "if the soul is to know God, it must know Him outside time and place, since God is neither in this or that, but One and above them." Only through "unknowing," emptying oneself, could one come to experience the divine. Yet God was also present in individual human souls, and to a degree in every creature, all of which God called into being before the beginning of time. Within each soul there was what Eckhart called a "little spark," an innermost essence that allows the soul — with God's grace and Christ's redemptive action — to come to God. "Our salvation depends upon our knowing and recognizing the Chief Good which is God Himself," preached Eckhart; "the Eye with which I see God is the same Eye with which God sees me." "I have a capacity in my soul for taking in God entirely," he went on, a capacity that was shared by all humans, not simply members of the clergy or those with special spiritual gifts. Although Eckhart did not reject church sacraments or the hierarchy, he frequently stressed that union with God was best accomplished through quiet detachment and simple prayer rather than pilgrimages, extensive fasts, or other activities: "If the only prayer you said in your whole life was 'thank you,' that would suffice."*

Eckhart's unusual teachings led to charges of heresy in 1327, which Eckhart denied. The pope — who was at this point in Avignon — presided over a trial condemning him, but Eckhart appears to have died during the course of the proceedings or shortly thereafter. His writings were ordered destroyed, but many survived, and his teachings continued to be spread by his followers.

In the last few decades, Meister Eckhart's ideas have been explored and utilized by philosophers and mystics in other religious traditions, including Buddhism, Hinduism, and neo-paganism, as well as by Christians. Books of his sermons sell widely for their spiritual insights, and quotations from them — including the one above about thank-you prayers — can be found on coffee mugs, tote bags, and T-shirts.

A sixteenth-century woodcut of Meister Eckhart teaching. (Visual Connection Archive)

QUESTIONS FOR ANALYSIS

1. Why might Meister Eckhart's preaching have been viewed as threatening by the leaders of the church?

2. Given the situation of the church in the late Middle Ages, why might mysticism have been attractive to pious Christians?

Meister Eckhart's Sermons, trans. Claud Field (London: n.p., 1909).

burning their castles, raping their wives and daughters, and killing or maiming their horses and cattle. Artisans, small merchants, and parish priests joined the peasants. Urban and rural groups committed terrible destruction, and for several weeks the nobles were on the defensive. Then the upper class united to repress the revolt with merciless ferocity. Thousands of the "Jacques," innocent as well as guilty, were cut down. That forcible suppression of social rebellion, without any effort to alleviate its underlying causes, served to drive protest underground.

The 1381 **English Peasants' Revolt** involved thousands of people. Its causes were complex and varied from place to place. In general, though, the thirteenth century had witnessed the steady replacement of labor services by cash rents, and the Black Death had drastically cut the labor supply. As a result, peasants demanded higher wages and fewer manorial obligations. Their lords countered

English Peasants' Revolt
Revolt by English peasants in 1381 in response to changing economic conditions.

in 1351 with the Statute of Laborers, a law freezing wages and binding workers to their manors:

Whereas to curb the malice of servants who after the pestilence were idle and unwilling to serve without securing excessive wages, it was recently ordained . . . that such servants, both men and women, shall be bound to serve in return for salaries and wages that were customary . . . five or six years earlier.[11]

This attempt to freeze wages and social mobility could not be enforced, but a huge gap remained between peasants and their lords, and the peasants sought release for their economic frustrations in revolt. Economic grievances combined with other factors. The south of England, where the revolt broke out, had been subjected to destructive French raids during the Hundred Years' War. The English government did little to protect the south, and villagers grew increasingly frightened and insecure. Moreover, decades of aristocratic violence against the

Map 12.3 Fourteenth-Century Revolts In the later Middle Ages, peasant and urban uprisings were endemic, as common as factory strikes in the industrial world. The threat of insurrection served to check unlimited exploitation.

weak peasantry had bred hostility and bitterness. Social and religious agitation by the popular preacher John Ball fanned the embers of discontent. Ball's famous couplet calling for a return to the social equality that had existed in the Garden of Eden — "When Adam delved and Eve span; / Who was then the gentleman?" — reflected real revolutionary sentiment.

The English revolt was ignited by the reimposition of a tax on all adult males. Despite widespread opposition to the tax in 1380, the royal council ordered the sheriffs to collect it again in 1381 on penalty of a huge fine. Beginning with assaults on the tax collectors, the uprising in England followed a course similar to that of the Jacquerie in France. Castles and manors were sacked. Manorial records were destroyed. Many nobles, including the archbishop of Canterbury who had ordered the collection of the tax, were murdered. The center of the revolt lay in the highly populated and economically advanced south and east, but sections of the north also witnessed rebellions (see Map 12.3).

The boy-king Richard II (r. 1377–1399) met the leaders of the revolt, agreed to charters ensuring peasants' freedom, tricked them with false promises, and then crushed the uprising with terrible ferocity. In the aftermath of the revolt, the nobility tried to restore the labor obligations of serfdom, but they were not successful, and the conversion to money rents continued. The English Peasants' Revolt did not bring social equality to England, but rural serfdom continued to decline, and it disappeared in England by 1550.

Urban Conflicts

In Flanders, France, and England, peasant revolts often blended with conflicts involving workers in cities. Unrest also occurred in Italian, Spanish, and German cities. The revolts typically flared in urban centers, where the conditions of work were changing for many people. In the thirteenth century craft guilds had organized the production of most goods, with masters, journeymen, and apprentices working side by side. In the fourteenth century a new system evolved to make products on a larger scale. Capitalist investors hired many households, with each household performing only one step of the process. Initially these investors were wealthy bankers and merchants, but eventually shop masters themselves embraced the system. This promoted a greater division within guilds between wealthier masters and the poorer masters and journeymen they hired. Some masters became so wealthy from the profits of their workers that they no longer had to work in a shop themselves, nor did their wives and family members, though they still generally belonged to the craft guild.

While capitalism provided opportunities for some artisans to become investors and entrepreneurs, especially in cloth production, for many it led to a decrease in income and status. Guilds sometimes responded to crises by opening up membership, as they did in some places immediately after the Black Death, but they more often responded to competition by limiting membership to existing guild families, which meant that journeymen who were not master's sons or who could not find a master's widow or daughter to marry could never become masters themselves. They remained journeymen their entire lives, losing their sense of solidarity with the masters of their craft. Resentment led to rebellion over economic issues.

Urban uprisings were also sparked by issues involving honor, such as employers' requiring workers to do tasks they regarded as beneath them. As their actual status and economic prospects declined and their work became basically wage labor, journeymen and poorer masters emphasized skill and honor as qualities that set them apart from less-skilled workers.

Guilds increasingly came to view the honor of their work as tied to an all-male workplace. When urban economies were expanding in the High Middle Ages, the master's wife and daughters worked alongside him, and female domestic servants also carried out productive tasks. (See "Listening to the Past: Christine de Pizan, Advice to the Wives of Artisans," page 362.) Masters' widows ran shops after the death of their husbands. But in the fourteenth century a woman's right to work slowly eroded. First, masters' widows were limited in the amount of time they could keep operating a shop or were prohibited from hiring journeymen; then female domestic servants were excluded from any productive tasks; then the number of daughters a master craftsman could employ was limited. When women were allowed to work, it was viewed as a substitute for charity.

Sex in the City

Peasant and urban revolts and riots had clear economic bases, but some historians have suggested that late medieval marital patterns may have also played a role in unrest. In northwestern Europe, people believed that couples should be economically independent before they married, so both spouses spent long periods as servants or workers in other households, saving money and learning skills, or they waited until their own parents had died and the family property was distributed.

The most unusual feature of this pattern was the late age of marriage for women. Unlike in earlier time periods and in most other parts of the world, a woman in late medieval northern and western Europe entered marriage as an adult and took charge of running a household immediately. She was thus not as dependent on her husband or mother-in-law as was a woman who married at a younger age. She had fewer pregnancies than

impetuous than cautious, for fortune is a woman, and if one wishes to keep her down, it is necessary to beat her and knock her down."[5]

The Prince is often seen as the first modern guide to politics, though Machiavelli was denounced for writing it, and people later came to use the word *Machiavellian* to mean cunning and ruthless. Medieval political philosophers had debated the proper relation between church and state, but they regarded the standards by which all governments were to be judged as emanating from moral principles established by God. Machiavelli argued that governments should instead be judged by how well they provided security, order, and safety to their populace. A ruler's moral code in maintaining these was not the same as a private individual's, for a leader could—indeed, should—use any means necessary. Machiavelli put a new spin on the Renaissance search for perfection, arguing that ideals needed to be measured in the cold light of the real world. This more pragmatic view of the purposes of government, and Machiavelli's discussion of the role of force and cruelty, was unacceptable to many.

Even today, when Machiavelli's more secular view of the purposes of government is widely shared, scholars debate whether Machiavelli actually meant what he wrote. Most regard him as realistic or even cynical, but some suggest that he was being ironic or satirical, showing princely government in the worst possible light to contrast it with republicanism. He dedicated *The Prince* to the new Medici ruler of Florence, however, so any criticism was deeply buried within what was, in that era of patronage, essentially a job application.

Christian humanists
Northern humanists who interpreted Italian ideas about and attitudes toward classical antiquity and humanism in terms of their own religious traditions.

Christian Humanism

In the last quarter of the fifteenth century, students from the Low Countries, France, Germany, and England flocked to Italy, absorbed the "new learning," and carried it back to their own countries. Northern humanists shared the ideas of Ficino and Pico about the wisdom of ancient texts, but they went beyond Italian efforts to synthesize the Christian and classical traditions to see humanist learning as a way to bring about reform of the church and deepen people's spiritual lives. These **Christian humanists**, as they were later called, thought that the best elements of classical and Christian cultures should be combined. For example, the classical ideals of calmness, stoical patience, and broad-mindedness should be joined in human conduct with the Christian virtues of love, faith, and hope.

The English humanist Thomas More (1478–1535) began life as a lawyer, studied the classics, and entered government service. This left him time to write, and he became most famous for his controversial dialogue

Procession of the Magi This segment of a huge fresco covering three walls of a chapel in the Medici Palace in Florence shows members of the Medici family and other contemporary individuals in a procession accompanying the biblical three wise men (*magi* in Italian) as they brought gifts to the infant Jesus. The painting was ordered in 1459 by Cosimo and Piero de' Medici, who had just finished building the family palace in the center of the city. Reflecting the self-confidence of his patrons, artist Bennozzo Gozzoli places the elderly Cosimo and Piero at the head of the procession, accompanied by their grooms. The group behind them includes Pope Pius II (in the last row in a red hat that ties under the chin) and the artist (in the second to last row in a red hat with gold lettering). (Scala/Art Resource, NY)

Utopia (1516), a word More invented from the Greek words for "nowhere." *Utopia* describes a community on an island somewhere beyond Europe where all children receive a good education, primarily in the Greco-Roman classics, and adults divide their days between manual labor or business pursuits and intellectual activities. The problems that plagued More's fellow citizens, such as poverty and hunger, have been solved by a beneficent government. Because private property promoted inequality and greed, profits from business and property are held in common. There is religious toleration, and order and reason prevail. Because Utopian institutions are perfect, however, dissent and disagreement are not acceptable.

More's purposes in writing *Utopia* have been just as debated as have Machiavelli's in *The Prince*. Some view it as a revolutionary critique of More's own hierarchical and violent society, some as a call for an even firmer hierarchy, and others as part of the humanist tradition of satire. It was widely read by learned Europeans in the Latin in which More wrote it, and later in vernacular translations, and its title quickly became the standard word for any imaginary society.

Better known by contemporaries than Thomas More was the Dutch humanist Desiderius Erasmus (dez-ih-DARE-ee-us ih-RAZ-muhs) (1466?–1536) of Rotterdam. His fame rested largely on his exceptional knowledge of Greek and the Bible. Erasmus's long list of publications includes *The Education of a Christian Prince* (1504), a book combining idealistic and practical suggestions for the formation of a ruler's character through the careful study of Plutarch, Aristotle, Cicero, and Plato; *The Praise of Folly* (1509), a satire of worldly wisdom and a plea for the simple and spontaneous Christian faith of children; and, most important, a critical edition of the Greek New Testament (1516). In the preface to the New Testament, Erasmus explained the purpose of his great work: "I wish that even the weakest woman should read the Gospel—should read the epistles of Paul. And I wish these were translated into all languages, so that they might be read and understood, not only by Scots and Irishmen, but also by Turks and Saracens."[6]

Two fundamental themes run through all of Erasmus's work. First, education is the means to reform, the key to moral and intellectual improvement. The core of education ought to be study of the Bible and the classics. Second, the essence of Erasmus's thought is, in his own phrase, "the philosophy of Christ." By this Erasmus meant that Christianity is an inner attitude of the heart or spirit. Christianity is not formalism, special ceremonies, or law; Christianity is Christ—his life and what he said and did, not what theologians have written.

The Printed Word

The fourteenth-century humanist Petrarch and the sixteenth-century humanist Erasmus had similar ideas about many things, but the immediate impact of their ideas was very different because of one thing: the printing press with movable metal type. The ideas of Petrarch were spread slowly from person to person by hand copying. The ideas of Erasmus were spread quickly through print, in which hundreds or thousands of identical copies could be made in a short time.

Printing with movable metal type developed in Germany in the 1440s as a combination of existing technologies. Several metal-smiths, most prominently Johann Gutenberg, recognized that the metal stamps used to mark signs on jewelry could be covered with ink and used to mark symbols onto a surface, in the same way that other craftsmen were using carved wood stamps to print books. (This woodblock printing technique originated in China and Korea centuries earlier.) Gutenberg and his assistants made stamps—later called *type*—for every letter of the alphabet and built racks that held the type in rows. This type could be rearranged for every page and so used over and over.

Printing Press In this reproduction of Gutenberg's printing press, metal type sits in a frame ready to be placed in the bottom part of the press, with a leather-covered ink ball nearby for spreading ink on the type. Paper was then placed over the type, and a heavy metal plate brought down onto the paper with a firm pull of the large wooden handle, a technology adapted from wine presses. (Erich Lessing/Art Resource, NY)

Picturing the Past

Tax Collectors New types of taxes, and more effective methods of tax collection, were essential to the growth of Renaissance states, but were often highly unpopular. In this painting from about 1540 the Dutch artist Marinus van Reymerswaele depicts two tax collectors as they count their take and record it in a ledger. Tax collectors were men of middling status, but here they are wearing clothing more appropriate for nobles. (Erich Lessing/Art Resource, NY)

ANALYZING THE IMAGE What elements of the men's clothing suggest wealth? How would you describe the expressions on their faces? What does the painting suggest about the artist's opinion of tax collectors?

CONNECTIONS In Spain converso tax collectors were widely resented. What were some of the reasons behind this resentment? What public event was an outgrowth of this hatred, and what were its aims?

To complete this activity online, go to the Online Study Guide at bedfordstmartins.com/mckaywest.

secretly adhering to Jewish beliefs and performing rites of the Jews."[11] Investigations and trials began immediately, as officials of the Inquisition looked for conversos who showed any sign of incomplete conversion, such as not eating pork.

Recent scholarship has carefully analyzed documents of the Inquisition. Most conversos identified themselves as sincere Christians; many came from families that had received baptism generations before. In response, officials of the Inquisition developed a new type of anti-Semitism. A person's status as a Jew, they argued, could not be changed by religious conversion, but was in the person's blood and was heritable, so Jews could never be true Christians. In what were known as "purity of blood" laws, having pure Christian blood became a requirement for noble status. Ideas about Jews developed in Spain were important components in European concepts of race, and discussions of "Jewish blood" later expanded into notions of the "Jewish race."

In 1492, shortly after the conquest of Granada, Isabella and Ferdinand issued an edict expelling all practicing Jews from Spain. Of the community of perhaps 200,000 Jews, 150,000 fled. Many Muslims in Granada were forcibly baptized and became another type of New Christian investigated by the Inquisition. Absolute religious orthodoxy and purity of blood served as the theoretical foundation of the Spanish national state.

The Spanish national state rested on marital politics as well as military victories and religious courts. In 1496 Ferdinand and Isabella married their second daughter Joanna, heiress to Castile, to the archduke Philip, heir to the Burgundian Netherlands and the Holy Roman Empire. Philip and Joanna's son, Charles V (r. 1519–1556), thus succeeded to a vast inheritance. When Charles's son Philip II joined Portugal to the Spanish crown in 1580, the Iberian Peninsula was at last politically united.

Saint Dominic Presiding over an Auto-da-Fe
In this 1495 painting the Spanish artist Pedro Berruguete shows an auto-da-fe, a public ritual of penance for those found guilty of religious crimes. In the foreground, the guilty wear tall hats with their crimes described on them, while above them two men are about to be burned at the stake. Technically execution did not happen at the auto-da-fe, but rather at a later secular execution, although the two events sometimes blended into one another. Berruguete portrays Saint Dominic, the founder of the Dominican order, as presiding over this trial, although autos-da-fe were not common until centuries after Dominic's death in 1221. (Museo del Prado, Madrid/Institut Amatller d'Art Hispànic)

LOOKING BACK LOOKING AHEAD

THE ART HISTORIAN Giorgio Vasari, who first called this era the Renaissance, thought that his contemporaries had both revived the classical past and gone beyond it. Vasari's judgment was echoed for centuries, as the art, architecture, educational ideas, social structures, and attitude toward life of the Renaissance were set in sharp contrast with those of the Middle Ages: whereas the Middle Ages were corporate and religious, the Renaissance was individualistic and secular. More recently, historians and other scholars have stressed continuity as well as change. Families, kin networks, guilds, and other corporate groups remained important in the Renaissance, and religious belief remained firm. This re-evaluation changes our view of the relationship between the Middle Ages and the Renaissance. It may also change our view of the relationship between the Renaissance and the dramatic changes in religion that occurred in Europe in the sixteenth century. Those religious changes, the Reformation, used to be viewed as a rejection of the values of the Renaissance and a return to the intense concern with religion of the Middle Ages. This idea of the Reformation as a sort of counter-Renaissance may be true to some degree, but there are powerful continuities as well. Both movements looked back to a time they regarded as purer and better than their own, and both offered opportunities for strong individuals to shape their world in unexpected ways.

CHAPTER REVIEW

■ **What economic and political developments in Italy provided the setting for the Renaissance? (p. 374)**

In the commercial revival of the Middle Ages, ambitious merchants amassed great wealth, especially in the city-states of northern Italy. These city-states were communes in which all citizens shared power, but political instability led to their transformation into signori or oligarchies. As their riches and power grew, signori and oligarchs displayed their wealth in great public buildings as well as magnificent courts — palaces where they lived and conducted business. Political rulers, popes, and powerful families hired writers, artists, musicians, and architects through the system of patronage, which allowed for a great outpouring of culture.

■ **What were the key ideas of the Renaissance, and how were they different for men and women and for southern and northern Europeans? (p. 378)**

The Renaissance was characterized by self-conscious awareness among fourteenth- and fifteenth-century Italians, particularly scholars and writers known as humanists, that they were living in a new era. Key to this attitude was a serious interest in the Latin, and later the Greek, classics, especially the works of Cicero and Plato. Humanists also believed in striving for perfection, and they greatly admired individuals who exhibited the quality of virtù, the ability to shape the world around them to their will. These qualities are evident in political theory developed during the Renaissance, particularly that of Machiavelli. Humanists opened schools for boys and young men to train them for active lives of public service, but they had doubts about whether humanist education was appropriate for women. Some self-taught women did argue that study of the classics should not be limited to men. In northern Europe, religious concerns among humanists were more pronounced, and adherents came to be known as Christian humanists. Well-known writers such as Thomas More of England and Desiderius Erasmus of Rotterdam set out plans for the reform of church and society. Their ideas reached a much wider audience than those of early humanists because of the development of the printing press with movable metal type, which revolutionized communication.

■ **How did changes in art reflect new Renaissance ideals? (p. 387)**

Artistic patronage in the early Renaissance was primarily provided by groups such as guilds, but in the later Renaissance individuals increasingly supported the arts as a way of glorifying themselves and their families. At the same time, humanist interest in the classical past and in the individual shaped Renaissance art in terms of style and subject matter. Painting became more naturalistic, and the individual portrait emerged as a distinct artistic genre. Perspective was pioneered in painting, and balance and harmony became hallmarks of Italian architecture. Art in Italy became more secular and classical, with more works focused on pagan gods and goddesses. In northern Europe, where humanist thinking was more connected to Christian ideals, art retained a more religious tone. The style of mannerism evolved, which exaggerated the color and musculature of painted figures in order to provide more drama and emotion. Artists began to understand themselves as having a special creative genius, though they were still expected to undergo extensive technical training, and they continued to produce works on order for patrons, who often determined the content and form. Women were largely excluded from the major arts, as were most people from working families, and art itself was created for consumption mainly by an elite minority.

■ **What were the key social hierarchies in Renaissance Europe, and how did ideas about hierarchy shape people's lives? (p. 393)**

Social hierarchies in the Renaissance built on those of the Middle Ages, with the addition of new features that evolved into the modern social hierarchies of race, class, and gender. In the fifteenth century black slaves entered Europe in sizable numbers for the first time since the collapse of the Roman Empire. Europeans saw Africans as inferior, and they felt that contact with Christians would serve to improve the lives of blacks, even as slaves. The medieval hierarchy of orders based on function in society intermingled with a new hierarchy based on wealth, with new types of elites becoming more powerful through political and marital alliances. Noble families that were experiencing declining wealth could rebuild their fortunes by integrating with the newly rich. The Renaissance debate about women led to discussions of women's character and questioning of whether women could serve effectively as rulers. There was little debate, however, that among the nonruling classes, both men and women were expected to fit neatly into "natural" roles, with men as heads of households and women as subordinate; any deviation from this pattern was seen as a threat to societal order.

■ **How did the nation-states of western Europe evolve in this period? (p. 397)**

With taxes provided by business people, kings in western Europe established armies to maintain greater peace and order, both essential for trade, and feudal monarchies gradually evolved in the direction of nation-states. French kings benefited from opportunistic marriages and an alliance with the pope, and English kings used Machiavellian methods to crush the nobility. Spain used similar practices, though unification came more slowly, and Spanish rulers focused intently on expelling practicing Jews from their country.

Suggested Reading

Clark, Samuel. *State and Status: The Rise of the State and Aristocratic Power*. 1995. Discusses the relationship between centralizing states and the nobility.

Earle, T. F., and K. J. P. Lowe, eds. *Black Africans in Renaissance Europe*. 2005. Includes essays discussing many aspects of ideas about race and the experience of Africans in Europe.

Eisenstein, Elizabeth. *The Printing Press as an Agent of Change: Communications and Cultural Transformations in Early Modern Europe*. 1979. The definitive study of the impact of printing.

Ertman, Thomas. *The Birth of Leviathan: Building States and Regimes in Medieval and Early Modern Europe*. 1997. A good introduction to the creation of nation-states.

Grafton, Anthony, and Lisa Jardine. *From Humanism to the Humanities: Education and the Liberal Arts in Fifteenth and Sixteenth Century Europe*. 1986. Discusses humanist education and other developments in Renaissance learning.

Hale, J. R. *The Civilization of Europe in the Renaissance*. 1994. A comprehensive treatment of the period, arranged thematically.

Harbison, Craig. *The Mirror of the Artist: Northern Renaissance Art in Its Historical Context*. 1995. The best introduction to the art of northern Europe.

Hartt, Frederick, and David Wilkins. *History of Italian Renaissance Art*, 6th ed. 2008. Comprehensive survey of painting, sculpture, and architecture in Italy.

Holmes, George, ed. *Art and Politics in Renaissance Italy*. 1993. Treats the art of Florence and Rome against a political background.

Jardine, Lisa. *Worldly Goods: A New History of the Renaissance*. 1998. Discusses changing notions of social status, artistic patronage, and consumer goods.

Johnson, Geraldine. *Renaissance Art: A Very Short Introduction*. 2005. Excellent brief survey that includes male and female artists, and sets the art in its cultural and historical context.

King, Ross. *Machiavelli: Philosopher of Power*. 2006. Brief biography that explores Machiavelli's thought in its social and political context.

Lubkin, Gregory. *A Renaissance Court: Milan Under Galeazzo Maria Sforza*. 1994. A wonderful study of one of the most important Renaissance courts.

Man, John. *Gutenberg Revolution: The Story of a Genius and an Invention That Changed the World*. 2002. Presents a rather idealized view of Gutenberg, but has good discussions of his milieu and excellent illustrations.

McConica, James. *Erasmus*. 1991. A sensitive treatment of the leading northern humanist.

Nauert, Charles. *Humanism and the Culture of Renaissance Europe*, 2d ed. 2006. A thorough introduction to humanism throughout Europe.

Netanyahu, Benzion. *The Origins of the Inquisition in Fifteenth Century Spain*. 1995. An analysis of issues relating to the expulsion of the Jews.

Wiesner-Hanks, Merry E. *Women and Gender in Early Modern Europe*, 3d ed. 2008. Discusses all aspects of women's lives and ideas about gender.

Key Terms

Renaissance (p. 374)
patronage (p. 374)
communes (p. 375)
popolo (p. 375)
signori (p. 376)
courts (p. 376)
humanism (p. 378)
virtù (p. 379)
Christian humanists (p. 384)
debate about women (p. 396)
New Christians (p. 401)

Notes

1. In Gertrude R. B. Richards, *Florentine Merchants in the Age of the Medici* (Cambridge: Harvard University Press, 1932).
2. In James Bruce Ross and Mary Martin McLaughlin, *The Portable Renaissance Reader* (New York: Penguin, 1953), p. 27.
3. Ibid., pp. 480–481, 482, 492.
4. Niccolò Machiavelli, *The Prince*, trans. Leo Paul S. de Alvarez (Prospect Heights, Ill.: Waveland Press, 1980), p. 101.
5. Ibid., p. 149.
6. Quoted in F. Seebohm, *The Oxford Reformers* (London: J. M. Dent & Sons, 1867), p. 256.
7. Quoted in Lauro Martines, *Power and Imagination: City-States in Renaissance Italy* (New York: Vintage Books, 1980), p. 253.
8. Quoted in J. Devisse and M. Mollat, *The Image of the Black in Western Art*, vol. 2, trans. W. G. Ryan (New York: William Morrow, 1979), pt. 2, pp. 187–188.
9. Stuttgart, Württembergische Hauptstaatsarchiv, Generalreskripta, A38, Bü. 2, 1550; trans. Merry Wiesner-Hanks.
10. Denys Hay, ed. and trans., *The Anglia Historia of Polydore Vergil, AD 1485–1537*, book 74 (London: Camden Society, 1950), p. 147.
11. Quoted in Benzion Netanyahu, *The Origins of the Inquisition in Fifteenth Century Spain* (New York: Random House, 1995), p. 921.

For practice quizzes and other study tools, visit the Online Study Guide at **bedfordstmartins.com/mckaywest**.

For primary sources from this period, see *Sources of Western Society*, **Second Edition**.

For Web sites, images, and documents related to topics in this chapter, visit Make History at **bedfordstmartins.com/mckaywest**.

14
Reformations and Religious Wars

1500–1600

Calls for reform of the Christian church began very early in its history. Throughout the centuries, men and women believed that the early Christian church represented a golden age, akin to the golden age of the classical past celebrated by Renaissance humanists. When Christianity became the official religion of the Roman Empire in the fourth century, many believers thought that the church had abandoned its original mission, and they called for a return to a church that was not linked to the state. Throughout the Middle Ages individuals and groups argued that the church had become too wealthy and powerful and urged monasteries, convents, bishoprics, and the papacy to give up their property and focus on service to the poor. Some asserted that basic teachings of the church were not truly Christian and that changes were needed in theology as well as in institutional structures and practices. The Christian humanists of the late fifteenth and early sixteenth centuries urged reform, primarily through educational and social change. What was new in the sixteenth century was the breadth of acceptance and the ultimate impact of the calls for reform. This acceptance was due not only to religious issues and problems within the church, but also to political and social factors. In 1500 there was one Christian church in western Europe to which all Christians at least nominally belonged. One hundred years later there were many, a situation that continues today. ■

Erich Lessing/Art Resource, NY

Religious Violence in Urban Life. This 1590 painting shows Catholic military forces, including friars in their robes, processing through one of the many towns affected by the French religious wars that followed the Reformation.

CHAPTER PREVIEW

The Early Reformation
■ What were the central ideas of the reformers, and why were they appealing to different social groups?

The Reformation and German Politics
■ How did the political situation in Germany shape the course of the Reformation?

The Spread of Protestant Ideas
■ How did Protestant ideas and institutions spread beyond German-speaking lands?

The Catholic Reformation
■ How did the Catholic Church respond to the new religious situation?

Religious Violence
■ What were the causes and consequences of religious violence, including riots, wars, and witch-hunts?

The Early Reformation

What were the central ideas of the reformers, and why were they appealing to different social groups? ■

In early sixteenth-century Europe a wide range of people had grievances with the church. Educated laypeople such as Christian humanists and urban residents, villagers and artisans, and church officials themselves called for reform. This widespread dissatisfaction helps explain why the ideas of an obscure professor from a new and not very prestigious German university found a ready audience. Within a decade of his first publishing his ideas (using the new technology of the printing press), much of central Europe and Scandinavia had broken with the Catholic Church, and even more radical concepts of the Christian message were being developed and linked to calls for social change.

anticlericalism Opposition to the clergy.

pluralism The clerical practice of holding more than one church benefice (or office) at the same time and enjoying the income from each.

The Christian Church in the Early Sixteenth Century

If external religious observances are an indication of conviction, Europeans in the early sixteenth century were deeply pious. Villagers participated in processions honoring the local saints. Merchants and guild members made pilgrimages to the great shrines, such as Saint Peter's in Rome, and paid for altars in local churches. Men and women continued to remember the church in their wills. People of all social groups devoted an enormous amount of their time and income to religious causes and foundations.

Despite — or perhaps because of — the depth of their piety, many people were also highly critical of the Roman Catholic Church and its clergy. The papal conflict with the German emperor Frederick II in the thirteenth century, followed by the Babylonian Captivity and the Great Schism, badly damaged the prestige of church leaders, and the fifteenth-century popes' concentration on artistic patronage and building up family power did not help matters. Papal tax collection methods were attacked orally and in print. Some criticized the papacy itself as an institution, and even the great wealth and powerful courts of the entire church hierarchy. Some groups and individuals argued that certain doctrines taught by the church, such as the veneration of saints and the centrality of the sacraments, were incorrect. They suggested measures to reform institutions, improve clerical education and behavior, and alter basic doctrines.

Occasionally these reform efforts had some success, and in at least one area, Bohemia (the modern-day Czech Republic), they led to the formation of a church independent of Rome a century before Luther (see Chapter 12).

In the early sixteenth century court records, bishops' visitations of parishes, and popular songs and printed images show widespread **anticlericalism**, or opposition to the clergy. The critics concentrated primarily on three problems: clerical immorality, clerical ignorance, and clerical **pluralism** (the practice of holding more than one church office at a time), with the related problem of absenteeism. Charges of clerical immorality were aimed at a number of priests who were drunkards, neglected the rule of celibacy, gambled, or indulged in fancy dress. Charges of clerical ignorance were motivated by barely literate priests who simply mumbled the Latin words of the Mass by rote without understanding their meaning. Many priests, monks, and nuns lived pious lives of devotion, learning, and service and had strong support from the laypeople in their areas, but everyone also knew (and repeated) stories about lecherous monks, lustful nuns, and greedy priests.

In regard to absenteeism and pluralism, many clerics held several benefices, or offices, simultaneously, but they seldom visited the benefices, let alone performed the spiritual responsibilities those offices entailed. Instead, they collected revenues from all of them and hired a poor priest, paying him just a fraction of the income to fulfill the spiritual duties of a particular local church. Many Italian officials in the papal curia, the pope's court in Rome, held benefices in England, Spain, and Germany. Revenues from those countries paid the Italian clerics' salaries, provoking not only charges of absenteeism but also nationalistic resentment aimed at the upper levels of the church hierarchy, which was increasingly viewed as foreign. This was particularly the case in Germany, where the lack of a strong central government to negotiate with the papacy meant that demands for revenue were especially high.

There was also local resentment of clerical privileges and immunities. Priests, monks, and nuns were exempt from civic responsibilities, such as defending the city and paying taxes. Yet religious orders frequently held large amounts of urban property, in some cities as much as one-third. City governments were increasingly determined to integrate the clergy into civic life by reducing their privileges and giving them public responsibilities. Urban leaders wanted some say in who would be appointed to high church offices, rather than having this decided far away in Rome. This brought city leaders into opposition with bishops and the papacy, which for centuries had stressed the independence of the church from lay control and the distinction between members of the clergy and laypeople.

Martin Luther

By itself, widespread criticism of the church did not lead to the dramatic changes of the sixteenth century. Those resulted from the personal religious struggle of a German university professor and priest, Martin Luther (1483–1546). Luther was born at Eisleben in Saxony. At considerable sacrifice, his father sent him to school and then to the University of Erfurt, where he earned a master's degree with distinction. Luther was to proceed to the study of law and a legal career, which for centuries had been the stepping-stone to public office and material success. Instead, however, a sense of religious calling led him to join the Augustinian friars, a religious order whose members often preached to, taught, and assisted the poor. (Religious orders were groups whose members took vows and followed a particular set of rules.) Luther was ordained a priest in 1507 and after additional study earned a doctorate of theology. From 1512 until his death in 1546, he served as professor of the Scriptures at the new University of Wittenberg. Throughout his life, he frequently cited his professorship as justification for his reforming work.

Martin Luther was a very conscientious friar, but his scrupulous observance of religious routine, frequent confessions, and fasting gave him only temporary relief from anxieties about sin and his ability to meet God's demands. Through his study of Saint Paul's letters in the New Testament, he gradually arrived at a new understanding of Christian doctrine. His understanding is often summarized as "faith alone, grace alone, Scripture alone." He believed that salvation and justification come through faith. Faith is a free gift of God's grace, not the result of human effort. God's word is revealed only in Scripture, not in the traditions of the church.

At the same time that Luther was engaged in scholarly reflections and professorial lecturing, Pope Leo X authorized the sale of a special Saint Peter's indulgence to finance his building plans in Rome. The archbishop who controlled the area in which Wittenberg was located, Albert of Mainz, was an enthusiastic promoter of this indulgence sale. For his efforts, he received a share of the profits in order to pay off a debt he had incurred in order to purchase a papal dispensation allowing him to become the bishop of several other territories as well.

What exactly was an **indulgence**? According to Catholic theology, individuals who sin could be reconciled to God by confessing their sins to a priest and by doing an assigned penance, such as praying or fasting. But beginning in the twelfth century learned theologians increasingly emphasized the idea of purgatory, a place where souls on their way to Heaven went to make further amends for their earthly sins. Both earthly penance and time in purgatory could be shortened by drawing on what was termed the "treasury of merits." This was a collection of all the virtuous acts that Christ, the apostles, and the saints had done during their lives. People thought of it as a sort of strongbox, like those in which merchants carried coins. An indulgence was a piece of parchment (later, paper), signed by the pope or another church official, that substituted a virtuous act from the treasury of merits for penance or time in purgatory. The papacy and bishops had given Crusaders such

> **indulgence** A document issued by the Catholic Church lessening penance or time in purgatory, widely believed to bring forgiveness of all sins.

Selling Indulgences A woodcut advertising Johann Tetzel's sale of indulgences in 1517, which shows him blessed by the Holy Spirit in the form of a dove, while people run to buy, as the rhyme here puts it, "grace and forgiveness for your sins, for you, your parents, wife, and child." Indulgences were often printed fill-in-the-blank forms. This indulgence (upper left), purchased in 1521, has space for the indulgence seller's name at the top, the buyer's name in the middle, and the date at the bottom. (woodcut: akg-images; indulgence: Visual Connection Archive)

indulgences, and by the later Middle Ages they were offered for making pilgrimages or other pious activities and also sold outright (see Chapter 10).

Albert's indulgence sale, run by a Dominican friar named Johann Tetzel who mounted an advertising blitz, promised that the purchase of indulgences would bring full forgiveness for one's own sins or release from purgatory for a loved one. One of the slogans—"As soon as coin in coffer rings, the soul from purgatory springs"—brought phenomenal success, and people traveled from miles around to buy indulgences.

Luther was severely troubled that many people believed they had no further need for repentance once they had purchased indulgences. In 1517 he wrote a letter to Archbishop Albert on the subject and enclosed in Latin his "Ninety-five Theses on the Power of Indulgences." His argument was that indulgences undermined the seriousness of the sacrament of penance, competed with the preaching of the Gospel, and downplayed the importance of charity in Christian life. After Luther's death, biographies reported that the theses were also nailed to the door of the church at Wittenberg Castle on October 31, 1517. Such an act would have been very strange—they were in Latin and written for those learned in theology, not for normal churchgoers—but it has become a standard part of Luther lore.

Whether the theses were posted or not, they were quickly printed, first in Latin and then in German translation. Luther was ordered to come to Rome, although because of the political situation in the empire, he was able instead to engage in formal scholarly debate with a representative of the church, Johann Eck, at Leipzig in 1519. He refused to take back his ideas and continued to develop his calls for reform, publicizing them in a series of pamphlets in which he moved further and further away from Catholic theology. Both popes and church councils could err, he wrote, and secular leaders should reform the church if the pope and clerical hierarchy did not. There was no distinction between clergy and laypeople, and requiring clergy to be celibate was a fruitless attempt to control a natural human drive. Luther clearly understood the power of the new medium of print, and so authorized the publication of his works.

The papacy responded with a letter condemning some of Luther's propositions, ordering that his books be burned, and giving him two months to recant or be excommunicated. Luther retaliated by publicly burning the letter. By 1521, when the excommunication was supposed to become final, Luther's theological issues had become interwoven with public controversies about the church's wealth, power, and basic structure. The papal legate wrote of the growing furor, "All Germany is in revolution. Nine-tenths shout 'Luther' as their war cry; and the other tenth cares nothing about Luther, and cries 'Death to the court of Rome.'"[1] In this highly charged atmosphere, the twenty-one-year-old emperor Charles V held his first diet (assembly of the nobility, clergy, and cities of the Holy Roman Empire) in the German city of Worms, and summoned Luther to appear. Luther refused to give in to demands that he take back his ideas. "Unless I am convinced by the evidence of Scripture or by plain reason," he said, "I cannot and will not recant anything, for it is neither safe nor right to go against conscience."[2] His appearance at the Diet of Worms in 1521 created an even broader audience for reform ideas, and throughout central Europe other individuals began to preach and publish against the existing doctrines and practices of the church, drawing on the long tradition of calls for change as well as on Luther.

Protestant Thought

The most important early reformer other than Luther was the Swiss humanist, priest, and admirer of Erasmus, Ulrich Zwingli (ZWIHN-glee) (1484–1531). Zwingli announced in 1519 that he would preach not from the church's prescribed readings but, relying on Erasmus's New Testament, go right through the New Testament "from A to Z," that is, from Matthew to Revelation. Zwingli was convinced that Christian life rested on the Scriptures, which were the pure words of God and the sole basis of religious truth. He went on

The Ten Commandments Lucas Cranach the Elder, the court painter for the elector of Saxony, painted this giant illustration of the Ten Commandments (more than 5 feet by 11 feet) for the city hall in Wittenberg in 1516, just at the point that Luther was beginning to question Catholic doctrine. Cranach was an early supporter of Luther, and many of his later works depict the reformer and his ideas. Paintings were used by both Protestants and Catholics to teach religious ideas. (Lutherhalle, Wittenberg/The Bridgeman Art Library)

to attack indulgences, the Mass, the institution of monasticism, and clerical celibacy. In his gradual reform of the church in Zurich, he had the strong support of the city authorities, who had long resented the privileges of the clergy.

The followers of Luther, Zwingli, and others who called for a break with Rome came to be called Protestants. The word **Protestant** derives from the protest drawn up by a small group of reforming German princes at the Diet of Speyer in 1529. The princes "protested" the decisions of the Catholic majority, and the word gradually became a general term applied to all non-Catholic western European Christians.

Protestant The name originally given to Lutherans, which came to mean all non-Catholic Western Christian groups.

Luther, Zwingli, and other early Protestants agreed on many things. First, how is a person to be saved? Traditional Catholic teaching held that salvation is achieved by both faith and good works. Protestants held that salvation comes by faith alone, irrespective of good works or the sacraments. God, not people, initiates salvation. (See "Listening to the Past: Martin Luther, *On Christian Liberty*," page 414.) Second, where does religious authority reside? Christian doctrine had long maintained that authority rests both in the Bible and in the traditional teaching of the church. For Protestants, authority rested in the Bible alone. For a doctrine or issue to be valid, it had to have a scriptural basis. Because of this, most Protestants rejected Catholic teachings about the sacraments—the rituals that the church had defined as imparting God's benefits on the believer (see Chapter 10)—holding that only baptism and the Eucharist have scriptural support.

Third, what is the church? Protestants held that the church is a spiritual priesthood of all believers, an invisible fellowship not fixed in any place or person, which differed markedly from the Roman Catholic practice of a hierarchical clerical institution headed by the pope in Rome. Fourth, what is the highest form of Christian life? The medieval church had stressed the superiority of the monastic and religious life over the secular. Protestants disagreed and argued that every person should serve God in his or her individual calling.

Protestants did not agree on everything, and one important area of dispute was the ritual of the Eucharist (also called communion, the Lord's Supper, and, in Catholicism, the Mass). Catholicism holds the dogma of transubstantiation: by the consecrating words of the priest during the Mass, the bread and wine become the actual body and blood of Christ. In opposition, Luther believed that Christ is really present in the consecrated bread and wine, but this is the result of God's mystery, not the actions of a priest. Zwingli understood the Eucharist as a memorial in which Christ was present in spirit among the faithful, but not in the bread and wine. The Colloquy of Marburg, summoned in 1529 to unite Protestants, failed to resolve these differences, though Protestants reached agreement on almost everything else.

The Appeal of Protestant Ideas

Pulpits and printing presses spread the Protestant message all over Germany, and by the middle of the sixteenth century people of all social classes had rejected Catholic teachings and had become Protestant. What was the immense appeal of Luther's religious ideas and those of other Protestants?

Educated people and many humanists were much attracted by Luther's ideas. He advocated a simpler personal religion based on faith, a return to the spirit of the early church, the centrality of the Scriptures in the liturgy and in Christian life, and the abolition of elaborate ceremonies—precisely the reforms the Christian humanists had been calling for. The Protestant insistence that everyone should read and reflect on the Scriptures attracted literate and thoughtful city residents. This included many priests and monks who left the Catholic Church to become clergy in the new Protestant churches. In addition, townspeople who envied the church's wealth and resented paying for it were attracted by the notion that the clergy should also pay taxes and should not have special legal privileges. After Zurich became Protestant, the city council taxed the clergy and placed them under the jurisdiction of civil courts.

Scholars in many disciplines have attributed Luther's fame and success to the invention of the printing press, which rapidly reproduced and made known his ideas. Many printed works included woodcuts and other illustrations, so that even those who could not read could grasp the main ideas. (See "Living in the Past: Uses of Art in the Reformation," page 418.) Equally important was Luther's incredible skill with language, as seen in his two catechisms (compendiums of basic religious knowledge) and in hymns that he wrote for congregations to sing. Luther's linguistic skill, together with his translation of the New Testament into German in 1523, led to the acceptance of his dialect of German as the standard written version of the German language.

Both Luther and Zwingli recognized that for reforms to be permanent, political authorities as well as concerned individuals and religious leaders would have to accept them. Zwingli worked closely with the city council of Zurich, and city councils themselves took the lead in other cities and towns of Switzerland and south Germany. They appointed pastors whom they knew had accepted Protestant ideas, required them to swear an oath of loyalty to the council, and oversaw their preaching and teaching.

Luther lived in a territory ruled by a noble—the elector of Saxony—and he also worked closely with political authorities, viewing them as fully justified in as-

Picturing the Past

Domestic Scene The Protestant notion that the best form of Christian life was marriage and a family helps explain its appeal to middle-class urban men and women, such as those shown in this domestic scene. The engraving, titled "Concordia" (harmony), includes the biblical inscription of what Jesus called the greatest commandment — "You shall love the Lord your God with all your heart and all your soul and your neighbor as yourself" (Deuteronomy 6; Matthew 22) — on tablets at the back. The large covered bed at the back was both a standard piece of furniture in urban homes and a symbol of proper marital sexual relations. (Mary Evans Picture Library)

ANALYZING THE IMAGE What are the different family members doing? What elements of this image suggest that this is a pious, Christian family?

CONNECTIONS How do the various family roles shown here support the Protestant ideal of marriage and family?

To complete this activity online, go to the Online Study Guide at bedfordstmartins.com/mckaywest.

serting control over the church in their territories. Indeed, he demanded that German rulers reform the papacy and its institutions, and he instructed all Christians to obey their secular rulers, whom he saw as divinely ordained to maintain order. Individuals may have been convinced of the truth of Protestant teachings by hearing sermons, listening to hymns, or reading pamphlets, but a territory became Protestant when its ruler, whether a noble or a city council, brought in a reformer or two to reeducate the territory's clergy, sponsored public sermons, and con-

fiscated church property. This happened in many of the states of the Holy Roman Empire during the 1520s.

The Radical Reformation and the German Peasants' War

While Luther and Zwingli worked with political authorities, some individuals and groups rejected the idea that church and state needed to be united. Beginning in the 1520s, they sought instead to create a voluntary

Martin Luther, *On Christian Liberty*

LISTENING TO THE PAST

The idea of liberty has played a powerful role in the history of Western society and culture, but the meaning and understanding of liberty has undergone continual change and interpretation. In the Roman world, where slavery was a basic institution, liberty meant the condition of being a free man, independent of obligations to a master. In the Middle Ages possessing liberty meant having special privileges or rights that other persons or institutions did not have. A lord or a monastery, for example, might speak of his or its liberties, and citizens in London were said to possess the "freedom of the city," which allowed them to practice trades and own property without interference.

The idea of liberty also has a religious dimension, and the reformer Martin Luther formulated a classic interpretation of liberty in his treatise On Christian Liberty *(sometimes translated as* On the Freedom of a Christian*), arguably his finest piece. Written in Latin for the pope but translated immediately into German and published widely, it contains the main themes of Luther's theology: the importance of faith, the relationship of Christian faith and good works, the dual nature of human beings, and the fundamental importance of Scripture. Luther writes that Christians were freed from sin and death through Christ, not through their own actions.*

❝ A Christian man is the most free lord of all, and subject to none; a Christian man is the most dutiful servant of all, and subject to everyone. Although these statements appear contradictory, yet, when they are found to agree together, they will do excellently for my purpose. They are both the statements of Paul himself, who says, "Though I be free from all men, yet have I made myself a servant unto all" (I Corinthians 9:19) and "Owe no man anything but to love one another" (Romans 13:8). Now love is by its own nature dutiful and obedient to the beloved object. Thus even Christ, though Lord of all things, was yet made of a woman; made under the law; at once free and a servant; at once in the form of God and in the form of a servant.

Let us examine the subject on a deeper and less simple principle. Man is composed of a twofold nature, a spiritual and a bodily. As regards the spiritual nature, which they name the soul, he is called the spiritual, inward, new man; as regards the bodily nature, which they name the flesh, he is called the fleshly, outward, old man. The Apostle speaks of this: "Though our outward man perish, yet the inward man is renewed day by day" (II Corinthians 4:16). The result of this diversity is that in the Scriptures opposing statements are made concerning the same man, the fact being that in the same man these two men are opposed to one another; the flesh lusting against the spirit, and the spirit against the flesh (Galatians 5:17).

We first approach the subject of the inward man, that we may see by what means a man becomes justified, free, and a true Christian; that is, a spiritual, new, and inward man. It is certain that absolutely none among outward things, under whatever name they may be reckoned, has any influence in producing Christian righteousness or liberty, nor, on the other hand, unrighteousness or slavery. This can be shown by an easy argument. What can it profit to the soul that the body should be in good condition, free, and full of life, that it should eat, drink, and act according to its pleasure, when even the most impious slaves of every kind of vice are prosperous in these matters? Again, what harm can ill health, bondage, hunger, thirst, or any other outward evil, do to the soul, when even the most pious of men, and the freest in the purity of their conscience, are harassed by these things? Neither of these states of things has to do with the liberty or the slavery of the soul.

And so it will profit nothing that the body should be adorned with sacred vestment, or dwell in holy places, or be occupied in sacred offices, or pray, fast, and abstain from certain meats, or do whatever works can be done through the body and in the body. Something widely different will be necessary for the justification and liberty of the soul, since the things I have spoken of can be done by an impious person, and only hypocrites are produced by devotion to these things. On the other hand, it will not at all injure the soul that the body should be clothed in profane raiment, should dwell in profane places, should eat and drink in the ordinary fashion, should not pray aloud, and should leave undone all the things above mentioned, which may be done by hypocrites.

. . . One thing, and one alone, is necessary for life, justification, and Christian liberty; and that is the most Holy Word of God, the Gospel of Christ, as He says, "I am the resurrection and the life; he that believeth in me shall not die eternally" (John 9:25), and also, "If the Son shall make you free, ye shall be free indeed" (John 8:36), and "Man shall not live by bread alone, but by every word that proceedeth out of the mouth of God" (Matthew 4:4).

Let us therefore hold it for certain and firmly established that the soul can do without everything except the Word of God, without which none at all of its wants is provided for. But, having the Word, it is rich and wants for nothing, since that is the Word of life, of truth, of light, of peace, of justification, of salvation,

On effective preaching, especially to the uneducated, Luther urged the minister "to keep it simple for the simple."
(Church of St. Marien, Wittenberg/The Bridgeman Art Library)

of joy, of liberty, of wisdom, of virtue, of grace, of glory, and of every good thing. . . .

But you will ask, "What is this Word, and by what means is it to be used, since there are so many words of God?" I answer, "The Apostle Paul (Romans 1) explains what it is, namely the Gospel of God, concerning His Son, incarnate, suffering, risen, and glorified through the Spirit, the Sanctifier." To preach Christ is to feed the soul, to justify it, to set it free, and to save it, if it believes the preaching. For faith alone, and the efficacious use of the Word of God, bring salvation. "If thou shalt confess with thy mouth the Lord Jesus, and shalt believe in thine heart that God hath raised Him from the dead, thou shalt be saved" (Romans 9:9); . . . and "The just shall live by faith" (Romans 1:17). . . .

But this faith cannot consist of all with works; that is, if you imagine that you can be justified by those works, whatever they are, along with it. . . . Therefore, when you begin to believe, you learn at the same time that all that is in you is utterly guilty, sinful, and damnable, according to that saying, "All have sinned, and come short of the glory of God"

(Romans 3:23). . . . When you have learned this, you will know that Christ is necessary for you, since He has suffered and risen again for you, that, believing on Him, you might by this faith become another man, all your sins being remitted, and you being justified by the merits of another, namely Christ alone.

. . . [A]nd since it [faith] alone justifies, it is evident that by no outward work or labour can the inward man be at all justified, made free, and saved; and that no works whatever have any relation to him. . . . Therefore the first care of every Christian ought to be to lay aside all reliance on works, and strengthen his faith alone more and more, and by it grow in knowledge, not of works, but of Christ Jesus, who has suffered and risen again for him, as Peter teaches (I Peter 5). 🔅

QUESTIONS FOR ANALYSIS

1. What did Luther mean by liberty?
2. Why, for Luther, was Scripture basic to Christian life?

Source: *Luther's Primary Works*, ed. H. Wace and C. A. Buchheim (London: Holder and Stoughton, 1896). Reprinted in *The Portable Renaissance Reader*, ed. James Bruce Ross and Mary Martin McLaughlin (New York: Penguin Books, 1981), pp. 721–726.

❝ Let everyone who can smite, slay, and stab [the peasants], secretly and openly, remembering that nothing can be more poisonous, hurtful or devilish than a rebel. ❞

—MARTIN LUTHER

community of believers separate from the state, as they understood it to have existed in New Testament times. In terms of theology and spiritual practices, these individuals and groups varied widely, though they are generally termed "radicals" for their insistence on a more extensive break with prevailing ideas. Some adopted the baptism of believers—for which they were given the title of "Anabaptists" or rebaptizers by their enemies—while others saw all outward sacraments or rituals as misguided. Some groups attempted communal ownership of property, living very simply and rejecting anything they thought unbiblical. Some reacted harshly to members who deviated, but others argued for complete religious toleration and individualism.

Religious radicals were often pacifists and refused to hold office or swear oaths, which marked them as societal outcasts and invited fanatical hatred and bitter persecution. Both Protestant and Catholic authorities felt threatened by the social, political, and economic implications of their religious ideas, and by their rejection of a state church, which the authorities saw as key to maintaining order. In Saxony, in Strasbourg, and in the Swiss cities, radicals were either banished or cruelly executed by burning, beating, or drowning. Their community spirit and heroism in the face of martyrdom, however, contributed to the survival of radical ideas. Later, the Quakers, with their pacifism; the Baptists, with their emphasis on inner spiritual light; the Congregationalists, with their democratic church organization; and in 1787 the authors of the U.S. Constitution, with their opposition to the "establishment of religion" (state churches), would all trace their origins, in part, to the radicals of the sixteenth century.

Radical reformers sometimes called for social as well as religious change, a message that German peasants heard. In the early sixteenth century the economic condition of the peasantry varied from place to place but was generally worse than it had been in the fifteenth century and was deteriorating. Crop failures in 1523 and 1524 aggravated an explosive situation. Nobles had aggrieved peasants by seizing village common lands, by imposing new rents and requiring additional services, and by taking the peasants' best horses or cows whenever a head of household died. The peasants made demands that they believed conformed to the Scriptures, and they cited radical thinkers as well as Luther as proof that they did.

Luther wanted to prevent rebellion. Initially he sided with the peasants, blasting the lords for robbing their subjects. But when rebellion broke out, peasants who expected Luther's support were soon disillusioned. Freedom for Luther meant independence from the authority of the Roman church; it did not mean opposition to legally established secular powers.

As for biblical support for the peasants' demands, he maintained that Scripture had nothing to do with earthly justice or material gain, a position that Zwingli supported. Firmly convinced that rebellion would hasten the end of civilized society, Luther wrote the tract *Against the Murderous, Thieving Hordes of the Peasants*: "Let everyone who can smite, slay, and stab [the peasants], secretly and openly, remembering that nothing can be more poisonous, hurtful or devilish than a rebel."[3] The nobility ferociously crushed the revolt. Historians estimate that more than seventy-five thousand peasants were killed in 1525.

The German Peasants' War of 1525 greatly strengthened the authority of lay rulers. Not surprisingly, the Reformation lost much of its popular appeal after 1525, though peasants and urban rebels sometimes found a place for their social and religious ideas in radical groups. Peasants' economic conditions did moderately improve, however. For example, in many parts of Germany, enclosed fields, meadows, and forests were returned to common use.

Marriage and Sexuality

Luther and Zwingli both believed that a priest's or nun's vows of celibacy went against human nature and God's commandments, and that marriage brought spiritual advantages and so was the ideal state for nearly all human beings. Luther married a former nun, Katharina von Bora (1499–1532), and Zwingli married a Zurich widow, Anna Reinhart (1491–1538). Both women quickly had several children. Most other Protestant reformers also married, and their wives had to create a new and respectable role for themselves—pastor's wife—to overcome being viewed as simply a new type of priest's concubine. They were living demonstrations of their husband's convictions about the superiority of marriage to celibacy, and they were expected to be models of wifely obedience and Christian charity.

Though they denied that marriage was a sacrament, Protestant reformers stressed that it had been ordained by God when he presented Eve to Adam, served as a "remedy" for the unavoidable sin of lust, provided a site for the pious rearing of the next generation of God-fearing Christians, and offered husbands and wives companionship and consolation. A proper marriage was one that reflected both the spiritual equality of men and

Martin Luther and Katharina von Bora Lucas Cranach the Elder painted this double marriage portrait to celebrate Luther's wedding in 1525 to Katharina von Bora, a former nun. The artist was one of the witnesses at the wedding and, in fact, had presented Luther's marriage proposal to Katharina. Using a go-between for proposals was very common, as was having a double wedding portrait painted. This particular couple quickly became a model of the ideal marriage, and many churches wanted their portraits. More than sixty similar paintings, with slight variations, were produced by Cranach's workshop and hung in churches and wealthy homes. (Uffizi, Florence/Scala/Art Resource, NY)

women and the proper social hierarchy of husbandly authority and wifely obedience.

Protestants did not break with medieval scholastic theologians in their idea that women were to be subject to men. Women were advised to be cheerful rather than grudging in their obedience, for in doing so they demonstrated their willingness to follow God's plan. Men were urged to treat their wives kindly and considerately, but also to enforce their authority, through physical coercion if necessary. European marriage manuals used the metaphor of breaking a horse for teaching a wife obedience, though laws did set limits on the husband's power to do so. A few women took Luther's idea about the priesthood of all believers to heart. Argula von Grumbach, a German noblewoman, wrote religious pamphlets supporting Protestant ideas, asserting, "I am not unfamiliar with Paul's words that women should be silent in church but when I see that no man will or can speak, I am driven by the word of God when he said, he who confesses me on earth, him will I confess, and he who denies me, him will I deny."[4] No sixteenth-

century Protestants officially allowed women to be members of the clergy, however, though monarchs such as Elizabeth I of England and female territorial rulers of the states of the Holy Roman Empire did determine religious policies just as male rulers did.

Protestants saw marriage as a contract in which each partner promised the other support, companionship, and the sharing of mutual goods. Because, in Protestant eyes, marriage was created by God as a remedy for human weakness, marriages in which spouses did not comfort or support one another physically, materially, or emotionally endangered their own souls and the surrounding community. The only solution might be divorce and remarriage, which most Protestants came to allow. Protestant allowance of divorce differed markedly from Catholic doctrine, which viewed marriage as a sacramental union that, if validly entered into, could not be dissolved (Catholic canon law allowed only separation with no remarriage). Although it was a dramatic legal change, divorce did not have a dramatic impact on newly Protestant areas. Because marriage was the cornerstone

England, too, had a strong monarchy, but the king broke from the Catholic Church for other reasons (see page 423). The Holy Roman Empire, in contrast, included hundreds of largely independent states. Against this background of decentralization and strong local power, Martin Luther had launched a movement to reform the church. Two years after he published the "Ninety-five Theses," the electors of the Holy Roman Empire chose as emperor a nineteen-year-old Habsburg prince who ruled as Charles V (r. 1519–1556). The course of the Reformation was shaped by this election and by the political relationships surrounding it.

The Rise of the Habsburg Dynasty

War and diplomacy were important ways that states increased their power in sixteenth-century Europe, but so was marriage. Royal and noble sons and daughters were important tools of state policy. The benefits of an advantageous marriage stretched across generations, a process that can be seen most dramatically with the Habsburgs. The Holy Roman emperor Frederick III, a Habsburg who was the ruler of most of Austria, acquired only a small amount of territory—but a great deal of money—with his marriage to Princess Eleonore

of Portugal in 1452. He arranged for his son Maximilian to marry Europe's most prominent heiress, Mary of Burgundy, in 1477; she inherited the Netherlands, Luxembourg, and the County of Burgundy in what is now eastern France. Through this union with the rich and powerful duchy of Burgundy, the Austrian house of Habsburg, already the strongest ruling family in the empire, became an international power. The marriage of Maximilian and Mary angered the French, however, who considered Burgundy French territory, and inaugurated centuries of conflict between the Austrian house of Habsburg and the kings of France.

Maximilian learned the lesson of marital politics well, marrying his son and daughter to the children of Ferdinand and Isabella, the rulers of Spain, much of southern Italy, and eventually the Spanish New World empire. His grandson Charles V (1500–1558) fell heir to a vast and incredibly diverse collection of states and peoples, each governed in a different manner and held together only by the person of the emperor (Map 14.1). Charles's Italian adviser, the grand chancellor Gattinara, told the young ruler, "God has set you on the path toward world monarchy." Charles not only believed this but also was convinced that it was his duty to maintain the political and religious unity of Western Christendom.

Fresco of Pope Clement VII and the Emperor Charles V In this double portrait, artist Giorgio Vasari uses matching hand gestures to indicate agreement between the pope and the emperor, though the pope's red hat and cape make him the dominant figure. Charles V remained loyal to Catholicism, though the political situation and religious wars in Germany eventually required him to compromise with Protestants. (Palazzo Vecchio, Florence/Scala/Art Resource, NY)

Religious Wars in Switzerland and Germany

In the sixteenth century the practice of religion remained a public matter. The ruler determined the official form of religious practice in his (or occasionally her) jurisdiction. Almost everyone believed that the presence of a faith different from that of the majority represented a political threat to the security of the state, and few believed in religious liberty.

Luther's ideas appealed to German rulers for a variety of reasons. Though Germany was not a nation, people did have an understanding of being German because of their language and traditions. Luther frequently used the phrase "we Germans" in his attacks on the papacy. Luther's appeal to national feeling influenced many rulers otherwise confused by or indifferent to the complexities of the religious matters. Some German rulers

were sincerely attracted to Lutheran ideas, but material considerations swayed many others to embrace the new faith. The rejection of Roman Catholicism and adoption of Protestantism would mean the legal confiscation of lush farmlands, rich monasteries, and wealthy shrines. Thus many political authorities in the empire used the religious issue to extend their financial and political power and to enhance their independence from the emperor.

Charles V was a vigorous defender of Catholicism, so it is not surprising that the Reformation led to religious wars. The first battleground was Switzerland, which was officially part of the Holy Roman Empire, though it was really a loose confederation of thirteen largely autonomous territories called "cantons." Some cantons remained Catholic, and some became Protestant, and in the late 1520s the two sides went to war. Zwingli was killed on the battlefield in 1531, and both sides quickly decided

Map 14.1 The Global Empire of Charles V, ca. 1556 Charles V exercised theoretical jurisdiction over more European territory than anyone since Charlemagne. He also claimed authority over large parts of North and South America (see Map 15.2 on page 452), though actual Spanish control was weak in much of the area.

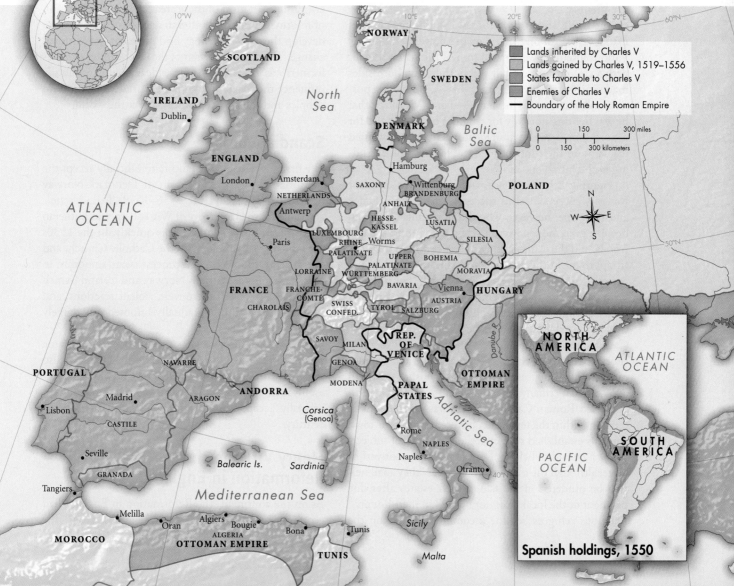

that a treaty was preferable to further fighting. The treaty basically allowed each canton to determine its own religion and ordered each side to give up their foreign alliances, a policy of neutrality that has been characteristic of modern Switzerland.

Trying to halt the spread of religious division, Charles V called an Imperial Diet in 1530, to meet at Augsburg. The Lutherans developed a statement of faith, later called the Augsburg Confession, and the Protestant princes presented this to the emperor. (The Augsburg Confession remains an authoritative statement of belief for many Lutheran churches.) Charles refused to accept it and ordered all Protestants to return to the Catholic Church and give up any confiscated church property. This demand backfired, and Protestant territories in the empire—mostly northern German principalities and southern German cities—formed a military alliance. The emperor could not respond militarily, as he was in the midst of a series of wars with the French: the Habsburg-Valois wars (1521–1559), fought in Italy along the eastern and southern borders of France and eventually in Germany. The Ottoman Turks had also taken much of Hungary and in 1529 were besieging Vienna.

The 1530s and early 1540s saw complicated political maneuvering among many of the powers of Europe. Various attempts were made to heal the religious split with a church council, but stubbornness on both sides made it increasingly clear that this would not be possible and that war was inevitable. Charles V realized that he was fighting not only for religious unity, but also for a more unified state, against territorial rulers who wanted to maintain their independence. He was thus defending both church and empire.

Fighting began in 1546, and initially the emperor was very successful. This success alarmed both France and the pope, however, who did not want Charles to become even more powerful. The pope withdrew papal troops, and the Catholic king of France sent money and troops to the Lutheran princes. Finally, in 1555 Charles agreed to the Peace of Augsburg, which, "in order to bring peace into the holy empire," officially recognized Lutheranism. The political authority in each territory was permitted to decide whether the territory would be Catholic or Lutheran and was ordered to let other territories "enjoy their religious beliefs, liturgy, and ceremonies as well as their estates in peace." Most of northern and central Germany became Lutheran, while the south remained Roman Catholic. There was no freedom of religion within the territories, however. Princes or town councils established state churches to which all subjects of the area had to belong. Dissidents had to convert or leave, although the treaty did order that "they shall neither be hindered in the sale of their estates after due payment of the local taxes nor injured in their honor."[5] Religious refugees became a common feature on the roads of the empire, though rulers did not always let their subjects leave as easily as the treaty stipulated.

The Peace of Augsburg ended religious war in Germany for many decades. His hope of uniting his empire under a single church dashed, Charles V abdicated in 1556 and moved to a monastery, transferring power over his holdings in Spain and the Netherlands to his son Philip and his imperial power to his brother Ferdinand.

The Spread of Protestant Ideas

How did Protestant ideas and institutions spread beyond German-speaking lands? ■

States within the Holy Roman Empire were the earliest territories to accept the Protestant Reformation, but by the later 1520s and 1530s religious change came to Denmark-Norway, Sweden, England, France, and eastern Europe. In most of these areas, a second generation of reformers built on Lutheran and Zwinglian ideas to develop their own theology and plans for institutional change. The most important of the second-generation reformers was John Calvin, whose ideas would profoundly influence the social thought and attitudes of European peoples and their descendants all over the world.

Scandinavia

The first area outside the empire to officially accept the Reformation was the kingdom of Denmark-Norway under King Christian III (r. 1536–1559). Danish scholars studied at the University of Wittenberg, and Lutheran ideas spread into Denmark very quickly. In the 1530s the king officially broke with the Catholic Church, and most clergy followed. The process went smoothly in Denmark, but in northern Norway and Iceland (which Christian also ruled) there were violent reactions, and Lutheranism was only gradually imposed on a largely unwilling populace.

In Sweden, Gustavus Vasa (r. 1523–1560), who came to the throne during a civil war with Denmark, also took over control of church personnel and income. Protestant ideas spread, though the Swedish church did not officially accept Lutheran theology until later in the century.

Henry VIII and the Reformation in England

As on the continent, the Reformation in England had economic and political as well as religious causes. The

Allegory of the Tudor Dynasty The unknown creator of this work intended to glorify the virtues of the Protestant succession; the painting has no historical reality. Henry VIII (seated) hands the sword of justice to his Protestant son Edward VI. The Catholic Queen Mary and her husband Philip of Spain (left) are followed by Mars, god of war, signifying violence and civil disorder. At right the figures of Peace and Plenty accompany the Protestant Elizabeth I, symbolizing England's happy fate under her rule. (Yale Center for British Art, Paul Mellon Collection/The Bridgeman Art Library)

impetus for England's break with Rome was the desire of King Henry VIII (r. 1509–1547) for a new wife, though ultimately his own motives also combined personal, political, social, and economic elements.

Henry VIII was married to Catherine of Aragon, the daughter of Ferdinand and Isabella and widow of Henry's older brother Arthur. Marriage to a brother's widow went against canon law, and Henry had been required to obtain a special papal dispensation to marry Catherine. The marriage had produced only one living heir, a daughter, Mary. By 1527 Henry decided that God was showing his displeasure with the marriage by denying him a son, and he appealed to the pope to have the marriage annulled. He was also in love with a court lady-in-waiting, Anne Boleyn, and assumed that she would give him the son he wanted. Normally an annulment would not have been a problem, but the troops of Emperor Charles V were in Rome at that point, and Pope Clement VII was essentially their prisoner. Charles V was the nephew of Catherine of Aragon and thus was

vigorously opposed to an annulment, which would have declared his aunt a fornicator and his cousin Mary a bastard. The pope stalled.

With Rome thwarting his matrimonial plans, Henry decided to remove the English church from papal jurisdiction. In a series of measures during the 1530s, Henry used Parliament to end the authority of the pope and make himself the supreme head of the church in England. Some opposed the king and were beheaded, among them Thomas More, the king's chancellor and author of *Utopia* (see Chapter 13). When Anne Boleyn failed twice to produce a male child, Henry VIII charged her with adulterous incest and in 1536 had her beheaded. His third wife, Jane Seymour, gave Henry the desired son, Edward, but she died in childbirth. Henry went on to three more wives.

Theologically, Henry was conservative, and the English church retained such traditional Catholic practices and doctrines as confession, clerical celibacy, and transubstantiation. Between 1535 and 1539, however, under the influence of his chief minister, Thomas Cromwell, Henry decided to dissolve the English monasteries because he wanted their wealth. Working through Parliament, the king ended nine hundred years of English monastic life, dispersing the monks and nuns and confiscating their lands. Their proceeds enriched the royal treasury, and hundreds of properties were sold to the middle and upper classes, the very groups represented in Parliament. The dissolution of the monasteries did not achieve a more equitable distribution of land and wealth; rather, the redistribution of land strengthened the upper classes and tied them to both the Tudor dynasty and the new Protestant church.

The nationalization of the church and the dissolution of the monasteries led to important changes in government administration. Vast tracts of formerly monastic land came temporarily under the Crown's jurisdiction, and new bureaucratic machinery had to be developed to manage those properties. Cromwell reformed and centralized the king's household, the council, the secretariats, and the Exchequer. New departments of state were set up. Surplus funds from all departments went into a liquid fund to be applied to areas where there were deficits. This balancing resulted in greater efficiency and economy, and Henry VIII's reign saw the growth of the modern centralized bureaucratic state.

Did the religious changes under Henry VIII have broad popular support? Some English people had been dissatisfied with the existing Christian church before Henry's measures, and Protestant literature circulated. Traditional Catholicism exerted an enormously strong and vigorous hold over the imagination and loyalty of the people, however. Most clergy and officials accepted Henry's moves, but all did not quietly acquiesce. In 1536 popular opposition in the north to the religious changes led to the Pilgrimage of Grace, a massive rebellion that proved the largest in English history. The "pilgrims" accepted a truce, but their leaders were arrested, tried, and executed. Recent scholarship points out that people rarely "converted" from Catholicism to Protestantism overnight. People responded to an action of the Crown that was played out in their own neighborhood—the closing of a monastery, the ending of Masses for the dead—with a combination of resistance, acceptance, and collaboration. Some enthusiastically changed to Protestant forms of prayer, for example, while others recited Protestant prayers in church while keeping pictures of the Catholic saints at home.

Loyalty to the Catholic Church was particularly strong in Ireland. Ireland had been claimed by English kings since the twelfth century, but in reality the English had firm control of only the area around Dublin, known as the Pale. In 1536, on orders from London, the Irish parliament, which represented only the English landlords and the people of the Pale, approved the English laws severing the church from Rome. The Church of Ireland was established on the English pattern, and the (English) ruling class adopted the new reformed faith. Most of the Irish people remained Roman Catholic, thus adding religious antagonism to the ethnic hostility that had been a feature of English policy toward Ireland for centuries (see Chapter 12). Irish armed opposition to the Reformation led to harsh repression by the English. Catholic property was confiscated and sold, and the profits were shipped to England. The Roman church was essentially driven underground, and the Catholic clergy acted as national as well as religious leaders.

Upholding Protestantism in England

In the short reign of Henry's sickly son, Edward VI (r. 1547–1553), Protestant ideas exerted a significant influence on the religious life of the country. Archbishop Thomas Cranmer simplified the liturgy, invited Protestant theologians to England, and prepared the first *Book of Common Prayer* (1549), which was later approved by Parliament. In stately and dignified English, the *Book of Common Prayer* included the order for all services and prayers of the Church of England.

The equally brief reign of Mary Tudor (r. 1553–1558) witnessed a sharp move back to Catholicism. The devoutly Catholic daughter of Catherine of Aragon, Mary rescinded the Reformation legislation of her father's reign and restored Roman Catholicism. Mary's marriage to her cousin Philip II of Spain, son of the emperor Charles V, proved highly unpopular in England, and her execution of several hundred Protestants further alienated her subjects. During her reign, about a thousand Protestants fled to the continent. Mary's death raised to the throne her sister Elizabeth, Henry's daughter with Anne Boleyn, who had been raised a Protestant. Her reign from 1558 to 1603 inaugurated the beginnings of religious stability.

At the start of Elizabeth's reign sharp differences existed in England. On the one hand, Catholics wanted a Roman Catholic ruler. On the other hand, a vocal number of returning exiles wanted all Catholic elements in the Church of England eliminated. The latter, because they wanted to "purify" the church, were called "Puritans."

Shrewdly, Elizabeth chose a middle course between Catholic and Puritan extremes. She referred to herself as the "supreme governor of the Church of England," using the term *governor* instead of the traditional *head* because this allowed Catholics to remain loyal to her without denying the pope. She required her subjects to attend services in the Church of England or risk a fine, but she did not interfere with their privately held beliefs. As she put it, she did not "want to make windows into men's souls." The Anglican Church, as the Church of England was called, moved in a moderately Protestant direction. Services were conducted in English, monasteries were not re-established, and clergymen were (grudgingly) allowed to marry. But the church remained hierarchical, with archbishops and bishops, and services continued to be elaborate, with the clergy in distinctive robes, in contrast to the simpler services favored by many continental Protestants.

Toward the end of the sixteenth century Elizabeth's reign was threatened by European powers attempting to re-establish Catholicism. Philip II of Spain had hoped that his marriage to Mary Tudor would reunite England with Catholic Europe, but Mary's death ended those plans. Another Mary—Mary, Queen of Scots—provided a new opportunity. Mary was Elizabeth's cousin, but she was Catholic. Mary was next in line to the English throne, and Elizabeth imprisoned her because she worried—quite rightly—that Mary would become the center of Catholic plots to overthrow her. In 1587 Mary became implicated in a plot to assassinate Elizabeth, a conspiracy that had Philip II's full backing. When the English executed Mary, the Catholic pope urged Philip to retaliate.

Philip prepared a vast fleet to sail from Lisbon to Flanders, where a large army of Spanish troops was stationed because of religious wars in the Netherlands (see page 435). The Spanish ships were to escort barges carrying some of the troops across the English Channel to attack England. On May 9, 1588, *la felicíssima armada*—"the most fortunate fleet," as it was ironically called in official documents—composed of more than 130 vessels, sailed from Lisbon harbor. The **Spanish Armada** met an English fleet in the channel before it reached Flanders. The English ships were smaller, faster, and more maneuverable, and many of them had greater firing power than their Spanish counterparts. A combination of storms and squalls, spoiled food and rank water, inadequate Spanish ammunition, and, to a lesser extent, English fire ships that caused the Spanish to scatter gave England the victory. On the journey home many Spanish ships went down in the rough seas around Ireland; perhaps 65 ships managed to reach home ports.

The battle in the English Channel has frequently been described as one of the decisive battles in world history. In fact, it had mixed consequences. Spain soon rebuilt its navy, and after 1588 the quality of the Spanish fleet improved. The war between England and Spain dragged on for years. Yet the defeat of the Spanish Armada prevented Philip II from reimposing Catholicism on England by force. In England the victory contributed to a David and Goliath legend that enhanced English national sentiment.

Spanish Armada The fleet sent by Philip II of Spain in 1588 against England as a religious crusade against Protestantism. Weather and the English fleet defeated it.

The Institutes of the Christian Religion Calvin's formulation of Christian doctrine, which became a systematic theology for Protestantism.

Calvinism

In 1509, while Luther was preparing for a doctorate at Wittenberg, John Calvin (1509–1564) was born in Noyon in northwestern France. As a young man he studied law, which had a decisive impact on his mind and later his thought. In 1533 he experienced a religious crisis, as a result of which he converted to Protestantism.

Calvin believed that God had specifically selected him to reform the church. Accordingly, he accepted an invitation to assist in the reformation of the city of Geneva. There, beginning in 1541, Calvin worked assiduously to establish a Christian society ruled by God through civil magistrates and reformed ministers. Geneva became the model of a Christian community for Protestant reformers.

To understand Calvin's Geneva, it is necessary to understand Calvin's ideas. These he embodied in ***The Institutes of the Christian Religion***, published first in 1536 and in its final form in 1559. The cornerstone of Calvin's theology was his belief in the absolute sovereignty and omnipotence of God and the total weakness of humanity. Before the infinite power of God, he asserted, men and women are as insignificant as grains of sand.

Calvin did not ascribe free will to human beings because that would detract from the sovereignty of God. Men and women cannot actively work to achieve salvation; rather, God in his infinite wisdom decided at the beginning of time who would be saved and who damned. This viewpoint constitutes the theological

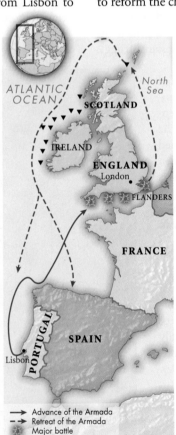

The Route of the Spanish Armada, 1588

ATLANTIC OCEAN

North Sea

SCOTLAND

IRELAND

ENGLAND
London

FLANDERS

FRANCE

PORTUGAL   SPAIN

Lisbon

→ Advance of the Armada
--▶ Retreat of the Armada
✳ Major battle
▼ Shipwreck

principle called **predestination**. Calvin explained his view:

> Predestination we call the eternal decree of God, by which he has determined in himself, what he would have become of every individual. . . . For they are not all created with a similar destiny; but eternal life is foreordained for some, and eternal damnation for others. . . . To those whom he devotes to condemnation, the gate of life is closed by a just and irreprehensible, but incomprehensible, judgment. How exceedingly presumptuous it is only to inquire into the causes of the Divine will; which is in fact, and is justly entitled to be, the cause of everything that exists. . . . For the will of God is the highest justice; so that what he wills must be considered just, for this very reason, because he wills it.[6]

Many people consider the doctrine of predestination, which dates back to Saint Augustine and Saint Paul, to be a pessimistic view of the nature of God. But "this terrible decree," as even Calvin called it, did not lead to pessimism or fatalism. Rather, the Calvinist believed in the redemptive work of Christ and was confident that God had elected (saved) him or her. Predestination served as an energizing dynamic, giving a person the strength to undergo hardships in the constant struggle against evil.

predestination The teaching that God has determined the salvation or damnation of individuals based on his will and purpose, not on their merit or works.

In his reform of Geneva, Calvin had several remarkable assets, including complete mastery of the Scriptures and exceptional eloquence. He also understood the importance of institutions and established the Genevan Consistory, a body of laymen and pastors, "to keep watch over every man's life [and] to admonish amiably those whom they see leading a disorderly life" and provide "medicine to turn sinners to the Lord."[7]

Although all municipal governments in early modern Europe regulated citizens' conduct, none did so with the severity of Geneva's Consistory under Calvin's leadership. Absence from sermons, criticism of ministers, dancing, card playing, family quarrels, and heavy drinking were all investigated and punished by the Consistory.

Serious crimes and heresy were handled by the civil authorities, which, with the Consistory's approval, sometimes used torture to extract confessions. Between 1542 and 1546 alone seventy-six persons were banished from Geneva, and fifty-eight were executed for heresy, adultery, blasphemy, and witchcraft (see page 435). Among them was the Spanish humanist and refugee Michael Servetus, who was burned at the stake for denying the scriptural basis for the Trinity, rejecting child baptism, and insisting that a person under twenty cannot commit a mortal sin, all of which were viewed as threats to society.

Religious refugees from France, England, Spain, Scotland, and Italy visited Calvin's Geneva, and many of the most prominent exiles from Mary Tudor's England stayed. Subsequently, the church of Calvin—often termed "Reformed"—served as the model for the Presbyterian church in Scotland, the Huguenot church in France (see page 433), and the Puritan churches in England and New England.

Calvinism became the compelling force in international Protestantism. The Calvinist ethic of the "calling" dignified all work with a religious aspect. Hard work, well done, was pleasing to God. This doctrine encouraged an aggressive, vigorous activism, and Calvinism became the most dynamic force in sixteenth- and seventeenth-century Protestantism.

Calvinism spread on the continent of Europe, and also found a ready audience in Scotland. There as elsewhere,

Young John Calvin This oil painting of the reformer as a young man captures his spiritual intensity and determination, qualities that the artist clearly viewed as positive. (Bibliothèque de Genève, Département iconographique)

❝ Predestination we call the eternal decree of God, by which he has determined in himself, what he would have become of every individual. ❞

—JOHN CALVIN

political authority was the decisive influence in reform. The monarchy was weak, and factions of virtually independent nobles competed for power. King James V and his daughter Mary, Queen of Scots (r. 1560–1567), staunch Catholics and close allies of Catholic France, opposed reform, but the Scottish nobles supported it. One man, John Knox (1505?–1572), dominated the reform movement, which led to the establishment of a state church.

Knox was determined to structure the Scottish church after the model of Geneva, where he had studied and worked with Calvin. In 1560 Knox persuaded the Scottish parliament, which was dominated by reform-minded barons, to end papal authority and rule by bishops, substituting governance by presbyters, or councils of ministers. The Presbyterian Church of Scotland was strictly Calvinist in doctrine, adopted a simple and dignified service of worship, and laid great emphasis on preaching.

The Reformation in Eastern Europe

While political and economic issues determined the course of the Reformation in western and northern Europe, ethnic factors often proved decisive in eastern Europe, where people of diverse backgrounds had settled in the later Middle Ages. In Bohemia in the fifteenth century, a Czech majority was ruled by Germans. Most Czechs had adopted the ideas of Jan Hus, and the emperor had been forced to recognize a separate Hussite church (see Chapter 12). Yet Lutheranism appealed to Germans in Bohemia in the 1520s and 1530s, and the nobility embraced Lutheranism in opposition to the Catholic Habsburgs. The forces of the Catholic Reformation (see page 428) promoted a Catholic spiritual revival in Bohemia, and some areas reconverted. This complicated situation would be one of the causes of the Thirty Years' War in the early seventeenth century.

By 1500 Poland and the Grand Duchy of Lithuania were jointly governed by king, senate, and diet (parliament), the two territories retained separate officials, judicial systems, armies, and forms of citizenship. The combined realms covered almost 500,000 square miles, making Poland-Lithuania the largest European polity. A population of only about 7.5 million people was very thinly scattered over that land.

The population of Poland-Lithuania was also very diverse; Germans, Italians, Tartars, and Jews lived with Poles and Lithuanians. Such peoples had come as merchants, invited by medieval rulers because of their wealth or to make agricultural improvements. Each group spoke its native language, though all educated people spoke Latin. Luther's ideas took root in Germanized towns but were opposed by King Sigismund I (r. 1506–1548) as well as by ordinary Poles, who held strong anti-German feeling. The Reformed tradition of John Calvin, with its stress on the power of church elders, appealed to the Polish nobility, however. The fact that Calvinism originated in France, not in Germany, also made it more attractive than Lutheranism. But doctrinal differences among Calvinists, Lutherans, and other groups prevented united opposition to Catholicism, and a Counter-Reformation gained momentum. By 1650, due to the efforts of Stanislaus Hosius (1505–1579) and those of the Jesuits (see page 431), Poland was again staunchly Roman Catholic.

Hungary's experience with the Reformation was even more complex. Lutheranism was spread by Hungarian students who had studied at Wittenberg, and sympathy for it developed at the royal court of King Louis II in Buda. But concern about "the German heresy" by the Catholic hierarchy and among the high nobles found expression in a decree of the Hungarian diet in 1523 that "all Lutherans and those favoring them . . . should have their property confiscated and themselves punished with death as heretics."[8]

Before such measures could be acted on, a military event on August 26, 1526, had profound consequences for both the Hungarian state and the Protestant Reformation there. On the plain of Mohács in southern Hungary, the Ottoman sultan Suleiman the Magnificent inflicted a crushing defeat on the Hungarians, killing King Louis II, many of the nobles, and more than sixteen thousand ordinary soldiers. The Hungarian kingdom was then divided into three parts: the Ottoman Turks absorbed the great plains, including the capital, Buda; the Habsburgs ruled the north and west; and Ottoman-supported Janos Zapolya held eastern Hungary and Transylvania.

The Turks were indifferent to the religious conflicts of Christians, whom they regarded as infidels. Christians of all types paid extra taxes to the sultan, but kept their faith. Many Magyar (Hungarian) nobles accepted Lutheranism; Lutheran schools and parishes headed by men educated at Wittenberg multiplied; and peasants

The Battle of Mohács Massed armies on both sides confront each other in this Turkish illustration of the Battle of Mohács. In the right panel, Suleiman in a white turban sits on a black horse surrounded by his personal guard, while his soldiers fire muskets and large cannon at the enemy. In the left panel the Europeans are in disarray, and their weapons are clearly inferior. (Topkapi Saray Museum)

welcomed the new faith. The majority of people were Protestant until the late seventeenth century, when Hungarian nobles recognized Habsburg (Catholic) rule and Ottoman Turkish withdrawal in 1699 led to Catholic restoration.

The Catholic Reformation

How did the Catholic Church respond to the new religious situation? ■

Between 1517 and 1547 Protestantism made remarkable advances. Nevertheless, the Roman Catholic Church made a significant comeback. After about 1540 no new large areas of Europe, other than the Netherlands, accepted Protestant beliefs (Map 14.2). Many historians see the developments within the Catholic Church after the Protestant Reformation as two interrelated move-

ments, one a drive for internal reform linked to earlier reform efforts, and the other a Counter-Reformation that opposed Protestants intellectually, politically, militarily, and institutionally. In both movements, the papacy, new religious orders, and the Council of Trent that met from 1545 to 1563 were important agents.

Papal Reform and the Council of Trent

Renaissance popes and their advisers were not blind to the need for church reforms, but they resisted calls for a general council representing the entire church, and feared that any transformation would mean a loss of power, revenue, and prestige. This changed beginning with Pope Paul III (pontificate 1534–1549), when the papal court became the center of the reform movement rather than its chief opponent. The lives of the pope and his reform-minded cardinals, abbots, and bishops were models of

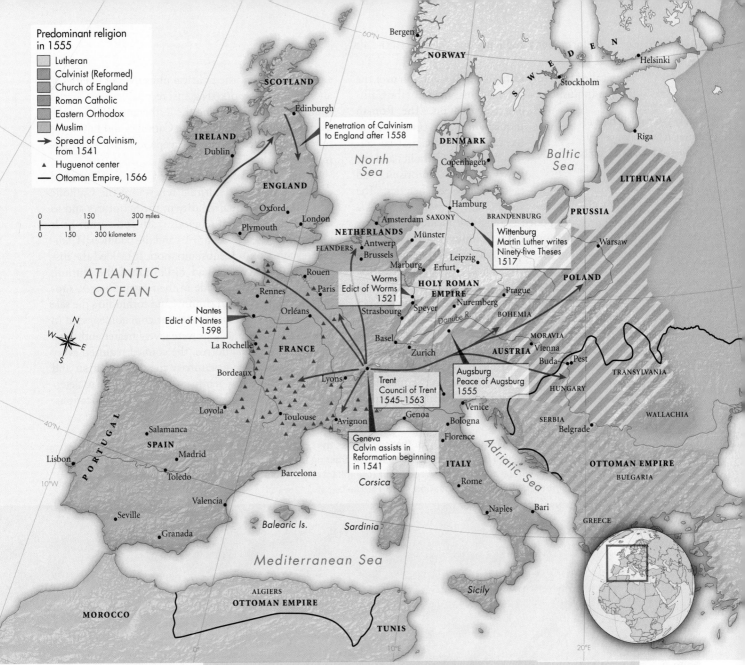

Predominant religion in 1555

- Lutheran
- Calvinist (Reformed)
- Church of England
- Roman Catholic
- Eastern Orthodox
- Muslim
- → Spread of Calvinism, from 1541
- ▲ Huguenot center
- — Ottoman Empire, 1566

0 150 300 miles
0 150 300 kilometers

Penetration of Calvinism to England after 1558

Wittenburg
Martin Luther writes
Ninety-five Theses
1517

Worms
Edict of Worms
1521

Nantes
Edict of Nantes
1598

Trent
Council of Trent
1545–1563

Augsburg
Peace of Augsburg
1555

Geneva
Calvin assists in
Reformation beginning
in 1541

Mapping the Past

Map 14.2 Religious Divisions in Europe, ca. 1555 The Reformations shattered the religious unity of Western Christendom. The situation was even more complicated than a map of this scale can show. Many cities within the Holy Roman Empire, for example, accepted a different faith than the surrounding countryside; Augsburg, Basel, and Strasbourg were all Protestant, though surrounded by territory ruled by Catholic nobles.

ANALYZING THE MAP Which countries were the most religiously diverse in Europe? Which were the least diverse?

CONNECTIONS Where was the first arena of religious conflict in sixteenth-century Europe, and why did it develop there and not elsewhere? To what degree can nonreligious factors be used as an explanation for the religious divisions in sixteenth-century Europe?

To complete this activity online, go to the Online Study Guide at bedfordstmartins.com/mckaywest.

decorum and piety, in contrast to Renaissance popes who concentrated on building churches and enhancing the power of their own families. Paul III and his successors supported improvements in education for the

clergy, the end of simony (the selling of church offices), and stricter control of clerical life.

In 1542 Pope Paul III established the Supreme Sacred Congregation of the Roman and Universal Inquisition, often called the **Holy Office**, with jurisdiction over the Roman Inquisition, a powerful instrument of the Catholic Reformation. The Roman Inquisition was a committee of six cardinals with judicial authority over all Catholics and the power to arrest, imprison, and execute suspected heretics. The Holy Office published the *Index of Prohibited Books*, a catalogue of forbidden reading that included works by Christian humanists such as Erasmus as well as by Protestants. Within the Papal States, the Inquisition effectively destroyed heresy, but outside the papal territories, its influence was slight.

Holy Office The official Roman Catholic agency founded in 1542 to combat international doctrinal heresy.

Pope Paul III also called a general council, which met intermittently from 1545 to 1563 at Trent, an imperial city close to Italy. It was called not only to reform the Catholic Church but also to secure reconciliation with the Protestants. Lutherans and Calvinists were invited to participate, but their insistence that the Scriptures be the sole basis for discussion made reconciliation impossible. In addition, the political objectives of Charles V and France both worked against reconciliation: Charles wanted to avoid alienating the Lutheran nobility in the empire, and France wanted the Catholics and Lutherans to remain divided in order to keep Germany decentralized and weak.

Nonetheless, the decrees of the Council of Trent laid a solid basis for the spiritual renewal of the Catholic Church. It gave equal validity to the Scriptures and to tradition as sources of religious truth and authority. It reaffirmed the seven sacraments and the traditional Catholic teaching on transubstantiation. It tackled the disciplinary matters that had disillusioned the faithful, requiring bishops to reside in their own dioceses, suppressing pluralism and simony, and forbidding the sale of indulgences. Clerics who kept concubines were to give them up, and bishops were given greater authority. In a highly original decree, the council required every diocese to establish a seminary for the education and training of the clergy. Seminary professors were to determine whether candidates for ordination had vocations,

Church of the Gesù Begun in 1568 as the mother church for the Jesuit order, the Church of the Gesù conveyed a sense of drama, motion, and power through its lavish decorations and shimmering frescoes. Gesù served as a model for Catholic churches elsewhere in Europe and the New World, their triumphant and elaborate style reflecting the dynamic and proselytizing spirit of the Catholic Reformation. (The Art Archive/Corbis)

Rosary Beads Rosaries were loops of beads designed to help Catholics count a set sequence of prayers that became more common during the Catholic Reformation. Rosaries with fancier beads, such as the one shown here, were often worn around the neck or looped through the belt, serving as a fashion item as well as a devotional aid. (Image © Cleveland Museum of Art, acc. # 1952.277)

genuine callings to the priesthood. This was a novel idea, since from the time of the early church, parents had determined their sons' (and daughters') religious careers. For the first time, great emphasis was laid on preaching and instructing the laity, especially the uneducated.

One decision had especially important social consequences for laypeople. The Council of Trent stipulated that for a marriage to be valid, the marriage vows had to be made publicly before a priest and witnesses. Trent thereby ended the widespread practice of private marriages in Catholic countries, curtailing the number of denials and conflicts that inevitably resulted from marriages that took place in secret.

Although it did not achieve all of its goals, the Council of Trent composed decrees that laid a solid basis for the spiritual renewal of the church. The doctrinal and disciplinary legislation of Trent served as the basis for Roman Catholic faith, organization, and practice through the middle of the twentieth century.

New Religious Orders

The establishment of new religious orders within the church reveals a central feature of the Catholic Reformation. Most of these new orders developed in response to one crying need: to raise the moral and intellectual level of the clergy and people. (See "Individuals in Society: Teresa of Ávila," page 432.) Education was a major goal of the two most famous orders.

The Ursuline order of nuns, founded by Angela Merici (1474–1540), attained enormous prestige for the education of women. The daughter of a country gentleman, Angela Merici worked for many years among the poor, sick, and uneducated around her native Brescia in northern Italy. In 1535 she established the first women's religious order concentrating exclusively on teaching young girls, with the goal of re-Christianizing society by training future wives and mothers. After receiving papal approval in 1565, the Ursulines rapidly spread to France and the New World.

The Society of Jesus, or **Jesuits**, founded by Ignatius Loyola (1491–1556) played a powerful international role in strengthening Catholicism in Europe and spreading the faith around the world.

While recuperating from a severe battle wound in his legs, Loyola studied books about Christ and the saints and decided to give up his military career and become a soldier of Christ. During a year spent in seclusion, prayer, and asceticism, he gained insights that went into his great classic, *Spiritual Exercises* (1548). This work, intended for study during a four-week period of retreat, set out a training program of structured meditation designed to develop spiritual discipline and allow one to meld one's will with that of God. Loyola introduces his program by noting:

> **Jesuits** Members of the Society of Jesus, founded by Ignatius Loyola, whose goal was the spread of the Roman Catholic faith.

> By the term "Spiritual Exercises" is meant every method of examination of conscience, of meditation, of contemplation, of vocal and mental prayer, and of other spiritual activities. For just as taking a walk, journeying on foot, and running are bodily exercises, so we call Spiritual Exercises every way of preparing and disposing the soul to rid itself of all inordinate attachments, and, after their removal, of seeking and finding the will of God in the disposition of our life for the salvation of our soul.[9]

Just as do today's physical trainers, Loyola provides daily exercises that build in intensity over the four weeks of the program, and charts on which the exerciser can track his progress.

Loyola was a man of considerable personal magnetism. After study at universities in Salamanca and Paris, he gathered a group of six companions and in 1540 secured papal approval of the new Society of Jesus. The first Jesuits, recruited primarily from wealthy merchant

Teresa of Ávila

INDIVIDUALS IN SOCIETY

HER FAMILY DERIVED FROM TOLEDO, center of the Moorish, Jewish, and Christian cultures in medieval Spain. Her grandfather, Juan Sanchez, made a fortune in the cloth trade. A New Christian (a convert from Judaism or Islam), he was accused of secretly practicing Judaism. He endured the humiliation of a public repentance and moved his family south to Ávila. Beginning again, he recouped his wealth and, perhaps hoping to hide his

status as a convert, bought noble status. Juan's son Alzonzo Sanchez de Cepeda married a woman of thoroughly Christian background, giving his family an aura of impeccable orthodoxy. The third of their nine children, Teresa, became a saint and in 1970 was the first woman declared a Doctor of the Church, a title given to a theologian of outstanding merit.

At age twenty, inspired more by the fear of Hell than the love of God, Teresa (1515–1582) entered the Carmelite Convent of the Incarnation in Ávila. Most of the nuns were daughters of Ávila's leading citizens; they had entered the convent because of family decisions about which daughters would marry and which would become nuns. Their lives were much like those of female family members outside the convent walls, with good food, comfortable surroundings, and frequent visits from family and friends. Teresa was frequently ill, but she lived quietly in the convent for many years. In her late thirties, she began to read devotional literature intensely and had profound mystical experiences — visions and voices in which Christ chastised her for her frivolous life and friends. She described one such experience in 1560:

> It pleased the Lord that I should see an angel. . . . Short, and very beautiful, his face was so aflame that he appeared to be one of the highest types of angels. . . . In his hands I saw a long golden spear and at the end of an iron tip I seemed to see a point of fire. With this he seemed to pierce my heart several times so that it penetrated to my entrails. When he drew it out . . . he left me completely afire with the great love of God.*

Teresa responded with a new sense of purpose and resolved to found a reformed house. Four basic principles guided the new convent. First, poverty was to be fully observed, symbolized by the nuns' being barefoot, with charity and the nuns' own work supporting the community. Second, the convent must keep strict enclosure, with no visitors allowed, even if they were the convent's wealthy supporters. Third, the convent was to have an egalitarian atmosphere in which class distinctions were forbidden and all sisters, including those of aristocratic background, shared the manual chores. The discriminatory measures common in Spanish society that applied to New Christians were also not to be prac-

ticed. Fourth, like Ignatius Loyola and the Jesuits, Teresa placed great emphasis on obedience, especially to one's confessor.

Between 1562 and Teresa's death in 1582, she founded or reformed fourteen other houses of nuns, traveling widely to do so. Teresa thought of the new religious houses she founded as answers to the Protestant takeover of Catholic churches elsewhere in Europe. From her brother, who had obtained wealth in the Spanish colonies, she learned about conditions in Peru and instructed her nuns "to pray unceasingly for the missionaries working among the heathens." Through prayer, Teresa wrote, her nuns could share in the exciting tasks of evangelization and missionary work otherwise closed to women. Her books, along with her five hundred surviving letters, show her as a practical and down-to-earth woman as well as a mystic and a creative theologian.

Seventeenth-century cloisonné enamelwork illustrating Teresa of Ávila's famous vision of an angel piercing her heart. (By gracious permission of Catherine Hamilton Kappauf)

QUESTIONS FOR ANALYSIS

1. How did convent life in Ávila reflect the values of sixteenth-century society, and how did Teresa's reforms challenge these?

2. How is the life of Teresa of Ávila typical of developments in the Catholic Reformation? How is her life unusual?

*The Autobiography of St. Teresa of Ávila, trans. and ed. E. A. Peers (New York: Doubleday, 1960), pp. 273–274.

and professional families, saw the Reformation as a pastoral problem, its causes and cures related not to doctrinal issues but to people's spiritual condition. Reform of the church, as Luther and Calvin understood that term, played no role in the future the Jesuits planned for themselves. Their goal was "to help souls."

The Society of Jesus developed into a highly centralized, tightly knit organization. In addition to the traditional vows of poverty, chastity, and obedience, professed members vowed special obedience to the pope. Flexibility and the willingness to respond to the needs of time and circumstance formed the Jesuit tradition, which proved attractive to many young men. The Jesuits achieved phenomenal success for the papacy and the reformed Catholic Church, carrying Christianity to India and Japan before 1550 and to Brazil, North America, and the Congo in the seventeenth century. Within Europe the Jesuits brought southern Germany and much of eastern Europe back to Catholicism. Jesuit schools adopted the modern humanist curricula and methods, educating the sons of the nobility as well as the poor. As confessors and spiritual directors to kings, Jesuits exerted great political influence.

Religious Violence

What were the causes and consequences of religious violence, including riots, wars, and witch-hunts? ■

In 1559 France and Spain signed the Treaty of Cateau-Cambrésis (CAH-toh kam-BRAY-sees), which ended the long conflict known as the Habsburg-Valois wars. Spain was the victor. France, exhausted by the struggle, had to acknowledge Spanish dominance in Italy, where much of the fighting had taken place. However, true peace was elusive, and over the next century religious differences led to riots, civil wars, and international conflicts. Especially in France and the Netherlands, Protestants and Catholics used violent actions as well as preaching and teaching against each other, for each side regarded the other as a poison in the community that would provoke the wrath of God. Catholics continued to believe that Calvinists and Lutherans could be reconverted; Protestants persisted in thinking that the Roman church should be destroyed. Catholics and Protestants alike feared people of other faiths, whom they often saw as agents of Satan. Even more, they feared those who were explicitly identified with Satan: witches living in their midst. This era was the time of the most virulent witch persecutions in European history, as both Protestants and Catholics tried to make their cities and states more godly.

French Religious Wars

The costs of the Habsburg-Valois wars, waged intermittently through the first half of the sixteenth century, forced the French to increase taxes and borrow heavily. King Francis I (r. 1515–1547) also tried two new devices to raise revenue: the sale of public offices and a treaty with the papacy. The former proved to be only a temporary source of money: once a man bought an office he and his heirs were exempt from taxation. But the latter, known as the Concordat of Bologna (see page 399), gave the French crown the right to appoint all French bishops and abbots, ensuring a rich supplement of money and offices. Because French rulers possessed control over appointments and had a vested financial interest in Catholicism, they had no need to revolt against Rome.

Significant numbers of those ruled, however, were attracted to the Reformed religion of Calvinism. Initially, Calvinism drew converts from among reform-minded members of the Catholic clergy, industrious city dwellers, and artisan groups. Most French Calvinists (called **Huguenots**) lived in major cities, such as Paris, Lyons, and Rouen. When King Henry II (r. 1547–1559) died in 1559—accidentally shot in the face at a tournament celebrating the Treaty of Cateau-Cambrésis—perhaps one-tenth of the population had become Calvinist.

Huguenots French Calvinists.

The feebleness of the French monarchy was the seed from which the weeds of civil violence sprang. The three weak sons of Henry II who occupied the throne could not provide the necessary leadership, and they were often dominated by their mother, Catherine de' Medici. The French nobility took advantage of this monarchical weakness. Just as German princes in the Holy Roman Empire had adopted Lutheranism as a means of opposition to Emperor Charles V, so French nobles frequently adopted Protestantism as a religious cloak for their independence. Armed clashes between Catholic royalist lords and Calvinist antimonarchical lords occurred in many parts of France. Both Calvinists and Catholics believed that the others' books, services, and ministers polluted the community. Preachers incited violence, and religious ceremonies such as baptisms, marriages, and funerals triggered it.

Calvinist teachings called the power of sacred images into question, and mobs in many cities took down and smashed statues, stained-glass windows, and paintings, viewing this as a way to purify the church. Though it was often inspired by fiery Protestant sermons, this iconoclasm, or destruction of religious images, is an example of ordinary men and women carrying out the Reformation themselves. Catholic mobs responded by defending images, and crowds on both sides killed their opponents, often in gruesome ways.

A savage Catholic attack on Calvinists in Paris on Saint Bartholomew's Day, August 24, 1572, followed the usual pattern. The occasion was the marriage ceremony of the king's sister Margaret of Valois to the Protestant Henry of Navarre, which was intended to help reconcile Catholics and Huguenots. Instead, Huguenot wedding guests in Paris were massacred, and other Protestants were slaughtered by mobs. Religious violence spread to the provinces, where thousands were killed. This Saint Bartholomew's Day massacre led to a civil war that dragged on for fifteen years. Agriculture in many areas was destroyed; commercial life declined severely; and starvation and death haunted the land.

What ultimately saved France was a small group of moderates of both faiths, called **politiques**, who believed that only the restoration of strong monarchy could reverse the trend toward collapse. The politiques also favored accepting the Huguenots as an officially recognized and organized group. The death of Catherine de' Medici, followed by the assassination of King Henry III, paved the way for the accession of Henry of Navarre (the unfortunate bridegroom of the Saint Bartholomew's Day massacre), a politique who became Henry IV (r. 1589–1610).

Henry's willingness to sacrifice religious principles to political necessity saved France. He converted to Catholicism but also issued the **Edict of Nantes** in 1598, which granted liberty of conscience and liberty of public worship to Huguenots in 150 fortified towns. The reign of Henry IV and the Edict of Nantes prepared the way for French absolutism in the seventeenth century by helping restore internal peace in France.

politiques Catholic and Protestant moderates who held that only a strong monarchy could save France from total collapse.

Edict of Nantes A document issued by Henry IV of France in 1598, granting liberty of conscience and of public worship to Calvinists, which helped restore peace in France.

The Netherlands Under Charles V

In the Netherlands, what began as a movement for the reformation of the church developed into a struggle for Dutch independence. Emperor Charles V had inherited the seventeen provinces that compose present-day Belgium and the Netherlands (see page 420). Each was self-governing and enjoyed the right to make its own laws and collect its own taxes. The provinces were united politically only in recognition of a common ruler, the emperor. The cities of the Netherlands made their living by trade and industry.

In the Low Countries as elsewhere, corruption in the Roman church and the critical spirit of the Renaissance provoked pressure for reform, and Lutheran ideas took root. Charles V had grown up in the Netherlands, however, and he was able to limit their impact. But Charles V abdicated in 1556 and transferred power over the Netherlands to his son Philip II, who had grown up in Spain. Protestant ideas spread.

By the 1560s Protestants in the Netherlands were primarily Calvinists. Calvinism's intellectual seriousness, moral gravity, and emphasis on any form of labor well done appealed to urban merchants, financiers, and artisans. Whereas Lutherans taught respect for the powers that be, Calvinism tended to encourage opposition to political authorities who were judged to be ungodly.

Iconoclasm in the Netherlands Calvinist men and women break stained-glass windows, remove statues, and carry off devotional altarpieces. Iconoclasm, or the destruction of religious images, is often described as a "riot," but here the participants seem very purposeful. Calvinist Protestants regarded pictures and statues as sacrilegious and saw removing them as a way to purify the church. (The Fotomas Index/The Bridgeman Art Library)

When Spanish authorities attempted to suppress Calvinist worship and raised taxes in the 1560s, rioting ensued. Calvinists sacked thirty Catholic churches in Antwerp, destroying the religious images in them in a wave of iconoclasm. From Antwerp the destruction spread. Philip II sent twenty thousand Spanish troops under the duke of Alva to pacify the Low Countries. Alva interpreted "pacification" to mean ruthless extermination of religious and political dissidents. On top of the Inquisition, he opened his own tribunal, soon called the "Council of Blood." On March 3, 1568, fifteen hundred men were executed. To Calvinists, all this was clear indication that Spanish rule was ungodly and should be overthrown.

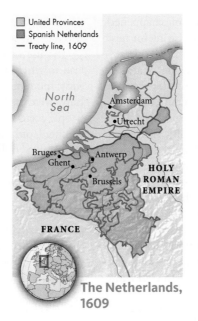

☐ United Provinces
■ Spanish Netherlands
— Treaty line, 1609

North Sea

Amsterdam
•Utrecht

Bruges•
Ghent•   •Antwerp
        •Brussels   HOLY ROMAN EMPIRE

FRANCE

The Netherlands, 1609

Between 1568 and 1578 civil war raged in the Netherlands between Catholics and Protestants and between the seventeen provinces and Spain. Eventually the ten southern provinces, the Spanish Netherlands (the future Belgium), came under the control of the Spanish Habsburg forces. The seven northern provinces, led by Holland, formed the **Union of Utrecht** and in 1581 declared their independence from Spain. The north was Protestant; the south remained Catholic. Philip did not accept this, and war continued. England was even drawn into the conflict, supplying money and troops to the northern United Provinces. (Spain launched an unsuccessful invasion of England in response; see page 425.) Hostilities ended in 1609 when Spain agreed to a truce that recognized the independence of the United Provinces.

The Great European Witch-Hunt

The relationship between the Reformation and the upsurge in trials for witchcraft that occurred at roughly the same time is complex. Increasing persecution for witchcraft actually began before the Reformation in the 1480s, but it became especially common about 1560, and the mania continued until roughly 1660. Religious reformers' extreme notions of the Devil's powers and the insecurity created by the religious wars contributed to this increase. Both Protestants and Catholics tried and executed witches, with church officials and secular authorities acting together.

The heightened sense of God's power and divine wrath in the Reformation era was an important factor in the witch-hunts, but so was a change in the idea of what a witch was. Nearly all premodern societies believe in witchcraft and make some attempts to control witches, who are understood to be people who use magical forces. In the later Middle Ages, however, many educated Christian theologians, canon lawyers, and officials added a demonological component to this notion of what a witch was. For them, the essence of witchcraft was making a pact with the Devil. Witches were no longer simply people who used magical power to get what they wanted, but rather people used by the Devil to do what he wanted. Witches were thought to engage in wild sexual orgies with the Devil, fly through the night to meetings called sabbats that parodied Christian services, and steal communion wafers and unbaptized babies to use in their rituals. Some demonological theorists also claimed that witches were organized in an international conspiracy to overthrow Christianity. Witchcraft was thus spiritualized, and witches became the ultimate heretics, enemies of God.

Trials involving this new notion of witchcraft as diabolical heresy began in Switzerland and southern Germany in the late fifteenth century, became less numerous in the early decades of the Reformation when Protestants and Catholics were busy fighting each other, and then picked up again in about 1560. Scholars estimate that during the sixteenth and seventeenth centuries between 100,000 and 200,000 people were officially tried for witchcraft and between 40,000 and 60,000 were executed.

Union of Utrecht
The alliance of seven northern provinces (led by Holland) that declared its independence from Spain and formed the United Provinces of the Netherlands.

Though the gender balance varied widely in different parts of Europe, between 75 and 85 percent of those tried and executed were women. Ideas about women and the roles women actually played in society were thus important factors shaping the witch-hunts. Some demonologists expressed virulent misogyny, or hatred of women, and particularly emphasized women's powerful sexual desire, which could be satisfied only by a demonic lover. Most people viewed women as weaker and so more likely to give in to an offer by the Devil. In both classical and Christian traditions, women were associated with nature, disorder, and the body, all of which were linked with the demonic. Women's actual lack of power in society and gender norms about the use of violence meant that they were more likely to use scolding and cursing to get what they wanted instead of taking people to court or beating them up. Curses were generally expressed (as they often are today) in religious terms; "go to Hell" was calling on the powers of Satan. Women also had more contact with areas of life in which bad things happened unexpectedly, such as preparing food or caring for new mothers, children, and animals.

Legal changes also played a role in causing, or at least allowing for, massive witch trials. One of these was a change from an accusatorial legal procedure to an inquisitorial procedure. In the former, a suspect knew the accusers and the charges they had brought, and an accuser could in turn be liable for trial if the charges were not proven. In the latter, legal authorities themselves brought the case. This change made people much more willing to accuse others, for they never had to take personal responsibility for the accusation or face the accused person's relatives. Areas in Europe that did not make this legal change saw very few trials. Inquisitorial procedure involved intense questioning of the suspect, often with torture. Torture was also used to get the names of addi-

tional suspects, as most lawyers firmly believed that no witch could act alone.

The use of inquisitorial procedure did not always lead to witch-hunts. The most famous inquisitions in early modern Europe, those in Spain, Portugal, and Italy, were in fact very lenient in their treatment of people accused of witchcraft. The Inquisition in Spain executed only a handful of witches, the Portuguese Inquisition only one, and the Roman Inquisition none, though in each of these there were hundreds of cases. Inquisitors believed in the power of the Devil and were no less misogynist than other judges, but they doubted very much whether the people accused of witchcraft had actually made pacts with the Devil that gave them special powers. They viewed such people not as diabolical Devil-worshipers but as superstitious and ignorant peasants who should be educated

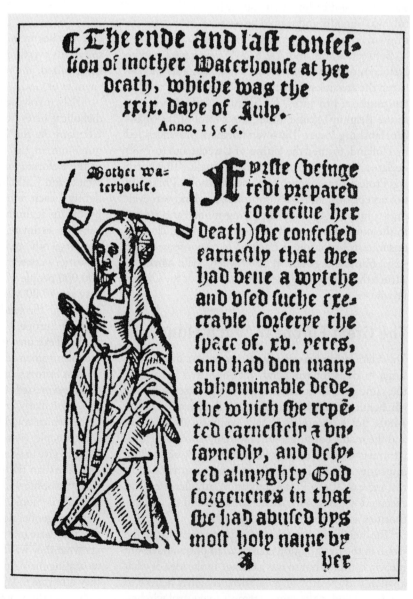

Witch Pamphlet This printed pamphlet presents the confession of "Mother Waterhouse," a woman convicted of witchcraft in England in 1566, who describes her "many abominable deeds" and "execrable sorcery" committed over fifteen years, and asks for forgiveness right before her execution. Enterprising printers often produced cheap, short pamphlets during witch trials, knowing they would sell, sometimes based on the actual trial proceedings and sometimes just made up. They both reflected and helped create stereotypes about what witches were and did. (The Granger Collection, New York)

rather than executed. Thus most people brought up before the Inquisition for witchcraft were sent home with a warning and a penance.

Most witch trials began with a single accusation in a village or town. Individuals accused someone they knew of using magic to spoil food, make children ill, kill animals, raise a hailstorm, or do other types of harm. Tensions within families, households, and neighborhoods often played a role in these accusations. Women number very prominently among accusers and witnesses as well as among those accused of witchcraft because the actions witches were initially charged with, such as harming children or curdling milk, were generally part of women's sphere. A woman also gained economic and social security by conforming to the standard of the good wife and mother and by confronting women who deviated from it.

Once a charge was made, the suspect was brought in for questioning. One German witch pamphlet from 1587 described a typical case:

> Walpurga Hausmännin . . . upon kindly questioning and also torture . . . confessed . . . that the Evil One indulged in fornication with her . . . and made her many promises to help her in her poverty and need. . . . She promised herself body and soul to him and disowned God in heaven. . . . She destroyed a number of cattle, pigs, and geese . . . and dug up [the bodies] of one or two innocent children. With her devil-paramour and other playfellows she has eaten these and used their hair and their little bones for witchcraft.

Confession was generally followed by execution. In this case, Hausmännin was "dispatched from life to death by burning at the stake . . . her body first to be torn five times with red-hot irons."[10]

Detailed records of witch trials survive for many parts of Europe. They have been used by historians to study many aspects of witchcraft, but they cannot directly answer what seems to us an important question: did people really practice witchcraft and think they were witches? They certainly confessed to evil deeds and demonic practices, sometimes without torture, but where would we draw the line between reality and fantasy? Clearly people were not riding through the air on pitchforks, but did they think they did? Did they actually invoke the Devil when they were angry at a neighbor, or was this simply in the minds of their accusers? Trial records cannot tell us, and historians have answered these questions very differently, often using insights from psychoanalysis or the study of more recent victims of torture in their explanations.

After the initial suspect had been questioned, and particularly if he or she had been tortured, the people who had been implicated were brought in for questioning. This might lead to a small hunt, involving from five to ten suspects, and it sometimes grew into a much larger hunt, what historians have called a "witch panic." Panics were most common in the part of Europe that saw the most witch accusations in general: the Holy Roman Empire, Switzerland, and parts of France. Most of this area consisted of very small governmental units that were jealous of each other and, after the Reformation, were divided by religion. The rulers of these small territories often felt more threatened than did the monarchs of western Europe, and they saw persecuting witches as a way to demonstrate their piety and concern for order. Moreover, witch panics often occurred after some type of climatic disaster, such as an unusually cold and wet summer, and they came in waves.

In large-scale panics a wider variety of suspects were taken in—wealthier people, children, a greater proportion of men. Mass panics tended to end when it became clear to legal authorities, or to the community itself, that the people being questioned or executed were not what they understood witches to be, or that the scope of accusations was beyond belief. Some from their community might be in league with Satan, they thought, but not this type of person and not as many people as this.

As the seventeenth century ushered in new ideas about science and reason, many began to question whether witches could make pacts with the Devil or engage in the wild activities attributed to them. Doubts about whether secret denunciations were valid or torture would ever yield truthful confessions gradually spread among the same type of religious and legal authorities who had so vigorously persecuted witches. Prosecutions for witchcraft became less common and were gradually outlawed. The last official execution for witchcraft in England was in 1682, though the last one in the Holy Roman Empire was not until 1775.

" Walpurga Hausmännin . . . dug up [the bodies] of one or two innocent children. With her devil-paramour and other playfellows she has eaten these and used their hair and their little bones for witchcraft. "

—GERMAN WITCH PAMPHLET

LOOKING BACK LOOKING AHEAD

ALONG WITH THE RENAISSANCE, the Reformation is often seen as a key element in the creation of the "modern" world. This radical change contained many elements of continuity, however. Sixteenth-century reformers looked back to the early Christian church for their inspiration, and many of their reforming ideas had been advocated for centuries. Most Protestant reformers worked with political leaders to make religious changes, just as early church officials had worked with Emperor Constantine and his successors as Christianity became the official religion of the Roman Empire in the fourth century. The spread of Christianity and the spread of Protestantism were accomplished not only by preaching, persuasion, and teaching, but also by force and violence. The Catholic Reformation was carried out by activist popes, a church council, and new religious orders, just as earlier reforms of the church had been.

Just as they linked with earlier developments, the events of the Reformation were also closely connected with what is often seen as the third element in the "modern" world: European exploration and colonization. Only a week after Martin Luther stood in front of Charles V at the Diet of Worms declaring his independence in matters of religion, Ferdinand Magellan, a Portuguese sea captain with Spanish ships, was killed in a group of islands off the coast of Southeast Asia. Charles V had provided the backing for Magellan's voyage, the first to circumnavigate the globe. Magellan viewed the spread of Christianity as one of the purposes of his trip, and later in the sixteenth century institutions created as part of the Catholic Reformation, including the Jesuit order and the Inquisition, would operate in European colonies overseas as well as in Europe itself. The islands where Magellan was killed were later named the Philippines, in honor of Charles's son Philip, who sent the ill-fated Spanish Armada against England. Philip's opponent Queen Elizabeth was similarly honored when English explorers named a huge chunk of territory in North America "Virginia" as a tribute to their "Virgin Queen." The desire for wealth and power was an important motivation in the European voyages and colonial ventures, but so was religious zeal.

CHAPTER REVIEW

■ **What were the central ideas of the reformers, and why were they appealing to different social groups? (p. 408)**

By the early sixteenth century many lay Christians and members of the clergy had grown disillusioned with the church's wealth and certain practices, particularly its sale of indulgences and church offices. People were also critical of the immorality, ignorance, and absenteeism that they perceived among the clergy, and for centuries many individuals and groups had called for reform. Amid this background Luther and other Protestants developed a new understanding of Christian doctrine that emphasized faith, the power of God's grace, and the centrality of the Bible. Protestant ideas were attractive to educated people and urban residents, among whom anticlericalism had become widespread, and the new concepts spread rapidly among many groups through preaching, hymns, and the printing press. Most Protestant reformers worked with rulers to bring about religious change, but more radical thinkers and the German peasants wanted political and social, as well as religious, changes. Both radicals and the peasants were put down harshly. The Protestant reformers did not break with medieval ideas about the proper gender hierarchy, though they did elevate the status of marriage and viewed orderly households as the key building blocks of society.

■ **How did the political situation in Germany shape the course of the Reformation? (p. 419)**

Beginning in 1519 the Habsburg emperor Charles V ruled almost half of Europe along with Spain's overseas colonies. Within the empire his authority was limited, however, and local princes, nobles, and cities actually held most power. This decentralization allowed the Reformation to spread as local rulers assumed religious authority. Charles remained firmly Catholic, and in the late 1520s religious wars began in central Europe. The papacy and Catholic kings of France initially supported Charles V's cause, but they withdrew support when he began gaining too much ground. The wars were brought to an end with the Peace of Augsburg in 1555, which officially recognized Lutheranism and allowed rulers in each territory to choose whether their territory would be Catholic or Lutheran.

■ How did Protestant ideas and institutions spread beyond German-speaking lands? (p. 422)

Outside of Germany, Protestantism spread first to Scandinavia and then elsewhere in northern Europe. In England, Henry VIII's desire for an annulment triggered the split with Rome, and a Protestant church was established, first differing little from Catholicism in terms of theology and later, under Queen Elizabeth, breaking more firmly with Catholic practice. The printing press and increased literacy of European society, as well as the growing number of universities, allowed Protestant ideas to spread rapidly into France and eastern Europe. In all these areas, a second generation of reformers built on Lutheran and Zwinglian ideas to develop their own theology and plans for institutional change. The most important of the second-generation reformers was John Calvin, whose ideas would come to shape Christianity over a much wider area than did Luther's.

■ How did the Catholic Church respond to the new religious situation? (p. 428)

By the 1530s the papacy was leading a movement for reform within the church and countering Protestant challenges. Catholic doctrine was reaffirmed at the Council of Trent, and reform measures such as the opening of seminaries for priests, the insistence on morality for the clergy, and a ban on holding multiple church offices were introduced. New religious orders such as the Jesuits and the Ursulines spread Catholic ideas through teaching, and in the case of the Jesuits through missionary work.

■ What were the causes and consequences of religious violence, including riots, wars, and witch-hunts? (p. 433)

Religious differences led to riots, civil wars, and international conflicts in the later sixteenth century. In France and the Netherlands, Calvinist Protestants and Catholics used violent actions against one another, and religious differences mixed with political and economic grievances. Long civil wars resulted, with that in the Netherlands becoming an international conflict. War ended in France with the Edict of Nantes in which Protestants were given some civil rights, and in the Netherlands with a division of the country into a Protestant north and Catholic south. The era of religious wars was also a time of the most extensive witch persecutions in European history, as both Protestants and Catholics tried to rid their cities and states of people they regarded as linked to the Devil.

Suggested Reading

Bossy, John. *Christianity in the West, 1500–1700.* 1985. A lively brief overview.

Gordon, Bruce. *John Calvin.* 2009. Situates Calvin's theology and life within the context of his relationships and the historical events of his time.

Haigh, Christopher. *English Reformations: Religion, Politics, and Society under the Tudors.* 1998. Explores the religious views and practices of ordinary English people as well as of the political elite.

Hendrix, Scott. *Luther.* 2009. A brief introduction to his thought, in the Abingdon Pillars of Theology series.

Holt, Mack P. *The French Wars of Religion, 1562–1629.* 1995. A thorough survey designed for students.

Hsia, R. Po-Chia. *The World of Catholic Renewal, 1540–1770.* 1998. Situates the Catholic Reformation in a global context and provides coverage of colonial Catholicism.

Karant-Nunn, Susan C., and Merry E. Wiesner-Hanks, eds. and trans. *Luther on Women: A Sourcebook.* 2003. An extensive collection of Luther's writings on marriage, women, and sexuality.

Levack, Brian. *The Witchhunt in Early Modern Europe*, 3d ed. 2007. A good introduction to the witch-hunts, with helpful bibliographies of the vast literature on witchcraft.

Levi, Anthony. *Renaissance and Reformation: The Intellectual Genesis.* 2002. Surveys the ideas of major Reformation figures against the background of important political issues.

Lindbergh, Carter. *The European Reformations.* 1996. A thorough discussion of the Protestant Reformation and some discussion of Catholic issues.

Monter, William E. *Calvin's Geneva.* 1967. Shows the effect of Calvin's reforms on the social life of the Swiss city.

O'Malley, John W. *Trent and All That: Renaming Catholicism in the Early Modern Era.* 2000. Provides an excellent historiographical review of the literature, and explains why and how early modern Catholicism influenced early modern European history.

Roper, Lyndal. *The Holy Household: Women and Morals in Reformation Augsburg.* 1991. An important study in local religious history as well as the history of gender and the family.

Shagan, Ethan. *Popular Politics and the English Reformation.* 2003. Analyzes the process of the Reformation in local areas.

Wheatcroft, Andrew. *The Habsburgs: Embodying Empire.* 1995. A solid study of political developments surrounding the Reformation.

Key Terms

anticlericalism (p. 408)
pluralism (p. 408)
indulgence (p. 409)
Protestant (p. 412)
Spanish Armada (p. 425)
The Institutes of the Christian Religion (p. 425)
predestination (p. 426)
Holy Office (p. 430)
Jesuits (p. 431)
Huguenots (p. 433)
politiques (p. 434)
Edict of Nantes (p. 434)
Union of Utrecht (p. 435)

Notes

1. Quoted in Owen Chadwick, *The Reformation* (Baltimore: Penguin Books, 1976), p. 55.
2. Quoted in E. H. Harbison, *The Age of Reformation* (Ithaca, N.Y.: Cornell University Press, 1963), p. 52.
3. Quoted in S. E. Ozment, *The Age of Reform, 1250–1550: An Intellectual and Religious History of Late Medieval and Reformation Europe* (New Haven, Conn.: Yale University Press, 1980), p. 284.
4. Ludwig Rabus, *Historien der heyligen Außerwolten Gottes Zeugen, Bekennern und Martyrern* (n.p., 1557), fol. 41. Trans. Merry Wiesner-Hanks.

5. From Henry Bettenson, ed., *Documents of the Christian Church*, 2d ed. (London: Oxford University Press, 1963), pp. 301–302.
6. J. Allen, trans., *John Calvin: The Institutes of the Christian Religion* (Philadelphia: Westminster Press, 1930), bk. 3, chap. 21, para. 5, 7.
7. Quoted in E. William Monter, *Calvin's Geneva* (New York: John Wiley & Sons, 1967), p. 137.
8. Quoted in David P. Daniel, "Hungary," in *The Oxford Encyclopedia of the Reformation*, vol. 2, ed. H. J. Hillerbrand (New York: Oxford University Press, 1996), p. 273.
9. *The Spiritual Exercise of St. Ignatius of Loyola*, trans. Louis J. Puhl, S.J. (Chicago: Loyola University, 1951), p. 1.
10. From *the Fugger News-Letters*, ed. Victor von Klarwell, trans. P. de Chary (London: John Lane, The Boley Head Ltd., 1924), quoted in James Bruce Ross and Mary Martin McLaughlin, *The Portable Renaissance Reader* (New York: Penguin, 1968), pp. 258, 260, 262.

For practice quizzes and other study tools, visit the Online Study Guide at **bedfordstmartins.com/mckaywest**.

For primary sources from this period, see *Sources of Western Society*, **Second Edition**.

For Web sites, images, and documents related to topics in this chapter, visit Make History at **bedfordstmartins.com/mckaywest**.

15

European Exploration and Conquest

1450–1650

National Gallery, London/Art Resource, NY

Before 1450 Europeans were relatively marginal players in a centuries-old trading system that linked Africa, Asia, and Europe. Elites everywhere prized Chinese porcelains and silks, while wealthy members of the Celestial Kingdom, as China called itself, wanted ivory and black slaves from Africa, and exotic goods and peacocks from India. African people wanted textiles from India and cowrie shells from the Maldives in the Indian Ocean. Europeans craved Asian silks and spices but they had few desirable goods to offer their trading partners.

The European search for better access to Asian trade led to a new overseas empire in the Indian Ocean and the accidental discovery of the Western Hemisphere. Within a few decades European colonies in South and North America would join this worldwide web. Europeans came to dominate trading networks and political empires of truly global proportions. The era of globalization had begun.

Global contacts created new forms of cultural exchange, assimilation, conversion, and resistance. Europeans struggled to comprehend the peoples and societies they found and sought to impose European cultural values on them. New forms of racial prejudice emerged, but so did new openness and curiosity about different ways of life. Together with the developments of the Renaissance and the Reformation, the Age of Discovery — as the period of European exploration and conquest from 1450 to 1650 is known — laid the foundations for the modern world. ■

Life in the Age of Discovery. A detail from an early-seventeenth-century Flemish painting depicting maps, illustrated travel books, a globe, a compass, and an astrolabe. The voyages of discovery revolutionized Europeans' sense of space and inspired a passion among the wealthy for collecting objects related to navigation and travel.

CHAPTER PREVIEW

World Contacts Before Columbus

What was the Afro-Eurasian trading world before Columbus? ■

Columbus did not sail west on a whim. To understand his and other Europeans' explorations, we must first understand late medieval trade networks. Historians now recognize that a type of world economy, known as the Afro-Eurasian trade world, linked the products and people of Europe, Asia, and Africa in the fifteenth century. The West was not the dominant player before Columbus, and the European voyages derived from a desire to share in and control the wealth coming from the Indian Ocean.

The Trade World of the Indian Ocean

The Indian Ocean was the center of the Afro-Eurasian trade world. Its location made it a crossroads for commercial and cultural exchange between China, India, the Middle East, Africa, and Europe (Map 15.1). From

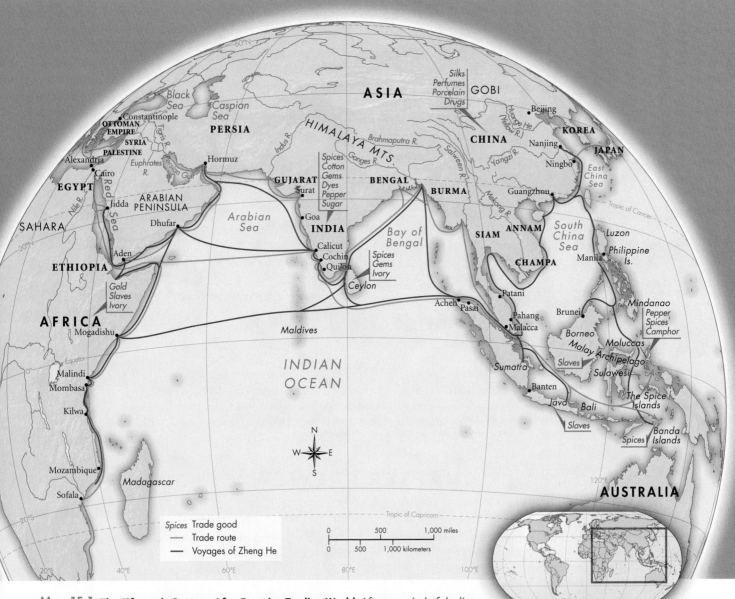

Map 15.1 The Fifteenth-Century Afro-Eurasian Trading World After a period of decline following the Black Death and the Mongol invasions, trade revived in the fifteenth century. Muslim merchants dominated trade, linking ports in East Africa and the Red Sea with those in India and the Malay Archipelago. Chinese Admiral Zheng He's voyages (1405–1433) followed the most important Indian Ocean trade routes, in the hope of imposing Ming dominance of trade and tribute.

the seventh through the fourteenth centuries, the volume of this trade steadily increased, declining only during the years of the Black Death.

Merchants congregated in a series of multicultural, cosmopolitan port cities strung around the Indian Ocean. Most of these cities had some form of autonomous self-government. Mutual self-interest had largely limited violence and attempts to monopolize trade. The most developed area of this commercial web was in the South China Sea. In the fifteenth century the port of Malacca (muh-LAH-kuh) became a great commercial entrepôt (AHN-truh-poh), a trading post to which goods were shipped for storage while awaiting redistribution to other places. To Malacca came Chinese porcelains, silks, and camphor (used in the manufacture of many medications); pepper, cloves, nutmeg, and raw materials such as sandalwood from the Moluccas; sugar from the Philippines; and Indian textiles, copper weapons, incense, dyes, and opium.

The Mongol emperors opened the doors of China to the West, encouraging Europeans like the Venetian trader and explorer Marco Polo to do business there. Marco Polo's tales of his travels from 1271 to 1295 and his encounter with the Great Khan fueled Western fantasies about the exotic Orient. After the Mongols fell to the Ming Dynasty in 1368, China entered a period of agricultural and commercial expansion, population growth, and urbanization. By the end of the dynasty in 1644, the Chinese population had tripled to between 150 million and 200 million. The city of Nanjing had one million inhabitants, making it the largest city in the world, while the new capital, Beijing, had more than six thousand inhabitants, larger than any European city. Historians agree that China had the most advanced economy in the world until at least the start of the eighteenth century.

China also took the lead in exploration, sending Admiral Zheng He's fleet along the trade web as far west as Egypt. From 1405 to 1433, each of his seven expeditions involved hundreds of ships and tens of thousands of men. In one voyage alone, Zheng He sailed more than 12,000 miles, compared to Columbus's 2,400 miles on his first voyage some sixty years later.[1] Court conflicts and the need to defend against renewed Mongol encroachment led to the abandonment of the expeditions after the deaths of Zheng He and the emperor. China's turning away from external trade opened new opportunities for European states to claim a decisive role in world trade.

Another center of trade in the Indian Ocean was India, the crucial link between the Persian Gulf and the Southeast Asian and East Asian trade networks. The

1443	Portuguese establish first African trading post at Arguin
1492	Columbus lands in the Americas
1511	Portuguese capture Malacca from Muslims
1518	Spanish king authorizes slave trade to New World colonies
1519–1522	Magellan's expedition circumnavigates the world
1521	Cortés conquers the Mexica Empire
1533	Pizarro conquers the Inca Empire
1602	Dutch East India Company established

subcontinent had ancient links with its neighbors to the northwest: trade between South Asia and Mesopotamia dates back to the origins of human civilization. Romans had acquired cotton textiles, exotic animals, and other luxury goods from India. Arab merchants who circumnavigated India on their way to trade in the South China Sea established trading posts along the southern coast of India, where the cities of Calicut and Quilon became thriving commercial centers. India was an important contributor of goods to the world trading system; much of the world's pepper was grown there, and Indian cotton textiles were highly prized.

The Trading States of Africa

Africa also played an important role in the world trade system before Columbus. By 1450 Africa had a few large and developed empires along with hundreds of smaller states. From 1250 until its defeat by the Ottomans in 1517, the Mamluk Egyptian empire was one of the most powerful on the continent. Its capital, Cairo, was a center of Islamic learning and religious authority as well as a hub for Indian Ocean trade goods. Sharing in Cairo's prosperity was the African highland state of Ethiopia, a Christian kingdom with scattered contacts with European rulers. On the east coast of Africa Swahili-speaking city-states engaged in the Indian Ocean trade, exchanging ivory, rhinoceros horn, tortoise shells, and slaves for textiles, spices, cowrie shells, porcelain, and other goods. Peopled by confident and urbane merchants, cities like Mogadishu and Mombasa were known for their prosperity and culture.

Another important African contribution to world trade was gold. In the fifteenth century most of the gold that reached Europe came from Sudan in West Africa and from the Akan (AH-kahn) peoples living near present-day Ghana (GAH-nuh). Transported across the Sahara by Arab and African traders on camels, the gold was sold in the ports of North Africa. Other trading routes led to the Egyptian cities of Alexandria and Cairo, where the Venetians held commercial privileges.

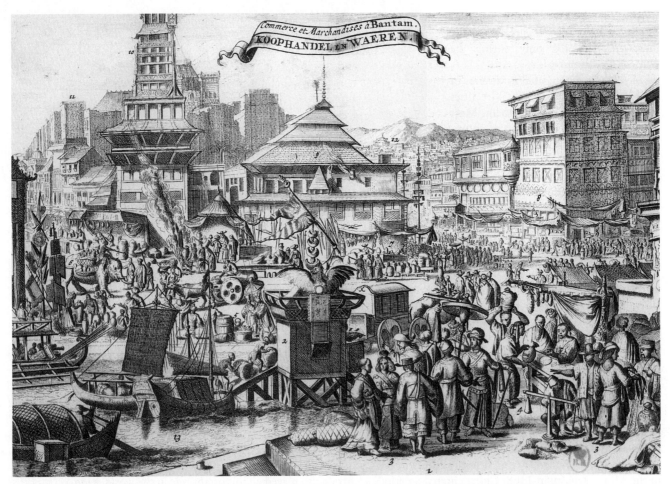

The Port of Banten in Western Java Influenced by Muslim traders and emerging in the early sixteenth century as a Muslim kingdom, Banten evolved into a thriving entrepôt. The city stood on the trade route to China and, as this Dutch engraving suggests, in the seventeenth century the Dutch East India Company used Banten as an important collection point for spices purchased for sale in Europe. (Archives Charmet/The Bridgeman Art Library)

Nations inland that sat astride the north-south caravan routes grew wealthy from this trade. In the mid-thirteenth century the kingdom of Mali emerged as an important player on the overland trade route. Malian ruler Mansa Musa reportedly discussed sending vessels to explore the Atlantic Ocean, which suggests that not only the Europeans envisaged westward naval exploration. In later centuries the diversion of gold away from the trans-Sahara routes would weaken the inland states of Africa politically and economically.

Gold was one important object of trade; slaves were another. Slavery was practiced in Africa, as virtually everywhere else in the world, before the arrival of Europeans. Arabic and African merchants took West African slaves to the Mediterranean to be sold in European, Egyptian, and Middle Eastern markets and also brought eastern Europeans—a major element of European slavery—to West Africa as slaves. In addition, Indian and Arabic merchants traded slaves in the coastal regions of East Africa.

Legends about Africa also played an important role

in Europeans' imagination of the outside world. They long cherished the belief in a Christian nation in Africa ruled by a mythical king, Prester John, who was believed to be a descendant of one of the three kings who visited Jesus after his birth.

The Ottoman and Persian Empires

The Middle East served as an intermediary for trade between Europe, Africa, and Asia and was also an important supplier of goods for foreign exchange, especially silk and cotton. Two great rival empires, the Persian Safavids (sah-FAH-vidz) and the Turkish Ottomans, dominated the region. Persian merchants could be found in trading communities as far away as the Indian Ocean. Persia was also a major producer and exporter of silk.

The Persians' Shi'ite Muslim faith clashed with the Ottomans' adherence to Sunnism. Economically, the two competed for control over western trade routes to the East. Under Sultan Mohammed II (r. 1451–1481), the Ottomans captured Europe's largest city, Constantinople, in May 1453. Renamed Istanbul, the city became the capital of the Ottoman Empire. By the mid-sixteenth century the Ottomans controlled the sea trade in the eastern Mediterranean, Syria, Palestine, Egypt, and the rest of North Africa, and their power extended into Europe as far west as Vienna.

Ottoman expansion frightened Europeans. The Ottoman armies seemed nearly invincible and the empire's desire for expansion limitless. In France in the sixteenth century, twice as many books were printed about the Turkish threat as about the American discoveries. The strength of the Ottomans helps explain some of the missionary fervor Christians brought to new territories. It also raised economic concerns. With trade routes to the east in the hands of the Ottomans, Europeans needed to find new trade routes.

Genoese and Venetian Middlemen

Compared to the riches and vibrancy of the East, Europe constituted a minor outpost in the world trading system. European craftsmen produced few products to rival the fine wares and expensive spices of Asia. In the late Middle Ages, the Italian city-states of Venice and Genoa controlled the European luxury trade with the East.

In 1304 Venice established formal relations with the sultan of Mamluk Egypt, opening operations in Cairo, the gateway to Asian trade. Venetian merchants specialized in expensive luxury goods like spices, silks, and carpets, which they obtained from middlemen in the eastern Mediterranean and Asia Minor. A little went a long way. Venetians purchased no more than five hundred tons of spices a year around 1400, but with a profit of about 40 percent. The most important spice was pepper, grown in India and Indonesia, which composed 60 percent of the spices they purchased in 1400.[2]

The Venetians exchanged Eastern luxury goods for European products they could trade abroad, including Spanish and English wool, German metal goods, Flemish textiles, and silk cloth made in their own manufactures with imported raw materials. Eastern demand for such goods was low. To make up the difference, the Venetians earned currency in the shipping industry and through trade in firearms and slaves. At least half of what they traded with the East took the form of precious metal, much of it acquired in Egypt and North Africa. When the Portuguese arrived in Asia in the late fifteenth century, they found Venetian coins everywhere.

Venice's ancient rival was Genoa. In the wake of the Crusades, Genoa dominated the northern route to Asia through the Black Sea. Expansion in the thirteenth and fourteenth centuries took the Genoese as far as Persia and the Far East. In 1291 they sponsored an expedition into the Atlantic in search of India. The ships were lost,

The Taking of Constantinople by the Turks, April 22, 1453 The Ottoman conquest of the capital of the Byzantine Empire in 1453 sent shock and despair through Europe. Capitalizing on the city's strategic and commercial importance, the Ottomans made it the center of their empire. (Bibliothèque nationale de France)

and their exact destination and motivations remain unknown. This voyage reveals the long roots of Genoese interest in Atlantic exploration.

In the fifteenth century, with Venice claiming victory in the spice trade, the Genoese shifted focus from trade to finance and from the Black Sea to the western Mediterranean. Located on the northwestern coast of Italy, Genoa had always been active in the western Mediterranean, trading with North African ports, southern France, Spain, and even England and Flanders through the Strait of Gibraltar. When Spanish and Portuguese voyages began to expore the western Atlantic (see pages 451–456), Genoese merchants, navigators, and financiers provided their skills to the Iberian monarchs, whose own subjects had much less commercial experience. The Genoese, for example, ran many of the sugar plantations established on the Atlantic islands colonized by the Portuguese. Genoese merchants would eventually help finance Spanish colonization of the New World in return for a share in the profits.

A major element of both Venetian and Genoese trade was slavery. Merchants purchased slaves, many of whom were fellow Christians, in the Balkans. The men were sold to Egypt for the sultan's army or sent to work as agricultural laborers in the Mediterranean. Young girls, who made up the majority of the trade, were sold in western Mediterranean ports as servants or concubines. After the loss of the Black Sea—and thus the source of slaves—to the Ottomans, the Genoese sought new supplies of slaves in the West, taking the Guanches (indigenous peoples from the Canary Islands), Muslim prisoners and Jewish refugees from Spain, and by the early 1500s both black and Berber Africans. With the growth of Spanish colonies in the New World, Genoese and Venetian merchants would become important players in the Atlantic slave trade.

Italian experience in colonial administration, slaving, and international trade and finance served as a model for the Iberian states as they pushed European expansion to new heights. Mariners, merchants, and financiers from Venice and Genoa—most notably Christopher Columbus—played a crucial role in bringing the fruits of this experience to the Iberian Peninsula and to the New World.

The European Voyages of Discovery

How and why did Europeans undertake ambitious voyages of expansion? ■

As we have seen, Europe was by no means isolated before the voyages of exploration and its "discovery" of the New World. But because they did not produce many products desired by Eastern elites, Europeans were modest players in the Indian Ocean trading world. As Europe recovered after the Black Death, new European players entered the scene with new technology, eager to spread Christianity and to undo Italian and Ottoman domination of trade with the East. A century after the plague, Iberian explorers began the overseas voyages that helped create the modern world, with staggering consequences for their own continent and the rest of the planet.

Causes of European Expansion

European expansion had multiple causes. By the middle of the fifteenth century, Europe was experiencing a revival of population and economic activity after the lows of the Black Death. This revival created demands for luxury goods, especially spices, from the East. The fall of Constantinople and subsequent Ottoman control of trade routes created obstacles to fulfilling these demands. Europeans needed to find new sources of precious metal to trade with the Ottomans or trade routes that bypassed the Ottomans.

Why were spices so desirable? Introduced into western Europe by the Crusaders in the twelfth century, pepper, nutmeg, ginger, mace, cinnamon, and cloves added flavor and variety to the monotonous European diet. Spices evoked the scent of the Garden of Eden and of divinity itself; they seemed a marvel and a mystery. They were used not only as flavorings for food, but also for anointing oil and incense in religious rituals and as perfumes, medicines, and dyes in daily life. Take, for example, cloves, for which Europeans found many uses. If picked green and sugared, the buds could be transformed into jam; if salted and pickled, cloves became a flavoring for vinegar. Cloves sweetened the breath. When added to food or drink, they were thought to stimulate the appetite and clear the intestines and bladder. When crushed and powdered, they were a medicine rubbed on the forehead to relieve head colds and applied to the eyes to strengthen vision. Taken with milk, they were believed to enhance sexual pleasure.

Religious fervor was another important catalyst for expansion. The passion and energy ignited by the Christian reconquista (reconquest) of the Iberian Peninsula encouraged the Portuguese and Spanish to continue the Christian crusade. Just seven months separated the Spanish conquest of Granada, the last remaining Muslim state on the Iberian Peninsula, and Columbus's departure across the Atlantic. Overseas exploration was in some ways a transfer of religious zeal, enthusiasm for conquest, and certainty of God's blessing to new non-Christian territories. Since the remaining Muslim states, such as the mighty Ottoman Empire, were too strong to defeat, Iberians turned their attention elsewhere.

Combined with eagerness for profits and to spread Christianity was the desire for glory and the urge to chart new waters. Scholars have frequently described the European discoveries as a manifestation of Renaissance curiosity about the physical universe—the desire to know more about the geography and peoples of the world. The detailed journals kept by such voyagers as Christopher Columbus and Antonio Pigafetta (a survivor of Magellan's world circumnavigation) attest to their wonder and fascination with the new peoples and places they visited.

❝ I have come to win gold, not to plow the fields like a peasant. ❞

—HERNANDO CORTÉS

Individual explorers combined these motivations in unique ways. Christopher Columbus was a devout Christian who was increasingly haunted by messianic obsessions in the last years of his life. As Portuguese explorer Bartholomew Diaz put it, his own motives were "to serve God and His Majesty, to give light to those who were in darkness and to grow rich as all men desire to do." When the Portuguese explorer Vasco da Gama reached the port of Calicut, India, in 1498 and a native asked what he wanted, he replied, "Christians and spices."[3] The bluntest of the Spanish **conquistadors** (kahn-KEES-tuh-dorz), Hernando Cortés, announced as he prepared to conquer Mexico, "I have come to win gold, not to plow the fields like a peasant."[4]

Eagerness for exploration was heightened by a lack of opportunity at home. After the reconquista, young men of the Spanish upper classes found their economic and political opportunities greatly limited. The ambitious turned to the sea to seek their fortunes.

Whatever the reasons, the voyages were made possible by the growth of government power. The Spanish monarchy was stronger than before and in a position to support foreign ventures. In Portugal explorers also looked to the monarchy, to Prince Henry the Navigator in particular (page 451), for financial support and encouragement. Like voyagers, monarchs shared a mix of motivations, from the desire to please God to the desire to win glory and profit from trade. Competition among European monarchs was an important factor in encouraging the steady stream of expeditions that began in the late fifteenth century.

Ordinary sailors were ill paid, and life at sea meant danger, overcrowding, unbearable stench, and hunger. For months at a time, 100 to 120 people lived and worked in a space of 1,600 to 2,000 square feet. A lucky sailor would find enough space on deck to unroll his sleeping mat. Horses, cows, pigs, chickens, rats, and lice accompanied them on the voyages. As one scholar concluded, "traveling on a ship must have been one of the most uncomfortable and oppressive experiences in the world."[5]

> **conquistador** Spanish for "conqueror"; Spanish soldier-explorers, such as Hernando Cortés and Francisco Pizarro, who sought to conquer the New World for the Spanish crown.

Men choose to join these miserable crews to escape poverty at home, to continue a family trade, to win a few crumbs of the great riches of empire, or to find better lives as illegal immigrants in the colonies. Many orphans and poor boys were placed on board as young pages and had little say in the decision. Women also paid a price for the voyages of exploration. Left alone for months or years at a time, and frequently widowed, sailors' wives struggled to feed their families. The widow of a sailor lost on Magellan's 1519 voyage had to wait until 1547 to collect her husband's salary from the Spanish crown.[6]

The people who stayed at home had a powerful impact on the process. Royal ministers and factions at court influenced monarchs to provide or deny support for exploration. The small number of people who could read served as a rapt audience for tales

The Travels of Sir John Mandeville The author of this tale claimed to be an English knight who traveled extensively in the Middle East and Asia from the 1320s to the 1350s. Although historians now consider the work a skillful fiction, it had a great influence on how Europeans understood the world at the time. This illustration, from an edition published around 1410, depicts Mandeville approaching a walled city on the first stage of his voyage to Constantinople. (© British Library Board)

caravel A small, maneuverable, three-mast sailing ship developed by the Portuguese in the fifteenth century that gave the Portuguese a distinct advantage in exploration and trade.

Ptolemy's *Geography*
A second-century-c.e. work that synthesized the classical knowledge of geography and introduced the concepts of longitude and latitude. Reintroduced to Europeans in 1410 by Arab scholars, its ideas allowed cartographers to create more accurate maps.

of fantastic places and unknown peoples. Cosmography, natural history, and geography aroused enormous interest among educated people in the fifteenth and sixteenth centuries. One of the most popular books of the time was the fourteenth-century text *The Travels of Sir John Mandeville*, which purported to be a firsthand account of the author's travels in the Holy Land, Egypt, Ethiopia, the Middle East, and India and his service to the Mamluk sultan of Egypt and the Mongol Great Khan of China. Although we now know the stories were fictional, these fantastic tales of cannibals, one-eyed giants, men with the heads of dogs, and other marvels were believed for centuries and constituted the core of many Europeans' knowledge of such places. Christopher Columbus took a copy of Mandeville and the equally popular and more reliable *The Travels of Marco Polo* on his voyage in 1492.

Technology and the Rise of Exploration

Technological developments in shipbuilding, weaponry, and navigation provided another impetus for European expansion. Since ancient times, most seagoing vessels had been narrow, open boats called galleys, propelled largely by slaves or convicts manning the oars. Though well suited to the placid waters of the Mediterranean, galleys could not withstand the rough winds and uncharted shoals of the Atlantic. The need for sturdier craft, as well as population losses caused by the Black Death, forced the development of a new style of ship that would not require much manpower to sail. In the course of the fifteenth century, the Portuguese developed the **caravel**, a small, light, three-mast sailing ship. Though somewhat slower than the galley, the caravel held more cargo. Its triangular lateen sails and sternpost rudder also made the caravel a much more maneuverable vessel. When fitted with cannon, it could dominate larger vessels.

Great strides in cartography and navigational aids were also made during this period. Around 1410 Arab scholars reintroduced Europeans to **Ptolemy's *Geography***. Written in the second century c.e. by a Helle-

Ptolemy's *Geography* The recovery of Ptolemy's *Geography* in the early fifteenth century gave Europeans new access to ancient geographical knowledge. This 1486 world map, based on Ptolemy, is a great advance over medieval maps but contains errors with significant consequences for future exploration. It shows a single continent watered by a single ocean, with land covering three-quarters of the world's surface. Africa and Asia are joined with Europe, making the Indian Ocean a landlocked sea and rendering the circumnavigation of Africa impossible. The continent of Asia is stretched far to the east, greatly shortening the distance from Europe to Asia via the Atlantic. (Giraudon/Art Resource, NY)

nized Egyptian, the work synthesized the geographical knowledge of the classical world. Ptolemy's work provided significant improvements over medieval cartography, showing the world as round and introducing the idea of latitude and longitude to plot position accurately. It also contained crucial errors. Unaware of the Americas, Ptolemy showed the world as much smaller than it is, so that Asia appeared not very distant from Europe to the west. Based on this work, cartographers fashioned new maps that combined classical knowledge with the latest information from mariners. First the Genoese and Venetians, and then the Portuguese and Spanish, took the lead in these advances.

The magnetic compass enabled sailors to determine their direction and position at sea. The astrolabe, an instrument invented by the ancient Greeks and perfected by Muslim navigators, was used to determine the altitude of the sun and other celestial bodies. It permitted mariners to plot their latitude, that is, their precise position north or south of the equator.

Like the astrolabe, much of the new technology that Europeans used on their voyages was borrowed from the East. Gunpowder, the compass, and the sternpost rudder were Chinese inventions. The lateen sail, which allowed European ships to tack against the wind, was a product of the Indian Ocean trade world and was brought to the Mediterranean on Arab ships. Advances in cartography also drew on the rich tradition of Judeo-Arabic mathematical and astronomical learning in Iberia. Sometimes assistance to Europeans came from humans rather than instruments. The famed explorer Vasco da Gama employed a local Indian pilot to guide his expedition from the East African coast to India. In exploring new territories, European sailors thus called on techniques and knowledge developed over centuries in China, the Muslim world, and the Indian Ocean.

The Portuguese Overseas Empire

For centuries Portugal was a small and poor nation on the margins of European life whose principal activities were fishing and subsistence farming. It would have been hard for a European to predict Portugal's phenomenal success overseas after 1450. Yet Portugal had a long history of seafaring and navigation. Blocked from access to western Europe by Spain, the Portuguese turned to the Atlantic and North Africa, whose waters they knew better than did other Europeans. Nature favored the Portuguese: winds blowing along their coast offered passage to Africa, its Atlantic islands, and, ultimately, Brazil.

In the early phases of Portuguese exploration, Prince Henry (1394–1460), a younger son of the king, played a

leading role. A nineteenth-century scholar dubbed Henry "the Navigator" because of his support for the study of geography and navigation and for the annual expeditions he sponsored down the western coast of Africa. Although he never personally participated in voyages of exploration, Henry's involvement ensured that Portugal did not abandon the effort despite early disappointments.

The Portuguese Fleet Embarked for the Indies The image below shows a Portuguese trading fleet in the late fifteenth century bound for the riches of the Indies. Between 1500 and 1635 over nine hundred ships sailed from Portugal to ports on the Indian Ocean, in annual fleets composed of five to ten ships. Portuguese sailors used astrolabes, such as the one pictured at left, to accurately plot their position. (fleet: British Museum/HarperCollins Publishers/The Art Archive; astrolabe: Courtesy of the Trustees of the British Museum)

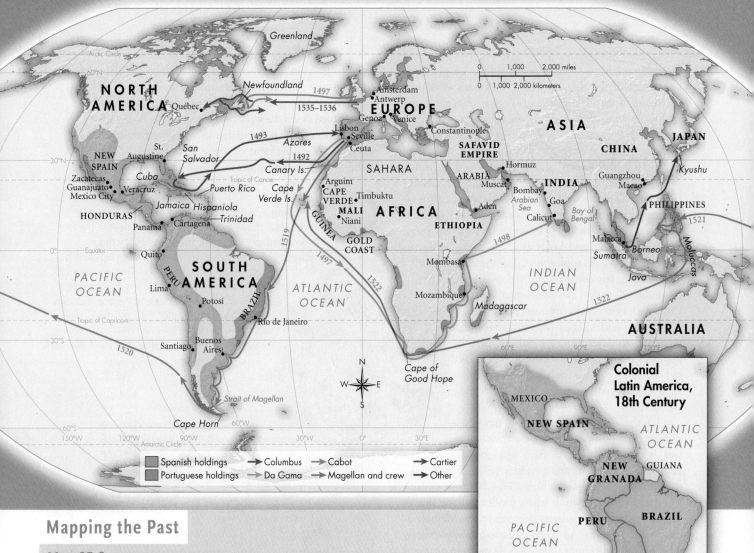

Mapping the Past

Map 15.2 Overseas Exploration and Conquest in the Fifteenth and Sixteenth Centuries The voyages of discovery marked a dramatic new phase in the centuries-old migrations of European peoples. This map depicts the voyages of the most significant European explorers of this period.

ANALYZING THE MAP Consider the routes and dates of the voyages shown. How might have the successes of the earlier voyages contributed to the later expeditions? Which voyage had the most impact and why?

CONNECTIONS Do you think the importance of these voyages was primarily economic, political, or cultural? Why?

To complete this activity online, go to the Online Study Guide at bedfordstmartins.com/mckaywest.

The objectives of Portuguese exploration policy included desires for military glory; crusades to Christianize Muslims and to locate a mythical Christian king of Africa, Prester John; and the quest to find gold, slaves, and an overseas route to the spice markets of India. Portugal's conquest of Ceuta, an Arab city in northern Morocco, in 1415 marked the beginning of European overseas expansion. In the 1420s, under Henry's direction, the Portuguese began to settle the Atlantic islands of Madeira (ca. 1420) and the Azores (1427). In 1443 they founded their first African commercial settlement at Arguin in North Africa. By the time of Henry's death in 1460, his support for exploration was vindicated by thriving sugar

plantations on the Atlantic islands, the first arrival of enslaved Africans in Portugal (see page 465), and new access to African gold.

The Portuguese next established trading posts and forts on the gold-rich Guinea coast and penetrated into the African continent all the way to Timbuktu (Map 15.2). By 1500 Portugal controlled the flow of African gold to Europe. The golden century of Portuguese prosperity had begun.

The Portuguese then pushed farther south down the west coast of Africa. In 1487 Bartholomew Diaz rounded the Cape of Good Hope at the southern tip, but storms and a threatened mutiny forced him to turn back. A decade later Vasco da Gama succeeded in rounding the Cape while commanding a fleet of four ships in search of a sea route to India. With the help of an Indian guide, da Gama reached the port of Calicut in India. Overcoming local hostility, he returned to Lisbon loaded with spices and samples of Indian cloth. He had failed to forge any trading alliances with local powers, and Portuguese arrogance ensured the future hostility of Muslim merchants who dominated the trading system. Nonetheless, de Gama proved the possibility of lucrative trade with the East via the Cape route. Thereafter, a Portuguese convoy set out for passage around the Cape every March.

Lisbon became the entrance port for Asian goods into Europe, but this was not accomplished without a fight. Muslim-controlled port city-states had long controlled the rich spice trade of the Indian Ocean, and they did not surrender it willingly. Portuguese cannon blasted open the port of Malacca in 1511, followed by Calicut, Ormuz, and Goa. The bombardment of these cities laid the foundation for Portuguese imperialism in the sixteenth and seventeenth centuries.

In March 1493, between the voyages of Diaz and da Gama, Spanish ships under a triumphant Genoese mariner named Christopher Columbus (1451–1506), in the service of the Spanish crown, entered Lisbon harbor. Spain also had begun the quest for an empire.

The Problem of Christopher Columbus

Christopher Columbus is a controversial figure in history—glorified by some as the brave discoverer of America, vilified by others as a cruel exploiter of Native Americans. Rather than judging Columbus by debates and standards of our time, it is more important to understand him in the context of his own time. First, what kind of man was Columbus, and what forces or influences shaped him? Second, in sailing westward from Europe, what were his goals? Third, did he achieve his goals, and what did he make of his discoveries?

In his dream of a westward passage to the Indies, Columbus embodied a long-standing Genoese ambition to circumvent Venetian domination of eastward trade, which was now being claimed by the Portuguese. Columbus was very knowledgeable about the sea. He had worked as a mapmaker, and he was familiar with such fifteenth-century Portuguese navigational developments as *portolans*—written descriptions of the courses along which ships sailed—and the use of the compass as a nautical instrument. As he implied in his *Journal*, he had acquired not only theoretical but also practical experience: "I have spent twenty-three years at sea and have not left it for any length of time worth mentioning, and I have seen every thing from east to west [meaning he had been to England] and I have been to Guinea [North and West Africa]."[7] His successful thirty-three-day voyage to the Caribbean owed a great deal to his seamanship.

Columbus was also a deeply religious man. He began the *Journal* of his voyage to the Americas in the form of a letter to Ferdinand and Isabella of Spain:

On 2 January in the year 1492, when your Highnesses had concluded their war with the Moors who reigned in Europe, I saw your Highnesses' banners victoriously raised on the towers of the Alhambra, the citadel of the city, and the Moorish king come out of the city gates and kiss the hands of your Highnesses and the prince, My Lord. And later in that same month, on the grounds of information I had given your Highnesses concerning the lands of India . . . your Highnesses decided to send me, Christopher Columbus, to see these parts of India and the princes and peoples of those lands and consider the best means for their conversion.

Columbus had witnessed the Spanish conquest of Granada and shared fully in the religious and nationalistic fervor surrounding that event. Like the Spanish rulers and most Europeans of his age, he understood Christianity as a missionary religion that should be carried to places where it did not exist. He viewed himself as a divine agent: "God made me the messenger of the new heaven and the new earth of which he spoke in the Apocalypse of St. John . . . and he showed me the post where to find it."[8]

What was the object of this first voyage? Columbus gave the answer in the very title of the expedition, "The Enterprise of the Indies." He wanted to find a direct ocean trading route to Asia. Rejected for funding by the Portuguese in 1483 and by Ferdinand and Isabella in 1486, the project finally won the backing of the Spanish monarchy in 1492. The Spanish crown named Columbus viceroy over any territory he might discover and gave him one-tenth of the material rewards of the journey. Inspired by the stories of Mandeville and Marco Polo, Columbus dreamed of reaching the court of the Mongol emperor, the Great Khan (not realizing that the Ming Dynasty had overthrown the Mongols in 1368). Based on Ptolemy's *Geography* and other texts, he expected to pass the islands of Japan and then land on the east coast of China.

How did Columbus interpret what he had found, and in his mind did he achieve what he had set out to do? Columbus's small fleet left Spain on August 3, 1492. He landed in the Bahamas, which he christened San Salvador, on October 12, 1492. Columbus believed he had found some small islands off the east coast of Japan. On encountering natives of the islands, he gave them some beads and "many other trifles of small value," pronouncing them delighted with these gifts and eager to trade. In a letter he wrote to Ferdinand and Isabella on his return to Spain, Columbus described the natives as handsome, peaceful, and primitive people whose body painting reminded him of the Canary Islands natives.

scope of his achievement: to have found a vast continent unknown to Europeans, except for a fleeting Viking presence centuries earlier. He could not know that the scale of his discoveries would revolutionize world power, raising issues of trade, settlement, government bureaucracy, and the rights of native and African peoples.

Later Explorers

The Florentine navigator Amerigo Vespucci (veh-SPOO-chee) (1454–1512) realized what Columbus had not. Writing about his discoveries on the coast of modern-day Venezuela, Vespucci stated: "Those new regions which we found and explored with the fleet . . . we may rightly call a New World." This letter, titled *Mundus Novus* (The New World), was the first document to describe America as a continent separate from Asia. In recognition of Amerigo's bold claim, the continent was named for him. (When later cartographers realized that Columbus had made the discovery first, it was too late to change the maps.)

To settle competing claims to the Atlantic discoveries, Spain and Portugal turned to Pope Alexander VI. The resulting **Treaty of Tordesillas** (tor-duh-SEE-yuhs) in 1494 gave Spain everything to the west of an imaginary line drawn down the Atlantic and Portugal everything to the east. This arbitrary division worked in Portugal's favor when in 1500 an expedition led by Pedro Alvares Cabral, en route to India, landed on the coast of Brazil, which Cabral claimed as Portuguese territory.

The search for profits determined the direction of Spanish exploration and expansion into South America. With insignificant profits from the Caribbean compared to the enormous riches that the Portuguese were reaping in Asia, Spain renewed the search for a western passage to Asia. In 1519 Charles V of Spain (and the Holy Roman Empire) sent the Portuguese mariner Ferdinand Magellan (1480–1521) to find a sea route to the spices of the Moluccas off the southeast coast of Asia. Magellan sailed southwest across the Atlantic to Brazil, and after a long search along the coast he located the treacherous straits that now bear his name (see Map 15.1). The new ocean he sailed into after a rough passage through the straits seemed so peaceful that Magellan dubbed it the Pacific, from the Latin word for peaceful. He was soon to realize his mistake. His fleet sailed north up the west coast of South America and then headed west into the immense expanse of the Pacific toward the Malay Archipelago.

Treaty of Tordesillas The 1494 agreement giving Spain everything to the west of an imaginary line drawn down the Atlantic and giving Portugal everything to the east.

World Map of Diogo Ribeiro, 1529 This map integrates the wealth of new information provided by European explorers in the decades after Columbus's 1492 voyage. Working on commission for the Spanish king Charles V, mapmaker Diogo Ribeiro incorporated new details on Africa, South America, India, the Malay Archipelago, and China. Note the inaccuracy in his placement of the Moluccas, or Spice Islands, which are much too far east. This "mistake" was intended to serve Spain's interests in trade negotiations with the Portuguese. (Biblioteca Apostolica Vaticana)

> ❝ Those new regions which we found and explored with the fleet . . . we may rightly call a New World. ❞

—**AMERIGO VESPUCCI**

Some of these islands were conquered in the 1560s and named the "Philippines" for Philip II of Spain.

Terrible storms, disease, starvation, and violence haunted the expedition. Magellan had set out with a fleet of five ships and around 270 men. Sailors on two of the ships attempted mutiny on the South American coast; one ship was lost, and another ship deserted and returned to Spain before even traversing the straits. The trip across the Pacific took ninety-eight days, and the men survived on rats and sawdust. Magellan himself was killed in a skirmish in the Philippines. The expedition had enough survivors to man only two ships, and one of them was captured by the Portuguese. One ship with only eighteen men returned to Spain from the east by way of the Indian Ocean, the Cape of Good Hope, and the Atlantic in 1522. The voyage—the first to circumnavigate the globe—had taken close to three years.

Despite the losses, this voyage revolutionized Europeans' understanding of the world by demonstrating the vastness of the Pacific. The earth was clearly much larger than Columbus had believed. Although the voyage made a small profit in spices, the westward passage to the Indies was too long and dangerous for commercial purposes. Spain soon abandoned the attempt to oust Portugal from the Eastern spice trade and concentrated on exploiting her New World territories.

The English and French also set sail across the Atlantic during the early days of exploration in search of a northwest passage to the Indies. In 1497 John Cabot, a Genoese merchant living in London, aimed for Brazil but discovered Newfoundland. The next year he returned and explored the New England coast. These forays proved futile, and the English established no permanent colonies in the territories they explored. One hundred years later, English efforts to find a passage to Asia focused on the extreme north. Between 1576 and 1578, Martin Frobisher made three voyages in and around the Canadian bay that now bears his name. Frobisher hopefully brought a quantity of ore back to England with him, but it proved to be worthless.

Early French exploration of the Atlantic was equally frustrating. Between 1534 and 1541 Frenchman Jacques Cartier made several voyages and explored the St. Lawrence region of Canada, searching for a passage to the wealth of Asia. His exploration of the St. Lawrence was halted at the great rapids west of the present-day island of Montreal; he named the rapids "La Chine" in the optimistic belief that China lay just beyond. When this hope proved vain, the French turned to a new source of profit within Canada itself: trade in beavers and other furs. As had the Portuguese in Asia, French traders bartered with local peoples, who maintained control over their trade goods. French fishermen also competed with Spanish and English for the teeming schools of cod they found in the Atlantic waters around Newfoundland. Fishing vessels salted the catch on board and brought it back to Europe, where a thriving market for fish was created by the Catholic prohibition of eating meat on Fridays and during Lent.

Spanish Conquest in the New World

In 1519, the year Magellan departed on his worldwide expedition, the Spanish sent an exploratory expedition from their post in Cuba to the mainland under the command of the brash and determined conquistador Hernando Cortés (1485–1547). Accompanied by six hundred men, sixteen horses, and ten cannon, Cortés was to launch the conquest of the **Mexica Empire**. Its people were later called the Aztecs, but now most scholars prefer to use the term *Mexica* to refer to them and their empire.

The Mexica Empire was ruled by Montezuma II (r. 1502–1520) from his capital at Tenochtitlán (tay-noch-teet-LAHN), now Mexico City. Larger than any European city of the time, it was the heart of a sophisticated civilization with advanced mathematics, astronomy, and engineering, with a complex social system, and with oral poetry and historical traditions.

Cortés landed on the coast of the Gulf of Mexico on April 21, 1519. The Spanish camp was soon visited by delegations of unarmed Mexica leaders bearing gifts and news of their great emperor. Impressed by the wealth of the local people, Cortés decided to cut his ties with Spain. He founded the settlement of Vera Cruz and burned his ships to prevent any disloyal followers from returning to Cuba. Cortés soon began to realize that he could exploit internal dissension within the empire to his own advantage. The Mexica state religion necessitated constant warfare against neighboring peoples to secure captives for religious sacrifices and laborers for agricultural and building projects. Conquered peoples were required to pay products of their agriculture and craftsmanship as tribute to the Mexica state through their local chiefs.

Mexica Empire Also known as the Aztec Empire, a large and complex Native American civilization in modern Mexico and Central America that possessed advanced mathematical, astronomical, and engineering technology.

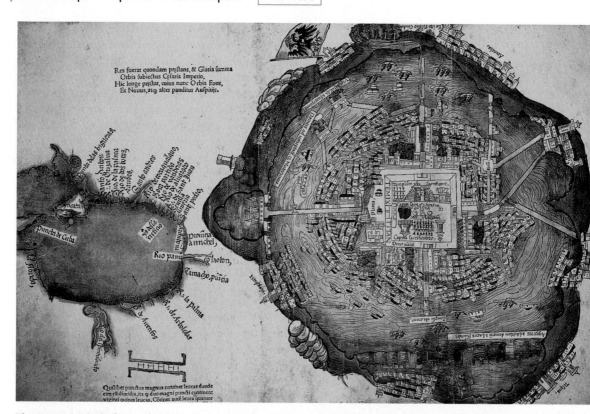

The Aztec Capital of Tenochtitlán Occupying a large island, Tenochtitlán was laid out in concentric circles. The administrative and religious buildings were at the heart of the city, which was surrounded by residential quarters. Cortés himself marveled at the city in his letters: "The city is as large as Seville or Cordoba. . . . There are bridges, very large, strong, and well constructed, so that, over many, ten horsemen can ride abreast. . . . The city has many squares where markets are held. . . . There is one square . . . where there are daily more than sixty thousand souls, buying and selling. In the service and manners of its people, their fashion of living was almost the same as in Spain, with just as much harmony and order." (The Newberry Library)

Cortés quickly forged an alliance with the Tlaxcalas and other subject kingdoms, which chafed under the tribute demanded by the Mexica. In October a combined Spanish-Tlaxcalan force occupied the city of Cholula, second largest in the empire and its religious capital, and massacred many thousands of inhabitants. Strengthened by this display of power, Cortés made alliances with other native kingdoms. In November 1519, with a few hundred Spanish men and some six thousand indigenous warriors, Cortés marched on Tenochtitlán.

Montezuma refrained from attacking the Spaniards as they advanced toward his capital and welcomed Cortés and his men into Tenochtitlán. Historians have often condemned the Mexica ruler for vacillation and weakness. Certainly other native leaders did attack the

Invasion of Tenochtitlán, 1519–1521

→ Cortés's original route, 1519
→ Cortés's retreat, 1520
→ Cortés's return route, 1520–1521

Gulf of Mexico

Texcoco
Otumba
Zautla
Jalapa
Tlaxcala
Cholula
Veracruz
Tenochtitlán

Spanish. But Montezuma relied on the advice of his state council, itself divided, and on the dubious loyalty of tributary communities. Historians have largely discredited one long-standing explanation, that he feared the Spaniards as living gods. This idea seems to have been a myth spread by Spanish missionaries and their converts after the fact, as a way of justifying and explaining the conquest. Montezuma's long hesitation proved disastrous. When Cortés—with incredible boldness—took Montezuma hostage, the emperor's influence over his people crumbled.

During the ensuing attacks and counterattacks, Montezuma was killed. The Spaniards and their allies escaped from the city and began gathering forces and making new alliances against the Mexica. In May 1520 Cortés led a second assault on

Picturing the Past

Doña Marina Translating for Hernando Cortés During His Meeting with Montezuma In April 1519 Doña Marina (or La Malinche as she is known in Mexico) was among twenty women given to the Spanish as slaves. Fluent in Nahuatl (NAH-wha-tuhl) and Yucatec Mayan (spoken by a Spanish priest accompanying Cortés), she acted as an interpreter and diplomatic guide for the Spanish. She had a close relationship with Cortés and bore his son, Don Martín Cortés, in 1522. This image was created by Tlaxcalan artists shortly after the conquest of Mexico and represents one indigenous perspective on the events. (The Granger Collection, New York)

ANALYZING THE IMAGE What role does Doña Marina (far right) appear to be playing in this image? Does she appear to be subservient or equal to Cortés (right, seated)? How did the painter indicate her identity as non-Spanish?

CONNECTIONS How do you think the native rulers negotiating with Cortés might have viewed her? What about a Spanish viewer of this image? What does the absence of other women here suggest about the role of women in these societies?

To complete this activity online, go to the Online Study Guide at bedfordstmartins.com/mckaywest.

Tenochtitlán at the head of an army of approximately 1,000 Spanish and 75,000 native warriors.[10] Spanish victory in late summer 1521 was hard-won and greatly aided by the effects of smallpox, which had weakened and reduced the Mexica population. After the defeat of Tenochtitlán, Cortés and other conquistadors began the systematic conquest of Mexico. Over time, a series of indigenous kingdoms gradually fell under Spanish domination, although not without decades of resistance.

More surprising than the defeat of the Mexicas was the fall of the remote **Inca Empire**. Perched more than 9,800 feet above sea level, the Incas were isolated from other indigenous cultures and knew nothing of the Mexica civilization or its

Inca Empire The vast and sophisticated Peruvian empire centered at the capital city of Cuzco that was at its peak from 1438 until 1532.

LIVING IN THE PAST

MANY STUDENTS ARE AWARE of the devastating effects of European diseases on peoples of the New World and of the role of gunpowder and horses in the conquest of native civilizations. They may be less aware of how New World foodstuffs transformed Europeans' daily life.

Prior to Christopher Columbus's voyages, many common elements of today's European diet were unknown in Europe. It's hard to imagine Italian pizza without tomato sauce or Irish stew without potatoes, yet tomatoes and potatoes were both unknown in Europe before 1492. Additional crops originating in the Americas included many varieties of beans, squash, pumpkins, avocados, and peppers.

One of the most important of such crops was maize (corn), first introduced to Europe by Columbus in 1493. Because maize gives a high yield per unit of land, has a short growing season, and thrives in climates too dry for rice and too wet for wheat, it proved an especially important crop for Europeans. By the late seventeenth century the crop had become a staple in Spain, Portugal, southern France, and Italy, and in the eighteenth century it became one of the chief foods of southeastern Europe. Even more valuable was the nutritious white potato, which slowly spread from west to east — to Ireland, England, and France in the seventeenth century, and to Germany, Poland, Hungary, and Russia in the eighteenth, contributing everywhere to a rise in population. Ironically, the white potato reached New England from old England in the early eighteenth century.

Europeans' initial reaction to these crops was often fear or hostility. Adoption of the tomato and the potato was long hampered by belief that they were unfit for human consumption and potentially poisonous. Both plants belong to the deadly nightshade family, and both contain poison in their leaves and stems. It took time and persuasion for these plants to win over tradition-minded European peasants, who

Saint Diego of Alcala Feeding the Poor (1645–1646), by Bartolome Esteban Murillo, the first dated European depiction of the potato in art. (Joseph Martin/akg-images)

Incan women milking goats, from a collection of illustrations by a Spanish bishop that offers a valuable view of life in Peru in the 1780s. (Oronoz)

The first European scientific illustration of maize appeared in 1542, a half century after it was introduced to the continent. (The LuEsther T. Mertz Library, NYBG/Art Resource, NY)

used potatoes mostly as livestock feed. During the eighteenth-century Enlightenment, scientists and doctors played an important role in popularizing the nutritive benefits of the potato.

Columbus himself contributed to misconceptions about New World foods when he mistook the chili pepper for black pepper, one of the spices he had hoped to find in the Indies. The Portuguese quickly began exporting chili peppers from Brazil to Africa, India, and Southeast Asia along the trade routes they dominated. The chili pepper arrived in North America through its place in the diet of enslaved Africans.

European settlers introduced various foods to the native peoples of the New World, including rice, wheat, lettuce, and onions. Perhaps the most significant introduction to the diet of Native Americans came via the meat and milk of the livestock that the early conquistadors brought with them, including cattle, sheep, and goats.

The foods of the Columbian exchange traveled a truly global path. They provided important new sources of nutrition to people all over the world, as well as creating new and beloved culinary traditions. French fries with ketchup, anyone?

QUESTIONS FOR ANALYSIS

1. Why do you think it was so difficult for Europeans to accept new types of food, even when they were high in nutritional quality?

2. What do these illustrations suggest about the importance of the Columbian exchange?

3. List the foods you typically eat in a day. How many of them originated in the New World, and how many in the Old World? How does your own life exemplify the outcome of the Columbian exchange?

Crete, Sicily, and Cyprus had the warm and wet climate needed for growing sugar cane. When Genoese and other Italians colonized the Canary Islands and the Portuguese settled on the Madeira Islands, sugar plantations came to the Atlantic.

Sugar was a particularly difficult and demanding crop to produce for profit. Seed-stems were planted by hand, thousands to the acre. When mature, the cane had to be harvested and processed rapidly to avoid spoiling, forcing days and nights of work with little rest. Moreover, its growing season is virtually constant, meaning that there is no fallow period when workers could recuperate from the arduous labor. The demands of sugar production were only increased with the invention of roller mills to crush the cane more efficiently. Yields could be augmented, but only if a sufficient labor force was found to supply the mills. Europeans solved the labor problem by forcing first native islanders and then enslaved Africans to provide the backbreaking work.

Sugar gave New World slavery its distinctive shape. Columbus himself, who spent a decade in Madeira, brought sugar plants on his voyages to "the Indies." The transatlantic slave trade began in 1518 when Spanish king Charles I authorized traders to bring African slaves to New World colonies. The Portuguese brought the first slaves to Brazil around 1550; by 1600 four thousand were being imported annually. After its founding in 1621, the Dutch West India Company, with the full support of the United Provinces, transported thousands of Africans to Brazil and the Caribbean, mostly to work on sugar plantations. In the late seventeenth century, with the chartering of the Royal African Company, the English got involved.

European sailors found the Atlantic passage cramped and uncomfortable, but conditions for African slaves were lethal. Before 1700, when slavers decided it was better business to improve conditions, some 20 percent of slaves died on the voyage.[16] The most common cause of death was from dysentery induced by poor quality food and water, intense crowding, and lack of sanitation. Men were often kept in irons during the passage, while women and girls were considered fair game for sailors. To increase profits, slave traders packed several hundred captives on each ship. One slaver explained that he removed his boots before entering the slave hold because he had to crawl over the slaves' packed bodies.[17] On sugar plantations, death rates among slaves from illness and exhaustion were extremely high, leading to a constant stream of new shipments of slaves from Africa.

In total, scholars estimate that European traders embarked over 10 million African slaves across the Atlantic from 1518 to 1800 (of whom roughly 8.5 million disembarked), with the peak of the trade occurring in the eighteenth century.[18] By comparison, only 2 to 2.5 million Europeans migrated to the New World during the same period. Enslaved Africans worked in an infinite variety of occupations: as miners, soldiers, sailors, servants, and artisans and in the production of cotton, rum, indigo, tobacco, wheat, corn, and, most predominantly, sugar.

Spanish Silver and Its Economic Effects

The sixteenth century has often been called Spain's golden century, but silver mined in the Americas was the true source of Spain's incredible wealth. In 1545, at an altitude of fifteen thousand feet, the Spanish discovered an extraordinary source of silver at Potosí (poh-toh-SEE) (in present-day Bolivia) in territory conquered from the Inca Empire. The frigid place where nothing grew had been unsettled. A half century later 160,000 people lived there, making it about the size of the city of London. By 1550 Potosí yielded perhaps 60 percent of all the silver mined in the world. From Potosí and the mines at Zacatecas (za-kuh-TAY-kuhhs) and Guanajuato (gwah-nah-HWAH-toh) in Mexico, huge quantities of precious metals poured forth. To protect this treasure from French and English pirates, armed convoys transported it to Spain each year. Between 1503 and 1650, 35 million pounds of silver and over 600,000 pounds of gold entered Seville's port. Spanish predominance, however, proved temporary.

In the sixteenth century Spain experienced a steady population increase, creating a sharp rise in the demand for food and goods. Spanish colonies in the Americas also demanded consumer goods that were not produced in the colonies, such as cloth and luxury goods. Since Spain had expelled some of its best farmers and businessmen—the Muslims and Jews—in the fifteenth century, the Spanish economy was suffering and could not meet the new demands. The excess of demand over supply led to widespread inflation. The result was a rise in production costs and a further decline in Spain's productive capacity.

Did the flood of silver bullion from America cause the inflation? Prices rose most steeply before 1565, but bullion imports reached their peak between 1580 and 1620. Thus silver did not cause the initial inflation. It did, however, exacerbate the situation, and, along with the ensuing rise in population, the influx of silver significantly contributed to the upward spiral of prices. Inflation severely strained government budgets. Several times between 1557 and 1647, Spain's King Philip II and his successors wrote off the state debt, thereby undermining confidence in the government and leaving the economy in shambles. After 1600, when the population declined, prices gradually stabilized.

As Philip II paid his armies and foreign debts with silver bullion, Spanish inflation was transmitted to the rest of Europe. Between 1560 and 1600 much of Europe

INDIVIDUALS IN SOCIETY

DURING THE LONG WARS OF THE RECONQUISTA, Muslims and Christians captured each other in battle and used the defeated as slaves. As the Muslims were gradually eliminated from Iberia in the fifteenth and sixteenth centuries, the Spanish and Portuguese turned to the west coast of Africa for a new supply of slaves. Most slaves worked as domestic servants, rather than in the fields. Some received specialized training as artisans.

Not all people of African descent were slaves, and some experienced both freedom and slavery in a single lifetime. The life and career of Juan de Pareja (pah-REH-huh) illustrates the complexities of the Iberian slave system and the heights of achievement possible for those who achieved freedom.

Pareja was born in Antequera, an agricultural region and the old center of Muslim culture near Seville in southern Spain. Of his parents we know nothing. Because a rare surviving document calls him a "mulatto," one of his parents must have been white and the other must have had some African blood. In 1630 Pareja applied to the mayor of Seville for permission to travel to Madrid to visit his brother and "to perfect his art." The document lists his occupation as "a painter in Seville." Since it

Velázquez, *Juan de Pareja*, 1650. (The Metropolitan Museum of Art, Fletcher Fund, Rogers Fund, and Bequest of Miss Adelaide Milton de Groot (1876–1967), by exchange, supplemented by gifts from friends of the Museum, 1971. [1971.86]. Image copyright © The Metropolitan Museum of Art)

mentions no other name, it is reasonable to assume that Pareja arrived in Madrid a free man. Sometime between 1630 and 1648, however, he came into the possession of the artist Diego Velázquez (1599–1660); Pareja became a slave.

How did Velázquez acquire Pareja? By purchase? As a gift? Had Pareja fallen into debt or committed some crime and thereby lost his freedom? We do not know. Velázquez, the greatest Spanish painter of the seventeenth century, had a large studio with many assistants. Pareja was set to grinding powders to make colors and to preparing canvases. He must have demonstrated ability because when Velázquez went to Rome in 1648, he chose Pareja to accompany him.

In 1650, as practice for a portrait of Pope Innocent X, Velázquez painted Pareja. The portrait shows Pareja dressed in fine clothing and gazing self-confidently at the viewer. Displayed in Rome in a public exhibition of Velázquez's work, the painting won acclaim from his contemporaries. That same year, Velázquez signed the document that gave Pareja his freedom, to become effective in 1654. Pareja lived out the rest of his life as an independent painter.

What does the public career of Pareja tell us about the man and his world? Pareja's career suggests that a person of African descent might fall into slavery and yet still acquire professional training and work alongside his master in a position of confidence. Moreover, if lucky enough to be freed, a former slave could exercise a profession and live his own life in Madrid. Pareja's experience was far from typical for a slave in the 1600s, but it reminds us of the myriad forms that slavery took in this period.

QUESTIONS FOR ANALYSIS

1. Since slavery was an established institution in Spain, speculate on Velázquez's possible reasons for giving Pareja his freedom.
2. To what extent was Pareja a marginal person in Spanish society? Was he an insider or an outsider to Spanish society?

Sources: Jonathan Brown, *Velázquez: Painter and Courtier* (New Haven, Conn.: Yale University Press, 1986); *Grove Dictionary of Art* (New York: Macmillan, 2000); Sister Wendy Beckett, *Sister Wendy's American Collection* (New York: Harper Collins Publishers, 2000), p. 15.

In many ways, though, it was not Spain but China that controlled the world trade in silver. The Chinese demanded silver for their products and for the payment of imperial taxes. China was thus the main buyer of world silver, absorbing half the world's production. The silver market drove world trade, with New Spain and Japan being mainstays on the supply side and China dominating the demand side. The world trade in silver is one of the best examples of the new global economy that emerged in this period.

The Birth of the Global Economy

With the Europeans' discovery of the Americas and their exploration of the Pacific, the entire world was linked for the first time in history by seaborne trade. The opening of that trade brought into being three successive commercial empires: the Portuguese, the Spanish, and the Dutch.

The Portuguese were the first worldwide traders. In the sixteenth century they controlled the sea route to India (see Map 15.3). From their fortified bases at Goa on the Arabian Sea and at Malacca on the Malay Peninsula, ships carried goods to the Portuguese settlement at Macao in the South China Sea. From Macao Portuguese ships loaded with Chinese silks and porcelains sailed to the Japanese port of Nagasaki and to the Philippine port of Manila, where Chinese goods were exchanged for Spanish silver from New Spain. Throughout Asia the Portuguese traded in slaves — sub-Saharan Africans, Chinese, and Japanese. The Portuguese exported horses from Mesopotamia and copper from Arabia to India; from India they exported hawks and peacocks for the Chinese and Japanese markets. Back to Portugal they brought Asian spices that had been purchased with textiles produced in India and with gold and ivory from East Africa. They also shipped back sugar from their colony in Brazil, produced by enslaved Africans whom they had transported across the Atlantic.

Coming to empire a few decades later than the Portuguese, the Spanish were determined to claim their place in world trade. The Spanish Empire in the New World was basically a land empire, but across the Pacific the Spaniards built a seaborne empire centered at Manila in the Philippines. The city of Manila served as the transpacific bridge between Spanish America and China. In Manila, Spanish traders used silver from American mines to purchase Chinese silk for European markets. The European demand for silk was so huge that in 1597, for example, 12 million pesos of silver, almost the total value of the transatlantic trade, moved from Acapulco in New Spain to Manila (see Map 15.3). After 1640 the Spanish silk trade declined in the face of stiff competition from Dutch imports.

Philip II, ca. 1533 This portrait of Philip II as a young man and crown prince of Spain is by the celebrated artist Titian, court painter to Philip's father, Charles V. After taking the throne, Philip became another great patron of the artist. (Museo Nacional del Prado, Madrid)

experienced large price increases. Prices doubled and in some cases quadrupled. Spain suffered most severely, but all European countries were affected. Because money bought less, people who lived on fixed incomes, such as nobles, were badly hurt. Those who owed fixed sums of money, such as the middle class, prospered because in a time of rising prices, debts lessened in value each year. Food costs rose most sharply, and the poor fared worst of all.

In the seventeenth century the Dutch challenged the Spanish and Portuguese Empires. Drawing on their commercial wealth and long experience in European trade, the Dutch emerged by the end of the century as the most powerful worldwide seaborne trading power. The Dutch Empire was built on spices. In 1599 a Dutch fleet returned to Amsterdam carrying 600,000 pounds of pepper and 250,000 pounds of cloves and nutmeg. Those who had invested in the expedition received a 100 percent profit. The voyage led to the establishment in 1602 of the Dutch East India Company, founded with the stated intention of capturing the spice trade from the Portuguese.

The Dutch set their sights on gaining direct access to and control of the Indonesian sources of spices. The Dutch fleet, sailing from the Cape of Good Hope in

Goods from the Global Economy Spices from Southeast Asia were a driving force behind the new global economy, and among the most treasured European luxury goods. They were used not only for cooking but also as medicines and health tonics. This fresco (center) shows a fifteenth-century Italian pharmacist measuring out spices for a customer. After the discovery of the Americas, a wave of new items entered European markets, silver foremost among them. The incredibly rich silver mines at Potosí (modern-day Bolivia) were the source of this eight-reale coin (left) struck at the mine during the reign of Charles II. Such coins were the original "pieces of eight" prized by pirates and adventurers. Soon Asian and American goods were mixed together by enterprising tradesmen. The mid-seventeenth-century Chinese teapot (right) was made of porcelain with the traditional Chinese design prized in the West, but with a silver handle added to suit European tastes. (teapot: Private Collection/Paul Freeman/The Bridgeman Art Library; coin: Hoberman Collection/SuperStock; spice shop: Alfredo Dagli Orti/The Art Archive)

Africa and avoiding the Portuguese forts in India, steered directly for the Sunda Strait in Indonesia (see Map 15.3). In return for assisting Indonesian princes in local squabbles and disputes with the Portuguese, the Dutch won broad commercial concessions. Through agreements, seizures, and outright war, they gained control of the western access to the Indonesian archipelago in the first half of the seventeenth century. Gradually, they acquired political domination over the archipelago itself. By the 1660s the Dutch had managed to expel the Portuguese from Ceylon and other East Indian islands, thereby establishing control of the lucrative spice trade.

Not content with challenging the Portuguese in the Indian Ocean, the Dutch also aspired to a role in the Americas. Founded in 1621 in a period of war with Spain, the Dutch West India Company aggressively sought to open trade with North and South America and capture Spanish territories there. The company captured or destroyed hundreds of Spanish ships, seized the Spanish silver fleet in 1628, and captured portions of Brazil and the Caribbean. The Dutch also successfully interceded in the transatlantic slave trade, bringing much of the west coast of Africa under Dutch control. Ironically, the nation that was known throughout Europe as a bastion of tolerance and freedom came to be one of the principal operators of the slave trade starting in the 1640s.

Dutch efforts to colonize North America were less successful. The colony of New Netherland, governed from New Amsterdam (modern-day New York City), was hampered by lack of settlement and weak governance and was easily captured by the British in 1664.

Changing Attitudes and Beliefs

How did new ideas about race and the works of Montaigne and Shakespeare reflect the encounter with new peoples and places? ■

The age of overseas expansion heightened Europeans' contacts with the rest of the world. These contacts gave birth to new ideas about the inherent superiority or inferiority of different races, in part to justify European participation in the slave trade. Cultural encounters also inspired more positive views. The essays of Michel de Montaigne epitomized a new spirit of skepticism and cultural relativism, while the plays of William Shakespeare reflected the efforts of one great writer to come to terms with the cultural complexity of his day.

New Ideas About Race

At the beginning of the transatlantic slave trade, most Europeans would have thought of Africans, if they thought of them at all, as savages because of their eating habits, morals, clothing, and social customs and as barbarians because of their language and methods of war. Despite lingering belief in a Christian Ethiopia under the legendary Prester John, they grouped Africans into the despised categories of pagan heathens and Muslim infidels. Africans were certainly not the only peoples subject to such dehumanizing attitudes. Jews were also viewed as an alien group that was, like Africans, naturally given to sin and depravity. More generally, elite people across Europe were accustomed to viewing the peasant masses as a lower form of humanity. They scornfully compared rustic peasants to dogs, pigs, and donkeys and even reviled the dark skin color peasants acquired while laboring in the sun.[19]

As Europeans turned to Africa for new sources of slaves, they drew on and developed ideas about Africans' primitiveness and barbarity to defend slavery and even argue that enslavement benefited Africans by bringing the light of Christianity to heathen peoples. In 1444 an observer defended the enslavement of the first Africans by Portuguese explorers as necessary for their salvation "because they lived like beasts, without any of the customs of rational creatures, since they did not even know what were bread and wine, nor garments of cloth, nor life in the shelter of a house; and worse still was their ignorance, which deprived them of knowledge of good, and permitted them only a life of brutish idleness."[20] Compare this with an early seventeenth-century Englishman's complaint that the Irish "be so beastly that they are better like beasts than Christians."[21]

Over time, the institution of slavery fostered a new level of racial inequality. In contrast to peasants, Jews, and the Irish, Africans gradually became seen as utterly distinct from and wholly inferior to Europeans. From rather vague assumptions about non-Christian religious beliefs and a general lack of civilization, Europeans developed increasingly rigid ideas of racial superiority and inferiority to safeguard the growing profits gained from plantation slavery. Black skin became equated with slavery itself as Europeans at home and in the colonies convinced themselves that blacks were destined by God to serve them as slaves in perpetuity.

Support for this belief went back to the Greek philosopher Aristotle's argument that some people are naturally destined for slavery and to biblical associations between darkness and sin. A more explicit justification was found in the story of Noah's curse upon Canaan. According to the Bible, Ham defied his father's ban on sexual relations on the ark and further

❝ They lived like beasts, without any of the customs of rational creatures, since they did not even know what were bread and wine, nor garments of cloth, nor life in the shelter of a house. **❞**

—EUROPEAN OBSERVER

enraged Noah by entering his tent and viewing his father unclothed. To punish Ham, Noah cursed Ham's son Canaan and all his descendants to be the "servant of servants." Biblical genealogies listing Ham's sons as those who peopled North Africa and Cush were read to mean that all inhabitants of those regions bore Noah's curse. From the sixteenth century onward, this story was often cited as justification for the enslavement of an entire race.

After 1700 the emergence of new methods of observing and describing nature led to the use of science to define race. From referring to a nation or an ethnic group, henceforth "race" would mean biologically distinct groups of people, whose physical differences produced differences in culture, character, and intelligence. Biblical justifications for inequality thereby gave way to supposedly scientific ones.

Michel de Montaigne and Cultural Curiosity

Racism was not the only possible reaction to the new worlds emerging in the sixteenth century. Decades of religious fanaticism, bringing civil anarchy and war, led both Catholics and Protestants to doubt that any one faith contained absolute truth. Added to these doubts was the discovery of peoples in the New World who had radically different ways of life. These shocks helped produce ideas of skepticism and cultural relativism in the sixteenth and seventeenth centuries. Skepticism is a school of thought founded on doubt that total certainty or definitive knowledge is ever attainable. The skeptic is cautious and critical and suspends judgment. Cultural relativism suggests that one culture is not necessarily superior to another, just different. Both notions found expression in the work of Frenchman Michel de Montaigne (duh mahn-TAYN) (1533–1592).

Montaigne developed a new literary genre, the essay—from the French *essayer*, meaning "to test or try"—to express his thoughts and ideas. Published in 1580, Montaigne's *Essays* consisted of short personal reflections drawing on his extensive reading in ancient texts, his experience as a government official, and his own moral judgment. Intended to be accessible to ordinary people, Montaigne wrote in French rather than Latin and in an engaging conversational style.

Montaigne's essay "Of Cannibals" reveals the impact of overseas discoveries on one thoughtful European's consciousness. In contrast to the prevailing views of the time, he rejected the notion that one culture is superior to another. Speaking of native Brazilians, he wrote:

> I find that there is nothing barbarous and savage in this nation [Brazil], . . . except, that everyone gives the title of barbarism to everything that is not according to his usage; as, indeed, we have no other criterion of truth and reason, than the example and pattern of the opinions and customs of the place wherein we live. . . . They are savages in the same way that we say fruits are wild, which nature produces of herself and by her ordinary course; whereas, in truth, we ought rather to call those wild whose natures we have changed by our artifice and diverted from the common order.[22]

In his own time and throughout the seventeenth century, few would have agreed with Montaigne's challenge to ideas of European superiority or his even more radical questioning of the superiority of humans over animals. The publication of his ideas, however, contributed to a basic shift in attitudes. Montaigne inaugurated an era of doubt. "Wonder," he said, "is the foundation of all philosophy, research is the means of all learning, and ignorance is the end."[23]

William Shakespeare and His Influence

In addition to the essay as a literary genre, the period fostered remarkable creativity in other branches of literature. England—especially in the latter part of Queen Elizabeth I's reign and in the first years of her successor, James I (r. 1603–1625)—witnessed remarkable literary expression. The terms *Elizabethan* and *Jacobean* (referring to the reign of James) are used to designate the English music, poetry, prose, and drama of this period.

The undisputed master of the period was the dramatist William Shakespeare, whose genius lay in the originality of his characterizations, the diversity of his plots,

Titus Andronicus With classical allusions, fifteen murders and executions, a Gothic queen who takes a black lover, and incredible violence, this early Shakespearean tragedy (1594) was a melodramatic thriller that enjoyed enormous popularity with the London audience. The shock value of a dark-skinned character on the English stage is clearly shown in this illustration. (Reproduced by permission of the Marquess of Bath, Longleat House, Warminster, Wilts)

his understanding of human psychology, and his unsurpassed gift for language. Born in 1564 to a successful glove manufacturer in Stratford-on-Avon, Shakespeare grew into a Renaissance man with a deep appreciation of classical culture, individualism, and humanism. Such plays as *Julius Caesar* and *Antony and Cleopatra* deal with classical subjects and figures. Several of his comedies have Italian Renaissance settings. His history plays, including *Richard III* and *Henry IV*, express English national consciousness. Shakespeare's later tragedies, including *Hamlet*, *Othello*, and *Macbeth*, explore an enormous range of human problems and are open to an almost infinite variety of interpretations.

Like Montaigne, Shakespeare's work reveals the impact of the new discoveries and contacts of his day. The title character of *Othello* is described as a "Moor of Venice." In Shakespeare's day, the term "moor" referred to Muslims of Moroccan or North African origin, including those who had migrated to the Iberian Peninsula. It could also be applied, though, to natives of the Iberian Peninsula who converted to Islam or to non-Muslim Berbers in North Africa. To complicate things even more, references in the play to Othello as "black" in skin color have led many to believe that Shakespeare intended him

to be a sub-Saharan African, and he is usually depicted as such in modern performances. This confusion in the play reflects the uncertainty in Shakespeare's own day about racial and religious classifications.

The character of Othello is both vilified in racist terms by his enemies and depicted as a brave warrior, a key member of the city's military leadership, and a man capable of winning the heart of an aristocratic white woman. In contrast to the prevailing view of Moors as inferior, Shakespeare presents Othello as a complex human figure, whose only crime is to have "loved [his wife] not wisely, but too well." Shakespeare's play thus demonstrates both the intolerance of contemporary society and the possibility for some individuals to look beyond racial stereotypes.

Shakespeare's last play, *The Tempest*, displays a similar interest in race and race relations. The plot involves the stranding on an island of sorcerer Prospero and his daughter Miranda. There Prospero finds and raises Caliban, a native of the island, whom he instructs in his own language and religion. After Caliban's attempted rape of Miranda, Prospero enslaves him, earning the rage and resentment of his erstwhile pupil. Modern scholars often note the echoes between this play and the realities of imperial conquest and settlement in Shakespeare's day. It is no accident, they argue, that the poet portrayed Caliban as a monstrous dark-skinned island native who was best-suited for slavery. Shakespeare himself borrows words from Montaigne's essay "Of Cannibals," suggesting that he may have intended to criticize, rather than endorse, racial intolerance. Shakespeare's work shows us one of the finest minds of the age grasping to come to terms with the racial and religious complexities around him.

LOOKING BACK LOOKING AHEAD

JUST THREE YEARS SEPARATED the posting of Martin Luther's "Ninety-five Theses" in 1517 from Ferdinand Magellan's discovery of the Pacific Ocean in 1520. Within a few short years, the religious unity of western Europe and its notions of terrestrial geography were shattered. Old medieval certainties about Heaven and earth collapsed. In the ensuing decades, Europeans struggled to come to terms with religious difference at home and the multitudes of new peoples and places they encountered abroad. These processes were intertwined, as Puritans and Quakers fled religious persecution at home to colonize the New World and the new Jesuit order proved its devotion to the pope by seeking Catholic converts across the globe. While some Europeans were fascinated and inspired by this new diversity, too often the result was violence. Europeans endured decades of civil war between Protestants and Catholics, and indigenous peoples suffered massive population losses as a result of European warfare, disease, and exploitation. Tragically, both Catholic and Protestant religious leaders condoned the African slave trade that was to bring suffering and death to millions of Africans.

Even as the voyages of discovery contributed to the fragmentation of European culture, they also belonged to longer-term processes of state centralization and consolidation. The new monarchies of the Renaissance produced stronger and wealthier governments capable of financing the huge expenses of exploration and colonization. Competition to gain overseas colonies became an integral part of European politics. Spain's investment in conquest proved spectacularly profitable and yet, as we will see in Chapter 16, the ultimate result was a weakening of its power. Other European nations took longer to realize financial gain, yet over time the Netherlands, England, and France reaped tremendous profits from colonial trade, which helped them build modernized, centralized states. The path from medieval Christendom to modern nation-states led through religious warfare and global encounter.

CHAPTER REVIEW

■ **What was the Afro-Eurasian trading world before Columbus? (p. 444)**

Prior to Columbus's voyages, well-developed trade routes linked the peoples and products of Africa, Asia, and Europe. The Indian Ocean was the center of the Afro-Eurasian trade world, ringed by cosmopolitan commercial cities such as Mombasa in Africa, Calicut in India, and Malacca in Southeast Asia. Chinese silk and porcelain were desired by elites throughout the trading system. The Ottoman and Persian Empires produced textiles and other goods for the world market, while also serving as intermediaries for trade between East and West. Venetian and Genoese merchants brought spices, silks, and other luxury goods into western Europe from the East. Overall, Europeans played a minor role in the Afro-Eurasian trading world because they did not produce many products desired by Eastern elites.

■ **How and why did Europeans undertake ambitious voyages of expansion? (p. 448)**

In the sixteenth and seventeenth centuries Europeans gained access to large parts of the globe for the first time. A revival of populations and economies after the time of the Black Death created markets for spices and other goods from the East. In addition to searching for routes that would undo the Italian and Ottoman dominance of trade in the East, Europeans were motivated by intellectual curiosity, driving ambition, religious zeal, and a lack of opportunities at home. The revived monarchies of the sixteenth century now possessed sufficient resources to back ambitious seafarers like Christopher Columbus and Vasco da Gama. Technological developments such as the invention of the caravel and magnetic compass enabled Europeans to undertake ever more ambitious voyages.

■ **What was the impact of European conquest on the peoples and ecologies of the New World? (p. 461)**

In the aftermath of conquest, the Spanish established new forms of governance to dominate native peoples and exploit their labor. The arrival of Europeans also brought enormous population losses to native communities, primarily through the spread of infectious diseases. Women played an important role in creating new colonial societies, both through the union of native and African women with European men and through the migration of European women to the colonies. The Age of Discovery sparked a complex exchange of germs, flora, and fauna between the Old and New Worlds, which is known as the "Columbian exchange." Europeans brought familiar crops and livestock to the Americas, and brought home new ones, some of which became staples of the European diet.

■ **How was the era of global contact shaped by new commodities, commercial empires, and forced migrations? (p. 464)**

One of the most important consequences of the Age of Discovery was the creation of the first truly global economy in the sixteenth and seventeenth centuries. Tragically, a major component of global trade was the transatlantic slave trade, in which Europeans transported many millions of Africans to labor in horrific conditions in the mines and sugar plantations of the New World. The discovery of extraordinarily rich silver mines in New Spain brought enormous wealth to the Spanish crown, but little economic development. European nations vied for supremacy in global trade, with early Portuguese success in India and Asia being challenged first by the Spanish and then by the Dutch, who successfully imposed control of trade with the East in the mid-seventeenth century.

■ **How did new ideas about race and the works of Montaigne and Shakespeare reflect the encounter with new peoples and places? (p. 472)**

Increased contact with the outside world led Europeans to develop new ideas about cultural and racial difference. Europeans had long held negative attitudes toward Africans; as the slave trade grew, they began to express more rigid notions of racial inequality and to claim that Africans were inherently suited for slavery. Most Europeans shared such views, with some important exceptions. In his essays, Michel de Montaigne challenged the idea that natives of the Americas were inferior barbarians, while William Shakespeare's plays contain ambivalent attitudes toward complex non-European characters.

Suggested Reading

Crosby, Alfred W. *The Columbian Exchange: Biological and Cultural Consequences of 1492.* 30th anniversary ed. 2003. An innovative and highly influential account of the environmental impact of Columbus's voyages.

Elliot, J. H. *Empires of the Atlantic World: Britain and Spain in America, 1492–1830.* 2006. A masterful account of the differences and similarities between the British and Spanish Empires in the Americas.

Fernández-Armesto, Felip. *Columbus.* 1992. An excellent biography of Christopher Columbus.

Greenblatt, Stephen. *Marvelous Possessions: The Wonder of the New World.* 1991. Describes the cultural impact of New World discoveries on Europeans.

Menard, Russell. *Sweet Negotiations: Sugar, Slavery and Plantation Agriculture in Early Barbados.* 2006. Explores the intertwined history of sugar plantations and slavery in seventeenth-century Barbados.

Northrup, David, ed. *The Atlantic Slave Trade*. 1994. Collected essays by leading scholars on many different aspects of the slave trade.

Pérez-Mallaína, Pablo E. *Spain's Men of the Sea: Daily Life on the Indies Fleet in the Sixteenth Century*. 1998. A description of recruitment, daily life, and career paths of ordinary sailors and officers in the Spanish fleet.

Pomeranz, Kenneth, and Steven Topik. *The World That Trade Created: Society, Culture and the World Economy, 1400 to the Present*. 1999. The creation of a world market presented through rich and vivid stories of merchants, miners, slaves, and farmers.

Restall, Matthew. *Seven Myths of Spanish Conquest*. 2003. A re-examination of common ideas about why and how the Spanish conquered native civilizations in the New World.

Scammell, Geoffrey V. *The World Encompassed: The First European Maritime Empires, c. 800–1650*. 1981. A detailed overview of the first European empires, including the Italian city-states, Portugal, and Spain.

Schmidt, Benjamin. *Innocence Abroad: The Dutch Imagination and the New World, 1570–1670*. 2001. Examines changing Dutch attitudes toward the New World, from criticism of the cruelty of the Spanish conquest to eagerness for their own overseas empire.

Subrahamanyam, Sanjay. *The Career and Legend of Vasco da Gama*. 1998. A probing biography that places Vasco da Gama in the context of Portuguese politics and society.

Notes

1. Thomas Benjamin, *The Atlantic World: Europeans, Africans, Indians and Their Shared History, 1400–1900* (Cambridge, U.K.: Cambridge University Press, 2009), p. 56.
2. G. V. Scammell, *The World Encompassed: The First European Maritime Empires, c. 800–1650* (Berkeley: University of California Press, 1981), pp. 101, 104.
3. Quoted in C. M. Cipolla, *Guns, Sails, and Empires: Technological Innovation and the Early Phases of European Expansion, 1400–1700* (New York: Minerva Press, 1965), p. 132.
4. Quoted in F. H. Littell, *The Macmillan Atlas: History of Christianity* (New York: Macmillan, 1976), p. 75.
5. Pablo E. Pérez-Mallaína, *Spain's Men of the Sea: Daily Life on the Indies Fleet in the Sixteenth Century* (Baltimore: Johns Hopkins University Press, 1998), p. 133.
6. Ibid., p. 19.
7. Quoted in F. Maddison, "Tradition and Innovation: Columbus' First Voyage and Portuguese Navigation in the Fifteenth Century," in *Circa 1492: Art in the Age of Exploration*, ed. J. A. Levenson (Washington, D.C.: National Gallery of Art, 1991), p. 69.
8. Quoted in R. L. Kagan, "The Spain of Ferdinand and Isabella," in *Circa 1492: Art in the Age of Exploration*, ed. J. A. Levenson (Washington, D.C.: National Gallery of Art, 1991), p. 60.
9. Peter Hulme, *Colonial Encounters: Europe and the Native Caribbean, 1492–1797* (London and New York: Methuan, 1986), pp. 22–31.
10. Benjamin, *The Atlantic World*, p. 141.
11. Ibid., pp. 35–59.
12. Quoted in C. Gibson, ed., *The Black Legend: Anti-Spanish Attitudes in the Old World and the New* (New York: Knopf, 1971), pp. 74–75.
13. Quoted in L. B. Rout, Jr., *The African Experience in Spanish America* (New York: Cambridge University Press, 1976), p. 23.
14. Cited in Geoffrey Vaughn Scammell, *The First Imperial Age: European Overseas Expansion, c. 1400–1715* (London and New York: Routledge, 2002), p. 62.
15. Ibid., p. 432.
16. Herbert S. Klein, "Profits and the Causes of Mortality," in David Northrup, ed., *The Atlantic Slave Trade* (Lexington, Mass.: D. C. Heath and Co., 1994), p. 116.
17. Malcolm Cowley and Daniel P. Mannix, "The Middle Passage," in David Northrup, ed., *The Atlantic Slave Trade* (Lexington, Mass.: D. C. Heath and Co., 1994), p. 101.
18. Voyages: The Trans-Atlantic Slave Trade Database, http://www.slavevoyages.org/tast/assessment/estimates.faces (accessed May 9, 2009).
19. Paul Freedman, *Images of the Medieval Peasant* (Stanford, Calif.: Stanford University Press, 1999).
20. Quoted in James H. Sweet, "The Iberian Roots of American Racist Thought," *The William and Mary Quarterly*, Third Series, Vol. 54, No. 1 (Jan. 1997), p. 155.
21. Quoted in Sean J. Connolly, *Contested Island: Ireland, 1460–1630* (Oxford: Oxford University Press, 2007), p. 397.
22. C. Cotton, trans., *The Essays of Michel de Montaigne* (New York: A. L. Burt, 1893), pp. 207, 210.
23. Ibid., p. 523.

Key Terms

conquistador (p. 449)
caravel (p. 450)
Ptolemy's *Geography* (p. 450)
Treaty of Tordesillas (p. 456)
Mexica Empire (p. 457)
Inca Empire (p. 459)
viceroyalties (p. 461)
encomienda system (p. 461)
Columbian exchange (p. 463)

For practice quizzes and other study tools, visit the Online Study Guide at **bedfordstmartins.com/mckaywest**.

For primary sources from this period, see ***Sources of Western Society*, Second Edition**.

For Web sites, images, and documents related to topics in this chapter, visit Make History at **bedfordstmartins.com/mckaywest**.

16
Absolutism and Constitutionalism

ca. 1589–1725

The seventeenth century was a period of crisis and transformation in Europe. Agricultural and manufacturing slumps led to food shortages and shrinking population rates. Religious and dynastic conflicts led to almost constant war, visiting violence and destruction on ordinary people and reshaping European states. Armies grew larger than they had been since the time of the Roman Empire, resulting in new government bureaucracies and higher taxes. Despite these obstacles, European states succeeded in gathering more power, and by 1680 much of the unrest that originated with the Reformation was resolved.

These crises were not limited to western Europe. Central and eastern Europe experienced even more catastrophic dislocation, with German lands serving as the battleground of the Thirty Years' War and borders constantly vulnerable to attack from the east. In Prussia and in Habsburg Austria absolutist states emerged in the aftermath of this conflict. Russia and the Ottoman Turks also developed absolutist governments. The Russian and Ottoman Empires seemed foreign and exotic to western Europeans, who saw them as the antithesis of their political, religious, and cultural values. While absolutism emerged as the solution to crisis in many European states, a small minority adopted a different path, placing sovereignty in the hands of privileged groups rather than the Crown. Historians refer to states where power was limited by law as "constitutional." The two most important seventeenth-century constitutionalist states were England and the Dutch Republic. Constitutionalism should not be confused with democracy. The elite rulers of England and the Dutch Republic pursued familiar policies of increased taxation, government authority, and social control. Nonetheless, they served as influential models to onlookers across Europe as a form of government that checked the power of a single ruler. ■

Life in Absolutist France. King Louis XIV receives foreign ambassadors to celebrate a peace treaty. The king grandly occupied the center of his court, which in turn served as the pinnacle for the French people and, at the height of his glory, for all of Europe.

CHAPTER PREVIEW

Seventeenth-Century Crisis and Rebuilding
■ What were the common crises and achievements of seventeenth-century European states?

Absolutism in France and Spain
■ What factors led to the rise of the French absolutist state under Louis XIV, and why did absolutist Spain experience decline in the same period?

Absolutism in Austria and Prussia
■ How did the rulers of Austria and Prussia transform their nations into powerful absolutist monarchies?

The Development of Russia and the Ottoman Empire
■ What were the distinctive features of Russian and Ottoman absolutism?

Alternatives to Absolutism in England and the Dutch Republic
■ How and why did the constitutional state triumph in the Dutch Republic and England?

Baroque Art and Music
■ What was the baroque style in art and music, and where was it popular?

Seventeenth-Century Crisis and Rebuilding

What were the common crises and achievements of seventeenth-century European states? ■

Historians often refer to the seventeenth century as an "age of crisis." After the economic and demographic growth of the sixteenth century, Europe faltered into stagnation and retrenchment. This was partially due to climate changes beyond anyone's control, but it also resulted from bitter religious divides, increased governmental pressures, and war. Overburdened peasants and city-dwellers took action to defend themselves, sometimes profiting from conflicts to obtain relief. In the long run, however, governments proved increasingly able to impose their will on the populace. The period witnessed spectacular growth in army size as well as new forms of taxation, government bureaucracies, and increased state sovereignty.

Peasant Life in the Midst of Economic Crisis

In the seventeenth century most Europeans lived in the countryside. The hub of the rural world was the small peasant village centered on a church and a manor. Life was in many ways circumscribed by the village, although we should not underestimate the mobility induced by war, food shortage, fortune-seeking, and religious pilgrimage.

In western Europe, a small number of peasants in each village owned enough land to feed themselves and had the livestock and ploughs necessary to work their land. These independent farmers were leaders of the peasant village. They employed the landless poor, rented out livestock and tools, and served as agents for the noble lord. Below them were small landowners and tenant farmers who did not have enough land to be self-sufficient. These families sold their best produce on the market to earn cash for taxes, rent, and food. At the bottom were the rural workers who worked as dependent

An English Food Riot Nothing infuriated ordinary women and men more than the idea that merchants and landowners were withholding grain from the market in order to push high prices even higher. In this cartoon an angry crowd hands out rough justice to a rich farmer accused of hoarding. (Courtesy of the Trustees of the British Museum)

laborers and servants. In eastern Europe, the vast majority of peasants toiled as serfs for noble landowners and did not own land in their own right (see page 482).

Rich or poor, east or west, bread was the primary element of the diet. The richest ate a white loaf, leaving brown bread to those who could not afford better. Peasants paid stiff fees to the local miller for grinding grain into flour and sometimes to the lord for the right to bake bread in his oven. Bread was most often accompanied by a soup made of roots, herbs, beans, and perhaps a small piece of salt pork. An important annual festival in many villages was the killing of the family pig. The whole family gathered to help, sharing a rare abundance of meat with neighbors and carefully salting the extra and putting down the lard. In some areas, menstruating women were careful to stay away from the kitchen for fear they might cause the lard to spoil.

European rural society lived on the edge of subsistence. Because of the crude technology and low crop yield, peasants were constantly threatened by scarcity and famine. In the seventeenth century a period of colder and wetter climate throughout Europe, dubbed the "little ice age" by historians, meant a shorter farming season with lower yields. A bad harvest created food shortages; a series of bad harvests could lead to famine. Recurrent famines significantly reduced the population of early modern Europe. Most people did not die of outright starvation, but rather of diseases brought on by malnutrition and exhaustion. Facilitated by the weakened population, outbreaks of bubonic plague continued in Europe until the 1720s.

The Estates of Normandy, a provincial assembly, reported on the dire conditions in northern France during an outbreak of plague in which disease was compounded by the disruption of agriculture and a lack of food:

Of the 450 sick persons whom the inhabitants were unable to relieve, 200 were turned out, and these we saw die one by one as they lay on the roadside. A large number still remain, and to each of them it is only possible to dole out the least scrap of bread. We only give bread to those who would otherwise die. The staple dish here consists of mice, which the inhabitants hunt, so desperate are they from hunger. They devour roots which the animals cannot eat; one can, in fact, not put into words the things one sees. . . . We certify to having ourselves seen herds, not of cattle, but of men and women, wandering about the fields between Rheims and Rhétel, turning up the earth like pigs

Chronology

ca. 1500–1650	Consolidation of serfdom in eastern Europe
1533–1584	Reign of Ivan the Terrible in Russia
1589–1610	Reign of Henry IV in France
1598–1613	Time of Troubles in Russia
1620–1740	Growth of absolutism in Austria and Prussia
1642–1649	English civil war, which ends with execution of Charles I
1643–1715	Reign of Louis XIV in France
1653–1658	Military rule in England under Oliver Cromwell (the Protectorate)
1660	Restoration of English monarchy under Charles II
1665–1683	Jean-Baptiste Colbert applies mercantilism to France
1670	Charles II agrees to re-Catholicize England in secret agreement with Louis XIV
1670–1671	Cossack revolt led by Stenka Razin
ca. 1680–1750	Construction of baroque palaces
1682	Louis XIV moves court to Versailles
1682–1725	Reign of Peter the Great in Russia
1683–1718	Habsburgs push the Ottoman Turks from Hungary
1685	Edict of Nantes revoked
1688–1689	Glorious Revolution in England
1701–1713	War of the Spanish Succession

to find a few roots; and as they can only find rotten ones, and not half enough of them, they become so weak that they have not strength left to seek food.[1]

Given the harsh conditions of life, industry also suffered. The output of woolen textiles, one of the most important European manufactures, declined sharply in the first half of the seventeenth century. Food prices were high, wages stagnated, and unemployment soared. This economic crisis was not universal: it struck various regions at different times and to different degrees. In the middle decades of the century, Spain, France, Germany, and England all experienced great economic difficulties; but these years were the golden age of the Netherlands.

The urban poor and peasants were the hardest hit. When the price of bread rose beyond their capacity to pay, they frequently expressed their anger by rioting. In towns they invaded bakers' shops to seize bread and resell it at a "just price." In rural areas they attacked convoys taking grain to the cities. Women often led these actions, since their role as mothers gave them some impunity in authorities' eyes. Historians have labeled this vision of a world in which community needs predominate over competition and profit a moral economy.

The Return of Serfdom in the East

While economic and social hardship was common across Europe, important differences existed between east and west. In the west the demographic losses of the Black Death allowed peasants to escape from serfdom as they acquired enough land to feed themselves and the livestock and ploughs necessary to work their land. In eastern Europe seventeenth-century peasants had largely lost their ability to own land independently. Eastern lords dealt with the labor shortages caused by the Black Death by restricting the right of their peasants to move to take advantage of better opportunities elsewhere. In Prussian territories by 1500 the law required that runaway peasants be hunted down and returned to their lords. Moreover, lords steadily took more and more of their peasants' land and arbitrarily imposed heavier and heavier labor obligations. By the early 1500s lords in many eastern territories could command their peasants to work for them without pay for as many as six days a week.

The gradual erosion of the peasantry's economic position was bound up with manipulation of the legal system. The local lord was also the local prosecutor, judge, and jailer. There were no independent royal officials to provide justice or uphold the common law. The power of the lord reached far into serfs' everyday lives. Not only was their freedom of movement restricted, but they required permission to marry or could be forced to marry. Lords could reallocate the lands worked by their serfs at will or sell serfs apart from their families. These conditions applied even on lands owned by the church.

Between 1500 and 1650 the consolidation of serfdom in eastern Europe was accompanied by the growth of commercial agriculture, particularly in Poland and eastern Germany. As economic expansion and population growth resumed after 1500, eastern lords increased the production of their estates by squeezing sizable surpluses out of the impoverished peasants. They then sold these surpluses to foreign merchants, who exported them to the growing cities of wealthier western Europe. The Netherlands and England benefited the most from inexpensive grain from the east.

It was not only the peasants who suffered in eastern Europe. With the approval of kings, landlords systematically undermined the medieval privileges of the towns and the power of the urban classes. Instead of selling products to local merchants, landlords sold directly to foreigners, bypassing local towns. Eastern towns also lost their medieval right of refuge and were compelled to return runaways to their lords. The population of the towns and the urban middle classes declined greatly. This development both reflected and promoted the supremacy of noble landlords in most of eastern Europe in the sixteenth century.

The Thirty Years' War

In the first half of the seventeenth century, the fragile balance of life was violently upturned by the ravages of the Thirty Years' War (1618–1648). The Holy Roman Empire was a confederation of hundreds of principalities, in-

Estonian Serfs in the 1660s The Estonians were conquered by German military nobility in the Middle Ages and reduced to serfdom. The German-speaking nobles ruled the Estonian peasants with an iron hand, and Peter the Great reaffirmed their domination when Russia annexed Estonia. (Mansell Collection/Time Life Pictures/Getty Images)

Soldiers Pillage a Farmhouse Billeting troops among civilian populations during the Thirty Years' War caused untold hardships. In this late-seventeenth-century Dutch illustration, brawling soldiers take over a peasant's home, eat his food, steal his possessions, and insult his family. Peasant retaliation sometimes proved swift and bloody. (Rijksmuseum-Stichting Amsterdam)

dependent cities, duchies, and other polities loosely united under an elected emperor. The uneasy truce between Catholics and Protestants created by the Peace of Augsburg in 1555 deteriorated as the faiths of various areas shifted. Lutheran princes felt compelled to form the Protestant Union (1608), and Catholics retaliated with the Catholic League (1609). Each alliance was determined that the other should make no religious or territorial advance. Dynastic interests were also involved; the Spanish Habsburgs strongly supported the goals of their Austrian relatives: the unity of the empire and the preservation of Catholicism within it.

The war is traditionally divided into four phases. The first, or Bohemian, phase (1618–1625) was characterized by civil war in Bohemia between the Catholic League and the Protestant Union. In 1620 Catholic forces defeated Protestants at the Battle of the White Mountain. The second, or Danish, phase of the war (1625–1629) — so called because of the leadership of the Protestant king Christian IV of Denmark (r. 1588–1648) — witnessed additional Catholic victories. The Catholic imperial army led by Albert of Wallenstein swept through Silesia, north to the Baltic, and east into Pomerania, scoring smashing victories. Habsburg power peaked in 1629. The emperor issued the Edict of Restitution, whereby all Catholic properties lost to Protestantism since 1552 were restored, and only Catholics and Lutherans were allowed to practice their faiths.

The third, or Swedish, phase of the war (1630–1635) began with the arrival in Germany of the Swedish king

Gustavus Adolphus (r. 1594–1632) and his army. The ablest administrator of his day and a devout Lutheran, he intervened to support the empire's Protestants. The French chief minister, Cardinal Richelieu, subsidized the Swedes, hoping to weaken Habsburg power in Europe. Gustavus Adolphus won two important battles but was fatally wounded in combat. The final, or French, phase of the war (1635–1648) was prompted by Richelieu's concern that the Habsburgs would rebound after the death of Gustavus Adolphus. Richelieu declared war on Spain and sent military as well as financial assistance. Finally, in October 1648 peace was achieved.

The 1648 **Peace of Westphalia** that ended the Thirty Years' War marked a turning point in European history. For the most part, conflicts fought over religious faith receded. The treaties recognized the independent authority of more than three hundred German princes (Map 16.1), reconfirming the emperor's severely limited authority. The Augsburg agreement of 1555 became permanent, adding Calvinism to Catholicism and Lutheranism as legally permissible creeds. The north German states remained Protestant; the south German states, Catholic.

> **Peace of Westphalia** The name of a series of treaties that concluded the Thirty Years' War in 1648 and marked the end of large-scale religious violence in Europe.

The Thirty Years' War was probably the most destructive event for the central European economy and society prior to the world wars of the twentieth century. Perhaps one-third of urban residents and two-fifths of

Map 16.1 Europe After the Thirty Years' War This map shows the political division of Europe after the Treaty of Westphalia (1648) ended the war. Which country emerged from the Thirty Years' War as the strongest European power? What dynastic house was that country's major rival in the early modern period?

the rural population died, leaving entire areas depopulated. Trade in southern German cities, such as Augsburg, was virtually destroyed. Agricultural areas suffered catastrophically. Many small farmers lost their land, allowing nobles to enlarge their estates and consolidate their control.[2]

Achievements in State-Building

In this context of economic and demographic depression, monarchs began to make new demands on their people. Traditionally, historians have distinguished between the "absolutist" governments of France, Spain, central Europe, and Russia and the constitutionalist governments of England and the Dutch Republic.

Whereas absolutist monarchs gathered all power under their personal control, English and Dutch rulers were obliged to respect laws passed by representative institutions. More recently, historians have emphasized commonalities among these powers. Despite their political differences, all these states shared common projects of protecting and expanding their frontiers, raising new taxes, consolidating central control, and competing for the new colonies opening up in the New and Old Worlds.

Rulers who wished to increase their authority encountered formidable obstacles. Some were purely material. Without paved roads, telephones, or other modern technology, it took weeks to convey orders from the central government to the provinces. Rulers also suffered from lack of information about their realms, making it impossible to police and tax the population effectively. Local power structures presented another serious obstacle. Nobles, the church, provincial and national assemblies, town councils, guilds, and other bodies held legal privileges, which could not easily be rescinded. In some kingdoms many people spoke a language different from the Crown's, further diminishing their willingness to obey its commands.

Nonetheless, over the course of the seventeenth century both absolutist and constitutional governments achieved new levels of central control. This increased authority focused in four areas in particular: greater taxation, growth in armed forces, larger and more efficient bureaucracies, and the increased ability to compel obedience from their subjects. Over time, centralized power added up to something close to sovereignty. A state may be termed sovereign when it possesses a monopoly over the instruments of justice and the use of force within clearly defined boundaries. In a sovereign state, no system of courts, such as ecclesiastical tribunals, competes with state courts in the dispensation of justice; and private armies, such as those of feudal lords, present no threat to central authority. While seventeenth-century states did not acquire total sovereignty, they made important strides toward that goal.

Warfare and the Growth of Army Size

The driving force of seventeenth-century state-building was warfare, characterized by dramatic changes in the size and style of armies. Medieval armies had been raised by feudal lords for particular wars or campaigns, after which the troops were disbanded. In the seventeenth century monarchs took command of recruiting and maintaining armies—in peacetime as well as wartime. Kings deployed their troops both inside and outside the country in the interests of the monarchy. Instead of serving their own interests, army officers were required to be loyal and obedient to the monarchs who commanded them. New techniques for training and deploying soldiers meant a rise in the professional standards of the army.

Along with professionalization came an explosive growth in army size. The French took the lead, with the army growing from roughly 125,000 men in the Thirty Years' War to 340,000 at the end of the seventeenth century.[3] This growth was caused in part by changes in the style of armies. Mustering a royal army took longer than simply hiring a mercenary band, giving enemies time to form coalitions. For example, the large coalitions Louis XIV confronted (see page 492) required him to fight on multiple fronts with huge armies. In turn, the relative size and wealth of France among European nations allowed Louis to field enormous armies and thereby to pursue the ambitious foreign policies

The Professionalization of the Swedish Army Swedish king Gustavus Adolphus, surrounded by his generals, gives thanks to God for the safe arrival of his troops in Germany during the Thirty Years' War. A renowned military leader, the king imposed constant training drills and rigorous discipline on his troops, which contributed to their remarkable success in the war. (Photo courtesy of The Army Museum, Stockholm)

that caused his alarmed neighbors to form coalitions against him.

The death toll during war for noble officers, who personally led their men in battle, was startlingly high. The paramount noble value of honor outshone concerns for safety or material benefit. Nobles had to purchase their positions in the army and supply horses, food, uniforms, and weapons for themselves and their troops. Royal stipends did not begin to cover these expenses. The only legacy an officer's widow received was the debt incurred to fund her husband's military career. It was not until the 1760s that the French government assumed the costs of equipping troops.

Other European powers were quick to follow the French example. The rise of absolutism in central and eastern Europe led to a vast expansion in the size of armies. Great Britain followed a similar, albeit distinctive pattern. Instead of building a land army, the British focused on naval forces and eventually built the largest navy in the world.

Popular Political Action

In the seventeenth century increased pressures of taxation and warfare turned neighborhood riots over the cost of bread into armed uprisings. Popular revolts were extremely common in England, France, Spain, Portugal, and Italy in the mid-seventeenth century. In 1640 Philip IV of Spain faced revolt in Catalonia, the economic center of his realm. At the same time he struggled to put down uprisings in Portugal and in the northern provinces of the Netherlands. In 1647 the city of Palermo, in Spanish-occupied Sicily, exploded in protest over food shortages caused by a series of bad harvests. Fearing public unrest, the city government subsidized the price of bread, attracting even more starving peasants from the countryside. When Madrid ordered an end to subsidies, municipal leaders decided to lighten the loaf rather than raise prices. Not fooled by this change, local women led a bread riot, shouting "Long live the king and down with the taxes and the bad government!" As riot transformed to armed revolt, insurgency spread to the rest of the island and eventually to Naples on the mainland. Apart from affordable food, rebels demanded the suppression of extraordinary taxes and participation in municipal government. Some dreamed of a republic in which noble tax exemptions would be abolished. Despite initial successes, the revolt lacked unity and strong leadership and could not withstand the forces of the state.

In France urban uprisings became a frequent aspect of the social and political landscape. Beginning in 1630 and continuing on and off through the early 1700s, major insurrections occurred at Dijon, Bordeaux (bor-DOH), Montpellier, Lyons, and Amiens. All were characterized by deep popular anger and violence directed at outside officials sent to collect taxes. These officials were sometimes seized, beaten, and hacked to death. For example, in 1673 Louis XIV's imposition of new taxes on legal transactions, tobacco, and pewter ware provoked an uprising in Bordeaux.

Municipal and royal authorities often struggled to overcome popular revolt. They feared that stern repressive measures, such as sending in troops to fire on crowds, would create martyrs and further inflame the situation, while forcible full-scale military occupation of a city would be very expensive. The limitations of royal authority gave some leverage to rebels. To quell riots, royal edicts were sometimes suspended, prisoners released, and discussions initiated.

By the beginning of the eighteenth century, this leverage had largely disappeared. Municipal governments were better integrated into the national structure, and local authorities had prompt military support from the central government. People who publicly opposed royal policies and taxes received swift and severe punishment.

Absolutism in France and Spain

What factors led to the rise of the French absolutist state under Louis XIV, and why did absolutist Spain experience decline in the same period? ■

In the Middle Ages jurists held that as a consequence of monarchs' coronation and anointment with sacred oil, they ruled "by the grace of God." Law was given by God; kings "found" the law and acknowledged that they must respect and obey it. Kings in absolutist states amplified these claims, asserting that, as they were chosen by God, they were responsible to God alone. They claimed exclusive power to make and enforce laws, denying any other institution or group the authority to check their power. In France the founder of the Bourbon monarchy, Henry IV, established foundations upon which his successors Louis XIII and Louis XIV built a stronger, more centralized French state. Louis XIV is often seen as the epitome of an "absolute" monarch, with his endless wars, increased taxes and economic regulation, and glorious palace at Versailles. In truth, his success relied on collaboration with nobles, and thus his example illustrates both the achievements and the compromises of absolutist rule.

As French power rose in the seventeenth century, the glory of Spain faded. Once the fabulous revenue from American silver declined, Spain's economic stagnation could no longer be disguised, and the country faltered under weak leadership.

The Foundations of Absolutism

Louis XIV's absolutism had long roots. In 1589 his grandfather Henry IV (r. 1589–1610), the founder of the Bourbon dynasty, acquired a devastated country. Civil wars between Protestants and Catholics had wracked France since 1561. Poor harvests had reduced peasants to starvation, and commercial activity had declined drastically. "Henri le Grand" (Henry the Great), as the king was called, promised "a chicken in every pot" and inaugurated a remarkable recovery.

He did so by keeping France at peace during most of his reign. Although he had converted to Catholicism, he issued the Edict of Nantes, allowing Protestants the right to worship in 150 traditionally Protestant towns throughout France. He sharply lowered taxes and instead charged royal officials an annual fee to guarantee the right to pass their positions down to their heirs. He also improved the infrastructure of the country, building new roads and canals and repairing the ravages of years of civil war. Despite his efforts at peace, Henry was murdered in 1610 by a Catholic zealot, setting off a national crisis.

After the death of Henry IV his wife, the queen-regent Marie de' Medici, headed the government for the nine-year-old Louis XIII (r. 1610–1643). In 1628 Armand Jean du Plessis—Cardinal Richelieu (1585–1642)—became first minister of the French crown. Richelieu's maneuvers allowed the monarchy to maintain power within Europe and within its own borders despite the turmoil of the Thirty Years' War.

Cardinal Richelieu's political genius is best reflected in the administrative system he established to strengthen royal control. He extended the use of intendants, commissioners for each of France's thirty-two districts who were appointed directly by the monarch, to whom they were solely responsible. They recruited men for the army, supervised the collection of taxes, presided over the administration of local law, checked up on the local nobility, and regulated economic activities in their districts. As the intendants' power increased under Richelieu, so did the power of the centralized French state.

Under Richelieu, the French monarchy also acted to repress Protestantism. Louis personally supervised the siege of La Rochelle, an important port city and a major commercial center with strong ties to Protestant Holland and England. After the city fell in October 1628, its municipal government was suppressed. Protestants retained the right of public worship, but the Catholic liturgy was restored. The fall of La Rochelle was one step in the removal of Protestantism as a strong force in French life.

Richelieu did not aim to wipe out Protestantism in the rest of Europe, however. His main foreign policy goal was to destroy the Catholic Habsburgs' grip on territories that surrounded France. Consequently, Richelieu supported Habsburg enemies, including Protestants. In 1631 he signed a treaty with the Lutheran king Gustavus Adolphus promising French support against the Habsburgs in the Thirty Years' War. For the French cardinal, interests of state outweighed religious considerations.

Richelieu's successor as chief minister for the next child-king, the four-year-old Louis XIV, was Cardinal Jules Mazarin (1602–1661). Along with the regent, Queen Mother Anne of Austria, Mazarin continued Richelieu's centralizing policies. His struggle to increase royal revenues to meet the costs of war led to the uprisings of 1648–1653 known as the **Fronde**. A *frondeur* was originally a street urchin who threw mud at the passing carriages of the rich, but the word came to

be applied to the many individuals and groups who opposed the policies of the government. In Paris, magistrates of the Parlement of Paris, the nation's most important court, were outraged by the Crown's autocratic measures. These so-called robe nobles (named for the robes they wore in court) encouraged violent protest by the common people. During the first of several riots, the queen mother fled Paris with Louis XIV. As rebellion spread outside Paris and to the sword nobles (the traditional warrior nobility), civil order broke down completely. In 1651 Anne's regency ended with the declaration of Louis as king in his own right. Much of the rebellion died away, and its leaders came to terms with the government.

The violence of the Fronde had significant results for the future. The twin evils of noble rebellion and popular riots left the French wishing for peace and for a strong monarch to reimpose order. This was the legacy that Louis XIV inherited in 1661 when he assumed personal rule of the largest and most populous country in western Europe at the age of twenty-three. Humiliated by his flight from Paris, he was determined to avoid any recurrence of rebellion.

Louis XIV and Absolutism

In the reign of Louis XIV (r. 1643–1715), the longest in European history, the French monarchy reached the peak of absolutist development. In the magnificence of his court and the brilliance of the culture that he presided over, Louis dominated his age. Religion, Anne, and Mazarin all taught Louis the doctrine of the divine right of kings: God had established kings as his rulers on earth, and they were answerable ultimately to him alone. Kings were divinely anointed and shared in the sacred nature of divinity, but they could not simply do as they pleased. They had to obey God's laws and rule for the good of the people. To symbolize his central role in the divine order, when he was fifteen years old Louis danced at a court ballet dressed as the sun, thereby acquiring the title of the "Sun King."

In addition to parading his power before the court, Louis worked very hard at the business of governing. He ruled his realm through several councils of state and insisted on taking a personal role in many of the councils' decisions. He selected councilors from the recently ennobled or the upper middle class because he believed "that the public should know, from the rank of those whom I chose to serve me, that I had no intention of sharing power with them."[4] Despite increasing financial problems, Louis never called a meeting of the Estates General. The nobility, therefore, had no means of united expression or action. Nor did Louis have a

> **Fronde** A series of violent uprisings during the early reign of Louis XIV triggered by growing royal control and oppressive taxation.

Laud attempted to impose two new elements on church organization in Scotland: a new prayer book, modeled on the Anglican *Book of Common Prayer*, and bishoprics. The Presbyterian Scots rejected these elements and revolted. To finance an army to put down the Scots, King Charles was compelled to summon Parliament in November 1640.

Charles had ruled from 1629 to 1640 without Parliament, financing his government through extraordinary stopgap levies considered illegal by most English people. For example, the king revived a medieval law requiring coastal districts to help pay the cost of ships for defense, but he levied the tax, called "ship money," on inland as well as coastal counties. Most members of Parliament believed that such taxation without consent amounted to despotism. Consequently, they were not willing to trust the king with an army. Moreover, many supported the Scots' resistance to Charles's religious innovations. Accordingly, this Parliament, called the "Long Parliament" because it sat from 1640 to 1660, enacted legislation that limited the power of the monarch and made government without Parliament impossible.

In 1641 the Commons passed the Triennial Act, which compelled the king to summon Parliament every three years. The Commons impeached Archbishop Laud and then threatened to abolish bishops. King Charles, fearful of a Scottish invasion—the original reason for summoning Parliament—reluctantly accepted these measures.

The next act in the conflict was precipitated by the outbreak of rebellion in Ireland, where English governors and landlords had long exploited the people. In 1641 the Catholic gentry of Ireland led an uprising in response to a feared invasion by anti-Catholic forces of the British Long Parliament.

Without an army, Charles I could neither come to terms with the Scots nor respond to the Irish rebellion. After a failed attempt to arrest parliamentary leaders, Charles left London for the north of England. There, he recruited an army drawn from the nobility and its cavalry staff, the rural gentry, and mercenaries. In response, Parliament formed its own army, the New Model Army, composed of the militia of the city of London and country squires with business connections. During the spring of 1642 both sides prepared for war. In July a linen weaver became the first casualty of the

Protectorate The English military dictatorship (1653–1658) established by Oliver Cromwell following the execution of Charles I.

The English Civil War, 1642–1649

Parliamentarians
Royalists
Major battle

civil war during a skirmish between royal and parliamentary forces in Manchester.

The English civil war (1642–1649) pitted the power of the king against that of the Parliament. After three years of fighting, Parliament's New Model Army defeated the king's armies at the Battles of Naseby and Langport in the summer of 1645. Charles, though, refused to concede defeat. Both sides jockeyed for position, waiting for a decisive event. This arrived in the form of the army under the leadership of Oliver Cromwell, a member of the House of Commons and a devout Puritan. In 1647 Cromwell's forces captured the king and dismissed members of the Parliament who opposed his actions. In 1649 the remaining representatives, known as the "Rump Parliament," put Charles on trial for high treason. Charles was found guilty and beheaded on January 30, 1649, an act that sent shock waves around Europe.

Cromwell and Puritanical Absolutism in England

With the execution of Charles, kingship was abolished. The question remained of how the country would be governed. One answer was provided by philosopher Thomas Hobbes (1588–1679). Hobbes held a pessimistic view of human nature and believed that, left to themselves, humans would compete violently for power and wealth. The only solution, as he outlined in his 1651 treatise *Leviathan*, was a social contract in which all members of society placed themselves under the absolute rule of a monarch, who would maintain peace and order. Hobbes imagined society as a human body in which the monarch served as head and individual subjects together made up the body. Just as the body cannot sever its own head, so Hobbes believed that society could not, having accepted the contract, rise up against its king. Deeply shocked by Charles's execution, he utterly denied the right of subjects to rebellion.

Hobbes's longing for a benevolent absolute monarch was not widely shared in England. Instead, a commonwealth, or republican government, was proclaimed. Theoretically, legislative power rested in the surviving members of Parliament, and executive power was lodged in a council of state. In fact, the army that had defeated the king controlled the government, and Oliver Cromwell controlled the army. Though called the **Protectorate**, the rule of Cromwell (1653–1658) constituted military dictatorship.

"The Royall Oake of Brittayne" The chopping down of this tree, as shown in this cartoon from 1649, signifies the end of royal authority, stability, and the rule of law. As pigs graze (representing the unconcerned common people), being fattened for slaughter, Oliver Cromwell, with his feet in Hell, quotes Scripture. This is a royalist view of the collapse of Charles I's government and the rule of Cromwell. (Courtesy of the Trustees of the British Museum)

The army prepared a constitution, the Instrument of Government (1653), that invested executive power in a lord protector (Cromwell) and a council of state. It provided for triennial parliaments and gave Parliament the sole power to raise taxes. But after repeated disputes, Cromwell dismissed Parliament in 1655, and the instrument was never formally endorsed. Cromwell continued the standing army and proclaimed quasi-martial law. He divided England into twelve military districts, each governed by a major general. Reflecting Puritan ideas of morality, Cromwell's state forbade sports, kept the theaters closed, and rigorously censored the press.

On the issue of religion, Cromwell favored some degree of toleration, and the Instrument of Government gave all Christians except Roman Catholics the right to practice their faith. Cromwell had long associated Catholicism in Ireland with sedition and heresy, and led an army there to reconquer the country in August

1649. One month later, his forces crushed a rebellion at Drogheda and massacred the garrison. After Cromwell's departure for England, atrocities worsened. The English banned Catholicism in Ireland, executed priests, and confiscated land from Catholics for English and Scottish settlers. These brutal acts left a legacy of Irish hatred for England.

Cromwell adopted mercantilist policies similar to those of absolutist France. He enforced a Navigation Act (1651) requiring that English goods be transported on English ships. The act was a great boost to the development of an English merchant marine and brought about a short but successful war with the commercially threatened Dutch. Cromwell also welcomed the immigration of Jews because of their skills, and they began to return to England after four centuries of absence.

The Protectorate collapsed when Cromwell died in 1658 and his ineffectual son succeeded him. Fed up with military rule, the English longed for a return to civilian government and, with it, common law and social stability. By 1660 they were ready to restore the monarchy.

The Restoration of the English Monarchy

The Restoration of 1660 brought to the throne Charles II (r. 1660–1685), eldest son of Charles I, who had been living on the continent. Both houses of Parliament were also restored, together with the established Anglican Church. The Restoration failed to resolve two serious problems, however. What was to be the attitude of the state toward Puritans, Catholics, and dissenters from the established church? And what was to be the relationship between the king and Parliament?

Test Act Legislation, passed by the English parliament in 1673, to secure the position of the Anglican Church by stripping Puritans, Catholics, and other dissenters of the right to vote, preach, assemble, hold public office, and attend or teach at the universities.

To answer the first question, Parliament enacted the **Test Act** of 1673 against those outside the Church of England, denying them the right to vote, hold public office, preach, teach, attend the universities, or even assemble for meetings. But these restrictions could not be enforced. When the Quaker William Penn held a meeting of his Friends and was arrested, the jury refused to convict him.

In politics Charles II was determined to avoid exile by working well with Parliament. This intention did not last, however. Finding that Parliament did not grant him an adequate income, in 1670 Charles entered into a secret agreement with his cousin Louis XIV. The French king would give Charles two hundred thousand pounds annually, and in return Charles would relax the laws against Catholics, gradually re-Catholicize England, and convert to Catholicism himself. When the details of this treaty leaked out, a great wave of anti-Catholic sentiment swept England.

When James II (r. 1685–1688) succeeded his brother, the worst English anti-Catholic fears were realized. In violation of the Test Act, James appointed Roman Catholics to positions in the army, the universities, and local government. When these actions were challenged in the courts, the judges, whom James had appointed, decided in favor of the king. The king was suspending the law at will and appeared to be reviving the absolutism of his father and grandfather. He went further. Attempting to broaden his base of support with Protestant dissenters and nonconformists, James granted religious freedom to all.

Seeking to prevent the return of Catholic absolutism, a group of eminent persons in Parliament and the Church of England offered the English throne to James's Protestant daughter Mary and her Dutch husband,

Prince William of Orange. In December 1688 James II, his queen, and their infant son fled to France and became pensioners of Louis XIV. Early in 1689 William and Mary were crowned king and queen of England.

Constitutional Monarchy and Cabinet Government

The English call the events of 1688 and 1689 the "Glorious Revolution" because it replaced one king with another with a minimum of bloodshed. It also represented the destruction, once and for all, of the idea of divine-right monarchy. William and Mary accepted the English throne from Parliament and in so doing explicitly recognized the supremacy of Parliament. The revolution of 1688 established the principle that sovereignty, the ultimate power in the state, was divided between king and Parliament and that the king ruled with the consent of the governed.

The men who brought about the revolution framed their intentions in the Bill of Rights (1689), which was formulated in direct response to Stuart absolutism. Law was to be made in Parliament; once made, it could not be suspended by the Crown. Parliament had to be called at least once every three years. The independence of the judiciary was established, and there was to be no standing army in peacetime. Protestants could possess arms, but the Catholic minority could not. No Catholic could ever inherit the throne. Additional legislation granted freedom of worship to Protestant dissenters, but not to Catholics.

The Glorious Revolution and the concept of representative government found its best defense in political philosopher John Locke's *Second Treatise of Civil Government* (1690). Locke (1632–1704) maintained that a government that oversteps its proper function — protecting the natural rights of life, liberty, and property — becomes a tyranny. By "natural" rights Locke meant rights basic to all men because all have the ability to reason. (His idea that there are natural or universal rights equally valid for all peoples and societies was especially popular in colonial America.) Under a tyrannical government, the people have the natural right to rebellion. On the basis of this link, he justified limiting the vote to property owners. (American colonists also appreciated his arguments that Native Americans had no property rights since they did not cultivate the land and, by extension, no political rights because they possessed no property.)

The events of 1688 and 1689 did not constitute a democratic revolution. The revolution placed sovereignty in Parliament, and Parliament represented the upper classes. The age of aristocratic government lasted at least until 1832 and in many ways until 1928, when women received full voting rights.

In the course of the eighteenth century, the cabinet

system of government evolved. The term *cabinet* derives from the small private room in which English rulers consulted their chief ministers. In a cabinet system, the leading ministers, who must have seats in and the support of a majority of the House of Commons, formulate common policy and conduct the business of the country. During the administration of one royal minister, Sir Robert Walpole, who led the cabinet from 1721 to 1742, the idea developed that the cabinet was responsible to the House of Commons. The Hanoverian king George I (r. 1714–1727) normally presided at cabinet meetings throughout his reign, but his son and heir, George II (r. 1727–1760), discontinued the practice. The influence of the Crown in decision making accordingly declined. Walpole enjoyed the favor of the monarchy and of the House of Commons and came to be called the king's first, or "prime," minister. In the English cabinet system, both legislative power and executive power are held by the leading ministers, who form the government.

England's brief and chaotic experiment with republicanism under Oliver Cromwell convinced its people of the advantages of a monarchy, albeit with strong checks on royal authority. The eighteenth-century philosopher David Hume went so far as to declare that he would prefer England to be peaceful under an absolute monarch than in constant civil war as a republic. These sentiments would have found little sympathy among the proud burghers of the Dutch Republic.

The Dutch Republic in the Seventeenth Century

In the late sixteenth century the seven northern provinces of the Netherlands fought for and won their independence from Spain. The independence of the Republic of the United Provinces of the Netherlands was recognized in 1648 in the treaty that ended the Thirty Years' War. In this period, often called the "golden age of the Netherlands," Dutch ideas and attitudes played a profound role in shaping a new and modern worldview. At the same time, the United Provinces developed its own distinctive model of a constitutional state.

Jan Steen, *The Merry Family*, 1668 In this painting from the Dutch golden age, a happy family enjoys a boisterous song while seated around the dining table. Despite its carefree appearance, the painting was intended to teach a moral lesson. The children are shown drinking wine and smoking, bad habits they have learned from their parents. The inscription hanging over the mantelpiece (upper right) spells out the message clearly: "As the Old Sing, so Pipe the Young." (Gianni Dagli Orti/The Art Archive)

Glückel of Hameln

INDIVIDUALS IN SOCIETY

IN 1690 A JEWISH WIDOW IN THE SMALL GERMAN TOWN OF HAMELN in Lower Saxony sat down to write her autobiography. She wanted to distract her mind from the terrible grief she felt over the death of her husband and to provide her twelve children with a record "so you will know from what sort of people you have sprung, lest today or tomorrow your beloved children or grandchildren came and know naught of their family." Out of her pain and heightened consciousness, Glückel (1646–1724) produced an invaluable source for scholars.

She was born in Hamburg two years before the end of the Thirty Years' War. In 1649 the merchants of Hamburg expelled the Jews, who moved to nearby Altona, then under Danish rule. When the Swedes overran Altona in 1657–1658, the Jews returned to Hamburg "purely at the mercy of the Town Council." Glückel's narrative proceeds against a background of the constant harassment to which Jews were subjected — special papers, permits, bribes — and in Hameln she wrote, "And so it has been to this day and, I fear, will continue in like fashion."

When Glückel was "barely twelve," her father betrothed her to Chayim Hameln. She married at age fourteen. She describes him as "the perfect pattern of the pious Jew," a man who stopped his work every day for study and prayer, fasted, and was scrupulously honest in his business dealings. Only a few years older than Glückel, Chayim earned his living dealing in precious metals and in making small loans on pledges (pawned goods). This work required his constant travel to larger cities, markets, and fairs, often in bad weather, always over dangerous roads. Chayim consulted his wife about all his business dealings. As he lay dying, a friend asked if he had any last wishes. "None," he replied. "My wife knows everything. She shall do as she has always done." For thirty years Glückel had been his friend, full business partner, and wife. They had thirteen children, twelve of whom survived their father, eight then unmarried. As Chayim had foretold, Glückel succeeded in launching the boys in careers and in providing dowries for the girls.

Although no images of Glückel exist, Rembrandt's *The Jewish Bride* suggests the mutual devotion that Glückel and her husband felt for each other. (Rijksmuseum-Stichting Amsterdam)

Glückel's world was her family, the Jewish community of Hameln, and the Jewish communities into which her children married. Her social and business activities took her across Europe, from Amsterdam to Berlin, from Danzig to Vienna, so her world was not narrow or provincial. She took great pride that Prince Frederick of Cleves, later king of Prussia, danced at the wedding of her eldest daughter. The rising prosperity of Chayim's businesses allowed the couple to maintain up to six servants.

Glückel was deeply religious, and her culture was steeped in Jewish literature, legends, and mystical and secular works. Above all, she relied on the Bible. Her language, heavily sprinkled with scriptural references, testifies to a rare familiarity with the Scriptures.

Students who would learn about seventeenth-century business practices, the importance of the dowry in marriage, childbirth, Jewish life, birthrates, family celebrations, and even the meaning of life can gain a good deal from the memoirs of this extraordinary woman who was, in the words of one of her descendants, the poet Heinrich Heine, "the gift of a world to me."

Source: *The Memoirs of Glückel of Hameln* (New York: Schocken Books, 1977).

QUESTIONS FOR ANALYSIS

1. Consider the ways in which Glückel of Hameln was both an ordinary and an extraordinary woman of her times. Would you call her a marginal or a central person in her society?

2. How might Glückel's successes be attributed to the stabilizing force of absolutism in the seventeenth century?

Rejecting the rule of a monarch, the Dutch established a republic, a state in which power rested in the hands of the people and was exercised through elected representatives. Other examples of republics in early modern Europe included the Swiss Confederation and several autonomous city-states of Italy and the Holy Roman Empire. Among the Dutch, an oligarchy of wealthy businessmen called "regents" handled domestic affairs in each province's Estates (assemblies). The provincial Estates held virtually all the power. A federal assembly, or States General, handled foreign affairs and war, but it did not possess sovereign authority. All issues had to be referred back to the local Estates for approval, and each of the seven provinces could veto any proposed legislation. Holland, the province with the largest navy and the most wealth, usually dominated the republic and the States General.

In each province, the Estates appointed an executive officer, known as the **stadholder**, who carried out ceremonial functions and was responsible for military defense. Although in theory freely chosen by the Estates and answerable to them, in practice the reigning prince of Orange usually held the office of stadholder in several of the seven provinces of the Republic. This meant that tensions always lingered between supporters of the House of Orange and those of the staunchly republican Estates, who suspected the princes of harboring monarchical ambitions. When one of them, William III, took the English throne in 1688 with his wife, Mary, the republic simply continued without stadholders for several decades.

> **stadholder** The executive officer in each of the United Provinces of the Netherlands, a position often held by the princes of Orange.

The political success of the Dutch rested on their phenomenal commercial prosperity. The moral and ethical bases of that commercial wealth were thrift, frugality, and religious toleration. Although there is scattered evidence of anti-Semitism, Jews enjoyed a level of acceptance and assimilation in Dutch business and general culture unique in early modern Europe. (See "Individuals in Society: Glückel of Hameln," at left.) In the Dutch Republic, toleration paid off: it attracted a great deal of foreign capital and investment.

The Dutch came to dominate the shipping business by putting profits from their original industry—herring fishing—into shipbuilding. They boasted the lowest shipping rates and largest merchant marine in Europe, allowing them to undersell foreign competitors (see Chapter 15). Trade and commerce brought the Dutch the highest standard of living in Europe, perhaps in the world. Salaries were high, and all classes of society ate well. A scholar has described the Netherlands as "an island of plenty in a sea of want." Consequently, the Netherlands experienced very few of the food riots that characterized the rest of Europe.[11]

countries in the later seventeenth and the eighteenth centuries. The personal success of scientists and scholars depended on making new discoveries, and science became competitive. Second, as governments intervened to support and sometimes direct research, the new scientific community became closely tied to the state and its agendas. National academies of science were created under state sponsorship in London in 1662, Paris in 1666, Berlin in 1700, and later across Europe. At the same time, scientists developed a critical attitude toward established authority that would inspire thinkers to question traditions in other domains as well.

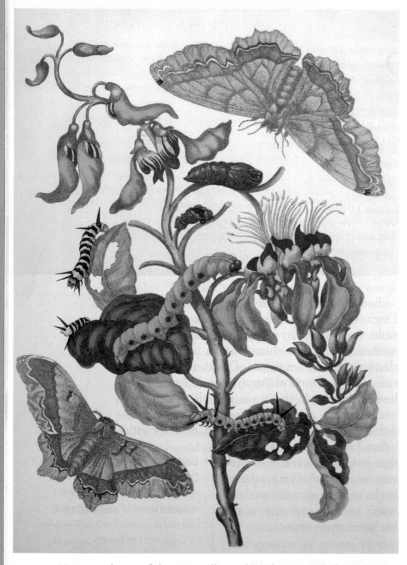

Metamorphoses of the Caterpillar and Moth Maria Sibylla Merian (1647–1717), the stepdaughter of a Dutch painter, became a celebrated scientific illustrator in her own right. Her finely observed pictures of insects in the South American colony of Surinam introduced many new species. For Merian, science was intimately tied with art: she not only painted but also bred caterpillars and performed experiments on them. Her two-year stay in Surinam, accompanied by a teenage daughter, was a daring feat for a seventeenth-century woman. (Bildarchiv Preussischer Kulturbesitz/Art Resource, NY)

Some things did not change in the scientific revolution. Scholars have recently analyzed representations of femininity and masculinity in the scientific revolution and have noted that nature was often depicted as a female, whose veil of secrecy needed to be stripped away and penetrated by male experts. New "rational" methods for approaching nature did not question traditional inequalities between the sexes—and may have worsened them in some ways. When Renaissance courts served as centers of learning, talented noblewomen could find niches in study and research. The rise of a professional scientific community raised barriers for women because the new academies that furnished professional credentials did not accept female members. (This continued for a long time. Marie Curie, the first person to win two Nobel prizes, was rejected by the French Academy of Science in 1911 because she was a woman.[8])

There were, however, a number of noteworthy exceptions. In Italy, universities and academies did offer posts to women, attracting some foreigners spurned by their own countries. Women across Europe were allowed to work as makers of wax anatomical models and as botanical and zoological illustrators. Women were also very much involved in informal scientific communities, attending salons, participating in scientific experiments, and writing learned treatises. Some female intellectuals were recognized as full-fledged members of the philosophical dialogue. In England, Margaret Cavendish, Anne Conway, and Mary Astell all contributed to debates about Descartes's mind-body dualism, among other issues. Descartes himself conducted an intellectual correspondence with the princess Elizabeth of Bohemia, of whom he stated: "I attach more weight to her judgment than to those messieurs the Doctors, who take for a rule of truth the opinions of Aristotle rather than the evidence of reason."[9]

The scientific revolution had few consequences for economic life and the living standards of the masses until the late eighteenth century. True, improvements in the techniques of navigation facilitated overseas trade and helped enrich states and merchant companies. But science had relatively few practical economic applications. Thus the scientific revolution of the seventeenth century was first and foremost an intellectual revolution. For more than a hundred years its greatest impact was on how people thought and believed.

Finally, there is the question of the role of religion in the development of science. Just as some historians have argued that Protestantism led to the rise of capitalism, others have concluded that Protestantism was a fundamental factor in the rise of modern science. According to this view, Protestantism, particularly in its Calvinist varieties, made scientific inquiry a question of individual conscience, not of religious doctrine. The Catholic Church, in contrast, supposedly suppressed scientific theories that conflicted with its teachings and thus discouraged scientific progress. The truth is more complicated. All Western religious authorities—Catholic, Protestant, and Jewish—opposed the Copernican system to a greater or lesser extent until about 1630, by which time the scientific revolution was definitely in progress. The Catholic Church was initially less hostile than Protestant and Jewish religious leaders, and Italian scientists played a crucial role in scientific progress right up to the trial of Galileo in 1633. Thereafter, the Counter-Reformation church became more hostile to science, a change that helped account for the decline of science in Italy (but not in Catholic France) after 1640. At the same time, Protestant countries such as the Netherlands and Denmark became quite "pro-science," especially countries that lacked a strong religious authority capable of imposing religious orthodoxy on scientific questions.

This was certainly the case with Protestant England after 1630. English religious conflicts became so intense that the authorities could not impose religious unity on anything, including science. The work of Bacon's many followers during Oliver Cromwell's commonwealth (see Chapter 16) helped solidify the independence of science. Bacon advocated the experimental approach precisely because it was open-minded and independent of preconceived religious and philosophical ideas. Neutral and useful, science became an accepted part of life and developed rapidly in England after about 1640.

Medicine, the Body, and Chemistry

The scientific revolution, which began with the study of the cosmos, soon inspired renewed study of the microcosm of the human body. For many centuries the ancient Greek physician Galen's explanation of the body carried the same authority as Aristotle's account of the universe. According to Galen, the body contained four humors: blood, phlegm, black bile, and yellow bile. Illness was believed to result from an imbalance of humors, which is why doctors frequently prescribed bloodletting to expel excess blood.

Swiss physician and alchemist Paracelsus (1493–1541) was an early proponent of the experimental method in medicine and pioneered the use of chemicals and drugs to address what he saw as chemical, rather than humoral, imbalances. Another experimentalist, Flemish physician Andreas Vesalius (1516–1564) studied anatomy by dissecting human bodies, often those of executed criminals. In 1543, the same year Copernicus published *On the Revolutions*, Vesalius issued his masterpiece, *On the Structure of the Human Body*. Its two hundred precise drawings revolutionized the understanding of human anatomy. The experimental approach also led English royal physician William Harvey (1578–1657) to discover the circulation of blood through the veins and arteries in 1628. Harvey was the first to explain that the heart worked like a pump and to explain the function of its muscles and valves.

Irishman Robert Boyle (1627–1691) founded the modern science of chemistry. Following Paracelsus's lead, he undertook experiments to discover the basic

ANDREAE VESALII.

AN. ÆT. XXVIII.

M.D.XLII.

Frontispiece to *De Humani Corporis Fabrica* (On the Structure of the Human Body) The frontispiece to Vesalius's pioneering work, published in 1543, shows him dissecting a corpse before a crowd of students. This was a revolutionary new hands-on approach for physicians, who usually worked from a theoretical, rather than a practical, understanding of the body. Based on direct observation, Vesalius replaced ancient ideas drawn from Greek philosophy with a much more accurate account of the structure and function of the body. (© SSPL/Science Museum/The Image Works)

elements of nature, which he believed was composed of infinitely small atoms. Boyle was the first to create a vacuum, thus disproving Descartes's belief that a vacuum could not exist in nature, and he discovered Boyle's law (1662), which states that the pressure of a gas varies inversely with volume.

The Enlightenment

How did the new worldview affect the way people thought about society and human relations? ■

The scientific revolution was the single most important factor in the creation of the new worldview of the eighteenth-century **Enlightenment**. This worldview, which has played a large role in shaping the modern mind, grew out of a rich mix of diverse and often conflicting ideas. For the writers who espoused them, these ideas competed vigorously for the attention of a growing public of well-educated but fickle readers, who remained a minority of the population.

Enlightenment The influential intellectual and cultural movement of the late seventeenth and eighteenth centuries that introduced a new worldview based on the use of reason, the scientific method, and progress.

rationalism A secular, critical way of thinking in which nothing was to be accepted on faith, and everything was to be submitted to reason.

Despite the diversity, three central concepts stand at the core of Enlightenment thinking. The most important and original idea was that the methods of natural science could and should be used to examine and understand all aspects of life. This was what intellectuals meant by *reason*, a favorite word of Enlightenment thinkers. Nothing was to be accepted on faith; everything was to be submitted to **rationalism**, a secular, critical way of thinking. A second important Enlightenment concept was that the scientific method was capable of discovering the laws of human society as well as those of nature. Thus was social science born. Its birth led to the third key idea, that of progress. Armed with the proper method of discovering the laws of human existence, Enlightenment thinkers believed, it was at least possible for human beings to create better societies and better people.

The Emergence of the Enlightenment

Loosely united by certain key ideas, the European Enlightenment (ca. 1690–1789) was a broad intellectual and cultural movement that gained strength gradually and did not reach its maturity until about 1750. Yet it was the generation that came of age between the publication of Newton's *Principia* in 1687 and the death of Louis XIV in 1715 that tied the crucial knot between the scientific revolution and a new outlook on life. Talented writers of that generation popularized hard-to-understand scientific achievements for the educated elite.

A new generation came to believe that the human mind itself is capable of making great progress. Medieval and Reformation thinkers had been concerned primarily with the abstract concepts of sin and salvation. The humanists of the Renaissance had emphasized worldly matters (especially art and literature), but their inspiration came from the classical past. Enlightenment thinkers came to believe that their era had gone far beyond antiquity and that intellectual progress was very possible.

The excitement of the scientific revolution also generated doubt and uncertainty, contributing to a widespread crisis in late-seventeenth-century European thought. In the wake of the devastation wrought by the Thirty Years' War, some people asked whether ideological conformity in religious matters was really necessary. Others skeptically asked if religious truth could ever be known with absolute certainty and concluded that it could not. This was a new development because many seventeenth-century scientists, Catholic and Protestant, believed that their work exalted God and helped explain his creation to fellow believers.

The most famous of these skeptics was Pierre Bayle (1647–1706), a French Huguenot who despised Louis XIV and found refuge in the Netherlands. Bayle critically examined the religious beliefs and persecutions of the past in his *Historical and Critical Dictionary* (1697). Demonstrating that human beliefs had been extremely varied and very often mistaken, he concluded that nothing can ever be known beyond all doubt, a view known as skepticism. His very influential *Dictionary* was reprinted frequently in the Netherlands and in England and was found in more private libraries of eighteenth-century France than any other book.

As they questioned religious teachings and traditions, some early Enlightenment philosophers became interested in Judaism. They read Jewish scripture mostly in the abstract to help define what true religion should be like. Some Jewish scholars participated in the early Enlightenment movement. The philosopher Baruch Spinoza (1632–1677) was excommunicated by the relatively large Jewish community of Amsterdam for his controversial religious ideas. Rejecting his youthful support for Descartes, Spinoza came to believe that mind and body are united in one substance and that God and nature were two names for the same thing. He envisioned a deterministic universe in which good and evil were merely relative values. Few of Spinoza's radical writings were published during his lifetime, but he is now recognized as among the most original thinkers of the early Enlightenment.

The rapidly growing travel literature on non-European lands and cultures was another cause of

Popularizing Science The frontispiece illustration of Fontenelle's *Conversations on the Plurality of Worlds* (1686) invites the reader to share the pleasures of astronomy with an elegant lady and an entertaining teacher. The drawing shows the planets revolving around the sun. (By permission of the Syndics of Cambridge University Library)

questioning among thinkers. In the wake of the great discoveries, Europeans were learning that the peoples of China, India, Africa, and the Americas all had their own very different beliefs and customs. Europeans shaved their faces and let their hair grow. Turks shaved their heads and let their beards grow. In Europe a man bowed before a woman to show respect. In Siam a man turned his back on a woman when he met her because it was disrespectful to look directly at her. Countless similar examples discussed in travel accounts helped change the perspective of educated Europeans. They began to look at truth and morality in relative, rather than absolute, terms. If anything was possible, who could say what was right or wrong?

Out of this period of intellectual turmoil came John Locke's *Essay Concerning Human Understanding* (1690), often viewed as the first major text of the Enlightenment. In this work Locke (1632–1704) brilliantly set forth a new theory about how human beings learn and form

their ideas. Whereas Descartes based his deductive logic on the conviction that certain first premises, or innate ideas, are imbued in all humans by God, Locke insisted that all ideas are derived from experience. The human mind at birth is like a blank tablet, or tabula rasa on which the environment writes the individual's understanding and beliefs. Human development is therefore determined by education and social institutions, for good or for evil. Locke's essay contributed to the theory of sensationalism, the idea that all human ideas and thoughts are produced as a result of sensory impressions. With his emphasis on the role of perception in the acquisition of knowledge, Locke provided a systematic justification of Bacon's emphasis on the importance of observation and experimentation. The *Essay Concerning Human Understanding* passed through many editions and translations and, along with Newton's *Principia*, was one of the dominant intellectual inspirations of the Enlightenment.

The Influence of the Philosophes

By the time Louis XIV died in 1715, many of the ideas that would soon coalesce into the new worldview had been assembled. Yet Christian Europe was still strongly attached to its established political and social structures and its traditional spiritual beliefs. By 1775, however, a large portion of western Europe's educated elite had embraced many of the new ideas. This acceptance was the work of the **philosophes** (fee-luh-zawfz), a group of influential intellectuals who proudly proclaimed that they, at long last, were bringing the light of knowledge to their ignorant fellow creatures.

> **philosophes** A group of French intellectuals who proclaimed that they were bringing the light of knowledge to their fellow creatures in the Age of Enlightenment.

Philosophe is the French word for "philosopher," and it was in France that the Enlightenment reached its highest development. There were at least three reasons for this. First, French was the international language of the educated classes in the eighteenth century, and France was still the wealthiest and most populous country in Europe. Second, although French intellectuals were not free to openly criticize either church or state, they were not as strongly restrained as intellectuals in eastern and east-central Europe. Third, the French philosophes made it their goal to reach a larger audience of elites, many of whom were joined together in the eighteenth-century concept of the "republic of letters"—an imaginary transnational realm of the well-educated.

Knowing that published attacks on society and the church would probably be banned or burned, the philosophes circulated their most radical works in manuscript form. To appeal to the public and get around the censors, they wrote novels and plays, histories and philosophies, dictionaries and encyclopedias, all filled with

Voltaire and Philosophes This painting belongs to a series commissioned by Catherine the Great to depict daily life at the philosopher's retreat at Ferney in Switzerland. It shows Voltaire seated at the dinner table surrounded by his followers, including *Encyclopedia* editors Diderot and d'Alembert. The scene is imaginary, for Diderot never visited Ferney. (Photo by permission of the Voltaire Foundation, University of Oxford)

satire and double meanings to spread their message to an eager audience.

One of the greatest philosophes, the baron de Montesquieu (mahn-tuhs-KYOO) (1689–1755), brilliantly pioneered this approach in *The Persian Letters*, an extremely influential social satire published in 1721. This work consisted of amusing letters supposedly written by two Persian travelers, Usbek and Rica, who as outsiders see European customs in unique ways and thereby allow Montesquieu a vantage point for criticizing existing practices and beliefs.

Like many Enlightenment philosophes, Montesquieu saw relations between men and women as highly representative of the overall social and political system. He used the oppression of women in the Persian harem, described in letters from Usbek's wives, to symbolize Eastern political tyranny. At the end of the book, the rebellion of Usbek's harem against the cruel eunuchs he left in charge demonstrates that despotism must ultimately fail. Montesquieu also used the Persians' observations of habitual infidelity among French wives and the strength of female power behind the throne to poke fun at European social and political customs. As Rica remarks:

The thing is that, for every man who has any post at court, in Paris, or in the country, there is a woman through whose hands pass all the favours and sometimes the injustices that he does. These women are all in touch with one another, and compose a sort of commonwealth whose members are always busy giving each other mutual help and support.[10]

Montesquieu was exaggerating, but he echoed other critics of the informal power women gained in an absolutist system, where royal mistresses and female courtiers could have more access to the king than government ministers (see Chapter 16). Having gained fame by using wit as a weapon against cruelty and superstition, Montesquieu settled down on his family estate to study history and politics. His interest was partly personal, for, like many members of the French robe nobility, he was disturbed by the growth in royal absolutism under Louis XIV. But Montesquieu was also inspired by the example of the physical sciences, and he set out to apply the critical method to the problem of government in *The Spirit of Laws* (1748). The result was a complex comparative study of republics, monarchies, and despotisms—a great pioneering inquiry in the emerging social sciences.

> ❝ The thing is that, for every man who has any post at court, in Paris, or in the country, there is a woman through whose hands pass all the favours and sometimes the injustices that he does. ❞

—**Montesquieu**

Showing that forms of government were shaped by history, geography, and customs, Montesquieu focused on the conditions that would promote liberty and prevent tyranny. He argued for a separation of powers, with political power divided and shared by a variety of classes and legal estates holding unequal rights and privileges. Admiring greatly the English balance of power among the king, the houses of Parliament, and the independent courts, Montesquieu believed that in France the thirteen high courts—the *parlements*—were frontline defenders of liberty against royal despotism. Apprehensive about the uneducated poor, Montesquieu was clearly no democrat, but his theory of separation of powers had a great impact on the constitutions of the young United States in 1789 and of France in 1791.

The most famous and in many ways most representative philosophe was François Marie Arouet, who was known by the pen name Voltaire (vohl-TAIR) (1694–1778). In his long career, this son of a comfortable middle-class family wrote more than seventy witty volumes, hobnobbed with kings and queens, and died a millionaire because of shrewd business speculations. His early career, however, was turbulent, and he was arrested on two occasions for insulting noblemen. Voltaire moved to England for three years in order to avoid a longer prison term in France, and there he came to share Montesquieu's enthusiasm for English liberties and institutions.

Returning to France and soon threatened again with prison in Paris, Voltaire had the great fortune of meeting Gabrielle-Emilie Le Tonnelier de Breteuil, marquise du Châtelet (SHAH-tuh-lay) (1706–1749), a gifted woman from the high aristocracy with a passion for science. Inviting Voltaire to live in her country house at Cirey in Lorraine and becoming his long-time companion (under the eyes of her tolerant husband), Madame du Châtelet studied physics and mathematics and published scientific articles and translations, including the first—and only—translation of Newton's *Principia* into French. Excluded from the Royal Academy of Sciences because she was a woman, Madame du Châtelet had no doubt that women's limited role in science was due to their unequal education. She once wrote that if she were a ruler, "I would reform an abuse which cuts off, so to speak, half the human race. I would make women participate in all the rights of humankind, and above all in those of the intellect."[11]

While living at Cirey, Voltaire wrote various works praising England and popularizing English scientific progress. Newton, he wrote, was history's greatest man, for he had used his genius for the benefit of humanity. "It is," wrote Voltaire, "the man who sways our minds by the prevalence of reason and the native force of truth, not they who reduce mankind to a state of slavery by force and downright violence . . . that claims our reverence and admiration."[12] In the true style of the Enlightenment, Voltaire mixed the glorification of science and reason with an appeal for better individuals and institutions.

Yet, like almost all of the philosophes, Voltaire was a reformer, not a revolutionary, in social and political matters. He pessimistically concluded that the best one could hope for in the way of government was a good monarch, since human beings "are very rarely worthy to govern themselves." He lavishly praised Louis XIV

Madame du Châtelet The marquise du Châtelet was fascinated by the new world system of Isaac Newton. She helped spread Newton's ideas in France by translating his *Principia* and by influencing Voltaire, her companion for fifteen years until her death. (Giraudon/Art Resource, NY)

❝ I must enlighten my people, cultivate their manners and morals, and make them as happy as human beings can be, or as happy as the means at my disposal permit. ❞

—FREDERICK THE GREAT

up its territory. Despite invasions from all sides, Frederick fought on with stoic courage. In the end he was miraculously saved: Peter III came to the Russian throne in 1762 and called off the attack against Frederick, whom he greatly admired.

The terrible struggle of the Seven Years' War tempered Frederick's interest in territorial expansion and brought him to consider how more humane policies for his subjects might also strengthen the state. Thus Frederick went beyond a superficial commitment to Enlightenment culture for himself and his circle. He tolerantly allowed his subjects to believe as they wished in religious and philosophical matters. He promoted the advancement of knowledge, improving his country's schools and permitting scholars to publish their findings. Moreover, Frederick tried to improve the lives of his subjects more directly. As he wrote his friend Voltaire, "I must enlighten my people, cultivate their manners and morals, and make them as happy as human beings can be, or as happy as the means at my disposal permit."

The legal system and the bureaucracy were Frederick's primary tools. Prussia's laws were simplified, torture of prisoners was abolished, and judges decided cases quickly and impartially. Prussian officials became famous for their hard work and honesty. After the Seven Years' War ended in 1763, Frederick's government energetically promoted the reconstruction of agriculture and industry in his war-torn country. Frederick himself set a good example. He worked hard and lived modestly, claiming that he was "only the first servant of the state." Thus Frederick justified monarchy in terms of practical results and said nothing of the divine right of kings.

Frederick's dedication to high-minded government went only so far, however. While he condemned serfdom in the abstract, he accepted it in practice and did not free the serfs on his own estates. He accepted and extended the privileges of the nobility, who remained the backbone of the army and the entire Prussian state.

In reforming Prussia's bureaucracy, Frederick drew on the principles of **cameralism**, the German science of public administration that emerged in the decades following the Thirty Years' War. Influential throughout the German lands, cameralism held that monarchy was the best of all forms of government, that all elements of society should be placed at the service of the state, and that, in turn, the state should make use of its resources and authority to improve society. Predating the Enlightenment, cameralist interest in the public good was usually inspired by the needs of war. Cameralism shared with the Enlightenment an emphasis on rationality, progress, and utilitarianism; in the eighteenth century, they overlapped a lot.

Catherine the Great of Russia

Catherine the Great of Russia (r. 1762–1796) was one of the most remarkable rulers of her age, and the French philosophes adored her. Catherine was a German princess from Anhalt-Zerbst, an insignificant principality sandwiched between Prussia and Saxony. Her father commanded a regiment of the Prussian army, but her mother was related to the Romanovs of Russia, and that proved to be Catherine's opening to power.

At the age of fifteen Catherine's Romanov connection made her a suitable bride for the heir to the Russian throne. It was a mismatch from the beginning, but her *Memoirs* made her ambitions clear: "I did not care about Peter, but I did care about the crown." When her husband Peter III came to power during the Seven Year's War, his decision to withdraw Russian troops from the coalition against Prussia alienated the army. Catherine profited from his unpopularity to form a conspiracy to depose her husband. In 1762 Catherine's lover Gregory Orlov and his three brothers, all army officers, murdered Peter, and the German princess became empress of Russia.

Catherine had drunk deeply at the Enlightenment well. Never questioning that absolute monarchy was the best form of government, she set out to rule in an enlightened manner. She had three main goals. First, she worked hard to continue Peter the Great's effort to bring the culture of western Europe to Russia (see Chapter 16). To do so, she imported Western architects, sculptors, musicians, and intellectuals. She bought masterpieces of Western art and patronized the philosophes. An enthusiastic letter writer, she corresponded extensively with Voltaire and praised him as the "champion of the human race." When the French government banned the *Encyclopedia*, she offered to publish it in St. Petersburg, and she sent money to Diderot when he needed it. With these actions, Catherine won good press in the West for herself and for her country. Moreover, this intellectual ruler, who wrote plays and loved good talk, set the tone for the entire Russian nobility. Peter the Great westernized Russian armies, but it was Catherine who westernized the imagination of the Russian nobility.

cameralism View that monarchy was the best form of government, that all elements of society should serve the monarch, and that, in turn, the state should use its resources and authority to increase the public good.

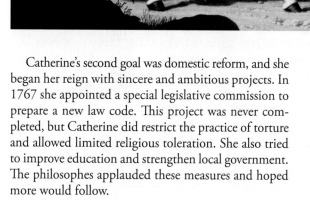

Catherine's second goal was domestic reform, and she began her reign with sincere and ambitious projects. In 1767 she appointed a special legislative commission to prepare a new law code. This project was never completed, but Catherine did restrict the practice of torture and allowed limited religious toleration. She also tried to improve education and strengthen local government. The philosophes applauded these measures and hoped more would follow.

Such was not the case. In 1773 a common Cossack soldier named Emelian Pugachev sparked a gigantic uprising of serfs, very much as Stenka Razin had done a century earlier (see Chapter 16). Proclaiming himself the true tsar, Pugachev issued orders abolishing serfdom, taxes, and army service. Thousands joined his cause, slaughtering landlords and officials over a vast area of southwestern Russia. Pugachev's untrained forces eventually proved no match for Catherine's noble-led army. Betrayed by his own company, Pugachev was captured and savagely executed.

Pugachev's rebellion put an end to any intentions Catherine might have had about reforming the system. The peasants were clearly dangerous, and her empire rested on the support of the nobility. After 1775 Catherine gave the nobles absolute control of their serfs, and she extended serfdom into new areas, such as Ukraine. In 1785 she formalized the nobility's privileged position, freeing nobles forever from taxes and state service. Under Catherine the Russian nobility attained its most exalted position, and serfdom entered its most oppressive phase.

Catherine's third goal was territorial expansion, and in this respect she was extremely successful. Her armies subjugated the last descendants of the Mongols and the Crimean Tartars, and began the conquest of the Caucasus (KAW-kuh-suhs). Her greatest coup by far was the partition of Poland (Map 17.1). When, between 1768 and 1772, Catherine's armies scored unprecedented victories against the Turks and thereby threatened to disturb the balance of power between Russia and Austria in eastern Europe, Frederick of Prussia obligingly came forward with a deal. He proposed that Turkey be let off easily and that Prussia, Austria, and Russia each compensate itself by taking a gigantic slice of the weakly ruled Polish territory. Catherine jumped at the chance. The first partition of Poland took place in 1772. Subsequent

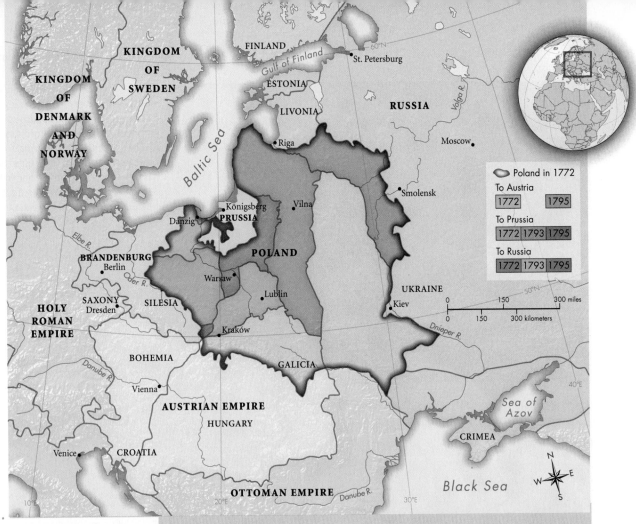

Mapping the Past

Map 17.1 **The Partition of Poland, 1772–1795** In 1772 war between Russia and Austria threatened over Russian gains from the Ottoman Empire. To satisfy desires for expansion without fighting, Prussia's Frederick the Great proposed that parts of Poland be divided among Austria, Prussia, and Russia. In 1793 and 1795 the three powers partitioned the remainder, and the ancient republic of Poland vanished from the map.

ANALYZING THE MAP Of the three powers that divided the kingdom of Poland, which benefited most? How did the partition affect the geographical boundaries of each state, and what was the significance? What border with the former Poland remained unchanged? Why do you think this was the case?

CONNECTIONS Why was Poland vulnerable to partition in the latter half of the eighteenth century? What does it say about European politics at the time that a country could simply cease to exist on the map? Could that happen today?

To complete this activity online, go to the Online Study Guide at bedfordstmartins.com/mckaywest.

partitions in 1793 and 1795 gave away the rest of Polish territory, and the ancient republic of Poland vanished from the map.

The Austrian Habsburgs

Another female monarch, Maria Theresa (r. 1740–1780) of Austria, set out to reform her nation, although traditional power politics was a more important motivation for her than were Enlightenment teachings. A devout mother and wife who inherited power from her father, Charles VI, Maria Theresa was a remarkable but old-fashioned absolutist. Her more radical son, Joseph II (r. 1780–1790), drew on Enlightenment ideals, earning the title of "revolutionary emperor."

Emerging from the long War of the Austrian Succession in 1748 with the serious loss of Silesia, Maria Theresa was determined to introduce reforms that would make the state stronger and more efficient. First, she introduced measures aimed at limiting the papacy's political influence in her realm. Second, a whole series of administrative reforms strengthened the central

Maria Theresa The empress and her husband pose with twelve of their sixteen children at Schönbrunn palace in this family portrait by court painter Martin Meytens (1695–1770). Joseph, the heir to the throne, stands at the center of the star on the floor. Wealthy women often had very large families, in part because they, unlike poor women, seldom nursed their babies. (Réunion des Musées Nationaux/Art Resource, NY)

bureaucracy, smoothed out some provincial differences, and revamped the tax system, taxing even the lands of nobles, previously exempt from taxation. Third, the government sought to improve the lot of the agricultural population, cautiously reducing the power of lords over their hereditary serfs and their partially free peasant tenants.

Coregent with his mother from 1765 onward and a strong supporter of change, Joseph II moved forward rapidly when he came to the throne in 1780. Most notably, Joseph abolished serfdom in 1781, and in 1789 he decreed that peasants could pay landlords in cash rather than through compulsory labor on their land. This measure was violently rejected not only by the nobility but also by the peasants it was intended to help, because they lacked the necessary cash. When a disillusioned

Joseph died prematurely at forty-nine, the entire Habsburg empire was in turmoil. His brother Leopold II (r. 1790–1792) canceled Joseph's radical edicts in order to re-establish order. Peasants once again were required to do forced labor for their lords.

Despite differences, Joseph II and the other eastern European absolutists of the later eighteenth century combined old-fashioned state-building with the culture and critical thinking of the Enlightenment. In doing so, they succeeded in expanding the role of the state in the life of society. They perfected bureaucratic machines that were to prove surprisingly adaptive and capable of enduring into the twentieth century. Their failure to implement policies we would recognize as humane and enlightened—such as abolishing serfdom—may reveal inherent limitations in Enlightenment

Moses Mendelssohn and the Jewish Enlightenment

INDIVIDUALS IN SOCIETY

IN 1743 A SMALL, HUMPBACKED JEWISH BOY with a stammer left his poor parents in Dessau (DE-sow) in central Germany and walked eighty miles to Berlin, the capital of Frederick the Great's Prussia. According to one story, when the boy reached the Rosenthaler (ROH-zuhn-taw-lehr) Gate, the only one through which Jews could pass, he told the inquiring watchman that his name was Moses and that he had come to Berlin "to learn." The watchman laughed and waved him through. "Go Moses, the sea has opened before you."*

In Berlin the young Mendelssohn studied Jewish law and eked out a living copying Hebrew manuscripts in a beautiful hand. But he was soon fascinated by an intellectual world that had been closed to him in the Dessau ghetto. There, like most Jews throughout central Europe, he had spoken Yiddish—a mixture of German, Polish, and Hebrew. Now, working mainly on his own, he mastered German; learned Latin, Greek, French, and English; and studied mathematics and Enlightenment philosophy. Word of his exceptional abilities spread in Berlin's Jewish community (the dwelling of 1,500 of the city's 100,000 inhabitants). He began tutoring the children of a wealthy Jewish silk merchant, and he soon became the merchant's clerk and later his partner. But his great passion remained the life of the mind and the spirit, which he avidly pursued in his off hours.

Gentle and unassuming in his personal life, Mendelssohn was a bold thinker. Reading eagerly in Western philosophy since antiquity, he was, as a pious Jew, soon convinced that Enlightenment teachings need not be opposed to Jewish thought and religion. He concluded that reason could complement and strengthen religion, although each would retain its integrity as a separate sphere.† Developing his idea in his first great work, "On the Immortality of the Soul" (1767), Mendelssohn used the neutral setting of a philosophical dialogue between Socrates and his followers in ancient Greece to argue that the human soul lived forever. In refusing to bring religion and critical thinking into conflict, he was strongly influenced by contemporary German philosophers who argued similarly on behalf of Christianity. He reflected the way the German Enlightenment generally supported established religion, in contrast to the French Enlightenment, which attacked it.

Mendelssohn's treatise on the human soul captivated the educated German public, which marveled that a Jew could have written a philosophical masterpiece. In the excitement, a Christian zealot named Lavater challenged Mendelssohn in a pamphlet to accept Christianity or to demonstrate how the Christian faith was not "reasonable." Replying politely but passionately, the Jewish philosopher affirmed that his studies had only strengthened him in his faith, although he did not seek to convert anyone not born into Judaism. Rather, he urged toleration in religious matters and spoke up courageously against Jewish oppression.

Orthodox Jew and German philosophe, Moses Mendelssohn serenely combined two very different worlds. He built a bridge from the ghetto to the dominant culture over which many Jews would pass, including his novelist daughter Dorothea and his famous grandson, the composer Felix Mendelssohn.

QUESTIONS FOR ANALYSIS

1. How did Mendelssohn seek to influence Jewish religious thought in his time?
2. How do Mendelssohn's ideas compare with those of the French Enlightenment?

Lavater (right) attempts to convert Mendelssohn, in a painting of an imaginary encounter by Moritz Oppenheim. (Collection of the Judah L. Magnes Museum, Berkeley)

*H. Kupferberg, *The Mendelssohns: Three Generations of Genius* (New York: Charles Scribner's Sons, 1972), p. 3.

†D. Sorkin, *Moses Mendelssohn and the Religious Enlightenment* (Berkeley: University of California Press, 1996), pp. 8 ff.

thinking about equality and social justice, rather than in their execution of Enlightenment programs. The fact that leading philosophes supported rather than criticized eastern rulers' policies suggests some of the blinders of the era.

Jewish Life and the Limits of Enlightened Absolutism

Perhaps the best example of the limitations of enlightened absolutism are the debates surrounding the possible emancipation of the Jews. Europe's small Jewish populations lived under highly discriminatory laws. For the most part, Jews were confined to tiny, overcrowded ghettos, were excluded by law from most business and professional activities, and could be ordered out of a kingdom at a moment's notice. Still, a very few did manage to succeed and to obtain the right of permanent settlement, usually by performing some special service for the state. Many rulers relied on Jewish bankers for loans to raise armies and run their kingdoms. Because of their large and closely knit diaspora, Jewish merchants and traders were prominent in international trade.

In the eighteenth century, an Enlightenment movement known as the **Haskalah** emerged from within the European Jewish community, led by the Prussian philosopher Moses Mendelssohn (1729–1786). (See "Individuals in Society: Moses Mendelssohn and the Jewish Enlightenment," at left.) Christian and Jewish Enlightenment philosophers, including Mendelssohn, began to advocate for freedom and civil rights for European Jews. In an era of reason, tolerance, and universality, they argued, restrictions on religious grounds could not stand. The Haskalah accompanied a period of controversial social change within Jewish communities, in which rabbinic controls loosened and heightened interaction with Christians took place.

Arguments for tolerance won some ground. The British Parliament passed a law allowing naturalization of Jews in 1753, but later repealed the law due to public outrage. The most progressive reforms took place under Austrian emperor Joseph II. Among his liberal edicts of the 1780s were measures intended to integrate Jews more fully into society, including eligibility for military service, admission to higher education and artisanal trades, and removal of requirements for special clothing or emblems. Welcomed by many Jews, these reforms raised fears among traditionalists of assimilation into the general population.

Many monarchs refused to entertain the idea of emancipation. Although he permitted freedom of religion to his Christian subjects, Frederick the Great of Prussia firmly opposed any general emancipation for the Jews, as he did for the serfs. Catherine the Great, who acquired most of Poland's large Jewish population when she annexed part of that country in the late eighteenth century, similarly refused. In 1791 she established the Pale of Settlement, a territory including parts of modern-day Poland, Latvia, Lithuania, Ukraine, and Belorussia, in which most Jews were required to live. Jewish habitation was restricted to the Pale until the Russian Revolution in 1917.

The first European state to remove all restrictions on the Jews was France under the French Revolution. Over the next hundred years, Jews gradually won full legal and civil rights throughout the rest of western Europe. Emancipation in eastern Europe took even longer and aroused more conflict and violence.

Haskalah The Jewish Enlightenment of the second half of the eighteenth century, led by the Prussian philosopher Moses Mendelssohn.

The Pale of Settlement, 1791

LOOKING BACK LOOKING AHEAD

HAILED AS THE ORIGIN of modern thought, the scientific revolution must also be seen as a product of its past. Medieval universities gave rise to important new scholarship, and the ambition and wealth of Renaissance patrons nurtured intellectual curiosity. Religious faith also impacted the scientific revolution, inspiring thinkers to understand the glory of God's creation, while bringing censure and personal tragedy to others. Natural philosophers following Copernicus pioneered new methods of observing and explaining nature while drawing on centuries-old traditions of mysticism, astrology, alchemy, and magic.

The Enlightenment ideas of the eighteenth century were a similar blend of past and present; they could serve as much to bolster authoritarian regimes as to inspire revolutionaries to fight for individual rights and liberties. Although the Enlightenment fostered critical thinking about everything from science to religion, the majority of Europeans, including many prominent thinkers, remained devout Christians.

The achievements of the scientific revolution and the Enlightenment are undeniable. Key Western values of rationalism, human rights, and open-mindedness were born from these movements. With their new notions of progress and social improvement, Europeans would embark on important revolutions in industry and politics in the centuries that followed. Nonetheless, others have seen a darker side. For these critics, the mastery over nature permitted by the scientific revolution now threatens to overwhelm the earth's fragile equilibrium, and the Enlightenment belief in the universal application of reason can lead to arrogance and intolerance, particularly intolerance of other people's spiritual, cultural, and political values. Such vivid debate about the legacy of these intellectual and scientific developments testifies to their continuing importance in today's world.

CHAPTER REVIEW

■ What was revolutionary in the new attitudes toward the natural world? (p. 520)

Decisive breakthroughs in astronomy and physics in the seventeenth century demolished the medieval synthesis of Aristotelian philosophy and Christian theology. One of the most notable discoveries was that the sun, not the earth, was the center of the galaxy. Although the early scientists considered their ideas to be in line with religion, their discoveries ran counter to long-held beliefs about the design of the universe by the Creator; therefore, Copernicus, Kepler, Galileo, and others were branded as heretics. Meanwhile, Bacon promoted the experimental method that drew conclusions based on empirical evidence, and Descartes championed deductive reasoning that speculated truths based on known principles. These two important methods eventually combined to form the modern scientific method that relies on both experimentation and reason. Following these early innovators, Newton devised the law of universal gravitation, which for the first time synthesized the orbiting planets of the solar system with the motion of objects on earth. These scientific breakthroughs had only limited practical consequences at the time, but their impact on intellectual life was enormous, nurturing a new critical attitude in many disciplines. In addition, an international scientific community arose, and state-sponsored academies, which were typically closed to women, advanced scientific research.

■ How did the new worldview affect the way people thought about society and human relations? (p. 530)

Interpreting scientific findings and Newtonian laws in a manner that was both antitradition and antireligion, Enlightenment philosophes extolled the superiority of rational, critical thinking. This new method, they believed, promised not just increased knowledge but even the discovery of the fundamental laws of human society. Believing that all aspects of life were open to question and skepticism, Enlightenment thinkers opened the doors to religious tolerance, representative government, and general intellectual debate. One important downside of the new scientific method was that it led to the classification of human races, with white Europeans placing themselves at the top of a new racial hierarchy.

What impact did new ways of thinking have on political developments and monarchical absolutism? (p. 541)

The ideas of the Enlightenment were an inspiration for monarchs, particularly absolutist rulers in central and eastern Europe who saw in them important tools for reforming and rationalizing their governments. Their primary goal was to strengthen their states and increase the efficiency of their bureaucracies and armies. Enlightened absolutists believed that these reforms would ultimately improve the lot of ordinary people, but this was not their chief concern. With few exceptions, they did not question the institution of serfdom. The fact that leading philosophes supported rather than criticized Eastern rulers' policies suggests some of the limitations of the era. Christian and Jewish Enlightenment thinkers argued in favor of emancipating Europe's small Jewish population. Some reforms took place, but full emancipation did not take place until the nineteenth century in the West and even later in the East.

Suggested Reading

Alexander, John T. *Catherine the Great: Life and Legend.* 1989. The best biography of the famous Russian tsarina.

Beales, Derek. *Joseph II.* 1987. A fine biography of the reforming Habsburg ruler.

Delborgo, James, and Nicholas Dew, eds. *Science and Empire in the Atlantic World.* 2008. A collection of essays examining the relationship between the scientific revolution and the imperial expansion of European powers across the Atlantic.

Ellis, Markman. *The Coffee-House: A Cultural History.* 2004. An engaging study of the rise of the coffeehouse and its impact on European cultural and social life.

Eze, E. Chukwudi, ed. *Race and the Enlightenment: A Reader.* 1997. A pioneering source on the origins of modern racial thinking in the Enlightenment.

Goodman, Dena. *The Republic of Letters: A Cultural History of the Enlightenment.* 1994. An innovative study of the role of salons and salon hostesses in the rise of the Enlightenment.

MacDonogh, Giles. *Frederick the Great.* 2001. An outstanding biography of the Prussian king.

Osler, Margaret J., ed. *Rethinking the Scientific Revolution.* 2000. A collection of essays focusing on new historical approaches to the scientific revolution.

Outram, Dorinda. *The Enlightenment,* 2d ed. 2006. An outstanding and accessible introduction to Enlightenment debates that emphasizes the Enlightenment's social context and global reach.

Shapin, Steven. *The Scientific Revolution.* 2001. A concise and well-informed general introduction to the scientific revolution.

Sorkin, David. *Moses Mendelssohn and the Religious Enlightenment.* 1996. A brilliant study of the Jewish philosopher and of the role of religion in the Enlightenment.

Notes

1. H. Butterfield, *The Origins of Modern Science* (New York: Macmillan, 1951), p. viii.
2. Quoted in A. G. R. Smith, *Science and Society in the Sixteenth and Seventeenth Centuries* (New York: Harcourt Brace Jovanovich, 1972), p. 97.
3. Quoted in Butterfield, *The Origins of Modern Science*, p. 47.
4. Ibid., p. 120.
5. Quoted in John Freely, *Aladdin's Lamp: How Greek Science Came to Europe Through the Islamic World* (New York: Knopf, 2009), p. 206.
6. Ibid., p. 217.
7. Ibid., p. 225.
8. L. Schiebinger, *The Mind Has No Sex? Women in the Origins of Modern Science* (Cambridge, Mass.: Harvard University Press, 1989), p. 2.
9. Jacqueline Broad, *Women Philosophers of the Seventeenth Century* (Cambridge, U.K.: Cambridge University Press, 2003), p. 17.
10. Montesquieu, *Persian Letters*, trans. C. J. Betts (London: Penguin Books), 1993, p. 197.
11. Schiebinger, *The Mind Has No Sex?* p. 64.
12. Quoted in L. M. Marsak, ed., *The Enlightenment* (New York: John Wiley & Sons, 1972), p. 56.
13. Quoted in G. L. Mosse et al., eds., *Europe in Review* (Chicago: Rand McNally, 1964), p. 156.
14. Quoted in P. Gay, "The Unity of the Enlightenment," *History* 3 (1960): 25.
15. Quoted in G. P. Gooch, *Catherine the Great and Other Studies* (Hamden, Conn.: Archon Books, 1966), p. 149.
16. See E. Fox-Genovese, "Women in the Enlightenment," in *Becoming Visible: Women in European History*, 2d ed., ed. R. Bridenthal, C. Koonz, and S. Stuard (Boston: Houghton Mifflin, 1987), esp. pp. 252–259, 263–265.
17. Jean Le Rond d'Alembert, *Eloges lus dans les séances publiques de l'Académie française* (Paris, 1779), p. ix, quoted in Mona Ozouf, "'Public Opinion' at the End of the Old Regime," *The Journal of Modern History* 60, Supplement: Rethinking French Politics in 1788 (September 1988): S9.
18. Quoted in Emmanuel Chukwudi Eze, ed., *Race and the Enlightenment: A Reader* (Oxford: Blackwell, 1997), p. 33.

Key Terms

natural philosophy (p. 520)
Copernican hypothesis (p. 522)
experimental method (p. 524)
law of inertia (p. 524)
law of universal gravitation (p. 526)
empiricism (p. 526)
Cartesian dualism (p. 527)
Enlightenment (p. 530)
rationalism (p. 530)
philosophes (p. 531)
reading revolution (p. 535)
salons (p. 536)
rococo (p. 537)
public sphere (p. 537)
enlightened absolutism (p. 543)
cameralism (p. 544)
Haskalah (p. 549)

For practice quizzes and other study tools, visit the Online Study Guide at **bedfordstmartins.com/mckaywest**.

For primary sources from this period, see *Sources of Western Society*, **Second Edition**.

For Web sites, images, and documents related to topics in this chapter, visit Make History at **bedfordstmartins.com/mckaywest**.

Glossary

abbess/prioress Head of a convent for women. (p. 297)

abbot/prior Head of a monastery for men. (p. 298)

acropolis An elevated point within a city on which stood temples, altars, and public monuments. (p. 61)

Agincourt The location near Arras in Flanders where an English victory in 1415 led to the reconquest of Normandy. (p. 350)

agora A public square or marketplace that was a political center of Greece. (p. 61)

al-Andalus The part of the Iberian Peninsula under Muslim control in the eighth century, encompassing most of modern-day Spain. (p. 211)

anticlericalism Opposition to the clergy. (p. 408)

apostolic succession The doctrine that all bishops can trace their spiritual ancestry back to Jesus' apostles. (p. 180)

Arianism A theological belief that originated with Arius, a priest of Alexandria, denying that Christ was divine and co-eternal with God the Father. (p. 178)

Babylonian Captivity Period from 587 to 538 B.C.E. during which the survivors of a Babylonian attack on the southern kingdom of Judah were exiled in Babylonia. The term was later used to refer to the period from 1309 to 1376 when the popes resided in Avignon rather than in Rome. (pp. 38, 355)

barbarians From the Greek word meaning people who don't speak Greek; Romans used the term to describe any tribes of people who were not Greco-Roman. (p. 150)

barracks emperors The name of the period in the middle of the third century when many military commanders ruled the Roman Empire. (p. 171)

Beguines Groups of laywomen seeking to live religious lives in the growing cities of Europe. (p. 333)

Black Death Plague that first struck Europe in 1347 and killed perhaps one-third of the population. (p. 341)

Book of the Dead An Egyptian book that preserved ideas about death and the afterlife; it explains that the soul leaves the body to become part of the divine after death. (p. 21)

boyars The highest-ranking members of the Russian nobility. (pp. 232, 498)

Bronze Age The period in which the production and use of bronze implements became basic to society; bronze made farming more efficient and revolutionized warfare. (p. 25)

caliph A successor, as chosen by a group of Muhammad's closest followers. (p. 211)

cameralism View that monarchy was the best form of government, that all elements of society should serve the monarch, and that, in turn, the state should use its resources and authority to increase the public good. (p. 544)

canon law Church law, which had its own courts and procedures. (p. 255)

caravel A small, maneuverable, three-mast sailing ship developed by the Portuguese in the fifteenth century that gave the Portuguese a distinct advantage in exploration and trade. (p. 450)

Cartesian dualism Descartes's view that all of reality could ultimately be reduced to mind and matter. (p. 527)

catacombs Huge public underground cemeteries; the Roman catacombs offered refuge in times of persecution and include early pagan and Christian art. (p. 168)

cathedral The church of a bishop and the administrative headquarters of a diocese. (p. 326)

chivalry Code of conduct originally devised by the clergy to transform the crude and brutal behavior of the knightly class. (p. 290)

Christendom The term used by early medieval writers to refer to the realm of Christianity. (p. 269)

Christian humanists Northern humanists who interpreted Italian ideas about and attitudes toward classical antiquity and humanism in terms of their own religious traditions. (p. 384)

Cistercians Religious order founded in the late eleventh century that adopted an austere lifestyle and tried to separate from feudal power structures. (p. 294)

civilization A large-scale system of human political, economic, and social organization; civilizations include laws that govern, a code of manners and social conduct, and scientific, philosophical, and theological beliefs that explain the larger world. (p. 4)

civitas The city and surrounding territory that served as a basis of the administrative system in the Frankish kingdoms, based on Roman models. (p. 216)

college of cardinals A special group of high clergy with the authority and power to elect the pope and the responsibility to govern the church when the office of the pope is vacant. (p. 252)

Columbian exchange The exchange of animals, plants, and diseases between the Old and the New Worlds. (p. 463)

comitatus A war band of young men in a barbarian tribe who were closely associated with the king, swore loyalty to him, and fought with him in battle. (p. 187)

comites A senior official or royal companion, later called a count, who presided over the civitas. (p. 216)

commercial revolution The transformation of the European economy as a result of changes in business procedures and growth in trade. (p. 312)

common law A body of English law established by King Henry II's court that in the next two or three centuries became common to the entire country. (p. 249)

Common Peace A political concept created in the fourth century B.C.E. to prevent war based on the idea that the states of Greece should live together in peace and freedom, each enjoying its own laws and customs. (p. 85)

communes Sworn associations of free men in Italian cities led by merchant guilds that sought political and economic independence from local nobles. (p. 375)

conciliarists People who believed that the authority in the Roman church should rest in a general council composed of clergy, theologians, and laypeople, rather than in the pope alone. (p. 356)

confraternities Voluntary lay groups organized by occupation, devotional preference, neighborhood, or charitable activity. (p. 357)

conquistador Spanish for "conqueror"; Spanish soldier-explorers, such as Hernando Cortés and Francisco Pizarro, who sought to conquer the New World for the Spanish crown. (p. 449)

constitutionalism A form of government in which power is limited by law and balanced between the authority and power of the government on the one hand and the rights and liberties of the subject or citizen on the other hand; could include constitutional monarchies or republics. (p. 506)

constitutional monarchy A monarchy in which the power of the ruler is restricted by the constitution and the laws of the nation. (p. 147)

consuls The two chief Roman magistrates; elected for one-year terms, consuls along with the senate ran the affairs of the state. (p. 125)

Copernican hypothesis The idea that the sun, not the earth, was the center of the universe. (p. 522)

Cossacks Free groups and outlaw armies originally comprising runaway peasants living on the borders of Russian territory from the fourteenth century onward. By the end of the sixteenth century they had formed an alliance with the Russian state. (p. 498)

courts Magnificent households and palaces where the signori and the most powerful merchant oligarchs required political business to be conducted. (p. 376)

Covenant A formal agreement between Yahweh and the Hebrew people that if the Hebrews worshiped Yahweh as their only god, he would consider them his chosen people and protect them from their enemies. (p. 38)

craft guild A band of producers that regulated most aspects of production. (p. 307)

Crusades Holy wars sponsored by the papacy for the recovery of the Holy Land from the Muslims from the late eleventh to the late thirteenth centuries. (p. 255)

cuneiform Sumerian form of writing; the term describes the wedge-shaped strokes of the stylus. (p. 11)

debate about women Debate among writers and thinkers in the Renaissance about women's qualities and proper role in society. (p. 396)

Delian League A free naval alliance under the leadership of Athens aimed at liberating Ionia from Persian rule. (p. 69)

democracy A type of Greek government in which all people, without regard to birth or wealth, administered the work-

ings of government; in practice, only people granted citizenship participated. (p. 62)

diocese An administrative unit in the later Roman Empire; adopted by the Christian church as the territory under the authority of a bishop. (p. 176)

Domesday Book A general inquiry about the wealth of his lands ordered by William of Normandy; it is a valuable source of social and economic information about medieval England. (p. 242)

Dominicans The followers of Dominic, officially known as the Preaching Friars. (p. 331)

Edict of Nantes A document issued by Henry IV of France in 1598, granting liberty of conscience and of public worship to Calvinists, which helped restore peace in France. (p. 434)

empiricism A theory of inductive reasoning that calls for acquiring evidence through observation and experimentation rather than reason and speculation. (p. 526)

encomienda system A system whereby the Spanish crown granted the conquerors the right to forcibly employ groups of Indians; it was a disguised form of slavery. (p. 461)

English Peasants' Revolt Revolt by English peasants in 1381 in response to changing economic conditions. (p. 360)

enlightened absolutism Term coined by historians to describe the rule of eighteenth-century monarchs who, without renouncing their own absolute authority, adopted Enlightenment ideals of rationalism, progress, and tolerance. (p. 543)

Enlightenment The influential intellectual and cultural movement of the late seventeenth and eighteenth centuries that introduced a new worldview based on the use of reason, the scientific method, and progress. (p. 530)

Epicureanism A practical philosophy founded by Epicurus, it argued that the principal good of human life is pleasure. (p. 109)

Exchequer The bureau of finance established by Henry I; the first institution of the governmental bureaucracy of England. (p. 242)

excommunication A penalty used by the Christian church that meant being cut off from the sacraments and all Christian worship. (p. 253)

experimental method The approach, pioneered by Galileo, that the proper way to explore the workings of the universe was through repeatable experiments rather than speculation. (p. 524)

federalism A political system developed by Greek states that banded together in leagues and marshaled their resources to defend themselves from outside interference, while remaining independent in their internal affairs. (p. 63)

feudalism A political system in which a vassal was promised protection and material support by a lord in return for his loyalty, aid, and military assistance. (p. 234)

fief A piece of land granted by a feudal lord to a vassal in return for service and loyalty. (p. 234)

First Punic War A war between Rome and Carthage in which Rome emerged the victor after twenty-three years of fighting (264–241 B.C.E.). (p. 128)

First Triumvirate A political alliance among Caesar, Crassus, and Pompey in which they agreed to advance one another's interests. (p. 139)

five good emperors The five Roman emperors (Nerva, Trajan, Hadrian, Antoninus Pius, and Marcus Aurelius) who created an unparalleled period of peace and prosperity. (p. 155)

Five Pillars of Islam The five practices Muslims must fulfill according to the shari'a, or sacred law, including the profession of faith, prayer, fasting, giving alms to the poor, and pilgrimage to Mecca. (p. 210)

flagellants People who believed that the plague was God's punishment for sin and sought to do penance by flagellating (whipping) themselves. (p. 347)

forum A public meeting place in ancient Rome. (p. 122)

franchise The right to vote or hold Roman office. (p. 124)

Franciscans The followers of Francis and his mission of simplicity, humility, and devotion. (p. 331)

friars Men belonging to certain religious orders who did not live in monasteries but out in the world. (p. 332)

Fronde A series of violent uprisings during the early reign of Louis XIV triggered by growing royal control and oppressive taxation. (p. 487)

Gauls The Roman name for the Celts, a people who swept aside a Roman army and sacked Rome around 390 B.C.E. (p. 123)

Gentiles Non-Jews. (p. 168)

gladiators Criminals, slaves, and sometimes free men who fought each other or wild animals to the death in Roman arenas as public entertainment. (p. 158)

Gothic An architectural style typified by pointed arches and large stained-glass windows. (p. 326)

Great Famine A terrible famine in 1315–1322 that hit much of Europe after a period of climate change. (p. 340)

Great Schism The division, or split, in church leadership from 1378 to 1417 when there were two, then three, popes. (p. 355)

Great Silk Road The name of the major trading route to the east, so called because silk was one of the most prominent goods trafficked along it. (p. 107)

Hammurabi's law code A proclamation in the language of the land issued by the Babylonian king Hammurabi to establish law and justice; it inflicted harsh punishments, but was pervaded by a sense of responsibility to the people. (p. 17)

Hanseatic League A mercantile association of towns begun in northern Europe in the thirteenth century that allowed for mutual protection and security. (p. 311)

Haskalah The Jewish Enlightenment of the second half of the eighteenth century, led by the Prussian philosopher Moses Mendelssohn. (p. 549)

hegemony Political domination over other states. (p. 85)

heliocentric theory The theory of Aristarchus that the earth and planets revolve around the sun. (p. 111)

Hellenistic The new culture that arose when Alexander overthrew the Persian Empire and began spreading Hellenism, the Greek culture, language, thought, and way of life. (p. 95)

helots State serfs who worked the land. (p. 65)

heresy The denial of a basic doctrine of faith. (pp. 167, 178)

Holy Office The official Roman Catholic agency founded in 1542 to combat international doctrinal heresy. (p. 430)

Holy Roman Empire The loose confederation of principalities, duchies, cities, bishoprics, and other types of regional governments stretching from Denmark to Rome and from Burgundy to Poland. (p. 245)

hoplites The heavily armed infantry who were the backbone of the Greek army. (p. 62)

Huguenots French Calvinists. (p. 433)

humanism A program of study designed by Italians that emphasized the critical study of Latin and Greek literature with the goal of understanding human nature. (p. 378)

imperator A Roman title given to a general after a major victory that came to mean "emperor." (p. 147)

Inca Empire The vast and sophisticated Peruvian empire centered at the capital city of Cuzco that was at its peak from 1438 until 1532. (p. 459)

Indo-European Peoples who speak a language from a large family of languages that includes English, most of the languages of modern Europe, Greek, Latin, Persian, and Sanskrit. (p. 26)

indulgence A document issued by the Catholic Church lessening penance or time in purgatory, widely believed to bring forgiveness of all sins. (pp. 258, 409)

infidel A disparaging term used for a person who does not believe in a particular religion. (p. 213)

Inquisition Court established in the 1230s by the papacy with power to investigate and try individuals for heresy and other religious crimes. (p. 265)

Institutes of the Christian Religion, The Calvin's formulation of Christian doctrine, which became a systematic theology for Protestantism. (p. 425)

irrigation A system of watering land and draining it to prevent buildup of salt in the soil; the solution to the problem of arid climates and scant water supplies. (p. 10)

Jacquerie A massive uprising by French peasants in 1358 protesting heavy taxation. (p. 358)

janissary corps The core of the sultan's army, composed of slave conscripts from non-Muslim parts of the empire; after 1683 it became a volunteer force. (p. 504)

Jesuits Members of the Society of Jesus, founded by Ignatius Loyola, whose goal was the spread of the Roman Catholic faith. (p. 431)

Junkers The nobility of Brandenburg and Prussia, they were reluctant allies of Frederick William in his consolidation of the Prussian state. (p. 495)

Kievan Rus A confederation of Slavic territories, with its capital at Kiev, ruled by descendants of the Vikings. (p. 229)

law of inertia A law formulated by Galileo that states that motion, not rest, is the natural state of an object, that an object continues in motion forever unless stopped by some external force. (p. 524)

law of universal gravitation Newton's law that all objects are attracted to one another and that the force of attraction is proportional to the object's quantity of matter and inversely proportional to the square of the distance between them. (p. 526)

lay investiture The selection and appointment of church officials by secular authority. (p. 253)

ma'at The Egyptian belief in a cosmic harmony that embraced truth, justice, and moral integrity; it gave the pharaohs the right and duty to govern. (p. 22)

Magna Carta A peace treaty intended to redress the grievances that particular groups had against King John, later viewed as the source of English rights and liberty more generally. (p. 250)

manorialism A system in which residents of manors, or farming villages, provided work and goods for their lord in exchange for protection. (p. 234)

mercantilism A system of economic regulations aimed at increasing the power of the state based on the belief that a nation's international power was based on its wealth, specifically its supply of gold and silver. (p. 489)

merchant guild A band of merchants that prohibited nonmembers from trading in the town. (p. 305)

Messiah The savior of Israel, who according to apocalyptic predictions would destroy the Roman Empire and usher in a period of peace and plenty for the Jews; Christians believed that Jesus was the Messiah but that he would establish a spiritual kingdom, not an earthly one. (p. 165)

Mexica Empire Also known as the Aztec Empire, a large and complex Native American civilization in modern Mexico and Central America that possessed advanced mathematical, astronomical, and engineering technology. (p. 457)

millet system A system used by the Ottomans whereby subjects were divided into religious communities with each millet (nation) enjoying autonomous self-government under its religious leaders. (p. 505)

Minoan A flourishing and vibrant culture on Crete around 1650 B.C.E.; the palace was the center of political and economic life, the most important one being Knossos. (p. 58)

monarchy Type of government in which a king rules; common during the Mycenaean period. (p. 62)

monotheism The belief in one universal god. (p. 26)

Mycenaean A Greek society that developed around 1650 B.C.E. when a powerful group centered at Mycenae spread its culture over the less-advanced native population. (p. 58)

mystery religions Cults that arose in the second century B.C.E. incorporating aspects of Greek and Eastern religions and involving secret rituals and the promise of life after death. (p. 108)

natural law A Stoic concept that a single law that was part of the natural order of life governed all people. (p. 110)

natural philosophy An early modern term for the study of the nature of the universe, its purpose, and how it functioned; it encompassed what we would call "science" today. (p. 520)

Neolithic period The period between 11,000 and 4000 B.C.E., when the development of agriculture and the domestication of animals enabled peoples to establish permanent settlements. (p. 6)

New Christians A fourteenth-century term for Jews and Muslims who accepted Christianity; in many cases they included Christians whose families had converted centuries earlier. (p. 401)

nobility A small group of people at the top of the medieval social structure who held most of the social and political power. (p. 290)

oblates Children who were given to monasteries as offerings or permanent gifts. (p. 281)

oligarchy A type of Greek government in which a small group of wealthy citizens, not necessarily of aristocratic birth, ruled. (p. 62)

open-field system System in which the arable land of a manor was divided into two or three fields without hedges or fences to mark individual holdings. (p. 277)

Orthodox church Eastern Christian church in the Byzantine Empire. (p. 201)

pagans All those who believed in the Greco-Roman gods; non-Christians. (p. 166)

Paleolithic period The time between 400,000 and 11,000 B.C.E., when early peoples began making primitive stone tools, survived by hunting and gathering, and dwelled in temporary shelters. (p. 5)

patriarchal Societies in which most power is held by older adult men, especially those from the elite groups. (p. 14)

patricians The Roman aristocracy; wealthy landowners who held political power. (p. 124)

patronage Financial support of writers and artists by cities, groups, and individuals, often to produce specific works or works in specific styles. (p. 374)

pax Romana A period of Roman security, order, harmony, flourishing culture, and expanding economy during the first and second centuries C.E. (p. 146)

Peace of Utrecht A series of treaties, from 1713 to 1715, that ended the War of the Spanish Succession, ended French expansion in Europe, and marked the rise of the British Empire. (p. 492)

Peace of Westphalia The name of a series of treaties that concluded the Thirty Years' War in 1648 and marked the end of large-scale religious violence in Europe. (p. 483)

Petrine Doctrine A doctrine stating that the popes (the bishops of Rome) were the successors of Saint Peter and therefore heirs to his highest level of authority as chief of the apostles. (p. 181)

pharaoh The leader of religious and political life in the Old Kingdom, he commanded the wealth, resources, and people of Egypt. (p. 21)

philosophes A group of French intellectuals who proclaimed that they were bringing the light of knowledge to their fellow creatures in the Age of Enlightenment. (p. 531)

plebeians The common people of Rome. (p. 124)

pluralism The clerical practice of holding more than one church benefice (or office) at the same time and enjoying the income from each. (p. 408)

polis Generally interpreted to mean city-state, it was the basic political and institutional unit of Greece. (p. 61)

politiques Catholic and Protestant moderates who held that only a strong monarchy could save France from total collapse. (p. 434)

polytheism The worship of several gods; this was the tradition of the Mesopotamian and Egyptian religions. (p. 12)

popolo Disenfranchised common people in Italian cities who resented their exclusion from power. (p. 375)

Praetorians Imperial bodyguard created by the Roman emperor Augustus. (p. 154)

predestination The teaching that God has determined the salvation or damnation of individuals based on his will and purpose, not on their merit or works. (p. 426)

primogeniture An inheritance system in which the oldest son inherits all land and noble titles. (p. 243)

principate Period from the reign of Augustus to the crisis of the third century with a government ruled by a princeps, or first citizen, who was in theory first among equals. (p. 146)

Protectorate The English military dictatorship (1653–1658) established by Oliver Cromwell following the execution of Charles I. (p. 508)

Protestant The name originally given to Lutherans, which came to mean all non-Catholic Western Christian groups. (p. 412)

Ptolemy's *Geography* A second-century-c.e. work that synthesized the classical knowledge of geography and introduced the concepts of longitude and latitude. Reintroduced to Europeans in 1410 by Arab scholars, its ideas allowed cartographers to create more accurate maps. (p. 450)

public sphere An idealized intellectual space that emerged in Europe during the Enlightenment, where the public came together to discuss important issues relating to society, economics, and politics. (p. 537)

Puritans Members of a sixteenth- and seventeenth-century reform movement within the Church of England that advocated purifying it of Roman Catholic elements, such as bishops, elaborate ceremonials, and wedding rings. (p. 507)

Qur'an The sacred book of Islam. (p. 209)

rationalism A secular, critical way of thinking in which nothing was to be accepted on faith, and everything was to be submitted to reason. (p. 530)

reading revolution The transition in Europe from a society where literacy consisted of patriarchal and communal reading of religious texts to a society where literacy was commonplace and reading material was broad and diverse. (p. 535)

reconquista The Christian term for the conquest of Muslim territories in the Iberian Peninsula by Christian forces. (p. 248)

regular clergy Men and women who lived in monastic houses and followed sets of rules, first those of Benedict and later those written by other individuals. (p. 181)

relics Bones, articles of clothing, or other objects associated with the life of a saint. (p. 197)

religious orders Groups of monastic houses following a particular rule. (p. 294)

Renaissance A French word meaning "rebirth," first used by art historian and critic Giorgio Vasari to refer to the rebirth of the culture of classical antiquity. (p. 374)

representative assemblies Deliberative meetings of lords and wealthy urban residents that flourished in many European countries between 1250 and 1450 and were the precursors to the English parliament, German diets, and Spanish cortes. (p. 354)

republicanism A form of government in which there is no monarch and power rests in the hands of the people as exercised through elected representatives. (p. 506)

rococo A popular style in Europe in the eighteenth century, known for its soft pastels, ornate interiors, sentimental portraits, and starry-eyed lovers protected by hovering cupids. (p. 537)

Romanesque An architectural style with rounded arches and small windows. (p. 326)

Royal Road The main highway created by the Persians; it spanned 1,677 miles from Greece to Iran. (p. 49)

runic alphabet Writing system developed in some barbarian groups that helps to give a more accurate picture of barbarian society. (p. 185)

sacraments Certain rituals defined by the church in which God bestows benefits on the believer through grace. (p. 185)

salons Regular social gatherings held by talented and rich Parisian women in their homes, where philosophes and their followers met to discuss literature, science, and philosophy. (p. 536)

Scholastics University professors who developed a method of thinking, reasoning, and writing in which questions were raised and authorities cited on both sides of a question. (p. 321)

Sea Peoples Foreign invaders who destroyed the Hittite and Egyptian empires in the thirteenth century B.C.E. (p. 29)

Second Punic War A war fought between Carthage, led by Hannibal, and Rome (218–201 B.C.E.); Roman victory meant that the western Mediterranean would henceforth be Roman. (p. 129)

Second Triumvirate A pact between Augustus and two of Caesar's lieutenants, Marc Antony and Lepidus; together they hunted down and defeated Caesar's murderers. (p. 139)

secular clergy Priests and bishops who staffed churches where people worshiped and were not cut off from the world. (p. 182)

senate Originating under the Etruscans as a council of noble elders who advised the king, the Roman senate advised the magistrates; over time its advice came to have the force of law. (p. 124)

serfs Peasants bound to the land by a relationship with a feudal lord. (p. 235)

signori Government by one-man rule in Italian cities such as Milan. (p. 376)

simony The buying and selling of church offices, officially prohibited but often practiced. (p. 251)

sovereign An independent, autonomous state run by its citizens and free of outside interference. (p. 98)

Spanish Armada The fleet sent by Philip II of Spain in 1588 against England as a religious crusade against Protestantism. Weather and the English fleet defeated it. (p. 425)

stadholder The executive officer in each of the United Provinces of the Netherlands, a position often held by the princes of Orange. (p. 513)

Statute of Kilkenny Laws issued in 1366 that discriminated against the Irish, forbidding marriage between the English and the Irish, requiring the use of the English language, and denying the Irish access to ecclesiastical offices. (p. 367)

Stoicism The most popular of Hellenistic philosophies, it considered nature an expression of divine will; people could be happy only when living in accordance with nature. (p. 110)

Struggle of the Orders A conflict in 494–287 B.C.E. in which the Roman plebeians wanted real political representation and safeguards against patrician domination and the right to intermarry and climb up the social hierarchy. (p. 126)

sultan The ruler of the Ottoman Empire; he owned all the agricultural land of the empire and was served by an army and bureaucracy composed of highly trained slaves. (p. 504)

sumptuary laws Laws that regulated the value and style of clothing and jewelry that various social groups could wear, as well as the amount they could spend on celebrations. (p. 315)

Test Act Legislation passed by the English parliament in 1673 to secure the position of the Anglican Church by stripping Puritans, Catholics, and other dissenters of the right to vote, preach, assemble, hold public office, and attend or teach at the universities. (p. 510)

tetrarchy Diocletian's four-part division of the Roman Empire. (p. 176)

three orders, the Model of the divisions of society in the High Middle Ages into those who pray, those who fight, and those who work. (p. 274)

tournament An arena for knights to compete on horseback, giving them valuable battle experience. (p. 291)

Treaty of Tordesillas The 1494 agreement giving Spain everything to the west of an imaginary line drawn down the Atlantic and giving Portugal everything to the east. (p. 456)

Treaty of Verdun Treaty signed in 843 by Charlemagne's grandsons dividing the Carolingian empire into three parts and setting the pattern for political boundaries in Europe still in use today. (p. 226)

tribunes Plebeian-elected officials in the Roman Empire; tribunes brought plebeian grievances to the senate for resolution and protected plebeians from the arbitrary conduct of patrician magistrates. (p. 126)

troubadours Poets who wrote and sang lyric verses celebrating love, desire, beauty, and gallantry. (p. 326)

Tyche The Greek goddess of fate or chance; an unpredictable and sometimes malicious force. (p. 108)

tyranny Rule by one man who used his wealth or other powers to seize the government unconstitutionally. (p. 62)

Unam Sanctam An official letter issued by Pope Boniface VIII claiming that all Christians were subject to the pope. (p. 334)

Union of Utrecht The alliance of seven northern provinces (led by Holland) that declared its independence from Spain and formed the United Provinces of the Netherlands. (p. 435)

vassal A warrior who swore loyalty and service to a noble in exchange for land, protection, and support. (p. 234)

vernacular literature Writings in the author's local dialect, that is, in the everyday language of the region. (p. 323)

viceroyalties The name for the four administrative units of Spanish possessions in the Americas: New Spain, Peru, New Granada, and La Plata. (p. 461)

villa A Roman country estate that was the primary unit of organized political life in the provinces. (p. 161)

virtù The quality of being able to shape the world according to one's own will. (p. 379)

wergeld Compensatory payment for death or injury set in many barbarian law codes. (p. 187)

Yahweh The Hebrew god that appeared to Moses on Mount Sinai and made a covenant with the Hebrews; in medieval Latin he became known as Jehovah. (p. 37)

Zoroastrianism Persian religion whose gods, Ahuramazda, god of good and light, and Ahriman, god of evil and dark, were locked in a battle for the human race; the religion emphasized the individual's responsibility to choose between good and evil. (p. 51)

▪ Index

Persians and, 49–51
Rome and, 161
Seleucids and, 102
Aspasia, 81, 81*(i)*
Aspendos, Turkey, 161–162
Assemblies. *See also* Estates (assemblies)
  representative, 354
  in Rome, 124–125
  in Spain, 248
Assimilation
  of barbarians, 195
  in Near East, 34–35
  in New France, 463
Assyria and Assyrian Empire, 17*(i)*, 32, 42–47,
    43*(m)*, 48*(m)*
  Alexander in, 93
  Babylon and, 16
  government and culture of, 46–47
  Israel and, 38
  Jewish surrender to, 43*(i)*
  lion hunt in, 44–45*(b)*, 46*(i)*
Astell, Mary, 528
Astrolabe (instrument), 451
Astronomical clocks, 313*(i)*
Astronomy. *See also* Scientific revolution;
    Universe
  Aristotle and, 84, 111, 520, 520*(i)*, 521
  Brahe and, 522–523
  Copernicus and, 522
  exploration and, 451
  Galileo and, 525
  Newton and, 525–526
  Ptolemaic, 520–521
  scientific revolution and, 522
  sextants and, 523*(i)*
Astyages (Media), 50*(b)*
Atahualpa (Inca), 460
Athena (goddess), 73, 74–75, 79, 80, 82
Athena Nike (goddess), temple of, 73–74
Athens, 58, 66–67
  Acropolis of, 73, 75, 76*(i)*
  ancient, 76*(m)*
  arts in, 77–79
  daily life in, 77–79
  decline of, 97
  in Delian League, 69, 69*(m)*
  as democracy, 65
  empire of, 69–71
  government of, 66–67
  Great Plague at (430 B.C.), 74–75*(b)*,
    75*(i)*
  hegemony of Greece and, 85–86
  Peloponnesian War and, 71–73, 72*(m)*
  Sparta and, 71–73, 86
Athletics. *See* Sports
Atlantic Ocean region. *See also* Exploration
  Genoese exploration in, 447, 448
Atomist theory, Descartes and, 527
Aton (god), 26, 27*(b)*
Atrahasis (Mesopotamia), myth of, 10
Attica, 58, 72, 82
Attila (Huns), 191
Audiencia, 460
Augsburg Confession, 422
Augustine of Canterbury, 196
Augustine of Hippo (Saint), 184–185, 284
Augustinian friars, 409

Augustus (**Octavian,** Rome), 138*(b)*,
    139–142, 140–141*(b)*, 146–154
  constitutional monarchy of, 144
  as imperator, 146*(i)*, 147
  Res Gestae of, 146, 148–149*(b)*, 148*(i)*,
    149*(i)*
  successors to, 154–156
Austria
  absolutism in, 494–495
  France and, 420
  growth to 1748, 496*(m)*
  Habsburgs and, 420, 483, 495, 546–549
  Jews in, 549
  Rome and, 150
Authority. *See* Power (authority)
Autobiography, in Renaissance, 380
Autocracy, in Russia, 498
Auto-da-fe, 403*(i)*
Avaris (city), Hyksos in, 25
Avars, 191, 199, 219
Avebury, 9
Aventine Hill (Rome), 120*(m)*, 121
Avicenna, 215
Avignon, pope in, 310, 355–357
Ay Khanoum (Hellenistic city), 97
Azores, 452
Aztecs, 457–459

Baal (god), 37
Babylon and Babylonians, 16–19, 28*(m)*. *See
    also* Neo-Babylonians
  Assyrians and, 46
  Chaldeans in, 32
  Cyrus and, 51*(b)*
  Hammurabi and, 10, 17–19, 18*(i)*
  Hittites in, 28
Babylonian Captivity
  of Catholic Church, 355, 408
  of Hebrews, 38, 355
Bach, Johann Sebastian, 515
Bacon, Francis, 526, 527, 529
Bactria, 48*(m)*, 49, 93, 96–97
Baghdad, flood in (1831), 10
Bahamas, 453
Bailiffs, 276
Balance of power
  in Italian Renaissance, 376–378
  in Near East, 28*(m)*
  Peace of Utrecht and, 492
Balkan region
  Greek-speaking peoples in, 58
  Orthodox Christianity in, 228
  Ottomans and, 503–504
  slaves from, 448
Ball, John, 361
Baltic region, 267*(m)*
  Black Death and, 342
  Christianity in, 267
  migrations into, 275
  Russia and, 502
  in Thirty Years' War, 483
Banking, in Florence, 374–375
Bankruptcy, in Florence, 375
Banten, Java, 446*(i)*
Baptism
  infant, 288
  of Jews, 401–402

Baptistery (Florence), doors of, 387
Baptists, 416
Barbarians
  conversion of, 195–198
  Frankish kingdom and, 215
  migrations by, 187, 188–195, 189*(m)*
  race and, 540
  Rome and, 150, 155, 188, 198–199
  society of, 185–188
Barbarossa, Frederick. *See* Frederick I
    Barbarossa (Holy Roman Empire)
Barcelona, 394
Bards, barbarian, 188
Barons, English, 250
Baroque period, arts of, 514–515
Barracks emperors (Rome), 171
Basil (Saint), 181
Basilicas, 180, 326
Bath, England, 135*(i)*
Bath houses, 364*(i)*
Bathing, Roman, 135*(i)*
Battering ram, 71*(i)*
Battles. *See* specific battles and wars
Bavaria, 217, 219, 232
  Rome and, 150
Bayeux Tapestry, 240*(i)*
Bayle, Pierre, 530, 534
Beattie, James, 540
Beaver trade, 457
Becket, Thomas, 239*(i)*, 249, 258
Bede (Venerable), 189, 224, 225*(b)*, 225*(i)*
Bedouins, 208
Beguines, 333
Beijing (Peking), China, 445
Belarus (Belorussia), 549
Belgium. *See also* Netherlands
  Charles V and, 434
  Spanish Netherlands as, 434
Benedict of Nursia (Saint) and Benedictines,
    181–182, 182*(i)*
  library of, 212
  monasteries of, 294
  Rule of, 181, 182*(i)*
Benefices (offices), 408
Benet Biscop (Saint), 224
Beowulf, 226
Berbers, 211, 448
Bernard of Clairvaux (Saint), 263, 295, 296
Berruguete, Pedro, 403
Bible, 186*(i)*. *See also* New Testament; Old
    Testament
  Copernican hypothesis and, 522
  darkness, sin, and, 472–473
  in English, 356
  Gospels and, 166
  in Gothic language, 196
  Gutenberg, 386
  Hebrew, 36, 39, 40–41*(b)*, 41
  Mesopotamian myths and, 13
  Protestants and, 412
  Vulgate, 182
Biographies, in Renaissance, 380
Births and birthrate, medieval rituals and,
    288
Bishoprics, 266–267
Bishops, 180. *See also* Pope(s)
Bithus (Roman soldier), 164–165*(b)*

	Government	Society and Economy
3000 B.C.E.	Emergence of first cities in Mesopotamia, ca. 3000 Unification of Egypt; Archaic Period, ca. 3100–2600 Old Kingdom of Egypt, ca. 2660–2180 Dominance of Akkadian empire in Mesopotamia, ca. 2331–2200 Middle Kingdom in Egypt, ca. 2080–1640	Neolithic peoples rely on settled agriculture, while others pursue nomadic life, ca. 7000–3000 Expansion of Mesopotamian trade and culture into the modern Middle East and Turkey, ca. 2600
2000 B.C.E.	Babylonian empire, ca. 2000–1595 Code of Hammurabi, ca. 1790 Hyksos invade Egypt, ca. 1640–1570 Hittite Empire, ca. 1600–1200 New Kingdom in Egypt, ca. 1570–1075	First wave of Indo-European migrants, by ca. 2000 Extended commerce in Egypt, by ca. 2000 Horses introduced into western Asia, by ca. 2000
1500 B.C.E.	Third Intermediate Period in Egypt, ca. 1100–653 Unified Hebrew kingdom under Saul, David, and Solomon, ca. 1025–925	Use of iron increases in western Asia, by ca. 1300–1100 Second wave of Indo-European migrants, by ca. 1200 "Dark Age" in Greece, ca. 1100–800
1000 B.C.E.	Hebrew kingdom divided into Israel and Judah, 925 Assyrian Empire, ca. 900–612 Phoenicians found Carthage, 813 Kingdom of Kush conquers and reunifies Egypt, ca. 800–700 Roman monarchy, ca. 753–509 Medes conquers Persia, 710 Babylon wins independence from Assyria, 626 Dracon issues law code at Athens, 621 Solon's reforms at Athens, ca. 594 Cyrus the Great conquers Medes, founds Persian Empire, 550 Persians complete conquest of ancient Near East, 521–464 Reforms of Cleisthenes in Athens, 508	Phoenician seafaring and trading in the Mediterranean, ca. 900–550 First Olympic games, 776 Concentration of landed wealth in Greece, ca. 750–600 Greek overseas expansion, ca. 750–550 Beginning of coinage in western Asia, ca. 640
500 B.C.E.	Persian wars, 499–479 Struggle of the Orders in Rome, ca. 494–287 Growth of the Athenian Empire, 478–431 Peloponnesian War, 431–404 Rome captures Veii, 396 Gauls sack Rome, 390 Roman expansion in Italy, 390–290 Phillip II of Macedonia conquers Greece, 338 Conquests of Alexander the Great, 334–323 Punic Wars, 264–133 Reforms of the Gracchi, 133–121	Growth of Hellenistic trade and cities, ca. 330–100 Beginning of Roman silver coinage, 269 Growth of slavery, decline of small farmers in Rome, ca. 250–100 Agrarian reforms of the Gracchi, 133–121

Religion and Philosophy	Science and Technology	Arts and Letters
Growth of anthropomorphic religion in Mesopotamia, ca. 3000–2000	Development of wheeled transport in Mesopotamia, by ca. 3000	Egyptian hieroglyphic writing, ca. 3100
Emergence of Egyptian polytheism and belief in personal immortality, ca. 2660	Use of widespread irrigation in Mesopotamia and Egypt, ca. 3000	Sumerian cuneiform writing, ca. 3000
Spread of Mesopotamian and Egyptian religious ideas as far north as modern Turkey and as far south as central Africa, ca. 2600	Construction of Stonehenge monument in England, ca. 3000–1600	
	Construction of first pyramid in Egypt, ca. 2600	
Emergence of Hebrew monotheism, ca. 1700	Construction of first ziggurats in Mesopotamia, ca. 2000	*Epic of Gilgamesh*, ca. 1900
Mixture of Hittite and Near Eastern religious beliefs, ca. 1595	Widespread use of bronze in ancient Near East, ca. 1900	
	Babylonian mathematical advances, ca. 1800	
Exodus of the Hebrews from Egypt into Palestine, ca. 1300–1200	Hittites introduce iron technology, ca. 1400	Phoenicians develop alphabet, ca. 1400
Akhenaten imposes monotheism in Egypt, 1367–1350		Naturalistic art in Egypt under Akhenaten, 1367–1350
		Egyptian *Book of the Dead*, ca. 1300
Era of the prophets in Israel, ca. 1100–500	Babylonian astronomical advances, ca. 750–400	Homer, traditional author of *Iliad* and *Odyssey*, ca. 800
Beginning of the Hebrew Bible, ca. 950–800	Construction of Parthenon in Athens begins, 447	Hesiod, author of *Theogony* and *Works and Days*, ca. 800
Intermixture of Etruscan and Roman religious cults, ca. 753–509		Aeschylus, first significant Athenian tragedian, ca. 525–456
Growing popularity of local Greek religious cults, ca. 700 B.C.E.–337 C.E.		
Introduction of Zoroastrianism, ca. 600		
Babylonian Captivity of the Hebrews, 587–538		
Pre-Socratic philosophers, ca. 500–400	Hippocrates, formal founder of medicine, ca. 430	Sophocles, tragedian whose plays explore moral and political problems, ca. 496–406
Socrates executed, 399	Building of the Via Appia begins, 312	Herodotus, "father of history," ca. 485–425
Plato, student of Socrates, 427–347	Aristarchos of Samos, advances in astronomy, ca. 310–230	Euripides, most personal of the Athenian tragedians, ca. 480–406
Diogenes, leading proponent of cynicism, ca. 412–323	Euclid codifies geometry, ca. 300	Thucydides, historian of Peloponnesian War, ca. 460–440
Aristotle, student of Plato, 384–322	Herophilus, discoveries in medicine, ca. 300–250	Aristophanes, greatest Athenian comic playwright, ca. 445–386
Epicurus, founder of Epicurean philosophy, 340–270	Archimedes, works on physics and hydrologics, ca. 287–212	
Zeno, founder of Stoic philosophy, 335–262		
Emergence of Mithraism, ca. 300		
Greek cults brought to Rome, ca. 200		
Spread of Hellenistic mystery religions, ca. 200–100		

	Government	Society and Economy
100 B.C.E.	Dictatorship of Sulla, 88–79 B.C.E. Civil war in Rome, 88–31 B.C.E. Dictatorship of Caesar, 45–44 B.C.E. Principate of Augustus, 31 B.C.E.–14 C.E. "Five Good Emperors" of Rome, 96–180 C.E. "Barracks Emperors'" civil war, 235–284 C.E.	Reform of the Roman calendar, 46 B.C.E. "Golden age" of Roman prosperity and vast increase in trade, 96–180 C.E. Growth of serfdom in Roman Empire, ca. 200–500 C.E. Economic contraction in Roman Empire, ca. 235–284 C.E.
300 C.E.	Constantine removes capital of Roman Empire to Constantinople, ca. 315 Visigoths defeat Roman army at Adrianople, 378 Bishop Ambrose asserts church's independence from the state, 380 Odoacer deposes last Roman emperor in the West, 476 Clovis issues Salic law of the Franks, ca. 490	Barbarian migrations throughout western and northern Europe, ca. 378–600
500	Law code of Justinian, 529 Spread of Islam across Arabia, the Mediterranean region, Spain, North Africa, and Asia as far as India, ca. 630–733	Gallo-Roman aristocracy intermarries with Germanic chieftains, ca. 500–700 Decline of towns and trade in the West; agrarian economy predominates, ca. 500–1800
700	Charles Martel defeats Muslims at Tours, 732 Pippin III anointed king of the Franks, 754 Charlemagne secures Frankish crown, r. 768–814	Height of Muslim commercial activity with western Europe, ca. 700–1300
800	Imperial coronation of Charlemagne, Christmas 800 Treaty of Verdun divides Carolingian kingdom, 843 Viking, Magyar, and Muslim invasions, ca. 850–1000 Establishment of Kievan Rus, ca. 900	Invasions and unstable conditions lead to increase of serfdom in western Europe, ca. 800–900 Height of Byzantine commerce and industry, ca. 800–1000
1000	Seljuk Turks conquer Muslim Baghdad, 1055 Norman conquest of England, 1066 Penance of Henry IV at Canossa, 1077	Decline of Byzantine free peasantry, ca. 1025–1100 Growth of towns and trade in the West, ca. 1050–1300 *Domesday Book* in England, 1086
1100	Henry I of England, r. 1100–1135 Louis VI of France, r. 1108–1137 Frederick I of Germany, r. 1152–1190 Henry II of England, r. 1154–1189	Henry I of England establishes the Exchequer, 1130 Beginnings of the Hanseatic League, 1159

Religion and Philosophy	Science and Technology	Arts and Letters
Mithraism spreads to Rome, 27 B.C.E.–270 C.E. Life of Jesus, ca. 3 B.C.E.–29 C.E.	Engineering advances in Rome, ca. 100 B.C.E.–180 C.E.	Flowering of Latin literature: Virgil, 70–19 B.C.E.; Livy, ca. 59 B.C.E.–17 C.E.; Ovid, 43 B.C.E.–17 C.E.
Constantine legalizes Christianity, 312 Theodosius declares Christianity the official state religion, 380 Donatist heretical movement at its height, ca. 400 St. Augustine, *Confessions*, ca. 390; *The City of God*, ca. 425 Clovis adopts Roman Christianity, 496	Construction of Arch of Constantine, ca. 315	St. Jerome publishes Latin *Vulgate*, late 4th c. Byzantines preserve Greco-Roman culture, ca. 400–1000
Rule of St. Benedict, 529 Life of the Prophet Muhammad, ca. 571–632 Pope Gregory the Great publishes *Dialogues*, *Pastoral Care*, *Moralia*, 590–604 Monasteries established in Anglo-Saxon England, ca. 600–700 Publication of the Qur'an, 651 Synod of Whitby, 664	Using watermills, Benedictine monks exploit energy of fast-flowing rivers and streams, by 600 Heavy plow and improved harness facilitate use of multiple-ox teams; harrow widely used in northern Europe, by 600 Byzantines successfully use "Greek fire" in naval combat against Arab fleets attacking Constantinople, 673, 717	Boethius, *The Consolation of Philosophy*, ca. 520 Justinian constructs church of Santa Sophia, 532–537
Bede, *Ecclesiastical History of the English Nation*, ca. 700 Missionary work of St. Boniface in Germany, ca. 710–750 Iconoclastic controversy in Byzantine Empire, 726–843 Pippin III donates Papal States to the papacy, 756		Lindisfarne Gospel Book, ca. 700 *Beowulf*, ca. 700 Carolingian Renaissance, ca. 780–850
Foundation of abbey of Cluny, 909 Byzantine conversion of Russia, late 10th c.	Stirrup and nailed horseshoes become widespread in combat, 900–1000 Paper (invented in China, ca. 150) enters Europe through Muslim Spain, ca. 900–1000	Byzantines develop Cyrillic script, late 10th c.
Schism between Roman and Greek Orthodox churches, 1054 Lateran Council restricts election of pope to College of Cardinals, 1059 Pope Gregory VII, 1073–1085 Theologian Peter Abelard, 1079–1142 First Crusade, 1095–1099 Founding of Cistercian order, 1098	Arab conquests bring new irrigation methods, cotton cultivation, and manufacture to Spain, Sicily, southern Italy, by 1000 Avicenna, Arab scientist, d. 1037	Muslim musicians introduce lute, rebec (stringed instruments, ancestors of violin), ca. 1000 Romanesque style in architecture and art, ca. 1000–1200 *Song of Roland*, ca. 1095
Universities begin, ca. 1100–1300 Concordat of Worms ends investiture controversy, 1122 Height of Cistercian monasticism, 1125–1175	Europeans, copying Muslim and Byzantine models, construct castles with rounded towers and crenellated walls, by 1100	Troubadour poetry, especially of Chrétien de Troyes, circulates widely, ca. 1100–1200 *Rubaiyat of Umar Khayyam*, ca. 1120 Dedication of abbey church of Saint-Denis launches Gothic style, 1144

Government	Society and Economy
1100 (cont.) Thomas Becket, archbishop of Canterbury, murdered 1170 Philip Augustus of France, r. 1180–1223	
1200 Spanish victory over Muslims at Las Navas de Tolosa, 1212 Frederick II of Germany and Sicily, r. 1212–1250 Magna Carta, charter of English political and civil liberties, 1215 Louis IX of France, r. 1226–1270 Mongols end Abbasid caliphate, 1258 Edward I of England, r. 1272–1307 Philip IV (the Fair) of France, r. 1285–1314	European revival, growth of towns; agricultural expansion leads to population growth, ca. 1200–1300 Crusaders capture Constantinople (Fourth Crusade) and spur Venetian economy, 1204
1300 Philip IV orders arrest of Pope Boniface at Anagni, 1303 Hundred Years' War between England and France, 1337–1453 Political disorder in Germany, ca. 1350–1450 Merchant oligarchies or despots rule Italian city-states, ca. 1350–1550	"Little ice age," European economic depression, ca. 1300–1450 Black Death appears ca. 1347; returns intermittently until ca. 1720 Height of the Hanseatic League, 1350–1450 Peasant and working-class revolts: Flanders, 1328; France, 1358; Florence, 1378; England, 1381
1400 Joan of Arc rallies French monarchy, 1429–1431 Medici domination of Florence begins, 1434 Princes in Germany consolidate power, ca. 1450–1500 Ottoman Turks under Mahomet II capture Constantinople, May 1453 War of the Roses in England, 1455–1471 Establishment of the Inquisition in Spain, 1478 Ferdinand and Isabella complete reconquista in Spain, 1492 French invasion of Italy, 1494	Population decline, peasants' revolts, high labor costs contribute to decline of serfdom in western Europe, ca. 1400–1650 Flow of Balkan slaves into eastern Mediterranean, of African slaves into Iberia and Italy, ca. 1400–1500 Christopher Columbus reaches the Americas, 1492 Portuguese gain control of East Indian spice trade, 1498–1511
1500 Charles V, Holy Roman emperor, 1519–1556 Habsburg-Valois Wars, 1521–1559 Philip II of Spain, r. 1556–1598 Revolt of the Netherlands, 1566–1598 St. Bartholomew's Day massacre in France, 1572 English defeat of the Spanish Armada, 1588 Henry IV of France issues Edict of Nantes, 1598	Consolidation of serfdom in eastern Europe, ca. 1500–1650 Balboa discovers the Pacific, 1513 Magellan's crew circumnavigates the earth, 1519–1522 Spain and Portugal gain control of regions of Central and South America, ca. 1520–1550 Peasants' Revolt in Germany, 1524–1525 "Time of Troubles" in Russia, 1598–1613

Religion and Philosophy	Science and Technology	Arts and Letters
Aristotle's works translated into Latin, ca. 1140–1260 Third Crusade, 1189–1192 Pope Innocent III, height of the medieval papacy, 1198–1216	Underground pipes with running water and indoor latrines installed in some monasteries, such as Clairvaux and Canterbury Cathedral Priory, by 1100; elsewhere rare until 1800 Windmill invented, ca. 1180	
Founding of the Franciscan order, 1210 Fourth Lateran Council accepts seven sacraments, 1215 Founding of Dominican order, 1216 Thomas Aquinas, height of scholasticism, 1225–1274	*Notebooks* of architect Villard de Honnecourt, a major source for Gothic engineering, ca. 1250 Development of double-entry bookkeeping in Florence and Genoa, ca. 1250–1340 Venetians purchase secrets of glass manufacture from Syria, 1277 Mechanical clock invented, ca. 1290	*Parzifal, Roman de la rose, King Arthur and the Round Table* celebrate virtues of knighthood and chivalry, ca. 1200–1300 Height of Gothic style, ca. 1225–1300
Pope Boniface VIII declares all Christians subject to the pope in *Unam Sanctam*, 1302 Babylonian Captivity of the papacy, 1309–1376 Theologian John Wyclif, ca. 1330–1384 Great Schism in the papacy, 1378–1417	Edward III of England uses cannon in siege of Calais, 1346 Clocks in general use throughout Europe, by 1400	Paintings of Giotto mark emergence of Renaissance movement in the arts, ca. 1305–1337 Dante, *Divine Comedy*, ca. 1310 Petrarch develops ideas of humanism, ca. 1350 Boccaccio, *The Decameron*, ca. 1350 Jan van Eyck, Flemish painter, 1366–1441 Brunelleschi, Florentine architect, 1377–1446 Chaucer, *Canterbury Tales*, ca. 1387–1400
Council of Constance ends the schism in the papacy, 1414–1418 Pragmatic Sanction of Bourges affirms special rights of French crown over French church, 1438 Expulsion of Jews from Spain, 1492	Water-powered blast furnaces operative in Sweden, Austria, the Rhine Valley, Liège, ca. 1400 Leonardo Fibonacci's *Liber Abaci* popularizes use of Hindu-Arabic numerals, important in rise of Western science, 1402 Paris and largest Italian cities pave streets, making street cleaning possible, ca. 1450 European printing and movable type, ca. 1450	Height of Renaissance movement: Masaccio, 1401–1428; Botticelli, 1444–1510; Leonardo da Vinci, 1452–1519; Albrecht Dürer, 1471–1528; Michelangelo, 1475–1564; Raphael, 1483–1520
Machiavelli, *The Prince*, 1513 More, *Utopia*, 1516 Luther, *Ninety-five Theses*, 1517 Henry VIII of England breaks with Rome, 1532–1534 Merici establishes Ursuline order for education of women, 1535 Loyola establishes Society of Jesus, 1540 Calvin establishes theocracy in Geneva, 1541 Council of Trent shapes essential character of Catholicism until the 1960s, 1545–1563 Peace of Augsburg, official recognition of Lutheranism, 1555	Scientific revolution in western Europe, ca. 1540–1690: Copernicus, *On the Revolutions of the Heavenly Bodies*, 1543; Galileo, 1564–1642; Kepler, 1571–1630; Harvey, 1578–1657	Erasmus, *The Praise of Folly*, 1509 Castiglione, *The Courtier*, 1528 Baroque movement in arts, ca. 1550–1725: Rubens, 1577–1640; Velasquez, 1599–1660 Shakespeare, West's most enduring and influential playwright, 1564–1616 Montaigne, *Essays*, 1598

Government	Society and Economy
1600 Thirty Years' War begins, 1618 Richelieu dominates French government, 1624–1643 Frederick William, Elector of Brandenburg, r. 1640–1688 English Civil War, 1642–1649 Louis XIV, r. 1643–1715 Peace of Westphalia ends the Thirty Years' War, 1648 The Fronde in France, 1648–1660	Chartering of British East India Company, 1600 English Poor Law, 1601 Chartering of Dutch East India Company, 1602 Height of Dutch commercial activity, ca. 1630–1665
1650 Anglo-Dutch wars, 1652–1674 Protectorate in England, 1653–1658 Leopold I, Habsburg emperor, r. 1658–1705 English monarchy restored, 1660 Ottoman siege of Vienna, 1683 Glorious Revolution in England, 1688–1689 Peter the Great of Russia, r. 1689–1725	Height of mercantilism in Europe, ca. 1650–1750 Agricultural revolution in Europe, ca. 1650–1850 Principle of peasants' hereditary subjugation to their lords affirmed in Prussia, 1653 Colbert's economic reforms in France, ca. 1663–1683 Cossack revolt in Russia, 1670–1671
1700 War of the Spanish Succession, 1701–1713 Peace of Utrecht redraws political boundaries of Europe, 1713 Frederick William I of Prussia, r. 1713–1740 Louis XV of France, r. 1715–1774 Maria Theresa of Austria, r. 1740–1780 Frederick the Great of Prussia, r. 1740–1786	Foundation of St. Petersburg, 1701 Last appearance of bubonic plague in western Europe, ca. 1720 Growth of European population, ca. 1720–1789 Enclosure movement in England, ca. 1730–1830
1750 Seven Years' War, 1756–1763 Catherine the Great of Russia, r. 1762–1796 Partition of Poland, 1772–1795 Louis XVI of France, r. 1774–1792 American Revolution, 1775–1783 French Revolution, 1789–1799 Slave insurrection in Saint-Domingue, 1791	Growth of illegitimate births in Europe, ca. 1750–1850 Industrial Revolution in western Europe, ca. 1780–1850 Serfdom abolished in France, 1789
1800 Napoleonic era, 1799–1815 Haitian republic declares independence, 1804 Congress of Vienna re-establishes political power after defeat of Napoleon, 1814–1815 Greece wins independence from Ottoman Empire, 1830 French conquest of Algeria, 1830 Revolution in France, 1830 Great Britain: Reform Bill of 1832; Poor Law reform, 1834; Chartists, repeal of Corn Laws, 1838–1848 Revolutions in Europe, 1848	British takeover of India complete, 1805 British slave trade abolished, 1807 German Zollverein founded, 1834 European capitalists begin large-scale foreign investment, 1840s Great Famine in Ireland, 1845–1851 First public health law in Britain, 1848

Religion and Philosophy	Science and Technology	Arts and Letters
Huguenot revolt in France, 1625	Further development of scientific method: Bacon, *The Advancement of Learning*, 1605; Descartes, *Discourse on Method*, 1637	Cervantes, *Don Quixote*, 1605, 1615 Flourishing of French theater: Molière, 1622–1673; Racine, 1639–1699 Golden age of Dutch culture, ca. 1625–1675: Rembrandt van Rijn, 1606–1669; Vermeer, 1632–1675
Social contract theory: Hobbes, *Leviathan*, 1651; Locke, *Second Treatise on Civil Government*, 1690 Patriarch Nikon's reforms split Russian Orthodox Church, 1652 Test Act in England excludes Roman Catholics from public office, 1673 Revocation of Edict of Nantes, 1685 James II tries to restore Catholicism as state religion, 1685–1688	Tull (1674–1741) encourages innovation in English agriculture Newton, *Principia Mathematica*, 1687	Construction of baroque palaces and remodeling of capital cities, central and eastern Europe, ca. 1650–1725 Bach, great late baroque German composer, 1685–1750 Enlightenment begins, ca. 1690: Fontenelle, *Conversations on the Plurality of Worlds*, 1686; Voltaire, French philosopher and writer whose work epitomizes Enlightenment, 1694–1778 Pierre Bayle, *Historical and Critical Dictionary*, 1697
Wesley, founder of Methodism, 1703–1791 Montesquieu, *The Spirit of Laws*, 1748	Newcomen develops steam engine, 1705 Charles Townsend introduces four-year crop rotation, 1730	
Hume, *The Natural History of Religion*, 1755 Rousseau, *The Social Contract* and *Emile*, 1762 Fourier, French utopian socialist, 1772–1837 Papacy dissolves Jesuits, 1773 Smith, *The Wealth of Nations*, 1776 Church reforms of Joseph II in Austria, 1780s Kant, *What Is Enlightenment?*, 1784 Reorganization of church in France, 1790s Wollstonecraft, *A Vindication of the Rights of Women*, 1792 Malthus, *Essay on the Principle of Population*, 1798	Hargreaves's spinning jenny, ca. 1765 Arkwright's water frame, ca. 1765 Watt's steam engine promotes industrial breakthroughs, 1780s Jenner's smallpox vaccine, 1796	*Encyclopedia*, edited by Diderot and d'Alembert, published 1751–1765 Classical style in music, ca. 1770–1830: Mozart, 1756–1791; Beethoven, 1770–1827 Wordsworth, English romantic poet, 1770–1850 Romanticism in art and literature, ca. 1790–1850
Napoleon signs Concordat with Pope Pius VII regulating Catholic Church in France, 1801 Spencer, Social Darwinist, 1820–1903 Comte, *System of Positive Philosophy*, 1830–1842 Height of French utopian socialism, 1830s–1840s List, *National System of Political Economy*, 1841 Nietzsche, radical and highly influential German philosopher, 1844–1900 Marx, *Communist Manifesto*, 1848	First railroad, Great Britain, 1825 Faraday studies electromagnetism, 1830–1840s	Staël, *On Germany*, 1810 Balzac, *The Human Comedy*, 1829–1841 Delacroix, *Liberty Leading the People*, 1830 Hugo, *The Hunchback of Notre Dame*, 1831

	Government	**Society and Economy**
1850	Second Empire in France, 1852–1870 Crimean War, 1853–1856 Britain crushes Great Rebellion in India, 1857–1858 Unification of Italy, 1859–1870 U.S. Civil War, 1861–1865 Bismarck leads Germany, 1862–1890 Unification of Germany, 1864–1871 Britain's Second Reform Bill, 1867 Third Republic in France, 1870–1940	Crédit Mobilier founded in France, 1852 Japan opened to European influence, 1853 Russian serfs emancipated, 1861 First Socialist International, 1864–1871
1875	Congress of Berlin, 1878 European "scramble for Africa," 1880–1900 Britain's Third Reform Bill, 1884 Dreyfus affair in France, 1894–1899 Spanish-American War, 1898 South African War, 1899–1902	Full property rights for women in Great Britain, 1882 Second Industrial Revolution; birthrate steadily declines in Europe, ca. 1880–1913 Social welfare legislation, Germany, 1883–1889 Second Socialist International, 1889–1914 Witte directs modernization of Russian economy, 1892–1899
1900	Russo-Japanese War, 1904–1905 Revolution in Russia, 1905 Balkan wars, 1912–1913	Women's suffrage movement, England, ca. 1900–1914 Social welfare legislation, France, 1904, 1910; Great Britain, 1906–1914 Agrarian reforms in Russia, 1907–1912
1914	World War I, 1914–1918 Armenian genocide, 1915 Easter Rebellion, 1916 U.S. declares war on Germany, 1917 Bolshevik Revolution, 1917–1918 Treaty of Versailles, World War I peace settlement, 1919	Planned economics in Europe, 1914 Auxiliary Service Law in Germany, 1916 Bread riots in Russia, March 1917
1920	Mussolini seizes power in Italy, 1922 Stalin comes to power in U.S.S.R., 1927 Hitler gains power in Germany, 1933 Rome-Berlin Axis, 1936 Nazi-Soviet Non-Aggression Pact, 1939 World War II, 1939–1945	New Economic Policy in U.S.S.R., 1921 Dawes Plan for reparations and recovery, 1924 Great Depression, 1929–1939 Rapid industrialization in U.S.S.R., 1930s Start of Roosevelt's New Deal in U.S., 1933
1940	United Nations founded, 1945 Decolonization of Asia and Africa, 1945–1960s Cold War begins, 1947 Founding of Israel, 1948 Communist government in China, 1949 Korean War, 1950–1953 De-Stalinization of Soviet Union under Khrushchev, 1953–1964	Holocaust, 1941–1945 Marshall Plan enacted, 1947 European economic progress, ca. 1950–1970 European Coal and Steel Community founded, 1952 European Economic Community founded, 1957
1960	Building of Berlin Wall, 1961 U.S. involvement in Vietnam War, 1964–1973 Student rebellion in France, 1968	Civil rights movement in U.S., 1960s Stagflation, 1970s Feminist movement, 1970s

Religion and Philosophy	Science and Technology	Arts and Letters
Decline in church attendance among working classes, ca. 1850–1914 Mill, *On Liberty*, 1859 Pope Pius IX, *Syllabus of Errors*, denounces modern thoughts, 1864 Marx, *Das Capital*, 1867 Doctrine of papal infallibility, 1870	Modernization of Paris, ca. 1850–1870 Great Exhibition in London, 1851 Freud, founder of psychoanalysis, 1856–1939 Darwin, *On the Origin of Species*, 1859 Pasteur develops germ theory of disease, 1860s Suez Canal opened, 1869 Mendeleev develops periodic table, 1869	Realism in art and literature, ca. 1850–1870 Flaubert, *Madame Bovary*, 1857 Tolstoy, *War and Peace*, 1869 Impressionism in art, ca. 1870–1900 Eliot (Mary Ann Evans), *Middlemarch*, 1872
Growth of public education in France, ca. 1880–1900 Growth of mission schools in Africa, 1890–1914	Emergence of modern immunology, ca. 1875–1900 Electrical industry: lighting and streetcars, ca. 1880–1900 Trans-Siberian Railroad, 1890s Marie Curie, discovery of radium, 1898	Zola, *Germinal*, 1885 Kipling, "The White Man's Burden," 1899
Separation of church and state in France, 1901–1905 Hobson, *Imperialism*, 1902 Schweitzer, *Quest of the Historical Jesus*, 1906	Planck develops quantum theory, ca. 1900 First airplane flight, 1903 Einstein develops theory of special relativity, 1905–1910	Modernism in art and literature, ca. 1900–1929 Conrad, *Heart of Darkness*, 1902 Cubism in art, ca. 1905–1930 Proust, *Remembrance of Things Past*, 1913–1927
Keynes, *Economic Consequences of the Peace*, 1919	Submarine warfare introduced, 1915 Ernest Rutherford splits atom, 1919	Spengler, *The Decline of the West*, 1918
Emergence of modern existentialism, 1920s Revival of Christianity, 1920s–1930s Wittgenstein, *Essay on Logical Philosophy*, 1922 Heisenberg's principle of uncertainty, 1927	"Heroic age of physics," 1920s First major public radio broadcasts in Great Britain and U.S., 1920 First talking movies, 1930 Radar system in England, 1939	Gropius, Bauhaus, 1920s Dadaism and surrealism, 1920s Woolf, *Jacob's Room*, 1922 Joyce, *Ulysses*, 1922 Eliot, *The Waste Land*, 1922 Remarque, *All Quiet on the Western Front*, 1929 Picasso, *Guernica*, 1937
De Beauvoir, *The Second Sex*, 1949 Communists fail to break Catholic Church in Poland, 1950s	U.S. drops atomic bombs on Japan, 1945 Big Science in U.S., ca. 1945–1965 Watson and Crick discover structure of DNA molecule, 1953 Russian satellite in orbit, 1957	Cultural purge in Soviet Union, 1946–1952 Van der Rohe, Lake Shore Apartments, 1948–1951 Orwell, *1984*, 1949 Pasternak, *Doctor Zhivago*, 1956 "Beat" movement in U.S., late 1950s
Second Vatican Council announces sweeping Catholic reforms, 1962–1965 Pope John II, 1978–2005	European Council for Nuclear Research founded, 1960 Space race, 1960s	The Beatles, 1960s Solzhenitsyn, *One Day in the Life of Ivan Denisovich*, 1962

Government	Society and Economy
1960 (cont.) Soviet tanks end Prague Spring, 1968 Détente between U.S. and U.S.S.R., 1970s Soviet occupation of Afghanistan, 1979–1989	Collapse of postwar monetary system, 1971 OPEC oil price increases, 1973, 1979
1980 U.S. military buildup, 1980s Solidarity in Poland, 1980 Unification of Germany, 1989 Revolutions in eastern Germany, 1989–1990 Persian Gulf War, 1990–1991 Dissolution of Soviet Union, 1991 Civil war in Yugoslavia, 1991–2001 Separatist war breaks out in Chechnya, 1991	Growth of debt in the West, 1980s Economic crisis in Poland, 1988 Maastricht Treaty proposes monetary union, 1990 European Community becomes European Union, 1993 Migration to western Europe increases, 1990s
2000 Terrorist attacks on U.S., Sept. 11, 2001 War in Afghanistan begins, 2001 War in Iraq begins, 2003	Euro enters circulation, 2002 Voters reject new European Union constitution, 2005 Immigrant riots in France, 2005, 2009 Worldwide financial crisis begins, 2008

Religion and Philosophy	Science and Technology	Arts and Letters
	Russian cosmonaut first to orbit globe, 1961 American astronaut first person on moon, 1969	Carson, *Silent Spring*, 1962 Friedan, *The Feminine Mystique*, 1963 Servan-Schreiber, *The American Challenge*, 1967
Revival of religion in Soviet Union, 1985– Growth of Islam in Europe, 1990s Fukuyama proclaims "end of history," 1991	Reduced spending on Big Science, 1980s Computer revolution continues, 1980s–1990s U.S. Genome Project begins, 1990 First World Wide Web server and browser, 1991 Pentium processor invented, 1993 First genetically cloned sheep, 1996	Solzhenitsyn returns to Russia, 1994; dies 2008 Author Salman Rushdie exiled from Iran, 1989 Gehry, Guggenheim Museum, Bilbao, 1997
Ramadan, *Western Muslims and the Future of Islam*, 2004 Conservative elected as Pope Benedict XVI, 2005	Growing concern about global warming, 2000s First hybrid car, 2003 Copenhagen Summit on climate change, 2009	Movies and books exploring clash between immigrants and host cultures popular: *Bend It Like Beckham*, 2002; *The Namesake*, 2003; *White Teeth*, 2003; *The Class*, 2008

THE CONTEMPORARY WORLD

Greenland
(Den.)

ICELAND

UNITED
KINGDOM

IRELAND

FRANCE

SPAIN

Alaska
(U.S.)

CANADA

PORTUGAL

UNITED STATES

ATLANTIC
OCEAN

Azores
(Port.)

MOROCCO

Bermuda (U.K.)

Canary Is.
(Sp.)

Hawaii (U.S.)

Western Sahara
(Mor.)

MEXICO

BAHAMAS

DOMINICAN
REPUBLIC

HAITI

Puerto Rico (U.S.)

ST. KITTS AND NEVIS

ANTIGUA AND BARBUDA

DOMINICA

ST. VINCENT AND THE GRENADINES

BARBADOS

GRENADA

TRINIDAD AND TOBAGO

MAURITANIA

CUBA

JAMAICA

BELIZE

GUATEMALA

HONDURAS

EL SALVADOR

NICARAGUA

COSTA RICA

PANAMA

Guadeloupe (Fr.)

Martinique (Fr.)

ST. LUCIA

CAPE
VERDE

SENEGAL

MALI

GAMBIA

GUINEA-BISSAU

GUINEA

BURKINA FASO

SIERRA LEONE

LIBERIA

CÔTE D'IVOIRE

GHANA

VENEZUELA

GUYANA

SURINAME

French Guiana (Fr.)

COLOMBIA

ECUADOR

Galápagos Is.
(Ec.)

PACIFIC OCEAN

Equator

BRAZIL

PERU

SAMOA

BOLIVIA

TONGA

PARAGUAY

CHILE

ATLANTIC
OCEAN

URUGUAY

ARGENTINA

Easter I.
(Chile)

0   1,500   3,000 miles

0   1,500   3,000 kilometers

Falkland Is.
(U.K.)

80°N

60°N

40°N

20°N

0°

20°S

40°S

60°S

80°S

60°W   40°W   120°W   100°W   80°W   60°W   40°W   20°W

ARCTIC OCEAN

NORWAY
SWEDEN
FINLAND
DEN.
NETH.
GERMANY
BEL.
LUX.
SWITZ.
SLN.
IITALY
CR.
B.H.
MO. KO.
ALB.
MAC.
GREECE
TUNISIA
MALTA
ESTONIA
LATVIA
LITHUANIA
BELARUS
POLAND
CZ.
SLK.
AUS.
HUNG.
ROMANIA
SE.
BULGARIA
UKRAINE
MOLDOVA
GEORGIA
ARMENIA
TURKEY
CYPRUS
ISRAEL
LEBANON
SYRIA
West Bank
Gaza Strip
JORDAN
AZERBAIJAN

RUSSIAN FEDERATION

KAZAKHSTAN

UZBEKISTAN
TURKMENISTAN
KYRGYZSTAN
TAJIKISTAN

MONGOLIA

N. KOREA
S. KOREA
JAPAN

CHINA

PACIFIC OCEAN

IRAQ
IRAN
AFGHANISTAN
PAKISTAN
KUWAIT
BAHRAIN
SAUDI ARABIA
QATAR
UNITED ARAB
EMIRATES
OMAN

NEPAL
BHUTAN
BANGLADESH
INDIA
MYANMAR
(BURMA)
LAOS
VIETNAM
THAILAND
CAMBODIA

Taiwan

GERIA
LIBYA
EGYPT

NIGER
CHAD
SUDAN
ERITREA
YEMEN
DJIBOUTI

NIGERIA
OGO
ENIN
CAMEROON
EQ.
INEA
GABON
CONGO
CENTRAL
AFRICAN REP.
ETHIOPIA
SOMALIA

MALDIVES
SRI
LANKA

BRUNEI
MALAYSIA
SINGAPORE

PHILIPPINES

Mariana Is.
(U.S.)
Guam
(U.S.)

MARSHALL
IS.

PALAU

FEDERATED STATES
OF MICRONESIA

NAURU
KIRIBATI

SÃO
TOMÉ
PRÍNCIPE
RWANDA
UGANDA
KENYA
DEM. REP. OF
THE CONGO
BURUNDI
TANZANIA
COMOROS
SEYCHELLES

INDIAN OCEAN

INDONESIA

TIMOR
LESTE

PAPUA
NEW
GUINEA

SOLOMON
IS.

TUVALU

ANGOLA
ZAMBIA
MALAWI

MADAGASCAR
MAURITIUS

VANUATU
FIJI

NAMIBIA
ZIMBABWE
BOTSWANA

AUSTRALIA

New Caledonia
(Fr.)

SOUTH
AFRICA
MOZAMBIQUE
SWAZILAND
LESOTHO

Tasmania
(Aust.)

NEW
ZEALAND

ANTARCTICA

20°E   40°E   60°E   80°E   100°E   120°E   140°E   160°E

ABBREVIATIONS

ALB.	ALBANIA
AUS.	AUSTRIA
BEL.	BELGIUM
B.H.	BOSNIA AND HERZEGOVINA
CR.	CROATIA
CZ.	CZECH REPUBLIC
DEN.	DENMARK
HUNG.	HUNGARY
KO.	KOSOVO
LUX.	LUXEMBOURG
MAC.	MACEDONIA
MO.	MONTENEGRO
NETH.	NETHERLANDS
SE.	SERBIA
SLK.	SLOVAKIA
SLN.	SLOVENIA
SWITZ.	SWITZERLAND

About the Authors

John P. McKay (Ph.D., University of California, Berkeley) is professor emeritus at the University of Illinois. He has written or edited numerous works, including the Herbert Baxter Adams Prize–winning book *Pioneers for Profit: Foreign Entrepreneurship and Russian Industrialization, 1885–1913* (1970) and *Tramways and Trolleys: The Rise of Urban Mass Transport in Europe* (1976). He most recently contributed to *Imagining the Twentieth Century* (1997).

Bennett D. Hill (Ph.D., Princeton University), late of the University of Illinois, was the history department chair from 1978 to 1981. He published *English Cistercian Monasteries and Their Patrons in the Twelfth Century* (1968), *Church and State in the Middle Ages* (1970), and numerous articles and reviews, and was one of the contributing editors to *The Encyclopedia of World History* (2001). A Benedictine monk of St. Anselm's Abbey in Washington, D.C., he was also a visiting professor at Georgetown University.

John Buckler (Ph.D., Harvard University) taught history at the University of Illinois. Published books include *Theban Hegemony, 371–362 B.C.* (1980), *Philip II and the Sacred War* (1989), and *Aegean Greece in the Fourth Century B.C.* (2003). With Hans Beck, he most recently published *Central Greece and the Politics of Power in the Fourth Century* (2007).

Clare Haru Crowston (Ph.D., Cornell University) teaches at the University of Illinois, where she is currently associate professor of history. She is the author of *Fabricating Women: The Seamstresses of Old Regime France, 1675–1791* (2001), which won the Berkshire and Hagley Prizes. She edited two special issues of the *Journal of Women's History* (vol. 18, nos. 3 and 4), has published numerous journal articles and reviews, and is a past president of the Society for French Historical Studies and a former chair of the Pinkney Prize Committee.

Merry E. Wiesner-Hanks (Ph.D., University of Wisconsin–Madison) taught first at Augustana College in Illinois, and since 1985 at the University of Wisconsin–Milwaukee, where she is currently UWM Distinguished Professor in the department of history. She is the coeditor of the *Sixteenth Century Journal* and the author or editor of more than twenty books, most recently *The Marvelous Hairy Girls: The Gonzales Sisters and Their Worlds* (2009) and *Gender in History* (2nd ed., 2010). She currently serves as the Chief Reader for Advanced Placement World History.

Joe Perry (Ph.D., University of Illinois at Urbana-Champaign) is associate professor of modern German and European history at Georgia State University. He has published numerous articles and is author of the recently published book *Christmas in Germany: A Cultural History* (2010). His current research interests include issues of consumption, gender, and television in East and West Germany after World War II.